DEVIANTS
VOLUNTARY ACTORS IN A HOSTILE WORLD

ACKNOWLEDGMENTS

BASIC BOOKS, INC., PUBLISHERS: Figure 2, "Organization of the Lupollo Numbers Enterprise, (page 95), from *A Family Business: Kinship and Social Control in Organized Crime,* by Francis A. J. Ianni with Elizabeth Reuss-Ianni, © 1972 by Russell Sage Foundation, New York.

CBS NEWS: "The Trouble with Rock," as broadcast over the CBS Television Network on August 11, 1974. Copyright © 1974 CBS, Inc. All rights reserved.

DOUBLEDAY & COMPANY, INC.: Vincent Teresa, with Thomas C. Renner, *My Life in the Mafia.* Copyright © 1973 by Doubleday & Company, Inc.

HARPER & ROW, PUBLISHERS, INC.: Chart adapted from pages 112–115 and excerpts from *Theft of the Nation* by Donald R. Cressey. Copyright © 1969 by Donald R. Cressey. By permission of Harper & Row, Publishers, Inc.

ALFRED A. KNOPF, INC.: Gus Tyler, "The Crime Corporation." In Abraham S. Blumberg, ed., *Current Perspectives on Criminal Behavior: Original Essays on Criminology.* Copyright © 1974, Alfred A. Knopf, Inc.

G. P. PUTNAM'S SONS: John Kobler, *Capone: The Life and World of Al Capone.* Copyright © 1971 by G. P. Putnam's Sons. Also, Peter Maas, *The Valachi Papers.* Copyright 1968 by G. P. Putnam's Sons.

UNIVERSITY OF TEXAS PRESS: Material in the section on Crime and Delinquency by Edwin I. Megargee is drawn in large part from Chapter 2 of C. M. Rosenquist and E. I. Megargee, *Delinquency in Three Cultures.* Copyright © 1969 by The Hogg Foundation for Mental Health. By permission of the publisher, University of Texas Press.

Manufactured in the United States of America

Published simultaneously in Canada

Library of Congress Catalog Card Number 76-57979

ISBN 0-382-18029-1

To the children:
Fred, Pat, Brad, Johanna, Eric Sagarin

And the parents:
Fred and Filomena Montanino

Preface

Books on the general subject of deviance, and on specific categories of deviant people, have become so abundant that we learned, with a bit of surprise, that gaps remained for new writers and editors to fill. In the present book, we have limited ourselves to what we call "voluntary deviants," as distinguished from those, the physically disabled and the mentally retarded, for example, who had no control over and no responsibility for what befell them. It was our aim to place the entire concept of voluntary deviance within the framework of responsibility, and then to look at major types of people coping with a world in which they are viewed with hostility. Who are these voluntary deviants, what are the sources of their problems in life, how did they arrive at the point of embracing deviant life styles, how does society react to them? These are some of the questions that we attempt to answer in the following pages.

In this book we examine ten types of voluntary deviants—prostitutes, alcoholics, drug addicts, white collar criminals, sex deviants, organized or syndicate crime figures, and others—by presenting an overview of each problem as it exists in America today. It is our hope that the substantive studies found here will contribute to the testing, refinement, and development of other ongoing work in the area of deviance.

Enough of a red carpet; now open the door and proceed inside.

Edward Sagarin
Fred Montanino

Contents

ONE
Deviants: voluntarism and responsibility

FRED MONTANINO
Yale University

EDWARD SAGARIN
City College of New York

As definitions of deviance are studied, one can logically conclude that the most significant distinction that can be drawn among various people described by sociologists as deviant is the voluntarism of their behavior. This is not voluntarism in the sense of a desire to be reviled by society (there is no doubt a little of this, a sort of psychic masochism with psychopathological overtones), but rather of a conscious decision to embrace a path or status that will lead to social hostility.

The lists of deviant people, the deviant categories, and some of the definitions of deviance, by a general consensus among sociologists, cover a wide spectrum of people and behavior, having in common only that large and sometimes powerful forces in the society are hostile, antagonistic, and react legally or socially by punishment, ostracism, gossip, ridicule, or in some other manner that shows that these persons are held in poor esteem. Erving Goffman (1963) has covered this range very nicely in the one word *stigma*, and he includes among the stigmatized the criminal as well as the physically handicapped. In fact, he goes a step further and includes the racially ostracized, who have what he terms a *tribal stigma.*

A series of studies, such as contained in this book, of persons involved in voluntary rather than involuntary deviance, immediately brings into focus a number of questions. There is the problem of etiology and motivation: Why do people pursue activities that they have been taught are contrary to the norms of society and that they know will bring forth the reaction of a hostile world? Also, the problem of responsibility arises: What is meant by that term, and to what extent should people be required to assume responsibility for actions that they have voluntarily embraced? Interwoven with both of these questions is the issue of degree: To what extent is an action voluntary, and are some more voluntary than others? Finally, is there less responsibility and less voluntarism for what one *is*, rather than for what one *does*, and is there a pervasive confusion between identity and action?

Voluntarism, like involuntarism, is a matter of degree. In looking over the persons and activities described in this book, one will find at one end of a spectrum persons who undertake their behavior with a great degree of voluntarism: the syndicate criminals, the white collar and upperworld criminals, and the dealers in pornography, as well as the adulterers and "fornicators." At the other end, there are those whose actions are somewhat less voluntaristic; these persons who for economic, psychological, or other reasons become prostitutes, indulge in violent and often uncontrollable behavior, or end up among the suicide statistics. But there are still other problems. In alcoholism and drug addiction, for example, and to a smaller extent in other areas of deviance, what may start as a purely voluntaristic act continues in a far less voluntary matter. If anything, this is the crux of the definition of habit and addiction: It is what is meant by the expression "getting hooked."

The fact that an action—or a course of action for that matter—is voluntary does not necessarily mean that there is pride in the mind of the performer. Those who are participants in political and religious deviant movements, atheists, snake cultists, or splinter-group nationalists who practice terrorism, may very well be proud of their acts and happy about their membership in these subcultures. If they fail to own up to their actions in public or in court (as sometimes they do), it is not out of shame but for the protection of themselves and the movements that they have embraced. Others are far less proud, and their concealment of their actions (while it may also serve the cause of self-protection) is often the inevitable result of having no sense of self-righteousness. Such persons are likely to have an acute awareness that there were forces around them, social and personal, that brought them to the point of doing what they now do, despite the enormous hostility that they face.

In the view of many, though, putting the blame on external forces is nothing short of a cop-out. Responsibility, as Jean-Paul Sartre has stated, is itself freedom because it implies choice. The problem for many social scientists may well be to determine the causes of many forms of deviance: that is, to locate the roots of the activities in familial, social, and other relationships, in blocked opportunities, differential associations, cultural transmission, unresolved childhood problems, conflicts of norms and of interest groups, and the like. For the individual, however, the problem is to decide whether to blame events in infancy and childhood, people around in the hostile world, an ambience of decadence, or other forces for one's patterns in life, or to decide to exercise control over these patterns oneself.

INVOLUNTARY DEVIANCE

The freedom to make decisions for oneself implies that one has accepted responsibility for status and actions. Those who cannot make such decisions and whose status has incited social hostility can be termed the *involuntary deviants*. These would include the physically handicapped (except in the rare case of a self-inflicted wound or in failure to obtain assistance that is available), the mentally retarded and brain damaged, perhaps some instances of the mentally ill, and— despite the sympathy that is intermingled with the hostility—probably the terminally ill. These are examples of what can be termed *nonresponsibility* (to be clearly distinguished from *irresponsibility*) for one's status in society. In these instances, there are two separable factors: (1) the condition itself and (2) the social reaction to it, particularly the stigmatizing activities of normals.[1]

So far as the condition is concerned, those so afflicted may blame their wretched and disvalued state of existence on pure accident, tough luck, or some other circumstances beyond their control. Even an actor who had control and performed in a manner that could have been avoided, as a drunken driver who gets into an accident and is physically disabled, has not chosen the physical disability, although he was responsible for the act that led to it. The involuntary deviants, in short, cannot be said to desire the disvalued traits, or to value their state of existence, or to derive gratification for their behavior, all of which are somewhat counterposed to social norms and expectations. These persons can be described as the purest of society's victims, disvalued not for what they choose *to do* but for what they have no choice *in being;* not for their violation of formal codes of conduct but for their inability to satisfy informal, unspoken expectations held by the mass of society's normals.

There is a further distinction that can be made here: The disvaluation of the involuntary deviants arises not from disapproval of others but from the discomfort that others fall susceptible to in their presence. Their disability has not been consciously acquired, it is totally unwelcomed, and it is often burdensome beyond the imagination of normals, except perhaps for an intimate family member whose life revolves around the care of such a person. Unlike the case of more voluntary states, there is an ominous specter of permanence for those involuntarily afflicted. Yet, should recovery prove possible, they become fully embraced in the world of normals, a pleasant fate that usually does not await those who return to the normative path after a period of voluntary deviance. For the involuntary deviants, the former condition leaves few social scars, an indication that normals perceive their nonresponsibility for their status.

The involuntary deviant disvalues the condition that is the source of the stigmatization. Only rarely is it put forth that the state of disability is as desirable an existence as that recognized as normal.[2] Among the involuntary deviants, there is frequently found a commitment of over-conformity to normative statuses, at least to those that are capable of being attained and enacted. In some respects, this may be an attempt to compensate for others in which the deficiency is unavoidable and the handicap cannot be overcome. One who embraces an overconforming stance is seeking affirmation from those who are normal. When such a pattern is followed, there may be avoidance of others who are similarly situated and commonly affected. In short, those with involuntary handicaps may often become, in essence, "voluntary conformists" who require that their affiliation with and conformation to normative cultural prescriptions be met with acceptance and encouragement, not frustration and rejection.

Most types of involuntary deviance do not lend themselves to concealment of the disvalued characteristic, but such a situation is possible. There emerges, then, what Goffman (1963) terms the discredited and the discreditable. In the case of the latter, a course of everyday activities arises that is part of a strategy designed by the deviant actor for navigating in the world of normals. The success of such coping strategies is a function of the visibility and sometimes the severity of the condition itself and of the degree of social hostility against it.

Clearly, the responsibility for stigmatization of the involuntary deviants lies with the society of normals. The serious social student of this phenomenon is concerned with two factors: the nature of the societal reaction, and the manner of coping with life under such conditions. The various statuses that fall under the rubric of involuntarism are not subject to discouragement but rather to prevention. Further, involuntary deviance is not subject to social control in the sense that the latter operates for crime, delinquency, or even adultery; but only the control of avoidance, separation, or institutionalization of the affected individuals. Hostile and negative sentiments cannot be marshaled in order to implement a program that will prevent the proliferation of involuntary deviance; only a program for the abatement of hostility toward those affected will serve to lessen the suffering of people so affected. So that, despite the many similarities between the involuntary and voluntary deviants in terms of the mechanisms by which they cope both with life and the censure of hostile others, the two major groupings are sufficiently dissimilar to be worthy of separate study.

VOLUNTARY DEVIANCE

One would expect that in the case of voluntary deviance, which entails more freedom of choice on the part of the actor, there would be a tendency to provide categorizations that involve a lesser degree of permanence. Nevertheless, this is not always the case. Unlike the involuntary deviants, who are thus classified on the basis of rather permanent and undeniable aspects of their existence, the voluntary deviants are judged on the basis of their activities and actions. The very fact that these are activities, and that they have been chosen, implies that they need not be permanent but can be renounced at any time. Nevertheless, there are many instances in which a more or less permanent personality imputation is placed upon the deviant; it has been suggested that this is due at least in part to the nature of the language (Sagarin, 1975, 1976). In speech, there is a tendency to talk of people as *being* when one actually means *doing*, a tendency to confer on individuals permanent personalities or identities on the basis of certain acts that they commit, especially if such acts are among those that are considered aberrant.

A very special type of mistaken identity occurs when permanence is attributed to acts that may or may not occur frequently, or that may have occurred only once (yet for which one is detected and consequently labeled). The notion of identity, popularized by Erik Erikson and given high value by the resurgence of ethnic and racial identity movements after World War II, has a different flavor when conferred and accepted by oneself on the basis of the nature of one's behavior. For a pattern of behavior is almost invariably susceptible to change, but the transformation of it in the mind of the actor from *doing* to *being* tends to exclude the avenue of change as an alternate road to follow.

When persons commit crimes, have homosexual encounters, or perform countless other deviant acts, they are referred to as criminals, homosexuals, and the like. A woman who performs sexually in an indiscriminate manner for pay is called a prostitute, a person who imbibes alcohol in excess is labeled an alcoholic, and one who ingests illegal narcotic drugs for the purpose of altering consciousness or experiencing euphoria is tagged a drug addict. But they *are* such types of persons, it will be argued, and if they are, then is it not better that they be so categorized? The argument here is that the freedom to choose, to continue or to discontinue, is greater if persons are conceptualized as *doing*—and hence having the power to stop doing, if they so decide—rather than *being*.

When the concept of latency is introduced into the categorization of people and their acts, as is done all too often, then one can be considered by the normals and even by oneself to have a deviant identity not only on the basis of what one has done but also, in the absence of the actions, on the basis of what one secretly wishes, or has the conscious or unconscious potential to become, or would like to have done but has repressed the desire. It has been argued that to the extent that one

comes to be identified as being deviant and accepts the i
oneself as such, imprisonment in that identity or in that
Socially, a situation arises where it becomes tempting, convenient, ..
well-nigh inescapable to fail to associate with others so identified, and
in many ways one is pushed into becoming what others believe one to
be. However, the identification itself, whether negative or positive,
does not have to be accepted as an identity but can be viewed as a
pattern of activities or conduct. Seen in this light, it no longer appears to
be as immutable as in the case of involuntary deviants; and once it is
not seen by the deviant or others as immutable, it tends to lose its
permanent hold.

Voluntaristic activities are those in which an actor has a certain
amount of freedom of choice to continue in or to depart from the
disvalued state, and to the extent that this freedom of choice exists, the
actor bears a greater responsibility for his place in society.

ON THE MATTER OF COPING

The coping strategies for human survival that are exhibited by those
who can be considered voluntary deviants differ markedly from those of
the involuntary deviants. Here, the concept of self-justification
becomes crucial; it may even exist in the face of the deviant actor's
condemnatory statements and sentiments about his own behavior. One
who commits deviant acts must be able to limit the internal conflict that
may arise over the commission of the act or over the deviant career of
which that act forms a part, particularly if that career is at an early stage.
Self-justifications, rationalizations, excuses, explanations—what Marvin Scott and Stanford Lyman (1963) summarize under the heading of
"accounts"—are all forms of antideviance neutralization and are functions of the degree of voluntarism associated with the aberrant
behavior.

The white collar criminal, the adulterer, the pornographer, and to
some extent the syndicate criminal are likely to search for some forms of
self-justifications in an effort to cope with their deviant conduct. These
categories of activities are extremely voluntaristic, and to this extent it
would prove difficult to place the blame for their occurrence on a wider
social milieu, on forces within oneself and beyond one's controls, or on
psychological problems.

The adulterer, for example, may justify his actions by a firmly held belief that such activity is a matter of personal privacy, having little to do with the wider society, and that it is certainly harmless to those whom it does not concern. In many such instances, basic morality and notions of monogamy may be challenged as outmoded, unrealistic, and generally useless. In any event, the adulterous action is viewed as a matter of personal conscience and not public interest. Yet adultery itself is a mixed bag, as the performer of the act must know. The adulterer may even think of his action as beneficial under certain circumstances, such as when it arises out of sexual dissatisfaction in an otherwise permanent and monogamous relationship. The adulterer can see his act as being the cement that holds his marriage together, very much as Kingsley Davis (1937) viewed prostitution, in that both activities offer opportunities for sexual outlet that do not compete with and threaten the permanence of the family. The introduction of distrust, furtive patterns, sexual jealousy with potential for disruption of a family, and prevarication is part of the price that the voluntary deviant must pay for embarking on the adulterous path.

White collar criminals may view their activities as merely extensions of "business ethics" that dictate the value of the pursuit of individual success. They may point to the entrepreneurial system and the widespread practices of cutting corners, cheating, and generally engaging in unethical business conduct that reach to the highest levels of corporate, political, and military life. These criminals abandon individual morality and responsibility to become part of the systemic decay rather than be engulfed by it, and they consider their only mistake to be in getting caught at what everyone else is doing. Indeed, such individuals may point to the lenient treatment that white collar criminals experience at the hands of the judiciary and interpret this as a sign of implicit approval or even encouragement. In such an atmosphere, white collar criminals need not view themselves as adding to the decay that they daily witness all around them; in fact, they may even be part of the condemnation of that decay.

Somewhere between the businessman and the sex deviant one can place those who promote pornography and prostitution and the many others who cater to what have been called "the vices." It is not known to what extent these persons believe their activities to be detrimental or immoral, but they cannot avoid the onus of having voluntarily chosen their businesses and lifestyles. They can gain some comfort, if their conscience and morals require it, from the thought that they are providing a service that would certainly be flourishing if they were to disappear from the scene. Their coping may become a matter of separating their business lives from their personal lives, for some of them have respectable and legitimate reputations that they have built up in circles where their deviant behavior is unknown. If they condemn the behavior in which they indulge and live a somewhat schizoid existence, then the problem of coping becomes twofold: on the one hand, to keep the two lives separate, and on the other, to find internal justifications.

This separation of two aspects of one's life is probably more apparent in the syndicate criminal, particularly the most successful. He leads a dual existence, for the fruits of his illegal labors bring him wealth, prestige, and respectability and allow him to enter respectable areas of endeavor. To safeguard his legitimate place in society, he may expend enormous sums of money on legal counsel; recruit support from semi-legitimate, marginal, although not criminal associates who hold positions of responsibility in social control agencies; and indulge, even ostentatiously, in philanthropic and religious activities. From these contacts and the encouragement that the system provides, he justifies his own lifestyle; yet he often does not want to pass the business down to his own sons and will not permit or tolerate his type of deviant conduct in his own backyard.

Clearly, a person needs to justify normal violations only in those instances where freedom of choice is provided and where the responsibility accompanying that freedom is somehow felt to be violated.

BLAMING SOCIETY: VIOLENCE AND PROSTITUTION

When attention is turned to less voluntaristic activities, such as prostitution and the subculture of violence, condemnation of society rather than condemnation of self may provide the rationale and justification for an actor's entrance into and continued participation in such patterns.

The juveniles, especially those who belong to the "conflict" mode of street gang, the warriors that value "heart" and street-fighting skills, are often depicted as in some manner "trapped" in that mode of existence. Richard Cloward and Lloyd Ohlin (1960) find the roots for the existence of such groups in the frustration that arises from the unsuccessful efforts of youths to achieve success goals through legitimate and normative means, as well as from their lack of access to the illegitimate means of achieving material success (that is, access to utilitarian criminal means). Such violent youth gangs were said to flourish in inner-city areas, in slum dwellings that were disorganized and decayed and marked by changing industrial land use patterns and weak community bonds. For a time, it appeared that these types of gangs had gone into a decline, but by the mid-1970s there were signs of resurgence, or perhaps the decline had been illusory.

A somewhat different stance is taken by Albert Cohen (1955), who views such violent modes of adaptation as a result of status frustration, which is prevalent among lower- and working-class children who cannot rise to a middle-class status, although they have internalized the values and aspirations for such upward mobility. They are frustrated, rejected, and ill-equipped to compete with their middle-class counterparts; yet they seek status, which ultimately can only be gained through setting their own standards. These, of course, must be standards in which they have the means and capability to achieve success.

Like Gresham Sykes and David Matza (1957), Cohen sees that various techniques of neutralization allow the conflict-oriented juveniles, those who embrace violence, to continue in their disvalued patterns and statuses in the face of the severe hostility that they encounter from the world of normals (although, of course, not from their peers). To this, Cloward and Ohlin (1960) add another factor: alienation. When youths become alienated from the mainstream of society, they need not neutralize their actions after the fact, because alienation has allowed them to withdraw their sentiments from normative prescriptions before the aberrant acts were committed.

In either view, members of what Marvin Wolfgang and Franco Ferracuti (1967) have called a subculture of violence are likely to blame the society rather than themselves for any frustrations that are encountered. Whatever truth there may be in the facts of squalor, poverty, and other social conditions that have generated violence, the mode of violent adaptation that ensues is the responsibility of those who adopt it. Embracing the subculture of violence—whether to survive, to show contempt for the normative society, or to secure limited neighborhood social amenities—is, in the last analysis, subject to discretion and personal control. To find the cause for such action in social conditions is

not the same as to place blame on society. That discretion is
proven by the renunciation of the violent mode of behavi
years, whether this be in favor of embracing normative roles in the
community or of developing yet another form of deviant adaptation.

Prostitutes may also point to the society of which they are a part in an
effort to account for their deviant careers. Disadvantaged socioeconomic positions, coupled with rather restricted legitimate avenues for
the achievement of success goals, do provide strong impediments and
considerable discouragement to those who would pursue normative
patterns. The prostitute is said to rationalize her own behavior quite
frequently with a rather distorted analogy in which she compares
herself to the housewife who does essentially the same thing, only for a
"regular John," her husband. She may point out that her services do
harm to no one, least of all the John, and in this way she cautiously
ignores those who would point to the destructive and negative career
contingencies of her own occupation.

The defense of her life that the prostitute may offer (to herself, for few
others ask her to defend herself, and the problem is largely one of
coping with self-image) ignores the pitfalls of maladjustment, self-
degradation, and abuse that to many observers are the cornerstones of
her existence. She does not view accepting money for sexual favors as
an impediment to the development of stable and adjusted emotional
relationships. Instead, she often equates such a practice to that of
sharing dinner and a night out, a commonplace occurrence in the
development of a meaningful and emotionally rewarding relationship
between a man and a woman.

And so her list of justifications and rationales could continue. Ultimately, they serve the purpose not of making "the profession" respectable but of allowing the participant to continue in this disvalued behavior with a self-proclaimed air of self-worth and respectability. It allows
her to endure negative evaluations and permits her to continue working, free of internal conflicts that would otherwise arise at various
junctions in her career.

ADDICTION: VOLUNTARISM AND ITS INVERSION

Despite widespread misconception, one is not born an alcoholic or
drug addict.[3] The voluntary nature of drug use is highlighted by the fact

that one must learn to become a user and must develop contacts for the procurement of the drug (especially in the case of such illegal commodities as heroin). In addition, knowledge of the proper way of using the drug to gain the greatest amount of pleasure with the least potential for danger must also be learned, as Howard Becker (1963) has carefully explained for marijuana.

While the opportunities for such learning processes are not difficult to find, they must nonetheless be searched out and sought after in order that one may successfully arrive at the state of being addicted. No doubt the roads to addiction (including alcoholism) are trodden by many who have developed proclivities for the deviance in the course of interaction in the normative society. For many, it appears to be a road of escape, whether temporary or permanent. If there is a common ideology that addicts learn to embrace in interaction with one another, it may well revolve around escapism. In other instances, addiction may be used as a prerequisite for assimilation into various subcultures, such as the youth gangs of an inner city, a student subculture, or even skid row.

Perhaps more in the case of illegal drugs than alcohol, an expenditure of enormous effort on the part of addicts is required to maintain their existence. The price of illegal drugs and the impediments to obtaining them require a constant and continuous hustle on the part of the addict. To what extent is the effort motivated by the physical addiction, once it is developed? Even if the addict or alcoholic started out on a voluntary basis, it can be contended that there is an element of involuntarism in the continuation of their patterns of conduct. In other words, if the concept of addiction is meaningful, then breaking the habit or going cold turkey is just not the same as deciding not to rob another bank after successfully doing so on a few previous occasions.

There is a continuum between the voluntary and the involuntary act, and certainly the later stages of addiction are not at the voluntaristic end of this spectrum. In fact, the concept that addiction is less than voluntary is indicated by the proliferation of medical and community-health treatment facilities, which often include both physical and psychological therapy, that have the aim of returning the addict to the mainstream of society. Yet, even this is recognition of the impermanence of addiction. The responsibility for taking the step toward breaking the habit lies with the individual (although society also has its responsibility: to make such facilities for a change available and possible and to welcome the formerly addicted into its ranks). Whatever measures are offered by social services, they are useless unless the addict has reached a point of determination to shed the addiction, and this itself implies a recognition of the voluntarism of the addiction and hence of the responsibility of the participant.

The perpetuation of addiction, despite its disvaluation, may be achieved by cloaking it in secrecy. Very often the addict is capable of obviating detection, although this often requires great expenditure of energy. Should addiction reach the point of visibility, or become generally known to significant persons in the life of the addict, the euphoria, the physical dependence, the fear of withdrawal, and the anxiety at the thought of returning to the world of normals, particularly normals in the know, may prove to be hurdles too formidable to face.

In certain instances, the addict may be reluctant to accept the reality of the addiction, often preferring to believe that the habit has not reached proportions beyond control. Psychological, physical, and social decay may accrue from addiction before a person realizes the extent to which heroin, alcohol, or some other substance has a grip on him. Despite this, the ultimate decision of whether to continue the behavior is a matter that rests with the addict. Greater aid (that is, aid to resist and overcome) may be required in the latter stages of addiction than at the start, but only the recognition of the voluntarism of the addiction will succeed in making it voluntary.

In other words, there is in addiction both voluntarism and some degree of involuntarism, the former being greater in earlier stages. The involuntarism that develops in the course of addiction takes on the form of psychological and physiological dependence. Yet such a condition is not irreversible, not beyond correction, and is far from hopeless. Only the definition of it in terms of irreversibility can possibly make it so. It is not an easy task, but the addict and the alcoholic, in the last analysis, have freedom of choice: whether to inject the next dose, whether to take the next drink. One can say no, face up to the responsibility of accounting for one's own state of existence, and do something about it. Or one can continue to deny this responsibility, pointing to forces, both interpersonal and social as well as psychological, that impinge on and impel a person to continue. This is to succumb to an escape from responsibility. If this is sometimes an easier alternative, it is also one that proves detrimental and dysfunctional not only for the individuals and intimate others around them but for the society of which they remain a part.

COMPULSIVITY AND PSYCHOPATHOLOGY

The problem of deviance and responsibility reaches a point of complexity when one deals with psychological and perhaps psychopathological states. Some persons apparently are driven to deviant behavior by compulsions, which by definition means that they are not in control of what they do. Even American criminal law recognized, as early as 1884, in the "irresistible impulse" rulings, that responsibility is diminished unless a person is capable of knowing right from wrong and also capable of doing that which is right and abstaining from acts that that person knows are wrong. There is a violent personality that borders on, if it does not belong to, such categories as the psychopathic and criminally insane. While it is doubtful that compulsive and uncontrollable behavior accounts for a great deal of violence or for sizable proportions of such deviance as juvenile delinquency or prostitution, there may be more such instances in some areas of sexuality, some cases of alcoholism and drug addiction, and certainly suicide.

The problem of how to view persons subject to compulsion can be answered in part by placing such persons in the mid-area of the continuum between voluntarism and involuntarism. A more effective answer, however, is to define these as voluntary states. This can lead to the overcoming of those forms of deviance that bring about suffering both for the deviant and others (such as victims), and at the same time it can provide the deviant with greater freedom of choice. Such a definition is not meant to be a delusion or an arbitrary categorization under another semantic label. The goal here is to help persons obtain control over their behavior by urging them not to capitulate to the idea that there are "evil forces" or "inner demands" that are beyond their ability to handle.

DEVIANCE, RESPONSIBILITY, AND VOLUNTARISM

In this book, two concepts are interwoven: deviance and voluntarism. By deviants and deviance are meant persons and behavior, respectively, that incite negative social reaction or that bring negative evaluation from significant others or significant portions of society. By voluntarism is meant the deliberate and purposive achievement of such states of being or patterns of behavior. It is hoped that the focus on these two interrelated and often interdependent themes will provide enhanced understanding both of the concept of deviance and of its individual manifestations. Such an understanding should lead one to work toward several social goals: (1) diminished hostility toward those forms of behavior presently defined as deviant that are not hurtful to the society and probably not to the persons involved; (2) diminished occurrence of some forms of deviance through the perception by those involved of the potential for control over their own lives; (3) enhanced social control over such forms of deviance as are beyond the levels of tolerance of the society, by rejection of the notion of diminished responsibility; and (4) greater freedom of all persons to choose the path of their own lives.

NOTES

1. The word *normals* and the adjective *normal* are here used in the sociological sense as they are employed by Goffman (1963), rather than in any psychological or value-judgmental manner. They simply refer to others who do not have the stigmatizing trait, characteristic, or attribute.

2. A dwarf has been known to make such a statement, but harboring such a belief may be reassuring and may ease the burdens of the stigmatized life.

3. The newborn can be addicted as a result of activities of the mother during pregnancy, but this accounts for a negligible amount of total drug addiction.

BIBLIOGRAPHY

Becker, Howard S. *Outsiders: Studies in the Sociology of Deviance.* New York: The Free Press, 1963.

Cloward, Richard A., and Lloyd E. Ohlin. *Delinquency and Opportunity: A Theory of Delinquent Gangs.* Glencoe, Ill.: The Free Press, 1960.

Cohen, Albert K. *Delinquent Boys: The Culture of the Gang.* Glencoe, Ill.: The Free Press, 1955.

Davis, Kingsley. "The Sociology of Prostitution." *American Sociological Review,* 1937, 2:744–755.

Goffman, Erving. *Stigma: Notes on the Management of Spoiled Identity.* Englewood Cliffs, N.J.: Prentice-Hall, 1963.

Sagarin, Edward. *Deviants and Deviance: An Introduction to the Study of Disvalued People and Behavior.* New York: Praeger, 1975.

Sagarin, Edward. "The High Personal Cost of Wearing a Label." *Psychology Today,* 1976, 9:25–31.

Scott, Marvin B., and Stanford M. Lyman. "Accounts." *American Sociological Review,* 1963, 33:46–62.

Sykes, Gresham M., and David Matza. "Techniques of Neutralization: A Theory of Delinquency." *American Sociological Review,* 1957, 22:644–670.

Wolfgang, Marvin E., and Franco Ferracuti. *The Subculture of Violence: Towards an Integrated Theory in Criminology.* London: Tavistock, 1967.

TWO

Crime and delinquency

EDWIN I. MEGARGEE
Florida State University

Every three seconds a light blinks under a large clock in the lobby of the J. Edgar Hoover Building in Washington, D.C. According to official FBI statistics, this signifies that somewhere in the United States a serious crime has taken place. The light blinks day and night, 19 times a minute, 1,140 times an hour, 27,360 times a day. At the end of the year, when new crime statistics have been collected, the clock is stopped and reprogrammed to blink at a faster rate. In the 15-year period from 1960 through 1975, the blinking light was speeded up 203 percent to keep pace with the increase in the reported number of serious crimes (Federal Bureau of Investigation, 1975). In that same period the population of the United States increased only 18 percent.

FBI personnel and criminologists know that the Crime Clock seriously underestimates the amount of crime in the United States. A survey undertaken by the National Opinion Research Corporation for the President's Commission on Law Enforcement and Administration of Justice (1967) indicated that the actual rate of forcible rape was three-

and-one-half times greater than the reported rate, burglaries were three times as frequent, and aggravated assaults and larcenies of fifty dollars or more were twice the official rate.

THE COST OF CRIME IN THE UNITED STATES

The cost of crime in the United States is so vast that it defies calculation. The official FBI statistics indicate that well over $1 billion worth of goods were stolen in 1972. But this is only the tip of the iceberg. Most people thinking of crime only consider the holdups and shootings that are reported in their newspapers—events that typically happen to someone else. Data collected by the President's Commission (1967), however, show that every day each of us is a victim of less obvious crimes. Embezzlement and shoplifting are rarely reported in the official statistics; nevertheless, about two cents out of *every* retail dollar we spend goes to pay the cost of such thefts. Many of us share in the $100 million annually swindled from the public for unnecessary auto repairs or suffer some of the $1.8 billion annual loss due to drunken driving. And how is one to place a dollar value on the cost to society of the 20,600 murders and the 452,720 aggravated assaults that take place yearly (Kelley, 1973)?

THE SEARCH FOR AN ANSWER TO THE CRIME PROBLEM

People have been seeking answers to the crime problem throughout recorded history. The theme of crime and punishment pervaded the Book of Genesis just as it now dominates our televisions and newspapers. Over the centuries wise men, judges, priests, and philosophers have struggled to find a solution to the problem.

Now, with the development of psychology, psychiatry, and sociology, society is turning to behavioral scientists for answers. As the FBI statistics point up, though, even present-day insights are ineffective against crime.

The main reason for this failure is that all too often simplistic solutions of "more this" or "less that" are proposed—more psychologists, police, community programs, street lights, jobs; less poverty, racism, judicial leniency, dirty movies, restrictive laws. Unfortunately the simple answer to the problems of crime and delinquency is that there is no simple answer. If in our search for simplicity we minimize the complexity of the problem, it is unlikely that any substantial progress will be made.

Even when our understanding of behavior is much farther advanced than it is today, behavioral scientists will still have difficulty in accounting for criminal behavior because "crime" is a legal rather than a scientific term. Suppose one individual picks up a gun and shoots another. This is a fairly clear-cut bit of behavior, and even in our present state of knowledge we can often understand why such an act took place, how it could have been prevented, and what might be done to forestall its happening again. But has a *crime* taken place? That depends on other factors outside the realm of behavioral science. For an act to be a crime it must be "prohibited by public law for the protection of the public, and made punishable by the state in a judicial proceeding in its own name" (Marshall & Clark, 1970). There are numerous circumstances in which it is not illegal for one individual to shoot another—warfare, self-defense, the carrying out of a legal order of execution, to name a few.

In determining whether or not an act is criminal it is not enough to establish that the behavior that occurred was prohibited by the penal code. It must also be established that the perpetrator had a *criminal intent*. If the person doing the shooting was a five-year-old child or an individual who was mentally incapable of discerning that harm would result from the shooting, then no crime would have taken place.

Even with a relatively simple situation such as one person shooting another, it can be seen that many factors outside the psychological realm determine whether or not a crime has taken place. The situation is much more complex with other behaviors. Sometimes whether an act is legal or illegal depends on age, locale, or point in time. There are many behaviors that are legal for adults, such as drinking, staying out late, spending the night away from home, or failing to attend school, that could result in a juvenile's arrest. In 1970, a physician in New York could legally terminate a pregnancy at the request of the mother but a colleague in Connecticut would be committing a felony by doing so. After the Supreme Court decision (1973) legalizing abortion, the physician in Connecticut would no longer be committing a crime by terminating a pregnancy. Even if behavioral scientists can someday write equations that would predict the occurrence of these behavioral acts—staying away from home, terminating a pregnancy, giving beer to a nineteen-year-old—how is it possible for the scientist to predict whether crimes will be committed when the definition of what constitutes a crime is so arbitrary?

The general public is just beginning to become aware of the shortcomings of simplistic explanations of crime and delinquency. The author suspects that this is directly related to the fact that the middle class has only recently had to confront the fact that "respectable" people engage in criminal behavior. As long as drug abuse and riots were confined to the nation's ghettos, it was easy for Middle America to attribute the drug problem to black "dope fiends" or riots to anarchists or communists (McGuire & Megargee, 1974). When their own sons and daughters were arrested for using marijuana or participating in demonstrations, their natural reaction was to protest that despite this behavior, their children were not "common criminals." But if someone who breaks the law is not a criminal, then who is?

During the Nixon administration, the question of what constitutes criminal behavior was brought into sharper focus for the public at large The Watergate burglary and subsequent coverup, the activities of former Vice-President Spiro Agnew, and later the pardon of former President Richard Nixon raised such fundamental questions as to whether all citizens are equal in the eyes of the law and what constitutes a crime in our society. Is illegal behavior legal when authorized by a president, as John Ehrlichman contended? A poor black youth who violates federal laws by stealing a Social Security check from a mailbox is commonly regarded as a criminal, but opinions differ on the guilt of wealthy middle-aged politicians who file fraudulent income-tax returns.

PROBLEMS IN STUDYING CRIME SCIENTIFICALLY

The scientific study of crime and criminals would not appear to pose great difficulties. To determine what factors are associated with the incidence of crime, one would suppose a sociologist would simply examine the variation in crime rates as a function of locale, street lighting, unemployment, the phase of the moon, or whatever. Since society collects and cages criminals, psychologists literally have a "captive population" to respond to tests or answer questionnaires. This is fine if the sociologist is only interested in *reported crime* or the psychologist is concerned only with the characteristics of *imprisoned* criminals. However, most behavioral scientists are concerned with studying *all* criminal behavior, not just with those crimes that happen to be officially recorded or with those miscreants unfortunate enough to be imprisoned. There is good reason to believe that recorded crime and convicted criminals are not representative of the total domain of illegal behavior. If this is so, unless investigators are very careful to point out the limitations of their studies, their results may actually retard progress because it is better to have no answer than an erroneous one.

A report by the President's Commission on Law Enforcement and Administration of Justice (1967) showed how selective factors operate at each stage of the criminal justice process so that the imprisoned criminal cannot be regarded as representative of anyone but other imprisoned criminals. We already have noted that, according to the President's Commission, only one third to one half of the crimes committed are reported to the police. For the 2,780,000 serious (or *index*) offenses known to the police in 1965, only 177,000 people were formally charged with committing them; of these, 160,000 were convicted. Of those convicted, 63,000, or less than 9 percent of those originally arrested, were sent to prison. It can be seen that imprisoned criminals, who are the subjects typically studied, represent a very small and highly biased sample of the population of people committing illegal acts. The more intelligent, skilled, and experienced criminals are most likely to avoid detection. Of those identified by the police, those with the best connections, the greatest financial resources, the most stable work and family backgrounds, the fewest prior offenses, and the whitest skins are most likely to avoid arrest, conviction, and imprisonment.

How can this "criminal justice funnel" distort our understanding of crime and delinquency? Several theories of criminal behavior attribute crime to social class factors. Walter Miller (1958) argued that lower-class culture has certain focal concerns that serve to generate gang delinquency. Robert Merton (1938) and Richard Cloward and Lloyd Ohlin (1960) pointed out how limitations on the legitimate opportunities for success that are open to lower-class boys lead them to choose illegitimate avenues. Albert Cohen (1955) attributed gang delinquency to a deviant subculture arising from the conflict between lower-class behavior patterns and the reward systems imposed in middle-class schools. All of these explanations are predicated on the tacit assumption that juvenile delinquency is primarily a lower-class phenomenon. If one examines the official data, this appears to be the case. Clifford Shaw and Henry McKay (1942) demonstrated how the rate of crime increases from the suburb to the inner-city ghetto. Demographic studies of institutions for delinquents show an overrepresentation of lower-class children. But is this because lower-class children actually have greater criminal propensities, or because a lower-class child who commits a deviant act is more apt to be detected, apprehended, adjudicated, and incarcerated than a middle-class child who engages in similar behavior?

GENERAL THEORIES OF CRIME AND DELINQUENCY

Theories of Innate, Inherited Characteristics as Causes of Crime and Delinquency
The earliest and most enduring class of theories attributed criminality to some innate characteristic of the individual. These theories, like those of Sigmund Freud and Charles Darwin, grew out of the belief of many nineteenth-century scientists in biological determinism. Some regarded criminal tendencies themselves as being inherited; others attributed criminality to some intervening innate trait such as defective intelligence.

These theories have probably had more empirical testing than have any other class of criminological theories. Sample sizes, which frequently have run into the thousands, have been larger, too. As is often the case in human genetic research, however, these investigations have been hindered by sampling problems and, in some cases, by problems of measurement. Consequently, none of these theoretical positions can be considered established despite the large masses of data that have been collected. These theoretical positions have been rejected by most of today's criminologists, who are mainly predisposed toward theories of environmental causation.

The Lombrosian Hypothesis.   One of the earliest constitutional theories was that of Cesare Lombroso (1836–1909), who hypothesized that certain criminals who behave in a savage fashion are, in fact, "atavistic reversals" or throwbacks to a more primitive form of man. Lombroso suggested that this hypothesis could be tested by comparing the physical characteristics of criminals and noncriminals. If criminals were indeed throwbacks, Lombroso predicted they would have more primitive somatic characteristics or *stigmata,* such as low sloping foreheads, than would noncriminals. Accordingly, Lombroso made numerous anthropological measurements of Italian criminals and soldiers and reported that he found a higher incidence of such peculiarities among the criminal samples. These studies were, of course, biased because the soldiers had previously had to pass a physical examination while the criminals had not.

In the present century, extensive investigations of Lombroso's hypotheses have been made by Charles Goring (1913) and Ernest Hooton (1939). Goring concluded that his investigation offered no support for the Lombrosian hypothesis; Hooton, who criticized Goring's procedure, felt that his own findings supported the Lombrosian position. Most modern criminologists, who share a strongly environmental orientation, criticize Lombroso's and Hooton's methods and cite Goring to prove that the Lombrosian position is untenable. The present writer agrees that since there are so many drawbacks to the sampling procedures used by Lombroso and Hooton, their conclusions cannot be accepted. At the same time it must be noted that an equally rigorous analysis reveals similar flaws in Goring's study.

The Criminal as a Biologically Inferior Organism.   Many of the environmentalist criminologists who accept Goring's work relatively uncritically seem unaware of the fact that although he rejected Lombroso's theory, he nevertheless maintained that criminality was the result of innate physical and mental inferiority. The hypothesis that the criminal is an inferior organism also has been put forth by other writers who have observed that delinquents tend to be less healthy than nondelinquents (Burt, 1944). The evidence on this matter, however, is contradictory. A number of studies have found no significant differences between the physical fitness of delinquents and nondelinquents;

in fact, some have even found the delinquents to be somewhat superior (cf. Rosenquist & Megargee, 1969).

The Relation Between Delinquency and Body Type. Constitutional psychiatrists such as Ernst Kretschmer and William Sheldon have suggested that there is a close link between physique and temperament. Sheldon, Emil Hartl, and Eugene McDermott (1949) devised a procedure for rating individual physiques and applied it to a sample of 200 young men who had gotten into various types of trouble with the law. As a result of this investigation, they concluded that physical inadequacy is a basic cause of crime and that eugenics offers the best long-term solution to the crime problem. The theories of Sheldon and his colleagues have been strongly criticized, and the methods used in their research have been challenged. Edwin Sutherland (1951) reanalyzed Sheldon, Hartl, and McDermott's data using what he felt was a more meaningful criterion of delinquency and found no significant differences between seriously delinquent and nondelinquent boys. However, Sheldon and Eleanor Glueck (1950, 1956) found that mesomorphs (boys with muscular builds) were overrepresented in their delinquent sample while ectomorphs (boys with slender, linear physiques) were underrepresented. This finding seems to be contrary to Cyril Burt's theory that delinquents are physically inferior. While the predominance of mesomorphs could be attributed to some genetic factor that causes both delinquency and mesomorphy, a social learning explanation that muscular boys are more likely to be rewarded for aggressiveness and thus to develop more antisocial habits is equally tenable and probably more parsimonious.

Delinquency as a Result of Glandular Malfunction. Another physiological theory of delinquency was the hypothesis that crime resulted from emotional disorders produced by malfunctions of the endocrine glands (Schlapp & Smith, 1928). While in some individual cases it is clear that disordered or criminal behavior has resulted from glandular imbalance, endocrinologists agree that there is no evidence to justify regarding endocrinological disorders as a necessary or sufficient explanation for criminal behavior (cf. Ashley-Montagu, 1941; Hoskins, 1941).

Delinquency as the Result of Mental Deficiency.   Still another physiological theory was the hypothesis that innate mental deficiency was the basic cause of crime and delinquency. This theory reached its zenith during the period from 1915 to 1930 when standardized intelligence tests were being developed. Investigators such as H. H. Goddard and F. H. Kuhlman examined numerous prisoners with the new intelligence tests and reported that a large proportion of them were "feebleminded." Later research demonstrated that this was an erroneous conclusion stemming from the fact that the new tests had not yet been adequately standardized for use with adults. Reanalyses of the data did not indicate that an extraordinarily high percentage of the inmate population was mentally retarded (Vold, 1958).

Although the notion that mental deficiency is the cause of delinquency has been dispelled, research does indicate that delinquents as a group do score significantly lower than nondelinquent groups on standard intelligence tests. Typically, delinquents do most poorly on tests stressing the verbal and conceptual abilities and best on nonlanguage or performance tests (Rosenquist & Megargee, 1969). Poor language skills and reasoning ability naturally make for poorer performance in school and increase the likelihood of difficulties in adjusting to the school situation; difficulties in adjusting to school in turn can result in educational retardation and a greater relative deficiency in conceptual skills. Thus, while the overlap between the IQ scores of delinquents and nondelinquents demonstrates that innate mental deficiency is not the primary cause of delinquency, it is also clear that learning disabilities, particularly in the verbal area, could be a significant factor in many individual cases.

Environmental Factors as an Explanation for Juvenile Delinquency
Sociologists and psychologists have tended to favor environmental rather than genetic factors as causes of crime and delinquency. The sociologists have mainly addressed themselves to the question of why recorded crime is more prevalent among underprivileged social groups, such as the poor, immigrants, and slum residents. They have sought the answers in terms of such social factors as the economic cycle, the conflict of different cultural groups, and differential law enforcement. Psychologists, meanwhile, have focused on the individual in an attempt to answer why one person in a given social group becomes delinquent

while another from similar circumstances does not, and to determine what function delinquent behavior serves within the individual's personality structure. To answer these questions they have focused on detailed analyses of the histories of individual delinquents and have placed primary emphasis on early childhood experiences and disturbed family relationships.

The Economic Cycle as a Cause of Crime and Delinquency. One of the earliest environmental theories sought to explain delinquency or crime in terms of fluctuations in the economy. In the nineteenth century, Georg Von Mayr demonstrated a positive correlation between the price of rye and offenses against the person in Bavaria from 1836 to 1861. However, Paul Wiers found a negative association between economic indices and the number of juvenile court cases in Detroit between 1921 and 1943 (Vold, 1958). A number of other scholars have also investigated the relationship between the economic cycle and the crime rate with equally contradictory results. The theory that poverty causes crime is intuitively appealing, particularly in the wake of widespread rioting and looting by the residents of poverty-stricken urban ghettos. However, this notion cannot account for middle-class or white-collar crime. Even among the poor it is debatable whether poverty causes crime directly or exacerbates other conditions that are conducive to delinquency, such as overcrowding, disease, and broken homes.

Deviant Subcultural Values as a Cause of Crime. According to another group of theories, what is normal behavior for some groups in society is rejected as criminal by members of the dominant middle-class culture. One of the earliest of these theorists was Thorsten Sellin, who focused on how such differences in conduct norms could lead to crime among certain subgroups. His classic example was a Sicilian immigrant who was incredulous at being arrested for murdering the seducer of his daughter "since he had merely defended his family honor in the traditional way" (Sellin, 1938, p. 68). Sellin recognized that differing conduct norms cannot explain all crime in our society and that other social, psychological, and physiological factors must also play a role. The leveling effect of mass communications media in the last decade, coupled with the decline in immigration, has undoubtedly done much to lessen the disparity between the values of different cultural groups in this country (Rosenquist & Megargee, 1969; Velez-Diaz & Megargee, 1970). However, research in Israel on culture conflict between Sephardic and European Jews has shown that elsewhere differing norms continue to be associated with criminal behavior (Shoham, 1962).

Gresham Sykes and David Matza (1957) disagree that criminal behavior stems from a different concept of what constitutes right and wrong. The very fact that many criminals and delinquents experience feelings of guilt and remorse, they argue, is evidence that they regard their behavior as reprehensible. They propose that instead of different moral principles, social classes differ in "techniques of neutralization"—rationalizations that excuse or justify deviant behavior for the perpetrator, if not for the society at large. Stealing may be wrong, but if a friend asks for help in a holdup, the principle that one should always help a buddy takes precedence. Similarly one can hold to commonly accepted social values while engaging in specific illegal acts if one can satisfy oneself that no one will suffer for it, that the victim deserves it, or that everyone else is doing it.

Although Sykes and Matza offered this analysis to account for lower-class behavior, one can readily see how such techniques of neutralization could be adopted by middle-class and white-collar criminals. If, for example, a public official is convinced that a certain contractor can do a good job on a public works project and that public office necessitates many personal expenses that cannot be charged to the state, then why would it be wrong to accept "personal contributions" from the contractor? After all, the contractor would no doubt have been awarded the contract anyhow, and the contributions make it possible to serve the public more effectively. In this manner a corrupt public official could convince himself that there is nothing really immoral or criminal about such kickbacks.

Walter Miller (1958), an anthropologist, has analyzed what he believes to be the focal concerns of the lower class. According to his analysis, the lower-class person is concerned with trouble, toughness, smartness, excitement, and autonomy. These concerns are seen as being conducive to the generation of gang delinquency. This conception differs from Sellin's in that instead of a basic disagreement as to what is right and wrong, the subculture is seen as having values that lead to behavior that both lower- and middle-class groups would probably classify as wrong.

The "differential association" theory advanced by Sutherland (1937) also falls into this general classification. According to Sutherland, much deviant behavior is simply learned from imitating deviant models, a position that anticipated modern social learning theory (Rotter, 1954). A high delinquency area is perpetuated as each successive cohort of teenagers is initiated into delinquent activities by the cohort ahead of them. The forcible recruitment of gang members through the "draft" would be another form of cultural transmission (Salisbury, 1958).

Sutherland suggested that delinquency originated in the subculture through cultural conflict that resulted from social disorganization. However, differential association can also explain middle-class deviance. The initiation of rookie policemen into "blue coat crime" (Stoddard, 1968) and the attempted coverups of such disparate activities as the My Lai massacre, the Cambodian bombing raids, and the so-called "White House Horrors" of 1972 could all fit into a differential association framework.

Delinquency as an Adolescent Crisis.   Another group of theorists has focused on the problems confronting the adolescent in Western society, suggesting that delinquency may result from the problems associated with this period of development. Erik Erikson (1950) has hypothesized that the critical conflict in early adolescence is between *ego identity* and *role diffusion* as the adolescent, faced with a changing body and ambiguous cultural expectations, strives for some definition of self. In the course of this crisis the adolescent may experiment with various roles and behaviors, including delinquent behavior. Herbert Bloch and Arthur Niederhoffer (1958) have pointed out how the ambiguity of the adolescent's role in Western society during the long period of physical maturity but economic dependence can lead to rebellious and delinquent behavior.

Social Conflict Theories
Another broad class of theories attributes crime to the conflict of social forces. One of the first such theorists was Robert Merton (1957), who noted that although American cultural mores demand that everyone should strive for status and material success, many lower-class individ-

uals find the socially approved paths to these goals blocked. For many, this inability to achieve socially approved goals by using legitimate means leads to a state of *anomie*, or normlessness, in which the ends become more important than the means. Consequently they resort to crime to achieve the money and respect that legitimate work cannot bring them.

Richard Cloward and Lloyd Ohlin (1960) adopted and embellished Merton's theory, adding to it elements of Sutherland's differential association approach. Like Merton, Cloward and Ohlin pointed to the disparity between the goals that lower-class children are expected to adopt and the inadequacy of the means for their attainment. "Faced with limitation on legitimate avenues of access to these goals, and unable to revise their aspirations downward, they experience intense frustration; the exploration of nonconformist alternatives may be the result" (Cloward & Ohlin, 1960, p. 86). During this period of exploration, differential association plays a critical role. A lower-class boy, frustrated by his inability to achieve wealth and status through legal means, will be more likely to turn to crime if he knows a successful professional criminal who might give him an opportunity to run numbers. As we shall see when we discuss typological approaches, Cloward and Ohlin suggested that if there are no such illegitimate opportunities available, the youth may be guided to the *conflict subculture* in which status is won through acts of violence. If he fails to succeed as a criminal, he may join the *retreatist subculture*, which features the use of drugs.

Some critics think Merton's theory implied that crime and delinquency are more goal-directed and rational than is actually the case. Both Merton's and Cloward and Ohlin's analyses have also been criticized for exaggerating the importance of social class while minimizing the importance of individual, familial, racial, and ethnic factors, and for overlooking the fact that among juveniles much delinquent behavior is caused by nothing more than a desire for fun and excitement (Caldwell, 1965). Moreover, while they may account for certain types of lower-class urban delinquency, other principles are necessary to explain criminal behavior among those who can take advantage of legitimate paths to success.

Albert Cohen (1955) also stressed the conflict between middle- and lower-class cultural expectations. The primary arena for this conflict, according to Cohen, is the school, in which the lower-class child is expected to behave according to middle-class standards and compete on middle-class terms. Despite their best efforts, many lower-class children find themselves faced with rejection and failure in this middle-class world. Therefore, they rebel and seek status among their peers, forming a subculture in which the middle-class value system is turned upside down. Thus, they reject the middle-class emphasis on self-control, conformity to authority, and reason and prize aggressiveness, sexuality, defiance, and malicious vandalism.

George Vold (1958) shifted the focus from the conflict of social forces to the conflict of special-interest groups. He pointed out that crimes associated with disputes between labor and mangement or with the efforts by civil rights groups to desegregate public facilities are not the product of the social forces or individual personality disturbances usually associated with crime. While Vold certainly did not hold that all crime is the by-product of such intergroup conflicts, he correctly maintained that the importance of this factor had been underestimated in other theoretical approaches.

Individual Psychopathology as a Cause of Delinquency

Psychologists[1] focus on the psychodynamics of the individual, and, as is usually the case, this microscopic examination reveals myriad complexities that may be overlooked in the sociologist's macroscopic study of large groups. The unique contribution of the psychologist has been the revelation of the role that unconscious motives may play in criminal and delinquent behavior. Most psychological theorists hold that delinquent acts are multiply determined. A boy who commits a rape may be motivated by the desire for sexual gratification, but the psychological examination might reveal that unresolved hostility against his mother, repressed fears of girls, and unconscious doubts regarding his own masculinity also influenced his behavior.

Many of the psychologists who have written about delinquency have shared a psychoanalytic frame of reference. While these investigators specialize in the detailed analysis of individual cases, they have noted some patterns that have recurred often enough to be worthy of comment. Sigmund Freud (1957) suggested that some offenders are driven by a sense of guilt that precedes and causes the antisocial behavior. Adelaide Johnson (1949) focused on the role parents play in unconsciously encouraging their children's delinquencies in order to satisfy their own repressed antisocial desires. Kate Friedlander (1947) described several neurotic patterns that may produce delinquent behavior, including acting out fantasies and using delinquent acts to satisfy unconscious aggressive desires.

The importance of neurotic motives in determining delinquency is a matter of some controversy. Because psychologists have cited psychopathology as a causal factor in *some* criminal behavior, some authorities, such as Judge David Bazelon (1973) have erroneously jumped to the conclusion that psychology attributes *all* criminal behavior to mental illness. There is still disagreement, however, over what proportion of the criminal and delinquent population should be classified as "disturbed" and what proportion as "normal"; much depends on the definitions employed.

Control and Containment Theories

Some sociologists have focused on both individual personality variables and social factors in their efforts to account for delinquent behavior. Albert Reiss (1951) suggested that criminal behavior results from a failure of both social and personal controls. In the absence of strong external social controls, the individual's internal inhibitions (conscience or superego) can prevent antisocial behavior. Similarly, strong social sanctions, such as the presence of a police officer, can often deter the undercontrolled individual.

Ivan Nye (1958) also focused on social factors that might contain or control delinquent tendencies. He differentiated four types of social control: (1) direct controls from discipline or punishment, (2) internalized controls or conscience, (3) indirect controls, which stem from the individual's desire not to disappoint parents or loved ones, and (4) the availability of alternative means of achieving goals. Nye maintained that the family is the primary agent of control, although controls can also be exercised by peers, institutions, such as the school or a church, and significant adults, such as teachers or national heroes.

While Nye felt that deficient social control was the factor underlying most crime and delinquency, he has been careful to point out that this cannot account for all types of delinquency. He specifically stated that his theory did not account for compulsive or neurotic crime or for the socialized crime learned in a delinquent subculture.

Reiss' and Nye's emphasis on the interaction of personality and the social setting contributed to Walter Reckless' development of containment theory. Reckless (1961) hypothesized that a favorable self-concept acts as an insulator against the pressures toward deviance found in a social environment conducive to delinquency. A favorable self-concept comes about primarily from being reared in a nurturing milieu, such as a family setting with affectionate, interested, well-socialized parents. Reckless also posited the existence of an *individual factor* that may facilitate or impede the development of a positive self-concept. He described environmental factors from which this individual factor may develop, but the possibility of innate differences, such as individual differences in temperament or arousal thresholds, is implicit in his formation. Like Reiss, Reckless specified that his containment theory does not apply to neurotic or psychopathic behaviors.

Multiple Factor Approaches

It has seemed to many that in the absence of adequate empirical data regarding crime and delinquency, theorists have rushed to fill the vacuum with theoretical explanations. The multiple factor approach, on the other hand, contrasted groups of delinquents and nondelinquents on an array of variables to determine which seemed to be more conducive to the development of deviant lifestyles. Lists of those variables that characterized the delinquents were then published.

Cohen has been particularly vehement in his criticism of this approach: " ... a multiple factor approach is not a theory; it is an abdication of the quest for a theory" (Cohen, 1970, p. 124). Opponents of multiple factor approaches feel that there is a tendency to describe each observed case as being unique so that there are no general laws or testable hypotheses. A related objection is that multiple factor theorists seem to explain each case on a post hoc basis.

The difficulty with multiple factor approaches, as Cohen points out, is that the theorists often fail to specify how variations in the factors they have identified are associated with the occurrence of the deviant behavior. A set of theoretical principles or laws relating the factors to one another is needed so that predictions can be made and tested. The furthest that multiple factor theorists have gone toward specifying such laws is to indicate that the likelihood of delinquent behavior increases as a function of the net sum of prodelinquent minus antidelinquent factors. According to Cohen:

... this assumption implies (1) that the inherent pathogenic (or benefi-cent tendency) of each factor in the actor's milieu is independent of the other factors which accompany it and (2) that these tendencies are independent of the actor's personality or the meanings of the factors to the actors. There is no other conclusion to be drawn from a list of concrete circumstances labeled, without qualification, causes of delin-quency (1970, p. 125).

Moreover, the interactions among variables need to be spelled out. For example, delinquents have been found to come from broken homes more often than nondelinquents. However, it is not enough to cite this fact as indicating that broken homes cause delinquency. Not all chil-dren from broken homes become delinquents or criminals. What deter-mines whether a child from a broken home becomes a delinquent? What about the broken home is pathogenic? Is it the absence of the father, as Miller (1958) suggested? Or is it the trauma associated with the dissolution of the home? It is questions such as these that suggest further research. For example, Carl Rosenquist and Edwin Megargee (1969) compared homes broken by the death of a parent (in which there was parental absence but presumably no acrimony) and those broken by divorce or separation. Delinquency was not related to parental deaths, but it was associated with divorce or separation. This suggested that it was the disharmony rather than parental absence that was condu-cive to delinquency.

Problems with General Theories

Many of the general theories that have been offered have been attempts to account for certain aspects of crime and delinquency that have been assumed to be fundamental. Some of the constitutional theories proba-bly originated in the observation that delinquents seemed to come from "bad stock" insofar as there was an above-average incidence of mental illness, criminality, and other forms of social pathology in their families. (Of course, unless the child has been reared by foster parents, such observations offer equally cogent evidence for environmental influ-ences.) Similarly, the reader has no doubt noted the emphasis on slum conditions and lower-class cultural patterns in many of the environ-mental theories. This stems from the observation that there is a higher incidence of officially recorded delinquent and criminal behavior in disorganized lower-class urban areas and that an inordinate number of the youths in training schools come from broken homes.

As we noted at the outset, however, there is increasing doubt regarding the validity of these observations. To be sure a disproportionate number of blacks and lower-class people are convicted of crimes, but is this because they are more likely to engage in criminal behavior? Or does it reflect the biases of the criminal justice system? Is the high percentage of youths from broken homes found in training schools because broken homes cause delinquency or because judges are apt to feel that a child from a broken home is more in need of institutional care than an equally deviant child from a stable home? Alex Thio recently charged: "In research strategy, students of deviance tend to follow the conventional stereotyped lead in tracking down deviance, focusing on the deviance of the powerless class but relatively neglecting the deviance of the powerful. As a result, they either explicitly or implicitly suggest that the powerless are generally more deviant than the powerful" (1973, p. 1).

Such concerns have led to some research aimed at determining the generality and validity of such observations. Nye (1958) used anonymous self-reports of illegal behaviors as his operational definition of deviance among high school students, and Edwin Megargee, George Parker, and Robert Levine (1971) used scores on the socialization scale of the California Psychological Inventory in their research on university students. Both investigations showed broken homes and familial discord to be associated with deviance. These studies indicate that the patterns that have been observed are probably not *solely* artifacts of bias in the criminal justice system. Nevertheless, Thio is absolutely correct in insisting that scholars should devote as much attention to deviance by the powerful as they do to deviance of the powerless. Indeed, since the behavior of the powerful is usually vastly more far-reaching in its effects and since so little has been done to date, research on their deviance deserves even higher priority.

It would not be surprising if such research demonstrated that the factors that have been assumed to be fundamental characteristics of criminals are revealed as being class-specific. Quite different patterns may be found among upper-class delinquents and criminals. As Robert MacIver stated: "Since crime, as a category of social action, has no inherent universal property, we cannot expect to find, in the variety of persons who are convicted of crimes, any one psychological or physiological type, any character trait whatever that differentiates them all from other persons" (1942, p. 89). This statement illustrates what many consider to be the chief drawback to the theoretical explanations presented thus far: the fact that they attempt to be too inclusive. Anomie, heredity, defective intelligence, deviant role models could all influence *some* individuals to engage in some types of criminal behavior, but none of these factors is a necessary or sufficient explanation of the total crime problem. All delinquents are not "sick" and any attempt to attribute all criminal behavior to psychopathology is doomed to failure. But this does not mean illness cannot lead some individuals to commit criminal acts. The fact that a given factor is not *the* cause of crime and delinquency does not mean that it cannot be *a* cause of criminal behavior.

Most scholars have abandoned any hope of deriving a general theory of crime and delinquency by studying adjudicated delinquents and criminals. As the biases within the criminal justice system have become more apparent, a number of sociologists have shifted their attention away from the individual offender to study the interactions between the individual and the establishment that result in the individual being labeled as a delinquent. In so doing they have found many similarities between the processing of criminals and other "social deviants," such as mental patients. This interactionist perspective will be examined in the next section.

The other trend has been in the opposite direction. Instead of expanding their viewpoint to include all those whom society regards as misfits, other scientists have tried to narrow the focus of their investigations, hoping to delineate types of illegal behavior for which specific causes and effective means of intervention may be found. A survey of these typological approaches will be presented in the following section.

THE INTERACTIONIST PERSPECTIVE

Labeling and Its Consequences

It is abundantly clear that only a small fraction of those engaging in illegal behavior ever see the inside of a prison cell. Interactionists examine the transactions between individuals and society that lead some to be officially labeled as transgressors and others who have engaged in the same behavior to remain respected members of the community. This shifts the focus from the alleged transgressors to the forces of social control. To the interactionist, a criminal is not someone who has committed certain prohibited acts but instead a person whom society has branded a criminal.

According to this "labeling" viewpoint, Nathaniel Hawthorne's famous character Hester Prynne did not become a social deviant when she took a lover to her bed but when the community affixed the scarlet letter "A" to her dress. This viewpoint is best expressed by Howard Becker in his oft-cited statement:

> Social groups create deviance by making the rules whose infractions constitute deviance, and by applying those rules to particular people and labeling them as outsiders. From this point of view, deviance is *not* a quality of the act the person commits, but rather a consequence of the application by others of rules and sanctions to an "offender." The deviant is one to whom that label has successfully been applied; deviant behavior is behavior that people so label (1964, pp. 8–9).

This applies not only to criminals but also to others that society labels as deviants—homosexuals, psychotics, radicals, alcoholics, and so forth (Megargee, 1973).

The social interaction does not, of course, end with the affixing of a label and the mustering of the forces of social control. Such "degradation ceremonies" cause a reaction in the accused, who may respond by denying the label as in the neutralization techniques described by Sykes and Matza (1957). Such efforts are rarely successful in expunging the label, for, according to Harold Garfinkel:

> The work of the denunciation effects the recasting of the objective character of the perceived other: the other person becomes in the eyes of his condemners literally a different and new person ... the former identity stands as accidental; the new identity is the "basic reality." What he is now is what, "after all," he was all along (1956, pp. 421f.).

The validity of this assertion was demonstrated in a recent incident in which federal narcotics agents mistakenly raided the wrong house and held a terrorized couple at gunpoint while they ransacked the premises in a vain search for drugs. Despite the fact that it was publicly acknowledged that the agents had made an error and searched the wrong house, public castigation of the innocent victims was so great that they were forced to leave and assume new identities in a new community. People felt that "where there's smoke there's fire" and continued to treat them as drug users, official denials notwithstanding.

Our self-images are largely based on the reactions of others. Mary Vecchio, the runaway teenager who received widespread publicity after being photographed kneeling over the body of a slain Kent State student, was recently interviewed after pleading "no contest" to prostitution charges. She said, "When people already think the worst of you, you just think negatively about yourself, and act that way" (Tallahassee *Democrat*, 1973, p. 6). Thus a label may be a self-fulfilling prophecy.

The implications for crime and, particularly, delinquency are clear. If a young person who engages in some disapproved behavior is caught up in the criminal justice system, officially labeled a "juvenile delinquent," and placed in an institution with other "juvenile delinquents," he may begin to regard himself as "bad" and model his behavior after that of the other "bad" people in his milieu. Thus programs designed to identify and treat potential delinquents might paradoxically end up by fostering *more* deviant behavior than would have occurred without the program. It is this process that Edwin Lemert had in mind when he wrote: " . . . the older sociology . . . tended to rest heavily upon the idea that deviance leads to social control. I have come to believe that the reverse idea, i.e., social control leads to deviance, is equally tenable . . ." (1967, p.v).

Primary and Secondary Deviance
At this point in the interactionist's argument some readers feel they have ventured into a topsy-turvy world in which one cannot tell the "good guys" from the "bad guys." Inmates of institutions are seen as persecuted victims of an unjust society, and their therapists are viewed as repressive lackeys perpetuating the power of a corrupt establishment.

Some of this confusion can be eliminated by adopting Lemert's distinction between "primary" and "secondary" deviance. Primary deviance is the original behavior that led to the individual being labeled. Secondary deviance is the behavior adopted by the individual to cope with the resulting societal reaction. For example, because of antagonistic feelings against his father, intellectual inadequacy, and the desire to impress his peers, a boy might act out and defy school authorities. As a result of this *primary deviance* he may be labeled a troublemaker and suspended from school. The school suspension in turn might result in anger and boredom, and, without a high school diploma, the young man might find it impossible to obtain employment. Since his "better-adjusted" peers are in school during the day, he is apt to find himself spending more time with older boys or with others who have been similarly cast out. If someone in the group suggests they "borrow" a car or "rip off" a store, he might go along with the idea. This behavior resulting from the school suspension is *secondary deviance*. If it leads to his arrest and incarceration in an institution where he develops a full-fledged criminal self-concept or becomes homosexual, these too would be secondary deviances. Lemert's distinction between primary and secondary deviance thereby enables us to appreciate the effects of labeling without falling into the trap of asserting that *all* criminal behavior stems from societal stigmatization.

Reading the interactionist literature, one may receive the impression that labeling effects are always negative. There is no logical or psychological reason, though, why the application of a *positive* label cannot lead to growth and thereby become a self-fulfilling prophecy. This notion is implicit in the common assertion that Harry S Truman "grew into" the presidency. Application of positive labels is the basis for self-enhancement programs as diverse as Couéism ("every day in every way I am getting better and better") and Rogerian psychotherapy. In institutional settings positive labeling is central to programs in which inmates are given responsibilities and expected to live up to them.

The growth of the interactionist perspective (which no doubt gained impetus from the social protest movements of the 1960s, during which time many social scientists had an opportunity to view the criminal justice system from the "consumer's" standpoint) has led to greater concern for maintaining the human dignity of offenders and attempting to cope with primary deviance in ways that will forestall the development of criminal identities. Recently the Commonwealth of Massachusetts closed all its training schools because it appeared that they were doing more harm than good. The money thus saved was supposed to provide community-based services and opportunities to enable those youths who had formerly been locked up to succeed on the outside. Other states are closely examining the Massachusetts experiment; if it succeeds, there will be an increased emphasis on community-based corrections, if only for reasons of economy. Similar developments are taking place in the care of the mentally retarded and the mentally ill.

The interactionist perspective has restored much-needed balance to a system that had tended to look only at the criminal's offenses against society while ignoring society's offenses against the criminal. The labeling approach, however, offers little insight into the causes of primary deviance. Progress in this area seems most likely to come about through the study of individuals from all strata of society who engage in asocial and antisocial behavior, with the view toward delineating specific syndromes.

TYPOLOGICAL APPROACHES

Offense-Based Typologies

The offense is one of the few bits of data that is routinely recorded regarding each and every offender, and it is not surprising that many investigators have attempted to discover whether similar patterns of criminal activity stemmed from similar background factors and would respond to the same treatment.

Although it is easy to start with the offense, the problem is where to stop. The FBI *Uniform Crime Index* lists some 29 different crimes; its British counterpart records 195! Obviously a typological system with this many classifications would be too unwieldy to have practical utility.

Therefore this array of offenses is often grouped into a fourfold classification scheme of (1) crimes against persons (such as murder, rape, and assault), (2) crimes against property (such as larceny, fraud, and burglary), (3) crimes against the self (such as drug usage), and (4) crimes against public decency (such as soliciting and vagrancy).

This taxonomic system is not very useful because the differences within the four categories are greater than those between them. For example, among men convicted of violent crimes against the person, the present writer has found two vastly different personality types, the overcontrolled and the undercontrolled. Each type has its own distinctive lifestyle, personality dynamics, and developmental history, and they require diametrically opposite methods of treatment (Megargee, 1966).

Clinard and Quinney's Typology

Marshall Clinard and Richard Quinney have criticized offense-based typologies as follows:

> This method of classifying criminals suffers from a number of disadvantages. For example, (1) it tells nothing about the person and the circumstances associated with the offense, nor does it consider the social context of the criminal act, as in the case of rape or the theft of an auto; (2) it creates a false impression of specialization by implying that criminals confine themselves to the kind of crime for which they happen to be caught or convicted; (3) it is a common practice in order to secure easy convictions to allow offenders to receive a reduced sentence by "plea copping" or pleading guilty to a lesser charge that may only slightly resemble the original charge or offense; (4) because the legal definition of a criminal act varies according to time and place, the legal classification of crime presents problems for comparative analysis; and (5) most important of all, the use of legal categories in a classification assumes that offenders with a certain legal label, such as burglars, robbers, auto thieves, and rapists, are all of the same type or are a product of a similar process (1973, p. 3).

In order to arrive at potentially useful legalistic typologies, most criminologists have found it necessary to introduce such variables as professionalism, motivation, social class, and personality dynamics. The resulting systems soon cease to be purely legalistic. One of the most refined such systems is that introduced by Clinard and Quinney in 1967 and revised in 1973. Their scheme encompasses not only the legal aspects of selected offenses but also the criminal career of the offender, group support for the illegal behavior, the correspondence between the criminal behavior and legitimate patterns, and the response of society and the criminal justice system. On the basis of these five dimensions, Clinard and Quinney (1973) postulated nine criminal behavior systems, which are summarized below.

(1) *Violent personal criminal behavior.* This includes the ancient crimes of homicide, assault, and forcible rape. Except for certain subcultures there is no group support for these offenses, and they are typically committed for personal reasons, in violation of society's mores.

(2) *Occasional property criminal behavior.* These offenses violate the laws protecting the material interests of the propertied class. They tend to be individual offenses with little group support. The offenders are committed to the general values of society despite violating its high regard for private property.

(3) *Conventional criminal behavior.* These offenders violate the same laws protecting property as the preceding group, but they begin their careers early, often as members of gangs or slum groups whose norms support theft for economic gain. The self-concept varies and vacillates, but there is at least a partial commitment to crime as a way of life. These offenders have incorporated the materialistic goals of society but not its high regard for the sanctity of private property.

(4) *Professional criminal behavior.* These offenders are distinguished more by their personality characteristics than by the specific laws they violate. They engage in highly specialized offenses requiring considerable technical skill and often the aid of an accomplice. Their motivation is economic gain, and they associate mainly with other professional criminals. They have considerable status among criminals, and their low visibility leads to a high degree of public tolerance.

(5) *Public order criminal behavior.* Although many of these offenses, such as prostitution, drug use, and homosexual behavior, are victimless arrangements between consenting adults, it is easier for society acting through its elected representatives to outlaw than to condone them. These offenders do not regard themselves as criminals; they are often supported by clearly defined deviant subcultures. There is a large correspondence with legitimate behavior patterns.

(6) *Political criminal behavior.* This category includes both crimes

against the government and crimes by the government. The offenders do not consider themselves criminal or identify with a criminal lifestyle. Their behavior is strongly supported, and indeed may be considered heroic, by members of their particular reference groups.

(7) *Occupational criminal behavior.* This category includes consumer frauds, embezzlement, professional malpractice, and the like. The offenders accept the conventional values of society but do not regard themselves or their behavior as criminal. Their rationalizations are often supported by their occupational groups and regarded as normal business practice.

(8) *Corporate criminal behavior.* These offenses by business concerns violate the laws established to regulate corporate behavior in such areas as corporate mergers (to protect against trusts), food and drugs (to assure purity and safeness of use), and sales and advertising (to protect against fraud). The offenders typically have high status in their corporations and regard the offenses as being necessary for business. This attitude is often supported by others in business.

(9) *Organized criminal behavior.* This behavior violates traditional laws against gambling, prostitution, and the like, as well as more recently enacted statutes opposing organized crime. The perpetrators have a well-developed criminal self-concept and pursue crime as a career. They are supported by the structure of organized crime, and although condemned by society at large, their acquisitive behavior is consistent with many American values.

Clinard and Quinney describe these nine types in considerable detail and summarize the research on each pattern. If one is interested in how different sorts of criminals operate and relate to society at large, their taxonomy is illuminating and valuable. However, there are few insights as to how one might cope with these patterns. There are no prescriptions for the differential treatment that should be afforded the conventional criminal as opposed to the professional, or the occupational offender as distinguished from the corporate. There is also little indication of the origin of these patterns, so it would be difficult to use them as a guide to prevention. Moreover, when one attempts to classify an individual offender, problems quickly arise because many offenders stubbornly refuse to confine their behavior to a single pattern.

Sociological Typologies

The three systems to be reviewed here are only meant to represent the large number of sociological classificatory schemes that have been proposed over the decades. An entire book would be required simply to review the full array of systems, much less to evaluate them. It will be seen that social structure plays a more prominent role in these schemes, and hypotheses as to the origin of these patterns are often made. These systems also reflect more of a traditional "establishment" point of view, focusing as they do on lower-class patterns, with less of Clinard and Quinney's emphasis on white-collar patterns.

Cloward and Ohlin's Typology.   Whereas offense-based systems are typically devoid of causal explanations, Cloward and Ohlin's (1960) tripartite division of juvenile delinquents stems directly from an integration of two theoretical explanations of the origin of delinquent behavior: Merton's social conflict theory and Sutherland's differential-association explanation.

Just as legitimate achievement depends on having the adequate skills and good connections, so too does illegitimate success. If a boy has the "good fortune" to live in an area where crime is prevalent and he makes a good impression on the neighborhood pimp or pusher, he may get a chance for part-time employment. If he has the necessary skills, this may lead to bigger and better things as he works his way up in the organization, fulfilling many of the elements of the American dream, which, in large measure, he shares. It is this pattern that leads to what Cloward and Ohlin termed the *criminal orientation,* a category that conforms most closely to Clinard and Quinney's "organized" and "professional" criminal patterns and also overlaps to some extent with their "conventional" criminal pattern.

But what if illegitimate opportunities are as scarce as legitimate ones? Or what if the youth is given a chance and found wanting? According to Cloward and Ohlin:

> Those adolescents in disorganized urban areas who are oriented toward achieving higher position but are cut off from institutionalized channels, criminal as well as legitimate, must rely on their own resources for solving this problem of adjustment. Under these circumstances, tendencies toward aberrant behavior become intensified and magnified. The

adolescents seize upon the manipulation of violence as a route to status not only because it provides a way of expressing pent-up angers and frustrations, but also because they are not cut off from access to violent means by vicissitudes of birth (1960, p. 175).

Thus a lack of access to both legitimate and illegitimate means leads, according to Cloward and Ohlin's analysis, to a pattern of violence that they term the *conflict orientation.*

Status, however, is a scarce commodity, and some lower-class adolescents are unable to achieve it by any means, legitimate, illegitimate, or violent. Some may revise their aspirations downwards, but according to Cloward and Ohlin, those who are unable to do so blame their own personal inadequacies and shortcomings for their chronic failure. In such a situation the individual may gain a *retreatist orientation,* joining a subculture in which social rejects tune out and turn on to drugs.

Thus, according to Cloward and Ohlin's analysis, three distinct subcultures—criminal, conflict, and retreatist—emerge from differential opportunities and access to legitimate and illegitimate avenues to success. The implication is that the provision of adequate opportunities to realize aspirations would be effective in preventing the development of these patterns. Moreover, providing potential delinquents with criminal associates by locking them up with older delinquents in a training school would appear to be conducive to the development of criminal patterns.

Ferdinand's Social Typology.   In formulating his system, Theodore Ferdinand (1966) considered the social structure of the delinquent group, the degree of alienation from the community as a whole, and the socioeconomic status of the delinquent individuals, along with the pattern of delinquent behavior resulting from the interaction of these factors.

The result was a typology delineating six distinctive patterns of social types:

(1) *Mischievous-Indulgent.* This group consists of hedonistic upper-class youths, weakly organized in terms of structure, who are somewhat alienated from more conventional peers and adults. They indulge their appetites but do so with style and taste.

(2) *Aggressive-Exploitative*. These lower-upper-class and upper-middle-class youths are well organized into clubs and gangs. Their delinquent activities, which consist mainly of proving themselves by competing in sports, drinking, and sexual exploits, rarely come to the attention of adults, and they are only minimally alienated from the community.

(3) *Criminal*. These loosely organized upper-lower-class and upwardly mobile lower-lower-class youths are apprentices in crime, learning the skills and techniques of adult criminals in the community.

(4) *Fighting*. Rejected by and alienated from the community, these upper-lower-class and upwardly mobile lower-lower-class youths are tightly organized into closely knit gangs with a formal hierarchical structure. Their major emphasis is on conflict and development of warrior skills.

(5) *Theft*. This group, which is also made up of upper-lower-class and upwardly mobile lower-class youths, engages in hedonistic behaviors including stealing for excitement, vandalism toward schools, and other forms of appetite indulgence. Loosely organized according to friendship cliques, they can be assaultive when challenged. They are not seriously alienated from or rejected by the immediate community.

(6) *Disorganized Acting-out*. This type, according to Ferdinand, is found in the lower-lower-class. The behavior consists of impulsive aggression, theft, and use of narcotics for hedonism rather than escape. The general orientation is toward immediate need-gratification. The social structure is so loose as to be virtually nonexistent, and the behavior is not easily differentiated from the normal adult patterns found in this class.

Thus it can be seen that Ferdinand's social typology incorporates many of the elements of Cloward and Ohlin's but expands their system to include lower-lower-class and upper-middle-class patterns.

Gibbons' Typology. Don Gibbons (1965) constructed a system that some regard as the most inclusive ever devised by a sociologist (Caldwell & Black, 1971). This scheme, describing role-career patterns, incorporates offense data, background variables, self-image and attitudes, and the interracial setting. Nine categories result.

(1) *The predatory gang delinquent.* Coming from a lower-class background with inadequate parental care and exposed early to delinquent models, this individual has extensive contacts with police and courts because of repeated thefts of a serious nature. His antisocial attitudes and delinquent self-image are reinforced by delinquent friends.

(2) *The conflict gang delinquent.* This lower-class, urban, male member of a violent gang thinks himself "tough" rather than criminal and regards society with cynicism rather than hostility.

(3) *The casual gang delinquent.* Although he engages in many delinquent activities with his peers, this working-class youth regards himself as a nondelinquent who likes to have fun. His parents are conventional and concerned, and he generally has only infrequent contacts with the criminal justice system.

(4) *The casual nongang delinquent.* This middle-class youth who has few contacts with police thinks of himself as being nondelinquent. His associates have a similar self-image and are regarded as nondelinquent by adults. He takes part in relatively few transgressions, and those he does commit are of a minor nature.

(5) *The auto-thief joyrider.* Coming from a well-integrated, middle-class family with a good discipline and supervision, his delinquency consists of stealing cars with his friends to have fun and to demonstrate that he is tough.

(6) *The heroin user.* This lower-class slum dweller with a conventional family background associates almost exclusively with a drug-using subculture. He regards himself not as a delinquent but as a persecuted addict and has many contacts with police and courts.

(7) *The overly aggressive delinquent.* This type engages in meaningless solitary assaults on peers and occasional adults. Severely rejected by his parents and having few, if any, close friends, he regards himself as the victim of society's hostility rather than as a delinquent. This individual, who may be the product of any social class, typically has numerous contacts with the criminal justice system.

(8) *The female delinquent*. Delinquent girls are usually involved in sexual behavior, which is often a manifestation of their hostility toward one or both parents and other authorities. Not restricted to any social class, these girls typically come from tense homes and have numerous contacts with the criminal justice system.

(9) *The "behavior problem" delinquent*. This type, who is a lone wolf, has conventional attitudes toward society and commits few offenses. He comes from any class, and his family situation is often unusual. The offenses he does commit are bizarre and often quite serious.

Psychiatric Typologies

Whereas sociology is primarily concerned with group phenomena and social variables, psychiatry and psychology focus on the individual. Moreover, whereas sociology is an academic discipline, psychiatrists and clinical psychologists are actively involved in the application of their findings to prevention and treatment.

There is a popular misconception that mental health professionals regard all criminals as being "sick" or "disturbed." As we shall see, this is a false impression. Criminal behavior is first and foremost *human* behavior, and the full range of human traits and foibles can be found among those who engage in crime. Criminals are no more immune to psychoses, neuroses, and behavior disorders than anyone else. If a criminal is disturbed, it is possible that his neurosis or psychosis plays a role in his criminal behavior, just as a student or professor's psychological problems can influence his scholarly activity. Since it is the disturbed criminals who are typically referred to psychiatrists and psychologists, it is natural that these professions should be particularly concerned with the problems posed by the disturbed offender. However, this does not mean that most mental health professionals regard psychological disorders as the only, or even the major, cause of crime.

Psychoanalytic Formulations

Psychoanalysts were among the first behavioral scientists to turn their attention to criminal behavior. They were especially interested in the extent to which neuroses in general and unconscious sexual conflicts in particular, might cause criminal behavior.

Abrahamsen's Typology. Abrahamsen (1960) distinguishes between *acute* and *chronic* criminals. Acute or momentary offenders are those who only commit an occasional offense under situational circumstances that are strongly conducive to crime. Their criminal behavior is only transitory, and because they have normal personality structures, they typically feel guilty and remorseful after the act. Acute offenders include *situational offenders*, who have been subjected to strong provocation or temptation, *associational offenders*, who identify with a family or peer group with strong criminal tendencies (as in Sutherland's differential association theory), and *accidental offenders*, who commit a crime through chance or mistake (as in the case of a hit-and-run driver).

Abrahamsen regards chronic or habitual offenders as being quite different from the acute because their deviant personality structures lead them to engage repeatedly in criminal activity. Abrahamsen divides chronic offenders into three subgroups: "(1) neurotic offenders, (2) offenders with neurotic character disorders and genuine psychopathic offenders, and (3) psychotic and mentally defective offenders" (1960, p. 127). The *neurotic offender's* criminal activity is contrary to his values (or, in analytic terminology, *ego-alien*). His inability to refrain from wrong-doing generates considerable anxiety and guilt. The offender with a *character disorder*, on the other hand, sees nothing wrong with his behavior. The *psychotic* or *mentally defective offender's* personality structure is so impaired by functional, organic, or toxic factors that he is unable to appreciate what he is doing or the fact that it is wrong.

These three types of chronic offenders suggest that Abrahamsen regards all habitual criminal behavior as being associated with some type of psychiatric disorder. According to Ferdinand (1966, p. 162), however, Abrahamsen also delineates in one of his works a fourth type that Ferdinand refers to as the *cultural delinquent*. This is an essentially normal individual who has grown up in and identified with a criminal way of life. This last type receives scant attention in the bulk of Abrahamsen's writings.

It can be seen that there are rather clear-cut treatment implications associated with this typological system. Acute offenders need little, if any, treatment aimed at inducing personality change. For the associational subtype, some form of foster home might be appropriate. The neurotic requires psychoanalytically oriented psychotherapy in Abrahamsen's opinion, whereas the psychotic would probably require psychiatric hospitalization.

Alexander and Staub's Typology. The psychoanalytic typological system advanced by Franz Alexander and Hugo Staub (1956) is similar to Abrahamsen's in many respects. They too divide their offenders into the acute and the chronic. Included in the acute category are *situational criminals,* whose impulsive offenses arise from some intense crisis, and *mistaken* or *accidental offenders,* who blunder into committing a criminal act by chance, as in the case of manslaughter.

In contrast with the acute offenders are the chronic criminals whose criminal behavior stems from basic personality characteristics. Alexander and Staub differentiate four types of chronic offenders. The *pathological criminal's* deviance stems from impairment of the central nervous system as a result of organic disease or toxic substances. Next is the *neurotic criminal,* with two subtypes: the *compulsive or symptomatic offender,* who engages in criminal acts that are alien to his otherwise normal values, and the *acting-out neurotic offender,* whose ego controls are overwhelmed by id impulses and who may be seeking punishment for unconscious guilt feelings.

The pathological and neurotic types' criminal acts are symptoms of their psychopathology. But there is no notable psychopathology in the final type of chronic offender. This is the *normal criminal,* who as a result of his association with other criminals has incorporated these deviant behavior patterns.

Psychiatric Nosology and Criminal Behavior
Psychiatry is a branch of medicine, and psychiatrists naturally follow the medical model of attempting to delineate homogeneous syndromes that might share a common etiology or respond to a similar course of treatment. This has resulted in a comprehensive nosological system for describing all the many people who might consult a psychiatrist.

It has been pointed out that there is no one-to-one correspondence between psychiatric disturbances and criminal behavior. Some types of mental disorders, however, are particularly likely to be associated with behavior patterns that have been outlawed by society. This includes sexual deviations such as exhibitionism and pedophilia and addiction to the use of illegal drugs. Brain impairments resulting from diseases such as syphilis or encephalitis, from the ingestion of toxic substances such as bromides or alcohol, or from injuries such as concussions, often result in impaired judgment, decreased frustration tolerance, and irritability. Patients with such disorders may be arrested for joyriding, aggravated assault, and even murder, as well as for violation of specific ordinances against public drunkenness or driving while intoxicated. Psychotic individuals typically lack adequate ego controls. In many cases this involves withdrawals into a fantasy world, but for some, such as paranoids, delusional patterns result that can lead to aggressive behavior. Psychotic depressions can result in suicide, sometimes preceded by homicide.

Whereas some mental disorders are conducive to illegal behavior, psychiatry has also delineated syndromes involving patterns of antisocial behavior or chronic conflicts with the law in the absence of any other demonstrable psychopathology. These include illegal behavior in response to stressful life circumstances, such as a prisoner of war who violates the code of military conduct by giving information to the enemy or the child who runs away from home after getting failing grades at school. Individuals who have learned a delinquent or criminal lifestyle by growing up in an atypical environment would also fall into this category.

For the criminologist, the most interesting psychiatric syndrome is the *psychopathic personality*, also referred to as the *antisocial personality* and the *sociopathic personality, antisocial type*. The psychopath is an excellent example of how the formation of syndromes leads to progress in the understanding of crime and delinquency.

The psychopath has been defined as " . . . an asocial, aggressive, highly impulsive person who feels little or no guilt, and is unable to form lasting bonds of affection with other human beings" (McCord & McCord, 1964, p. 3). This pattern of persistent, inadequately motivated, self-defeating, antisocial behavior occurs in bright individuals who lack the symptoms of such mental disorders as neuroses or psychoses. Indeed their *lack* of appropriate anxiety and guilt is their most distinguishing feature. Unable to accept blame, they never seem to learn from experience and continually repeat their mistakes.

The causes and treatment of psychopathy are still subjects of active debate and research. This behaviorally homogeneous group has been found to share distinctive family histories, patterns of autonomic responsivity, and deficits in avoidance conditioning. These observations have given rise to explanatory theories that in turn have suggested ways that the disorder might be prevented or treated. Research is currently proceeding to test these theories and treatment techniques.

The present writer feels that this syndrome approach is more likely to produce both short-term and long-term advances than are efforts to construct global taxonomies. It is unlikely to yield causal explanations for, or ways of coping with, *all* offenders, but it is more apt to promote rigorous research and valid answers about those characteristics that can be grouped into specific syndromes.

Psychological Typologies

Psychology integrates basic science and professional practice in a single discipline. This dual orientation is reflected in the typological systems that have been proposed by psychologists. As with the sociological typologies, there is an attempt to integrate the classification system with general theories of behavior. Moreover, psychologists attempt to validate the existence of their types by using them to formulate hypotheses and make predictions that can be empirically tested. Psychologists also share the psychiatrists' concern with applications and with treatment. But these treatment suggestions are also regarded as hypotheses that should be subjected to empirical testing and refinement.

Megargee's Typology of Assaultive Offenders.   Megargee (1966) suggests that assaultive offenders can be divided into at least two distinct types: (1) the *undercontrolled* or habitually aggressive individual with minimal inhibitions who acts out anger, hostility, or aggression on the slightest provocation, and (2) the *chronically overcontrolled* individual with excessive inhibitions who avoids expressing anger, hostility, or aggression at all costs.

Megargee explains the paradoxical assaultiveness of the overcontrolled type by suggesting that in the face of repeated provocation and frustration, aggressive instigation slowly accumulates through a process of temporal summation until in some cases it eventually overwhelms even the overcontrolled individual's massive defenses against aggressive behavior. At this point the resulting act is apt to be one of extreme, even homicidal, violence.

A number of investigations tend to bear out this hypothesis. Megargee, Patrick Cook, and Gerald Mendelsohn (1967) have devised a scale for the widely used Minnesota Multiphasic Personality Inventory (MMPI), to aid in the identification of the chronically overcontrolled type. This scale, called the *Overcontrolled Hostility (O-H) Scale,* has been subjected to a number of validation studies. Although the *O-H* scale is a useful aid in differentiating overcontrolled from undercontrolled assaultive offenders, it should be used in conjunction with case history data for accurate diagnosis (Haven, 1972).

Megargee and others who have studied this dimension have suggested quite different treatment strategies for the two types. Whereas undercontrolled assaultive offenders must learn to curb their habitual aggressiveness, overcontrolled individuals must be taught how to express their hostility in constructive ways that will help them to create a less frustrating milieu (Megargee, 1966). No systematic research has yet been done, however, to determine the effectiveness of these differential treatment strategies.

Whereas Megargee's research on overcontrolled and undercontrolled assaultive types represents a search for specific syndromes, the approaches we shall now turn to exemplify complete typological systems. Since they share a concern with delinquency prevention and treatment, though, they are pragmatic systems, designed to be used rather than merely admired.

Warren's Interpersonal Maturity Level Approach. Marguerite Warren and her colleagues have devised one of the most comprehensive and complex approaches to classification and treatment for the California Youth Authority. Their primary emphasis has been on developing differential treatment strategies to be used with different types of juvenile offenders.

Their system of offender classification rests upon the theory that individuals progress through seven successive stages of interpersonal maturity in the normal course of development. These stages extend from the completely immature newborn infant to a theoretical ideal of maturity that is only rarely, if ever, attained. At each stage certain crucial interpersonal problems must be coped with and resolved before the individual is able to progress to the next level (Sullivan, Grant, & Grant, 1957). Since not everyone is able to work through all the stages, some become fixated at various levels of development. According to this theory, the typical delinquent becomes stalled at a relatively immature developmental level. The exact characteristics and needs of the delinquent depend upon the level attained. Warren (1966, 1969) holds that most juvenile delinquents are to be found in levels two through four.

Although delinquents at any given level share important characteristics that set them off from those at other levels, there are important differences within levels that must be considered in prescribing differential treatment (Warren, 1966, 1969).

Discussions of treatment techniques too often focus on the tactics to be employed with specific syndromes and neglect such important issues as the personality characteristics of the change agent and the setting in which the treatment is to be conducted. Warren and her associates considered all these factors and classified treatment personnel and settings as well as delinquents. The outcome was a set of hypotheses that a particular subtype of delinquent should be in a certain type of setting (community, institution, etc.) working with a certain type of change agent (sympathetic, stern, etc.) who uses a particular treatment approach (supportive, confronting, etc.).

Research on the effectiveness of these differential treatment strategies has been an integral aspect of the program from the outset. However, even those readers unsophisticated in research methodology can appreciate the immensity of the evaluation task. It would take several lifetimes to test the effectiveness of several types of treatment, by several types of change agents, in several settings, for each of nine offender types.

Quay's Dimensions of Deviance.   Whereas Warren's system is rooted in a particular personality theory, Herbert Quay's (1970) approach to classification and treatment has an empirical basis and relies heavily on the statistical technique of factor analysis. Applied to the phenomenon of juvenile delinquency, his method can be used to help reveal dimensions underlying delinquent behavior and then to identify relatively homogeneous groups of delinquents. With this knowledge, the psychologist is able to devise different treatment strategies for each group. Prior to Quay's investigations, Lester Hewitt and Richard Jenkins (1946) and Jenkins and Sylvia Glickman (1947) had applied correlational techniques to lists of descriptive phrases culled from the case records of adjudicated delinquents and children referred to a child guidance clinic. Among the child guidance cases, they reported that the intercorrelations suggested the existence of three syndromes that they labeled *unsocialized aggressive, socialized delinquent,* and *overinhibited.* The adjudicated delinquents were also found to exhibit the unsocialized aggressive and socialized delinquent syndromes, but in place of the overinhibited category they found a pattern they preferred to label *disturbed.*

Quay replicated and extended these studies using factor analytic methods. He reported: "Factor analysis revealed that three factors, labeled 'unsocialized-psychopathic,' 'neurotic-disturbed,' and 'sub-cultural-socialized,' accounted for most of the variance. A fourth factor, called 'incompetent-immature,' was also found although it accounted for little of the variance" (1965, p. 154).

In a series of studies, Quay and his colleagues have explored and refined these dimensions and devised three objective and reliable instruments to assist in classifying individual delinquents according to their predominant mode. One instrument called the "Behavior Problem Checklist" (Quay & Peterson, 1967) is designed to be used by individuals who have had an opportunity to observe a child and note his characteristic behavior patterns. It can be used by teachers, parents, mental health professionals, and institutional personnel.

Quay and Peterson also devised a checklist to be used in analyzing the sorts of life history data that are typically found in case records. In addition, a 100-item true-false questionnaire, the Quay and Peterson Personal Opinion Study, was constructed to be responded to by the individual being classified.

These three instruments are each scored on three or four of the behavioral dimensions and the scores are combined to classify the individual into one of the four behavior categories based on their primary dimension of deviance.

The goal of this multidimensional behavioral classification system was to assist in the differential management and treatment of delinquent youths. Quay, along with Roy Gerard, Robert Levinson, Gilbert Ingram, and others, hypothesized the optimal way to treat youths falling into each of these four behavior categories. A number of these hypotheses were tested and refined at the United States Bureau of Prisons' National Training School for Boys in Washington, D.C. When the bureau opened the Robert F. Kennedy Youth Center at Morgantown, West Virginia, the institutional facilities and programs were designed so as to provide differential treatment based on the Quay system (Bureau of Prisons, 1970; Gerard, 1970; Quay & Parsons, 1970).

TREATMENT AND PREVENTION OF CRIME AND DELINQUENCY

Historical Patterns

Nothing reveals a social group's values and organization better than its treatment of those who violate its rules and mores. Over the centuries, as societies have grown more complex and man—for better or worse—has become more "civilized," the response toward criminals has changed, but not always as much or in the manner that everyone would like.

Response to Crime in Simple Nonliterate Societies. In simple preliterate societies, only acts that threaten the collective group *as a group* are considered "crimes" in the sense in which we have been using the word. Such acts include treason, misappropriation of communal property, witchcraft, or impious acts that might provoke the gods. Those who engage in such behavior are considered enemies of the tribe and are treated like any other enemies, being run off or put to death (Sutherland & Cressey, 1966).

Offenses against individuals, such as personal attack or theft of private property, are dealt with by the victims and their immediate families. This often leads to interfamilial blood feuds with each side seeking to inflict vengeance and suffering on the other. Such feuds are essentially private, with the rest of the social group acting as neutral bystanders. Similarly, when members of a family transgress against one another, the rest of the social group lets the family work the matter out for themselves.

Response to Crime in Complex Societies

PREVENTION OF RECIDIVISM. In the kingship period, which includes most of man's recorded history, " . . . disposition of wrongdoers became a public matter. The 'court' arose and was backed by the central authority. The reaction approached the punitive reaction as we now know it, for severe corporal punishments were inflicted by the group, but the notion that the pain imposed by the group has some value in itself was not necessarily present" (Sutherland & Cressey, 1966, p. 311).

Two dominant motives governed the response to crime: the desire to prevent recurrence and the thirst for retribution. The surest way to prevent recidivism is to eliminate the culprit, and many criminals accordingly were banished or put to death. Other early measures included mutilation and imprisonment. A thief's hand might be cut off to make it more difficult for him to steal in the future, or his forehead might be branded as a warning to potential victims.

As we can see from Old Testament accounts of the imprisonment of Samson, Daniel, Jeremiah, and Joseph, confinement has long been used, but in early times the primary motive was to remove the prisoner from society temporarily rather than to punish him (Caldwell, 1965).[2] According to Edwin Sutherland and Donald Cressey (1966, p. 310), the theory that the suffering involved in mutilation or confinement might lead the criminal to reform or might deter others from similar actions is relatively recent.

RETRIBUTION. However strong the goal of preventing recidivism, it has been inextricably mixed with a desire for retribution. Victims have craved revenge since man's earliest history, and centuries of civilization have had little impact on this aspect of human nature. Nowhere is the craving for vengeance clearer than in the ways man has executed offenders. Death alone would prevent recidivism, but, as Robert Caldwell has pointed out: " . . . it appears that men have exhausted their ingenuity in the destruction of the condemned criminal. . . . [M]ere killing has not always satisfied men's thirst for vengeance, so sometimes, as a hideous prelude to death, they have added the most fiendish and excruciating torture" (1965, p. 439).

Physical torture was not the only means of redressing a wrong. Often the offender was required to replace stolen property or compensate his victim in some fashion for the injuries he had suffered.³ In simple societies the victims or their families sought redress directly. As kings arose, they took over the general administration of justice in the areas they ruled. Pecuniary punishment continued to be used, but instead of compensating the victim, the funds went into the royal coffers. Fines and confiscated property thus became important sources of royal revenue.

Princes brought prisons, and no castle was complete without its dungeon. With the administration of justice reserved for the lord or seigneur, it was necessary to wait until the ruler or his representative appeared before an offense could be adjudicated. This took months, sometimes years, and prisons were used to confine the alleged malefactors until such time as justice could be meted out. Prisons were also used to confine those unwilling or unable to pay their fines or other debts. In essence, the debtor was held as a hostage rather than imprisoned as punishment.

The correctional literature is replete with accounts of deplorable conditions in these early institutions. Some writers have likened them to stables or kennels, but this analogy is inaccurate. In a kennel, dogs are provided with food, water, opportunities for exercise, and medical attention, and arrangements are made for the removal of body wastes. None of these conditions were to be found in early prisons. Moreover, in a kennel vicious animals are prevented from preying on the others, puppies are kept apart from adult dogs, and the animals are segregated by sex so that uncontrolled breeding does not occur. Not so in the jails. It is likely that most of those unfortunates confined in bridewells or the hulks during the eighteenth and even the nineteenth century would gladly have traded their lot for that of a foxhound in a nobleman's kennel.

DETERRENCE.   We can infer from history that even in early times men inflicted pain on offenders not simply for revenge but also to deter others from committing similar offenses. In 71 B.C., when Pompey captured 6,000 rebellious slaves who had followed Spartacus and plundered southern Italy, he could easily have wreaked vengeance and disposed of the rebels by having his legions put them to the sword. Instead he chose to crucify his captives all along his line of march from Capua to Rome. When one reflects upon the logistics and effort involved in guarding the prisoners, securing the necessary timber, and constructing and erecting 6,000 crosses, it is clear that Pompey would not have chosen such a dramatic and public form of execution if he had not believed that it would serve to deter every slave in Imperial Rome from emulating Spartacus.

REFORMATION OF THE CRIMINAL. The New Testament emphasized the redemption and rehabilitation of the sinner, and during the Middle Ages these motives were used to justify the punishments inflicted by the Church. "Vengeance is mine," the Lord has been quoted as saying, so during the Inquisition "heretics," such as Joan of Arc, were burned at the stake not to punish them but instead to induce them to renounce Satan so their souls could depart their bodies in a state of grace.

Only heretics and non-Christians could be executed by the Church, so, in contrast to the state, the medieval Church frequently resorted to imprisonment. Early records indicate that imprisonment, too, was aimed at inducing the offender to reform. For example, one "Brother John," who in 1283 ill-advisedly bit his prior on the finger, was ordered by his bishop to be kept " . . . in prison under iron chains in which he shall be content with bread, indifferent ale, pottage, and a pittance of meat or fish (which on the sixth day he shall do without) *until he is penitent*" (Ives, 1914, p. 44, quoted by Sutherland & Cressey, 1966, p. 324; italics supplied by present writer).

However, the state's response to criminal behavior continued to be governed by the traditional considerations of deterrence and retribution. The use of capital punishment and torture waxed and waned over the centuries. In England there were seventeen capital offenses in the early fifteenth century, about 350 in the late eighteenth century, and less than twenty again by the mid-nineteenth century (Sutherland & Cressey, 1966, p. 314ff.). During some periods, utilitarian considerations such as the need for able-bodied men to row the galleys or populate distant colonies dominated the methods used to cope with criminals.

Modern Methods of Dealing with Criminal Behavior

Punishment and Imprisonment. In the nineteenth and twentieth centuries there has been increasing concern over the rehabilitation of the criminal. This goal has been specifically embodied in many criminal codes. Although punitive techniques have persisted, their use is now justified by their alleged efficacy in reforming the offender and deterring others.

Although, as we have seen, reformation of the criminal had been a prime motive for the Church for centuries, it was the writings of such Rationalist philosophers as Voltaire, Rousseau, and Montesquieu that led to the use of punishment as an instrument of rehabilitation. They maintained that man is a rational creature who behaves in such a way as to receive the maximum pleasure for the minimum pain. Based on this principle, Cesare Beccaria, the founder of the so-called "Classical School" of criminology, suggested that for each criminal act the pleasure derived from it should be calculated and a definite penalty assigned to it such that the pain would just exceed the pleasure. This would deter the potential criminal from performing the act (Vold, 1958; Sutherland & Cressey, 1966). Indeed, Jeremy Bentham attempted to work out mathematical equations for the infliction of just the right amount of punishment.

The effectiveness of punishment depends not only on its severity but also on its certainty and swiftness. No matter how severe the penalty, it will never be an effective deterrent if most criminals are confident that they will never be punished or if the imposition of the punishment is in the remote future. Beccaria sought certainty by maintaining that fixed punishments should be levied on every offender without exception, no matter what that person's station in life.

After the French Revolution, Beccaria's proposals became the basis for the French Code of 1791. This code proved too inflexible, and it was soon modified to allow special treatment for lunatics, who could not be considered rational individuals, and young children. Moreover, it became recognized that some provision should be made for mitigating circumstances, thus opening the door to a consideration of the psychological and sociological context of the crime in determining punishment. This "neoclassical" position became the basis for the criminal justice system in Western society (Sutherland & Cressey, 1966).

Throughout the eighteenth and nineteenth centuries, punishment was still the modal response to crime, although, as already noted, the use of capital punishment and exile declined. For minor offenses public humiliation and degradation were often employed. Sometimes these involved "poetic punishments": A fishmonger convicted of selling spoiled smelts was paraded through the streets with his rotten wares draped around his neck; the "brank" or "dames' bridle" that immobilized the tongue was placed on the head of those found to be gossips or scolds (Caldwell, 1965). Many an offender was required to wear the initials of his offense affixed to his clothing (as in *The Scarlet Letter*) or branded on his body. Fines and restitution continued to be imposed, with those unable to pay being imprisoned.

As humanitarian concerns for the lot of convicted criminals increased and the use of corporal and capital punishment decreased, imprisonment came to be regarded as the best method of coping with crime. Imprisonment would offset the rewards of crime. During this enforced sabbatical the culprit would, according to the Rationalists, decide that criminal behavior was irrational and resolve to abandon it. In the interim, society would be protected from the criminal's depredations, his example would deter others, and the punishment would satisfy the public's thirst for retribution. Thus it seemed that prison would meet every social goal simultaneously.

Unfortunately, the multiplicity of objectives that made imprisonment seem so attractive to eighteenth and nineteenth century reformers today appears to be its chief drawback. The fact that society expects a prison to accomplish so many goals virtually ensures that it cannot succeed at all of them; indeed, the more an institution attempts to meet *every* societal expectation, the more it seems to fail to meet *any*. The first goal is protection of the public from the prisoners and of the inmates from one another. This goal requires tight security to make it difficult for the inmates to get out or for contraband to get in. Constant surveillance must be maintained, along with frequent shakedowns for weapons, drugs, and other prohibited articles. The officers must be watchful and wary, alert for the slightest hint of potential trouble and ready to move swiftly against anyone who seems to be a potential threat. Unfortunately, an attitude of suspicion and distrust is not conducive to the growth of personal maturity among the inmates. Moreover, the staff's expectation that all inmates are potentially dangerous seems to be a self-fulfilling prophecy. As the interactionist or labeling school of sociologists would predict, treating inmates as if they were constantly plotting escapes or rebellions fosters an atmosphere in which the inmates do in fact plot escapes and rebellions.

A better atmosphere for treatment is fostered by an attitude of mutual trust and respect. Work-release and study-release programs, for example, allow inmates to obtain on-the-job training or to take courses that are unavailable in the institution. They are trusted to behave themselves and return to the prison at night. Of course, to foster such an atmosphere and have such programs, it is necessary to sacrifice some of the external security and social segregation. But as Tom Runyon, who served twenty years before he died in prison, observed: "Each time needless discipline has been relaxed, each time they have been allowed to relax and respect themselves, I've seen men in this prison become better prisoners and better risks as ex-convicts. Each time I've seen men really trusted—not partly trusted, as on prison farms in other places with guards near—I've seen them try to deserve that trust" (Runyon, 1965).

Unfortunately, not every inmate accepts this responsibility, and it often takes only a few well-publicized failures—perhaps one rape by a study-release inmate—to destroy a program that may have benefited hundreds.

Similarly, to achieve retribution or deterrence, the prison should be as aversive as possible. However, if the staff is defined as the inmates' enemy and there are no rewards for appropriate behavior, the goals of retribution and rehabilitation are at odds. As many have pointed out, people should be sent to prison *as* punishment and not *for* punishment; nevertheless, the public is inclined to regard an institution with good facilities for education and recreation as a "country club."

Whereas the Classical and Neoclassical schools had emphasized man's rationality, the Positivist school had a much more mechanistic view of the nature of man. Founded by Lombroso in the late nineteenth century, the Positivist school reflects the movement away from the belief in man as a supremely rational being that followed the publication of Darwin's theory of evolution and that later received impetus from the works of Freud. Whereas the Classical school had maintained that the courts should focus on the offense and prescribe sentences only on the basis of the crime, the Positivist school maintained that the criminal and the circumstances that led to the crime should be the primary considerations, with the judge deciding what program would best meet the offender's particular needs.

Positivists have a jaundiced view of the effects of imprisonment.

They and their intellectual descendents argue that locking someone up and expecting that person to emerge reformed makes as much sense as locking an automobile with a faulty carburetor in the garage for a month and expecting it to start up immediately when it is finally used once again. The auto, like the inmate, would be more likely to deteriorate than improve under such circumstances.

Modern penologists agree that simply locking up a man or woman is likely to do that individual more harm than good. The effectiveness of a penal institution depends on what is done with and for the inmate during the period of incarceration. If positive rehabilitation does not take place, a penal institution can be a school for crime, an advanced education in criminal skills and techniques. It can be a retreat from the world in which a person unable to cope with life's demands finds refuge. It can be a breeding ground for hatred and alienation. Many emerge from prison more firmly committed to a life of crime than when they entered.

Although a prison sentence may retard some individuals' rehabilitation, society still demands the imprisonment of criminals, even though they may not pose a threat to the community. As mentioned earlier, imprisonment is seen by society to provide retribution and deterrence ("making an example"), two functions held to be more important than the competitive function of rehabilitation. For retribution, convicted criminals are thus segregated from society as a whole. Such segregation often works to the society's disadvantage, for it becomes extremely difficult for the 95 percent of imprisoned criminals who are eventually released from prison to resume useful places in society. Nevertheless, in the interim the public feels safer since the criminals are caged.

It is also questionable whether imprisonment really fulfills the function of deterrence as is generally supposed. Given the low apprehension and conviction rates, it is unlikely that many people are actually deterred from crime by the prospect of imprisonment. Tom Runyon, whose five-year bank robbery career was ended by a life sentence in 1937, recalled, "In a vague kind of way I felt sorry for convicts when I drove past a prison, but that was about the only time I thought of them" (1965, p. 637).

Instead of deterring would-be criminals, the present writer suspects that the punishment of lawbreakers serves more to reinforce noncriminals for their conformity. Who does not feel smug when seeing the speeder who roared past a moment before getting that richly deserved ticket? What scrupulous taxpayer does not want the Internal Revenue Service to punish the wealthy individual who has avoided paying income taxes? Whenever we see someone punished for something we refrained from doing, it reinforces us for being moral. On the other hand, the morale of a society suffers when it seems that some people are getting away with behavior that many regard as wrong.

Although imprisonment in and of itself seems to serve the ends of retribution and social solidarity more than the goal of rehabilitation, rehabilitative programs in prison settings can have a significant impact on many individuals. Merton suggested that many turn to crime because they lack the skills to achieve in socially legitimate ways. Educational and vocational training programs can change this. An individual who might never have had the opportunity to obtain a high school diploma or a college degree can earn both in many institutions. While schools in the community must gear themselves to the average student and work on a fixed schedule, correctional educational programs can move at the pace that is best for the individual inmate. In institutions with an industries program, inmates cannot only learn a skill but earn enough money to give them a good start after leaving. Prison art programs provide a spectacular example of the positive effects of acquiring a skill. Some inmates have discovered talents they had never suspected, achieved a following, and earned thousands of dollars from art sales while in the institution. With all this going for them when they leave, it would be surprising if they returned to holding up liquor stores or hotwiring cars.

Although not all criminality stems from psychopathology, there is no doubt that many criminals are disturbed and that this disturbance contributed to their offense. Through individual and group psychotherapy and counseling many of these problems can be resolved.

In the earlier sections of this chapter, it was noted how global conceptions of crime and delinquency have given way to the typological approach. In contemporary corrections it is recognized that criminals differ from one another and that a variety of approaches are required. One current trend is toward dividing the institution into relatively homogeneous subgroups and providing each with the program best suited to its needs.

It can be seen, therefore, that although imprisonment per se does not rehabilitate many individuals, programs provided in a prison setting can have a significant impact. Unfortunately the caliber of the educational, recreational, and therapeutic programs available at many institutions ranges from "inadequate" to "nonexistent." Thus, although rehabilitation is possible in institutional settings, some twentieth-century institutions still exist solely to serve the seventeenth-century goals of restraint and revenge.

Alternatives to Imprisonment. Confinement without effective programming is particularly deleterious for juvenile delinquents whose character and personality are still being molded, for better or for worse. The Commonwealth of Massachusetts recently surveyed its juvenile training-school system and concluded that it did more harm than good and failed to achieve anything more than custodial goals. As mentioned previously, Commissioner Jerome Miller decided in 1969 on the simple but radical answer of closing all the training schools. (See discussion on p. 40.)

More recently, the National Advisory Commission on Criminal Justice Standards and Goals went a step further and recommended:

> Each correctional agency administering State institutions for juvenile or adult offenders should adopt immediately a policy of not building new major institutions for juveniles under any circumstances, and not building new institutions for adults, unless an analysis of the total criminal justice and adult corrections systems produces a clear finding that no alternative is possible (1973, p. 357).

Many criminologists, including the present writer, disagree with this recommendation—feeling that legislatures will simply use it as an excuse to continue in their failure to provide adequate facilities for prisoners and build smaller minimum security institutions that lend themselves to treatment more than the large bastilles presently in operation. Some prisoners who pose distinct threats to society must be segregated. Others will continue to be confined because society demands their punishment. As long as we have penal institutions it is essential that we do our utmost to provide programs that will foster the positive personal growth of each inmate to the maximum extent possible.[4]

At the same time, there is no reason to confine those who do not need confinement. If intensive programs outside institutions can accomplish the goals of reform and rehabilitation better for nondangerous offenders and at less cost to society, then such programs should be instituted. These alternatives not only will help the individuals involved and their families, but they will also help institutional programs by relieving overcrowding. For these reasons, in recent years there has been an increasing reliance on community-based correctional programs such as pretrial diversion, probation, parole, and halfway houses (Warren, 1972).

PRETRIAL DIVERSION. We have seen how secondary deviance can stem from an individual being formally labeled a delinquent or criminal and being subjected to the sanctions of the criminal justice system. In addition to the negative effects on the individual's self-image, formal adjudication closes many doors. Convicted felons lose their civil rights, cannot be bonded, and are barred from many professions and occupations, including not only such obvious fields as law but also barbering, cosmetology, and many others.

To avoid these negative effects of the criminal justice system, *pretrial diversion* has been suggested for offenders who pose no serious threat to the community. In pretrial diversion, the accused voluntarily submits to treatment or rehabilitation. In return for cooperation, the charges are dropped. In this manner the accused obtains whatever benefits occur from the supervision or treatment program without being formally labeled as delinquent or criminal.At the same time, it eases the burden on the courts.

The problem with pretrial diversion is that it denies the accused the right to a court trial. Faced with the choice between informally submitting to treatment and facing trial, possible conviction, and a prison sentence, there is an all-but-irresistible temptation for innocent individuals to submit to treatment and forego their constitutional right to a speedy trial that could establish their innocence.

Although the proponents of pretrial diversion stress the benefits to the accused rather than the easing of the burdens on the court calendar, such a system is not the only way that formal adjudication can be avoided. The judge can withhold formal adjudication (labeling as a criminal) even for those who have been found guilty or have pleaded guilty in a court if they agree to cooperate in a rehabilitation program. Or, as we shall see next, they can be placed on probation, and if they complete probation successfully, the criminal convictions can be set aside. In this fashion clients can have the benefit of treatment without loss of their legal rights.

PROBATION. In probation, the imposition of a prison sentence is suspended, and offenders are allowed to remain in their communities under the supervision of probation officers as long as they behave according to conditions imposed by the court. Typically, these conditions stipulate that probationers must commit no new crimes, maintain regular employment or attend school faithfully, associate with no known criminals, and report regularly to their probation officers. Often special conditions are imposed, such as refraining from alcohol or participating in psychotherapy. Probationers usually must keep their probation officers informed of where they are living. An officer's permission must be obtained before making any change in residence, job, or marital status. As a general rule, the probationer must live a more upright life than other citizens.

If the offender successfully completes the period of probation, following all the rules for the prescribed length of time, the court will set the prison sentence aside. In many cases, particularly with juveniles, the original conviction will be expunged from the offender's record. On the other hand, if the probationer fails to live up to these conditions, or if the probation officer feels that the offender is not adjusting and poses a threat to the community, the officer may file a petition with the court asking that probation be rescinded. If the court agrees, the offender is taken into custody and the original sentence imposed.

Some judges will use a combination of prison or jail and probation. A five-year sentence may be imposed, with the first six months to be spent in jail and the remaining four-and-one-half years on probation. Some judges feel that this better indicates the gravity with which the court views the offense, provides the offender with additional motivation to abide by the conditions of probation, and demonstrates to the public that he is not "getting off scot-free."

The difference between probation and a simple suspended sentence is the supervision the client receives. Probably the major hindrance to effective probation is the enormous size to which probation officers' caseloads have grown in many jurisdictions. When caseloads range as high as 150, it is impossible for the officer to give more than a semblance of supervision; he is lucky if he can have even a brief talk with each of his probationers once a month. The President's Commission on Law Enforcement and Administration of Justice (1967) recommended average caseloads of thirty-five. However, in the present writer's opinion even caseloads of thirty-five are too high.

Probation is most apt to be helpful in the rehabilitation of the juvenile offender. Youngsters sent to a training school must perforce associate only with other delinquents. One would predict from differential association theory that this would be more apt to foster than to inhibit the development of a criminal career. Moreover, institutionalization labels a youngster as deviant, and, as we have seen from labeling theory, individuals often behave in accordance with societal expectations. Finally, the longer the period of removal from the community, the more difficulty the youth is likely to have readjusting after release from the institution. Merton's and Cloward and Ohlin's theories would predict that the more difficult it is to achieve desirable ends through socially approved channels, the more likely a person is to turn again to delinquency.

Probation may be able to achieve significant progress without these drawbacks. If a youngster's delinquency stems from inadequate supervision or the absence of an adequate adult role model, the supervising probation officer can do much to make up this deficit provided that adequate time is allowed for development of a close relationship with the client. When the probationer experiences difficulties with family, friends, school, or job, the caseworker can help in resolving these problems. Direct assistance in coping with significant figures in the client's real world provides a type of learning that it is impossible to obtain in an institution.

Research has identified certain key elements that determine whether or not probation is likely to be successful. The first, obviously, is the client. Some individuals are simply too dangerous, impulsive, or disturbed to be maintained in the community, and for them some form of institutional care is required. However, the data suggest that courts have generally been overly conservative in granting probation. The California Community Treatment Program has demonstrated that up to 80 percent of the delinquents once thought to require institutional care can be handled in the community if the proper conditions are provided.

A second key element is community resources. The more help a client receives from family, neighbors, teachers, employer, clergy, and the like, the better the prognosis.

A third key factor is caseload size. In the writer's opinion, reducing caseloads from 150 to 50 makes little difference. Even the difference between 50 and 25 is probably not as great as most suppose. The California Youth Authority's research has demonstrated that when caseloads are as low as 8, a change agent can have such a significant impact that it is possible to maintain youths in the community who would otherwise require institutionalization. Providing a probation officer for every eight delinquents is, of course, an expensive proposition, but one year of institutional care for eight youngsters would, in 1965, have cost $28,800, more than twice the average officer's annual salary (President's Commission on Law Enforcement and Administration of Justice, 1967).

The California Community Treatment Program (CTP), as we have seen, classifies clients according to their interpersonal maturity level and then seeks to match each type of delinquent with the most appropriate type of change agent. There are methodological problems in the evaluative research that make it difficult to determine exactly how effective this matching is (Beker & Heyman, 1972), but it makes sense that matching of clients with probation officers, if done correctly, should make probation even more effective.

HALFWAY HOUSES. Probation, even when it is operating properly, is no panacea. For various social and personal reasons, some individuals are simply unable to adjust rapidly enough to remain in the community. For some, a halfway house or community treatment center is the solution. Halfway houses help preserve community ties while providing closer supervision and greater structure than is possible on probation. In a halfway house, the offender lives with other offenders but typically goes to work or attends school in the community. There is much more freedom than there is in an institution; to succeed the offenders must learn how to resist the temptations that are ever-present in the community. However, they have more help from staff and peers than is available on conventional probation caseloads. Trained case-workers can help them find and maintain employment; others can show them how to manage their finances or teach them about credit so as to lessen some of the economic pressures that may have led them toward crime. There is usually an active and varied recreational program. This not only serves to keep the residents busy but ideally teaches them ways to use leisure time constructively so that when they are on the streets they will no longer need to play real-life games of "cops and robbers" to relieve boredom.

Most halfway houses have active group-counseling or therapy pro-grams. There is a strong tendency to favor the more active, challenging types of group treatment such as "Guided Group Interaction" and "Reality Therapy," in which offenders' rationalizations and excuses for their misdeeds and failures are actively challenged by the group (cf. Flackett & Flackett, 1970). This is most likely to be effective with the more manipulative and psychopathic offenders; they find it is difficult to "con" other "con artists" who have faced the same problems and used the same excuses. More neurotic, inadequate, or immature delin-quents may require more supportive forms of treatment.

Not all halfway houses are alternatives to prison. In addition to "halfway in" houses there are also "halfway out" houses, or community treatment centers that provide a reentry vehicle for convicts about to be paroled or released (Empey, 1967). In such open institutions, offenders can participate in community programs without coming under heavy peer pressure to smuggle drugs in or messages out, as they do in work-release programs in closed institutions. For those who have been segregated from community pressures, the community treatment center affords a chance to learn, with help, how to cope with all the many life problems that the institution handled for them—organizing their time, finding a place to live, obtaining credit, and so on.

PAROLE.   Only a small fraction of the inmates now confined in federal, state, and local institutions will live out their natural lives and die in prison. All the rest will be returned to the community at some time or other. About one third will be released when they have served out their sentences. Since they are released unconditionally, society has no more hold on them. One day they are in an institutional setting in which all the decisions are made for them; the next they are at the bus station with a new suit and a few dollars facing all the problems of going some place to start life anew. There is no one to help them find a job or resume their relations with their families, if any, or to supervise them during this difficult period of adjustment.

About two thirds, however, are released on parole. Such offenders are released before the end of their sentence on the understanding that they will abide by certain conditions until discharged from parole. Unlike those released on "flat time," parolees are supervised by correctional officials in the community. The parole officer has the dual role of helping the former inmate reenter society and making sure that no new crimes are committed while on parole. If the parolee is making a poor adjustment, is failing to abide by the conditions of parole or seems likely to get into additional trouble, the parole officer may, at his discretion, revoke the parole and have the inmate returned to the institution.

As we have pointed out with every aspect of the criminal justice system thus far, parole offers no panacea. All the problems faced by probation officers appear to be intensified when one is trying to work with someone who has just emerged from an institution.

No one can predict with absolute certainty whether a given inmate will succeed on parole. Parole boards must weigh the benefits against the possible risks. If a high proportion of their parolees are committing new offenses, then they are probably releasing too many before they are ready. These are the obvious failures that arouse public outcries. It is less generally realized that if a parole board has no such failures, then it is probably too conservative, retaining too many people in prison who could have succeeded in the community. It is a difficult task to balance the long- and short-term risks to society of releasing the marginal cases under supervision as opposed to keeping them in prison to be released without supervision when their sentences expire. Similarly, the costs of releasing some men who may commit new crimes must be balanced against the cost of keeping many other men in prison (and their families on the welfare rolls) when they could have become self-supporting citizens. As Caldwell has pointed out:

> Release on parole should not be based on any concept of clemency or be regarded as leniency, even though the prisoner is released before the

expiration of his sentence. Its chief purpose is to bridge the gap between the closely ordered life within an institution and the freedom of normal life in the community. It thus assumes that the period of confinement is only part of the correctional process and should be supplemented by a period of guidance and supervision in the community, and that the time immediately after release is a most crucial one in the adjustment of the offender. Parole, therefore, is not just a way of releasing prisoners. It is an integral part of the entire correctional program, and in it, as in all other aspects of this program, the interests of both society and the offender must be taken into consideration (1965, p. 667).

Treatment Approaches

Thus far in this section we have focused on the settings in which the task of offender rehabilitation can be accomplished. It is the people and the programs in these settings, however, that are the primary determinants of whether positive or negative changes take place.

The first step in treatment should be an assessment of the factors that led to the individual's current predicament and the design of a strategy to cope with these problems. This should be done as early as possible in the course of judicial processing, while the maximum number of options are available. Although personnel and programs are of paramount importance, some treatment strategies can be carried out more effectively in some settings than in others, so the choice of setting and legal status (for example, probation, prison, and the like) should be made so as to further the treatment goals, consistent of course with the societal need for protection.

Conceptually, it is possible to divide crime into primary and secondary deviance, that is, the criminal behavior that first brings an individual to the attention of the law and the subsequent criminal behavior that stems from involvement with the criminal justice system. A great deal of social reform is necessary to cope with the problem of secondary deviance. The writer, for example, has advocated fair-employment-practices legislation that would prohibit barring former felons from employment for which they are otherwise qualified. Even in formulating individual treatment plans, however, secondary deviance should be considered. A fragile, rather effeminate young man might learn a trade at an institution for adult felons, but he is also apt to be forced into a passive homosexual role by stronger convicts.

Turning to primary deviance, we have seen how a number of theorists have cited social problems as basic causes of criminal and delinquent behavior. Yet, in formulating individual treatment strategies we often behave as if the offenders are solely responsible for their behavior simply because they are here and can be dealt with, whereas society is somewhere "out there." One of the reasons institutions are not more successful is that they can work only with the offenders and not with the milieu from which they come. Insofar as community-based programs can deal to some extent with both individual and social factors, they have a somewhat better chance for success. Because of this, as well as to minimize both secondary deviance and expense, imprisonment should be reserved for those who present a clear and present danger to themselves or society.

Environmentally Based Programs. Environmental manipulation is designed to alter the circumstances of the offender's life and milieu so as to remove pressures toward deviance. With juvenile offenders, this might involve counseling the parents or working with school officials so as to foster an environment more conducive to growth. Foster-parent, big-brother, and some probation and parole programs are aimed at providing a stable, well-socialized adult with whom the child can identify. Such approaches are most apt to be effective with younger delinquents whose troubles stem from a lack of adequate role models.

Environmental manipulation is less apt to be used with individual adult offenders, although broad programs such as urban renewal, planned parenthood, and employment referral services have crime reduction as one goal. The major forms of environmental manipulation used with individual adults include finding employment for the offender and providing family counseling to help reduce marital stress that might lead to criminal behavior.

Individual Programs. Most treatment programs are aimed at individuals, attempting to help them change so that they can cope more effectively with their environment or, through their own efforts, escape from it. There are several ways in which this is traditionally done in both institutional and community-based settings.

EDUCATION. Merton (1957) and Cloward and Ohlin (1960) are among those who have cited the inability to achieve through culturally sanctioned means as a prime cause of criminal behavior. There is little doubt that the uneducated or untrained individual is poorly equipped to cope with a modern technological society; many offenders lack technological skills. Therefore a major treatment goal is often to provide offenders with academic and/or vocational training that will enable them to compete more successfully for gainful employment. Through such programs, both in institutional and community settings, many individuals who were unable or unwilling to learn in conventional educational settings have completed vocational-training, high-school-equivalency, and even college-degree programs.

Education does not, of course, immunize a person from criminal behavior. Most of those indicted in the Watergate conspiracy had college and graduate degrees, and college graduates currently have the dubious distinction of occupying three places on the FBI's "Ten Most Wanted Criminals" list. Nor does education guarantee a job especially if one carries the stigma of a prison sentence into the employment interview. Those who have invested great effort in securing a high school diploma only to be rejected yet again are apt to become even more alienated and bitter, particularly if they have been led to believe that education would open every door. Such disappointment can lead to secondary deviance.

Of course not every offender who participates in educational or vocational training does so with the idea of eventually seeking legitimate employment. One bank robber with whom the writer chatted recently is participating in an educational program to occupy his time in prison, but he intends to return to his former occupation when released.

Thus, as with any treatment approach, educational and vocational training can help to remove some of the road blocks to remaining "legit on the street," but they do not constitute a panacea.

PSYCHOTHERAPY.   Psychopathology, such as psychoses, neuroses, and personality disorders, seems to predispose some individuals to the commission of criminal offenses. In such instances, individual and group psychotherapy aimed at alleviating these conditions can reduce symptomatic criminal behavior.

Unfortunately, most psychotherapeutic approaches require some desire to change on the part of the client. Therapy can be viewed as the creation of an environment in which clients can grapple with their problems, but unless they are willing to invest the effort and the anguish that this entails, therapy is often doomed to failure. The bank robber mentioned above is a poor candidate for therapy because although he hates prison, he feels that the solution is to improve his bank-robbing technique. He has already decided that to ensure more cooperation from citizens and bank guards he will henceforth carry a submachine gun instead of a pistol. No doubt he will further refine his techniques through discussions with professional colleagues during this and future enforced sabbaticals.

Procedures and methods that originated in psychotherapeutic practice are also being used in efforts to help offenders not suffering from mental disturbances to learn how to anticipate the consequences of their behavior and control their impulses. Group therapy and counseling, guided group interaction, psychodrama, reality therapy, and other approaches are being used, often by paraprofessionals, in efforts to help offenders cope with the stresses of life in general and interpersonal interactions in particular. This can be viewed as part of a general social trend toward employing therapeutic techniques to enhance personal growth. To the extent that difficulties in interpersonal communication and understanding hinder the offender's adjustment, these techniques should help.

BEHAVIOR MODIFICATION. Behavior modification is a particular therapeutic approach that is based on the principles of operant conditioning; it has been applied in many settings beyond the residential psychiatric settings in which it originated. It is based on the principle that organisms repeat behavior that is rewarded, whereas unrewarded behavior will eventually be extinguished. The basic strategy is to arrange the environmental contingencies so that those behaviors that are considered desirable pay off more than those that are undesirable. Parents who praise their children when they are "good" and withhold approval when they are naughty are applying the basic principles of behavioral modification.

Since the active cooperation of the client is less essential than in traditional psychotherapy, many view behavior modification as being especially appropriate for correctional programs. It is most easily carried out in settings in which the staff, through token economies or other such means, can exercise a high degree of control over the environmental contingencies.

With the publication of books such as B. F. Skinner's *Beyond Freedom and Dignity* and the production of the motion picture *A Clockwork Orange,* behavior modification approaches with offenders in general and inmates in particular have been severely criticized. There appears to be a widespread misconception that behavior modification will reduce people to the status of Pavlovian automatons, robbed of their essential humanity. Partly because of this outcry, one correctional system recently abandoned a program aimed at using positive reinforcement to help socialize their most intractable offenders to the point where they could mingle freely with other inmates rather than having to be kept in strict segregation.

In deciding whether to institute a behavior modification program, several guidelines should be followed. Harsh and aversive conditioning should be avoided. Moreover, inmates should not be required to alter their behavior to secure basic necessities such as an adequate diet, shelter, exercise, and recreation. However, few would object to requiring them to earn extra privileges or small luxuries.

Behavior modification is a powerful technique, and there are instances in which abuses have occurred in the guise of treatment. Such abuses can best be avoided by submitting proposed behavior modification programs to disinterested professionals for peer review and by actively seeking the advice and suggestions of the offenders who will be participating in the program. In evaluating the desirability of a program, one should examine not only the proposed plan but also the alternatives and their effects. Those intractable inmates who were scheduled for the behavior modification program described above will now spend years in strict segregation for the protection of the rest of the inmate population. This regimen can be expected to have effects just as profound, although probably less desirable, than the operant reward system that had been planned.

MEDICAL TREATMENT.   Some illnesses, such as psychomotor epilepsy or temporal lobe tumors, can lead directly to violent behavior. In such cases medical treatment is necessary to restore the individual to health, and less violence may be an added benefit. In other individuals, the stress or problems engendered by a medical condition can lead toward crime. Someone who is disfigured, for example, may find it difficult to secure employment and may thus turn to theft. Cosmetic surgery may be beneficial. The narcotic addicts who are entering the criminal justice system in increasing numbers may also require medical attention.

More controversial are attempts to alter behavior directly through medical intervention. Attempts to change violent behavior through brain surgery or castration are deemed by most to go beyond the limits of rehabilitation and to constitute cruel and unusual punishment. Those Danish physicians who advocate castration of violent sex offenders maintain that this procedure is carried out only when all other remedies have been exhausted and the prisoner has voluntarily requested the operation. Nevertheless, one questions how voluntary a choice between castration and long-term confinement can be.

The use of tranquilizing medication is another controversial issue. Drugs may be used in institutional settings to make inmates more manageable, but many disapprove of efforts to influence the emotional reactivity and behavior of captives through chemical means. On the other hand, is this less ethical than withholding such medication and subjecting these individuals to greater stress and closer custody? What of the individual who cannot cope with community life unless he has medication to help withstand the stress? Should a judge or parole board insist on medication as a condition of probation or parole?

All of these ethical dilemmas are facets of the basic issue of how much control society has a right to exert over the minds and behavior of its members. Physicians would be well advised to prescribe for offenders as they would for their private patients and to submit potentially controversial treatment plans for disinterested peer review.

Treatment Personnel

Just as treatment programs are more important than the settings in which they take place, treatment personnel are more important than the programs. Self-centered, sadistic, or just plain stupid personnel can sabotage the best program. Unfortunately, dedicated, compassionate, and wise personnel cannot always salvage a poor program or overcome a miserable setting, although they can do a great deal to compensate for them.

Traditionally it has been the best-paid and least-available people— the psychologists, psychiatrists, chaplains, caseworkers, and teachers—

who have been considered "treatment personnel." There is now an increasing awareness that everyone who has contact with offenders from the time of their initial apprehension to their final discharge from the criminal justice system helps influence their attitudes and behavior. It is often those who are the most poorly trained with whom offenders have the most contact: the work supervisors, jailers, custodial personnel, and other inmates. The more these people can be actively involved in the treatment process, the more likely that process is to have positive rather than detrimental effects.

The common denominator for successful treatment personnel is their capacity to respect each offender's basic value as a human being no matter how much they disapprove of the behavior or attitudes that brought that person into custody. If the personnel offenders deal with have no respect for them as people, how can they come to respect themselves or others? Offenders are often told, "As you sow, so shall you reap." This applies to their keepers as well.

Primary Prevention

Thus far we have focused on society's response once a crime has been committed. In recent years, there has been increasing concern with ways of preventing the initial occurrence of criminal behavior. Historically, law enforcement has been regarded as the best way to combat crime. The Rationalists and others assumed that as the likelihood of detection, apprehension, and punishment increased, the incidence of crime would decrease. Within limits, this is correct, but the multiplicity of causes we have found for criminal and delinquent behavior suggests that no one approach is likely to eliminate crime. Moreover, as the population increases in size and complexity, the likelihood of a given individual ever going to prison for a crime decreases. Thus, the police, courts, and correctional agencies cannot be relied on as the sole answer to the crime problem.

Most of the environmental causes of crime that have been suggested imply ways that crime could be reduced. Theories citing familial discord point out that help might come from strengthening the family through casework or counseling or the provision of substitute families through foster homes or big brother programs. Social disorganization theories of gang delinquency have led to detached-worker programs in major cities and helped foster low-income housing projects, which, unfortunately, "have become those areas of our inner cities most susceptible to crime and vandalism" (Newman, 1973, p. xii). The community mental health movement was motivated by a desire to eliminate a number of forms of social pathology, including delinquency. As a result of theories such as Albert Cohen's, efforts have been made to train teachers to cope with disadvantaged children. Labeling theory has provided an incentive for pretrial diversion programs.

This multiplicity of approaches is healthy. Since a broad array of factors has been found to be associated with delinquent behavior patterns, a diverse attack on a number of fronts is most likely to be successful. With proper evaluative research, the most useful techniques can be retained and the others discarded. Thus far, however, evaluative research has been disappointing.

Many—perhaps most—social action programs are so concerned with implementing their particular approach that adequate data collection procedures and controls are not incorporated into the plan at the outset. Even when attempts are made to evaluate programs, it may be impossible to demonstrate a significant impact. This is partly because of the magnitude of the crime problem. It is unrealistic to think that any given program will have a significant impact on the local crime rate. Moreover, the complexity of many programs makes it virtually impossible to isolate the effects of any given factor. Sometimes, other contemporary social changes hopelessly confound the research program.

Research technology is beginning to catch up with these problems. Efforts are being made to ensure that demonstration and social-action projects collect the data that will be required to determine the effectiveness of these programs (Glaser, 1973). The use of quasi-experimental designs and sophisticated statistical methods can do much to help an investigator. But the members of the research team must have a voice in the design of the program at the outset if they are to evaluate it adequately at the end.

With the passage of the Omnibus Crime Control and Safe Streets Act of 1968 that created the Law Enforcement Assistance Administration (LEAA), the federal government began a massive infusion of funds into the criminal justice system at the state and national levels. At the outset, much of this money was spent on hardware such as improved communications systems. However, there appears to be an increasing realization of the need for basic research, as well as improved technology. Many of the more recent studies cited in this report were conducted under LEAA auspices.

For pedagogical reasons, the vast bulk of this paper has dealt with facts and theories about the causes of crime and the ways in which people have attempted to cope with it. However, the *people* who are involved are as important, if not more so, than the specific techniques that are employed. Great strides have been made in police training in recent years, but selection of good officer candidates based on sound research is even more important. It is unrealistic to expect a short training program to overcome twenty years or so of learning and personality development.

Increasingly, law enforcement, criminal justice, and corrections are becoming professions rather than trades. A number of schools of criminal justice that have been founded at various universities around the country are aimed at educating those who must administer the myriad criminal justice programs. Training programs in law enforcement and corrections have been instituted at many community colleges (Waldo, 1971). Such efforts to attract highly qualified personnel and to educate them to assume key roles in the criminal justice system and undertake the research for the future are likely to result in even more advances in the next half-century than will be obtained from the specific findings of many ongoing research projects.

EPILOGUE

The light on the crime clock in the J. Edgar Hoover building continues to blink, day and night, 19 times a minute, 1,140 times an hour, 27,360 times a day. In the six months that have passed since this chapter was begun, there have been 484,910 crimes of violence and 4,611,100 property crimes. Many have struggled with the task of understanding and coping with crimes. Despite our best efforts, crime continues at a greater rate in America than in many other industrial countries. As the President's Commission on Law Enforcement and Administration of Justice noted in 1967:

> Given enough time and money, specialists can do dramatic things. They
> can prolong human life. They can make deserts bloom. They can split

the atom. They can put men on the moon. However, specialists alone cannot control crime. Crime is a social problem that is interwoven with almost every aspect of American life; controlling it involves changing the way schools are run and classes are taught, the way cities are planned and houses are built, the way businesses are managed and workers are hired. Crime is a kind of human behavior; controlling it means changing the minds and hearts of men. Controlling crime is the business of every American institution. Controlling crime is the business of every American (1967, p. 288).

NOTES

1. *Psychologist* is used here as a generic term for all those who study individual as opposed to group behavior; in this sense it includes not only psychologists but also psychiatrists and psychoanalysts.

2. Caldwell (1965, p. 490) speculates that the earliest prisons were the stockades that cannibal tribes used as larders.

3. This, of course, continues to this day. Those who feel they have suffered at the hands of others can seek compensation through the civil courts.

4. It should be pointed out that this is a controversial position. Some of those who oppose institutions also oppose efforts to make them more humane and effective, reasoning that the more successful such programs are the more they are apt to perpetuate correctional institutions. In the hope of some day eliminating all confinement, they are apparently willing to write off the 200,000 felons currently confined.

BIBLIOGRAPHY

Abrahamsen, David. *The Psychology of Crime*. New York: Wiley, 1960.

Alexander, Franz, and Hugo Staub. *The Criminal, the Judge, and the Public*. Glencoe, Ill.: The Free Press, 1956.

Bazelon, David L. "Psychologists in Corrections: Are They Doing Good for the Offender or Well for Themselves?" In Stanley L. Brodsky, ed. *Psychologists in the Criminal Justice System*. Urbana, Ill.: University of Illinois Press, 1973, pp. 149–154.

Becker, Howard S., ed. *The Other Side: Perspectives on Deviance*. New York: The Free Press, 1964.

Beker, J., and D. Heyman. "A Critical Appraisal of the California Differential Treatment Typology of Juvenile Offenders." *Criminology*, 1972, 10:3–59.

Bloch, Herbert A., and Arthur Niederhoffer. *The Gang: A Study in Adolescent Behavior*. New York: Philosophical Library, 1958.

Bureau of Prisons. *Differential Treatment: A Way to Begin*. Washington, D.C.: U.S. Department of Justice, September 1970.

Burt, Cyril. *The Young Delinquent*, 4th ed. London: University of London Press, 1944.

Caldwell, Robert G. *Criminology*, 2nd ed. New York: Ronald Press, 1965.

Caldwell, Robert G., and James A. Black. *Juvenile Delinquency*. New York: Ronald Press, 1971.

Clinard, Marshall B., and Richard Quinney. *Criminal Behavior Systems: A Typology*, 2nd ed. New York: Holt, Rinehart and Winston, 1973.

Cloward, Richard A., and Lloyd E. Ohlin. *Delinquency and Opportunity: A Theory of Delinquent Gangs*. Glencoe, Ill.: The Free Press, 1960.

Cohen, Albert K. *Delinquent Boys: The Culture of the Gang*. Glencoe, Ill.: The Free Press, 1955.

Cohen, Albert K. "Multiple Factor Approaches." In Marvin E. Wolfgang, Leonard Savitz, and Norman Johnston, eds. *The Sociology of Crime and Delinquency*, 2nd ed. New York: Wiley, 1970, pp. 123–126.

Empey, LaMar T. *Alternatives to Incarceration*. J. D. Publication No. 9001. Washington, D.C.: U.S. Department of Health, Education, and Welfare, Office of Juvenile Delinquency and Youth Development, Social and Rehabilitation Source, 1967.

Erikson, Erik H. *Childhood and Society*. New York: Norton, 1950.

Federal Bureau of Investigation. *Crime in the United States: Uniform Crime Reports*, 1974. Washington, D.C.: U.S. Government Printing Office, 1975.

Ferdinand, Theodore N. *Typologies of Delinquency: A Critical Analysis*. New York: Random House, 1966.

Flackett, John M., and Gail Flackett. "Criswell House: An Alternative to

Institutional Commitment for the Juvenile Offender." *Federal Probation,* 1970, 34:30–37.

Freud, Sigmund. "Some Character-Types Met Within Psycho-analytic Work: (III) Criminals from a Sense of Guilt." In James Strachey, ed. *The Standard Edition of the Complete Psychological Works of Sigmund Freud,* vol. 14. London: Hogarth Press, 1957, pp. 332–333.

Friedlander, Kate. *The Psycho-analytical Approach to Juvenile Delinquency.* New York: International Universities Press, 1947.

Garfinkel, Harold. "Conditions of Successful Degradation Ceremonies." *American Journal of Sociology,* 1956, 61:420–424.

Gerard, Roy. "Institutional Innovations in Juvenile Corrections." *Federal Probation,* 1970, 34:37–44.

Gibbons, Don C. *Changing the Lawbreaker.* Englewood Cliffs, N.J.: Prentice-Hall, 1965.

Glaser, Daniel. *Routinizing Evaluation: Getting Feedback on Effectiveness of Crime and Delinquency Programs.* DHEW Publication No. (HSM) 73–9123. Rockville, Md.: National Institute of Mental Health, Center for Studies of Crime and Delinquency, 1973.

Glueck, Sheldon, and Eleanor Glueck. *Unraveling Juvenile Delinquency.* New York: The Commonwealth Fund, 1950.

Glueck, Sheldon, and Eleanor Glueck. *Physique and Delinquency.* New York: Harper, 1956.

Goring, Charles. *The English Convict: A Statistical Study.* London: His Majesty's Stationery Office, 1913.

Haven, H. "Descriptive and Developmental Characteristics of Chronically Overcontrolled Hostile Prisoners." *FCI Research Reports,* 1972, 4:1–40.

Hewitt, Lester E., and Richard L. Jenkins. *Fundamental Patterns of Maladjustment: The Dynamics of Their Origin.* Springfield, Ill.: State of Illinois, 1946.

Hooton, Ernest A. *The American Criminal, An Anthropological Study,* vol. 1, *The Native White Criminal of Native Parentage.* New York: Greenwood Press, 1939.

Hoskins, Roy G. *Endocrinology.* New York: Norton, 1941.

Jenkins, Richard L., and Sylvia Glickman. "Patterns of Personality Organization among Delinquents." *Nervous Child,* 1947, 6:329–339.

Johnson, Adelaide. "Sanctions for Super-ego Lacunae of Adolescence." In K. R. Eissler, ed., *Searchlights on Delinquency.* New York: International Universities Press, 1949.

Kelley, C. M. *Crime in the United States, 1972.* Washington: U.S. Government Printing Office, 1973.

Lemert, Edwin M. *Human Deviance, Social Problems, and Social Control.* Englewood Cliffs, N.J.: Prentice-Hall, 1967.

MacIver, Robert. *Social Causation.* New York: Ginn, 1942.

Marshall, William L., and William L. Clark. "The Legal Definition of Crime and Criminals." In Marvin E. Wolfgang, Leonard Savitz, and Norman Johnston, eds. *The Sociology of Crime and Delinquency,* 2nd ed. New York.: Wiley, 1970, pp. 15–21.

McCord, William, and Joan McCord. *The Psychopath—An Essay on the Criminal Mind.* Princeton, N.J.: Van Nostrand, 1964.

McGuire, Judith S., and Edwin I. Megargee. "Personality Correlates of Marijuana Use among Youthful Offenders." *Journal of Consulting and Clinical Psychology,* 1974, 42:124–133.

Megargee, Edwin I. "Undercontrolled and Overcontrolled Personality Types in Extreme Antisocial Aggression." *Psychological Monographs,* 1966, 80:1–29.

Megargee, Edwin I. "The Heuristic Value of the Concept of 'Social Deviance' for Psychologists." *Representative Research in Social Psychology,* 1973, 4:67–81.

Megargee, Edwin I., Patrick E. Cook, and Gerald A. Mendelsohn. "Development and Validation of an MMPI Scale of Assaultiveness in Overcontrolled Individuals." *Journal of Abnormal Psychology,* 1967, 72:519–528.

Megargee, Edwin I., George V. C. Parker, and Robert V. Levine. "The Relationship of Familial and Social Factors to Socialization in Middle-Class College Students." *Journal of Abnormal Psychology,* 1971, 77:76–89.

Merton, Robert. "Social Structure and Anomie." *American Sociological Review,* 1938, 3:672–682.

Merton, Robert K. *Social Theory and Social Structure.* Glencoe, Ill.: The Free Press, 1957.

Miller, Walter B. "Lower Class Culture as a Generating Milieu of Gang Delinquency." *Journal of Social Issues,* 1958, 14:5–19.

Montagu, M. F. Ashley. "The Biologist Looks at Crime." *Annals of the American Academy of Political and Social Science,* 1941, 218:46–57.

National Advisory Commission on Criminal Justice Standards and Goals. *Report on Corrections.* Washington, D.C.: U.S. Government Printing Office, 1973.

Newman, Oscar. *Architectural Design for Crime Prevention.* Washington, D.C.: U.S. Department of Justice, Law Enforcement Assistance Administration, National Institute of Law Enforcement and Criminal Justice, 1973.

Nye, F. Ivan. *Family Relationships and Delinquent Behavior.* New York: Wiley, 1958.

President's Commission on Law Enforcement and Administration of Justice. *The Challenge of Crime in a Free Society.* Washington, D.C.: U.S. Government Printing Office, 1967.

Quay, Herbert C. "Psychopathic Personality as Pathological Stimulation Seeking." *American Journal of Psychiatry*, 1965, 122:180–183.

Quay, Herbert C., and L. B. Parsons. *The Differential Behavioral Classification of the Juvenile Offender*. Washington, D.C.: U.S. Bureau of Prisons, 1970.

Quay, Herbert C., and D. R. Peterson. "A Brief Scale for Juvenile Delinquency." *Journal of Clinical Psychology*, 1967, 45:139–142.

Reckless, Walter C. *The Crime Problem*, 3rd ed. New York: Appleton-Century-Crofts, 1961.

Reiss, Albert J., Jr. "Delinquency as the Failure of Personal and Social Controls." *American Sociological Review*, 1951, 16:196–208.

Rosenquist, Carl M., and Edwin I. Megargee. *Delinquency in Three Cultures*. Austin, Tex.: University of Texas Press, 1969.

Rotter, Julian B. *Social Learning and Clinical Psychology*. Englewood Cliffs, N.J.: Prentice-Hall, 1954.

Runyon, Tom. "Prison Shocks." In Robert G. Caldwell. *Criminology*, 2nd ed. New York: Ronald Press, 1965, pp. 632–652.

Salisbury, Harrison E. *The Shook-up Generation*. New York: Harper & Row, 1958.

Schlapp, M. G., and E. H. Smith. *The New Criminology*. New York: Boni & Liveright, 1928.

Sellin, Thorsten. *Culture Conflict and Crime*. New York: Social Science Research Council, 1938.

Shaw, Clifford R., and Henry D. McKay. *Juvenile Delinquency and Urban Areas*. Chicago: University of Chicago Press, 1942.

Sheldon, William H., Emil M. Hartl, and Eugene McDermott. *Varieties of Delinquent Youth*. New York: Harper & Row, 1949.

Shoham, Shlomo. "The Application of the 'Culture Conflict' Hypothesis to the Criminality of Immigrants in Israel." *Journal of Criminal Law, Criminology, and Police Science*, 1962, 53:207–214.

Stoddard, Ellwyn, R. "The Informal 'Code' of Police Deviancy: A Group Approach to 'Blue-Coat Crime.' " *Journal of Criminal Law, Criminology, and Police Science*, 1968, 59:201–213.

Sullivan, Clyde, J. Douglas Grant, and Marguerite Q. Grant. "The Development of Interpersonal Maturity: Application to Delinquency." *Psychiatry*, 1957, 20:373–385.

Sutherland, Edwin H. *The Professional Thief*. Chicago: University of Chicago Press, 1937.

Sutherland, Edwin H. "Critique of Sheldon's Varieties of Delinquent Youth." *American Sociological Review*, 1951, 16:10–13.

Sutherland, Edwin H., and Donald R. Cressey. *Principles of Criminology*, 7th ed. Philadelphia: J. B. Lippincott, 1966.

Sykes, Gresham M., and David Matza. "Techniques of Neutralization: A Theory of Delinquency." *American Sociological Review*, 1957, 22:664–670.

Tallahassee *Democrat*, July 31, 1973, p. 6.

Thio, Alex. "Class Bias in the Sociology of Deviance." *The American Sociologist*, 1973, 8:1–12.

Vanderbeck, D. "A Construct Validity Study of the O-H (Overcontrolled Hostility) Scale of the MMPI, Using a Social Learning Approach to the Cartharsis Effect." *FCI Research Reports*, 1973.

Velez-Diaz, Angel, and Edwin I. Megargee. "An Investigation of Differences in Value Judgements Between Youthful Offenders and Nonoffenders in Puerto Rico." *Journal of Criminal Law, Criminology, and Police Science*, 1970, 61:549–553.

Vold, George B. *Theoretical Criminology*. New York: Oxford University Press, 1958.

Waldo, Gordon P. "Research and Training in Corrections: The Role of the University." *Federal Probation*, 1971, 35:57–62.

Warren, Marguerite Q. "Classification of Offenders as an Aid to Efficient Management and Effective Treatment." Report submitted to the President's Commission on Law Enforcement and Administration of Justice, Task Force on Corrections, 1966, pp. 8–12. Mimeographed.

Warren, Marguerite Q. "The Case for Differential Treatment of Delinquents." *Annals of the American Academy of Political and Social Science*, 1969, 381:47–59.

Warren, Marguerite Q. *Correctional Treatment in Community Settings: A Report of Current Research*. Rockville, Md.: National Institute of Mental Health, 1972.

THREE Criminal violence

DAVID F. LUCKENBILL
University of California, Santa Barbara

WILLIAM B. SANDERS
University of Florida

To speak of violence is to refer to acts of physical destruction that kill or injure people or that cause significant damage to property.[1] Violence includes everything from national wars and ghetto riots to political assassination and child beating. In some cases, violence may be intended, as when an executioner throws a switch, thus emitting a lethal gas into a chamber holding a condemned killer. In others, it may be unintended, as when a bombardier miscalculates his target and hits a small, allied village. Violence may be put to the service of one's personal interests, as when a mugger or rapist uses violence to secure money from or sexual access to the victim. On the contrary, it may be employed in the service of other people's interests, as when killers are employed to execute those who threaten the security of powerful criminal organizations or as in the 1900s when the militia and private

The authors wish to thank Donald R. Cressey, W. Clinton Terry, III, Don Zimmerman, and Rey Baca for their assistance in the preparation of this essay.

police put down the striking laborers to protect the interests of the powerful industrial barons. Violence may be criminal, as when students seek to oust their administration by assaulting buildings and people with rocks and bottles. Or it may be legitimate, as when the police shoot during a bank robbery or soldiers attack enemy positions in war.[2] The concern in this essay is with a particular brand of violence found in contemporary America: violence that is criminal and intentionally directed against people and property by those acting in their own interests.

Among the many social problems Americans recognize, criminal violence, such as murder, rape, juvenile gang wars, and ghetto riots, appears to be capturing the public's eye. Indeed, as John Conklin (1975, pp. 1–10, 26–30) observed, the 1960s witnessed the growing belief among the American public that the United States was engulfed in a wave of unprecedented criminal violence. This belief brought with it a heightened fear of victimization. In a comprehensive national survey, Louis Harris and his associates (1968) found that in the latter 1960s the number of people employed by private protection agencies had grown larger than all public police forces combined. They also found that people were increasingly fearful of walking the city streets in the evening hours, were purchasing greater numbers of firearms for protection, and were fortifying their homes against possible attack. In a survey of Baltimore residents, *Life* magazine (Rosenthal, 1969) ascertained that people were using their parks less frequently, were attending fewer nightspots, such as movies and restaurants, and were purchasing more locks, alarms, and other protective devices, all for fear of violent attack. This fear has been accompanied by increasing demands for immediate governmental action against criminal violence. In recent years, for instance, there has been growing support among the public for the continuance or reinstatement of capital punishment for various crimes of violence. Some people openly support violent police tactics against suspected muggers, rapists, rioters, and the like, while others support the increased use of psychosurgery to make violent offenders less harmful.

More often than not, people's understanding of the character of those very events they fear appears to be sketchy and often quite erroneous. Some popular conceptions of violence are that it is senseless and erratic in nature, that it is performed by unstable or deranged individuals, that interracial and interclass violence is common, and that victims rarely contribute to their own harm and death. Actually these ideas reflect exceptions rather than the general case; this points out that people's fears and suggested solutions may be based on widely held misconceptions. A white woman may have a gripping fear of sexual assault by a black; another person may fear being senselessly killed or assaulted by complete strangers. Yet these fears are as unrealistic as the responses that grow out of them: for instance, the wholesale use of psychotherapy to cure violent people or the use of official violence to eliminate criminal violence.

As is the case with some other kinds of human activities, people cannot readily consult existing academic research on violence for the validation of their beliefs or the answers to their questions. There is a surprising dearth of reliable information on assault, rape, and mugging, as well as on the history of American criminal violence. This is coupled with a lack of academic consensus over the findings of certain lines of investigation. What "causes" violence, for example, has been and continues to be a controversial issue.

The purpose of this chapter is to provide a sound and realistic understanding of contemporary criminal violence in the United States and then to use that understanding to suggest a means for reducing its occurrence. To these ends it would be useful first to place contemporary criminal violence within a cross-national and historical perspective and to examine the question of whether Americans, when compared to other peoples, are exceptionally violent. In the second and more extended section, the history of the nature of criminal violence will be described. The third section will delineate the character of the more notable forms of criminal violence found in contemporary America. The purpose here will be to secure an understanding of how such events are performed and what their situational facilitants are. In the final section the question of whether criminal violence can be reduced, as some seem to think, by the official violence of governmental bodies will be addressed.

VIOLENCE IN CONTEMPORARY AMERICA

Critics of the American scene seem justified in interpreting the tumult and violence of recent years to indicate that Americans are an incredibly violent people. In the 1960s the rate of American criminal homicide was more than twice that reported in Finland and between four and twelve times that found in such countries as Japan, Canada, England, and Norway.[3] The reported rate of criminal assault in the United States was twice that reported in England and Wales and eighteen times that of Canada; the rate of forcible rape surpassed that of Canada by three times and that of England and Wales by twelve times. With respect to the volume of civil strife—that is, nongovernmental collective violence within the political states, such as guerrilla terrorism, riots, violent protest, and the like—the United States surpassed other industrialized nations, including West Germany, the United Kingdom, and the Scandinavian countries, as well as the U.S.S.R. and Taiwan (Gurr, 1969).

While the United States may exceed the stable, modern nations of the western world in the volume of reported criminal violence, is it then reasonable to contend that this nation is *exceptionally* violent? Perhaps not. When compared to a variety of nations not restricted to the industrialized West, the scope of American violence is far from extraordinary. The rates of assaultive offenses pale when compared to those for countries such as Colmbia, Guatemala, Mexico, and South Africa (Wolfgang & Ferracuti, 1967, pp. 257–284). Such developing countries as India, Argentina, Korea, Bolivia, Indonesia, Venezuela, Iraq, and Guatemala significantly surpass the United States in the volume of political violence (Feierabend, Feierabend, & Nesvold, 1969, p. 626). Furthermore, other countries experience quite heavy losses from criminal violence centering about some types of conflict rarely experienced in contemporary America. Violence attendant to religious conflict, for example, is rare in contemporary America yet was commonplace at one point in India's history, as Stringfellow Barr aptly illustrates:

> I used to swear that Americans were peculiarly addicted to violence. But fourteen years ago I was shaken by an Indian professor named Dar, with whom I was dining in Delhi.
>
> "Mr. Barr," asked Mr. Dar, "you tell me you have now driven 7,500 miles in my country, visiting cities, towns, and villages. What is your liveliest impression of the Indian people?"
>
> "I think," I said, "it is their moving gentleness. In my country, people believe in getting tough."
>
> "Mr. Barr," said Mr. Dar, "I wish you had been in Delhi seven years ago, when all night and every night you would have heard the screams of victims while gentle Hindus and gentle Muslims murdered each other by the tens of thousands" (1973, p. 3).

Just as the United States is not exceptional with respect to the scope of criminal violence, neither does it appear that it is exceptional with respect to those conditions that account for surges in violence (Graham & Gurr, 1969, pp. 439–441). While every society experiences continuous change in its social, economic, and political spheres, it has been demonstrated that criminal violence (as well as progress) rises during periods of rapid, often unanticipated or disorderly, social change (Feierabend, Feierabend, & Nesvold, 1969; Hofstadter & Wallace, 1970; Bensman, 1971; Feierabend et al., 1971). It is during such periods that certain societal groups may experience increased anguish and disenchantment that they see as the result of a number of circumstances: limitations on their rightful opportunities to success and social mobility; deception by those in power; physical displacement; subjection to life conditions quite at odds with those previously enjoyed or anticipated; competition with other groups previously judged as inferior. In short, these periods result in problematic situations that may be resolved, under certain conditions, by the use of criminal violence.

The general variation between nations in the scope of criminal violence can be accounted for, in part, by the variation in the condition of rapid societal change and its attendant conflict. This is especially clear when political violence and civil strife are examined cross-nationally (Feierabend, Feierabend, & Nesvold, 1969; Gurr, 1969). Those nations that significantly exceed the United States in their level of civil strife are also engulfed in periods of widespread, disorderly modernization, especially in the realms of industrialization, urbanization, and politics.

While the United States, in contrast, has enjoyed a reasonable degree of stability in its political and economic institutions, there are certain racial and ethnic groups in contemporary America that are caught up in cycles of change resembling those experienced by many of the transitional nations of Africa and South America. Groups like the blacks, Chicanos, American Indians, students, prisoners, and others with little or no power have experienced some change in orientation. Through organizing, these groups have pressured governmental agencies to recognize their existence and guarantee equal access to opportunities that are available to others. At the same time, those groups in a relatively privileged and superordinate position have subjected the powerless to oppressive conditions fundamentally at odds with governmental guarantees. This strain served as a precondition to the violent protests, riots, and terrorism of the late 1960s and early 1970s (Hofstadter, 1970, p. 11). It was not the oppression and misery itself that brought these groups to collective anguish and eventual violence; rather it was the perception that, relative to other groups, they could not gain their rightful access to the normative opportunities for achieving legitimate collective ends (cf. Brinton, 1965, pp. 27–91). Marvin Wolfgang put it well:

> When men perceive oppression as their lot and know of others not oppressed, when ordered avenues of change are blocked by kings or legislators or some vague variety of any social system, the oppressed will either resign themselves to fate or rise up to taste the fruit of freedom, and having tasted will want the feast (1974, p. 249).

Finally, in comparison to the United States many modernized nations of the West appear relatively tranquil in their political, economic, and social development. Yet, they have not been without substantial strife and political violence in early periods of marked change (Hofstadter, 1970, pp. 6–9). The rapid movement from feudalism to national statehood, for example, found political terrorism, guerrilla warfare, assassination, and student protests to be commonplace in most European states (Bensman, 1971, pp. 374–375). Ethnic and economic conflict in Great Britian brought the massacre of some 12,000 or 15,000 English and Scotch settlers at the hands of the Irish in October 1641.

The point, Richard Hofstadter (1970, p. 6) argues, is that the United States, even with its considerable record of violence, appears not as some mutant monster among the peoples of the world but rather as a full-fledged and somewhat boisterous member of the fellowship of humankind.

HISTORY OF CRIMINAL VIOLENCE IN AMERICA

With the significant increases in assault and robbery in the 1960s, the United States witnessed bloody race riots in Los Angeles, Detroit, Tampa, and Cincinnati; violent skrimishes between civil rights advocates and prejudiced whites; battles between student protestors and police; and the assassinations of key political figures. As indicated before, with such events came the growing belief among the public that America is in an age of unprecedented violence. Indeed, critics of the

American scene have equated the violence of the 1960s with the decay of the nation and the morbidity of its people (Toch, 1969, p. 1). But is criminal violence new to the American scene as this might imply? Are Americans evolving into a belligerent, barbaric people? Does the seeming multitude of contemporary violence signify some growing pathology taking epidemic proportions among the masses?

Compared to the relatively tranquil 1950s, the 1960s did appear incredibly violent. Nevertheless, students of violence emphatically oppose contentions that the scope of violence reached unprecedented heights.[4] Just a scan of American history suggests that the violence defined today as criminal has been frequent, voluminous, and almost commonplace in our past (Hofstadter, 1970, p. 3). While the United States may have a history of violence, it does not have, as some imply, a "tradition" of violence—a long-held, customary use of violence for certain situations, shared by all or most societal members. This is so because "our violence lacks both an ideological and geographical center; it lacks cohesion; it has been too various, diffuse, and spontaneous to be forged into a single, sustained, inveterate hatred shared by entire social classes" (Hofstadter, 1970, p. 3). The United States has a history containing a multitude of qualitatively different kinds of violence— violence directed toward different kinds of goals, perpetrated by different kinds of people toward different kinds of targets—occurring in different periods and places. In some cases, the rich and poor alike engaged in violence; in others, it predominated among the poor. Sometimes certain forms of violence were considered by the community at large to be appropriate, possibly legitimate, and quite necessary; other times the same kinds of violence were deemed by the community to be criminal and senseless. In some cases, the particular forms of violence tied to certain times and places appear buried in the passing of those eras; in others, the styles, skills, attitudes, and justifications that permit violence appear to have been transmitted to future generations. It may be instructive, at this point, to comment on some of the more notable periods in which can be found violence that is today considered criminal.

Patriotic Violence in the Revolutionary Period
"Our nation was conceived and born in violence—in the violence of the Sons of Liberty and the patriots of the American port cities of the

1760s and 1770s" (Brown, 1969a, p. 46). During the Revolutionary period, the colonies experienced the widespread violence of political terrorism, guerrilla warfare, vigilantism, and the individual killing and assaulting of the British and their sympathizers. These violent patriots, composed of the rich and poor alike, were politically "weak," having little influence over the political and social control structures of the colonies under the English and Tories. Having little access to these legitimate structures, the patriots resorted to what the English considered the illegal use of personal and collective violence as a means of eliminating the binding command of the Crown.

Many colonists shared a perspective that considered physical violence a justifiable means for achieving collective autonomy and self-regulation. In fact, the Lockean-Jeffersonian philosophy, which formed the ideological base of our government in fundamental opposition to that of England, emphasized a person's right to physically fight for freedom. It was this ideology, which was set forth in the Declaration of Independence, that legitimized the terrorist activities and the revolutionary break with English rule (a break that cost the colonial rebels some 25,000 lives). Furthermore, this ideology, as well as the glorification of revolutionary violence, was used to justify sporadic occurrence of political terrorism and vigilantism well into the 1800s (Brown, 1969b, pp. 89–93).

The American Frontier and Justice by the Individual

The American experience of settling and "civilizing" a vast and untamed frontier, in a period that overlapped with the Revolutionary era and extended into the 1900s, witnessed perhaps the greatest amount of violence in the history of the nation. Individual and collective forms of violence, by both the rich and poor, were plentiful and diverse. Group rape of Indian and Mexican women by white men; gunfights; assaults on drunken cowboys for their gold and silver; lynch mobs and vigilantism; skirmishes over land and precious metals; violent conflict between settlers and native Indian and Mexican peoples; and wars between landowners and squatters, cattle barons and sheep herders or between open-range advocates and barbed-wire proponents—all these were commonplace during this period.

The character of the frontier was such that personal violence to achieve one's ends not only seemed appropriate but was often considered necessary (Bensman, 1971, p. 353), probably because of the unique character of the frontiersman. As Frederick Jackson Turner (1961, pp. 37–114) and his students explained, the frontiersman was an individualist, one without strong bonds to a family or community. At the core of his individualism were a set of liberal-capitalistic values and a materialistic philosophy that glorified property and personal holdings. Consequently, barriers to his acquisitions—such as Indian and Mexican inhabitants—as well as threats to his holdings—such as horse thieves and squatters—were exempt from governmental protection. Force was used to take what was there to be taken and to protect what was already his (Frantz, 1969, p. 120).

Violence may also have been deemed necessary because of the nature of frontier life. The frontier presented constant dangers that were never experienced by those inhabiting the urbanized cities of the times. Danger came from many directions. Frontier people faced angered Indians, Mexicans, and fellow settlers over land and stocks of wild game and horses; they had to protect themselves against bands of robbers, outlaws and fugitive criminals seeking refuge in a land of drifters. Furthermore, the frontier was a land in which danger could not be alleviated or eliminated by resorting to the legitimate political machinery or its agencies of social control (Bensman, 1971, p. 354; Conklin, 1975, pp. 187–194). Population movement outpaced the growth and strength of political structures, and consequently such structures were either nonexistent or had little in the way of enforcement agencies. If law enforcement did exist, it was typically inefficient or comprised of outlaws and skilled gunslingers no different than the criminals themselves.

The frontier people, whether rich or poor, had few alternatives to violence. They could flee in the face of adversity, yield to their advancing opponents, or engage in violence to take what was needed and to defend themselves (cf. Frantz, 1969). This latter course of conduct was invoked only too often. People would assemble into short-lived mobs to lynch suspected criminals, community deviants, or just unpopular opponents, justifying their action as a means of insuring future safety and achieving justice. Well-to-do community members would organize permanent vigilance committees for the purpose of rounding up known or suspected outlaws, holding kangaroo courts, and performing summary executions. The wealthier frontier people would hire gunslingers or cowhands for armed protection. Most others would individually take matters into their own hands by violently eliminating alleged transgressors.

The character of the frontiersman coupled with the contingencies of frontier life made physical violence an expedient and effective tool for resolving the problems of everyday living. As the frontier was slowly conquered and the political and law-enforcement agencies grew in strength, personal violence diminished.

Interracial Violence

Perhaps the earliest and most notable point of violence between whites and blacks was the Southern institution of slavery.[5] Slavery was a system of class rule in which blacks were an involuntary labor force for white plantation owners. While Christian morality did not condone human enslavement, blacks were simply not considered human. Instead, they were defined as godless heathens, members of a subspecies; given this justification, whites dismissed blacks as inferior creatures (Redding, 1950). Slaves lived as beasts of burden; not only were they housed as livestock, but they were literally branded and bred as stock. They were, in essence, "property," a material good to be bought and sold and bred to increase their owner's holdings.

Eugene Genovese (1974) proposes that slavery was based on an ideology of *paternalism:* Naturally subordinate beings should be cared for and protected by naturally superior beings. This ideology obligated the white masters to provide for their slaves. But, more important, it came to embrace a set of mutual obligations: Slaves were expected to work for their masters in exchange for protection and direction. This reciprocity, Genovese argues, implicitly recognized that slaves were in fact human and had certain rights. Thus, a paradox in defining slaves as inhuman (property) and human (with rights and obligations) was taking shape. Indeed, the law itself recognized slaves both as chattels and as human beings with the capacity for willed action. As the Civil War approached, this paradox accelerated with the steady decrease in slaves' opportunities for gaining freedom by purchase or manumission and with the steady improvement of their material conditions. That is, slaves lived a better life than in the seventeenth century yet suffered greater restrictions in the possibility of securing freedom.

Slaves were not fatalistic or apathetic toward their collective situation of relative deprivation, as is sometimes thought. Rather, their anger and resentment was generally submerged, finding expression in nonviolent resistance. There were, however, a number of instances in which white slaveowners and their families were beaten and killed and their property burned and destroyed at the hands of incensed slaves (Phillips, 1966). Perhaps the most famous collective uprising, which occurred in 1831, came to be known as the Nat Turner Rebellion. After killing the plantation owner and his family, Nat Turner gathered together fellow slaves to launch an attack against several other white slaveowners and their families. At the rebellion's end, some fifty white people were dead. This revolt exacerbated the growing paradox. On the one hand, new laws were passed, tightening the already totalitarian control of owners over slaves. On the other hand, there was further improvement in the slaves' material conditions, a response by whites to growing slave unrest. But such improvements did not calm the unrest. Consistent with the general thesis that collective violence of subjugated groups accompanies or follows improvement in material conditions, even more slave revolts followed. During this period there were an estimated 250 slave uprisings, far more than occurred in the seventeenth century when conditions were considerably poorer (Aptheker, 1966).

The character of interracial violence changed somewhat with the passing of the Civil War and the marked change in the status of blacks, from slaves to free people. Initially, such violence was in the form of terrorist activity by a group called the Ku Klux Klan. The Klan saw itself as the protector of Christianity, the white man's God-given dominance, and the Southern way of life. By 1871 the invisible empire of the Klan had a membership of over half a million, composed predominantly of poor whites and the remnants of the decaying Southern aristocracy. A Congressional investigation that year uncovered hangings, shootings, whippings, and mutilations in the thousands (Wolfgang, 1974, p. 250). Indeed, the Klan systematically punished any blacks (as well as many whites) considered to be "out of line" (Gillette & Tillinger, 1965). Thus, the Ku Klux Klan and the various groups to follow them (such as the White Caps) sought to maintain the antebellum system of white supremacy and black inferiority.

Less-organized mobs of whites also engaged in persecuting blacks in the post-slavery South. Like the activities of the Ku Klux Klan and other antiblack vigilance groups, the mob activity directed against threatening blacks was considered by Southern white communities as quite appropriate (even though it was technically criminal). Lynch mobs would be stirred into existence by some rumors that a black had overstepped the unwritten yet quite binding apartheid code of the South, usually by allegedly raping a white woman (Shibutani & Kwan, 1965, pp. 391–401). As the rumors spread, they would be embellished to the point that anyone believing them would think that blacks were raping scores of white women and were on the verge of overthrowing the white power structure of the South. In response to such "threats," whites would form short-lived mobs and rampage black neighborhoods, lynching known culprits and assaulting or killing those who stood in their way.

This type of violence was common around the turn of the century and up into the 1930s, when lynching declined and governmental police agencies grew in strength and dominance (cf. Brown, 1969b). The violence of these mobs, however, was no less brutal in the latter stages than at the outset, as can be seen in the following description of a lynching in Ocilla, Georgia, in January 1930.

> For more than an hour Irwin was tortured, his fingers and toes being cut off one by one. The rest of the gruesome treatment to which he was subjected was of a nature better left undescribed. (A doctor who was a member of the investigation committee said that even de Sade would never have been able to invent anything so terrible). Finally, he was strung up to a tree by the hands and slowly burnt (Nordholt, 1960, p. 223).

Nor was mob violence limited to the rural South. In the growing urban centers of the early 1900s, a host of interracial riots took place, including those of Atlanta (1906), St. Louis (1917), Chicago (1919), Tulsa (1921), and Detroit (1943) (Hofstadter & Wallace, 1970, pp. 204–258). These riots began as hastily organized groups of whites ventured into developing black neighborhoods, vandalizing property and attacking residents. The black communities were consequently provoked to counterviolence (Lupo, 1974).

The 1950s and early 1960s found whites individually and collectively attacking the blacks and their sympathizers engaged in the civil rights movement. Unlike during earlier periods, however, the violence directed toward aspiring blacks and their allies no longer had the air of legitimacy that whites had previously enjoyed. The 1965 riot in Watts heralded a new form of racial violence that continued for the remainder of the decade. The ghetto riots of the 1960s were not directly interracial, for only blacks participated. Yet, they were interracial in the sense that the violence was directed against the white power structure. Blacks took the offensive, reacting to such everyday events as police harassment, unwarranted arrests, or shooting of suspects—events symbolizing their repressed, subordinate status—by collectively attacking, burning, and looting the buildings and property of whites found in their neighborhoods.

The mid-1970s has witnessed yet another form of racial violence, this time stemming from the busing of school children so as to achieve racial equality in educational opportunities. In some cities court-ordered busing has been marked by interracial conflict and violence both by students and by parents (Lupo, 1974).

Migrants and Immigrants: Agents and Recipients of Conflict

During the latter 1800s and early 1900s, a sizable amount of violence was found among many of the migrant and immigrant groups entering expanding urban centers. The habitation of our major cities by new hordes of poor, dislocated people gave rise to friction both within the groups and between them and the longer established city people. On the one hand, these ethnic and racial minorities felt the bite of discrimination by the older members of the community, as well as the shock of operating in a new and alien land. On the other hand, enormous conflict arose between generations of such groups. Much to their immigrant parents' dismay, children would reject the old-country practices in favor of the American lifestyles of their coworkers and schoolmates.

Because many of the migrant and immigrant groups found the political and social control structures of the city to be inadequate to resolve such modes of conflict, they adhered to their imported perspectives and used violence as a justifiable means for achieving various goals. For instance, when an immigrant youth deviated from the Old World customs by acting "American," it was not uncommon for the man of the house to punish such deviance by whipping and beating the boy into tacit submission. Justice was also served by personal violence, as illustrated by Thorsten Sellin in a case where "a Sicilian father in New

Jersey killed the sixteen-year-old seducer of his daughter [and expressed] surprise at his arrest since he had merely defended his family honor in a traditional way" (1938, p. 68). Violence also served the youth of migrant and immigrant peoples. Males could build a reputation and achieve a measure of status and prestige among peers by aggressive sexuality toward the "tarnished" women of the neighborhood. These early ghetto residents had their own styles and skills of performing violence and attitudes and justifications that permit it. The characteristics of their violence, having been transmitted from one generation to the next, can still be found in the same urban ghettos of contemporary America that now house different minority groups (Bensman, 1971, p. 360).

Unlike earlier forms of violence—revolutionary, frontier, and anti-black—the violence exemplified by the migrants and immigrants who occupied the urban ghettos was regarded by the communities as criminal and oftentimes senseless, and public sentiment favoring violence generally receded as the 1900s wore on. Perhaps this was because the nation's machinery of political and social control was gaining strength. Many of the more prominent and influential members of the community now looked to the government as the effective agency for handling conflict. Whether in fact the support of personal violence by the community withdrew as a consequence of the increased strength and availability of legitimate forces of social control is debatable. Nonetheless, the increasing role of these agencies was accompanied by the public's diminishing support of face-to-face violence (cf. Brown, 1969b).

The Violence of Unionization

The violent struggles by workingmen to gain the rights of organization and unionization grew out of dehumanizing working conditions and indifferent management. At the turn of the century working conditions were not merely bad, they were deadly. In describing the steelworker's situation, Ovid Demaris has pointed out:

> He worked a twelve-hour shift seven days a week in temperatures that soared to 130 degrees. There was no time allowed for meals, no place to wash up and there was no compensation for frequent accidents. That the work [was] hazardous can be deduced from the fact that three hundred

men were killed and two thousand hurt on the job in various mills in the Pittsburgh area during the year before the [Homestead] strike [in July 1892] (1970, p. 150).

In the bloody and violent strike that followed many were killed and injured, yet the number harmed in the strike was far less than had been killed or injured the year before in the plants.

Through strikes workers sought to improve their working conditions, to increase their wages, and to secure recognition as a bargaining agent. However, management leaders saw it as their inalienable right to run their plants and treat their workers in any way they saw fit. Consequently the capitalists, with the aid of government and private police forces, attempted to suppress unionization and break up strikes by beating and killing workers. Such company action oftentimes brought fierce retaliation by striking workers. The Colorado Fuel and Iron Company strike of 1913–1914 was typical:

> [A] 15-hour battle between strikers and militiamen ended in the burning of the strikers' tent city during which 2 mothers and 11 children suffocated to death in the "Black Hole of Ludlow." Following this tragedy, maddened miners erupted in a 10-day rebellion which brought "anarchy and unrestrained class warfare" to a 250-mile area of southern Colorado before the entrance of Federal troops ended the violence (Brown, 1969a, p. 55).

Such violent strikes occurred around the country from 1877 through the 1930s, when the federal government instituted reforms regulating labor relations. Not only did the new laws help settle disputes, but they also demonstrated some governmental interest in and recognition of the workers' grievances. The government had not previously aided workers who wanted unionization. When labor violence was most fierce, the government was almost always on the side of industry. Troops or police were never sent in to protect strikers if the company being struck hired strikebreakers (scabs) and private police forces. Only if the workers appeared to be gaining the upper hand over management's forces, such as happened in the Homestead Steel Lockout in 1892 when the workers routed a force of Pinkerton men, did the government intervene, providing reinforcements for the company. This policy would continue far into the twentieth century.

Student Protest

Of final concern is the violence that overtook college and university campuses in the 1960s. Prior to this time loud parties and fraternity pranks had been the primary reasons that students got in trouble with the law. Beginning with the 1964 free speech movement in Berkeley, however, student-police confrontations took on an increasingly intense and violent character rarely seen in the United States (yet common in many European and Latin American countries for decades).

The new phase of student protest began at the University of California in Berkeley in reaction to new university regulations limiting political expression on campus. Berkeley students resisted by using nonviolent tactics such as sit-ins and mass gatherings borrowed from the civil rights movement (Rossman, 1971). When the police were called to break up the Berkeley demonstrations, some 800 students were arrested, none of whom resorted to violence.

As the war in Vietnam became a central issue among students, more and more demonstrations occurred with frequent clashes between police and student protestors. Passive resistance by students came to be regarded as a useless tactic since it seemed to have no effect on ending the war and a number of passive resisters had been beaten by police. To better resist the police, demonstrators began to take such measures as wearing motorcycle helmets and other kinds of protective headgear. Arrests were actively resisted, and various weapons (mainly rocks and bottles) were used against police. In their turn the police used such resistance to document their need for tougher tactics. An inevitable escalation of violence and militancy resulted.[6]

One of the most violent confrontations between protestors and police took place in Chicago at the 1968 Democratic National Convention. For a number of days before the convention, groups comprised mostly of students and former students had gathered. These groups represented a cross section of those involved in the antiwar movement. Some were supporters of Eugene McCarthy, a Democratic presidential candidate, others were antiwar activists, and still others were political radicals bent on disrupting the convention. To prevent such disruption, Mayor

Richard Daley of Chicago had alerted police and requested the assistance of the National Guard and Army to control the protestors. By the first day of the convention, the stage was set for the clash that was to follow (Stark, 1972, pp. 18–19).

As the convention got underway, demonstrations took place that for the most part were peaceful. In Grant Park and in front of the Conrad Hilton Hotel, however, the police attacked the demonstrators, beating and arresting literally scores of individuals (National Commission, 1969b, p. 1). Shown on television, the violence seemed largely the product of the legitimate yet rather dubious action of police rather than of the illegitimate action of demonstrators. Later, the police provided evidence that they had been attacked by rocks, knives, and other missiles that the television cameras had somehow missed. In spite of the provocation, the *Walker Report* still found reason to condemn the police action:

> [V]iolence [by the police] was made all the more shocking by the fact that it was often inflicted upon persons who had broken no law, disobeyed no order, made no threat. These included peaceful demonstrators, onlookers, and large numbers of residents who were simply passing through, or happened to live in the areas where confrontations were occurring (National Commission, 1969b, p. vii).

In subsequent student confrontations with the police, the violence was initiated by both police and protestors. In the 1970 riots at the University of California at Santa Barbara, the students burned a branch of the Bank of America and assaulted police with rocks, bottles, and slingshots. One student was shot and killed during one of these disturbances, and numerous students and professors were beaten, arrested, and confined. At Kent State University, Berkeley, and Jackson State University, students were killed in demonstrations. Widespread student protests resulting in violence diminished in the early 1970s; they would subsequently find only sporadic revival in moments of political and social tension.

Transmission of Violence Between Historical Periods

That the United States does not have a singular, highly valued tradition of violence shared by all societal members is not to suggest that the violence of certain times and places had no impact on the people of other times and places. Indeed, the vigilance committees found in the frontier and South would oftentimes cite the Declaration of Independence or the American Revolution as a basic justification for taking matters into their own hands and executing those deemed threatening to the community. The violence directed toward blacks by the Ku Klux Klan, White Caps, and lynch mobs after the Civil War certainly owed its occurrence to slavery, which had spawned and nurtured racial hostility and tolerance of violence to control blacks.

In a similar vein, many of the contemporary forms of criminal violence are indebted in part to the styles of, skills for, and attitudes favorable to violence that have been passed down among generations from several points in history (Graham & Gurr, 1969, pp. xiii–xiv, 624–628). For example, that segment of society accounting for much of the contemporary murder, rape, and assault is comprised primarily of male and minority group constituents of the lower socioeconomic class who inhabit the urban ghettos (Wolfgang & Ferracuti, 1967, pp. 155–163, 258–263). These people live and operate in the same neighborhoods as the early migrants and immigrants and have access to practices passed down, perhaps in altered form, through generations for handling particular situations arising out of the same kinds of life conditions—racial and ethnic discrimination, in-group conflict between generations, social immobility, and the like (cf. Cloward & Ohlin, 1960, pp. 144–160).

THEORETICAL EXPLANATIONS OF THE CHARACTER OF CRIMINAL VIOLENCE

The character of criminal violence has been explained from a variety of theoretical orientations, each of which emphasizes different units of analysis. Notable among these orientations are the biological and the psychodynamic, yet the sociological promises to offer a greater understanding of violence than either of these can provide.

The Biological Orientations
One popular biological approach examines the physiological basis of aggression. In recent years, it has been discovered that certain components of the body—the hypothalamus and neocortex of the brain, and the

endocrine glands—control rage and aggression. These are normal responses that these centers make when activated by *certain* kinds of stimuli of *certain* degrees of strength. Uncontrolled rage, explosive aggression, and irrational acts of violence can be explained as abnormal responses caused by defects or imbalances that allow *many* kinds of stimuli at *lower* degrees of strength to activate the centers (Buss, 1961).

A second biological approach argues that all animals, including humans, have an innate aggressive instinct. Konrad Lorenz (1966) is a renowned proponent of this theme. He contends that while aggression can emerge in various forms of violence, it springs from a basic innate drive. In describing this position, Marvin Wolfgang and Franco Ferracuti (1967, p. 192) suggest that aggression serves as a universal method among human beings for the spacing of individuals over the available territory, the selecting of the fittest to survive, and the making of social rank. The majority of biologists, however, oppose this view. Many argue that aggression is a response that has its basis not in the human biological constitution but instead in the human experience with an external environment. That is, people learn that an aggressive response should be elicited in the face of certain kinds of stimuli.

Psychodynamic Orientations

Criminal violence may also be explained through the psychodynamic-control approach. Essentially, this orientation considers behavior to be the product of two contending forces. On the one side are *impulses,* forces that direct individuals toward certain ends, such as gratification of hunger, thirst, and sex. On the other side are *controls,* "something inside the actor or in the situation of action that denies or forbids the expression of the impulse" (A. Cohen, 1966, p. 48). Two branches of this orientation are prominent in the explanation of violence.

The Psychoanalytic Model.

One branch, embracing a psychoanalytic model, holds that human beings have biologically rooted drives for sex and aggression and internal mechanisms, conceptually located in each person's psyche, for coping with such drives (cf. Chodorkoff & Baxter, 1969). Sigmund Freud (1947) suggested that the psyche could be analytically divided into three components: the id, the ego, and the superego. The *id* is that part of the psyche that contains human desires and impulses, including those of sex and aggression. It is the storehouse of the energy that propels human action toward the immediate satisfaction of desires and impulses. The *superego* is the social side of the psyche in that it incorporates society's rules. The *ego* might be considered the evaluator of human action. It both attends to the desires of the id and listens to the superego to learn the socially approved lines of action for reducing the tension created by those desires. Once the ego negotiates the conflict between the id and the superego, it responds with a line of action geared to satisfy the id in a socially acceptable manner.

Some psychoanalysts focus on the overly strong impulses of the id in the explanation of aggression. At times they assume some weakness in the control exerted by the superego and ego. For example, Freud (1922) suggested that human aggression was the actualization of the *death instinct*, a basic, inherent drive more or less comparable to those of hunger and thirst (cf. Mowrer & Kluckhohn, 1944, pp. 112–113). When this instinct takes on incredible strength, it overcomes the actor's internal controls and emerges in violence. In some cases this impulse would be directed toward the actor, taking such forms as suicide and masochism. But it is often balanced by the *life instinct*, which prevents self-destruction and often results in outwardly directed violence.

Other psychoanalysts have explained violence in terms of defective controls over impulses. Three defects in the control structure can be identified (cf. Megargee, 1969). First, an individual's ego may be weak. In this case, the person is unable to manage the impulses of the id or to evaluate the socially approved conduct dictated by the superego. Consequently, the ego is unable to defer gratification and transform impulses into socially approved conduct. At any instigation, then, the individual's actions will eventuate in aggression, thus bringing tension reduction. Second, the actor's superego may be underdeveloped. Here, aggressive impulses are carried out not because they cannot be managed through the dictates of the superego but because such impulses find no resistance or disapproval from the superego. Third, the actor's superego may be overdeveloped. In such cases, the superego will block any aggressive impulse of the id, no matter how minute; the consequence will be that tension is never reduced. As the aggressive impulses accumulate, they finally reach the upper threshold where the superego can no longer control them, and they emerge as uncontrolled, explosive outbursts of rage and destruction.

The Frustration-Aggression Theory.   A second branch of the psycho-dynamic-control orientation is the frustration-aggression theory. This very popular approach holds that when an actor is blocked in satisfying some end dictated by impulses (frustration), the result is some form of aggressive behavior (Mulvihill & Tumin, 1969, p. 434). In some cases, the obstacle to behavior may be internal. A psychoanalytic approach, for example, would suggest that the superego's interference with strong pleasure-seeking drives would be met with some form of aggression (Freud, 1925). John Dollard and his colleagues (1939), however, presented a more workable statement that shifted the emphasis to an external obstacle. They found that environmental or situational obstacles would produce aggression directed toward removing the source of frustration, thereby permitting the gratification of impulses.

The frustration-aggression principle has taken several directions in its history. Some considered the classic statement by Dollard and his colleagues to hold that all frustration brings aggression, and, conversely, that all aggression results from antecedent frustration.[7] This, however, was short-lived. Researchers found that not all aggression could be linked to antecedent frustrations and that if internal or external controls were strong enough, frustration would lead to responses other than outward and antisocial aggression. For example, aggression may be directed inward, taking such forms as suicide.

Most societal members have engaged in criminal violence at some point in life—fist fights, vandalism, battery against one's spouse, family, and friends. Middle and upper class members have learned to resolve situations of conflict systematically by calling the police, visiting psychiatrists, and by similar nonviolent measures. Many of the male and minority group members of the lower socioeconomic class living in the slums and ghettos, however, learn to handle certain kinds of friction by hitting and kicking, stabbing and shooting (Goode, 1969). As Wolfgang and Ferracuti (1967, pp. 154–155, 160–161) argue, these societal members share a cognitive perspective—a "subculture of violence"—learned through interaction with family and peers, in which violence for certain situations is rewarded while nonviolence for the same situations brings censure, ridicule, and ostracism.[8] Thus, violence is a permissible, if not expected, response to moments of insult, degradation, and establishing character (cf. Miller, 1958).[9] Wolfgang underlines the tenability of such contentions in his investigation of criminal homicide:

> The significance of a jostle, a slight derogatory remark, or the appearance of a weapon in the hands of an adversary are stimuli differentially perceived and interpreted by Negroes and whites, males and females. . . . A male is usually expected to defend the name and honor of his mother, the virtue of womanhood (even though his female companion for the evening may be an entirely new acquaintance and/or prostitute), and to accept no derogation about his race (even from a member of his own race), his age, or his masculinity. Quick resort to physical combat as a measure of daring, courage, or defense of status appears to be a cultural expectation, especially for lower socio-economic class males of both races (1958, pp. 168–169).

In situations of group rape, offenders may likewise feel obligated to satisfy their sexual needs and demonstrate manliness by means of violence, even when there may be misgivings:

> The leader of the male group . . . apparently precipitated and maintained the [sexual assault], despite misgivings, because of a need to fulfill the role that the other two men had assigned him. "I was scared when it began to happen," he says. "I wanted to leave but I didn't want to say it to the other guys—you know—that I was scared" (Blanchard in Griffin, 1971, p. 30).

It may be directed toward substitute objects, like the bedroom wall or a punching bag. Or it may be rendered harmless by sublimating aggression into such socially acceptable activities as athletic events.

Recent research suggests that an actor's response to frustration is learned rather than dependent upon the controls found in the psyche. Albert Bandura and Richard Walters (1959) marshal considerable proof that people learn what stimuli are frustrating and how to respond to those moments of frustration through a process of conditioning. According to this view, people act aggressively because they have been reinforced to be aggressive in response to frustrating stimuli. Those who attack substitute objects, sublimate aggression, or flee do so because they have been punished for direct aggression or reinforced for these other responses. As reinforcement contingencies change, so too will the types of responses.

The Sociological Orientation

Both the biological and psychodynamic orientations and their respective theories have provided a measure of knowledge for understanding the character of criminal violence. Skepticism is necessary, however, when approaching the contention that criminal violence is the *sole* result of certain innate drives or instincts or of idiosyncratic defects or abnormalities in internal control structures that compel people to be violent. A sociological orientation would argue that while people have the inherent capacity to be violent, such a capacity is shaped and directed by a variety of cultural and social processes (Wolfgang, 1967; Bohannon, 1969; Goode, 1972). People learn from others how and under what conditions different kinds of violence should be used, and their performance of violence is directed and shaped by specific others with whom they interact. Thus violence is a method for handling problematic situations that is learned through social interaction (Schrag, 1969).

In response to the American public's increased concern with criminal violence, behavioral and social scientists, through independent and government research (the latter under the auspices of the National Commission on the Causes and Prevention of Violence), have attempted to arrive at a more detailed understanding of violence. This research has taken two principal directions. The first has focused on the distribution (epidemiology) and modal characteristics of the more notable forms of violence. A second direction has attempted to provide specific answers to the question of why offenders commit various kinds of violence (etiology).

While both of these traditional lines of investigation provide a fund of information that is useful in paving the way to a better understanding of criminal violence, a third, yet neglected line of research holds the potential of providing an even richer understanding. Criminal homicide, assault, rape, mugging, vandalism, juvenile gang wars, and ghetto riots are *social acts* occurring within *social situations,* arenas of action where two or more actors mutually monitor one another and move with reference to the other's moves (Goffman, 1967, p. 167). Because these events are performed within social situations, one can anticipate that specific situational conditions and the performance of given roles by involved persons are necessary for the successful execution of the violent performances. This third line of investigation, then, would study violence at the level of the social situation, focusing on the patterns of situated conditions and roles common to particular kinds of events. The researcher asks, *How* is criminal violence performed? What situated conditions appear to facilitate violent events? What roles or patterns of conduct do the offenders, victims, and possible onlookers typically engage in during the performances? Are the actors mutually oriented to do violence, as would be found when two youngsters engage in a round of name calling and fighting on the playground? Or is the offenders' definition of the situation as one calling for violence forced on their unwilling situational colleagues? (This view is often promoted in media accounts of mass murders and political assassinations and generalized to other kinds of events.) If an audience is present, do its members condone the violence by cheering the offender to victory, or do they actively seek to deactivate the confrontation? In comparison to the more traditional lines of research, then, this mode of inquiry asks questions demanding fundamentally different answers.

Not only can this direction provide information not directly ascertained by the more traditional approaches, but it also suggests some reasonable methods for reducing violence. Too often researchers offer programs to reduce violence that simply treat the violent offender. Indeed, it is proposed that violent offenders can be "cured" and prevented from doing further violence by means of psychiatric therapy and counseling, prison rehabilitation, and the like. To this day, these methods have been of dubious value, for most treated subjects continue to engage in violence. If, however, one assumes that certain situated conditions and roles are important to the completion of violent events, then deactivating these conditions and roles should effectively lower the chances that an encounter will successfully escalate into violent behavior.

THE MAJOR FORMS OF PRESENT-DAY VIOLENCE

Since this situational approach promises to provide a very useful understanding of violence, the following examination of the character of major forms of contemporary criminal violence will follow the lead of Erving Goffman (1967, p. 3) and explore not merely men and their moments, as do theories focusing on the individual, but *moments and their men.* In the first part, the character of individual forms of criminal violence—face-to-face confrontations between an offender and victim as exemplified in homicide, assault, rape, and mugging—will be analyzed, with emphasis on the manner in which they are typically performed. This will be followed by an examination of the character of several forms of collective criminal violence. While in the final analysis collective forms also involve face-to-face confrontations, such events as vandalism, juvenile gang wars, ghetto riots, and prison violence are more typical as group-centered activities. That is, these events are generally characterized by being performed by people as collectivities for collective purposes, not by aggregates of individuals for individual purposes.

Individual Forms
While homicide, assault, rape, and mugging vary in terms of offenders' goals, victims' orientations, and the like, these individual forms of criminal violence occur within the same type of larger social occasion. A *social occasion* is a social affair or undertaking bounded in regard to time and place; within the occasion many situations form, dissolve, and re-form (Goffman, 1963, p. 18). Social occasions encompassing performances of criminal attacks share, at a minimum, two particular features.

First, research has shown that such occasions are typically *leisure-time* rather than *work-time.* That is, criminal attacks generally occur in the leisure hours: between the hours of 6 P.M. and 2 A.M., and especially on weekends and holidays. In addition, attacks predominate in leisure settings—in the home or in such public places as the tavern or street corner—rather than in one's place of employment.

The second feature is that these leisure-time occasions are "loosely" rather than "tightly" structured (cf. Goffman, 1963, pp. 198–215). That is, these occasions permit a wide range of activities that are defined by members as appropriate. An evening at home, for example, may find a person engaging in a number of suitable activities that would be seen as improper for other occasions. Or during an evening at the corner tavern it could be considered quite appropriate to solicit a barmaid, sing along with the jukebox, become drunk, or challenge all comers to arm wrestling. Such diversity of action is simply unacceptable in such tighter, formally structured occasions as funerals, weddings, or dinner parties.

It is hypothesized that individual forms of physical violence find greater occurrence in loosely structured occasions than in tighter, formally structured ones because violent escalation and consummation could be more easily defined as appropriate.

Although violent attacks generally occur within the context of loose, leisure-time occasions, these attacks take two fundamentally different forms. Typical cases of homicide and assault share some basic characteristics. First, these events are nonscheduled in time and place. That is, they generally develop within loosely structured occasions rather than being planned prior to them. Second, the violence is escalated by a character contest, a gamey confrontation in which the offender and victim attempt to save or establish face at the expense of each other by standing strong and steady in the face of adversity (Goffman, 1967, pp. 218–219, 238–257).[10] Third, the offender, victim, and, when present, audience, forge an explicit or implicit agreement that physical violence is a suitable if not required means for resolving questions of face.

The typical instance of forcible rape or mugging can be characterized along a different line. First, these events are usually scheduled in a one-sided manner. That is, the offender unilaterally structures both the time and place of attack, manipulating the victim during and after entrance to the setting. Second, each of these events are exploitative affairs, with the offenders forcing their definition of the situation on unwilling, dissenting victims. Finally, while the victim's moves direct those of the offender in the situation of attack, this type of performance, unlike that of some homicides or assaults, does not find the offender and victim interacting toward the agreement that violence is appropriate within the setting.

Criminal Homicide.   One of the most serious of all crimes is criminal homicide. While the public periodically considers the murder rate to be increasing by leaps and bounds, its occurrence, in comparison to that of other violent crimes, has been reasonably stable over several decades, despite a considerable rise since the beginning of the 1960s.[11] In 1974, the rate of homicide was 9.7 per 100,000 population, about 4 more per 100,000 than in 1960 yet far lower than in the mid-1930s. Criminal homicide is the unlawful taking of a human being's life by another person who, prior to the event, had the expressed intention of killing or seriously injuring the victim (cf. Morris & Howard, 1964). Manslaughter, however, is homicide without the intention of killing or rendering serious injury. Negligence or traffic accidents resulting in the victim's death are typically charged as manslaughter.

As with other collective transactions, criminal homicide is a developmental performance.[12] In addition, murder typically requires the contribution and shared orientation toward violence of both the offender and victim (Clinard & Quinney, 1973, pp. 40–42; Luckenbill, 1974).[13] Two cases presented by David Luckenbill (1974, p. 53) illustrate this point.

> *Case 49* The offender and victim were sitting on the back porch. He (offender) asked her (victim) while she was ironing if she would like to have sexual intercourse as her boyfriend was gone for the day. She stated, "I'm gunna tell Jack what you asked me for, you black son-of-a-bitch." The offender was angered, and stated, "Shut up, you bitch. If you tell him, I'll kill you, and don't call me no black son-of-a-bitch." This angered the victim. She rose, stated she was going to kill him, and ran to her room. The offender followed. In the room, the victim grabbed a pistol, turned, and shot the offender in the groin. He took the weapon from her and pumped four bullets into her.

> *Case 54* The male victim began to ridicule the female offender, calling her abusive names. The offender was angered by this and demanded that he "shut up." The victim, however, continued. Finally, the offender exclaimed, "I said shut up. If you don't shut up and stop it, I'm going to kill you and I mean it." He continued in the face of these threats. She rose from the chair, proceeded to the kitchen, grabbed a knife, and returned. Again she repeated her demand that the victim stop. The victim rose from the sofa, and swore at her stupidity for thinking she could hurt him, and continued laughing. She thrust the knife deep in his chest.

Such *situational improprieties* as the victim's insult or ridicule of the offender, flirtation with the offender's lover or spouse, or noncompliance with the offender's commands mark the first in a series of moves eventuating in the victim's death. Having noted the victim's inappropriate move, the offender retaliates. This *retaliation* may take a variety of forms, all of which suggest, either explicitly or implicitly, that physical violence may be necessary in the situation. In most cases retaliation comes in the form of threatening the victim with physical harm if apology, compliance, or flight is not forthcoming. In both of the above cases we find the offender threatening the victim with death if certain concessions are not made by the victim. At other times the offender may challenge the victim to fight, or the offender may respond with equally abusive or insulting gestures that are supported by a readiness to use force. In any case, retaliation represents an offender's attempt to maintain face in response to challenge or degradation by a victim.

The offender's move places the victim in a problematic and consequential position. The victim must either meet the challenge or back down from the offender's retaliation. Rather than the latter, which would be a display of weak character, the victim forges with the offender a *working consensus* that violence is a suitable means by which to resolve their conflict. In other words, the victim supports the improprieties and consequently escalates the confrontation. In many cases this support comes in the form of continuing the inappropriate activity under the offender's threat of harm or death.[14] In Case 54, for example, the male did not stop his insulting, degrading remarks after the female threatened to kill him if he continued. At other times the victim elicits a counterchallenge to the offender's threats, a move exemplified in Case 49. In yet other instances the victim responds with physical violence, immediately putting the offender on the defensive.[15]

Just as the offender and victim develop a mutual orientation toward the use of violence, so too does the audience to the event appear to share their working consensus. As the confrontation takes shape, the audience reacts in two ways. In over half of the cases involving bystanders reported by Luckenbill (1974), interested bystanders contributed to the escalation by actively encouraging the violent confrontation: for instance, by coaxing and daring the opponents, by supplying weapons, or by blocking the scuffle from interference by outsiders. In all other cases, onlookers assumed neutral roles, expressing neither encouragement nor discouragement. As Goffman (1969, p. 115) would suggest, such neutrality may be interpreted by opponents as a permissive stand toward their moves.

At this point of development, the offender and, not infrequently, the victim appear committed to themselves, the other, and their audience to carry through with their promised or implied violence. Since alternatives to violence have been reduced by the issuance of challenges, threats, or insults or by noncompliance, the only way the offender can avoid demonstrating weak character and losing face is to defeat the victim (Banitt, Katznelson, & Sheit, 1970).[16] Thus, it is at this point that weapons are secured by one or both and blows are exchanged, with one falling in defeat, the other rising to victory.

Once the victim falls, the offender exits the scene in regard to the victim and the moves of the audience. If the violent encounter occurred without an audience and the victim was a spouse, other relative, or close acquaintance of the offender, the offender will generally report his crime to police or to others who notify police. If the victim was merely a passing acquaintance or a complete stranger, however, the offender typically flees the situation, attempting to conceal his culpability.

Homicides generally occur before an audience. In these cases the offender acts in relation to the moves of that audience. When onlookers are supportive of the violence, then they support the offender's flight. They may suggest immediate departure, eliminate implicating evidence, not cooperate with police, and the like. When onlookers appear neutral to the confrontation, they are typically so shocked at the victim's demise that the offender is allowed to flee. When they are hostile to the violence, however, they usually restrain the offender until the arrival of the authorities and assist the fallen victim.

Assault.   In certain respects, assault and criminal homicide have similar characteristics. Assault may be defined as any physical attack that is done with the intent to kill, to inflict serious bodily injury, or to inflict simple injury, yet that falls short of death. This category includes aggravated assault, which typically requires medical treatment and hospitalization, and simple assault, which requires little treatment. In cases where assault occurs with other crimes like robbery, rape, or burglary, the assault is generally included in the greater offense. The concern in this discussion is with assaultive conduct aimed solely at injuring or killing, not meant as a means to some other criminal end.

Assaultive attacks are not as accurately reported as criminal homicide. Indeed, many child beatings and family disturbances go unreported. Nevertheless, the *Uniform Crime Reports* (Federal Bureau of Investigation, 1975) shows the minimal rate of assault as 214 per 100,000 population for 1974, an increase of 129 per 100,000 reported in 1960.[17] Assault is systematically performed by that segment of society that shares a subculture of violence. As in homicide, offenders are young, male minority group members of the lower classes of society. Their victims, while somewhat older, are similarly male minority group members of lower class background. In fact, in homicides, victims and offenders are often interlocked by kinship or other close relationship, so that assault is typically an intraclass, intraracial affair between members of a family or between close acquaintances.

Physical violence that eventuates in assault may be considered a strategy of action for demonstrating to others that one is not to be ridiculed, challenged, cheated, or pushed about. The manner in which such a strategy is implemented, however, varies. In one pattern of performance the victim contributes little to violent escalation and harm. Hans Toch offers the following as a case in point:

> I was with my boss's son and we'd been drinking wine and hitting all the bars and drinking whiskey too. . . . [There was this] loud-mouthed type. For some reason there, I just can't communicate with them at all. I have no patience with them. And he walked by me and poked me out of the way, walked right up front and I thought, "That's the way it goes," you know. I was mad, and we stood there for about, I guess, about ten minutes or something, and we were going to leave and he was coming back and he poked my boss's son out of the way, and he was coming like he was going to do it to me, and I just fired on him and decked him. And that was it (1969, pp. 94–95).

Or, to take the logical extreme, juveniles wishing to achieve a modicum of status in a new neighborhood may actually construct situations of assault. Lewis Yablonsky provides us with an example:

> [I]n one typical pattern . . . [the offender] will approach a stranger with the taunt, "What did you say about my mother?" An assault is then delivered upon the victim before he can respond to the question, which, of course, has no appropriate answer for preventing the attack (1962, pp. 208–209).

As David Pittman and William Handy (1964, p. 467) imply, the normal assault is not an explosive, passionate outburst of destruction; rather, it is the result of a period of intense, mutually oriented interaction between the offender and victim.[18] Marshall Clinard and Richard Quinney (1973, pp. 40–42) suggest that the typical assault consists of several stages. As with criminal homicide, assault begins when the offender defines the victim's actions as inappropriate or threatening. On the basis of this definition, the offender retaliates toward the victim in hope of restoring or establishing his questioned face. The retaliation generally takes the form of challenges or threats to do violence. For the conflict to eventuate in assault, moreover, the victim must move toward the offender to protect his integrity as a worthy opponent. Clearly, "if only one responds in a dispute, it is not likely to become violent" (Clinard & Quinney, 1973, p. 40). Thus, the victim in turn threatens to do violence if the offender does not back down. At this stage the violent encounter reaches a point of no return. Indeed, the opponents have little recourse but to initiate their violent attack or suffer the humiliation of a nonviolent defeat. Toch concludes that the "first moves increases the probability of violence; the reaction of the victim converts probability into certainty" (1969, p. 184).

Assaults between police and citizens may be useful in illustrating this sequence of moves. Toch found in his investigation that such assaults are the result of a series of face-saving moves by an officer and citizen who disagree on the very reason for their encounter (cf. McNamara, 1967; Hudson, 1970). Toch gives the following case as an example.

> This date while Reporting Officer was on routine patrol, I observed the suspect walking. Reporting Officer had not seen the suspect in some time and rolled the window on the radio car down and said to the suspect, "May I talk to you a minute Mr. S." With this the suspect with a large number of people around said in a very loud voice. "Kiss my a____ you mother f____." Reporting Officer got out of the radio car and told the suspect he was under arrest; at this point the suspect repeated the above phrase twice in a loud shouting voice as to attract a large number of people. At this point Reporting Officer grabbed suspect by the arm and told him he had been placed under arrest and attempted to get him to the radio car, so as to radio for patrol wagon. At this point suspect raised his right hand and struck Reporting Officer in the right shoulder, and had to be physically restrained (1969, p. 55).

In a typical case, an officer initiates the transaction by requesting the citizen's cooperation or by questioning him. The citizen, however, takes such a move as inappropriate because it is an affront to his autonomy and reputation. As James Hudson (1970) found, the citizen may be unwilling to accept what he perceives to be the role of suspect or criminal that the officer imputes to him. Consequently the citizen fails to comply. But the officer takes this refusal as a challenge to his authority and an indication of potential danger and violence (cf. Reiss, 1971, pp. 147–150). He moves from a verbal request to an order. The citizen resents such commands even more and escalates the confrontation by further noncompliance. Additionally, in many cases, including the above, noncompliance is accompanied by the use of abusive and threatening language. Now the officer is backed into a corner: He must either support his commands and maintain the authoritative character of his role or back down and lose face. His reaction is to maintain control of the situation by threatening or invoking arrest, supporting his moves by initiating physical restraint of the citizen. The citizen, however, to whom this attempted control is a cue of danger, takes defensive physical action. The battle ensues. The point is that each opponent contributes to the moves of the other by standing up to the other; the violence suggested in the officer's moves brings out a violent response of the citizen.

As with performances of criminal homicide, assaults involving police officers are also shaped by the stand of the audience (Toch, 1969). The mere presence of an audience of peers may require the citizen to stand up to the officer in order to display a courage and manliness that is important to his reputation (Bittner, 1970, p. 98). Similarly, the presence of onlookers requires the officer to take charge of the situation, to demonstrate to others that the authority vested in his position is something to be reckoned with. Moreover the audience may take an active role in escalating the violence. By jeering the officer, for example, the audience may stimulate his arrest of the citizen and cause him to escalate toward battle as a means of controlling the crowd (cf. Hudson, 1970, pp. 190–192). Similarly, its urging of an offender to stand up for himself requires that he not back down to "the man."

Forcible Rape. Forcible rape is the carnal knowledge of a woman by a man, carried out against her will and without her consent, extorted by means of force, threat or threat of force (Amir, 1971, p. 17).[19] Unlike criminal homicide or assault, forcible rape finds the male forcing on his victim a definition of the situation as one for sexual gratification. It is, then, an exploitative event in which the male obtains sexual satisfaction and gives in exchange physical and psychological injury (Weis & Borges, 1973, p. 80). It is perhaps the most frightening of criminal attacks in our society.

For 1974 the incidence of forcible rape was 26 for every 100,000 population, or roughly 52 for every 100,000 females.[20] This rate was more than a 150 percent increase from 1960. Such offenses are concentrated in those segments of society in which a subculture of violence is prevalent. Indeed, offenders and their victims are typically young, members of the lower and working classes, and of the same racial and ethnic background, this usually being black (Mulvihill & Tumin, 1969, p. 212). In contrast to homicide and assault, about half of all rapes occur between strangers rather than intimates or acquaintances (Mulvihill & Tumin, 1969, p. 249, note 62). Additionally, rape many times involves multiple offenders. Menachem Amir's study of Philadelphia disclosed that half of all rapes involved groups and pairs of offenders.

As with other criminal attacks under consideration, the performance of forcible rape is developmental in nature. In one of the most thorough studies of rape to date, Amir (1971) found the act to develop in four temporal stages.[21]

The first stage is the initial interaction of the offender and victim. This initial interaction, as well as the rape itself, is usually a planned event. The offender (or troupe of offenders) constructs the situation of the offense, awaiting the entrance of a suitable victim, or ventures forth to secure some particular victim for rape. In other instances the event may be partially planned, with the offender constructing the situation once initial interaction signifies potential sexual relations. Finally, the rape may be an "explosive" affair in which the offender takes advantage of a subdued victim. This latter, uncommon case is typical of felony rape: During the course of some crime like robbery, the offender decides to engage in sexual relations.

In many planned and partially planned rapes, the offender and victim may initially engage in positive interaction. Here, the offender and victim are acquainted or develop a friendly relationship that suggests to the offender the possibility of sexual relations. Friendly relations, moreover, can develop only in larger occasions that customarily permit positive relations. Thus, for example, there may be a friendly tone arising when offender and victim meet in a taproom or at a party. By contrast, in explosive and planned cases the initial interaction may be the offender's immediate use of force or intimidation to control the victim. This is found in occasions where striking up a friendly relationship with a stranger is difficult, such as walking the city streets, waiting for a bus, or strolling through the park (cf. Goffman, 1971). Thus, the offender will immediately take control through actual or threatened violence. Indeed, in situations where friendly relations are difficult to foster, force is deemed a suitable means to obtain control.

The second stage of the rape performance is the offender's further manipulation of the situation toward securing the victim in a "safe" scene. To do this the offender must maintain control of his victim through force or threat of force when the initial interaction was likewise forceful, or through friendly interaction and participation with the unknowing victim. More important, the offender must control the setting of the event. If the scene of the initial interaction is one that affords isolation and protection (this is found especially when the situation was planned and constructed), the offender may define the situation as ripe for immediate sexual assault. In other cases, however, the scene of initial interaction may afford little in terms of protection. The riskiness of these scenes is diminished by the offender's moving the victim to another setting. For example, in a tavern or at a party where initial interaction is friendly, the offender suggests to the victim that they move to a more secluded setting, such as his apartment or the country, where they may engage in more intimate conversation. On the victim's agreement, they depart. Or if the initial interaction is forceful, the offender coerces the victim to move. For example, a victim returning from shopping enters her car, only to find the offender crouched in the back seat. He draws a pistol and demands that she drive toward the country or he will kill her. Once in the secluded scene, the offender may commit the act without fear of outside interference.

Now the setting and the victim are under the offender's control. Once such control is achieved, the scene is set for the third stage of the performance, the sexual assault. When and how force is used to achieve sexual penetration varies among cases. Generally such variation depends on the orientation of the offender and victim to the situation as a whole. The interaction may have been of a friendly, consensual orientation in which both participants anticipated some potential sexual relationship. For example:

At 11 A.M., the offender saw the victim walking on the street near school. He slowed down his car, pulled along the curb, and asked the victim if she would like to ride around. She agreed, hopping in the front seat. After a short period of "cruising" the two decided to drive toward an oil company's lease fields, a heavily wooded and mountainous area. They parked on a deserted dirt road, listened to the radio and started necking. After "making out" for a while, the offender started petting the victim, removing her clothing in the course. She made no effort to resist. They continued necking for a period until the offender stated he wanted to screw. She refused, stating that she wanted to get back to school. He became angered and grabbed her. She wiggled from his hold, grasping the door handle to escape. As she opened the door to escape, the offender caught her by the neck and strangled her to semi-consciousness. He dragged her from the car, tore off her remaining clothes, and performed intercourse.[22]

Here, the offender initiated more sexually forceful overtures once the scene was made private. In the face of these forceful moves, the victim redefines the situation as one of disagreement and conflict and resists either verbally or physically. The offender, in turn, may interpret these moves as cues for continuance (Weis & Borges, 1973) or as rejection of his ability to successfully seduce a woman. He then initiates more aggression and brutality to gain cooperation, as well as to humiliate and degrade the woman (Amir, 1971).

On the other hand, the rape may develop from an initially violent or coercive encounter in which a forceful tone is continually present. One case presented by Susan Griffin illustrates this pattern:

I don't know how he got in; it was probably through the screen door. When I woke up, he was shaking my leg. . . . He started by saying that he wanted to sleep with me, and then got angrier and angrier, until he started to say, "I want pussy," "I want pussy." Then, I got scared and tried to push him away. That's when he started to force himself on me. It was awful. It was the most humiliating, terrible feeling. He was forcing my legs apart and ripping my clothes off. . . . I did fight him—he was slightly drunk and I was able to keep him away. I had taken judo a few years back, but I was afraid to throw a chop for fear that he'd kill me. I could see he was getting more and more violent. . . . Then he was hitting me again and somehow we pushed through the back door of the kitchen and onto the porch steps. We fell down the steps and that's when he started to strangle me. He was on top of me. He just went on until finally I lost consciousness (1971, p. 35).

In this kind of case the initial interaction is characterized by the presence or threat of violence. The use of force is a tool to insure the immediate control of the victim in a potentially troublesome setting. In many cases, though, a victim reacts by seeking to fight off and resist the attacker, and this resistance is generally met with an onslaught of physical force. Once the victim is under control, and consequently dazed or in a state of shock, the offender typically performs sexual penetration.

Other times, an offender may initiate the interaction with threats rather than physical force. The victim may submit without resistance to the offender's commands when they are accompanied by intimidation. She fears the physical harm and injury promised by the offender for noncompliance. Even in the above case, for example, the victim failed to use judo on her assailant for fear that he would kill her. The offender probably inflicts less physical harm when he does not encounter resistance.

Thus, in rape, as with other attacks, the offender's moves are dependent upon those of the victim. If in the initial encounter the victim appears friendly, then the offender may use that friendship to isolate the victim for sexual relations. If the victim appears from the start to be hostile and unwilling, then the offender may assert physical force or intimidation to control her. In the rape situation, the greater her resistance, the greater his force; the lesser her resistance, the lesser his force. These latter patterns were given substance by one convicted rapist:

Question: If you had a choice between a passive and aggressive woman, who would you prefer? Fred: Probably the passive one first. The aggressive one would be second choice. I'd be reluctant to rape the aggressive one because I want control of the situation. . . . The best thing to do if you get raped is to go along with it and let the man rape you. Those who get murdered usually resist. The more violent you resist, the more violent the attacker becomes (Winslow & Winslow, 1974, p. 307).

The final stage of the rape performance is the postrape action. Involvement of the victim does not end with the termination of sexual penetration. Some are held captive for a period of minutes to hours to be used for further sexual relations or to be *cooled out*. In cooling out the victim, the offender attempts to convince her that the forceful act was something other than a rape. Rather, it was an act of "love" in which he was just carried away by passion, alcohol, or some other intoxicant or by a misinterpretation in which he thought she wanted forceful lovemaking (Weis & Borges, 1973). In other cases the victim is transported to the place of initial interaction, to her home, or to some other isolated area. As a final alternative, she may simply be left at the scene of the crime.

Mugging.   Mugging is a popular term that has come to refer to a variety of criminal offenses occurring in our city streets. Assaults, homicides, rapes, and even child molesting have come under the popular conception of mugging. The criminal law has done little to remedy the ambiguity of the concept. For our purposes mugging will be considered as robbery with force or threat of force, committed on streets or in other public places. In 1974 there were some 208 reported robberies per 100,000 population. The *Uniform Crime Reports* (Federal Bureau of Investigation, 1975) estimates that half of these were street robberies, or muggings.

Mugging as a class of robbery has a unique character. Unlike rape, child beating, homicide, or assault, mugging is an event that does not usually take place between people of the same racial and socioeconomic class (Mulvihill & Tumin, 1969, p. 213). While offenders are generally black, male, and of lower-class background, their victims are often residents of other areas of the city and do not share their racial and class status. As Morton Hunt (1969) points out, this dissimilarity serves the offender well, for his identification by the victim is thus made difficult.

As with rape, mugging is typically a nonexplosive, scheduled event (cf. Conklin, 1972, pp. 79–101; Rubinstein, 1973, pp. 358–359). The offender or troupe of offenders hastily plans the performance in regard to time and setting. The troupe members may either construct or habituate a safe, isolated setting for commission of the offense. An obvious example is awaiting a passerby in a dark, isolated public park.

Or they may travel about the streets, by car or foot, in search of suitable targets located in a safe setting. Having agreed or decided on "scoring," a suitable target is selected. Muggers typically select people who can provide amounts of money that will suit their immediate purposes and who are vulnerable and can be easily defeated. In other words, people unable to fend for themselves, such as women, the elderly, drunks, and the physically weak, are often defined as appropriate targets.

Once the target is spotted in a protected setting, the offenders make their move. This is generally a swift and forceful strike that catches victims by surprise and, in effect, places them in powerless positions (Hunt, 1969, p. 41; LeJeune & Alex, 1973). In some cases offenders initiate interaction by verbally commanding the victims to come across with valuables or else face the dire consequences of harm or death. In other cases they initiate the encounter by immediately and forcefully overcoming the victims, giving them little choice and rendering possible resistance nil. The degree of force used in the strike varies with the nature and moves of each victim. In cases in which targets appear weak or put up little or no resistance, a minimum of force may be used. For example, a group of offenders may be driving about the city in search of a score. Spotting a lone woman, the driver drops two colleagues off on a nearby corner, and they dash toward the unsuspecting victim, shove her aside, and make off with her purse before she has a chance to realize her victimization (Conklin, 1972, pp. 70–71). Or the offenders may confront the victim, command his money with threats of injury or death for noncompliance, and brandish a weapon in support. For fear of harm, the shocked victim hands over his goods, securing at most a jostle or threat to keep quiet. Take the following as a case in point:

> When we started getting off the elevator he turned around and he said: "Give me ten dollars." I thought he wanted to borrow ten dollars. He said, "I don't want any trouble. Give me ten dollars." And I looked him up and down, and I see he had a knife in his hand. So I didn't let myself get knifed. I gave him the ten dollars and he got off (LeJeune & Alex, 1973, p. 267).

In cases where victims appear strong or put up resistance, greater force is generally used (cf. Conklin, 1972, pp. 101–102). As Jonathan Rubinstein observed:

A man always poses a greater problem because he may resist, and any money on him is likely to be in a pocket or in a wallet. . . . If the man resists, he must be subdued before the money can be obtained. The most common forms of mugging are against men at night, usually by several males who attack from the rear, rarely with any prior warning. Using surprise, they frequently smash the victim on the head with whatever is available—a piece of lead pipe, a table leg, anything that will stun him (1973, p. 359).

The case of Helmer, described by Hunt (1969, pp. 41–42), may be informative. In this case, the attackers stalked Helmer and cautiously awaited his entrance into the isolated building that housed his apartment:

Helmer had climbed two flights of stairs and was at the front door of his apartment. . . . As he got the door open he put the bunch of keys back in his pocket and started in; then from the stairway, to his left and behind, there was the sound of racing feet, and in an instant he was violently propelled inside and shoved, stumbling, half a dozen steps along the narrow hall to the kitchen doorway on the right side.

Here he lurched into the doorway and turned, gasping in astonishment and fear. The shapes of two young men were hard upon him, and a third was at the front door, in the background. Inexplicably and wordlessly, . . . one of the two took the bag of groceries from his unresisting hands and set it on the floor just outside the kitchen. The other, meanwhile, slipped into the kitchen behind Helmer, who wheeled around in panic, beginning to shout in a cracked, aging voice and flailing out at the intruder with his feeble old arms. Behind him, whoever had taken the groceries from him now pinioned his arms to his sides, at which Helmer shouted all the louder. Then suddenly the man in front of him had a knife in his hand, with which he struck at Helmer backhandedly and powerfully.

A moment later Helmer lay dead; his attackers rummaged through his shelves, drawers, and boxes in search of valuables.

Just as the event is scheduled by the offenders, so too is their departure. Exiting the situation may take a variety of forms. Helmer's attackers, for example, appeared to have structured their getaway. Once the victim had fallen to the blade of his attackers, the muggers fled the scene, each taking a different route. In other cases the offenders may have structured several avenues of escape. In a park, for example, they may have cased the setting and chosen a number of safe routes for vanishing. Or, if traveling by auto, the driver may keep the car out of sight of witnesses while partners score.

Thus, mugging is an offense marked by the characteristics of planning, speed, and surprise. The event is scheduled, the attack is swift, catching victims off guard, and escape is planned.

Collective Forms

Contrasted to individual forms of violence in which offenders victimize or exploit particular others, the violence found in vandalism, juvenile gang wars, ghetto riots, and prison conflicts has a collective character. A gang member, for example, may act violently because of gang pressure to perform as a member of the group. Similarly, during ghetto riots normally peaceful citizens are caught up in the action and behave in ways that they would ordinarily consider inappropriate for themselves.

Collective criminal violence, like the individual forms, may be differentiated along several dimensions. Collective violence can vary in the number of participants involved. While vandalism may involve only three of four offenders, a ghetto riot may involve several thousand inhabitants. There can be variance in the temporal span of the event. While a juvenile gang war may last only thirty minutes, a prison or ghetto riot may last several days. Collective violence can vary in goals. Vandalism is generally oriented toward such goals as recreation and competitive victories. Juvenile gang wars, ghetto riots, and prison riots, however, are oriented toward political ends. That is, such collective events have as their goal either effecting changes in the current power structure and allocation of valued goods, or maintaining the current system of power arrangements in the face of bitter opposition. To be sure, all violent transactions, whether they are individual or collective forms, have a power dimension: Some people comply with the desires of others for fear of what may occur if they do not, while others fight to determine whose desires will be honored at the expense of others (Lasswell, 1948, pp. 10–19). But unlike in muggings, most murders, and assaults, power is a major variable in juvenile gang wars, ghetto riots, prison riots, political terrorism and assassination, student protests, and labor-management violence. These are violent confrontations between those demanding change and those demanding maintenance of long-range power arrangements.

Vandalism.   Vandalism is "the deliberate defacement, mutilation, or destruction of private or public property" by one not having direct ownership of that property (Clinard & Wade, 1957, p. 494); it constitutes one of the most costly and destructive of criminal attacks in this society. In fact, in the fiscal year 1967–1968 vandalism brought over $813 million in damages to small businesses in the United States (U.S. Small Business Administration, 1969), and there is good reason to suspect that the damage was far greater by 1976. This criminal event accounted for more loss to small business than any other crime, including burglary, robbery, and employee theft.

Acts of vandalism are typified by certain characteristics. First, the juveniles involved are not entirely immersed in the subculture of violence (Clinard & Wade, 1958; Wade, 1967). Next, vandalism is a "group" activity (Wade, 1967; S. Cohen, 1968). Finally, because the victim is typically absent, he is necessarily at the mercy of the attackers. Their decision to destroy possessions cannot be influenced by the direct interaction or participation of the victim.

Andrew Wade (1967) has argued that performances of vandalism are processual. The idle moments of daily life provide for a variety of suggestions for destructive action. Chatting with peers about friends' enjoyable yet destructive activities may end in a proposal to follow suit in hope of finding excitement. Playful activities such as hitting a baseball may develop to the point where members smack the ball through apartment windows to hear the crash of shattering glass. Competition among peers may unfold to the point where destructive acts are criteria of achievement and victory. Suggestions of revenge on particular victims may provide the appropriate justification for slashing their tires or burning their homes. Or suggestions to protest the political and social climate may lead to the scrawling of obscenities on public monuments.

Once the suggestion for destruction and violence is made, the unstructured context of the situation is transformed. For example, one attacker's physical move may suggest a line of action for companions:

> Well, me and a couple of boy friends and a girl got in a car we had taken. We were going to stay there that night. She asked me if I had a knife. I

said, "Yeah." So she started cutting up the upholstery, ceiling and everything. After she quit cutting up, Joe got out of the car and went to the drugstore. I locked the door and wouldn't let him back in. So Raymond kicked out the window on the right side of the driver's seat. So Joe put his foot through the same window. Then I bent up the gearshift—took out the speedometer. Joe, he took the glove compartment, took it all apart. If I'd known she was going to cut it up, I wouldn't have given her the knife. I just took it away from her and started cutting up myself. So did Joe and Raymond (Wade, 1967, p. 101).

Thus, the proposal to initiate destruction serves to focus the group about a set of actions offering satisfaction and enjoyment to each individual.

In some cases, group members may not agree that the situation is ripe for violence, and dissenting members may be persuaded to join through jeering, challenging, and daring by assenting members. One juvenile described this persuasion:

He just picked up a rock and threw it. He didn't tell me he was going to do it. Those were $150 windows, something like that. He picked up a nice, big, juicy rock. He came and said, "Now it's your chance." Of course, the guys I ran around with, they call you "chicken." One guy dares another—calls him "chicken." Some guys can't take that. I took it as long as I could until I got into it. They said if you want to belong to our club, you got to break a window. We broke about eight windows that night (Wade, 1967, p. 102).

If conflict persists, however, we would expect the line of destructive action to cease. Thus, for a focused line of vandalism to develop, there must exist some agreement or working consensus among the individuals that such activity is currently appropriate.

Having achieved consensus, participants in the event enact and mutually embrace destructive roles. Whether such roles entail the wholesale shattering of windows, the slashing of new tires, or the devastating of classrooms, each move stimulates the others to continue. Such interstimulation, or circular reaction, raises and promotes the members' excitement in the course of the event. Nonparticipants to the affair engage in one of two roles relative to the participants. On the one hand, they may encourage and stimulate the actors' movements. On the other hand, they may remain neutral, neither discouraging nor encouraging the violence; such neutrality may be interpreted by the vandals as acceptance of the activity.

Thus, vandalism is a group-centered activity designed to focus attention on a set of actions deemed interesting and enjoyable (Sanders, 1976, pp. 95–105). While such events are criminal in character, involving physical damage and destruction, they are perceived by their perpetrators as noncriminal. Indeed, because stealing is not involved, vandals generally hold that their actions are just "pranks" or the result of "messing around." Yet these "fun" activities result in financial destruction that is greater than all other forms of juvenile delinquency combined (Clinard & Wade, 1958).

Juvenile Gang Violence. Delinquent gangs were romanticized in the musical *West Side Story* by the two gangs, the Jets and the Sharks. However, gang violence is hardly romantic, and members are not the last vestiges of knightly chivalry. Statistics of gang violence include 33 killings and 252 injuries in the first six months of 1969 in Chicago, and 257 shootings, 250 stabbings, and 205 gang fights between October 1962 and December 1968 in New York. In Boston on May 10, 1969, the police were called to handle gang activity 38 times in a 90-minute period; this is an average of one incident every 2½ minutes (W. Miller, 1969, p. 12). These bleak statistics are hardly romantic, and descriptions of gang violence are even more sobering.

A gang has been defined as "a group of urban adolescents who congregate recurrently at one or more nonresidential locales, with continued affiliation based on self-defined criteria of inclusion and exclusion" (W. Miller, 1969, p. 25). With such a broad definition it would seem that almost any group of juveniles, violent or not, who hang around together could be considered a gang. In fact, most gangs are not violent, and the major part of any gang's history is unlikely to include a great deal of violence.

Important to gang membership are the notions of *rep* and *heart*. *Rep* refers to the reputation held by either an individual gang member or the entire group (W. Miller, 1969, p. 24). The type of rep a gang achieves depends on the type of activity to which it is oriented. If oriented to the use of drugs, for example, it may achieve such reputations as "cool," "far-out" or "straight." An important element in reputation is heart (Cloward & Ohlin, 1960, p. 24). *Heart* is the willingness of a member to stick up for the gang and for fellow members in situations where reputation is made or lost; in short, it is "character" (cf. Goffman, 1967, p. 240). A gang member demonstrates heart, for example, when he keeps his cool while the gang robs a gas station, or when he keeps from informing police of his partners after his apprehension for the robbery. Unlike gangs oriented toward the use of drugs or various criminal ventures, some juvenile gangs are an integral part of the subculture of violence, where weakness is despicable and physical toughness a virtue (W. Miller, 1958). For a violent gang to build a rep and for its members to exhibit heart, violent physical combat is necessary and quite commonplace.

Several events can be found that initially facilitate gang warfare and that make or break reputations. One event that gangs typically define as troublesome, requiring their action, is the invasion of their home territory. Carl Werthman and Irving Piliavin (1967, pp. 57–62) point out that street corners are transformed in their meaning from "public places" to "hangouts," "territories," or "turfs," and gang members expect such places to be treated in the same way as one would treat a private home. In situations where one gang or its members trespass on the turf of another, they are inviting, either purposely or unwittingly, the immediate retaliation that a homeowner accords a prowler.

Identification as a gang member forces on the individual the obligation to defend the gang's honor and reputation in situations of insult (W. Miller, 1966). On the one hand, the degrading gestures of rival gang members toward the individual's colleagues may provoke an exchange of slanderous, insulting statements to the point where outsiders (police, shopkeepers, neighbors) intervene or the gangs exchange challenges, with promises of a future confrontation. On the other hand, the individual may defend gang honor, even at great odds, by initiating combat immediately upon degradation. In either case gestural affronts to reputation facilitate violent retaliation or its threat.

Identification as a gang member additionally forces on the individual the expectation that he will aid fellow members when they are attacked. Even in situations where a colleague provokes the attack—by invading another's turf or by degrading another's gang—an individual is obligated to render immediate assistance or join with fellows for immediate retaliation, rather than *rank out* (flee in the face of adversity).[23]

News of transgression travels to the "headquarters" of the offended gang. Here, observers or assaulted members recount to the group details of the incident. The gang collectively defines the event "as a violation of its rightful privileges, an affront to its honor, and a challenge to its 'rep'" (W. Miller, 1958, p. 17). Consequently, the gang is obligated to pursue a violent line of retaliation or lose its reputation. "Sessions of detailed planning now occur; allies are recruited if the size of [the offending gang] and its potential allies appears to necessitate larger numbers; strategy is plotted, and messengers dispatched" (W. Miller, 1958, p. 17). During planning and mobilization, members continually rehearse the provocative incident, heightening emotional commitment to the rather frightening end of full-scale battle. Prepared and committed, the gang enters "enemy territory." Sometimes the excursion brings warfare. But, as Walter Miller (1966) found, warfare is often avoided. The enemy cannot be located, for example, or the police appear and stop the confrontation. In such a case, the gang nevertheless defines its mission as accomplished and its honor avenged, for, as James Short and Fred Strodtbeck note, all that mattered was that they "had 'played the game' according to the standards of their community" (1964, p. 26).

Ghetto Riots.   Unlike the race riots that occurred in the 1800s and early 1900s, the ghetto riots of the 1960s were initiated by blacks, generally directed against property instead of people, and centered around grievances about poverty, discrimination, and repressive police action (Grimshaw, 1969). Racial segregation and oppression of blacks in the face of "official" equality was centrally at issue. In fact, the National Advisory Commission on Civil Disorders (1968) placed the blame for these riots squarely on white racism. The causes of such actions will not be dealt with here; rather the riot will be used as a resource for explaining the development of collective violence.

Ghetto riots are touched off by commonplace events that usually have no significance beyond their immediate occurrence. Quite often these events will take the form of a confrontation between white police and a black suspect. The Watts riot, for instance, began with the arrest of a drunken driver. In the 1967 Detroit riot a police raid on a "blind pig" (after-hours bar) was the spark that ignited the worst ghetto riot in the history of the United States (Hersey, 1968). Other incidents include the arrest of a youth for turning on a fire hydrant (Chicago, 1966), the chase of burglary suspects by police (Tampa, 1967), the arrest of a single protestor for blocking traffic (Cincinnati, 1967), and the arrest of a youth who tried to enter a bar (Atlanta, 1967).

These events have two things in common: (1) They serve as incidents that raise people's tension level (Goffman, 1961); and (2) they serve as noticeable gathering points for people. All arrests (and public investigations), of course, have the characteristic of creating tension and drawing curious onlookers. But in the context of the urban ghetto they come to be seen as signs of repression and discrimination since most of the police are white and the persons arrested are black. These points are illustrated by Robert Conot, who made the following observations of the events surrounding the incident that sparked the Watts riot:

"You motherfucking white cops, you're not taking me anywhere!" he screamed, whipping his body about as if he were half boxer, half dancer. There was a growl from the crowd, now about 100 in number. Many had just arrived, and, not having witnessed the beginning of the incident, had little knowledge of what the dispute was about. Marquette's defiance struck a responsive chord. The officers were white; they were outsiders; and, most of all, they were police. Years of reciprocal distrust, reciprocal contempt, and reciprocal insults had created a situation in which the residents assumed every officer to be in the wrong until he had proven himself right, just as the officers assumed every Negro guilty until he had proven his innocence. The people began to close in on the three highway patrolmen. What, a few minutes before, had seemed to be an entirely innocuous situation, was taking on an ugly tenor (1967, p. 14).

Violent riots could not occur without the willingness of the participants to believe inflammatory rumors. In the Watts riot, for example, a black woman barber was arrested when she interfered with the police who were arresting Marquette. At the time of arrest, she was wearing her barber's smock, leading some to believe that she was pregnant. As a consequence, the rumor that the police had brutalized and arrested a pregnant mother spread throughout Watts (Demaris, 1970, p. 214). Similarly, in the 1967 Tampa riot rumors spread that a police officer shot a youth who had his hands raised (National Advisory Commission,

1968, p. 22). Such rumors are used by ghetto residents as a resource for interpreting subsequent events between police and citizens. If the police are rumored to have beaten and shot people, there is justification for the people to burn, loot, and snipe. The police in their turn use these activities as justification for making indiscriminate arrests. In short, the rumors come to have a self-fulfilling character.

Several different approaches to account for collective behavior serve to explain the collective character of riots. The *convergence approach* sees collective behavior as the result of the coming together of people with similar predispositions (R. Turner, 1964, p. 392). If a number of people with like tendencies to violence simultaneously "converge," this convergence leads to violence. Thus, if blacks with similar frustrations and tendencies toward violent reactions to their situation converge, a riot may be sparked off by a seemingly trivial incident. A second explanation of collective behavior is known as the *contagion approach*. When aggregates are highly sensitized to one another, the actions of one person may be "contagious," spreading to the entire group (R. Turner, 1964, p. 394). Most of the incidents that have sparked ghetto violence began with a single event that proved to be contagious. Finally, the *emergent norm approach* explains collective behavior in terms of the failure of typical norms to order behavior and their replacement by "emergent norms" that allow collective violence (R. Turner, 1964, pp. 394–397). When the established social organization fails to provide normative guides for defining the situation, a void exists. Instead of reverting to individual psychological reactions, new norms emerge to direct collective action. The typical forms of ghetto riots suggest that norms do indeed emerge, as illustrated by a repetitive style in the riots that could not be accounted for in terms of idiosyncratic reactions.

Prison Violence.   Violence found in prisons takes a multitude of forms. There is individual conflict between inmates, as manifested in aggravated and simple assault, sexual assault, and murder. Fighting between conflicting inmate factions occurs, and these events are not unlike juveniles gang wars (cf. Minton, 1971, pp. 84–111). By and large, however, inmates attempt to avoid trouble and "do their own time" in a way that will minimize the already considerable pain of incarceration

(Irwin, 1970, p. 69). This point was clearly demonstrated by James Jacobs in his investigation of various members of four Chicago street gangs in Stateville Penitentiary:

> Unaffiliated inmate observers have found it remarkable that gangs which have been killing one another for years on the Chicago streets have been able to cooperate under the extraordinarily demanding prison conditions. G. B., leader of the Disciples [one street gang], has told me that the murderer of his mother is reputed to be among the inmates at Stateville but that he has taken no action to learn the individual's identity. For him to pursue a personal vendetta against a member of a rival gang could only result in the most disastrous consequences under the present circumstances of total confinement. There is an absolute consensus among the [gang] leadership that "international war" must be avoided at all costs (1974, p. 404).

Furthermore, those who routinely use violence as a means of coping with prison life are viewed as troublemakers by fellow inmates. Therefore, it cannot be said that those who enter prison are "socialized" into violence there. Many of the violent measures taken by inmates are defensive in nature, directed against the small minority of "gorillas" or "wolves" who employ violence in dealing with matters of everyday life.

The most spectacular form of prison violence, which is given a disproportionate amount of attention in relation to its frequency, is the riot or demonstration. In essence, prison riots are calculated uprisings directed at calling attention to prison conditions (Murton, 1976, pp. 80–81). But, as Donald Cressey points out, a prison riot is more than a conflict between "the keepers and the kept."[24] Rather, "a riot's possible benefits are greater for the 'old guard' among guards and inmates than for others" (1973, p. 141). A prison riot is something like antirevisionism or counterrevolution. It is the reaction of the "old regime" of guards and inmates to prison reform movements that disrupt established arrangements among guards and between guards and inmates and that take power from inmate elites—the "right guys" (merchants) and the "convicts" (politicians). To be sure, the direct benefits from uprisings usually include better food, visiting privileges, and other scarce goods and services. But it is important to note that such uprisings will generally stop or slow down a reformer's program; consequently, the privileged positions of the inmate elites will be maintained. Prison riots additionally serve the prison commissioner, for they provide the basis for arguing that more money is needed to run the institution adequately.

The pattern of violence in prison riots is fairly uniform (Cressey, 1973, p. 144). For the first few days there is a general upheaval as the "gorillas" take charge. They wreck buildings, engage in alcohol, sex, and drug orgies, collect hostages, and settle old grudges among themselves with knives and clubs (Cressey, 1972, p. 118). Then the leadership of the riot is assumed by the "right guys," assisted by the "convict" leaders who aspire to "right guy" status. This change in power is by no means uneventful. "At this juncture there is likely to be additional maiming and even an inmate murder or two—byproducts of the fight for leadership—and the persons maimed or murdered are likely to be either 'convicts' or 'gorillas'" (Cressey, 1973, p. 145). The stage is now set for the end of the uprising as the new leadership realizes and convinces the inmate population that any plan to escape is doomed to failure, given the public and official reaction to the event. The only hope is to bring to the public's attention a variety of deplorable conditions that allegedly "caused" the riot. Negotiations with the prison administration and other officials ensue. Since the demands of inmates are often in line with what the administration wants (e.g., larger budgets, better facilities, and the like), the end of the riot is virtually guaranteed.

As prisoners have become increasingly politicized and militant, a change in this pattern of events has taken place. The proportion of "gorillas" has increased, due perhaps to conceptions that they have been victimized by the oppression of the white establishment, and the proportion of "right guys" has diminished. "The recent shift of power from the 'right guys' to more militant inmates has done what prison reformers have rarely done—disrupted the privileged prison lives of 'thieves' and their allies" (Cressey, 1973, p. 147). The consequence may be a greater amount of violence in riots and its prolongation, for the transference of power to the "right guys" may not occur. The slaughter in the Attica riot was attributed to the fact that this transference did not take place.

METHODS OF DEACTIVATING VIOLENT SITUATIONS

Homicides and Assaults

One means of reducing the occurrence of homicide and some of the more serious assaults is by removing the situational equipment or props necessary for successful performance. In this regard the removal of such lethal weapons as firearms from the public's grasp is of paramount importance. Research has generally disclosed that homicide is typically performed with firearms (Pokorny, 1965; Hepburn & Voss, 1970), while serious assault is generally perpetrated with the use of knives, blunt objects, fists, and, to a lesser extent, firearms (Pittman & Handy, 1964). To be sure, if firearms were outlawed or confiscated upon entrance to loosely structured, leisure-time occasions, people could transform other situational props (such as pieces of wood or pipe, bricks, beer mugs, bottles, kitchen knives, and the like) into weapons or simply use their own bodies to bring harm or death to others. But as Clarence Schrag (1969, p. 1245) points out, firearms have a much greater killing potential than the other kinds of weapons typically used (cf. Yearwood, 1973). Hence, while the numbers of situations ending in violence may remain stable, the removal of such lethal props from the public's possession should lessen the numbers of killings and serious assaults while increasing the number of minor or simple assaults. In other words, fewer lives are lost at the expense of more bloodied noses and blackened eyes.

Because homicide and assault involve the contribution of the offender and victim and the implicit or explicit understanding among all parties that violence is a suitable means to resolve the conflict, we can hypothesize that these conditions are crucial to a successful performance. This assumption suggests that these attacks can be reduced by eliminating both the mutual contribution and the working consensus that violence is suitable. This can be done through several means. First, the victim's nonparticipation in escalating the event toward a violent confrontation may cool out the offender. In cases of homicide, for example, Luckenbill (1974, pp. 75–78) found that when a victim apologized, fled the scene, or backed down from the offender's threats or counterinsults, the offender generally withdrew without continuing escalation (cf. Goffman, 1967, pp. 242–243). Here, the victim gains life and limb at the expense of losing face; the offender gains face and demonstrates strong character. Second, if the offender interprets the victim's initial moves as mere kidding, the result of drunkeness or the like, and if he receives support in this interpretation from the audience, then he may be more willing to dismiss the affront or halt escalation (Luckenbill, 1974). Again the character contest is not given a chance to blossom into a confrontation in which opponents kill or maim. Finally, if an audience to the event openly discourages (or offers to mediate) the offender-victim conflict, this may stop the impending violence.

Open mediation, whether verbal or physical, should come early in the confrontation, for opponents committed to battle may turn violently on interfering members of the audience.[25] Intervention by onlookers may be especially crucial, for they can keep a victim's (or offender's) improprieties from the offender (or victim), can mediate by explaining to one that the other is drunk, crazy, or kidding or does not know what he is doing, or can make explicit the fact that neither opponent will lose face or character by backing down (Reiss, 1971, pp. 73–76). While the offender and victim may not readily wish to back down from each other, the audience is in a strategic position to provide opponents with the support needed to withdraw gracefully.

Forcible Rapes and Muggings
Because events of rape and mugging are one-sided attacks with offenders forcing themselves on unwilling victims, and because the police have been shown to be generally ineffective as preventive agents of social control (Reiss, 1971), action to reduce attacks becomes the responsibility both of potential victims and the citizenry as a whole. One way these attacks may be reduced is by removing potential victims from situations in which such attacks generally occur and by making these situations unsafe for attackers. A number of methods may achieve these conditions, several of which will be examined here.

For situations of rape and mugging, the removal of potential targets from dark and isolated city streets, alleyways, vacant lots, public parks, garages, hallways, and the like, especially in the late evening hours, would be useful. At the same time such hazardous settings could be made unsafe for attackers through better lighting of streets, parks, and buildings and the removal of such obstacles to vision as shrubs, trash cans, abandoned cars, or high grass (cf. Lofland, 1969, pp. 64–69). If particular classes of people who have been demonstrated to be probable victims—women in rape events, and women, the elderly, drunks, and the sick in mugging events—must venture into hazardous settings, they should act to reduce their vulnerability (cf. Csida & Csida, 1974, pp. 52–64). This could be accomplished, for example, if potential victims travel about the city with companions. Not only would traveling with friends, pets, or among groups lessen their attractiveness to any possible offenders, but it would also make hazardous situations neither private nor isolated and thereby unsafe for attackers. If walking alone, a possible victim could further guard against attack by avoiding dark and cluttered areas, walking near the curb and other well-traveled avenues, and restraining from hitchhiking or accepting rides from strangers. Attack could also be reduced by preventing an attacker's access to the safe situations under the victim's control. The fact that one is alone at particular times in isolated and private places, as the house or apartment, need not be made public.

If, however, people find themselves in a situation of actual attack, then certain lines of conduct may reduce their chances of serious injury. In regard to situations of rape it has been found that the more the victim resists her attacker, the more force the attacker uses. This suggests that for victims of both rape and mugging to escape serious injury, they should present their attackers with a minimum of resistance (unless they have expertise in the arts of self-defense). While this may suggest that one surrender to an attacker—which, in the case of rape, poses difficult ethical dilemmas as well as problems when the elements of "force," "resistance," and "cooperation" are debated in court—the point is that minimal resistance usually brings minimal physical harm.

Vandalism
Preventing situations of vandalism is very difficult. It would prove to be a formidable task to structure the leisure time of juveniles so as to preclude idle moments in which destructive activities are likely to develop. Nevertheless organized recreation for juveniles, including an array of playful and competitive situations, may be useful. To remove the objects of destruction from the grasp of vandals would be all but impossible. Indeed, one would have to eliminate windows, stop laying wet cement, construct impenetrable fences to surround valued property and goods, and the like. Yet some of this could be accomplished with

little effort. Fencing off valued goods, installing loud alarms, construct-ing additional lighting, and providing roving security guards would help to ward off juveniles looking for a good time.

Juvenile Gang Violence

Gang warfare may be reduced in a number of ways. On an immediate level, one can capitalize on a recent finding that gangs wish to avoid large-scale confrontations. Walter Miller (1966) emphatically argues that while gangs seek to enhance and maintain a "tough" reputation, they are rightfully fearful of war. Even the most hardened of members realize that war can easily bring serious injury and death. Conse-quently, although the gang is committed to avenge its honor, members are open to cues that permit an avoidance of fighting. For instance, they secretly inform police of impending skirmishes as a common technique to avoid war. Accepting the mediation by social workers attached to gangs or agreeing to have one representative from each gang engage in a "fair fight" are additional techniques used in avoiding massive con-frontations. Alternatives to violence for all situations of impending battle might involve the intervention by "concerned citizens" or spe-cial police units following gang activities, the mediation by social workers or others attached to gangs, or the provision of gym facilities for a boxing or wrestling match between gang representatives. Where nonviolent alternatives are not provided or appear unsuitable, violence is probable.

While social workers can act to defuse warfare situations, their very presence may serve to prevent such situations from ever occurring. A social worker attached to a gang serves as a symbol that the gang is so "tough," has such a reputation, that society recognizes its status as a group of power and strength (W. Miller, 1957; Short & Strodtbeck, 1964). This symbolization, in turn, replaces the need to do battle as a means of securing a rep and demonstrating heart. As a result, violence has been reduced among gangs with attached social workers. But when social workers are removed, the gang typically returns to violent battle as a means of reinstating its questioned, perhaps faltering reputation. While social workers may be useful in symbolizing the gang's tough-ness, hence reducing their need to engage in warfare, what is needed is not a substitution of the means by which a gang can demonstrate toughness but a reorientation of the group from the valuation of toughness.

Methods of reducing gang violence must take into account the position of violence in the lives of gang members. As Walter Miller (1958, p. 15) points out, all adolescents in America have a dominant concern with social status. Unlike other adolescents, however, the lower-class youths in violent gangs consider physical toughness and masculinity to be central criteria of status. Physical violence is deemed the suitable, and probably the only, means for achieving a tough reputation and demonstrating a strong, masculine character. Consequently, the way to reduce gang violence is to diminish the suitability of physical violence as a means of achieving status and prestige.

Such change may be accomplished in two ways. First, as Richard Cloward and Lloyd Ohlin (1960, pp. 171–178) would suggest, the social structure must be altered so that gang members have the opportunity to learn about *and* engage in nonviolent means for achieving standards of status other than those of toughness and masculine strength. They suggest that lower-class young people turn to violent gangs because they are restricted from access to the legitimate and illegitimate means to such other standards of status as monetary or occupational well-being. Thus, providing access to quality education, vocational training, summer jobs, and the like would essentially permit them to develop legitimate high-status careers. Second, and of equal import, gang members must be given social support for embracing nonviolent means to standards of status other than toughness and strength. It is one's "significant others," moreover, that provide the crucial support in learning nonviolent attitudes and engaging nonviolent means. Indeed, no matter how many opportunities are made available, if one's intimates fail to provide support for peaceful lines of conduct, an individual will remain violent.

Ghetto Riots
The National Advisory Commission on Civil Disorders (1968, p. 173) suggests several means for reducing ghetto riots. "Rumor centers" may be useful in stopping riots, for they serve to offset inflammatory rumors that spread and justify violence. However, the control of rumors only serves at best to cool off collective violence once it has begun. It is more important, the Commission argued, to attack the basic cause of ghetto violence, which is white racism. Were it not for the segregated housing patterns, there would be no black ghetto to begin with, and were there no ghetto, there would be no collective violence. There have been no

riots like those of Watts, Detroit, or Tampa where there are integrated communities. As racial discrimination subsides, so too will the violence in the ghettos.

Prison Violence

How to prevent the escalation of prison riots or bring them to an immediate end once they have begun is by no means clear. Few ideas have been advanced for dealing with prison violence. It has been suggested, though, that the miseries of incarceration may be minimized if diverse inmate factions collectively engage in "peaceful" confrontations that appeal to the public and bring its support. This seems to have worked well for Swedish prisoners and has brought them a reduction of many restrictions imposed by the state. This suggestion cuts to a more significant point: Inmates must share in political decisions affecting their lives. They must have the right to develop collective ends among themselves and to have these ends heard and appreciated by those acting for the state.

AN ARGUMENT AGAINST THE VIOLENT SUPPRESSION OF VIOLENCE

People often consider physical force authorized by the government as an effective means of countering the occurrence of criminal violence. In contemporary America, for example, physically confining a violent offender in a prison or mental hospital is considered an appropriate and sophisticated measure for rehabilitation. Capital punishment for murder and rape has also found support as an effective means for deterring others from committing similar offenses. The wholesale authorization of police, militia, or military force to crush political protest and terrorism, labor unrest, racial and student disturbances, juvenile gang wars, family fights, and barroom brawls has grown out of the public's concern with violence and politicians' promises to rid the streets of violent crime.

The use of legitimate violence to eliminate criminal violence, however, is not effective. There are many reasons for this. First, just as a victim of murder may contribute to the escalation of violence, so does legitimate violence frequently bring counterviolence (Skolnick, 1969, p. 345). It has been seen, in the discussions of racial, labor, and student violence, how strong measures by legitimate forces can bring about defensive moves by the protestors, resulting in escalation to full-scale battle. Second, there are instances in which the official use of force to suppress certain political and social protests may only result in the creation of martyrs and the formation of revolutionary terrorist groups bent on the violent promotion of their goals (Rose, 1969, pp. 27–45, 195–216). Third, while official agencies may put down violent events, such as family fights and gang wars, this show of force cannot be demonstrated to prevent the reappearance of further disturbances in another time and setting. Finally, the use of capital punishment to deter others from murder is likewise dubious. As William Chambliss observed, "The preponderance of evidence indicates that capital punishment does not act as a deterrent to murder" (1969, p. 361). This contention is based on several lines of evidence:

1. The fact that despite trends away from the use of capital punishment the murder rates have remained constant.

2. The fact that within the United States where one state has abolished capital punishment and another has not, the murder rate is no higher in the abolition state than the death-penalty state.

3. The fact that the possible consequences of the act of murder are apparently not considered by the murderer at the time of the crime (Chambliss, 1969, p. 361).

While considerable resources have been marshalled in the violent fight against criminal violence, people must recognize that other, non-violent means for handling such events exist. One can alter the situation of violence—the roles and facilitating conditions necessary for successful performances. These alterations, moreover, can immediately be put into effect by governmental officials. The government can also implement means of reducing violent confrontations by changing the social composition of potentially violent situations. For example, situations of murder, assault, juvenile gang wars, and ghetto riots may be reduced by providing trained specialists to mediate in altercations and situations of conflict. Providing the ghetto with rumor centers and liaisons with government and police personnel, attaching to gangs social workers and citizen volunteers, and providing such leisure-time places as taverns, amusement centers, cafes, and other public places with specialists trained to peacefully mediate conflict may prevent the escalation of hostilities and violence. Situations of rape and mugging may be countered by reducing the victim's vulnerability by the governmental provision of chaperone services, mass transit systems, access to police call boxes, and the like. Incentive programs to fill the city streets with pedestrians in the later evening hours—keeping businesses open longer, providing discounts to movies, restaurants, and amusements, or providing free entertainment—would similarly reduce the isolation and privacy needed for successful rape and mugging.

The government can alter the urban physical environment to reduce the occurrence of criminal violence. By means of increasing street lighting, tearing down abandoned buildings, clearing vacant lots, removing large obstacles to vision such as garbage cans and abandoned cars, and prohibiting open access to apartment buildings, garages, and the like, the number of isolated, dark settings offering safety to attackers could be reduced. Breaking up the ghetto and integrating its residents into prosperous urban neighborhoods (an enormous task to be sure) would thwart the development of riots by decreasing the chance of intense gathering points for incensed residents.

While altering the violent situation may break up the possibility of a successfully executed violent event, it does little to remedy the preconditions of violence. Serious efforts must be made to resolve the bitter oppression visited upon certain minorities during moments of rapid social change. Concurrently, people must be taught nonviolent means of dealing with problematic situations. For violence (criminal and legitimate) is, among other things, a strategy of action learned through a process of interaction with others. But just because one has learned this strategy does not mean that it will be implemented in all situations of conflict. Rather, to adapt the classic principles of Edwin Sutherland (1947), violence can only occur when the individual has learned attitudes favorable to criminal violence in excess to those favorable to nonviolence. Consequently, the object in reducing the occurrence of criminal violence is to impart attitudes favorable to nonviolence in excess of those favorable to violence. Adapting the scheme proposed by Donald Cressey (1955), violence can be reduced if people—children, teenagers, and adults—are rewarded for nonviolence in moments of conflict or need and punished through the withdrawal of rewards for violence. This learning process must take place not with sporadic sessions with psychiatrists or psychologists but through voluntary and continuous interaction with significant others who share a similar perspective toward the world and favor nonviolence.

Unqualified support must be given to the struggle against criminal violence if success is to be attained. One cannot glorify violence as part of the American character, on the one hand, and then, on the other, piously deplore it. One cannot simultaneously be in favor of violence as a means of social control and against it "in the streets." In short, the hypocrisy shown toward violence must end.

NOTES

1. *Violence* is not to be confused with *force*. "Acts of *force* are those which prevent the normal free action of movement of other persons, or which inhibit them through the threat of violence" (Hofstadter, 1970, p. 9). The concern in this chapter is with events of violence. Some actions, for instance rape, are considered violent yet may only involve force. Nevertheless, those events legally defined as violent will be treated as such, whether violence or force is used. The conceptual distinction, however, should be recognized.

2. For discussions of legitimate violence and that undertaken by the wealthy and politically powerful members of society, see the first two sections of Rose (1969), especially the articles by Newton Garver and Howard Zinn.

3. It is very difficult to ascertain with precision the rates of criminal violence within countries and to rank them on some scale of violence (Mulvihill & Tumin, 1969, pp. 13–42). There are many reasons for this: (1) the violence recorded in the United States may not be defined as criminal or important enough to be recorded in other countries; (2) all violence in the United States is not reported, recorded, or compiled; and (3) many nations simply have not developed recording or compilation methods or do not reveal their data. The rates referred to in this section are drawn primarily from Mulvihill and Tumin (1969, pp. 117–129).

4. As a matter of fact, Bittner (1970, pp. 36–47, 95) argues that Americans are apparently becoming increasingly nonviolent as history wears on. Indeed, convicted criminals are no longer executed in the public square, most events involving violence are defined as criminal, prisons are houses of "correction" rather than dungeons of torture and punishment, and some persons have suggested that capital punishment could be invoked in a humane manner (through drugs for example).

5. Gastril (1971) argues that the Southern culture of violence, one which accounts for more criminal violence than all other regions of the nation, owes a significant debt to the period of slavery, when hostility and toleration of physical violence with respect to racial matters thrived.

6. It is important to note that most student demonstrations did not involve violence. Of the more than 170 demonstrations that took place during 1967–1968, for example, only thirty-six involved violence, and only eight brought reported injuries.

7. While some consider the original statement by Dollard (1939) to hold that all frustration causes aggression, those authors say that they never held aggression to be the only response to frustration (N. Miller, 1941).

8. Many arguments have been raised to blame much of our contemporary violence on television and other mass media. This argument would be compelling were it not for the fact that violence was part of the American scene long before the advent of television. Furthermore, while all segments of society watch a good deal of television, only certain segments employ violence as a routine means of problem solving. This is not to condone television violence or to suggest that some violence is not imitative, but rather to point out the limitations of the argument.

9. It is suggested by Athens (1974) that there are several kinds of situations in which criminal violence is defined as appropriate and expected. These include situations interpreted as *requiring defense,* as *malefic* or extremely negative (based on the actions of a victim), and as *frustrative.* For a critique of the entire subculture of violence principle, see Ball-Rokeach (1973).

10. For events of homicide and assault, the terms of offender and victim may be somewhat elusive. In the typical case, the victim is the one who initiates the confrontation, and the offender is the one who stands up to the victim's insult or degrading gesture and terminates the encounter by killing or assaulting the victim. In some cases, however, the victim turns out to be the one who inflicts the fatal or harmful blow, and the offender falls in defeat. The victim is then playing an offender role. In this essay the victims are those who initiate violent confrontations.

11. The statistical rates of the various events are necessarily biased. Not all crimes of violence are reported to police. Of those that are reported, not all are defined by the police as criminal; even if they are so defined, they may nevertheless escape recording (as when husbands are not arrested for hitting their wives in a systematic fashion). Finally, not all police departments record events of violence in the same manner. Consequently, the rates given are general rather than precise.

12. The following discussion is based on Luckenbill (1974).

13. The contribution and coorientation of both the offender and victim are not to be confused with what researchers have termed *victim precipitation.* Victim precipitation refers to those events where the victim initiates the violent

action—fires the first shot, throws the first punch, and the like. Such a concept does not examine in depth the process that will be discussed here.

14. A victim who continues the inappropriate activity may not do so deliberately. In cases involving children, for example, the child may not have the ability to understand verbal language. Consequently, such commands as "shut up," "eat your dinner," or "be good"—backed with threats to hurt, spank, or kill—may not be understood by the victim. The offender, however, interprets this noncompliance as a conscious, purposive act of defiance and acts on the basis of this interpretation.

15. Assuming that victim precipitation is the victim's initiation of violence, Hepburn and Voss (1970) found that some 37 percent of their cases were victim-precipitated, Wolfgang's (1958) Philadelphia data found some 25 percent, and the President's Task Force found over 22 percent (Mulvihill & Tumin, 1969, p. 226).

16. This process of commitment is analyzed in Becker (1960) and in a discussion of *encapsulation* by Lofland (1969, pp. 50–60).

17. This rate is definitely minimal since simple assaults are not added into the rates given.

18. Pittman and Handy (1964, p. 467) found that over 70 percent of their cases were preceded by verbal arguments and altercations. Similarly, the Washington, D.C., survey made by the President's Commission on Causes and Prevention of Violence found 63 percent of the cases to be preceded by altercations (Mulvihill & Tumin, 1969, p. 234).

19. While it is not technically considered rape, men can be and have been sexually assaulted by other males. This is especially common in total institutions, such as jails and prisons.

20. Forcible rape is undoubtedly underreported. The *Uniform Crime Reports* (Federal Bureau of Investigation, 1975) for 1974 suggests that the true rate is probably ten times that officially recognized. Underreporting may be due to

several facts: (1) Some women may not recognize an event as rape, as when teenagers are forced to submit to the advances of their dates; (2) some women may not report their rape for fear of the stigma and embarrassment attached to being a rape victim; (3) some women may not report their rape for fear of the punishing experiences involved in police questioning and court appearances.

21. The following discussion is based on Amir (1971).

22. This case is drawn from the field notes that Luckenbill kept in June 1973.

23. In a preliminary statement Quicker (1974) suggests that even in female gangs, ranking out is reason for exclusion from membership.

24. The following discussion of prison riots is based on Cressey (1972, 1973).

25. Goode (1969, p. 969) finds that the police officer may be assaulted after the offender and victim begin to exchange blows. This would lead to the suggestion that profitable intervention should occur prior to the physical confrontation of the offender and victim.

BIBLIOGRAPHY

Amir, Menachem. *Patterns in Forcible Rape.* Chicago: University of Chicago Press, 1971.

Aptheker, Herbert. *Nat Turner's Slave Rebellion.* New York: Grove Press, 1966.

Athens, Lonnie. "The Self and the Violent Criminal Act." *Urban Life and Culture,* 1974, 3:98–112.

Ball-Rokeach, Sandra J. "Values and Violence: A Test of the Subculture of Violence Thesis." *American Sociological Review,* 1973, 39:736–749.

Bandura, Albert, and Richard Walters. *Adolescent Aggression.* New York: Ronald Press, 1959.

Banitt, Ruika, Shoshana Katznelson, and Shlomit Sheit. "The Situational Aspects of Violence: A Research Model." In Shlomo Shoham, ed. *Israel Studies in Criminology.* Tel Aviv, Israel: Gomeh Publishing House, 1970, pp. 241–258.

Barr, Stringfellow. "Violence and the Home of the Brave." In Irving Horowitz, ed. *The Troubled Conscience.* Palo Alto, Calif.: Freel, 1973, pp. 3–6.

Becker, Howard S. "Notes on the Concept of Commitment." *American Journal of Sociology,* 1960, 66:32–40.

Bensman, Joseph. "Social and Institutional Factors Determining the Level of Violence and Political Assassination in the Operation of Society: A Theoretical Discussion." In William J. Crotty, ed. *Assassinations and the Political Order.* New York: Harper & Row, 1971, pp. 345–387.

Bittner, Egon. *The Functions of the Police in Modern Society.* Rockville, Md.: National Institute of Mental Health, 1970.

Bohannon, Paul. "Cross-Cultural Comparison of Aggression and Violence." In Donald J. Mulvihill and Melvin M. Tumin, with Lynn A. Curtis. *Crimes of Violence,* appendix 25. A staff report to the National Commission on the Causes and Prevention of Violence. Washington, D.C.: U.S. Government Printing Office, 1969, pp. 1189–1239.

Brinton, Crane. *The Anatomy of Revolution,* rev. ed. New York: Random House, Vintage Books, 1965.

Brown, Richard Maxwell. "Historical Patterns of Violence in America." In Hugh Davis Graham and Ted Robert Gurr. *Violence in America: Historical and Comparative Perspectives,* vol. 1. A staff report to the National Commission on the Causes and Prevention of Violence. Washington, D.C.: U.S. Government Printing Office, 1969a, pp. 35–64.

Brown, Richard Maxwell. "The History of Extralegal Violence in Support of Community Values." In Thomas Rose, ed. *Violence in America.* New York: Random House, Vintage Books, 1969b, pp. 86–95.

Buss, Arnold H. *The Psychology of Aggression.* New York: John Wiley & Sons, 1961.

Chambliss, William J., ed. *Crime and the Legal Process.* New York: McGraw-Hill, 1969.

Chodorkoff, Bernard, and Seymour Baxter. "Psychiatric and Psychoanalytic Theories of Violence." In Donald J. Mulvihill and Melvin M. Tumin, with Lynn A. Curtis. *Crimes of Violence,* appendix 23. A staff report to the National Commission on the Causes and Prevention of Violence. Washington D.C.: U.S. Government Printing Office, 1969, pp. 1117–1162.

Clinard, Marshall, and Richard Quinney, eds. *Criminal Behavior Systems: A Typology,* 2nd ed. New York: Holt, Rinehart and Winston, 1973.

Clinard, Marshall, and Andrew Wade. "Toward the Delineation of Vandalism as a Subtype in Juvenile Delinquency." *Journal of Criminal Law, Criminology, and Police Science,* 1958, 48:493–499.

Cloward, Richard, and Lloyd Ohlin. *Delinquency and Opportunity: A Theory of Delinquent Gangs.* Glencoe, Ill.: The Free Press, 1960.

Cohen, Albert. *Deviance and Control.* Englewood Cliffs, N.J.: Prentice-Hall, 1966.

Cohen, Stanley. "The Politics of Vandalism: The Nature of Vandalism: Can It Be Controlled?" *New Society,* 1968, 12:872–878.

Conklin, John E. *Robbery and the Criminal Justice System.* Philadelphia: J. B. Lippincott, 1972.

Conklin, John E. *The Impact of Crime.* New York: Macmillan, 1975.

Conot, Robert. *Rivers of Blood, Years of Darkness.* New York: Bantam Books, 1967.

Cressey, Donald R. "Changing Criminals: The Application of the Theory of Differential Association." *American Journal of Sociology,* 1955, 61:116–120.

Cressey, Donald R. "A Confrontation of Violent Dynamics." *International Journal of Psychiatry,* 1972, 1:109–130.

Cressey, Donald R. "Adult Felons in Prison." In Lloyd E. Ohlin, ed. *Prisoners in America.* Englewood Cliffs, N.J.: Printice-Hall, 1973, pp. 117–150.

Crotty, William J. "Assassinations and Their Interpretations within the American Context." In William J. Crotty, ed. *Assassinations and the Political Order.* New York: Harper & Row, 1971, pp. 3–53.

Csida, June Bundy, and Joseph Csida. *Rape: How to Avoid It and What To Do About It If You Can't.* Chatsworth, Calif.: Books for Better Living, 1974.

Demaris, Ovid. *America the Violent.* New York: Penguin, 1970.

Dollard, John, and others. *Frustration and Aggression.* New Haven, Conn.: Yale University Press, 1939.

Federal Bureau of Investigation. *Crime in the United States: Uniform Crime Reports, 1974.* Washington, D.C.: U.S. Government Printing Office, 1975.

Feierabend, Ivo K., Rosalind L. Feierabend, and Betty Nesvold. "Social Change and Political Violence: Cross-National Patterns." In Hugh Davis Graham and Ted Robert Gurr. *Violence in America: Historical and Comparative Perspectives* vol. 2. A staff report to the National Commission on the Causes and Prevention of Violence. Washington, D.C.: U.S. Government Printing Office, 1969, pp. 497–535.

Feierabend, Ivo K., and others. "Political Violence and Assassination: A Cross-National Assessment." In William J. Crotty, ed. *Assassinations and the Political Order*. New York: Harper & Row, 1971, pp. 54–142.

Frantz, Joe B. "The Frontier Tradition: An Invitation to Violence." In Hugh Davis Graham and Ted Robert Gurr. *Violence in America: Historical and Comparative Perspectives*, vol. 1. A staff report to the National Commission on the Causes and Prevention of Violence. Washington, D.C.: U.S. Government Printing Office, 1969, pp. 101–119.

Freud, Sigmund. *Beyond the Pleasure Principle*. New York: Liveright, 1922.

Freud, Sigmund. "Mourning and Melancholia." In *Collected Papers*, vol. 4. London: Hogarth, 1925.

Freud, Sigmund. *The Ego and the Id*. London: Hogarth, 1947.

Gastril, Raymond D. "Homicide and a Regional Culture of Violence." *American Sociological Review*, 1971, 36:412–426.

Genovese, Eugene D. *Roll, Jordan, Roll: The World the Slaves Made*. New York: Pantheon Books, 1974.

Gillette, Paul J., and Eugene Tillinger. *Inside the Ku Klux Klan*. New York: Pyramid Press, 1965.

Goffman, Erving. *Encounters*. Indianapolis: Bobbs-Merrill, 1961.

Goffman, Erving. *Behavior in Public Places*. New York: The Free Press, 1963.

Goffman, Erving. *Interaction Ritual*. Garden City, N.Y.: Doubleday, 1967.

Goffman, Erving. *Strategic Interaction*. New York: Ballantine Books, 1969.

Goffman, Erving. *Relations in Public*. New York: Harper & Row, 1971.

Goode, William J. "Violence Between Intimates." In Donald J. Mulvihill and Melvin M. Tumin, with Lynn A. Curtis. *Crimes of Violence*, appendix 19. A staff report to the National Commission on the Causes and Prevention of Violence. Washington, D.C.: U.S. Government Printing Office, 1969, pp. 941–978.

Goode, William J. "The Place of Force in Human Society." *American Sociological Review*, 1972, 37:507–519.

Graham, Hugh Davis, and Ted Robert Gurr, *Violence in America: Historical and Comparative Perspectives*. A staff report to the National Commission on the Causes and Prevention of Violence. Washington, D.C.: U.S. Government Printing Office, 1969.

Griffin, Susan. "Rape: The All-American Crime." *Ramparts*, 1971, 10:26–35.

Grimshaw, Allen D., ed. *Racial Violence in the United States.* Chicago: Aldine, 1969.

Gurr, Ted Robert. "A Comparative Study of Civil Strife." In Hugh Davis Graham and Ted Robert Gurr. *Violence in America: Historical and Comparative Perspectives* vol. 2. A staff report to the National Commission on the Causes and Prevention of Violence. Washington, D.C.: U.S. Government Printing Office, 1969, pp. 443–486.

Harris, Louis, and others. *The American Public Looks at Violence.* A poll prepared for the National Commission on the Causes and Prevention of Violence. New York: The Commission, 1968.

Hepburn, John, and Harwin Voss. "Patterns of Criminal Homicide: A Comparison of Chicago and Philadelphia." *Criminology*, 1970, 8:21–45.

Hersey, John. *The Algiers Motel Incident.* New York: Alfred A. Knopf, 1968.

Hofstadter, Richard. "Reflections on Violence in the United States." In Richard Hofstadter and Michael Wallace, eds. *American Violence: A Documentary History.* New York: Random House, Vintage Books, 1970, pp. 3–43.

Hofstadter, Richard, and Michael Wallace, eds. *American Violence: A Documentary History.* New York: Random House, Vintage Books, 1970.

Hudson, James R. "Police-Citizen Encounters that Lead to Citizen Complaints." *Social Problems*, 1970, 18:179–193.

Hunt, Morton. *The Mugging.* New York: New American Library, Signet Books, 1969.

Irwin, John. *The Felon.* Englewood Cliffs, N.J.: Prentice-Hall, 1970.

Jacobs, James E. "Street Gangs Behind Bars." *Social Problems*, 1974, 21:395–409.

Lasswell, Harold D. *Power and Personality.* New York: W. W. Norton, 1948.

LeJeune, Robert, and Nicholas Alex. "On Being Mugged: The Event and Its Aftermath." *Urban Life and Culture*, 1973, 2:259–287.

Lofland, John. *Deviance and Identity.* Englewood Cliffs, N.J.: Prentice-Hall, 1969.

Lorenz, Konrad. *On Aggression.* Translated by Marjorie Wilson. New York: Bantam Books, 1966.

Luckenbill, David F. *Other People's Lives: The Social Organization of Criminal Homicide.* M.A. Thesis, University of California at Santa Barbara, 1974.

Lupo, Alan. "School Uproar in Boston." *Los Angeles Times*, September 22, 1974, pp. 1, 4.

McNamara, John H. "Uncertainties in Police Work: The Relevance of Police Recruit's Backgrounds and Training." In David Bordua, ed. *The Police: Six Sociological Essays.* New York: John Wiley & Sons, 1967, pp. 163–252.

Megargee, Edwin I. "The Psychology of Violence: A Critical Review of Theories of Violence." In Donald J. Mulvihill and Melvin M. Tumin, with Lynn

A. Curtis. *Crimes of Violence*, appendix 22. A staff report to the National Commission on the Causes and Prevention of Violence. Washington, D.C.: U.S. Government Printing Office, 1969, pp. 1037–1115.

Miller, N. E. "The Frustration-Aggression Hypothesis." *Psychological Review*, 1941, 48:337–342.

Miller, Walter B. "The Impact of a Community Group Work Program on Delinquent Corner Groups." *Social Service Review*, 1957, 31:390–406.

Miller, Walter B. "Lower Class Culture as a Generating Milieu of Gang Delinquency." *Journal of Social Issues*, 1958, 14:5–19.

Miller, Walter B. "Violent Crime in City Gangs." *Annals of the American Academy of Political and Social Science*, 1966, 343:97–112.

Miller, Walter B. "White Gangs." *Trans-action*, 1969, 6:11–26.

Minton, Robert L., Jr., ed. *Inside: Prison American Style*. New York: Random House, Vintage Books, 1971.

Morris, Norval, and Colin Howard. *Studies in Criminal Law*. London: Oxford University Press, 1964.

Mowrer, O. H., and Clyde Kluckhohn. "Dynamic Theory of Personality." In J. McV. Hunt, ed. *Personality and the Behavior Disorders*, vol. 1. New York: Ronald Press, 1944, pp. 69–135.

Mulvihill, Donald J., and Melvin M. Tumin, with Lynn A. Curtis. *Crimes of Violence*. A staff report to the National Commission on the Causes and Prevention of Violence. Washington, D.C.: U.S. Government Printing Office, 1969.

Murton, Thomas. *The Dilemma of Prison Reform*. New York: Holt, Rinehart and Winston, 1976.

National Advisory Commission on Civil Disorders. *Report*. Washington, D.C.: U.S. Government Printing Office, March 1968.

National Commission on the Causes and Prevention of Violence. *Violent Crime: Homicide, Assault, Rape, Robbery*. New York: George Braziller, 1969a.

National Commission on the Causes and Prevention of Violence. *Walker Report*. Submitted by the director of the Chicago team. Washington, D.C.: U.S. Government Printing Office, 1969b.

Nordholt, J. W. *The People that Walk in Darkness*. New York: Ballantine Books, 1960.

Phillips, Ulrich B. *American Negro Slavery*. Baton Rouge: Louisiana State University Press, 1966.

Pittman, David, and William Handy. "Patterns of Criminal Aggravated Assault." *Journal of Criminal Law, Criminology, and Police Science*, 1964, 55:462–470.

Pokorny, Alex D. "A Comparison of Homicide in Two Cities." *Journal of Criminal Law, Criminology, and Police Science*, 1965, 56:479–487.

Quicker, John C. "The Chicana Gang: A Preliminary Description." Paper presented at the annual meetings of the Pacific Sociological Association, San Jose, Calif., March 1974.

Redding, Saunders. *They Came in Chains*. Philadelphia: J. B. Lippincott, 1950.

Reiss, Albert J. *The Police and the Public*. New Haven, Conn.: Yale University Press, 1971.

Rose, Thomas, ed. *Violence in America: A Historical and Contemporary Reader*. New York: Random House, Vintage Books, 1969.

Rosenthal, Jack. "The Cage of Fear in Cities Beset by Crime." *Life*, 1969, 67:16–23.

Rossman, Michael. "Breakthrough in Berkeley." In Irving Horowitz, ed. *The Troubled Conscience*. Palo Alto, Calif.: Freel, 1971.

Rubinstein, Jonathan. *City Police*. New York: Farrar, Straus & Giroux, 1973.

Schrag, Clarence. "Critical Analysis of Sociological Theories." In Donald J. Mulvihill and Melvin M. Tumin, with Lynn A. Curtis. *Crimes of Violence*, appendix 26. A staff report to the National Commission on the Causes and Prevention of Violence. Washington, D.C.: U.S. Government Printing Office, 1969, pp. 1241–1289.

Sellin, Thorsten. *Culture Conflict and Crime*. Social Science Research Council, Bulletin No. 41. New York, 1938.

Shibutani, Tamotsu, and Kian M. Kwan. *Ethnic Stratification: A Comparative Approach*. New York: Macmillan, 1965.

Short, James F., and Fred L. Strodtbeck. "Why Gangs Fight." *Trans-action*, 1964, 1:25–29.

Skolnick, Jerome H. *The Politics of Protest*. New York: Ballantine Books, 1969.

Stark, Rodney. *Police Riots*. Belmont Calif.: Wadsworth, 1972.

Sutherland, Edwin H. *Principles of Criminology*, 4th ed. Philadelphia: J. B. Lippincott, 1947.

Sutherland, Edwin H., and Donald R. Cressey. *Criminology*, 8th ed. Philadelphia: J. B. Lippincott, 1970.

Toch, Hans. *Violent Men: An Inquiry into the Psychology of Violence*. Chicago: Aldine, 1969.

Turner, Frederick Jackson. *Frontier and Section: Seleted Essays of Frederick Jackson Turner*. Englewood Cliffs, N.J.: Prentice-Hall, 1961.

Turner, Ralph H. "Collective Behavior." In Robert Faris, ed. *Handbook of Modern Sociology*. Chicago: Rand McNally, 1964, pp. 382–423.

U.S. Small Business Administration. *Crime Against Small Business*. Senate Document 91–14. Washington, D.C.: 1969.

Wade, Andrew. "Social Processes in the Act of Juvenile Vandalism." In Marshall Clinard and Richard Quinney, eds. *Criminal Behavior Systems: A Typology*. New York: Holt, Rinehart and Winston, 1967, pp. 94–109.

Wallace, Samuel E. "Patterns of Violence in San Juan." In Walter C. Reckless and Charles L. Newman, eds. *Interdisciplinary Problems in Criminology: Papers of the American Society of Criminology, 1964.* Columbus, Ohio: Ohio State University Press, 1965, pp. 43–48.

Weis, Kurt, and Sandra Borges. "Victimology and Rape: The Case of the Legitimate Victim." *Issues in Criminology,* 1973, 8:71–115.

Werthman, Carl, and Irving Piliavin. "Gang Members and the Police." In David Bordua, ed. *The Police: Six Sociological Essays.* New York: John Wiley & Sons, 1967, pp. 56–98.

Winslow, Robert W., and Virginia Winslow. *Deviant Reality: Alternate World Views.* Boston: Allyn & Bacon, 1974.

Wolfgang, Marvin.*Patterns in Criminal Homicide.* Philadelphia: University of Pennsylvania Press, 1958.

Wolfgang, Marvin. *Crimes of Violence.* Report submitted to the President's Commission on Law Enforcement and Administration of Justice, 1967. Mimeographed.

Wolfgang, Marvin E. "Violent Behavior." In Abraham S. Blumberg, ed. *Current Perspectives on Criminal Behavior.* New York: Alfred A. Knopf, 1974, pp. 240–261.

Wolfgang, Marvin, and Franco Ferracuti. *The Subculture of Violence: Toward an Integrated Theory in Criminology.* London: Tavistock, 1967.

Yablonsky, Lewis. *The Violent Gang.* New York: Macmillan, 1962.

Yearwood, J. Homero. "Firearms and Interpersonal Relationships in Homicide: Some Cross-National Comparisons." Paper presented at American Society of Criminology meeting, New York, 1973.

Four
Syndicated crime in America

LOWELL L. KUEHN
The Evergreen State College

Many Americans view syndicated crime as far more romantic and respectable than other types of criminal behavior. While opinion polls register the public's increased sense of fear that one may be killed or robbed in the streets, that same public pays millions of dollars to read the latest Mafia exposé or view Hollywood accounts of organized crime exploits. American interest in organized crime may go beyond curiosity to approach envy. Thus, one reviewer noted with dismay that some readers of Mario Puzo's fictionalized rendering of syndicate life, *The Godfather,* were left with a yearning that they too could avail themselves of a secret, powerful organization to right their grievances (Pusateri, 1973).

Given the recent flood of fiction and nonfiction descriptions of associations variously labeled the Mafia, the Cosa Nostra, the Syndicate, or the Mob, one would suspect that the American public is quite knowledgeable about the operation of organized crime. There is, however, little hard evidence documenting such organizations, and the few reliable facts that are available have been blown out of proportion until myth supplants truth and rumor substitutes for research.

It is unfortunate that the facts about organized crime have become so distorted, for the truth is no less interesting than the fictitious beliefs that have gained wide attention. Organized crime is one of America's most significant social problems, and it is a phenomenon of considerable interest to students of criminology. This chapter is an effort to present a comprehensive review, free of myths and misconceptions, of what is known about organized crime.

A SOCIOLOGICAL APPROACH TO ORGANIZED CRIME

Organized Crime as a Social Problem

How much money is earned from organized crime operations is a matter of some conjecture, but there is no question that the profits are gained at a substantial cost to the American public. In order to earn an annual income of $40 billion—the estimate of the Research Institute of America (1968)—organized crime must be cheating government and legitimate business out of vast amounts of revenue and earnings. The ultimate losers are American citizens and consumers, who are asked to pay the higher prices and taxes prompted by the operations of organized crime.

John Conklin (1973) lists some of the more prominent costs of organized crime: money used to finance other costly illegal activities; the higher cost of illegal goods and services (whereas open competition would presumably drive the prices of vice down); and the corruption of government and law enforcement. But there are even more subtle costs. Thomas Schelling (1967) notes, for example, that organized crime's involvement in the management of labor sectors of business increases consumer prices for legitimate goods and services because the "overhead"—paying protection money, securing illegal union contracts, restraining competition, and price fixing—cuts into profits. Moreover, the consumer must pay higher taxes because organized crime pays none when it takes a bet or sells taxable goods like cigarettes or alcohol on the black market.

The social expense of organized crime also includes the financial loss from stolen property and the expenditures required to prevent, investigate, and insure such thefts. In a single year, one Wall Street brokerage house estimated a loss of at least $1 million in stolen, nontraceable, negotiable securities (Hammer, 1975, p. 347). Those losses are partly recouped by increasing prices to the consumer. Even though many crimes that are controlled by the syndicate are victimless offenses (in that the victim is a willing participant in the act, as in the case of a drug addict purchasing heroin), most of the consumers of what organized crime has to offer find themselves impoverished by the syndicate. No one can estimate the enormity of the loss assumed by the victims of these so-called victimless crimes. Bettors who consistently lose their paychecks to a bookie, narcotics addicts who must maintain a syndicate-nurtured habit, or indebted persons whose every negotiable resource is taken by a loan shark may represent the ultimate cost to society.

Organized Crime and Criminological Interest
Criminologists, like the general public, know very little about the operation of organized crime. Until this blank area is filled, efforts to produce a general theory of crime (or a theory of organized crime in particular) are doomed. Before empirically valid theories can be constructed, the data, facts, evidence, accounts, and observations must be collected.

The very nature of organized crime poses some intriguing criminological questions. These are crimes of special sociological interest, for numerous criminal partners rather than, as is typically the case, a single perpetrator or a loosely organized band are involved in the coordination of activities. How or why such organizations arise, and what structure they take, are important issues that will be addressed later on in this chapter.

The Problem of Defining "Organized Crime"
Some of the confusion surrounding the use of the term *organized crime* should be removed. In conventional discourse, organized crime has come to indicate illegal activities conducted by associations like the Mafia or Cosa Nostra. But those groups, and others of a similar nature, commit only a small number of the types of crime that can be called organized. Literally, and consistent with sociological usage, any act that

involves the coordination of two or more persons is organized. Hence, a pickpocket team or a delinquent gang could logically be included in a discussion of organized crimes.

Organization is just too ambiguous a word to be used to distinguish between several types of crime. For one thing, organization is not an attribute of crime so much as a characteristic of social interactions, both legal and illegal. That two or more interacting parties will adjust, coordinate, and organize their activities in relation to one another is practically a sociological truism, borne out by the example of basketball teams, factory assembly lines, persons who queue to board a bus, and illegal bookmaking operations.

In each instance, be it criminal or noncriminal, organization serves the purpose of facilitating social interaction by providing some order to determine who will do what, when, where, and upon whose authority. In business, where wasted effort and inefficiency decrease profit, coordination assures the speedy completion of each task with the minimum of oversights and duplications. The same is true in criminal organizations.

Organization has been called a "tool" or a weapon in the offender's arsenal that helps the criminal conceal operations and keep a step ahead of law enforcement (Cressey, 1972, pp. 97ff.). Without some coordination between several individuals, many crimes would be difficult to commit. Thus, organization keeps the risk of apprehension and the likelihood of profit and success within acceptable limits for any crime. Numerous examples of the benefits of organization are available: the gang delinquents who find safety in numbers for a crosstown war; pickpockets and shoplifting teams that earn greater profits from coordination; the operators of big con games who carefully orchestrate the roping and fleecing of a "mark" (Mack, 1973).

There have been suggestions that associations like the Mafia or Cosa Nostra are organized in a distinctive structure that differentiates them, without ambiguity, from other organizations of crime. Donald Cressey (1969), for example, notes some of the structural characteristics of criminal groups like the Cosa Nostra: an arrangement of roles in which authority is hierarchically determined; delegation of tasks in terms of a division of labor; clear delineation of channels of communication; official rules of operation and procedure; and possession of the greatest authority by members in the highest echelon of the structure, often because of their expertise. That description closely fits the conception of a *bureaucracy*, or a group rationally designed for the purpose of achieving a goal (Weber, 1947, pp. 329–341; Blau & Meyer, 1971).

Such organizations of crime presumably are markedly different from those fluid, amorphous structures of delinquents drawn together in a gang or from the unsophisticated coordination of a stickup team. But the attempt to merge conventional and sociological definitions of organized crime by designating Mafia-like activities as bureaucracies is only partly successful. For one thing, there is some evidence that the structure of such associations is far less formal and bureaucratic than has been suggested (see Ianni, 1972, 1974b). Furthermore, there are criminal activities not conducted by the Cosa Nostra that are just as bureaucratically organized, if not more so. The criminal activities of a legitimate business (such as the electrical price-fixing conspiracy of the mid-1950s, described by Gilbert Geis [1967]), white-collar crimes (Sutherland, 1949), and the operation of terrorist groups like the Symbionese Liberation Army would have to be included in any list of criminal organizations that are bureaucratically structured.

A useful way to distinguish between these various criminal bureaucracies may be in terms of their objectives. Groups like the Cosa Nostra are organized to earn a profit through the supply of illegal goods and services. A team of robbers provides no service except to themselves and those they support. Businesses, if they are legitimate, cannot obtain charters or licenses for operation if they plan to market illegal commodities, and terrorist groups are primarily interested in achieving political goals.

There have been two noteworthy efforts to clarify the definition of organized crime by specifying some of the characteristics of crime syndicates. Frederic Homer (1974) contends that organized crime is marked by four components: (1) a persistent set of interactions, (2) between some critical mass of persons—he suggests five or more individuals—(3) who are involved as producers and/or consumers of (4) certain criminal activities. Homer makes some useful distinctions, particularly in drawing attention to the fact that the boundary of criminal organizations goes beyond operatives who obtain and supply illegal goods and services to include the clientele who support those activities. Joseph Albini (1975) makes a similar effort at a definitional clarification, but he adds the specifications that organized crime is characterized by

(1) the structuring of a group with the purpose of supplying illegal goods and services on a continuous basis (2) where there is the potential for the use of force, intimidation, or threats and (3) the necessity of obtaining some protection or immunity from the legal structure to insure continued successful operations.

While both these efforts are steps forward in clearly specifying what organized crime is, neither leads to unambiguous distinctions between a number of closely related acts that may require quite different theoretical descriptions and explanations. For example, these definitions do not allow one to distinguish the activities of the Cosa Nostra from those of the Central Intelligence Agency, the White House Plumbers, corporate executives engaged in upperworld crime, or delinquent gangs. Homer (1974, p. 19) seems to anticipate a portion of this criticism when he notes that a difference should be drawn between units that act for political motives and groups that organize for economic gain.

The present author would go further and restrict a definition of organized crime to those groups of persons that are organized to earn a profit through the supply of illegal goods and services. A team of robbers provides no service except to themselves; legitimate businesses cannot obtain charters to market illegal commodities; and terrorist groups are interested in political gains rather than financial profit. Profit specifically obtained through the provision of goods and services that are in public demand but are legally prohibited seems to be what distinguishes organized crime syndicates from other forms of criminal organization.

The Problem of Naming Organized Crime
Yet another definitional problem must be considered before going any further. There is a confusing excess of labels used to describe organized crime. Some, like Mafia, Cosa Nostra, the Mob, and the Syndicate, have been mentioned already; others include cartel, confederation, the rackets, gang, underworld, and outfit. Each has its own etymological history. Some names refer to national variants of organized crime; thus, the Mafia or Cosa Nostra signifies the American version of secret criminal societies in Italy. Other labels reflect variations as to what organized crime is called in different regions of the United States. Still others are terms that have evolved in law enforcement and scholarly circles (Salerno & Tompkins, 1969).

Each label carries its own peculiar connotation, though the public is seldom aware of this. For simplicity and consistency, the term *syndicate* will be used throughout this chapter to designate criminal groups organized to achieve a profit through the supply of illegal goods and services to the public.

Methodological Difficulties in the Study of Organized Crime

Clearly, the seclusive and secretive nature of criminal syndicates precludes the use of many of the usual methods for gathering sociological data. Because any organization that wishes to conceal its activities from inquisitive agents of law enforcement is unlikely to reveal its inner workings to curious social scientists, criminologists must be prepared to work at some distance from their data and to make inferences on the basis of fragments of evidence. Thus, in summarizing his experiences while investigating the syndicates for the Organized Crime Task Force of the President's Commission on Law Enforcement and Administration of Justice, Cressey (1967b, 1969) draws a parallel between the criminologist who studies organized crime and the archaeologist who, from a shred of papyrus or a shard of pottery, must reconstruct lost cultures.

Actually, the factual evidence about organized crime that social scientists and legal investigators have been able to gather is considerably less substantial than the archaeologist's shards and shreds. A few members of organized crime syndicates have cooperated with law enforcement agencies, journalists, and anthropologists, and there are some cases where grand juries and congressional investigations have gained behind-the-scene glimpses of organized crime. But those rare observations comprise the sum total of the data criminologists must use. Furthermore, what information is available is none too reliable. The testimony of informers like Joseph Valachi or Vincent Teresa, or the journalistic collaboration of members of the Bonanno family with Gay Talese (1971), must be looked upon with suspicion. Valachi's low and insignificant position in the organization hardly made him privy to the operations at the top of the structure. Teresa and the Bonanno family may be able to provide a better view of the top, and Francis Ianni's reports on the Lupollo family (the fictitious name of the syndicate he studied) may lend a close-up view of family activities, but the reader should recall that the leader of another secretive society, the Black

Panthers, held to the maxim that those who knew didn't say, and those who said didn't know (Cleaver, 1967).

The distance from which sociologists have usually studied organized crime has had its consequences. By relying on secondary and tertiary accounts of syndicate activity, social scientists relinquish any opportunity to independently evaluate their findings according to the canons of science. The possibility for all sorts of distortion arises. In their review of much of the sociological literature concerning crime, John Galliher and James Cain (1974) find an abundance of unchecked folklore that presumably would not have seen print had sociologists studied the syndicates as closely as they investigate other social phenomena.

Furthermore, some reports, especially those prepared by governmental and law enforcement bodies, tend to exhibit a bias by focusing on the operations of criminals and thugs while overlooking the complicity of the upperworld of corrupt politicians, police, prosecutors, and judges (Chambliss, 1971). Legitimate businessmen who finance the syndicate and use its vice markets, and governmental officials whose dalliance permits organized crime's continued success, must be included in any accurate discussion of organized crime.

Finally, an ethnic bias enters many discussions of organized crime. The litany of Italian surnames in the history (and fiction) of American crime syndicates is unavoidable. But the frequency of those names should not lead to anti-Italian conclusions. The extreme involvement of some segments of Italian-American neighborhoods in syndicated crime occurred coincidentally with the rise of journalistic and social-scientific interest in organized crime. Had American curiosity prompted investigations fifty or a hundred years earlier, a myth of Irish or Jewish crime syndicates might have grown, and the problem might have been blamed on their homelands. Italians have made their own significant contribution to American organized crime, but so have most other immigrant groups in the United States.

Some social scientists, notably Francis Ianni (1972, 1974a, 1974b) and William Chambliss (1971), have done an excellent job of collecting data about organized crime through direct observation of syndicate activities. Indeed, Chambliss (1975, p. 39) finds a wealth of data but an absence of sociologists "on the streets." Until other sociologists follow their example, readers will have to be cautioned to accept all conclusions tentatively.

THE OPERATION OF ORGANIZED CRIME

The items offered for sale in the syndicate's catalog of illegal goods and services are diverse. Most criminal organizations limit their business to just a few services, much as legitimate retailers tend to market specialized merchandise. The variety in human tastes for the so-called vices, however, has led organized crime to seek profits in a number of different ways. Moreover, to protect those profits, organizations of crime frequently extend their operations beyond the supply of illegal goods and services to the control of competition and the corruption of law enforcement.

Loan Sharking

The return from loan-shark operations has increased steadily over the years until it has supplanted gambling in the top spot of the syndicate's earnings list (Conklin, 1973; Tyler, 1974). Loan sharking (sometimes called the *Shylock racket*) is the lending of money at illegal, usurious interest rates. Financing a loan, by itself, is not illegal, but it is against the law to charge interest rates above legally prescribed rates *(usury)*, to lend money to support illegal activities (as in the case of a loan to import narcotics), or to use violence, extortion, and other strong-arm tactics to collect from delinquent debtors.

Customary rates of interest on a note from a loan shark will range between 1 and 150 percent, compounded on the unpaid balance each *week*. The rate charged depends on the size of the loan, the intended use of the money, the likelihood that the borrower will default, and the relationship between the lender and the borrower (President's Commission, 1967, p. 3). Most money is lent at 20 percent per week (called a "6 for 5" because one dollar of interest is returned for each five dollars lent).

Obviously, such loans return an enormous profit in interest. For example, $1,000 borrowed at a weekly interest rate of 20 percent, compounded, would be worth $1,200 after one week, $2,073.60 after one month, and $10,699.30 at the end of three months. Even at those rates, there are always steady customers because, as Valachi told his biographer: "Jesus, if you gave to everybody who wanted money, you'd have to be the Bank of Rome" (Maas, 1968, p. 166).

Loan sharks draw their clientele from a special, and surprisingly large, segment of the population: those persons who lack the credit rating, contacts, or legitimate reason to obtain financing from banks. Thus, small-business owners who have exhausted all legitimate sources of capital may seek out the services of a loan shark. Many of the very high interest loans are made to support unusual activities, like bulk drug purchases, that can bring in large sums of money quickly. Few legitimate activities would return the fifteen to twenty times the original investment that is required to pay back such interest rates.

Highly profitable loans for illegal purposes glamorize the true nature of underworld banking. Loan sharking works best when the loans are used to yield a constant source of income by keeping the borrower in continual debt, and loan sharks try to develop and nurture the borrowing habit in customers who provide a lucrative weekly return. Gamblers are a particularly good clientele because they are often in debt, always in need of money to "get even," and often lucky enough to return all of their winnings to the lender. Accordingly, loan sharks follow all of the floating crap games in Manhattan just to make sure that they can instantaneously seize the winnings that cover past debts (Ianni, 1972, p. 97).

The very best loan-shark clients are persons employed in businesses or certain industries; these people can repay their loans by providing some special service to the syndicate. Small-business owners, for example, may be forced to turn over their establishments to the syndicate to be used as fronts for illegal operations, as places to conceal and "launder" money earned in other criminal activities, or as parasitical hosts from which every resource is taken as the company is run into bankruptcy.

To cancel their loans, employees in certain enterprises steal goods to be retailed on the syndicate's black market: pharmacists provide drugs, warehouse workers and truckers hijack goods ranging from expensive cameras to liquor and cigarettes, and employees of brokerage houses steal, and later sell, negotiable securities. Thus, Mark Furstenberg (1969, p. 934) reports the following wiretapped exchange between the employee of a Wall Street brokerage (JW) and the loan shark (NS) to whom the former owed $5,000:

> NS: Hey, by the way, the thought occurs to me. . . . If there was such a
> thing as stocks . . . say, for argument's sake, say the stock is in Al's

possession ... and Al wanted you to sell the stock ... can you handle that?

JW: Sure.

NS: Without his authority?

JW: No.

NS: Let's say that Al stole it. ...

JW: ... as long as it's signed on the back, I don't care.

NS: What if he, somebody, signed it on the back ... can you sell the stock?

JW: Sure.

NS: Maybe there's a shot of you getting out of this after all.[1]

If the debter has no other resource to offer, he may be impelled to work in the *boiler room,* a syndicate euphemism for a business where the debtor's wages can be illegally garnisheed (Albini, 1971, p. 275).

Ultimately, violence may have to be used to obtain payments from delinquent or uncooperative debtors. In those cases an "enforcer" may be used to threaten or assault the defaulting borrower.[2] One delinquent was told: "I know the school your kids go to; they can get hit by a car. Accidents do happen" (Tyler, 1974, p. 201). Another hapless debtor's shakedown was recorded on a police "bug" in which the sound of the enforcer slamming him into the wall is clearly audible, as is his threat: "I say you owe me three fucking hundred. Now I want my fucking money ... or I'll put you down the hill. Give it to me. Give it to me" (Cressey, 1969, p. 90).

The barest traces of organization are apparent in shylock operations. Initially, activities must be coordinated to obtain enough capital to open a bank. Usually some other criminal activity finances the new loan shark. Teresa (1973, pp. 31ff.), for example, reports coordinating his loan sharking with a confidence game that swindled money from businessmen. They would invest in "shares" of his loan-shark operation, and Teresa would later fail to repay his investors.

Some degree of organization is also visible in the division of labor between a loan shark, an enforcer, and the person who runs the boiler room. The shylock, for reasons of public relations or a lack of physical strength, may rely upon an expert in violence and strong-arm techniques to collect debts. Likewise, a loyal employee must be found to supervise the bookkeeping and garnishment of wages that makes for a successful boiler room.

It is also common to see some coordination between competing loan sharks in a community. Valachi provides a clue as to why the shylocks may coordinate their operations: "Sometimes I'm stuck, I don't have enough cash and I go to a shylock myself. He would charge me 10 percent, while I'm charging people 20 percent because he knows it is a solid loan" (Maas, 1968, p. 166). Thus, loan sharks come to rely upon each other for backup loans when their cash reserves dip. This mutual assistance pact is characteristic of the organization in other syndicate activities, especially bookmaking operations.

Gambling

As with loan sharking, an enormous public demand guarantees the involvement and the success of organized crime in gambling. Accurate estimates of the syndicate's profits from illegal betting are impossible, but a conservative guess is that organized crime grosses $20 billion from its gambling operations (President's Commission, 1967, p. 3). The services that are offered in any one community are varied, but they usually include cardrooms for small-stakes card games like stud poker; luxurious private clubs and casinos offering roulette, craps, high-stakes card games, and other games of chance; floating crap games designed to evade the discovery of the police; community lotteries in the forms of the numbers racket, policy, or *bolita;* bookmaking shops to take bets on sporting events; and warehouses to supply gambling paraphernalia like slot machines, punchboards, and gaming tables.

The reasons people gamble are diverse. Some subcultures may encourage gambling as a part of the lifestyle (Miller, 1958; Zola, 1963). In some communities gambling may be a method by which individuals set aside a small amount of money for "investment," almost as a kind of savings. In a study of the numbers racket, Ivan Light (1974) discovered that the probability is good that a gambler who bets two to three times a week for ten years will recover nearly 50 percent of all the money lost. While the rate of recovery (which is a net loss of 50%) cannot compare with a return from conventional methods of saving, there is a rationale to betting that encourages some people to play the numbers.

Whatever the motivation for gambling, the syndicate does not have to labor at enticing bettors into using their services. To turn a profit, gamblers need only provide a setting for the wagering and set the odds to favor the house, bookie, or numbers operator. As Gus Tyler has aptly observed: "All you need is a paper bag. If the first paper bag yields a profit, a new gambling entrepreneur is born" (1974, p. 200).

Syndicate odds are so favorable to the house that there is no question that gambling rackets will ultimately prosper. For example, the operator of a numbers game can expect to retain at least 40 percent of the money wagered because the payoff for correctly guessing any randomly selected three-digit number between 000 and 999 (1000 to 1 odds) is 600 to 1, or less. Unless several bettors select the correct number daily, the operator will pocket nearly half of all the money bet. Data collected on the numbers racket in New York City are instructive. In 1970 it was estimated that citizens of that metropolis placed $600 million on numbers bets (Fund for the City of New York, 1972, p. 9). The modal amount wagered was between ninety cents and one dollar. It is from just that type of lottery that Vito Genovese is alleged to have earned $30,000 to $40,000 weekly in Manhattan (Hammer, 1975, p. 275). In New York City it has been figured that in 1969 the operatives who collect the numbers earned an average annual salary of $9,600 (Light, 1974, p. 19), tax free. If, as has happened in some cases, the payoff number is fixed (after determining which combinations have been most heavily played), the margin of profit can be even greater.

While the profits to be earned from gambling can be enormous, one should not overlook the fact that operators may face heavy expenses that cut into those earnings. Because gambling requires some degree of organization of employees, the cut must be split a variety of ways to meet payrolls and other forms of overhead. By way of example, this author instituted a numbers game (played with toy money) as part of a nine-week course in organized crime.[3] There were nearly 250 students in that course, most of whom would place a bet three times a week. The profits were stupendous (only once during the quarter did anyone guess the correct number), but the organizational problems were staggering. It took five to ten minutes of each class period to record the bets and collect the money, and two to three hours each day for two students to keep the books. Altogether the numbers game required nearly thirty hours of work each week to stay in operation. This game was run under maximally favorable circumstances, but one can easily imagine the difficulty and the cost of having to conduct a small-scale numbers racket across several neighborhoods while law enforcement, competing lotteries, and some citizens are trying to close down the operation.

Gambling operators have a specific problem that clearly illustrates the necessity of some degree of coordination in a successful betting enterprise. The operator cannot control the public's bet, and frequently certain combinations of numbers will be played more often than would be expected if bets were randomly placed. Thus, several persons may pick 628 on June 28th or 217 after a 21 to 7 score in a noteworthy football game. If an over-bet number comes up, the odds will be so dramatically altered that the cost to pay off the winners at 600 to 1 will exceed the take from the losers.

Bookmakers face the same problem. Racetrack payoffs are determined on the basis of the total pool of money wagered on all horses in the race at the track. If a longshot (100 to 1) horse wins, the track is protected because the odds have been set to pay all the winners while leaving enough cash to cover the overhead and yield a profit. Since the bookmakers must pay track odds, if the distribution of their bets does not agree with the track's, there is a real possibility that the betting pool will be insufficient to cover the cost of paying certain winners.

Confronted with this problem, gambling entrepreneurs rely upon the structural device of the layoff bet. The layoff is an arrangement between bookies (or numbers operators) who place bets among themselves to balance the odds in their books in order to insure that highly wagered longshots can be paid. Much as insurance companies reinsure particularly risky policies with other insurance agents, gamblers will reinsure each other through layoff bets.

Valachi provides a good example of the layoff system in an anecdote from his days as a numbers operator:

> [T]here was this big payroll robbery in Brooklyn. I think it was at some ice cream company. Anyway they got away with $427,000. It was all over the front pages. . . . Now everybody has to play 427. We must have had $100 on it. If it hits, that means we get banged for $60,000. Naturally we can't pay off. . . . So, I call this fellow . . . to lay off the $100. But he . . . says "you are wasting the $100. If that number hits the way it is being played [all over town] nobody can pay off. But . . . I'll give you $40 on it" (Maas, 1968, p. 139).

In other words, Valachi bet $40 with a layoff bookie that would pay $24,000 of the $60,000 he would owe if number 427 were selected. He reports, with relief, that it did not hit that day.

In addition to a system of layoff bets, gambling operations require the coordination of a considerable number of workers. No single person could take all the bets, tabulate them, and make the payoffs in a single day, especially when, as in a large community, betting may involve thousands of transactions and millions of dollars. An idea of the complexity of gambling rackets can be seen in Ianni's diagram of a typical numbers enterprise in New York City (see Figure 1). Runners take the bets which are relayed through neighborhood collectors to a syndicate office (called a bank) that is tied to still another bank (called a wheel) at a higher level of collection and is ultimately connected to a regional bank. After the number is selected, the process reverses itself as payoffs are returned to the street. Hidden in this figure are the accountants, secretaries, messengers, enforcers, and other functionaries who are needed to keep the operation functioning.

Teresa, in noting all that was involved in fixing horse races, gives still another example of the complexity of some gambling operations and the coordination that is required between a number of persons:

> It required paying off exercise boys and stable hands to leave areas where horses were to be drugged. It meant reaching the right jockeys and cultivating the right owners. It meant dealing with the right people to obtain the most effective drugs. It also meant warning New England bookmakers working for the Office—so they would not get hurt by the heavy betting (1973, pp. 155–156).

It is not uncommon to find gambling rackets thus connected with other illegal activities. Teresa's example is vivid illustration of how the considerable profits from house odds can be increased by taking bets on sporting events whose outcomes have been fixed—in this case by drugging horses or bribing jockeys or owners to "throw" a race. Other types of fixing are often employed in other sports. For instance, *point shaving* is a common device used to manipulate the outcomes of football, baseball, and basketball games. Because bets are usually placed on the *spread* (the margin of points by which the winning team is expected to defeat the loser), bribing a field-goal kicker to miss an attempt, or threatening a

Figure 1. *The Organizational Structure of a Metropolitan Numbers Racket*

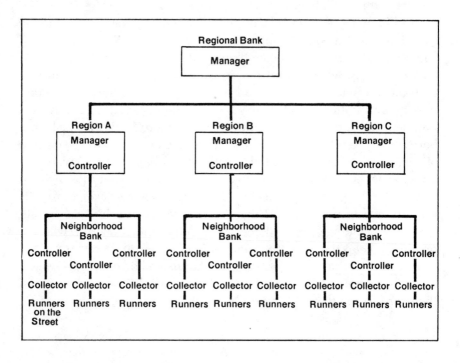

Source: Adapted from Figure 2. "Organization of the Lupollo Numbers Enterprise," (page 95) from *A Family Business: Kinship and Social Control in Organized Crime,* by Francis A. J. Ianni with Elizabeth Reuss-Ianni, © 1972 by Russell Sage Foundation, New York.

batter to convince him to have a bad night at the plate can result in final outcomes that are less than the spread. The bookmaker is thus ensured of a take of millions of dollars, rather than the smaller sums that may result without fixing (Merchant, 1973, pp. 103ff.).

There is some evidence that syndicate involvement in gambling extends beyond communities or regions to include nationwide operations. Thus, much of the money used to develop gambling resorts in Las Vegas, Reno, and the Caribbean came from investments by regional syndicates. During the boom of expansion after World War II—when, at the instigation of Benjamin Siegal, opulent gambling temples were built in the Nevada desert—financing came from figures like Chicago gangsters Sam Giancana and Tony Accardo and Eastern syndicate leaders Frank Costello, Meyer Lansky, and Sam Patriarcha (Messick & Goldblatt, 1972, pp. 149ff; Carpozi, 1973).

Several Nevada casinos have been accused of underreporting, or *skimming*, their profits in order to have a steady supply of cash and to avoid paying taxes. An indictment in 1969 alleged that one hotel, the Flamingo, skimmed $36 million between 1960 and 1967 (Hammer, 1975). That money probably represents only a small proportion of the untraceable cash that has been funneled from Las Vegas into syndicate operations since 1947.

The Supply of Illegal Goods
Humankind's infinite appetites, and attempts to legislate the satisfaction of those natural desires, have assured organized crime's success in supplying illegal goods to the public. A rich market for these goods inevitably follows attempts by the state to outlaw or restrict some commodity from public consumption. The items that have brought enormous profits to organized crime range from tires and petroleum products, to cigarettes, alcoholic beverages, foodstuffs, pornographic literature, and sex.

Any list of what the syndicates have offered for sale is ultimately misleading because human tastes and legal prohibitions vary over time. Some of the biggest moneymakers in the 1930s and 1940s could be purchased legally a few decades later, and conversely, it is impossible to predict which commodities will be outlawed or in such short supply so as to provide future profits. Few persons would have anticipated that the energy crisis of the mid-1970s would reach such severe proportions as to encourage black markets to supply gasoline and oil.

Historically, organized crime's most recognized product has been alcohol. The Volstead Act prohibited the sale of alcoholic beverages as of 1920, and in the thirteen years before it was repealed, bootleggers became millionaires. For example, Al Capone, who had been a small-time hoodlum and nightclub bouncer, earned enough money between 1926 and 1929 to purchase

> $20,000 worth of silverware, a gold-plated dinner service and personal ornaments, including thirty diamond belt buckles. His custom made suits ... his silk-monogrammed shirts ... [and other clothing] ... came to

about $7000. . . . His Chicago hotel bills ran between $1200 and $1500 a week . . . his telephone bills totalled $39,000 (Kobler, 1971, p. 285).

Another bootlegger who grew rich during Prohibition was Johnny Torrio, who joined with the son of a prominent Chicago brewer to market a low-quality beer that sold to Illinois tavern operators at $55 per barrel—plus protection (Landesco, 1929, p. 86). With devaluation and inflation, a similar quantity of beer could be obtained wholesale in the 1970s for $60, with a refund of one third for the return of the kegs. By today's standards Torrio was wholesaling beer at $330 per barrel. There can be little doubt of the allegations that Torrio and his partner earned $12 million *annually* between 1920 and 1924. Such stupendous profits as these enabled organized crime syndicates to finance other criminal activities long after the repeal of Prohibition ended the lucrative alcohol market.

Prostitution has yielded substantial profits for organized crime, but there is some evidence that it is a declining trade. The successful prosecution of several gangsters, especially Charles Luciano, under the Mann (White Slavery) Act and changes in sexual mores seem to have reduced the profitability of syndicate involvement in prostitution.

Sex, in one form or another, however, still earns a profit for organized crime. A series of ambiguous court decisions have made it lucrative and less risky for syndicates to invest their earnings from other activities to produce and distribute pornographic pictures, literature, and films (Hammer, 1975, p. 344). And many gangsters still recognize the effectiveness of using sexually alluring women to compromise jockeys into throwing horse races, to set up judges and politicians for extortion, and to lure suckers into con-games (Teresa, 1973.) Thus, to impress investors for his swindle, Teresa would hire prostitutes, introduce them to potential clients, and instruct the ladies to feign virtue and "let them think they're seducing you. Make them believe they're irresistible, but let them know that if it wasn't for Vinnie Teresa, you'd have never gone out with them" (Teresa, 1973, p. 233).

A lucrative enterprise for the syndicates is the operation of black markets that supply merchandise that is in demand by the public. This demand may result from heavy taxation that makes the legal purchase of the product undesirable. Taxes on gasoline, alcohol, tobacco products, and luxuries, among other items, greatly increase their costs to the consumer. The demand may also arise because of rationing, which is often imposed during times of warfare, when military needs for natural resources require a reduction in civilian consumption (Clinard, 1952). Rationing may severely limit the amount of a product that can be purchased, or it may make the product completely unavailable. Upon perceiving the demand, the criminal syndicates move to fill it, either by supplying counterfeit stamps with which the public can purchase restricted goods or by selling products at a price below that at which they can be purchased on the legal market. Organized crime is able to make huge profits from black market operations, for overhead is almost nil for stolen commodities marketed without paying sales taxes. Thus, Valachi reports that he was pleasantly surprised at the outcome of supplying bogus rationing stamps for gasoline during World War II: "I thought it was penny-ante stuff . . . then I find out how them pennies can mount up" (Maas, 1968, p. 195).

Much of the merchandise for the syndicate's black market is obtained through a hijacking network. The tie between black marketeering and hijacking demonstrates once again the necessity for some degree of organization in the operation of these kinds of rackets. Storehouses and distribution points must be arranged and staffed, cooperative truckers must be found and means of transport scheduled, and the flow of goods and the payroll must be monitored by bookkeepers and accountants.

Hijacking is big business. It is estimated that the city and state of New York annually lose $133 million in tax revenues from the sale of hijacked (untaxed) cigarette shipments from North Carolina (Albini, 1971, p. 296; *Los Angeles Times*, 1975). As Teresa makes clear in the quote below, some of the best customers for stolen goods are legitimate retailers who can thus obtain merchandise well below wholesale prices. Teresa is describing a system whereby a warehouseman who was in debt to a loan shark made it possible for hijacking teams to heist shipments of Polaroid film from a factory loading dock.

> One skid [a portable loading platform used by a forklift] . . . contained sixteen thousand . . . small packages of film, and each one of those sold for three bucks in the stores. We could sell skid loads for twenty-five to thirty grand all day. . . .

> The film was the hottest product the mob could lay its hands on. . . . There's no way to trace and there were businessmen standing in line waiting to buy our loads at half price (1973, pp. 136–137).

Similar fortunes have been made from the sale of stolen phonograph records and pirated (rerecorded) tapes. One estimate is that organized crime earned $250 million in 1973 from the sale of pirated recordings (McCaghy & Denisoff, 1973; CBS News, 1974; *Newsweek*, 1974; Ward, 1974).

Narcotics and other drugs have also yielded huge black market profits. However, because of active prosecution of laws regulating the drug trade and the severe legal penalties that are imposed upon conviction, some syndicates have restricted their involvement to the importation of raw drugs or the financing of street operations.[4] For years some Italian-American crime families avoided the drug market, for they believed that such business was below Mafia dignity (Talese, 1971, p. 139). It is probable that the potential profits may have lowered their resistance and assuaged their moral qualms in the last two decades.

The black market in drugs is believed to involve some of the most intricate and byzantine arrangements in organized crime. Unlike most syndicate offenses, the trade in narcotics is generally a truly international affair, as morphine and its derivatives are produced from poppies harvested in the Middle East then transported through the Mediterranean and across the Atlantic (Siragusa, 1966; Greene et al., 1973). Similar import routes have been discovered from Asia and Latin America, particularly Mexico.

The Mexican and South American connections have presumably given rise to an ingenious form of smuggling in which private pilots evade American air defenses to land their planes on abandoned airstrips, clearings, and dry lakebeds in the south and southwest. In 1975 it was believed that each day 150 such flights crossed the border to carry marijuana into the United States (Riverside *Press*, 1975). Cocaine and heroin are also believed to be commodities that are imported on a routine basis by high flying aerial smugglers piloting everything from Cessnas to surplus B-25s and Constellations.

In addition to the international connections that must be maintained, the black market in illegal drugs has to be organized so as to prevent criminal prosecution. Thus, after the drugs are imported, the syndicate leaves the refining, distribution, and sales to other groups. There is some evidence that Italian-American syndicates employ other ethnic groups (primarily blacks and Hispanics, who are eager to break into lucrative syndicate operations) to manage the riskier street operations (Ianni, 1974a). A typical structural feature of crime organizations is apparent here, for the syndicates employ a buffer, or construct a wide boundary between those who privately import the drugs and those who publicly sell them, to insure that there are several levels that must be exposed before syndicate leaders can be tied to criminal acts (Cressey, 1969, pp. 114–115).

Syndicate Involvement in Business, Labor Unions, and Politics

Involvement in business, labor, and government is a lucrative sideline for the syndicates, as each of those institutions may be corrupted to further and protect organized crime. Business and industry are a rich source of black market goods, unions can be manipulated as tools of extortion, and politicians whose agencies have the legal authority and means to destroy organized crime can be neutralized through bribery.

The line between businesses controlled by organized crime and respectable firms acting illegally is thin. In fact, some would suggest that the same values—an insatiable profit motive and a desire to eliminate competition—explain the existence of large corporations like General Motors and organizations of crime like the Cosa Nostra. In a capitalist society it is not surprising that organizations devised to supply vices will resemble the enterprises serving legitimate needs. George Vold's observation that "the underworld of crime and the upperworld of business and politics are . . . in many ways two sides of the same coin" (1958, p. 237) is a concise summary of the point of view that criminal syndicates are merely gross exaggerations of the free enterprise system.[5]

The acquisition of lawful firms and industries through illegal tactics represents one of the most common forms of involvement of organized crime in the business world. There are several ways in which takeovers can be accomplished. Moneys earned from illegal operations may be employed to purchase or gain a controlling interest in businesses, or stock or part ownership in a company may be accepted in lieu of payment for a gambling or loan-shark debt. Thus Valachi gained half interest in an upper-Manhattan restaurant as compensation for a debt owed him (Maas, 1968, p. 173). Extortion and threats may also be used to gain syndicate partnership in a legal operation.

Once infiltrated the firm can be used by the syndicate to finance or facilitate criminal activities. For example, loan sharks may seize and liquidate a business to cancel a loan (leaving the hapless owner bankrupt and broken). A New York meat wholesaler who could not repay his note to a syndicate shylock helplessly watched as an associate of Valachi's was installed as the new president of the firm. Peter Maas notes:

> In ten days they made $1,300,000. They did it by buying huge quantities of meat and poultry on credit and selling it immediately for cash at below market prices. Then, when they were through, they blithely ordered the thoroughly cowed firm to declare bankruptcy (1968, p. 293).

Businesses can also be maintained as fronts, with their activities and profits used to conceal other illegal operations. This often occurs on a small scale, as when a candy shop fronts for a bookmaker. But the Bonanno family of New York operated on a grander scale, hiding its operations behind trucking firms, auto repair shops, and a Wisconsin cheese factory (Talese, 1971). Fronts are especially useful in *laundering* money, or covering evidence that would allow it to be traced back to some criminal operation.[6] In one typical laundering operation, proceeds from gambling and shylock rackets were channeled to family-controlled real estate agencies and lawful finance companies; the funds were returned at a later date to the criminal enterprises (Ianni, 1972, p. 102). One informant has suggested that syndicate interests in jukebox and vending machines came about because operators of the numbers racket needed a front to bank their daily collection of thousands of nickels, dimes, and quarters without arousing suspicion.

Occasionally infiltrated businesses will be used to gain control of a legitimate market by merchandising the product in the same fashion as the vices. Businesses that are competitive to the syndicate's operation and that the syndicate does not wish to use to further its ends are simply run out of business. Meanwhile, a protection racket is used to force distributors to sell the syndicate product alone (Schelling, 1967, p. 116). Such force may take the form of threats, muggings, or the destruction of the business property. Through such techniques a monopoly may be achieved.

Protection practices were rampant during Prohibition, when protection was widely used and refined to an art, and the decades since repeal have seen little or no decline in this practice. In the 1960s a New Jersey syndicate entered the wholesale detergent business by intimidating store managers who refused to retail their soap. After several bombings in which employees of the A&P chain lost their lives, the plot was uncovered (Smith, 1967, pp. 103–104). More recently, artists under contract to some recording firms had their lives threatened unless their companies agreed to pay protection. One informant, an independent record producer, comments:

> I know that the Mafia . . . [is] intimidating a lot of super rock stars. They are threatening if he's a musician . . . to break his playing hand, and if he's a vocalist . . . to slit his throat. And they . . . in turn, are asking 25 percent of the artist's fees in kickbacks (CBS News, 1974).

At one time, when singer O. C. Smith's life was menaced because of unpaid gambling debts, an executive of CBS Records allegedly approached Cosa Nostra intermediaries to resolve the dispute peacefully (CBS News, 1974).

Syndicate involvement is not limited to the management of business and industry but extends to the control of labor unions. Labor racketeering takes two forms: thefts from union treasuries, retirement plans, and strike funds and extortion to threaten management into paying bribes or accepting union contracts.

The alliance that exists today between organized crime and some unions could not have been anticipated. Earlier in the twentieth century, organized crime profited from the supply of black market labor to break strikes (Cressey, 1969; Tyler, 1974) or goons to harass and assault labor organizers (Graham & Gurr, 1969). As recently as the 1950s some syndicates continued their antiunion activities, exemplified by the acid blinding of Victor Riesel, a newspaper columnist supportive of labor goals.

One union in particular, the International Brotherhood of Teamsters, Chauffeurs, Warehousemen, and Helpers, has been linked with shady operations. These activities came to light largely through Robert Kennedy's relentless investigation as chief counsel of the McClellan Committee, which studied the improper labor activities of Teamster Presidents Dave Beck and James Hoffa (Hoffa, 1975). Among the abuses of

Hoffa's stewardship of the union, it is alleged that he invested Teamster funds in companies whose employees were represented by the union and that he used his power to extort money from businesses holding Teamster contracts. Even after Hoffa's fall from power, controversy surrounded the investment of money collected from Teamsters who contribute to the Central States, Southeast and Southwest Areas Pension Fund. It is customary for retirement funds to invest their capital to increase the fund's value for pension holders, but some investigations have alleged that the Central States Fund has been associated with some highly speculative endeavors by individuals who are believed to have syndicate ties. It is believed that some Las Vegas casinos and the plush resort, Rancho La Costa, outside of San Diego were financed by Teamster money loaned to a number of entrepreneurs, some of whom, like Moe Dalitz, are suspected of having associations with organized crime (Bergman & Gerth, 1975).

With control of labor unions comes the potential to cripple the economy and wreck corporations by withdrawing the labor force that keeps business and industry functioning. Syndicate leaders recognize the potential for extortion by threatening to strike. A frequent goal of such strong-arm tactics is a "sweetheart contract" designed to bring greater profits to the labor leaders than to the workers (Salerno & Tompkins, 1969, p. 190). In return for abandoning the needs of the union, the corrupt leader can expect healthy kickbacks from corporate treasuries.

Contacts with both labor and government can enrich the syndicates, but corruption of politics does so in a different manner, by neutralizing those officials whose duty it is to enforce laws against organized crime. While no direct profit is reaped from an alliance between organizations of crime and government (in fact, bribes may represent a kind of overhead to the syndicates), the license to continue their operations free of interference is priceless.

Agents at every level of government can be of service to organized crime. Leaders of executive branches of state and local government can halt the investigation and prosecution of organized crime cases or provide clemency for racketeers who are snared; judges can disguise or acquit charges against gangsters or hand down lenient sentences; and legislators can kill laws that are unfavorable to the operation of the syndicates. Some claim that it will only be a matter of time before organized crime elects a president of the United States (Salerno, quoted in Hammer, 1974, p. 215).

Indeed, the scandals that led to the resignation of both Spiro Agnew and Richard Nixon illustrate that persons of high office may not be immune to the syndicate's inducements of money and power. Both before and after Nixon's resignation the press has printed allegations that he was on close terms with syndicate figures (Gerth, 1972; Nelson & Hazlett, 1973). Some point to the source of some of his campaign funding. Los Angeles mobster Mickey Cohen (1975) claims that he helped fund Nixon campaigns as early as 1945. Other critics have questioned the circumstances under which Jimmy Hoffa was pardoned by Nixon; they note Nixon's apparent close ties with Teamster President Frank Fitzsimmons, the support of the Teamsters in the 1972 election, and financial contributions ranging between $55,000 to $250,-000 to the Committee to Reelect the President (Nelson & Hazlett, 1973, p. 24; Hoffa, 1975, p. 78). Interestingly, one of the first public appearances Nixon made after leaving the White House was at a Rancho La Costa Teamster golf tournament hosted by Fitzsimmons.

Studies of governmental corruption show that organized crime survives best where there is a rather massive decay of community agencies (Gardiner, 1967; Chambliss, 1971).[7] Syndicate activities are not limited to a few corrupt cops and sinister thugs. Instead, Chambliss concludes that "[t]he people who run the organizations which supply the vices in American cities are members of business, political and law enforcement communities—not simply members of a criminal society" (1971, pp. 1172–1173). To overlook the involvement of "respectable" citizens, including influential clients who purchase vices, is to misunderstand completely the foundation of the syndicate's prosperity.

There is reason to believe that at one time the federal government contemplated using the syndicate's services by asking it to "put out a contract" on Fidel Castro. During the Kennedy administration some operatives in the Central Intelligence Agency went so far as to have Robert Maheu (a former Federal Bureau of Investigation agent who was at that time a high-placed employee of Howard Hughes) approach mobster John Roselli, who reported the plan to the head of the Chicago syndicate, Sam Giancana. The latter drew up plans to have Castro poisoned, but the Bay of Pigs invasion intervened, and the "hit" was cancelled (Schorr, 1976, p. 83).

One of the stories to come out of the Senate's recent investigation of CIA activities concerns John Kennedy's relationship with a Las Vegas showgirl, Judith Campbell. It is alleged that she was introduced to Frank Sinatra, who, in turn, introduced her to Kennedy on a visit to the Nevada resort. She and Kennedy remained friends for over a year, until the Secret Service learned of her association with Giancana and asked the President to stop communicating with her. Only a short time before Giancana was to go before the Senate committee investigating the CIA to testify on the matters of the Castro plot and the Campbell connection, he was shot to death under mysterious circumstances in his Chicago home (*Newsweek*, 1975a, 1975b).

While the consistent patronage of affluent members of the upper and middle class assures organized crime's vice profits, both William Chambliss and John Gardiner find a surprising naiveté among those members of the community who would like to halt the activities of the syndicates. These concerned citizens frequently launch reform movements, but whatever success they have is only temporary. In each instance, the reformers become complacent with the removal of the original threat; they fail to recognize that there has been no lessening of the syndicate's profits from their community's appetite for the vices (Gardiner, 1967, p. 78). Voting a corrupt politician out of office or incarcerating gangsters will fail as a method of controlling organized crime as long as the public demand for gambling, prostitution, drugs, and other illegal goods and services persists. A new cast of characters may step into the roles discarded by the disavowed crooks, but the clientele remains the same.

The area of corruption in many communities involves the police department. Interestingly, efforts to reach a middle ground between open licentiousness, where citizens can purchase whatever they want, and the full enforcement of the law is a ground for decay in many police agencies. A middle strategy, often called a *tolerance policy*, comes about for many reasons. For one thing, many of the offenses committed by criminal syndicates fall in the range of crimes without victims—that is, crimes marked by the willing participation of a person who would legally be considered the only victim but who does not become a complainant so as not to reveal his own participation in a criminal activity (Schur, 1965). Examples of such offenses include the procurer of a prostitute, the purchaser of drugs or other black market commodities, or borrowers of money from a loan shark. The end result is that the criminal justice system is often asked to enforce laws where the crime is committed with the cooperation of the putative victim.

The overabundance of laws that the police are asked to enforce contributes in part to explaining why tolerance policies emerge. There are simply more laws (and violations of those laws) than can be handled by the slim resources of most communities. In California, for example, a law enforcement officer is expected to be familiar with at least 650 state criminal codes, plus county and municipal ordinances, vehicle codes, health statutes, and the procedures of due process spelled out in the Constitution. This has been termed a "crisis of overcriminalization" (Kadish, 1967; see also Packer, 1968; Dobrovir, 1970).

The police and other law enforcement agencies cannot deal with all the criminal offenses that come to their attention, and they certainly cannot deal with those that do not, as in the case of victimless offenses. The usual solution to this problem, suggests Chambliss, is to

> do what any well managed bureaucracy would do under similar circumstances—they [the police] follow the line of least resistance. Using discretion inherent in their positions, they resolve the problem by establishing procedures which minimize organizational strain. . . . Typically this means that law enforcers adopt a tolerance policy towards the vices, selectively enforcing these laws only when it is to their advantage to do so (1971, p. 1154).

Thus, prostitution may be tolerated by restricting it to "red light" districts situated far from respectable residential or business areas, or cardrooms or bookmaking establishments may be given an informal license to operate.

Tolerance policies are not illegal and, by themselves, not corrupt. But the potential for corruption lurks wherever a policy of tolerance is pursued, for it places police officers in the position of choosing which laws will be enforced and against whom, independent of any *legal* criterion. What frequently evolves is a shakedown racket run by the police and willingly accepted by the syndicates, who forego a portion of their profits in bribes and payoffs to stay in business. The history of American municipal government is replete with examples of cities in which the police force has conducted a profitable alliance of this nature with organized crime. Seattle is only one example from hundreds.

Two years after a mayor had closed cardrooms across the city, Seattle instituted a tolerance policy to permit card playing at the discretion of the police.[8] Within six years an extensive network of police payoffs was discovered. A grand jury later alleged that some patrolmen were collecting $10 to $1,000 each month from operators of gambling establishments on their beats. Some portion of the payoffs (usually one third to one half) was passed up the chain of command as far, claimed the grand jury, as the chief of police. Several police officials were reported to have earned as much as $12,000 annually from the payoff system. Moreover, several prominent city officials, including the past county prosecutor, the president of the city council, and the county license director, were indicted for receiving bribes in the form of campaign contributions to cover up the corruption.[9] From the example of Seattle, it is apparent how quickly corruption can take hold under conditions of a tolerance policy.

THE STRUCTURE OF ORGANIZED CRIME

Each of the goods and services offered by criminal syndicates requires some degree of organization to be marketed profitably. Most demand too many simultaneous actions to be managed by a single perpetrator. A bookie could conceivably collect enough capital to start a one-person operation, but the profits become greater and the risks decline if the enterprise can be conducted on a larger scale with several actors coordinated in a division of labor.

Organization is a generic term that fails to specify which of many forms or structures comprise the group under discussion. Thus, both the United States and the People's Republic of China are organized political units, but their structures are quite different. Unfortunately, the kind of information that would clarify the structure of criminal organizations is lacking. Knowing some of their goals and problems, however, makes it possible to draw certain hypotheses about the kind of structure that would be needed to meet those exigencies. For example, a certain degree of flexibility and orderly procedure must be maintained if operations are to function efficiently and profitably. Secrecy must be built into the structure as long as the syndicates deal in illegal goods and services, and structural devices for monitoring and sanctioning employees who may compromise the organization's security will undoubtedly emerge.

The size of activities poses a particularly difficult management problem for some syndicates. Large structures often produce the biggest profits, but they also impede communication between different units, make it difficult for the organization to conceal its operation (and keep tabs on its employees), and destroy the syndicate's efficiency. William Bonanno discovered the truth of that proposition when he lost contact with his minions who were in hiding all over New York City during a gangland war. Bonanno told his confidant:

> This thing of ours is absolutely going to the dogs. . . . The Bonanno organization had lost two officers [who used the opportunity to defect to a rival gang] for which it had no comparable replacements. Its membership was now perhaps less than 200—it was impossible to figure because many men had recently disappeared from sight, taking prolonged summer vacations rather than remain in New York (Talese, 1971, p. 223).

Lacking hard evidence about the structural nature of criminal syndicates, there have been attempts to reconstruct the structure from the bits and pieces of data (much of it anecdotal) that do exist. Two notably ambitious efforts are the structural analysis by Cressey (1967a, 1969), derived from information collected for the President's Commission on Law Enforcement and Administration of Justice, and the model by Ianni (1972), produced from interactions with one cooperative syndicate over several years.

These analysts reach quite different conclusions as to the nature of the structure of criminal organizations. Cressey contends that the Cosa Nostra is nothing less than a formal organization, marked by a hierarchy of integrated positions arranged along a division of labor, with clear patterns of authority and centralized leadership and with formalized methods of recruitment, training, and social control. The bureaucratic structure described in its ideal form by Max Weber (1947) comes closest to resembling the phenomenon Cressey portrays. Accordingly, when searching for parallels to organized crime, Cressey continually relies upon examples drawn from big business, government, and military organizations.

Ianni (1972) rejects the image of a highly rational and bureaucratic formal organization; he instead describes criminal syndicates as "traditional social systems" quite similar to those of Italian-American kinship structures. He contends that organized crime families are just that:

structures that resemble families through being interconnected by blood, marriage, or church ritual (as in the case of baptismal or confirmation sponsorship. Furthermore, he asserts, "they [secret societies like the Mafia] are not rationally designed and consciously constructed; they are responsive to culture and are patterned by tradition" (Ianni, 1972, p. 153).

After studying black, Cuban, and Puerto Rican organized crime syndicates in New York and New Jersey, however, Ianni (1974a, 1974b) modified this position somewhat. He found these other syndicates to be organized in ways quite different from the familial pattern discovered among the Italian-Americans; there were different patterns of recruitment, authority, leadership, stability, and organization. He therefore suggested that in crime syndicates two basic forms of organization are apparent: associational networks and entrepreneurial networks.

Organized crime syndicates patterned as *associational networks* are marked by an emphasis on mutual trust and are bound together by a close interpersonal network that is often founded upon ties formed in earlier associations. Thus, friends who were members of the same childhood gang, or individuals who are brought together as part of a convict and inmate subculture in prison, pattern their criminal activities after the preestablished modes of interaction and organization (Ianni, 1974a, pp. 288–294). Similarly, kinship ties much like those described among Italian-American subcultures may form the bond for associational networks (p. 282).

The *entrepreneurial* model suggests to Ianni a "more advanced" form of organizational arrangement than the associational model, for it is based upon a network of individuals bound together in order to earn a mutual profit, an arrangement quite similar to a small business. While entrepreneurial associations possess a hierarchy of leadership and decision making that makes them more "bureaucratic" than associational networks, Ianni (1974a, pp. 294–295) stresses that such organizations are analogous to *small* businesses. The description of these small businesses of organized crime would suggest the existence of organizational patterns lying somewhere between the "big businesses" described by Cressey and Ianni's earlier description of the "traditional" Italian-American family.

The differences between Ianni and Cressey stem partly from the vantage point from which each draws his inference.[10] Cressey tends to see the formal, almost businesslike qualities of syndicate structure that would be highlighted in official reports gathered from law enforcement agencies, grand juries, and legislative investigations. Cressey's point of view is very much from the top of the structure looking down. Ianni, on the other hand has a view of the structure from the inside. He tends to emphasize the informal, clanlike nature of the syndicate that he became familiar with following years of interaction in the context of the family or friendship groups. While these are biases that affect the conclusions that each analyst eventually draws, neither view is totally right or wrong. Basing their conclusions on observations taken from quite different angles, each provides a partial answer to the nature of criminal syndicates.

For the student of organized crime, the analyses by Ianni and Cressey are useful guides. Their points of agreement and disagreement provide the most comprehensive glimpse of the syndicates to date. They address three issues: the extent of international involvement in organized crime; the interrelationship between different syndicates in the United States; and the characteristics of the structure that governs decision making, social control, recruitment, and socialization.

International Ties Among Crime Organizations

Both scholars agree that there is no evidence, despite the claims of some alarmists and romantics, that organized crime in America is controlled by some foreign syndicate. Nor do they believe that there is an international alliance of organization of crime headquartered in Italy. Criminal syndicates have never been the sole province of Italians or Sicilians. In American history, they supplanted other ethnic groups (most notably the Irish and Eastern European Jews) during the first part of the twentieth century. To restrict the onus of organized crime to Italians today is as erroneous as it would have been to lay the blame for the syndicates on the Irish (and their associations like the Sinn Fein or Brothers of Hibernia) or the Jews (and the Zionists) fifty years earlier.[11]

This is not to deny that there is a long history of secret criminal societies in southern Italy and Sicily. Groups like the Mafia and Camorra emerged to meet problems stemming from centuries of foreign domination, and the consequent lack of political autonomy among the natives, and from a passing of the traditional, feudal practices of land use and labor management (Albini, 1971, pp. 83–151; Hess, 1973).

Those societies exist today, but their operations seem unsophisticated and antiquated when compared to the complexity of the American organizations that manage a billion dollar vice market (Ianni, 1972, p. 37).

While there is no organizational tie between American syndicates and counterparts in southern Europe, it is likely that immigrants from those regions who engaged in organized crime were influenced by their cultural heritage after they came to the United States. Italian-American crime syndicates are not carbon copies of the Mafia or Camorra of their native lands (nor are they under the thrall of Palermo or Naples), but their structure may possess features that were transplanted to the United States. Furthermore, it appears that structuring the organization along family, village, or regional ties or following the lead of certain operations, like the Black Hand extortion racket popular at the turn of the century, may be traceable to Sicilian traditions (Glazer & Moynihan, 1963, p. 198; Albini, 1971, p. 192; Gambino, 1974, p. 294).

Immigrant awareness of the effectiveness of secret, criminal societies in their homelands may have predisposed some to employ similar tactics when faced by problems in America. The conditions of poverty and political alienation found by Italian immigrants to America were similar to those that spawned the Mafia in Sicily a few centuries earlier. As Luigi Barzini (1964, p. 253) notes, the Mafia is as much a state of mind to rationalize the use of illegal means to survive in a hostile environment as it is a criminal association found in the southern regions of Italy.

A Nationwide Confederation of Syndicates

The belief that American criminal syndicates are allied in a national network is less easily dismissed. Cressey contends, "In the United States, criminals have managed to put together an organization which is at once a nationwide illicit cartel and a nationwide confederation" (1969, p. 1). He recognizes that the term Cosa Nostra—literally "our thing"—is bound by time and culture, but he feels it accurately portrays the cross-country ties between Italian-American crime families. Cressey describes a system composed of twenty-four such families. Each family is organized around a single, patriarchal boss (sometimes called a *don* or *capo*), and the structures range in size from 20 to 800 members.

Cressey has a basis for these conclusions. His study of organized crime has revealed that a nationwide commission supposedly emerged during the 1930s to bring an end to the self-destructive warfare between families competing in the free-for-all market of Prohibition (Cressey, 1969, pp. 35ff.; Bloch & Geis, 1970, p. 196). Those ad hoc attempts at peace keeping have since evolved into what is called the *Consiglio d'Administrazione*, "made up of the rulers of the most powerful 'families' which are located in large cities" (Cressey, 1969, p. 111). At the time of writing, Cressey claimed there were eight such families, three from New York City, and one apiece from Buffalo, Newark, Philadelphia, Detroit, and Chicago. The commissioners, generally the dons of powerful families, frequently represent the interests of other families in nearby regions who lack their own seat on the central body. (There is some reason to believe that there are also regional committees that meet in councils. Thus, the five families that control New York City may meet to discuss issues of common relevance.)

The commission, acting as judge and jury, meets to resolve problems that arise between families and to set policy that will insure coordination between each of the organizations. An idea of what composes the commission's agenda may be gathered by considering the topics that were to be discussed at a meeting of some fifty syndicate leaders in Apalachin, New York, in 1956. According to Richard Hammer (1975, p. 273), the Commission was to ratify Vito Genovese's ascendance to the rank of "boss of the bosses" and to resolve the lingering animosities that followed that power grab. The commission also planned to consider keeping the membership books closed to new syndicate recruits and to reconsider the policy of staying out of the lucrative drug market.

The fieldwork focus of Ianni's research was, of course, unlikely to turn up evidence of such a commission. Thus he, with others, is skeptical of the existence of a national alliance of the syndicates. Gordon Hawkins (1969) argues persuasively that the evidence is too slim (or dubious—as in the case of an informer like Valachi) to support belief in such a phenomenon as the commission. Hawkins states:

> In the end, it is difficult to resist the conclusion that one is not dealing with an empirical phenomenon at all, but with an article of faith, transcending the contingent particularity of everyday experience and logically unassailable; one of those reassuring popular demonologies that . . .

the successful politician has to cherish and preserve and may, in the end, come to believe (1969, p. 51).

Ianni reaches much the same conclusion. He is not convinced, for example, that the clannish, traditional structure of organized crime families necessitates a central agency of management analogous to corporate activity. Why, he asks, should any family feel compelled to obey the directive of such a committee? Each family is an autonomous unit, and whatever power resides in the commission extends no further than each member. These families are not franchises in a corporate empire, to be directed by the will of a central office; instead, they are traditional family units who jealously guard their own business and keep their own counsel.

The different conclusions reached by Ianni and Cressey about a national alliance of criminal organizations undoubtedly reflect their unique vantage points and frames of reference. One need not accept a corporate model of organized crime to realize that an association may evolve to discuss problems common to persons engaged in the same kind of business. There are, after all, associations for swimming pool contractors, used-car sales managers, and sociologists. The existence of a group that meets to review matters of mutual concern does not mean that it functions as a governing body. It may indeed be true that the bloody history of unrestrained competition during Prohibition led the bosses of some families to meet with syndicate leaders from other regions. And those meetings may persist today. Cressey's account perhaps overestimates the degree of the commission's influence, but Ianni fails to note the utility of such a body for family operations.

The Internal Structure of an Organized Crime Family

Cressey and Ianni also disagree as to the way that individual syndicates are organized within themselves. It is Cressey's contention that a family is composed of a single patriarch who rules the family membership, which may number from 20 to 800 persons. Such a family is fictive in that the membership includes persons who have been recruited, or adopted, into the kinship system. *Compareggio*—the practice of crossing bloodlines to confer family status through godparenthood or sponsorship in church rituals—is a frequently employed mechanism of adoption (Cressey, 1969, p. 152; Ianni, 1972, p. 123).

Cressey sees the structure of a family as analogous to the organization of a business or industry, with the patriarch as president and the rest of the family in lower-management roles (see Figure 2). The patriarchal boss, or *capo,* is assisted by agents who carry out his directives and supervise the activities of underlings lower in the system. The under-boss, or *sottocapo,* acts as the vice president and executive officer for the *capo,* wielding great power over syndicate employees who receive orders from him. On the same level, but lacking the overall authority of the underboss, the *consigliere* is an advisor (much like a corporation's legal counsel) who reviews the implications of policy for the boss.

Figure 2. *The Structure of a Hypothetical Organized Crime Family*

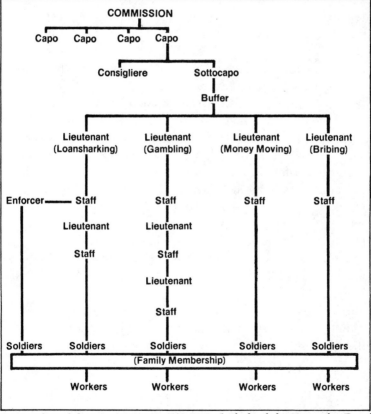

SOURCE: Adapted from pp. 112–115, 146–147 of *Theft of the Nation* by Donald R. Cressey. Copyright © 1969 by Donald R. Cressey. By permission of Harper & Row, Publishers, Inc.

At roughly the same level, the *buffer* acts as a communications conduit, passing orders down the line and routing information, questions, and money back to the policy-making levels. The buffer breaks any direct connection that would tie the criminal act of a syndicate employee to the *capo* or *sottocapo* who commanded the act. It is important that the buffer be a trusted and loyal member of the family because his cooperation with the police (or competing syndicates) could spell the end of the syndicate.

Lower in the structure are several levels of operatives. Each of the syndicate's operations is assigned to a different lieutenant. One may be entrusted with the special duties of moving money (e.g., supervising the laundering, investing, and banking of the syndicate's earnings), while another may become the corrupter, who has the responsibility of maintaining through bribery the family's ties with politicians and agents of the criminal justice system. At a slightly lower level, one family member may play the role of an enforcer, using strong-arm tactics to collect the organization's debts.

The depth of the organization below each lieutenant depends on the nature of the operation he commands. Gambling operations, for example, require many persons to complete the diverse chores necessary to that kind of racket. Others demand less complexity, and the layers between the lieutenant and the workers and soldiers in the field may be scant. In either case, the lieutenants will always have below them staff members who contribute special skills as bookkeepers, buffers, or foremen for each operation. Soldiers are employed to work on the street, supervising workers, numbers runners, prostitutes, truck drivers, and the employees who are needed to carry out each activity. Family membership rarely crosses the line between soldiers and workers (Cressey, 1969, p. 118).

Ianni rejects the view that the syndicates are organized bureaucratically and lists the structural differences in corporations and crime families. For one thing, formal organizations are structured in terms of positions and not persons. Thus, the duties and rights of the president of the United States are so clearly delineated that the organization (the nation) can swiftly replace an incumbent who dies or resigns. In syndicates like the Lupollo family, however, some members are indispensable because they possess special skills. Thus, the death of a family member who acts as a connection between the legal and illegal realms of the family may disorganize each unit because no immediate substitute could assume that role. Such indispensability of persons contradicts the premises of the theory of formal organizations.

Formal organizations are also supposed to be rationally organized, with persons rising to leadership because of their intelligence and expertise. But Ianni suggests that family standing and tradition play an equally important function in determining which family members will rule the syndicate. The rules that determine family authority give a good idea of the relative importance of education and aptitude:

1. The earlier the generation, the higher the rank. Thus, the oldest generation always commands the greatest amount of authority in the family, with the ultimate authority residing in the patriarch.

2. Because many persons may occupy the same generational level, those persons who are most closely related (by bloodline) to the patriarch will take precedence over other lineages.

3. Persons possessing some particular skill will rank above persons of the same generational level who are generalists (Ianni, 1972, p. 116).

Such a power structure has its closest comparison in the Old World extended family, in which power accrues to a person not because that is rational but because tradition demands it.

Ianni reports, however, that changes are taking place within the Lupollo family that represent a challenge to the traditional, patriarchal structure. Some of the younger members of the family feel that a proven record of achievement in business or politics—a very rational criterion in itself—is a better reason for granting power than generational and genealogical standing. Within the family, alliances have slowly arisen in which the most influential members are those persons whose interests go beyond the family and whose political and social outlook is considered less conservative or "Italian." If this trend continues, the corporate model may ultimately replace the traditional ways of allocating authority.

Again, Cressey and Ianni seem to be describing the same phenomenon from a different perspective. Working from the outside and compiling a list of positions in the structure (many of them gleaned from references in wiretapped conversations), Cressey tries to fit the pieces together and finds the most understandable arrangement to be a bureaucracy of almost military overtones. However, he seems to have lacked Ianni's insights as to the ways in which decisions are reached, or the traditional ways in which power is allocated among family relatives.

The differences between the two are so superficial as to suggest that Italian-American organized crime families are something of a structural hybrid, superimposing the rational, efficient model of American corporations over a structure patterned after the traditional, extended family of southern Europe. The synthesis of Old and New World values is apparent in the way in which new members are recruited into the syndicate. Cressey and Ianni both find that organization membership is restricted to family members—either actual or symbolic (through *compareggio*)—except at the very lowest levels (Cressey, 1969, pp. 151–152; Ianni, 1972, p. 63). From the successive ranks of sons, grandsons, cousins, nephews, and godsons, the syndicate's administrators are drawn. But consistent with the hybrid nature of the crime family, considerable selectivity enters into the process of deciding which of the many heirs will take power. Bloodline and tradition may define the pool from which administrative recruits are considered, but cold, organizational criteria like experience, intelligence, and performance in apprenticeships determine which candidates will ultimately be tapped for syndicate leadership.

Apprenticeships are a common device for evaluating the fitness of younger family members to assume more responsible positions in the syndicate. Thus Ianni reports:

> There is within the family a constant process of assessment of relatives who might be valuable adjuncts in the business . . . . A member of the family mentions a relative who is doing well in school or seems to have a sharp eye for business. The relative is given some minor supervisory position in one of the family businesses . . . . If he does well, he can expect to move ahead . . . under the protection of his kin sponsor (1972, pp. 132–133).

In a similar vein, Bill Bonanno recalls worrying that he might not measure up to the standards of his father, Joseph Bonanno, a New York *capo*. Arrested and jailed overnight after a youthful escapade, the son remembered with satisfaction that he had remained "cool" while in jail (Talese, 1971, p. 42).[12]

The question of whether persons rise to positions of power in the syndicate because of family influence or because of their ability should be answerable through historical analysis. Unfortunately, the reports of informants and the reconstructions of changes in family leadership provide no answer. For example, Homer (1974, p. 58) reports that New Jersey "boss" Sam Cavalcante's nephew Bobby Basile was given greater powers within the syndicate even though many family subordinates questioned Basile's abilities. On the other side of the question, Joseph Bonanno found that his effort to pass the leadership of his family to his son Bill was blocked by commission members who believed the son unqualified to assume leadership (Hammer, 1975, p. 285). These two contradictory examples probably show that it is erroneous to try to state conclusions about syndicate activities too concretely. No organization is purely bureaucratic or familial. Formal organizations outside of crime are replete with examples where nepotism or friendship predicted advancement, so it is not surprising that criminal syndicates may evidence similar anomalies.

Once having recruited and accepted members into the inner workings of the family, the syndicate must maintain strict control over those members. To protect itself from the attacks of competitors or law enforcement officials, the syndicate demands that complete obedience must follow a leader's commands and that absolute secrecy must cover each member's activities. Recruiting from within the family guarantees a loyalty bred of blood and tradition from most syndicate employees, but to assure conformity each new recruit learns a code of behavior.

The code seems to have evolved out of values expressed in the traditional Sicilian Mafia principles of *omerta*, or connivance (Cressey, 1967, p. 41), but elements of the code today are similar to norms spelled out in credos professed by American thieves and convicts. Such codes are not unique to the criminal world, for they can be found in almost any social grouping, ranging from college fraternities and sororities to craft guilds that attempt to control the behavior of their members.

Cressey and Ianni provide almost identical descriptions of the syndicate code. It is unwritten, but they claim it exhorts each family member (1) to be loyal to the family, placing one's personal or nuclear family needs after those of the syndicate; (2) to "act like a man," always behaving in a way that reflects the moral superiority of family members and never brings disgrace to the family; (3) to treat other family members honorably; and (4) to keep family operations secret, never discussing them with or reporting them to outsiders (Cressey, 1969, p. 171; Ianni, 1972, p. 139).

In his study of non-Italian syndicates, Ianni (1974b) found that there are similar but functionally different codes for the associational and entrepreneurial networks. Given the way in which both groups come to be organized, the differences are not surprising. The associational network code resembles the Italian-American in that it reaffirms the loyalty and pride that are part of family, friendship, gang, or prison ties. Within entrepreneurial networks, the code stresses the need of a small illegal business to have members that keep secrets, work competently and efficiently, and get along with coworkers.

Minor violations of the code are met with light, informal sanctions, and ridicule or public lectures are often sufficient to correct an erring family member. Thus, when Bill Bonanno's extramarital affair became too flagrant, his mother-in-law (the widow of a Profaci family member) cursed him at a family gathering (Talese, 1971, p. 84; for other examples see Ianni, 1972, pp. 148ff.). But protracted deviance, or activity that puts the family in an unfavorable public light, may be met with harsher sanctions. Apparently the commission or regional councils may be employed to act judicially, hearing the case of an errant family member and imposing penalties—often in the form of restricted rights within the family (Cressey, 1969, p. 213; also 1973). Bloodshed is the last resort, for, as Cressey (1973, p. 60) notes, the intense loyalty inspired by the code and family membership is far more effective than the threat of death in maintaining conformity.

Structural Changes in Organized Crime Families
In their analyses, Ianni and Cressey detect trends in the way that organizations of crime are evolving. It appears that the syndicates are using the moneys earned from illegal activities to finance respectable, legal businesses. Sons and grandsons of a syndicate patriarch embark on careers in those lawful activities, where the risks of imprisonment or public stigmatization are low. Ianni (1972) notes an increasing gap between the legal and illegal activities of the Lupollo family. The criminal enterprises continue and thrive, but the proportion of family members who follow careers in that sector grows smaller with each generation.

It would be erroneous to infer from these trends that organized crime will soon disappear. The families described by Ianni and Cressey are predominantly composed of the descendants of Italian immigrants. Their involvement in organized crime activities and their subsequent move toward legitimate business are merely reprises of a phenomenon that has occurred several times in American history with other immigrant groups.

SOME NOTES ON THE HISTORY OF ORGANIZED CRIME

Extensive information on the history of organized crime syndicates in America can be obtained from several sources that offer details on their rise and development.[13] Here a historical review of organized crime will suffice to highlight certain major issues that are relevant to this chapter.

Perhaps the most important thing to be learned from an overview of the syndicates is that organized crime has a much longer history than is generally recognized. There is a tendency to treat organized crime as a peculiarly American phenomenon that has only existed for the last hundred years. But looking at this form of criminal activity as it was defined earlier—syndicates organized to provide illegal goods and services for a profit—makes it apparent that organized crime is probably as old as both economic conceptions of personal profit and societal prohibitions against the use or consumption of certain goods or services.

By adopting a broader conception of what may be considered organized crime activity, one can see that some pre-twentieth century, non-American criminal acts resemble today's organized crime operations. The slave trade in the eighteenth and nineteenth centuries, a lucrative enterprise for shippers in America and Europe, is just one of many historical examples of smuggling that involved organization for profit through the provision of an illegal (in Great Britain and, after 1807, in the United States) product (Wright, 1973). In American history it is possible to identify epochs of smuggling. Over 150 years ago it was slaves. Fifty years ago it was bootleg liquor. Later it became narcotics from the Middle East and Latin America. The commodity changes, but the practice remains.

Historians of organized crime should develop a keener sensitivity to acts that may have comprised organized crime in earlier times. For another example drawn from American history, consider the practice of labor brokerage. By supplying labor to regions whose industries were expanding faster than the population, fortunes could be made. During the nineteenth century most immigrant groups encountered some form of labor brokerage. The *padrone* system among Italians is one of the best documented, but the practice was common among all ethnic groups who arrived hungry, impoverished, jobless, and unfamiliar with local customs (Gambino, 1974, p. 97). Newly arrived immigrants would be approached by someone from the old country, who, having been in the United States for some time, claimed to have connections that he would use to help his "brother" find a job. This would be done, and the immigrant would be thankful for the friendship that could speed success and prosperity in America. Only later would he realize that his "friend" received a commission (deducted from the laborer's wages) from construction teams and factories for supplying workers. It is estimated that by 1897 two thirds of the Italian labor force in New York City was in the control of the *padrone* system (Glazer & Moynihan, 1963, pp. 187ff.).

While immigrant labor brokerage systems are frequently cited as early examples of organized labor, there are other kinds of profitable trade in labor that also flourished during the nineteenth century. The example of *crimping* is particularly interesting because it represents a form of organized crime that has pretty much disappeared. Crimping or *shanghaiing* involved supplying sailing ships with seamen. Intolerable living conditions and long, arduous voyages made it difficult for ships to maintain a full complement of hands. The *press gangs* used to fill British warships during the first two decades of the century (Fowler, 1974) represent a kind of precedent for the crimps who would drug young, able-bodied men, carry them unconscious on board ship, and enlist them for a cruise. The hapless recruits would awake far out to sea, unable to do anything about their predicament except to make the best of it. Every major seaport had its crimps who would meet the sailing masters' need for "warm bodies" in return for a commission of $30 a head, plus expenses (Villiers, 1971, p. 164). (There were a few unscrupulous crimps who were known to have supplied ships with "cold bodies"—recently deceased men—by passing them off as unconscious.)

For the sociologist the history of organized crime in America is marked by an interesting phenomenon. From the nineteenth century one can follow a pattern of *ethnic succession* in the involvement and control of criminal syndicates by different immigrant groups. If the Irish dominated organized crime activities from the Civil War until the turn of the century, Jewish immigrants gained a share of the leadership through the Depression, and Italian syndicates have been foremost since Prohibition. It would be erroneous to take these rough historical boundaries as absolute, for Irish mobsters battled with Al Capone in Chicago, and some would claim that some syndicate activity is still directed by Jews today. But there is a clear pattern of one ethnic group supplanting or succeeding another in organized crime operations.

Most recently there has been increased activity by blacks and Puerto Ricans on the Eastern seaboard, while Chicanos have moved into the vice markets of the West and Southwest (Cressey, 1969; Salerno & Tompkins, 1969; Ianni, 1974a, 1974b; Tyler, 1974). Certainly there has been no reluctance among some leaders of these ethnic groups to use the rackets to gain political and economic equality. While still a congressman, controversial black minister Adam Clayton Powell summed up that point of view nicely when he proclaimed: "I am against numbers in any form. But until the day when numbers is wiped out in Harlem . . . I am going to fight for the Negro having the same chance as the Italian" (quoted in Cressey, 1969, p. 198).

Still, some sociologists have suggested that the pattern of ethnic succession may not be operating today. For one thing, the syndicate power of blacks and other ethnic minorities may be illusory, the result of Italian families leasing franchises for certain high-risk markets to other ethnic groups, while retaining the profits for themselves (Ianni, 1972, 1974a, 1974b). It may also be the case that the diminished influence of Italian syndicates is the legacy of a series of calamities that have occurred since the early 1960s (and even before), rather than the result of ethnic succession. Organized crime families have been the target of investigatory bodies like the Kefauver Commission in the 1950s, which investigated the role of organized crime in interstate commerce, the McClellan Committee in the 1960s, which held hearings on labor racketeering, and the President's Commission on Law Enforcement and Administration of Justice, which in 1967 issued a report with recommendations for controlling the syndicates. The find-

ings of these committees have spawned legislation making the collection of evidence and the prosecution of organized crime cases more
effective. Moreover, Robert Kennedy's tenure as attorney general set a
policy of active law enforcement that raised considerably the risk of
syndicate operations.

Arrests from the ill-timed Apalachin conference, stiffer penalties for
participation in drug trade, and the testimony of informers like Joseph
Valachi and Vincent Teresa depleted the Cosa Nostra of its leaders,
many of whom were at the middle-management level. Thus, as death
and old age cut into the ranks of the Italian-American patriarchs after
World War II, few substitutes remained to take up the reins. The
orderly succession to family power may have been short-circuited.

In reviewing the history of organized crime it becomes apparent that
the rise of the syndicates and the identification of the involvement of
certain groups in their activities may be functionally related to other
changes occurring in the society. For example, signs of increasing
crime activity that was attributed to an Italian-American "Mafia"
helped to fuel a xenophobic attitude in the American people. One
particular historical event that caught the attention of the press: the
assassination of New Orleans Superintendent of Police Peter Hennessey in 1890. Hennessey's involvement in a conflict between shipping
companies controlled by rival Italian-American families probably led to
his being gunned down outside his house by five assailants who were
identified (in Hennessey's dying words) as the "Dagoes." When members of one of the families were arrested, an open letter warned that
members of the other family members were the true culprits and that
the citizens of New Orleans should "wake up and think of your outrage
against justice if you don't want to be done in by the Mafia" (Albini,
1971, p. 161). The public responded by storming the jail and lynching
the prisoners. Thus the seed was planted in the American consciousness that a secret, dangerous Italian group lurked waiting to harm the
public (Ianni, 1972). Since this was a period of growing hostility toward
immigrant groups, the press and American xenophobes ballyhooed this
evidence of ethnic criminal involvement (Gambino, 1974). The death of
a New York police detective who was investigating the Mafia in Sicily a
few years later reinforced American fears with the result that

> to their horror, Italians in Chicago found themselves objects of open fear
> and contempt .... The word "Mafia" now appeared frequently in

Chicago's newspapers, and many . . . proclaimed the criminal inclinations of all Italians . . . . Americans concluded that the Mafia flourished wherever [Southern Italian and Sicilian] . . . immigrants lived (Nelli, 1969, pp. 374–375).

Another example demonstrates that the Volstead Act of 1919 was a significant turning point in the history of organized crime for the development of Italian-American syndicates. By restricting the sale of alcoholic beverages, the government provided the young, small, undercapitalized, and ambitious Italian gangs with a new and rich market. Since there was no established competition—no other ethnic group already monopolizing the market—Italians found that they could begin business without waiting for another syndicate to relinquish its control. Liquor and beer of any quality was in almost universal demand, so the Italian entrepreneurs could make enormous profits with minimum production costs. Prohibition represents a case where social change produced an advantage for one ethnic group trying to break into the operation of crime.

THEORIES OF ORGANIZED CRIME

There are several questions of theoretical interest to the student of organized crime. How can one identify the features of the social system that lead to the emergence of organized crime in some cultures? And— a corollary question—why does organized crime seem to emerge more frequently among certain ethnic groups? Finally, what psychological characteristics or motivations impel a person to embark upon a career in syndicated crime? These are all questions that attempt to isolate the variables that can help explain the occurrence and persistence of organized crime in the society or the participation in such crime by the individual.[14]

Theoretical Explanations for the Emergence of Organized Crime

The theories that have been proposed to explain why a society will support organized crime differ only in terms of which feature of the social system is seen as being most conducive to the syndicate's development. The ethnocultural theories hold that organized crime grows out of values that exist in the culture. On the other hand, the disorganization and deprivation theories contend that a breakdown or deficiency in some part of the social structure leads to the emergence of organizations of crime.

The thrust of ethnocultural theories is to identify the specific cultural values that encourage crime syndicates. Daniel Bell (1953) has made one of the clearest statements of this point of view. He argues that crime is "an American way of life." A central value that encourages the emergence of organized crime, notes Bell, is the belief that the state should regulate personal morality by declaring certain practices or goods to be criminal. Such control efforts generally fail and inevitably produce a market of persons who will pay dearly to have those goods. The taste for vices (partly refined by political interference in determining morality) combines with another powerful American value: the profit motive. Bell observes:

> Crime, in many ways, is a Coney Island mirror, caricaturing the morals and manners of a society. The jungle quality of the American business community, particularly at the turn of the . . . century was reflected in the mode of "business" practiced by the coarse gangster elements (1953, p. 132).

Echoing this view, George Vold contends that the criminal syndicate is distinct from noncriminal ones only in terms of the legality of the commodities that are sold. All fortunes are made in exactly the same way in a free enterprise system, be the enterprise in vices or lawful goods and services. Thus, Vold concludes that "organized crime must be thought of as a natural growth, or as an adjunct to our general system of private profit economy" (1958, p. 240).

In concert with these values, Humbert Nelli suggests that there is a tendency toward corruption in American society that facilitates the growth of organized crime. He notes that it is theoretically significant that Italian immigrants who settled in Latin America failed to develop equivalents to the Black Hand or Al Capone, yet their cousins in the United States formed powerful crime syndicates during the same period of time. The difference must be the result of some contaminating influence in American culture: "this environment, with its unparalleled economic opportunities, optimism, mobility, corruption, filth and violence" (Nelli, 1969, p. 379). Presumably, the example of corrupt politicians, robber barons, and amoral consumers showed the guileless Italian and Sicilian immigrants that wealth, power, security, and the American dream could be attained through crime.[15]

Unlike ethnocultural theories, disorganization and deprivation theories find the source of organized crime in the breakdown and malfunction of the system that provides access to goals valued throughout the society. Some of these theories hold that immigrants to the United States confronted a type of social disorganization akin to a condition called *anomie* (Durkheim, 1951; Merton, 1957). Thus, immigrants who expected to find jobs and security in America were rudely shocked because the avenues to wealth and social respectability were often closed, especially to those new arrivals who came from non-English speaking, non-Protestant countries or who were dark-skinned.

According to anomie theories, persons who find highly valued and tantalizing goals blocked may disregard the norms, mores, and laws that regulate behavior and employ other means, including illegal ones, to achieve socially approved ends. If wealth cannot be attained lawfully, a portion of the population may turn to stealing and other unlawful methods to gain financial security.

The conditions that immigrants found in America may have been anomic. Instead of jobs, they were faced with unemployment and exploitation at the hands of labor brokers. Instead of a home in the rich American countryside, many immigrant families shared cold-water flats in decrepit tenements. Instead of security from ill health, the new arrivals were weakened by malnutrition, intolerable working conditions, and the squalid surroundings of the ghetto. Italian immigrants in particular may have found the American dream hollow, for they arrived well after many of the best opportunities (especially farmlands and homesteads) had been seized by other immigrant groups (Glazer & Moynihan, 1963, p. 183; Cressey, 1969, p. 26). Arriving too late to share in America's bounty, the Italians found themselves limited to backbreaking labor in unskilled jobs and to life in the "Little Italy" ghettos that sprang up in America's largest cities (Wish, 1952, p. 244).

Out of these conditions of deprivation, Italian syndicates arose—as they had for other ethnic groups—to attain collectively the goals of security and prosperity that were barred to individuals. Singly, the Italian immigrants had little effect on American politics or economy, but they learned from the example of the Jews and the Irish that unified action could bring wealth and power. The self-help groups that emerged quickly learned that crime was an expedient way to earn enough money for survival and to have enough left over to insure the upward mobility of their sons and daughters.

Events of the last decade lend credence to deprivation theories. Those ethnic groups who are the most alienated from current American political and economic power—the blacks, the Spanish-speaking minorities—appear to be inheriting or seizing the syndicate operations that helped propel the Italians, Jews, and Irish to wealth and power fifty years earlier.

The paucity of evidence on organized crime prevents a full test of either of these theoretical positions. But the propositions of ethnocultural and deprivation theories have certain common postulates that outline which features of the culture and society provide a fertile breeding ground for organized crime. They are as follows:

1. Legislation outlawing some good or service

2. A public demand for such goods or services

3. A capitalist, free enterprise system that makes it profitable for persons to supply those illegal goods and services to an awaiting market

4. A group of persons who are willing (or predisposed, given their dreary economic and political prospects) to risk legal penalties to supply those goods and services

5. The existence of sufficient administrative acumen and coordination to make the marketing of those goods and services profitable.

Theories That Attempt to Explain Individual Involvement in Organized Crime

Efforts to explain why any individual chooses a career in organized crime are as diverse as the psychological explanations of motivation. In some cases, however, the choice is almost automatic: The sons and relatives of organized crime members are introduced into syndicate operations as soon as they demonstrate a true allegiance to the family code of loyalty, secrecy, and manliness.

Where there is no family connection, a significant predictor of involvement in organized crime is the existence of a syndicate in the community to provide opportunities to pursue that kind of career. Persons do not join a syndicate without the approval of the group leaders. As with many occupations, a period of apprenticeship must be served before applicants are allowed to pursue their chosen vocations. If there is no local crime syndicate, aspiring gangsters lack both the opportunities and role models to serve such apprenticeships. Consistent with that proposition, Irving Spergel (1964) finds that minimal involvement by youths in organized crime characterizes communities devoid of syndicates, while delinquents are employed as numbers runners, lookouts, and go-fors in neighborhoods where organizations of crime thrive.

The pattern of recruitment and socialization into the syndicates concurs with differential-association theories of crime (Sutherland & Cressey, 1974, p. 75ff.). Individuals pursue syndicate careers when their exposure to criminal values and definitions of the law exceeds their exposure to noncriminal lifestyles. Crime is learned, and differential-association theories hold that certain persons or groups are required as models and teachers if criminal values and skills are to be internalized.

The likelihood that persons will accept the values endorsed by gangsters is undoubtedly increased by conditions of poverty and deprivation. The image of the neighborhood gangster may be a significant factor in shaping the vocational plans of lower-class teenagers who perceive few legitimate opportunities. Thus, John Landesco commented many years ago:

> He [the young man of Chicago's lower-class ghettos] takes as his pattern the men in the neighborhood who have achieved success. His father, although virtuous in his grime, squalor and thrift, does not present as alluring an example to him as do some of the neighborhood gangsters. The men who frequent the . . . gambling houses are good-natured, well-dressed . . . sophisticated, and above all, they are American, in the eyes of the gang boy (1929, p. 210).

By "American," Landesco meant that the criminal had shed the stigma of his immigrant background and thus possessed the wealth and power consistent with the promises of the American dream. Surely today's poor are just as cognizant of the differential profits to be earned from joining the syndicates or from pursuing a lawful career.

THE CONTROL OF ORGANIZED CRIME

Methods of Control Presently in Use

There is a long history of local and nationwide efforts to eliminate organized crime in the United States. For many years the Department of Justice has been pursuing a "war" on the syndicates, but the effectiveness of that campaign has been minimal. Strategies used to control organized crime generally fall into one of four categories: tolerance policies, political reform, law enforcement, and legalization.

The deleterious effects of tolerance policies have already been described. By attempting to strike a balance between full law enforcement and the satisfaction of widespread public demand for some of the vices, tolerance policies inevitably degenerate into political corruption and police-operated protection rackets. Ultimately, tolerance breeds distrust and contempt of local law enforcement and government, and it often imposes crime upon citizens of one part of the city (usually the ghetto) by clustering vice dens in neighborhoods that do not have the political influence to effectively protest their presence (Chambliss, 1971).

Political reform and social action are also common responses to the discovery of organized crime in a community. But so long as the public continues to demand illegal goods and services, periodic efforts to "throw the bums out" will have only temporary success (Gardiner, 1967). The net result of the reforms is simply to bring about a changeover in the personalities who control the rackets; the structure and the market will persist independent of efforts to better community government.

Law enforcement encompasses several interrelated tasks, including legislation, arrest and prosecution, sanctioning, and intelligence gathering. Legislation involves the creation of laws and the setting of sanctions aimed at bringing a halt to criminal activity. For example, several states have increased the penalty for selling narcotics, while reducing the sanction for possession, in an effort to make the legal risks of the drug market offset the profits. Sanctions, however, can never bear the full responsibility for controlling organized crime (or, for that matter, any other type of crime), and they are effective only as long as they are surely and justly applied (Gibbs, 1968; Tittle, 1969). But, as America's history of capital punishment clearly demonstrates, even a penalty as severe as death is an ineffective deterrent when inconsistently employed. As long as the profits for supplying the vices remain high and the public endorses tolerance policies (for their own selfish reasons), persons will risk the criminal sanctions.

Cressey has suggested that it might be useful to produce legislation that would make it criminal "to be a member of an illicit crime syndicate." Presently it is not a crime (except under the cumbersome machinery of conspiracy legislation) to belong to an organization like the Mafia. The crime is in the perpetration of certain offenses like usury, drug sales, or gambling. Cressey recognizes that outlawing membership in criminal syndicates poses a potential problem of civil liberties, but he argues that those difficulties could be sidestepped if definitions of organized crime could be delineated as precisely as those of burglary or auto theft (Cressey, 1969, pp. 299–300).

Full enforcement and prosecution of the law as a strategy to eradicate organized crime suffers from its own defects. Enforcement depends on intelligence about criminal operations, and prosecution requires evidence to convince a jury or judge to convict. Both of those elements are frequently absent in organized crime cases, and arrests and convictions are therefore hard to obtain.

Information is hard to gather because syndicates conduct their operations in the strictest secrecy. The use of buffers to camouflage any direct connection between syndicate leaders and field operatives is only one device employed to throw investigators off the track. Indeed, it is likely that increased efforts to infiltrate syndicates or to gather information about them only produce further structural innovations to protect the syndicate's activities (Cressey, 1972).

Some of the crimes that are typical of most syndicate operations also work against law enforcement because they are crimes without victims. The loan shark's borrowers or the junkie's clients are willing victims; they are unlikely to seek legal remedy when they do not feel harmed or would rather not reveal their own criminal involvement to the police. Moreover, the existence of enforcers and the constant potential for violent retribution strongly encourage potential informers to be quiet.

In some cases active enforcement may lead to unexpected, undesirable outcomes, even increased criminality. The classic example is of course Prohibition, when the government created a rich market for the syndicates and every raid on distilleries only had the effect of further raising the price of bootleg liquor in the community. More recently, Operation Intercept, a tactic designed to halt the flow of marijuana into the United States from Mexico, temporarily succeeded in reducing marijuana markets on the West Coast, but it has been alleged that some of the consumers, not to be denied, turned to the use of other substances, particularly the more dangerous amphetamines and barbiturates still available on the streets (Kentfield, 1970).

A number of innovations have emerged to increase law enforcement's potential for gathering information about organized crime. Thus, telephone wiretaps (approved by a judge before their installation) and other technological advances are in current use, and no-knock provisions waive the necessity for police to warn inhabitants before they enter a house (Blakey, 1967, p. 93; Salerno & Tompkins, 1969, pp. 344ff.; Law Enforcement Assistance Administration, 1972; Hammer, 1974). These techniques, however, are only efficient in identifying the operators of the syndicates today; they cannot dismantle the syndicate itself so that it may not be reopened—under new management—tomorrow.

Attempts to outlaw the demand for the vices have produced such dreary results that there have been periodic suggestions to do away with laws regulating those acts altogether.[16] For example, New York City has operated an off-track betting franchise for horse races for several years; eleven states conduct lotteries to raise state revenues; Nevada allows casino gambling and, in some counties, prostitution; and Great Britain dispenses narcotics to registered addicts through public clinics that prescribe dosages that will maintain a habit without inducing withdrawal. Such legalization has a number of advantages. States have discovered that their treasuries can be supplemented by running or taxing an operation that had previously been a costly liability of law enforcement. In addition to fiscal gain, legalization allows the state to regulate the activities: to restrict the involvement of undesirable characters (as in the case of the Nevada Gaming Board's blacklist of organized crime figures who are barred from ownership of gambling resorts) or to legally inspect what would otherwise be a concealed operation (particularly important where venereal disease or adulterated drugs might pose a health problem).

Still legalization is not without its drawbacks, major among them being the public outcry by those who see legalization as a deterioration of the society's moral fabric. Moral issues involving one's relationship with other citizens (such as business contracts) can be resolved through legislation, but efforts to determine personal preferences in lifestyle legislatively have not been successful. Personal morality, as involved in most of the vices, is less a matter of political determination than of individual preference. But the thorniest problem surrounding legalization, as the current debates about abortion, homosexuality, and drug use illustrate, is that it is often hard to determine where the boundary should be drawn indicating those acts that are so harmful, debilitating, or perverse that they represent a true, criminal threat to the society.

Furthermore, legalization frequently fails to put organized crime out of business. State-controlled betting draws some trade, but bets placed with a bookie are unrecorded, and wins can be concealed from state and federal tax agencies. It is probably for this reason that off-track betting has not replaced the bookies in New York City (Merchant, 1973). Likewise, hijacking guarantees that the syndicates can always undersell private entrepreneurs who must meet an overhead of wages, taxes, and capital outlay before a profit is earned. Finally, legislation overlooks the diversity of human tastes. What is profitable for the syndicates in the future is often a matter of fads. As mentioned earlier, few persons would have anticipated that fortunes could be earned in the 1970s by trading in items like gasoline, fuel oil, and antifreeze.

In addition, it follows that if syndicates of crime are closely patterned after American corporations, they are as susceptible to failure as those legal businesses when faced by competition and the vagaries of modern economy (Vold, 1958, p. 242). Legalization increases the competition the syndicates must face by granting private or public franchises for the services that had been illegal. Presumably, legalization destroys the market for the syndicates in the same way that the end of Prohibition saw the demise of bootleggers in the face of competition from legitimate brewers and distillers.

Controlling Organized Crime in the Future

Sociological accounts of the syndicates—this one included—can easily portray organized crime as a social problem of enormous magnitude. But it is far more difficult for them to propound solutions to that problem. The frustration of seeking an answer may be what led such respected scholars as Schelling and Cressey to propose that the government of the United States "recognize" the Cosa Nostra and negotiate with them much as we deal with hostile foreign powers (Schelling, 1967, p. 123; Cressey, 1969, p. 323).

This call for something akin to a national tolerance policy, facetious as it may be, is fundamentally a recognition that a proclaimed war on organized crime has yet to work. In fact, the wartime psychology may have produced some significant drawbacks. The history of Project Intercept and the widespread use of devices that invade one's privacy are only two examples of instances where law enforcement's zeal to destroy organized crime may have initiated new problems and threatened civil liberties.

The search for solutions nevertheless continues. A useful task may be to look cross-culturally to see how other nations have tried to deal with organized crime. England may be a good point of comparison. Both J. A. Mack (1973) and Joseph Albini (1975) find British organized crime to be much less significant in scale than it is in the United States. Albini suggests that three factors may account for the differences in American and English organized crime. In England he finds (1) widespread legalization of goods and services demanded by the public, (2) passage of legislation, in most cases, only when it is known to be enforceable (thus eliminating laws that attempt to control acts that cannot be regulated), and (3) a court system whose personnel are selected and advanced on the basis of civil service criteria rather than public elections (Albini, 1975, p. 300).

Albini's observations may be instructive for those who want to bring organized crime under control. It may be possible, using England as an example, to construct certain conditions presumed to be associated with a reduction in organized crime. To his very tentative list, we might add active and full enforcement of the law, so that the profits of organized crime might be less than the legal risks. This seems to explain the drop in Italian-American syndicate involvement with the drug trade: It ceased to be profitable when compared to the costs of imprisonment.

To achieve this rather Utopian state of justice, certain changes would have to occur in the way that criminal justice currently operates. For one thing, it is clear that organized crime thrives with the collusion of law enforcement agents and prosecutors who can be compromised, co-opted, or threatened into tolerating syndicate activity. Albini's suggestion of civil service judges may point to the correct course of action. At least it reduces the possibility that agents of the court may become corrupted by seeking syndicate support for election. But beyond collusion, the effectiveness of the law to control organized crime activity may depend on the possibility of closing some of the loopholes in the justice system's operation that work against the swift and full enforcement of criminal laws and sanctions. For example:

(1) Legislatures (and the interest groups that foster legislation) should discontinue the practice of attempting to regulate behavior that is unenforceable. Acts that have no true victims to seek out prosecution or behaviors that reflect personal preferences, tastes, and moralities are probably best left to self, family, or church regulation.

(2) People must be made to recognize that it is their demand for illegal goods and services that assures the existence of organized crime. They should understand that they cannot condemn organized crime while at the same time they blithely use or consume the illegal goods and services that are the part and parcel of the syndicate.

(3) Participation in organized crime might be reduced if disenfranchised ethnic groups (who traditionally compose the backbone of syndicate leadership in the United States) were assimilated into American culture and allowed to achieve the promises of prosperity, freedom, and security. Those who would point to the recent limited disengagement of Italian-American families from syndicate control would be making an error if they assumed that the organized crime problem had passed. There are still many members of our society whose poverty and political alienation would allow them to justify their reliance on organized crime as a means for achieving some part of the American dream.

Any of the changes that might bring an end to organized crime are Utopian and highly unlikely. At best they are presumptions based on sketchy theories and explanations of the origin of criminal syndicates. A realistic approach to organized crime is probably best. It will remain a fact of modern, affluent societies as long as there is a profitable public demand for illegal goods and services.

NOTES

1. The ellipses are found in the original. Ellipses added by the present author will be so indicated.

2. For some lurid though perhaps apochryphal accounts of how a syndicate "hitman" operates, see Fisher (1973, 1974).

3. I would like to acknowledge the assistance of the graduate students at the University of California at Riverside who assisted in the operation of this mock numbers racket: Kerry Fine, Susan Hofacre, Donna Verska, Barbara Johnson, Mildred Pagelow, and Kathleen Brady.

4. The concern for security is not misplaced. Vito Genovese and a number of prominent New York gangsters were convicted by testimony provided by a Manhattan drug dealer who cooperated with federal prosecutors. From the testimony the prosecutors were able to trace the path of the dealer's drugs back to Genovese (Talese, 1971, p. 204).

5. Interestingly, illegal activities sometimes cease when a syndicate expands into the realm of legitimate business. For example, Ianni (1972, p. 88) reports that criminal activities and legal companies operated by different members of the Lupollo family thrived side by side and independently. Sometimes business is used as a legitimate outlet for relatives who wish to lead a respectable public life—enriched by the fortunes illegally earned by their forefathers (Cressey, 1969, p. 101; Anderson, 1965).

6. Ex-President Richard Nixon was well aware of the usefulness of a laundering front when he bemoaned on his tape of March 21, 1974, that the White House lacked the expertise to conceal, without danger of being traced, the use of campaign funds to buy the silence of Watergate spy E. Howard Hunt (White House, 1974).

7. Gardiner (1967) does observe, however, that the corruption manages to touch a few key persons without widespread involvement by a majority of employees of any one agency. He finds, for example, that no more than 10 percent of the police in the community he studied were on the syndicate's payroll.

8. Most of this account is drawn from reports in the Seattle *Times* during 1971 (see especially Corsaletti & Norton, 1971).

9. Interestingly, few of the indictments resulted in convictions.

10. There is a less subtle bias in both Cressey's and Ianni's analyses. Each focuses on Italian-American crime syndicates, and their conclusions tend to overemphasize certain qualities of the structure that may be unique to that ethnic group. This is apparent in their continued use of the names Cosa Nostra and Mafia and in the importance attached to the family, a phenomenon that may be typical of Italians (see Glazer & Moynihan, 1963, p. 198) but not other immigrant groups.

11. For a more detailed argument along these lines, see Bell (1960).

12. There is an implicit racist assumption here that should be rejected. Ianni's logic would suggest that any law-abiding member of a family of Italian heritage is a potential criminal collaborator with any member of the family who may be involved in criminal activity. This is not true.

13. See, for example, Asbury (1962); Sondern (1966); Talese (1971); Messick and Goldblatt (1972); Goddard (1974); Gosch (1974); Wolf (1974); Hammer (1975).

14. There is a series of other questions that are of interest to students of particular substantive areas of sociology and psychology. Thus, Cressey's and Ianni's analyses of the structure of organized crime is partly concerned with advancing sociology's understanding of the way that social units organize; they use criminal syndicates as an example in that substantive debate.

15. The opposite point of view, of course, is that Italian and Sicilian immigrants imported values that supported the development of criminal syndicates. Except for the finding that cultural heritage influenced the kind of structure that evolved (that is, the traditional family pattern of Italian-American syndicates), there is little empirical support for the hypothesis that organized crime can be traced to foreign sources.

16. It has been rumored that several of America's largest tobacco firms are prepared for the eventuality of marketing marijuana if it is legalized.

BIBLIOGRAPHY

Albini, Joseph L. *The American Mafia: Genesis of a Legend.* New York: Appleton-Century-Crofts, 1971.

Albini, Joseph L. "Mafia as Method: A Comparison between Great Britain and the U.S.A. Regarding the Existence and Structure of Types of Organized Crime." *International Journal of Criminology and Penology,* 1975, 3:295–305.

Anderson, Robert T. "From Mafia to Cosa Nostra." *American Journal of Sociology,* 1965, 71:302–310.

Aronson, Harvey. *The Killing of Joey Gallo.* New York: G. P. Putnam's Sons, 1973.

Asbury, Herbert. "Early Gangs of New York." In Gus Tyler, ed. *Organized Crime in America: A Book of Readings.* Ann Arbor, Mich.: University of Michigan Press, 1962, pp. 96–104.

Barzini, Luigi. *The Italians.* New York: Atheneum, 1964.

Bell, Daniel. "Crime as an American Way of Life." *Antioch Review,* 1953, 13:131–154.

Bell, Daniel. *The End of Ideology.* Glencoe, Ill.: The Free Press, 1960.

Bergman, Lowell, and Jeff Gerth. "La Costa." *Penthouse,* 1975, 6:47–48, 110–112.

Blakey, G. Robert. "Aspects of the Evidence Gathering Process in Organized Crime Cases." In President's Commission on Law Enforcement and Administration of Justice, Task Force on Organized Crime. *Task Force Report: Organized Crime,* appendix C. Washington, D.C.: U.S. Government Printing Office, 1967, pp. 80–113.

Blau, Peter M., and Marshall W. Meyer. *Bureaucracy in Modern Society,* 2nd ed. New York: Random House, 1971.

Bloch, Herbert A., and Gilbert Geis. *Man, Crime and Society,* 2nd ed. New York: Random House, 1970.

Carpozi, George, Jr. *Bugsy.* New York: Pinnacle Books, 1973.

CBS News. "The Trouble with Rock." Executive producer Leslie Midgley. As broadcast over the CBS Television Network, August 11, 1974.

Chambliss, William J. "Vice, Corruption, Bureaucracy, and Power." *Wisconsin Law Review,* 1971, pp. 1150–1173.

Chambliss, William J. "On the Paucity of Original Research on Organized Crime: A Footnote to Galliher and Cain." *The American Sociologist,* 1975, 10:36–39.

"Cigaret Smugglers Corner New York Market." *Los Angeles Times* (reprinted from *Newsday*), Feb. 23, 1975, 94:1, 8.

Cleaver, Eldridge. *Soul on Ice.* New York: McGraw-Hill, 1967.

Clinard, Marshall B. *The Black Market: A Study of White Collar Crime.* New York: Holt, Rinehart and Winston, 1952.

Cohen, Mickey. *Mickey Cohen: In My Own Words (The Underworld Autobiography of Mickey Cohen, as told to John Peer Nugent).* Englewood Cliffs, N.J.: Prentice-Hall, 1975.

Conklin, John E. "Introduction: Organized Crime and American Society." In John E. Conklin, ed. *The Crime Establishment: Organized Crime and American Society.* Englewood Cliffs, N. J.: Prentice-Hall, 1973, pp. 1–24.

Corsaletti, Lou, and Dee Norton. Seattle *Times,* July 28, 1971.

Cressey, Donald R. "The Functions and Structure of Criminal Syndicates." President's Commission on Law Enforcement and Administration of Justice, Task Force on Organized Crime. *Task Force Report: Organized Crime,* appendix A. Washington, D.C.: U.S. Government Printing Office, 1967a, pp. 25–60.

Cressey, Donald R. "Methodological Problems in the Study of Organized Crime as a Social Problem." *Annals of the American Academy of Political and Social Science,* 1967b, 374:101–112.

Cressey, Donald R. *Theft of the Nation: The Structure and Operations of Organized Crime in America.* New York: Harper & Row, 1969.

Cressey, Donald R. *Criminal Organization: Its Elementary Forms.* New York: Harper & Row, 1972.

Cressey, Donald R. "Advance Notice and Government Law within Criminal Confederations." *International Journal of Criminology and Penology,* 1973, 1:55–67.

Dobrovir, William A. "The Problem of Overcriminalization." In James S. Campbell, Joseph R. Sahid, and David P. Stang. *Law and Order Reconsidered.* A staff report to the National Commission on the Causes and Prevention of Violence. Washington, D.C.: U.S. Government Printing Office, 1970, pp. 551–570.

Durkheim, Emile. *Suicide.* Translated by John A. Spaulding and George Simpson. Glencoe, Ill.: The Free Press, 1951.

Fisher, Dave, and Joey. *Killer: Autobiography of a Mafia Hit Man.* Chicago: Playboy Press, 1973.

Fisher, Dave, and Joey. *Hit #29.* Chicago: Playboy Press, 1974.

Fowler, William M., Jr. "The Non-Volunteer Navy." *Proceedings of the U.S. Naval Institute,* 1974, 100:73–78.

Fund for the City of New York. *Legal Gambling in New York: A Discussion of Numbers and Sports Betting.* New York: The Fund, 1972.

Furstenberg, Mark H. "Violence and Organized Crime." In Donald J. Mulvihill and Melvin M. Tumin, with Lynn A. Curtis. *Crimes of Violence,* appendix 18. A staff report to the National Commission on the Causes and

Prevention of Violence. Washington, D.C.: U.S. Government Printing Office, 1969, pp. 911–939.

Galliher, John F., and James A. Cain. "Citation Support for the Mafia Myth in Criminology Textbooks." *The American Sociologist,* 1974, 9:68–74.

Gambino, Richard. *Blood of My Blood: The Dilemma of Italian-Americans.* Garden City, N. Y.: Doubleday, 1974.

Gardiner, John A., with David J. Olson. "Wincanton: The Politics of Corruption." President's Commission on Law Enforcement and Administration of Justice, Task Force on Organized Crime. *Task Force Report: Organized Crime,* appendix B. Washington, D.C.: U.S. Government Printing Office, 1967, pp. 61–79.

Geis, Gilbert. "The Heavy Electrical Equipment Antitrust Cases in 1961." In Marshall B. Clinard and Richard Quinney, eds. *Criminal Behavior Systems: A Typology.* New York: Holt, Rinehart and Winston, 1967, pp. 139–151.

Gerth, Jeff. "Nixon and the Mafia." *Sundance Magazine,* 1972, 1:32–42, 64–68.

Gibbs, Jack P. "Crime, Punishment and Deterrence." *Southwestern Social Science Quarterly,* 1968, 48:515–530.

Glazer, Nathan, and Daniel Moynihan. *Beyond the Melting Pot.* Cambridge, Mass.: M. I. T. Press, 1963.

Goddard, Donald. *Joey.* New York: Dell, 1974.

Gosch, Martin A., and Richard Hammer. *The Last Testament of Lucky Luciano.* Boston: Little, Brown, 1974.

Graham, Hugh Davis, and Ted Robert Gurr. *Violence in America: Historical and Comparative Perspectives,* vol. 2. A staff report to the National Commission on the Causes and Prevention of Violence. Washington, D.C.: U.S. Government Printing Office, 1969.

Greene, Robert W., and the staff and editors of *Newsday. The Heroin Trail.* Long Island, N. Y.: *Newsday,* 1973.

Hammer, Richard. "Playboy's History of Organized Crime, Part 12: The American Nightmare." *Playboy,* 1974, 21:126, 148, 204–216.

Hammer, Richard. *Playboy's Illustrated History of Organized Crime.* Chicago: Playboy Press, 1975.

Hawkins, Gordon. "God and the Mafia." *The Public Interest,* 1969, 14:24–38, 40–51.

Hess, Henner. *Mafia and Mafiosi: The Structure of Power.* Translated by Ewald Osers. Lexington, Mass.: Heath, 1973.

Hoffa, James. "Interview." *Playboy,* 1975, 22:73–96.

Homer, Frederic D. *Guns and Garlic: Myths and Realities of Organized Crime.* West Lafayette, Ind.: Purdue University Press, 1974.

Ianni, Francis A. J., with Elizabeth Reuss-Ianni. *A Family Business: Kinship and Social Control in Organized Crime.* New York: Russell Sage Foundation, 1972.

Ianni, Francis A. J. *Black Mafia: Ethnic Succession in Organized Crime.* New York: Simon & Schuster, 1974a.

Ianni, Francis A. J., with Elizabeth Reuss-Ianni. "New Mafia: Black, Hispanic, and Italian Styles." *Society,* 1974b, 11:26–39.

Kadish, Sanford. "The Crisis of Overcriminalization." *Annals of the American Academy of Political and Social Science,* 1967, 374:157–170.

Kentfield, Calvin. "Turning off the Tijuana Grass: Operation Intercept." *Esquire,* 1970, 73:8–16.

Kobler, John. *Capone: The Life and World of Al Capone.* New York: G. P. Putnam's Sons, 1971.

Landesco, John. *Organized Crime in Chicago.* Chicago: University of Chicago Press, 1929.

Law Enforcement Assistance Administration, Technical Assistance Division of the Office of Criminal Justice Administration. *Police Guide on Organized Crime.* Washington, D.C.: U.S. Government Printing Office, 1972.

Light, Ivan. "Numbers Gambling: A Financial Institution of the Ghetto." Paper presented to the Annual Conference on Gambling, Las Vegas, Nev., 1974.

Maas, Peter. *The Valachi Paper.* New York: G. P. Putnam's Sons, 1968.

Mack, J. A. "The 'Organised' and 'Professional' Labels Criticised." *International Journal of Criminology and Penology,* 1973, 1:103–116.

McCaghy, Charles H., and R. Serge Denisoff. "Pirates and Politics: An Analysis of Interest Group Conflict." In R. Serge Denisoff and Charles H. McCaghy, eds. *Deviance, Conflict, and Criminality.* Chicago: Rand McNally, 1973, pp. 297–309.

Merchant, Larry. *The National Football Lottery.* New York: Holt, Rinehart and Winston, 1973.

Merton, Robert K. *Social Theory and Social Structure,* rev. ed. Glencoe, Ill.: The Free Press, 1957.

Messick, Hank, and Burt Goldblatt. *The Mobs and the Mafia: The Illustrated History of Organized Crime.* New York: Ballantine Books, 1972.

Miller, Walter B. "Lower Class Culture as a Generating Milieu of Gang Delinquency." *Journal of Social Issues,* 1958, 14:5–19.

Nelli, Humbert S. "Italians and Crime in Chicago: The Formative Years, 1890–1920." *American Journal of Sociology,* 1969, 74:373–391.

Nelson, Jack, and Bill Hazlett. "Teamsters' Ties to Mafia—and to White House." *Los Angeles Times,* May 31, 1973, 92:1, 22–24.

Newsweek, June 17, 1974, pp. 86–87.

Newsweek, June 30, 1975a, pp. 17–18.

Newsweek, December 28, 1975b.

Packer, Herbert L. *The Limits of the Criminal Sanction*. Stanford, Calif.: Stanford University Press, 1968.

"Pot Smugglers Now Flying High, say Federal Officials." Riverside (Calif.) *Press*, June 5, 1975.

President's Commission on Law Enforcement and Administration of Justice, Task Force on Organized Crime. *Task Force Report: Organized Crime*. Washington, D.C.: U.S. Government Printing Office, 1967.

Pusateri, C. Joseph. "The Mafia Mania: Organized Crime and Wishful Thinking." *Christian Century*, 1973, 9:600–660.

Research Institute of America. *Protecting Your Business Against Organized Crime*. New York: The Institute, April 15, 1968, pp. 4–5.

Salerno, Ralph, and John S. Tompkins. *The Crime Confederation*. Garden City, N. Y.: Doubleday, 1969.

Schelling, Thomas C. "Economic Analysis of Organized Crime." President's Commission on Law Enforcement and Administration of Justice, Task Force on Organized Crime. *Task Force Report: Organized Crime*, appendix D. Washington, D.C.: U.S. Government Printing Office, 1967, pp. 114–126.

Schorr, Daniel. "My 17 Months on the CIA Watch: A Backstage Journal." *Rolling Stone*, 1976, 210:32–38, 80–98.

Schur, Edwin M. *Crimes without Victims: Deviant Behavior and Public Policy*. Englewood Cliffs, N. J.: Prentice-Hall, 1965.

Siragusa, Charles. *The Trail of the Poppy*. Englewood Cliffs, N. J.: Prentice-Hall, 1966.

Smith, Sandy. "Mobsters in the Marketplace: Money, Muscle, Murder." *Life*, Sept. 8, 1967, pp. 98–104.

Sondern, Frederic, Jr. *Brotherhood of Evil*. New York: Farrar, Straus, and Cudahy, 1966.

Spergel, Irving. *Racketville, Slumtown, and Haulberg*. Chicago: University of Chicago Press, 1964.

Sutherland, Edwin H. *White Collar Crime*. New York: Holt, Rinehart and Winston, 1949.

Sutherland, Edwin H., and Donald R. Cressey. *Criminology*, 9th ed. Philadelphia: J. B. Lippincott, 1974.

Talese, Gay. *Honor Thy Father*. New York: World Publishing, 1971.

Teresa, Vincent, with Thomas C. Renner. *My Life in the Mafia*. Garden City, N.Y.: Doubleday, 1973.

Tittle, Charles R. "Crime Rates and Legal Sanctions." *Social Problems*, 1969, 16:409–423.

Turkus, Burton B., and Sid Feder. *Murder, Inc*. London: Victor Gollancz, 1953.

Tyler, Gus. "The Crime Corporation." In Abraham S. Blumberg, ed. *Current Perspectives on Criminal Behavior: Original Essays on Criminology.* New York: Alfred A. Knopf, 1974, pp. 192–209.

Villiers, Alan. *The War with Cape Horn.* New York: Charles Scribner's Sons, 1971.

Vold, George B. *Theoretical Criminology.* New York: Oxford University Press, 1958.

Ward, Ed. "The Bootleg Blues: The Rise and Fall of Rubber Dubber Records." *Harpers,* 1974, 248:35–38.

Weber, Max. *The Theory of Social and Economic Organization.* New York: Oxford University Press, 1947.

White House, *Submission of Recorded Presidential Conversations to the Committee on the Judiciary of the House of Representatives by President Richard Nixon.* Washington, D.C.: U.S. Government Printing Office, 1974.

Wish, Harvey. *Society and Thought in Modern America.* New York: David McKay, 1952.

Wolf, George, with Joseph DiMona. *Frank Costello: Prime Minister of the Underworld.* New York: William Morrow, 1974.

Wright, Donald R. "Matthew Peary and the African Squadron." In Clayton R. Barrow, Jr., ed. *America Spreads Her Sails: U.S. Seapower in the 19th Century.* New York: Naval Institute Press, 1973, pp. 80–99.

Zola, Irving. "Observations on Gambling in a Lower Class Setting." *Social Problems,* 1963, 10:353–361.

FIVE White collar crime

CARL B. KLOCKARS
University of Delaware

White-collar crime may be defined approximately as a crime committed by a person of respectability and high social status in the course of his occupation (Sutherland, 1949).

There is no more controversial concept nor definition in the history of American criminology than this one by Edwin Sutherland. It has been hailed as deserving a Nobel Prize for its inventor, damned as a "blight on either a legal system or system of sociology that strives to be objective," and variously thought to warrant preservation, clarification, revision, or rejection in the opinions of some of the most talented scholars in the American criminological tradition. At the hands of its most enthusiastic interpreters it can be shown to imply a political, theoretical, and methodological revolution in the sociology of crime, while in actual practice it has had only a modest impact on criminological theory and still less of an effect on criminological research. By most standards of scientific definition it is deplorable, but it is also a concept that enjoys an international reputation in both scholarly and popular publications. French, French-Canadian, and German criminologists (Binder, 1962; Normandeau, 1965; Kellens, 1968; Pinatel, 1970) have accepted it in literal translation as *crime en col blanc* and *weisse-kragen kriminalität*. They have done so in spite of the fact, and this fact should be pointed out to anyone who wishes to examine the history of this ironic concept literally, that white-collar criminals wear jeans, uniforms, blue collars, stripes, pastels, ascots, coveralls, and dresses—or they wear nothing at all.

THE HISTORY OF WHITE COLLAR CRIME

The history of the concept, "white collar crime," is inseparable from the efforts of its architect and promoter, the dean of American criminology, Edwin H. Sutherland (1883–1950).[1] The only criminologist ever elected to the presidency of the American Sociological Association,* Sutherland began the career of "white collar crime" in his presidential address to that body in 1939. Between that time and 1949, when he published his monograph, *White Collar Crime,* Sutherland developed his concept and played out its implications in articles and addresses designed to challenge the dominant themes and ideas of his discipline. Sutherland sought, as we shall see, not only to criticize his criminological colleagues but also to challenge and mock them into confrontation with the mysteries of "white collar crime."

Sutherland began his 1939 presidential address with this modest declaration:

> This paper is concerned with crime in relation to business. . . . it is a comparison of crime in the upper or white-collar class, composed of respectable or at least respected business and professional men, and crime in the lower class, composed of persons of low socioeconomic status. This comparison is made for the purpose of developing the theories of criminal behavior, not for the purpose of muckraking or of reforming anything except criminology (1940, p. 1).

*To be precise, Sutherland was elected to the presidency of the American Sociological Society. The "Society" became an "Association" soon after it became fashionable to refer to such groups by their initials.

It was indeed an appropriate passage in which to give birth to the idea of white collar crime. It contains no real definition of the concept, one patent misrepresentation, and a grossly modest intimation of Sutherland's real ambition. Disclaimers notwithstanding, Sutherland would spend the next decade of his life muckraking with a passion. And what he really had in mind when he spoke of "developing" theories of criminal behavior and "reforming" criminology was the annihilation of half of its methodology, the disposal of almost all of its theory, and a substantial revision of its concept of crime.

Challenges to the Methodology of White Collar Crime

The Biases of Crime Statistics.   In leveling his critical guns on the criminological tradition, Sutherland first took aim at its methodology. In particular, he attacked the dependence of criminologists on the criminal statistics produced by the police, the adult criminal and juvenile courts, and the prisons. In 1939 these statistics showed unequivocally, as they still do today, that crime "*as popularly conceived and officially measured,* has a high incidence in the lower class and a low incidence in the upper class" (Sutherland, 1940, p. 1). Sutherland argued that these statistics, upon which most criminologists relied heavily as indices of crime, were biased in at least two major ways, both of which masked the extent of white collar criminality.

The first bias, Sutherland found, was that the most common collections of such statistics (for example, the FBI's *Uniform Crime Reports*) simply do not include the decisions of any bodies other than the adult criminal or juvenile courts. Even though supervisory boards, commissions, bureaus, or other administrative bodies deal with cases of fraud, misrepresentation, and dishonesty that might be tried in a criminal court, their decisions are not represented. Second, the respected and powerful members of the business class are able to influence in their own interest many of the operations of the criminal justice system. Pressure by such people affects decisions to investigate, arrest, prosecute, convict, and sentence. Sutherland was correct in these charges of bias. The first can be seen by inspection to be true, and the second has been supported by a great deal of research since Sutherland.

While both of these critiques struck directly at the class biases in official statistics, the sting of Sutherland's attack was against the way in which those biases were perpetuated by criminological researchers' dependence on them. If the class bias that Sutherland argued did exist, it threw into doubt all of the research that relied upon samples or populations of criminals arrested, charged, convicted, or imprisoned as accurately reflecting the true incidence of crime or the general characteristics of criminals. This included, of course, almost all the criminological research that had ever been done. Perhaps even more importantly, though, Sutherland's critique damaged irreparably the illusion of a tidy concept of crime. In his 1939 presidential address, he raised in complete seriousness (but answered only half seriously) the question: If you cannot trust reports from the police, criminal courts, or prisons to tell you who the criminals are, what can you trust?

The Concept of Crime.   The conventional understanding of "crime," and the notion of it with which most criminologists work, is that it is a violation of the criminal law. There are more elaborate definitions, of course, but the specification that a criminal law be violated is common to all of them. In his presidential address, Sutherland attacked the class biases inherent in the official police, criminal court, and prison statistics that reported violations of the criminal law. Had he stopped there it might be possible to agree with his loyal student Donald Cressey, (1961) that Sutherland did not wish to extend the concept of crime but merely to suggest an expansion of the sources of data that criminologists might use to compose a less class-biased portrait of it. However, Sutherland's suggestions in his initial address (1940), in his book, *White Collar Crime* (1949), and in various papers published between his first and last statements on this theme gave legally trained scholars (Tappan, 1947; Caldwell, 1958) cause to suspect that something far more radical was afoot.

In what was *apparently* a methodological critique of the operationalization of the concept of crime, Sutherland (1940, pp. 6–7) suggested four other types of data that criminologists should accept to balance the class bias in conventional statistics:

(1) Data from "other agencies than the criminal courts must be included." Sutherland had in mind the various bureaus and regulatory

agencies that supervise business practice: for instance, the Federal Trade Commission (FTC), Interstate Commerce Commission (ICC), and Food and Drug Administration (FDA).

(2) "[B]ehavior which would have a reasonable expectancy of conviction if tried in a criminal court or substitute agency should be defined as criminal." Sutherland sought to include as "criminal" civil court actions, such as stockholders' and patent infringement suits, and cases that were not criminally prosecuted because prosecution might interfere with civil actions for salvage or restitution.

(3) "[B]ehavior should be defined as criminal if conviction is avoided merely because of pressure which is brought to bear on the court or substitute agency." Sutherland argued that simply "because of the class bias of the courts and the power of their class to influence the implementation and administration of the law," white collar criminals should not escape the designation of "criminal" by criminologists.

(4) Finally, "persons who are accessory to a crime should be included among white-collar criminals as they are among other criminals." Here Sutherland observed that prosecution of white collar crime frequently stops with one offender. "Political graft," Sutherland noted, "almost always involved collusion between politicians and business men, but prosecutions are generally limited to politicians."

Although Sutherland (1940, 1945) himself stated that these recommendations were essentially methodological, such a claim is patently disingenuous. Even Sutherland's most modest recommendation, that decisions by agencies like the FTC, ICC, and FDA be used as evidence of criminal behavior, went well beyond what Sutherland knew to be the legal and social definition of crime. Perhaps the most startling evidence that Sutherland did know he was breaking new ground comes from a revelation from Cressey, who aided Sutherland in his research for the monograph *White Collar Crime* (1949). For this work, Sutherland selected seventy of the largest corporations in the United States and tabulated the decisions against them by various regulatory agencies of the government. He found that every corporation had at least one decision against it, and the average number of decisions was 14.0. Sutherland not only calls these seventy corporations "criminal" but "recidivists" and "habitual criminals" as well. Cressey, who was one of

Sutherland's research assistants at the time, reports that in his original manuscript Sutherland disclosed the identities of the corporations involved. When the attorneys for his publishers advised Sutherland that a libel suit might be lodged against him for calling the corporations "criminal," Sutherland withdrew the original manuscript and prepared a revised version that did not disclose the identities of the offending corporations (Cressey, 1961, p. viii).

Actually, the suggestion that criminologists use government agency and civil court data to supplement conventional crime statistics was one of Sutherland's most modest manipulations of the conventional concept of crime. Far more radical by comparison was his recommendation that criminologists should define behavior as criminal even though courts or substitute governmental agencies fail to do so because white collar criminals exert political pressure on them. Sutherland went even further by making the historical argument that the effect of white-collar-class pressure on the courts and legislatures has been cumulative. That is, although present-day courts may be less influenced by white collar political pressure than courts of earlier times, those earlier courts "established the precedents and rules of procedure of the present day courts. Consequently it is justifiable to interpret the actual or *potential* failures of conviction in the light of known facts regarding the pressures brought to bear on the agencies which deal with offenders" (Sutherland, 1940, p. 7, emphasis added). To act upon this suggestion of Sutherland's, criminological researchers would have to take it upon themselves not only to judge whether a particular failure to prosecute or convict was the product of influence, but also whether the *absence* of a law making an act a crime was the product of white-collar-class influence.*

The impact of Sutherland's suggestion was that it rendered problematic what criminologists before him had accepted as given. Crime could no longer be simply defined as that which the criminal law

---

*It might be possible to "excuse" this statement by Sutherland as a temporary megalomania brought on by his rise to the Olympian heights of the presidency of the American Sociological Society. However, eight years later, in the fourth edition of his textbook *Principles of Criminology*, he wrote:

> Some of the [white collar] offenses are not even a violation of the spirit of the law, for the parties concerned have been able by bribery and other means to prevent the enactment of laws to prohibit wrongful or injurious practices (1947, p. 37).

prohibits. Sutherland's demand, under the guise of a mere methodological critique, was for the study of the political history of laws and legislation, the sociological examination of the *structure* of lawmaking bodies, and the analysis of the conflicts of power and interest that could create, or block the creation of, a criminal law and, hence, a crime. Only recently has criminology begun to mature enough to accept Sutherland's most radical challenge to its concept of crime. This is all the more surprising since Sutherland laid the theoretical groundwork for revising the concept more than a quarter of a century ago.

Reform of Criminological Theory

Sutherland's apparently methodological critiques of the criminological tradition had behind them two direct and immediate conceptual reforms: the removal of the class biases in criminological research and the liberation of the concept of crime in ways that would make it historically, politically, and otherwise sociologically analyzable. In his presidential address and in other publications following it, Sutherland (1941, 1945, 1947, 1949, 1956) used these critiques in two major ways: (1) to attack the dominant theoretical perspectives in the criminological tradition, and (2) to suggest new orientations in criminological theory that would be able to accommodate the complexities of white collar crime.

Crime and Poverty.   Sutherland's attack on the dominant criminological theories of his time followed closely from his critique of class-biased data. By using such data, criminologists had developed theories that explained crime as caused either "by poverty or by personal and social characteristics associated with poverty, including feeblemindedness, psychopathic deviation, slum neighborhoods and 'deteriorated families'" (Sutherland, 1940, p. 1). Sutherland attacked the whole range of such theories, including those that were psychologically as well as sociologically based. Poverty and its pathologies, both social and psychological, he insisted, were *not* correlated with crime. In his view, theories making such a claim or elaborating on it were false and misleading for three reasons: First, they were an artifact of class-biased statistics; that is, the theories themselves were the source of the very association between crime and poverty that they asserted. Second, the association between poverty and poverty-related pathologies simply does not hold for a white collar crime; few white collar criminals come from broken homes, "deteriorated families," or slum neighborhoods. Third, where the association between poverty and its pathologies may exist is not with crime in general, but with particular types of crime; however, even this is difficult to establish because of the lack of comparative studies of white collar and conventional crime.

To appreciate the real impact of Sutherland's theoretical critique, it is necessary to understand that he was not simply attacking some cool scientific hypotheses. Instead, the theories relating crime and the pathologies of poverty summarized a complex of attitudes and ideas about crime that virtually amounted to an American cultural faith. The belief that poverty and its pathologies were the "cause of crime" was attractive to democratic, individualistic, and mobile Americans. On the one hand, it was a "hopeful" theory of crime. It suggested opportunities for action: slum renewal, psychological intervention, family therapy, and so on. On the other hand, it confirmed and supported the perception that criminals were fundamentally different from the "good people" in personal and social ways. Criminals were not like us; they were from the slums, from broken homes, from "deteriorated families," and they suffered from psychological, emotional, and personal pathologies that did not touch us. Sutherland knew that these themes surrounded the theories he was attacking and that to destroy the theories he would have to shake the attitudes that supported them. Taking on psychological-pathological theories of criminality, Sutherland chose to mock them into absurdity:

> Business leaders are capable, emotionally balanced, and in no sense pathological. We have no reason to think that General Motors has an inferiority complex or that the Aluminum Company of America has a frustration-aggression complex or that U.S. Steel has an Oedipus complex, or that the Armour Company has a death wish or that the DuPonts desire to return to the womb. The assumption that an offender must have some such pathological distortion of the intellect or the emotions seems to me absurd, and if it is absurd regarding the crimes of businessmen, it is equally absurd regarding the crimes of persons in the lower economic class (1956, p. 96).

Similarly, Sutherland knew that white collar crime was invisible crime. That is, it was crime that could rarely be seen clearly by its victims, hidden as it was in commission orders, civil actions, and bureau findings. To dramatize its presence, its costs, and its effects on the American society and economy, Sutherland often resorted to rhetorical devices that "stretched" the scientific accuracy of his data. On one occasion, after reviewing the "criminal records" of seventy of the largest U.S. corporations, Sutherland summarized his findings as follows:

> The statistics which I have presented are rather dry and may not mean much to the average student who is not a specialist in this field, but the prevalence of white-collar crimes by large corporations can be illustrated more concretely. If you consider the life of a person, you find that from the cradle to the grave he has been using articles which were sold or distributed in violation of the law. The professional criminals use the word "hot" to refer to an article which has been recently stolen. For the purpose of simplicity of statement, I wish to use this word to refer to articles manufactured by corporations, but I shall expand the meaning to include any official record without restricting it to recent times, and shall refer to a class of articles rather than articles manufactured by a particular concern. Using the word in this sense, we can say that a baby is assisted into this world with the aid of "hot" surgical instruments, rubbed with "hot" olive oil, wrapped in a "hot" blanket, weighed on "hot" scales. The father, hearing the good news, runs a "hot" flag up on his flag pole, goes to the golf course and knocks a "hot" golf ball around the course. The baby grows up, surrounded by such articles, and is finally laid to rest in a "hot" casket under a "hot" tombstone (1956, p. 81).

It is, of course, precisely this kind of statement that has prompted Geis (1974; Bloch & Geis, 1970) to label Sutherland a muckraker in the tradition of Frank Norris, Lincoln Steffens, Sinclair Lewis, and, currently, Martin Gross, Vance Packard, and Ralph Nader. For much of his work on white collar crime, Sutherland deserves such a title; like other muckrakers, he exposed the seamy, exploitative, and criminal behavior of respected people in high places and in positions of trust and responsibility. However, in calling Sutherland a muckraker, it is important to realize that muckraking was intimately related to the theoretical reforms he urged upon criminology, and that the word itself says too little rather than too much about the scope of Sutherland's work on white collar crime.

In the final chapters of *White Collar Crime,* Sutherland (1949) attempted to fit the concept of white collar crime into a theoretical perspective that would encourage further research. His theoretical attempts are of two types, the first dealing with a theory of how persons become white collar *criminals* and the second with the etiology of white collar *crime*.

White Collar Criminals.   Sutherland brought the explanation of white collar criminals under the umbrella of his own *differential association theory*. An extremely general approach to deviant behavior based upon learning theory, the differential association hypothesis is that "criminal behavior is learned in association with those who define such behavior favorably and in isolation from those who define it unfavorably, and that a person in an appropriate situation engages in such criminal behavior, if, and only if, the weight of the favorable definition exceeds the weight of the unfavorable definitions" (Sutherland, 1945, p. 234).

To support this hypothesis, Sutherland used case histories of white collar criminals who explained how their employers introduced them to favorable definitions of criminal and fraudulent business practices. A shoe salesman explained, for example, how he had been taught that being a "good" shoe salesman meant selling out-of-style or misfitting shoes rather than losing a sale. A used car salesman detailed how he was taught to fleece customers, misrepresent his company's guarantees, and even boast about doing so.

In addition, Sutherland's hypothesis required that he show that these codes of "good" business behavior were learned in isolation from "bad" definitions. He explains, for example, that governmental agencies that occasionally intervene to halt such practices do so timidly and with only modestly critical attitudes. The affinity between business and government is too strong to expect it to do otherwise. Business and government people are culturally similar. They are friends and relatives, seeking political support from, and enjoying financial interdependence with, one another. Many people leave government to go into business, and vice versa. Sutherland was describing that cultural, political, and economic set of interdependencies that has come to be known as the "military-industrial complex." At the level of explaining individual acts of white collar crime, the "military-industrial complex" was a set of friendships, "understandings," and sympathies that served to isolate and shield businessmen from unfavorable definitions of fraudulent and criminal business practices.

White Collar Crime.   Although Sutherland found it fairly easy to bring white collar *criminals* into the theoretical perspective of differential association, finding a suitable theory of white collar *crime* (an explanation from the point of view of society rather than the person) proved far more difficult. He had demolished the poverty/pathology theories, and as of 1949 the only major theoretical perspective from the point of view of society was called *social disorganization*. Social disorganization theory was of two types: *anomie* theory, which held that crime could be understood by the lack of authoritative and compelling norms of behavior, and *culture conflict* theory, which held that the norms and practices of different groups were in conflict and thus either failed to guide group members or led them into clashes with groups with other norms and practices.

Sutherland attempted to fit white collar crime under both branches of social disorganization theory. Under anomie theory he argued that white collar crime is complex, technical behavior that is not easily understood. Moreover, business practices had undergone tremendous changes in the late nineteenth and early twentieth centuries. Both of these factors, Sutherland claimed, created a normative void in the business world; the "ethics" of profit were unchecked and uncontrolled either because practices were too complex to be the focus of public outrage or too new for substitute ethical standards to have developed.

Within the culture conflict branch of social disorganization theory, Sutherland invented and introduced the concept of *differential social organization* to explain white collar crime. White collar business crime is organized crime. Neither the government nor the public had been able to produce organizations with the tight structure or the power and influence of corporations. Hence, white collar crime was rampant, ill-understood, and only occasionally punished. Therefore, Sutherland called for

> a clear cut opposition between the public and the government, on the one side, and the businessmen who violate the law, on the other. This clear cut opposition does not exist and the absence of this opposition is evidence of the lack of organization against white collar crime. What is, in theory, a war loses much of its conflict because of the fraternization between the two forces. White collar crimes continue because of this lack of organization on the part of the public (1949, pp. 255–256).

In the context of Sutherland's theory of white collar crime, it is now possible to see more clearly what his muckraking meant. His theory held that the criminality of businessmen was perpetuated by their isolation from definitions unfavorable to the exploitation of consumers. It also held that the only possible social response was an organization of the public and its government that would have power equal to that of the business community. Only then would a "fair" conflict over the creation of laws exist. Muckraking is precisely the action response to such a theory. It exposes to the public the apparently respectable facade of its targets, organizes public sentiments, and urges reforms. It reveals the processes by which those in positions of trust abuse that trust and informs those violators that large segments of the society will not tolerate their abuses. Like other muckrakers, Sutherland spoke simultaneously to two groups. To the violators his message was that their crimes would be revealed, their positions lost, and their respectability shattered. To the public he showed that failure to organize against white collar criminals would result in the continued exploitation of consumers, either because those who victimized them would not be apprehended or because laws that protected the public interest would not be enacted. In the first case there would be victims without criminals; in the second, victims without crimes.

The Heritage of Sutherland

Not surprisingly, Sutherland's attempts at a methodological, theoretical, and conceptual revolution in criminology produced a vigorous controversy. Frank Hartung predicted that "no general criminological research will in the future be able to ignore the implications of Sutherland's *White Collar Crime* . . ." (1953, p. 31). Later, Donald Newman called the concept of white collar crime the "most significant development in criminology since World War II" (1958, p. 745). If a Nobel Prize were given in criminology, Hermann Mannheim (1965, p. 470) suggested that Sutherland would have earned it for his work on white collar crime. But the strong praise for Sutherland from his sympathizers has been matched by the condemnation of him by his critics. Two issues have drawn the heaviest critical fire. The first involves the question, "What is a white collar criminal?" The second asks, "Is white collar crime 'crime'?"

What Is a White Collar Criminal?   Sutherland defined a white collar criminal as a person of high social status and respectability who commits a crime in the course of his occupation. This definition has five elements to it: crime, person, high status, respectability, and occupation. The most controversial element is the first, the assertion that white collar crime is crime. Let us reserve consideration of that question until after we have reviewed the other elements.

The least controversial element in the definition is that white collar crime must be committed in the course of one's occupation. A bank president who kills her husband in a marital dispute would not be considered a white collar criminal because her crime is not directly related to her business role. She would fit Sutherland's definition if she embezzled funds from her bank, condoned or practiced criminal misrepresentation of the interest rates charged by her bank, or otherwise criminally employed her position as a bank president. She would also be a white collar criminal, according to Sutherland, if, as a used-car dealer rather than a bank president, she swindled customers by misrepresenting her products, changing odometer readings, or engaging in other deceptive and fraudulent practices sanctioned by her employer.

This range in status and respectability, from bank president to used-car dealer, would have been acceptable to Sutherland, who talked about robber barons of the nineteenth century, seventy of the largest corporations in the United States, poor bank tellers, shoe sales clerks, car dealers, and minor appliance repairers all as white collar criminals. However, it raises a serious question: Given this wide range of occupations, how could Sutherland still keep respectability and high social status as defining elements of white collar crime? The answer of Gilbert Geis (1962, 1974), Earl Quinney (1964), Herbert Edelherz (1970), and a host of others is that he could not. Both Geis and Quinney have argued that references to high social status and respectability ought to be dropped from the definition of white collar crime, and that white collar crime ought to be redefined simply as *occupational* or *avocational crime*. Edelherz suggests revising the definition to include all nonviolent crime for gain![2]

These revisions would simplify the concept of white collar crime considerably, but at the same time they would resolve some of the ironies that have given the concept much of its impact and energy. Sutherland of course knew that high social status and respectability were not the most accurate descriptors of poor bank tellers, shoe sales clerks, and minor appliance repairmen. He included them in his discussions of white collar crime not because of *their* status and respectability but because they reflected the status and respectability of their employers who condoned their swindles, misrepresentations, and deceptions to customers. The issue for Sutherland was that white collar crime constituted a *violation of trust,* particularly the trust that consumers and the public feel for persons and institutions of respectability and high social status.

As Sutherland fully intended, the irony in his definition of white collar crime is that neither the element of respectability nor high social status should be taken seriously. It is precisely the point of Sutherland's concept and research (not to mention his muckraking) that white collar criminals are neither respectable nor socially honorable. Undoubtedly, the concept of occupational or avocational crime is simpler and clearer, but, as the history of criminology illustrates, it is all too easy to forget the irony of honored, respectable, trustworthy *criminals* unless we have a self-contradictory definition around as an irritating reminder.

Another controversy has centered around the ambiguities in Sutherland's use of "person" in his definition of white collar crime. Although it takes persons to commit criminal acts, the bulk of Sutherland's research and writing dealt with corporations, businesses, and occupational roles. Sutherland rarely spoke of particular persons but of car dealers, bank presidents, corporation officers, doctors, utility companies, and politicians. These are occupational *roles* and business *institutions,* not *persons* in the usual sense of that term. In fact, after reading *White Collar Crime,* one knows very little about persons who are white collar criminals but a good deal about the interests, conflicts, power, and abuses that are common to corporate or business life.

One way of resolving the ambiguities that surround "person" in the definition of white collar crime is to recall that Sutherland offered theories of white collar criminality at two levels of explanation: differential association at the individual level, and anomie and differential social organization at the levels of social structure and organization. As a concept, white collar crime delineates an area of human activity, and one can approach that area with theories and analyses at quite different levels of explanation. One can, for example, examine the personal histories of white collar criminals (Cressey, 1953; Levens, 1964); the differences between the nature of white collar and conventional crime (Robin, 1974); the affinities between criminality and certain types of business (R. Quinney, 1963; Klockars, 1974); the political structure that supports white collar crime (Graham, 1972; Chambliss, 1976); and the legal or administrative processes that respond or fail to respond to it (Kadish, 1963; Ball & Friedman, 1965; Geis, 1973). Each of these types of analyses requires theories of different types, some that have as their primary concern the person who is the white collar criminal and others that deal almost exclusively with institutions like legislative bodies, courts, and administrative agencies that control, or attempt to control, white collar crime.

With this much said about the ambiguities in four of the elements of Sutherland's definition of white collar crime, it is still possible to describe a white collar criminal as a criminal in the course of his occupation. His business position facilitates his criminal activities, providing him with an opportunity for certain types of crime, giving him trust and respectability that shield his criminality, and influencing to one degree or another those individuals and institutions that would seek to control, regulate, prohibit, or punish him. The white collar criminal can be an individual, a group of individuals, a business organization, or a corporate body enjoying a public trust and respectability that makes those who give that trust and believe in that respectability reluctant to define its behavior as *criminal*. A most fundamental question follows: "Is it?"

Is White Collar Crime "Crime"?   From a strictly legal point of view a criminal is a person who is found guilty in a criminal court, and a crime is an act punishable by a criminal court. From that same point of view only the machinery of a criminal court, governed by its complex of special rules, procedures, and precedents can determine if a crime has been committed or if a particular person is a criminal. This is, however, a purely formal definition and a fiction of the kind upon which lawyers thrive.

In actual practice people accept much less stringent evidence of the existence of crime and criminals than is required by the strict legal requirements of due process. The FBI, for example, publishes the *Uniform Crime Reports*, which lists "crimes known to the police," even though technically a crime does not exist until evidence of its existence has been proven in a criminal court. Perhaps even more to the point, most criminologists are not only willing to accept "crimes known to the police" data as a more accurate representation of the true incidence of crime than conviction data, but they also quite commonly accept sources such as life histories, interviews, and surveys of offenders and victims whose crimes were never reported or discovered.

The fact that criminologists have long used data other than criminal court convictions as evidence of crime should make us wary when critics of white collar crime passionately argue that *only those persons convicted in a criminal court* may be called criminal and that deviation from this use of the concept of crime is, to quote Sutherland's most passionate legal critic, lawyer-sociologist Paul Tappan, "courting disaster" (1947, p. 100). Tappan charges:

> Vague, omnibus concepts defining crime are a blight upon either a legal system or a system of sociology that strives to be objective. They allow judge, administrator, or—conceivably—sociologist, in an undirected, freely operating discretion, to attribute the status "criminal" to any individual or class which he conceives nefarious. This can accomplish no desirable objective, either politically or sociologically. . . . [The] law has defined with greater clarity and precision the conduct which is criminal than our anti-legalistic criminologists promise to do; it has moreover promoted a stability, a security and dependability of justice through its exactness, its so-called technicalities, and its moderation in inspecting proposals for change (1947, pp. 99–100).

Of course, what has Tappan so upset is not the use of life histories, questionnaires, interviews, or "crimes known to the police" as sources of data on crime, but Sutherland's bolder deviations, like his use of regulatory agency judgments as evidence of corporate white collar crime.

Those who have defended Sutherland's use of regulatory agency data as evidence of crime, have argued that, in one way or another, the actions of agencies like the Federal Trade Commission, Interstate Commerce Commission, and Food and Drug Administration are similar to those of a criminal court. The laws they enforce are at least partially penal. The punishments are different from those given to individual offenders, but that is a reflection of the difference in the punishability of the corporate offender, not in the essential criminality of its violation. Newman makes the case nicely:

> The emergence of the corporate criminal merely made imprisonment inappropriate as punishment, so other devices are used. New sanctions must be developed to meet new conditions of violation and new philosophies of law. It would be ridiculous to argue, for example, that a thief sent to prison today would not have been a thief by seventeenth century standards solely because he is not mutilated or branded (1958, p. 743).

Although Newman's analogy is attractive, it masks what is the real issue in the debate over whether white collar crime is crime. The debate is essentially a territorial dispute over the proper boundaries of the discipline of criminology, and white collar crime is a hegemonic concept. It seeks to bring under criminological consideration questions of why particular offenses and offenders are handled by administrative procedures that are less stigmatizing and less punitive than trial in a criminal court. It also tries to include those areas surrounding conventional legal concepts of crime and to determine whether laws that ought to be present have not been enacted because power and influence have been exercised to block them.

As is the case with any boundary dispute, political issues are as important as scientific ones. Tappan quite rightly detects that the opening of the boundaries of criminology beyond the limits set by criminal law can invite real abuses if the criminologist is free to "attribute the status of criminal to any individual or class which he conceives nefarious" (1947: p. 99).

Harold Pepinsky (1974) has recently suggested that white collar crime ought to be redefined as *exploitation*, a suggestion of exactly the kind Tappan had in mind when he spoke of abandoning the legal definition of crime as "courting disaster." On the other hand, if criminology limits itself to the strict legal definition of crime, it undoubtedly perpetuates a class bias in its theory and research and remains naive about the political character of the creation and administration of law.

One of the most common ways out of this dilemma is simply to define it away: to declare, for instance, that one's area of study is deviance, social problems, or social control rather than crime, criminology, or criminal justice. Although there is some differing opinion among scholars as to what each of these areas includes, it is possible to understand each as an attempt to deal with boundary problems of the discipline. It is also possible to see these choices of titles for one's area of study as political decisions. Pepinsky's suggestion of defining white collar crime as exploitation falls so far from any conventional use of the concept of crime that it is preposterous. However, if Pepinsky had defined his area of interest as social control, white collar crime would become at least plausible *evidence* of exploitation.

To answer here the question of whether or not white collar crime is crime would be presumptuous (if not criminal), for an answer to that question at any meaningful level involves ideological and political issues that go beyond the legitimate boundaries of this chapter. However, it must be recognized that in the following review of research in the white collar crime tradition, three themes constantly play against one another:

(1) There is a conflict between the powers that affect the discovery, stigmatization, criminalization, and prosecution of white collar criminals. The concept of white collar crime is particularly useful in leading the criminologist to areas immediately outside the boundaries of the criminal law, where conflict exists over whether or not certain behaviors ought to be legally controlled.

(2) Inseparable from any conflict analysis is some notion of justice that governs debate on the potential criminality or illegality of acts over which conflicting powers battle. White collar crime is a hegemonic concept, and inherent in it is an eye for abuse, victimization, and violation that falls outside the boundaries of contemporary legal prohibitions. "Abuse," "victimization," and "violation" are undoubtedly moral rather than legal terms in the context of much, though not all, white collar crime research.

(3) The themes of conflict and the question of the justice of claims by either side inevitably converge in the third theme of white collar crime, namely what ought to be done about it. Not *all* abuses, victimizations, violations, or even exploitations ought necessarily to be eliminated, if only for the reason that the many mechanisms for detection of such abuses and enforcement of laws preventing them are likely to be more

costly and abusive than the behaviors they are intended to control. Still less likely is the possibility of eliminating or controlling abuses by the rather clumsy and inevitably bureaucratic mechanisms of criminalizing them.

In the view of this writer, the weakest feature of white collar crime and the theories created to support it is *not* that it "becomes a propagandistic weapon which under the meretricious guise of science is to be used for the establishment of a new order" (Caldwell, 1959, p. 282), but that anchored as it is to the concept of crime, it intimates that a new and better order will be brought about by covering more acts with the criminal label.

RESEARCH IN THE WHITE COLLAR CRIME TRADITION

For many reasons, not the least of which are the ambiguities and ironies in the concept of white collar crime, there is a rather meager supply of adequate empirical studies of white collar criminality. Geis estimates that over the past two decades criminologists have produced an average of roughly "one original investigation annually plus an occasional reiteration of previous work and theory" (1974, p. 281). It would seem, however, that this very modest research productivity is in the process of changing in response to pressures of two types.

First, the consumer movement has generated a large and growing literature on white collar criminality. This literature generally lacks any type of adequate theoretical base, but popular reports of case after case of white collar criminality in the rhetoric of modern muckraking seem destined to force themselves into the criminological literature. Indeed, the most comprehensive, though now dated, bibliography on white collar crime "reviews materials which reflect the developments during the 1950s and 1960s in sharp and illegal practices of legal businesses and professions as they relate to the consumer" (Tompkins, 1967, p. v).

Second, the new criminology, social control, conflict criminology, and other Marxist and neo-Marxist approaches to criminology currently enjoy a significant following. Although comparatively little empirical research has come out of this perspective, and that which has emerged has rarely acknowledged its position in the mainstream of white collar crime, traditional studies of business, corporate, and professional criminality would be as polemically useful for neo-Marxist criminologists as they are for neo-Nader consumer advocates.

Before examining the more interesting contributions from conflict and consumer criminology as they bear upon white collar crime, one might begin with a review of some of the landmark studies that have established the concept of white collar crime within the mainstream of the criminological tradition.

Sutherland's White Collar Crime *(1949)*

The most influential study of white collar crime is Sutherland's pioneering monograph, *White Collar Crime.* The design of the study was exceedingly simple: compile the "criminal records" of seventy of the largest manufacturing, mining, and mercantile corporations in the United States. Sutherland chose his sample from a list of the two hundred largest American, "non-financial" corporations.[3] He excluded public utilities corporations, corporations in the transportation and communications industries, and the corporations in "one other industry," which he did not identify. He gathered his information on decisions against these seventy corporations from a variety of government sources, as well as from reports of violations in *The New York Times.* Counted as crimes were violations of the following types: "restraint of trade; misrepresentation in advertising; infringement of patents, trademarks and copyrights; unfair labor practices as defined by the National Labor Relations Law and a few decisions under other labor laws; rebates; financial fraud and violation of trust; violations of war regulations and some miscellaneous offenses" (Sutherland, 1949, p. 18).

The average age of the seventy corporations was forty-five years, and the period covered by the records of these corporations that Sutherland surveyed was roughly 1890–1945. In a 1948 speech Sutherland summarized his research findings as follows:

> This tabulation of the crimes of the 70 largest corporations in the United States gives a total of 980 adverse decisions. Every one of the 70 corporations has a decision against it, and the average number of decisions is 14.0. Of these 70 corporations, 98% are recidivists; that is, they have two or more adverse decisions. Several states have enacted habitual criminal laws, which define an habitual criminal as a person who has been convicted four times of felonies. If we use this number and do not

limit the convictions to felonies, 90% of the 70 largest corporations in the United States are habitual criminals. Sixty of the corporations have decisions against them for restraint of trade, 54 for infringements, 44 for unfair labor practices, 27 for rebates, and 43 for miscellaneous offenses (Sutherland, 1956, p. 80).

The main thrust of these findings was to demonstrate that crimes by corporations and corporate executives existed and were a regular part of business activities. It is obvious, however, that Sutherland oversold his findings in the above paragraph. The reference to corporations as habitual criminals and recidivists is a muckraking personification to dramatize and exaggerate his data. Corporations consist of thousands or even hundreds of thousands of employees and are not justifiably termed "recidivists" or "habitual criminals" on the basis of four convictions over a corporate life span that averages forty-five years. In fact, considering the amount of activity of the seventy largest corporations in the United States, their many employees, and the wide range of decisions—from patent infringement to misrepresentation in advertising—that Sutherland accepted as evidence of crime, one might well argue that four or even fourteen convictions is an exemplary record. The prime weakness in such a position, though, is exactly the weakness in Sutherland's comparison of the records of corporate offenders and those of individual criminals. While Sutherland's analogy between corporate and individual offenders buries the fact that corporate offenders include thousands and probably hundreds of thousands of occasions for offense, the defense of a corporation with "only" fourteen convictions assumes that the mechanisms of criminalization, detection, apprehension, and conviction are the same in their application to individual and corporate criminals.

Additionally, the personalization of corporate offenders as recidivists and habitual criminals is clearly a muckraking attempt to stigmatize corporate criminality in the same way that the individual, conventional offender is stigmatized by a conviction. Public reaction in the United States to corporate violation is quite mild compared to reactions toward conventional crimes like burglary, larceny, and robbery—an issue of no small importance in the reaction to the next sociological study of white collar criminality.

Hartung's "White Collar Offenses in the Wholesale Meat Industry in Detroit" (1950)

Quick on the heels of *White Collar Crime* came Hartung's study of "White Collar Offenses in the Wholesale Meat Industry in Detroit." Hartung tested four propositions in his study, all of which are grounded in Sutherland's previous works. He argued, first, that all of the 122 wholesale meat price violations handled by the Office of Price Administration (OPA) in Detroit between December 1942 and June 1946 were criminal in that they all involved violations of laws and were punished by actions that ranged from fine and imprisonment to warnings of license suspension. Second, Hartung found that only two persons involved in the total of 122 cases had any previous criminal record. This confirmed Sutherland's claim of the respectability of white collar criminals, at least as operationalized by lack of a criminal record. Third, Hartung found a kind of ripple effect in white collar crimes in the wholesale meat industry. That is, if one wholesaler sold meat for more than OPA ceiling prices, this would lead to violations at secondary wholesale and retail levels as well. This finding is consistent with a loose interpretation of differential association in that techniques for violation were learned in association with other white collar offenders.

Fourth, the 122 cases involved 195 types of price violations, which Hartung classified as either "Open Overceiling" (65 violations), "Evasive Overceiling" (58 violations), or "Record Keeping" (72 violations). What Hartung meant by open overceiling as opposed to evasive overceiling was that a violation of the first type usually involved no attempt to hide the violation, and this probably meant that the violation was unintentional. In the case of evasive overceiling violations, the company disguised its violations in an attempt to conceal them and thus intentionally to violate OPA regulations. Record keeping violations could have either been unintentional errors or conscious attempts to conceal evasive violations. Sixteen open overceiling violations were punished by orders suspending a company's right to deal in certain commodities for a stipulated period, a quite serious penalty. On this basis Hartung claimed that *"willfulness or deliberate intent is not essential to making a white collar offense a criminal act"* (1950, p. 32, emphasis added).

Hartung's research is important in the white collar crime tradition not only because it uses as evidence of crime OPA violations rather than conventional criminal court statistics, but also because it reaffirms Sutherland's denial of pathological elements in the personality or experience of white collar criminals. As Hartung commented in his best baiting rhetoric:

> Imagine what a cry of outraged ego would have electrified Congress if, upon establishing an evasive overcharge, the OPA had inquired into the businessman's love life to ascertain if he were frustrated or had investigated at what grade he had quit school or had measured his cephalic index and his mesomorphy or had tried to obtain any of the usual items that comprise the subject matter of current empirical studies of offenders (1950, p. 30).

In fact, Hartung went beyond Sutherland by claiming that one can become a white collar criminal *without criminal intent*. This claim in particular led Hartung into debate with Ernest W. Burgess, a past president of the American Sociological Society and one of the deans of American sociology. Burgess ruled that any sociological treatment of crime must define a criminal as "a person who regards himself as a criminal and is so regarded by society. He is the product of the criminal making process" (1950, p. 34). By "criminal making process" Burgess undoubtedly meant some special and probably "disorganized" or "defective" socialization, not the criminalization and legal labeling process a contemporary criminologist would be likely to mean by that phrase. The development of a labeling persective would not be introduced into the white collar crime tradition until other studies had examined the questions of whether or not a sociologically acceptable criminal has to define himself as such and whether or not society has to agree with that definition.

Cressey's Embezzlers

Within a few months of the appearance of Hartung's study, Cressey published "Criminal Violation of Financial Trust" (1950), a study of the social psychology of embezzlement that he later expanded into the now classic monograph, *Other People's Money* (1953). Cressey offered a theory of how people in positions of financial trust violated that trust. His theory, which was inductively developed from interviews with some 133 embezzlers and other trust violators, stressed the role of the "nonshareable problem." That is, employees found themselves with problems, often of the "wine, women or wagering" type, which they could not discuss with anyone. They "solved" these nonshareable problems by stealing from or defrauding their employers. Significantly, the embezzlers knew that their acts were criminal, and not merely technical, violations, but Cressey found that his embezzlers were able to create rationalizations for their "borrowing" of their employers' funds that to them justified their actions or diminished their responsibilities for them. Embezzlers hypothesize that reactions of others to their "borrowing" are much different from what they would be to *real* stealing or embezzlement. As Cressey pointed out: "It is because of an ability to hypothesize reactions which will not consistently and severely condemn his criminal behavior that the trusted person takes the role of what *we* have called the 'trust violator.' *He* often does not think of himself as playing that role, but instead thinks of himself as playing another role, such as that of a special kind of borrower or businessman" (1950, p. 743).

This finding by Cressey has an important bearing on the first requirement that Burgess imposed for the sociologically acceptable criminal— namely that he define himself as criminal. *Other People's Money* dealt with a class of acts that were unquestionably criminal. Not only is embezzlement a violation of the criminal law that is tried in criminal court, but Cressey interviewed his subjects as they sat in their cells at Joliet, Chino, and Terre Haute penitentiaries. While Cressey found that his embezzlers were willing to admit that what they had done was criminal, they accompanied that admission with explanations that neutralized the prohibitions and the moral sanctions against doing so.

Since *Other People's Money*, a number of studies have shown that juvenile, adult, and even adult-professional criminals often employ arguments that effectively neutralize the norms condemning their behavior (see, for example, Sykes & Matza, 1957; Matza, 1964; Scott & Lyman, 1968; Klockars, 1974). But even without the support of these additional studies, it was still clear that Burgess had set too high a requirement for a sociologically acceptable definition of the criminal. Cressey had chosen the single most difficult case against which to examine Burgess' requirement for a criminal self-definition. The victim of an embezzler is his employer, often a large corporation or organization with considerable ability to detect, prosecute, convict, and otherwise impress the embezzler with the criminality of his acts. If under these conditions the embezzler can still view his behavior "a) as essentially non-criminal, b) as justified, or c) as a part of a general irresponsibility for which he is not completely accountable" (Cressey, 1953, p. 93), then Burgess' first requirement for a sociologically acceptable definition of the criminal simply evaporates.

The second part of the Burgess declaration—the requirement that society must define the offender's behavior as criminal—was brought to test in two studies during the 1950s. The first is still the most comprehensive study of any form of white collar criminality, but it is also one of the most difficult to evaluate in terms of how it bears on the question of public attitudes toward white collar crime.

Clinard's Black Market (1952)

Marshall Clinard's study of violations of price control regulations in the United States during World War II supports most of the themes that have surrounded the concept of white collar criminality. Most of the price violators were "respectable" businessmen. Few had any previous encounters with the law. They were economically better off than conventional criminals and were better educated. Clinard's research demonstrated that there was no basis for the contention that any particular ethnic or immigrant group, race, or criminal organization caused, infiltrated, or organized the American black market, nor was there any evidence to show that any particular psychological pathologies infected the black market offender. Moreover, Clinard showed that black market activities were not associated with only certain commodities or particular industries. The black market existed across the entire horizon of the American business community, and it was within that community that Clinard found his explanation of the black market phenomenon.

Clinard found that the business community had an enormous hostility to government control and regulation of business, a similar antagonism and disrespect for the Office of Price Administration, which was charged with administering and enforcing price controls, and sympathy for, rather than condemnation of, price control violators. In trying to enforce price controls, the OPA found businessmen unwilling to testify against violators. The rule of silence that has come to be the hallmark of organized crime was the rule of the respectable business community during the World War II black market.

Clinard also found that the government contributed in various ways to the growth and extension of the black market. Enforcement, particularly during the early phase of price controls, was lax, confused, and uneven. Sanctions were weak, and the "sabotage of the government's efforts to control inflation by numerous vocal and irresponsible lobbyists and politicians, representing special interest rather than the consumer, helped to confuse rather than clarify the situation" (Clinard, 1952, p. 328).

Two interesting defenses of the black market businessman have often been given. It has been argued that the alternatives for those in business during World War II were either particpation in the black market or financial collapse. Clinard examined this argument and rejected it: "Generally, business made higher profits, business activity was at a higher level, and business failures were far lower under price and rationing controls than at any previous time, including 1929. While it is true that some business concerns suffered a loss of profits, they were a small minority, and the overall figures show large profits for business" (1952, p. 315).

The second defense of the black market businessman bears directly upon the question of public attitudes toward white collar crime. It is claimed that the general public rather than the businessman should bear the prime responsibility for creation of the black market. It takes two to make a market, and the businessman found himself under extraordinary pressure from consumers who were willing to buy with "no questions asked." Clinard attempted to show that there was considerable support for rationing and OPA price controls, but his demonstration is not particularly impressive. In the very same year (1945) that national surveys recorded the highest public support for government price controls (95 percent), a Gallup survey "showed that one person in five would condone black market buying on occasion" (Clinard, 1952, p. 93).

Clinard's results were clearly not strong enough to challenge Burgess' claim that white collar crime fell outside the purview of criminology because social norms condemning it were so weak compared to norms such as those condemning conventional crimes. The possibility existed, however, that the black market was a special kind of white collar offense in that it involved an exchange of illicit goods with willing buyers and sellers, a kind of consensual offense whose victims were not the buyer or the seller but "the country" and perhaps "the war effort." In an attempt to test the attitudes of the public on a less complicated white collar crime, Newman (1957) took on the Burgess challenge directly.

Newman's "Public Attitudes Toward a Form of White Collar Crime" (1957)

If *The Black Market* can be seen as a study in which the deck was stacked against finding norms severely condemning a form of white collar crime, Newman's study was an obvious attempt to stack it in just the opposite way. Newman asked a randomly selected sample of 205 people (178 of whom gave valid responses) what penalty ought to be given to violators in six sample cases. These were actual cases drawn from the files of a federal district attorney, abstracted with the names of the companies removed, and presented in questionnaire form. All of the cases involved adulteration of food. The following is a sample of the cases that he used.

> The _____ Dairy Products Company was found guilty of violating the Pure Food Law in that a pasteurized American cheese food that they manufactured and sold was found to contain maggots, cow hairs, cow manure, rodent hairs, and insect fragments. First offense" (Newman, 1957, p. 29).

Maggots, cow hairs, and insect fragments notwithstanding, Newman, who had hypothesized that people would choose penalties comparable to those for theft and burglary, found:

> The majority chose penalties less severe than a prison sentence. Fines, warnings, seizure of the product, and jail terms, in various combinations, were the most popular responses. In effect, respondents viewed food adulteration as more comparable to serious traffic violations than to burglary.

Newman thereupon concludes:

This can perhaps be taken as evidence in support of the position of Burgess and others that such violators are viewed as "law breakers" rather than criminals" (1957, p. 32).

For those who had allied themselves with the white collar crime revolution in criminology, Newman's findings must have constituted a grave disappointment. But should Newman have expected to find otherwise? Was it not Sutherland's original point that almost no one, including criminologists, took white collar crime very seriously? Were there not all kinds of good reasons, ranging from the status of the offenders to the complexity of the offenses, why public attitudes against white collar criminality should not be particularly strong?

A year after the publication of his study of public attitudes toward food adulteration, Newman (1958) published a superb essay reviewing the issues in the white collar crime controversy. In it he took up the Burgess argument but dealt with it as if his own findings never existed:

> [M]any white-collar violations are so complex and their effects so indirect that only an accountant or a lawyer can fully appreciate their criminal nature. Then, too, the victim of the white-collar offender is ordinarily that abstraction "the public," which means that the effects of the offense are diffuse and community resentment does not gain momentum. A murder is a clear-cut crime, usually involving one specific victim as well as a single, visible perpetrator. The violence, the directness of murder, engenders social solidarity against the criminal, particularly as long as the press reports every detail. But what of the formation of an illicit monopoly, with complex interlocking corporate structures? Even granting a crime has been committed, who is the criminal; who, the victim? Obviously, public resentment of such offenses must take a different form than in conventional criminal cases, but the very fact that laws forbidding monopoly exist argues for its cultural meaning as crime (Newman, 1958, p. 745).

Newman is undoubtedly correct in his comparison of the clarity of murder as opposed to the complexity of corporate crime. He is, however, less than candid as his argument applies to less complex and more direct crimes like manufacturing adulterated food. Few people would have difficulty understanding maggots, rat hair, and insect fragments in their cheese. But could it be that the majority of people questioned in his own 1957 study understood enough about the futility of jails and the difficulties of keeping food production sanitary to settle for less than a prison term for a dairy company executive's first offense?

Because Newman was unable to demonstrate that public attitudes toward even this particularly disgusting form of white collar crime came anywhere near the intensity of those condemning conventional crimes like larceny and burglary, his study marks a critical point in the focus of white collar crime research. Although Burgess wanted to exclude white collar crime from criminological consideration on the grounds that norms prohibiting them were not severe enough, the fact that those norms were not particularly strong simply lowered the requirements for theories explaining the acts of white collar criminals. It was no longer necessary to argue for defects in socialization, weakness in character, or faults in the personality of white collar criminals, any more than it would be necessary for traffic violators. Deviance is often its own reward, and norms from which both white collar criminals and traffic offenders deviate are just not strong enough to demand such explanations.

For instance, an important study by Richard Quinney (1963) found that prescription violations by retail pharmacists could be explained by their "business" rather than "professional" orientation to their work. Seventy-five percent of the pharmacists with a business-role orientation were prescription violators, while none of the pharmacists with a professional-role orientation were found to have violated prescription laws. Quinney suggests that the conflict between business and professional orientations may explain white collar criminality in many other professions in which both roles are found: dentistry, optometry, osteopathy, independent general medicine, clinical psychology, and accounting. In fact, virtually every study of white collar criminality finds support for the thesis that the rationales of white collar criminals are intimately related to values, practices, logics, and techniques that are common to the offender's business or occupation (Levens, 1964; Spencer, 1965; Geis, 1967; Klockars, 1974; Leff, 1976).

Although after Newman's 1957 findings of relatively mild public attitudes toward white collar crime criminological research began to develop theories of the association of crime and business, a more important development has occurred outside the boundaries of the formal academic discipline of criminology. That development involves the movement that seeks actively to change public attitudes toward white collar crimes, to organize and educate that public, and to harass, battle, badger, and otherwise make life miserable for white collar criminals and the law enforcement agencies that are lax in prosecuting them. The reference here is, of course, to the consumer movement and to the man who bears the same relationship to it as Sutherland does to white collar crime: Ralph Nader.

Consumer Criminology

Although the consumer movement originated outside of academic criminology and only occasionally draws upon criminological literature or consultants, its relationship to the themes and spirit of the white collar crime revolution in criminology is so strong that no review of white collar criminality can fail to consider it. But what is perhaps even more important to its being considered as part of the white collar crime research tradition is the indisputable fact that in the past decade it has produced a literature on white collar crime that is far more detailed than all the white collar crime research within the academic criminological tradition.

It will come as no surprise to anyone to say that much of that literature is controversial in its interpretations and does not meet accepted standards of scientific accuracy. A large portion of that literature, however—particularly the work of Nader and the law students, "Nader's Raiders," who spent their summer vacations working at his Center for Study of Responsive Law—should prove an inspiration to criminologists who have doubted that it was possible to get substantial information on the corruptions of big business and big government. Methodologically speaking, the secret of the success of Nader and his Raiders seems to be a combination of being on the scene in Washington, D.C., where access to government hearings, official agencies, lobbies, and other nonconventional sources of data on white collar crime abound, and of working very hard at collecting documents and pursuing sources. One group of Nader's Raiders produced a report documenting the laxity, inefficiency, and general ineffectiveness of the Federal Trade Commission in controlling many types of misrepresentation in advertising and other forms of consumer fraud. They reported that in spite of the fact that midway into their investigation the chairman of the FTC forbade his staff to give them any further interviews, they still found young attorneys on the FTC staff who were willing to talk. They had to learn, though, to suffer frequent refusals and continue to contrive to find information without giving up. In retrospect, they summarize their methodological animus in terms not normally found in research methods texts:

> Our collective naivete proved to be our strength: the more we were hampered in finding what we wanted to know the more we persisted. When we were called to testify in the spring of 1969 before the Senate Subcommittee on Executive Reorganization, Senator Abraham A. Ribicoff of Connecticut remarked: "Bureaucracy being what it is, I am fascinated by your ability to get in so deep and get so much information. I am sure that you gentlemen are the envy of the large number of reporters here" (Cox, Fellmeth, & Schulz, 1970, p. 3).

There is more to the relationship between the consumer movement and white collar crime research than the shared methodology of extracting data from hard-to-get-at, unconventional sources. Nader and Sutherland have both focused their principal attention on the corporate offender. Nader (1965b) was, in fact, propelled to national prominence with *Unsafe at Any Speed: The Designed-in Dangers of the American Automobile*, a book documenting abuses in the auto industry in general and focusing in particular on the death and carnage associated with General Motor's Corvair. The book became a best-seller (about half a million copies), and the sales were no doubt helped by disclosures that GM had hired detectives to find information that might be used to smear Nader. Nader continued his David and Goliath battles with the auto industry in other books and in his Raider reports (Nader, 1965a; Dodge et al., 1972). One of the most interesting of these reports, *What to Do With Your Bad Car: An Action Manual for Lemon Owners* (Nader, Dodge, & Hotchkiss, 1971), outlines strategies for fighting white collar criminals in the auto sales, manufacturing, and repair businesses.

After *Unsafe at Any Speed* Nader expanded his investigation of corporate white collar crime into areas other than the auto industry. Nader monographs and Nader-sponsored study-group investigations have appeared on general aviation crash safety (Bruce & Draper, 1970), land use in California (Fellmeth, 1972), nursing home frauds and abuses (Townsend, 1971), self-regulation in the medical profession (McCleery, 1971), domination of the state of Delaware by the DuPont family (Phelan & Pozen, 1972), adulteration of food products in the food-processing industry (Wellford, 1972), and corporate water (Fallows, 1971; Zwick & Benstock, 1971), and air pollution (Esposito & Silverman, 1970). These studies of corporate and business crime were complemented by a series of Nader-sponsored studies of some of the agencies that ought to have been enforcing and controlling that crime: the Federal Trade Commission (Cox, Fellmeth, & Schulz, 1970); the U.S. Bureau of Reclamation (Berkman & Viscusi, 1971); the Anti-Trust Enforcement Division of the Department of Justice (Green, Moore, & Wasserstein, 1972); and the Food and Drug Administration (Turner, 1970).

Nader and Sutherland also share a similarity in their political outlooks on the problems of white collar crime. Sutherland's satanic principle was *corporate socialism*, the control of society by business interests unchecked and unregulated by either organized public or government action. Sutherland saw that the appropriate political response to this situation was "organization on the part of the public" (1949, p. 256). With respect to this recommendation there can be no more perfect inheritor of the Sutherland spirit than Ralph Nader. It is, however, on the political dimension of his work that Nader has come under criticism. One of his original Raiders, Robert Fellmeth, notes, "Ralph's philosophy is ninth grade civics—just as defined by our forefathers and in the *Weekly Reader*" (McCarry, 1972). Nader has shown very little concern for the types of radical politics that one might think would develop from his repeated confrontation with the abuses of power, trust, and privilege that have been the constant targets of his attack. But perhaps the more critical feature of those confrontations is that, more often than not, Nader has won.

WHITE COLLAR CRIME AND CONTEMPORARY CRIMINOLOGICAL THEORY

While the consumer movement is waging its war outside the boundaries of academic criminology, a parallel, though smaller-scale, revolution has been occurring within. At least part of that revolution can be seen as a boundary dispute of the type described earlier in this chapter, particularly the attempts of those criminologists of the labeling perspective "to enlarge the area taken into consideration in the study of deviant phenomena by including in it activities of others than the allegedly deviant actor" (Becker, 1973, p. 180). Both empirically and theoretically, this perspective bears significantly on the white collar criminal's ability to resist the label "criminal," as well as the often modest efforts of law enforcement, legislative, and other governmental bodies to attach it to him.

An even more fundamental battle continues over whether white collar criminality is better comprehended from a functionalist perspective in the tradition of Emile Durkheim (1951) and Robert Merton (1957) or a conflict perspective in the tradition of Karl Marx.[4] Sutherland, as noted earlier, chose at least one explanation clearly of the functionalist variety, anomie, stressing the point that the rapid industrial development of the late nineteenth and twentieth centuries had left a normative void in many areas of business practice. What can be said, though, of his second explanatory concept, differential social organization, the explanation of white collar crime by the inequality in the battle between organized white collar crime and an unorganized public? On which side of the battle line should this concept fall—functionalist or conflict, Durkheim or Marx? For Sutherland, the muckraker, it clearly fell on the functionalist side. Sutherland believed in the possibility of a people outraged enough by white collar crime to organize against it and impress upon the business community its moral responsibilities. He also believed in a government that would respond to the demands of an organized public and actively criminalize, detect, and prosecute white collar crime. In short, for Sutherland the concept of differential social organization implied the hope of winning.

From the Marxist and neo-Marxist conflict perspectives, differential social organization would imply not a muckraker's fighting concept but the steady state at which a capitalist society rests. The distribution of power in society is a reflection of the distribution of property, and, at best, "reforms" within that system are merely visions of the falsely conscious. Chambliss (see Chambliss & Mankoff, 1976) has recently reminded us that government inspection of meat processing, ostensibly to correct unsanitary conditions in that industry, was actually a device to secure the interests of large meat-packing firms from smaller competitors.

It is appropriate to conclude this review of white collar crime with this final and fundamental controversy. Battles over the "true" meaning of differential social organization will no doubt continue, both within and outside of the formal boundaries of academic criminology. But it is important to remember that Sutherland, muckraker and criminologist, taught by his own example that both battles were inseparable. Whether in decades to come the more correct portrait of differential social organization will emerge from the functionalist perspective of Durkheim via Sutherland or the conflict perspective of Marx and his followers will depend upon the ability of Nader and others like him to organize the power of consumer criminology.

NOTES

1. In the text we will use quotation marks to make a distinction between the concept, "white collar crime," meaning the theoretical analysis developed by Sutherland about a particular type of crime and white collar crime (without quotation marks), which is a descriptive term applying to that crime as it occurs in society.

2. Actually, Edelherz offers a more elaborate redefinition of white collar crime: [T]he term . . . [can] be defined as *an illegal act or series of illegal acts committed by nonphysical means and by concealment or guile, to obtain money or property, to avoid the payment or loss of money or property, or to obtain business or personal advantage"* (Edelherz, 1970, p. 3).

3. Sutherland did not define what he meant by "non-financial" corporations. Noting the companies he chose to sample, however, it might be safely assumed that he meant those corporations based on the production and distribution of goods. "Financial" corporations such as banks, on the other hand, would be those dealing in money—circulating it, granting credit, and making investments.

4. In the writing of Marx himself the topic of crime is addressed in "The State and the Law" (1964a); in *Theories of Surplus Value* (1964b); in *The German Ideology* (1965); and in portions of *The Cologne Communist Trial* (1971). The "classical" Marxist perspective has been articulated most thoroughly in contemporary criminology by Gordon (1971) and Chambliss (Chambliss & Mankoff, 1976). Less orthodox Marxist or neo-Marxist positions are represented in Turk (1969), R. Quinney (1970), and Taylor, Walton, and Young (1973).

BIBLIOGRAPHY

Ball, Harry V., and Lawrence M. Friedman. "The Use of Criminal Sanctions in the Enforcement of Economic Legislation: A Sociological View." *Stanford Law Review*, 1965, 17:197–223.

Becker, Howard. *Outsiders: Studies in the Sociology of Deviance*. New York: The Free Press, 1973.

Berkman, Richard, and Kip Viscusi. *Damning the West: A Nader Task Force Report on the U.S. Bureau of Reclamation*. Washington, D.C.: Center for Study of Responsive Law, 1971.

Binder, M. "Weisse-kragen kriminalität." *Kriminalistik*, 1962, 16:251–255.

Bloch, Herbert A., and Gilbert Geis. *Man, Crime, and Society*, 2nd ed. New York: Random House, 1970.

Bruce, James, and John Draper, eds. *Crash Safety in General Aviation Aircraft*. Washington, D.C.: Center for Study of Responsive Law, 1970.

Burgess, Ernest W. "Concluding Comment." In Frank E. Hartung. "White-Collar Offenses in the Wholesale Meat Industry in Detroit." *American Journal of Sociology*, 1950, 56:34.

Caldwell, Robert G. "A Re-examination of the Concept of White-Collar Crime." *Federal Probation*, 1958, 22:30–36.

Caldwell, Robert G. "Book Review." *Journal of Criminal Law, Criminology, and Police Science*, 1959, 50:281–282.

Chambliss, William J. "The State and the Criminal Law." In William J. Chambliss and Milton Mankoff, eds. *Whose Law, What Order?* New York: John Wiley & Sons, 1976.

Clinard, Marshall B. *The Black Market: A Study of White Collar Crime*. New York: Rinehart, 1952.

Cox, Edward F., Robert C. Fellmeth, and John E. Schulz. *The Nader Report on the Federal Trade Commission*. New York: Grove Press, 1970.

Cressey, Donald R. "Criminal Violation of Financial Trust." *American Sociological Review*, 1950, 15:738–743.

Cressey, Donald R. *Other People's Money: A Study in the Social Psychology of Embezzlement*. Glencoe, Ill.: The Free Press, 1953.

Cressey, Donald R. "Foreword." In Edwin H. Sutherland. *White Collar Crime*. Hinsdale, Ill.: Dryden Press, 1961, pp. iii–xii.

Dodge, Lowell, and others. *Small on Safety: The Designed-in Dangers of the Volkswagen*. New York: Grossman Publishers, 1972.

Durkheim, Emile. *Suicide*. Glencoe, Ill.: The Free Press, 1951. (Originally published in 1897.)

Edelherz, Herbert. *The Nature, Impact and Prosecution of White Collar Crime*. Washington, D.C.: U.S. Government Printing Office, 1970.

Esposito, John C., and Larry J. Silverman. *Vanishing Air: The Ralph Nader Study Group Report on Air Pollution.* New York: Grossman Publishers, 1970.

Fallows, James M. *The Water Lords: Ralph Nader's Study Group Report on Industry and Environmental Crisis in Savannah, Georgia.* New York: Grossman Publishers, 1971.

Fellmeth, Robert C., ed. *Politics of Land: Ralph Nader's Study Group Report on Land Use in California.* New York: Grossman Publishers, 1972.

Geis, Gilbert. "Toward a Delineation of White-Collar Offenses." *Sociological Inquiry,* 1962, 32:159–171.

Geis, Gilbert. "The Heavy Electrical Equipment Antitrust Cases of 1961." In Gilbert Geis, ed. *White-Collar Criminal: The Offender in Business and the Professions.* New York: Atherton Press, 1967.

Geis, Gilbert. "Deterring Corporate Crime." In Ralph Nader and Mark J. Green, eds. *Corporate Power in America.* New York: Grossman Press, 1973, pp. 182–197.

Geis, Gilbert. "Avocational Crime." In Daniel Glaser, ed. *Handbook of Criminology.* Chicago: Rand McNally, 1974, pp. 273–298.

Gordon, David M. "Class and the Economics of Crime." *The Review of Radical Political Economics,* 1971, 3:51–72.

Graham, James M. "Amphetamine Politics on Capitol Hill." *Society,* 1972, 9:14–23.

Green, Mark J., Beverly Moore, Jr., and Bruce Wasserstein. *The Closed Enterprise System: Ralph Nader's Study Group Report on Anti-Trust Enforcement.* New York: Grossman Publishers, 1972.

Hartung, Frank E. "White Collar Offenses in the Wholesale Meat Industry in Detroit." *American Journal of Sociology,* 1950, 56:25–34.

Hartung, Frank E. "White Collar Crime: Its Significance for Theory and Practice." *Federal Probation,* 1953, 17:3–36.

Kadish, Sanford H. "Some Observations on the Use of Criminal Sanctions in Enforcing Economic Regulations." *University of Chicago Law Review,* 1963, 30:423–449.

Kellens, G. "Du 'Crime en Col Blanc' du 'Délit de Chevalier.'" *Annales de la Faculté du Droit de Liège,* 1968, 30:60–124.

Klockars, Carl B. *The Professional Fence.* New York: The Free Press, 1974.

Leff, Arthur Allen. *Swindling and Selling.* New York: The Free Press, 1976.

Levens, G. E. "101 British White Collar Criminals." *New Society,* 1964, 78:6–8.

Mannheim, Hermann. *Comparative Criminology.* Boston: Houghton Mifflin, 1965.

Marx, Karl. "The State and Law." In T. B. Bottomore and Maximillien Rubel, eds. *Kark Marx: Selected Writings in Sociology and Social Philosophy.* New York: McGraw-Hill, 1964a, pp. 215–230.

Marx, Karl. *Theories of Surplus Value,* vol. 1. London: Lawrence & Wishart, 1964b.

Marx, Karl. *The German Ideology.* London: Lawrence & Wishart, 1965.

Marx, Karl. *The Cologne Communist Trial.* London: Lawrence & Wishart, 1971.

Matza, David. *Delinquency and Drift.* New York: John Wiley & Sons, 1964.

McCarry, Charles. *Citizen Nader.* New York: Saturday Review Press, 1972.

McCleery, Robert S. *One Life—One Physician: An Inquiry into the Medical Profession's Performance in Self-Regulation.* Washington, D.C.: Public Affairs Press, 1971.

Merton, Robert. *Social Theory and Social Structure.* Glencoe, Ill.: The Free Press, 1957.

Nader, Ralph. *Automobile Design Hazards.* San Francisco: Bancroft-Whitney, 1965a.

Nader, Ralph. *Unsafe at Any Speed: The Designed-in Dangers of the American Automobile.* New York: Grossman Publishers, 1965b.

Nader, Ralph, Lowell Dodge, and Ralf Hotchkiss. *What to Do With Your Bad Car: An Action Manual for Lemon Owners.* New York: Grossman Publishers, 1971.

Newman, Donald J. "Public Attitudes Toward a Form of White Collar Crime." *Social Problems,* 1957, 4:228–232.

Newman, Donald J. "White Collar Crime." *Law and Contemporary Problems,* 1958, 23:735–753.

Normandeau, A. "Les Déviations en Affaires et la 'Crime en Col Blanc.'" *Review of International Criminal and Police Technology,* 1965, 19:247–258.

Pepinsky, Harold E. "From White Collar Crime to Exploitation." *Journal of Criminal Law and Criminology,* 1974, 55:208–214.

Phelan, James, and Robert Pozen. *The Company State: Ralph Nader's Study Group Report on DuPont in Delaware.* New York: Grossman Publishers, 1972.

Pinatel, J. "La Criminalité dans les Différents Cercles Sociaux." *Revue de Science Criminelle,* 1970, 25:677–684.

Quinney, Earl R. "The Study of White Collar Crime: Toward a Reorientation in Theory and Research." *Journal of Criminal Law, Criminology, and Police Science,* 1964, 55:208–214.

Quinney, Richard. "Occupational Structure and Criminal Behavior: Prescription Violations by Retail Pharmacists." *Social Problems,* 1963, 11:179–185.

Quinney, Richard. *The Social Reality of Crime.* Boston: Little, Brown, 1970.

Robin, Gerald D. "White-Collar Crime and Employee Theft." *Crime and Delinquency*, 1974, 20:251–262.

Scott, Marvin B., and Stanford M. Lyman. "Accounts." *American Sociological Review*, 1968, 33:46–62.

Spencer, John C. "White Collar Crime." In John C. Spencer, Tadeusz Grygier, and Howard Jones, eds.*Criminology in Transition.*London:Tavistock Publication, 1965, pp. 251–264.

Sutherland, Edwin H. "White-Collar Criminality." *American Sociological Review*, 1940, 5:1–12.

Sutherland, Edwin H. "Crime and Business." *The Annals of the American Academy of Political and Social Science*, 1941, 217:112–118.

Sutherland, Edwin H. "Is 'White-Collar Crime' Crime?" *American Sociological Review*, 1945, 10:132–139.

Sutherland, Edwin H. *Principles of Criminology*, 4th ed. Philadelphia: J. B. Lippincott, 1947.

Sutherland, Edwin H. "Crimes of Corporations." In Albert Cohen, Alfred Lindesmith, and Karl Schuessler, eds., *The Sutherland Papers*. Bloomington, Ind.: Indiana University Press, 1956. (This is the publication of a speech delivered in 1948.)

Sutherland, Edwin H. *White Collar Crime*. Hinsdale, Ill.: Dryden Press, 1949.

Sykes, Gresham, and David Matza. "Techniques of Neutralization." *American Sociological Review*, 1957, 22:667–669.

Tappan, Paul W. "Who Is the Criminal?" *American Sociological Review*, 1947, 12:96–102.

Taylor, Ian, Paul Walton, and Jack Young. *The New Criminology: For a Social Theory of Deviance*. Boston: Routledge & Kegan Paul, 1973.

Tompkins, Dorothy C. *White Collar Crime: A Bibliography*. Berkeley, Calif.: Institute of Government Studies, 1967.

Townsend, Claire. *Old Age: The Last Segregation (Ralph Nader's Study Group Report on Nursing Homes)*. New York: Grossman Publishers, 1971.

Turk, Austin. *Criminality and Legal Order*. Chicago: Rand McNally, 1969.

Turner, James S. *The Chemical Feast: Ralph Nader's Study Group Report on the Food and Drug Administration*. New York: Grossman Publishers, 1970.

Wellford, Harrison. *Sowing the Wind: A Report from Ralph Nader's Center for the Study of Responsive Law on Food Safety and the Chemical Harvest*. New York: Grossman Publishers, 1972.

Zwick, David, and Mary Benstock. *Water Wasteland: Ralph Nader's Study Group on Water Pollution*. New York: Grossman Publishers, 1971.

Drug abuse

WILLIAM BATES
Loyola University

BETTY CROWTHER
Southern Illinois University, Edwardsville

The use of various substances to change the patterns of human behavior and emotion is so old as to be lost in the legends of the people who first used them. Archaeologists have suggested that the earliest application of cultivated grain may have been for making beer. Mesopotamian tablets that date back to long before Christ lived show us that those early people understood the use of the opium poppy. Homer shows us that the early Greeks knew of the sleep-inducing properties of this flower and of some of the problems associated with its abuse. The relaxing properties of rauwolfia, from which our pharmacists extract reserpine, have been recognized by the physicians of India almost since the dawn of the history of that country.

In the New World other drugs were commonly used. The Indians of Texas and Mexico were aware of the effects of the mescal buttons from certain cacti long before Western medicine discovered that the buttons contained the drug we now call mescaline. The hallucinogenic effects of certain mushrooms have long been recognized not only in the New

World but also in the Old. It has even been suggested that the gospels were an elaborate way of cryptically telling initiates in drug use of the effects of these mushrooms (Allegro, 1970).[1]

In spite of such a widespread, popular familiarity with drugs throughout history, little has been written that offers a comprehensive discussion of drug use and abuse. Most research literature on this topic has usually focused on either a single drug or on a small, select population of users. Other writings consist of essays arguing a particular ethical or political position related to drug use. Therefore, this chapter will summarize the known effects, correlates, and incidence of use of the major families of drugs frequently abused in American society. For the most part, political and ethical issues involved either in drug use or in the laws relative to drugs have been avoided.

The number of substances that mankind can and has used to alter mood or perception is so vast that it would not be possible to treat all of them here. This discussion will thus restrict itself to those substances most commonly used in the United States. Specifically, alcohol, amphetamines, barbiturates, marijuana, hallucinogens, and opiates will be discussed in some detail. All of the drugs mentioned here are subject to control by federal law, and for many of them there are also state and local ordinances that attempt to control the use or distribution of the drugs.

Readers will first be familiarized with the terms that are needed for any discussion of drug abuse to take place, and they will also be introduced to the slang common to the drug subcultures. Next, the cultural context within which drug use takes place will be examined. Following this section will be a brief overview of the major drug categories and the pharmacological properties common to each. Finally, there will be a detailed discussion of each of the drugs with which this chapter is concerned.

THE LANGUAGE OF DRUG ABUSE

There are certain terms frequently used in the discussion of drugs. Several are scientific descriptions of the effect of drug use; many more compose the slang of the drug subcultures. The necessity of knowing the scientific words is obvious: Most scholarly works on drug abuse will assume reader familiarity with these words. The purpose of understanding slang expressions may seem more obscure—until the reader realizes that social scientists must "go to the streets" if their data is to accurately reflect present trends in the use of drugs.

Scientific Terminology

The term *physical dependence* means that after chronic usage of a drug at a specific dosage, the removal of the drug will cause physical signs that are specific for the drug. With opiates, for example, the specific signs include nausea, cramps, and gooseflesh. This specification of physical signs is important. Physical symptoms may accompany withdrawal from drugs having no physical dependence characteristics if the person has developed a psychological dependence on the drug. For example, a person who has grown habituated to a substance such as coffee may exhibit such signs as restlessness, headache, or an ill feeling if the substance is not available. These symptoms, however, are specific to the individual and not to the substance; they will not develop in every individual every time when the substance is not available. Often these psychological withdrawal symptoms are confused with the physical signs that occur when a person who is physically dependent on a drug cannot obtain that drug. Physical dependence, however, refers only to those drugs that cause a physiological change in the person. Furthermore, since psychological dependence can cause such changes, the signs exhibited upon withdrawal must be isolated as specific to that drug.

One can become *psychologically dependent* on any of the drugs discussed here. A psychological or psychic dependence is the feeling of needing a drug despite the fact that removal of the drug will not produce the characteristic physical signs of withdrawal. This is not to say that the individual will not suffer either mentally or physically if the drug is unavailable. It is possible for the person to become quite ill or depressed when the drug cannot be obtained. One must, however, differentiate physical symptoms of withdrawal that are caused by an imbalance in the system from physical symptoms that are psychic in origin.

A drug is said to produce *tolerance* if increased doses of the drug are required to produce the effect for which the drug is being used. For example, if a physician is giving morphine to control pain and finds that the dose must be increased over time to maintain the same control of pain, the patient is said to have become tolerant to the drug. This effect is well known in alcohol use, where the person who is accustomed to the substance can ingest larger quantities without showing the effects of alcohol than can a person who is not so accustomed to its use. Tolerance is a physical reaction to the drug in that the body seems to adapt to a specific dose of the drug. The psychological need for larger doses to produce greater "kicks" is not considered to be the development of tolerance for the drug. Only when one needs to increase the dose to obtain the same effect can one say that tolerance is developing.

Addiction is a difficult word to define in the drug literature. The dictionary's definition is suitably vague, saying it is "the state of being addicted; also habituation, especially to drugs." People who do drug research frequently prefer to restrict the term addiction to those drugs that can produce physical dependence and tolerance and to use the term *habituation* for those drugs that do not show this phenomenon. The World Health Organization has recommended that the term addiction be abandoned in favor of the phrase "dependence of the (name of the drug) type." Some individuals have attempted to restrict it to persons regularly ingesting a particular drug, while others define it in terms of the individual's perceived dependence on the drug. Perhaps the simplest definition is one that limits the term addict to those persons socially acknowledged as narcotic users. This would include all those persons who are known to law enforcement agencies as narcotic users and any person being treated for narcotic addiction or any person convicted of a crime involving narcotic use. Although this definition omits users who have never come to the attention of society and may include others who have never used narcotics, it provides a clear, easily operationalized definition of the addict in terms of a social definition, which may be a more important determinant of behavior than a definition based on use.[2]

The Slang of Drug Subcultures

Any subculture will eventually develop its unique vocabulary. The drug culture is no exception. Street terms have arisen for most of the drugs and for different behaviors associated with them.[3] Although, for the most part, the technical terms will be used and discussed in this chapter, a brief introduction to some of the slang may help the reader to place the information gained here in proper perspective.

A person who is intoxicated on alcohol is said to be "smashed," while a person "high" on marijuana is "stoned." Marijuana itself is called "pot," "grass," or "weed." A single marijuana cigarette is a "joint" or "reefer." High-quality marijuana may be called "gold" or "dynamite." The butt or end of a marijuana cigarette is a "roach," and the holders sold in head shops for it are "roach clips." If you want a large supply of marijuana, you buy a "key" (kilogram, or 2.2 pounds); smaller quantities of a "lid" (22 to 28 grams), a "nickel bag" (a $5 bag yielding from five to eight joints, also called a "matchbox"), or a "dime bag" (a $10 bag) are often purchased by the occasional user.

Amphetamines are usually referred to as "speed" or "uppers," and barbiturates, as "downers." A person using amphetamines regularly is called a "speed freak." The signs seen in the drug culture saying "Speed kills" do not refer to the automobile but rather to the effects of heavy amphetamine abuse.

Lysergic acid diethylamide is "LSD" or "acid" and is usually "dropped" or taken orally. Tom Wolfe (1969), who wrote about Ken Kesey and his merry pranksters, popularized the term "acid test," which is a colorful party at which persons attempt to accelerate the effect of LSD through visual and auditory stimuli. When you "trip" on acid, you may "freak out" or "flip out" or have a "bummer" or "bad trip." If so, it would mean that you have a panic reaction to, or a transitory psychosis from, the drug.

A heroin user is called a "junkie" because he uses "junk" or heroin. This drug is also commonly known as "H," "horse," or "smack." The user may "skin pop" (inject the drug under the skin) or "mainline" (inject the drug into the vein) the drug. At the beginning of his drug use he may "joy pop" or take the drug for pleasure without feeling the physical need for it, but then he will graduate to the state of being "hooked" or dependent on the drug.

A "head" is a drug user. This term is often qualified by the type of drug used, as, for example, an "acid head" or a "pot head." Having drugs in your possession is called "holding," and when you've disposed of the drugs, you are "clean." Your drug supply is your "stash."

Persons taking drugs by injection "hit up" or "shoot up" (inject) the drug. A shot is called a "fix," and the immediate effect is often termed a "flash" or a "rush." You may have a friend "tie off," which means to wrap a cord around the upper arm to distend the vein. A person who uses a needle ("fit" or "rig") to shoot may be a "needle freak," or one who appears to be addicted to the use of needles rather than the drug itself.

It is interesting to examine the differences in the use of slang terms. Although most of the terms presented here are so common as to be readily understood by nearly all persons using drugs, many terms are specific to an area of the country. There do appear to be some noticeable differences between terms used by narcotic addicts and those used in the student drug world. It appears to the authors that the youth tend to have more general meanings for some of the specific terms used by addicts. New terms are constantly appearing in the drug world, particularly as new drugs appear. For example, the authors first heard the term "angel dust" on the East Coast. In attempting to clarify its meaning, several members of the drug culture were contacted in both the East and Midwest. Apparently the term had multiple meanings even on the East Coast, and at the time persons in the Midwest had not heard of it. Now it seems to be most frequently used either to refer to "PCP" (phenylcyclidine hydrochloric acid) or to a mixture of heroin and cocaine; the meaning still depends on the region of the country where it is being used.

THE CULTURAL CONTEXT OF DRUG USE

The dictionary's definition of the word "abuse" is "to use improperly or injuriously." Neither the biological effects nor the extent of use can be given as a definition of abuse for it is the norms and laws of a society that provide the meanings of the words "improperly" or "injuriously" for any substance. To use the terminology of Emile Durkheim (1938), it is a social fact that a specific type of use of the substance is abuse if the public conscience defines the use of the substance as abuse. This point may be made clearer with some examples. In the United States, the sale of cannabis (marijuana) is forbidden by law. In American society, then, outside of rigorously controlled laboratory settings, all use of this drug is defined as abuse. In India, however, marijuana is used in the form of bhang as part of both Hindu and Sikh temple rituals. Among Moslem fakirs, cannabis is used as a means to long life and as an aid to prayer and an access to God. In Nepal it is used by priests of both Buddha and Shiva. Calcutta and Bombay have bazaars where the drug is sold for use in sweetmeats; this combination is considered a delicacy by some of the populace. In none of these societies is such marijuana use defined as abuse, nor is it considered a social problem.

Historically, other examples can be easily found to illustrate the social definition of the word *abuse*. Use of coffee was once defined as abuse in Arabia. The penalty of frequenting a coffee house was death. Tobacco smoking was outlawed in England when it was originally introduced. In Turkey in 1623, use of tobacco was punished by death. In each of these countries smoking later became accepted, and the penalties were abolished. Other societies have defined abuse in terms not of ingestion but of the effects. For example, the New England Puritans accepted the drinking of alcohol, but they severely punished drunkenness. In the United States up until 1914, the use of opiates without a prescription was an accepted fashion as long as the individual was able to function normally.

One might say that most, if not all, societies have some intoxicating substances that are socially acceptable. The use of these substances is controlled by social rituals that tend to define for the user not only the time, place, and amount of acceptable use but also the effects that the drug should produce. Use over the prescribed limits or out of the prescribed times will result in socially inflicted sanctions. Such sanctions will also be forthcoming if the user shows effects of the substances that are not socially acceptable.

When new intoxicants are introduced into a society, there are no socially accepted norms to define the proper occasions for use. The society therefore can define any use as abuse or go to the opposite extreme and provide no definition of abuse. Generally, no norms will be prescribed until after the drug has been accepted into the culture. When there are no socially defined limits of use, users must act on their own judgment, without the assistance of folk norms to control their intake. Since there are no socially defined effects, behavior in the period of intoxication is largely uncontrolled by social norms. One example of this can be seen in the introduction of distilled alcohol in American Indian culture. The drug was not part of the native heritage. In some tribes it became used frequently by people who were attempting to escape from tribal control. Their drinking generally resulted in intoxication that led to fighting and even to murderous assaults on others. In other Indian groups where alcohol was accepted into the culture and defined as a means of becoming happy, such violent results from drinking were not seen. In contemporary Indian groups where alcohol has been integrated according to the norms of the larger American society, the majority can use alcohol without continuing their drinking to the point of drunkenness.[4]

Another example is the introduction of marijuana to the United States. While the larger society did ultimately provide the definition that all use was abuse, such a definition was as good as none to the subcultures that originated the usage of this drug and persisted in its usage. Over the years a set of subcultural norms for marijuana use gradually evolved, but these norms would probably have remained restricted to the subcultures were it not for the fact that one of them—the college subculture—was a bridge to the larger society. As succeeding groups of college students left their subculture, they introduced norms for marijuana use that the larger society found acceptable to some extent. That the American culture is beginning to accept marijuana is evidenced by recent legislation in many states that decriminalizes the use of this drug. Complete acceptance of marijuana may occur in the future, when the society has more fully defined the time, place, and effects of its use, together with suitable users.

Some of the variables affecting the integration of the substance into the culture are availability, the method of introduction, and existing traditions for similar substances. Richard Blum (1969a) provides some evidence that availability affects the degree of use and acceptance into the culture. Cultivation and production of the substance is commonly a consequence of cultural acceptance but may also influence the rate of acceptance: As availability increases, use tends to increase. Further, when it is difficult to obtain one drug, another drug may be substituted in the pattern of use. For example, when marijuana became relatively scarce in 1968, there were reports that loco weed was being used as a substitute in the southwestern United States.

One of the major factors in the acceptance of a new drug is the method by which it is introduced into the culture. The social prestige of the individuals who introduce it or the prestige of the lending culture appears to be highly related to the degree of acceptance into the new culture. When John Hawkins introduced tobacco into England in 1565, it was poorly accepted by the people, but eight years later when Sir Francis Drake brought it again into the country, there was almost immediate acceptance. There has been some speculation that the prestige of Rome was a causal factor in the spread of wine use throughout parts of the Roman Empire. Supposedly a ruler in India started smoking tobacco because the Europeans who introduced it could do nothing foolish, and therefore it must be good. In general it may be said that when a new drug is introduced through the upper social classes or by persons having high prestige, the drug will have a greater possibility of being accepted throughout the culture. LSD is an excellent example of the downward diffusion of a new drug. This substance was first discovered in the laboratory and used by scientists and professionals in medical schools. Use then spread to other professors in the universities and paramedical hospital staff, all of whom have relatively high status in American culture. Later, LSD diffused downward to college and high school students at all social levels.

A new substance will not be integrated into a culture unless it can be fitted into the already existing norms and expectations. Blum (1969a) discusses two patterns of drug use in underdeveloped countries. In such places as India and Pakistan, marijuana has been incorporated into the traditional religious and medical practices without difficulty. In these countries the society does not define its use as abuse and does not see social problems arising from the use. In urbanized Africa, where marijuana use was not integrated into the cultural patterns and rituals already in existence, the opposite phenomenon is seen. Since use was there uncontrolled by social definitions, many adverse effects have been seen.[5]

When the behavioral effects of a drug reinforce or complement existing norms of the borrowing country, acceptance is often rapid. Alcohol use, for example, was readily accepted into the Latin culture, which prizes overt demonstrations of *machismo,* or manliness. H. B. M. Murphy (as quoted by Blum, 1969a) has suggested that cannabis will be relatively easily accepted into a society that places a high value on calm and passive behavior, but that it will be rejected by those societies that value action and aggressiveness. This principle in itself is not sufficient to determine acceptance, but it is one variable operating in this context.

If a substance is seen as filling a need in a society, as being useful for well-being, it will be accepted and integrated into the norms of the society. Coca was used by the Peruvian Indians to combat hunger, fatigue, and cold in the mountain regions. After being culturally defined as an aphrodisiac, mandrake became a popular element in love potions in Europe. African tribes used alcohol to guarantee themselves freedom from harm in battle. Anthropologists have suggested that the Native American Church uses peyote as a symbolic reaction against the larger American culture. Each of these drugs has been defined as useful in meeting existing felt needs of the using group. In other words, drug use tends to be interpreted by the using culture in terms that reinforce the existing norms and perceived needs of that culture.

The definition of drug use or abuse within a society is complicated by the fact that different patterns are acceptable for different people. Nearly all drug use is socially forbidden for some segment of a society. In ancient India, for example, a mistress was permitted to drink alcohol, while it was strictly forbidden for a legal wife. At the turn of the century in the United States, it was socially unacceptable for a woman to smoke, although men were permitted the use of tobacco. In our present society, the purchase of alcohol by children is prohibited by law. Within the Mexican-American culture in this country, the smoking of marijuana was widespread among the lower class but considered socially unacceptable for the middle and upper classes until its spread to college students (Bueno, 1970).

In summary, then, most societies have their own intoxicants for which use, abuse, and effects are controlled by definitions that exist in the culture. In the process of incorporating new intoxicants into the existing norms of the culture, definitions for acceptable use and abuse are developed.

HISTORICAL TRENDS IN AMERICAN ATTITUDES TOWARD DRUG USE

In one sense American society implements prevailing social attitudes towards drugs by imposing legal sanctions designed to control the use of such substances. Therefore, a study of the history of legal action concerning drugs will provide one measure of the society's response to the drug issue. Laws, however, are not passed simply in response to a perceived social need. International events, domestic problems, the concern of certain, small interest groups, or even the actions of a single individual may be the crucial ingredient determining legislative history. The process of formulating and passing the law can bring the public to an awareness of an issue that was never before considered. The actual enactment of the law itself can change or crystallize attitudes and behavior about a subject.

In the United States, attitudes with regard to drugs have undergone considerable change in the past one hundred years. At least as far back as 1878, medical literature reflected the concern of the medical profession for the problem of drug abuse. In the first sociology textbook, Albion Small and George Vincent (1894) discussed the problems arising from the misuse of alcohol and other substances. This long-standing recognition given to the drug problem by both medicine and sociology, however, was not shared by the general public. Although some states passed laws restricting opiate use before 1900, the public did not appear to consider the drug issue a problem until well into the twentieth century. Despite a growing awareness of the issue, the people were not actively concerned until near the middle of the century.

Around 1900 the United States was in the middle of a major social transformation from an agrarian to an industrial nation. At the same time the country was beginning to take an active interest in world events. These two factors—the industrialization of the country and its emergence as a world power—are considered to be the major factors that influenced the people's attitudes toward drug use and the legislation that was passed in the early 1900s.

The rapid growth of industry created the need for an expanded labor force that encouraged the immigration of people from many different nations. Each immigrant group tended to settle in a community of its own, and thus it was easy to identify certain behavior patterns as originating with certain groups. Thus, the Chinese introduced the habit of smoking opium into this country, while the Mexicans brought marijuana smoking. Even though opiates were widely used as an ingredient in patent medicines and marijuana was considered therapeutically useful, the general public came to associate the use of these drugs with ethnic minorities who had low status in this country. Early antidrug legislation appears to be directly related to the prejudice against such peoples.

The Spanish-American War of 1898 involved the United States directly in a drug problem when the country inherited the Spanish government's opium monopoly in the Philippines. This, plus other growing pressures led to the involvement of the United States in the first international drug conference at Shanghai in 1908. This conference

was followed by the Hague Conference in 1912, at which each participating country was urged to enact domestic legislation designed to
control drug use within its own boundaries. These international pressures, combined with a growing public awareness and vocal interest
groups crying for legislation, led to the passage of the Harrison Act in
1914.

Although the public supported the first antidrug laws passed during
the early 1900s, there appeared to be little widespread concern over the
problem. Most individuals considered the evils of drug use to be
isolated within the cultures of various minority groups. It is on record
that the Harrison Act was passed through Congress in a matter of
minutes and then was not even reported in *The New York Times*
summary of that session's work. At that time another drug, alcohol, was
the dominant concern in the public eye.

Still, the passage of the act did have at least two major effects on the
general public. In the first place, criminalizing drug use had a direct
effect on the user and probably an indirect effect on many other people.
There was a tremendous decline in opiate use immediately following
the enactment of the Harrison Act. Since the majority of opiate users
did not consider themselves to be criminals, they apparently changed
their behavior to conform with the law. This had the indirect effect of
making drug use more noticeable to others. The pattern of drug use
started changing in a way that tended to reinforce the general public's
view of such use. Although initially drug use had been associated with
lower-class minority groups, it now, quite realistically, became associated with lower-class criminal types living in urban slums. Thus, the
law had the direct effect of changing the recruitment patterns of opiate
users and the indirect effect of reinforcing existing prejudices against
lower-class persons who often belonged to minority ethnic groups.

The second major effect was more subtle and perhaps more influential to the development of the country as we know it today. Although
the Pure Food and Drug Act of 1906 was a federal regulation, most
direct attempts to control drug use had been a state rather than federal
concern. In the early 1900s most people thought that the federal government should not attempt to control individual behavior of this type.
By arguing that the law was a means of collecting federal revenue and
that the federal government had certain international obligations, the
federal government was able to pass a law that allowed it to restrict

individual freedom. Although the constitutionality of the law was debated in court cases for many years following the passage of the act, the precedent for controlling morality at the federal level had been set.

Apparently there was little active concern over any drug other than alcohol until the middle or late 1940s. Earlier, Harry J. Anslinger, head of the Federal Bureau of Narcotics, had campaigned to draw public awareness to the issue, and his success is evidenced by the passage of the Uniform Drug Act and the Marijuana Tax Act during the 1930s. For the most part, however, such legislation was passed quickly, without widespread opposition or support. It was not until the late 1940s, which saw a trend toward increased use of drugs by young people of all social classes, that Anslinger's campaign against the evils of drugs really began to have effect. The 1950s were characterized by an extreme punitive approach to drug use. In 1951 several states passed laws imposing mandatory minimum penalties for possession of marijuana and other drugs. The Narcotic Control Act of 1956 included some of the harshest penalties: for example, a minimum two-year penalty for possession of marijuana.

By the late 1950s and 1960s a negative reaction to this harsh punitive approach had set in. The American Medical Association, the American Bar Association, and other organizations publically announced that they felt that such an approach was unjust. In 1962, the Supreme Court declared that addiction was a disease rather than a crime. Maintenance clinics, which had first emerged in the late 1950s, began to increase in numbers. In 1966, the Narcotic Rehabilitation Act was passed. This act essentially supported the notion that addiction was a sickness and should not be treated as criminal behavior. In general, people were beginning to consider drug use as an act by a private individual who was sick rather than as an act against society.

An important attitudinal change emerged as drug use spread to youth of all social classes. It became impossible to ascribe drug use to disliked minorities when the problem could be found in the neighboring schoolyard. While the immediate reaction to this trend was the series of harsh sanctions imposed in the 1950s, a more durable change gradually became apparent. As the average American became more concerned with the immediate effects of this problem, the mass media coverage of the topic increased. The individual was exposed to the controversial drug issue though the newspaper, television, and radio, and more viewpoints were expressed by schools, PTAs, and the like. Regardless of the accuracy of the information presented, such exposure had the effect of making people aware of the issue. As the sensationalism of the initial presentations wore off, more and more scientific facts were included in such coverage. Since the prevailing view of scientists working in this area was that drug use is a disease, this orientation was incorporated into the media presentations.

The result of these events seems to be a change in the public's attitude toward drug use. There has been a trend toward more lenient and treatment-oriented responses to the drug problem. Although the typical American is not at present predisposed to legalize heroin, he does seem to be more receptive to laws that stress a treatment orientation (even though the effectiveness of all treatment programs has been questioned). Federal support for treatment facilities has been continually increasing. Maintenance clinics are now operating throughout the country. Possession of marijuana has already been decriminalized in six states. Court cases arguing the constitutionality of the law against possession are presently being fought. Enforcement of the laws is becoming more and more lax, often as the direct result of police policy. In general, the trend seems to be progressing toward a less punitive if not actually supportive position with regard to drug use.

AN OVERVIEW OF THE DRUGS

In the past opiates and marijuana have been classified legally as narcotics with use subject to the same penalties and regulations as the other drugs in that class. Under current federal law marijuana is no longer legally a narcotic but a dangerous drug. Legal classification has, however, tended to obscure the very real differences among the drugs listed. The physiological and psychological effects of marijuana and amphetamines, for example, are nearly opposite, and consequently they should not be lumped together in a single category. Unfortunately, the lay public does not often differentiate among the drug categories but rather groups them all together as "dope."

Therefore, this section is designed to provide the reader with a general overview of the different families of drugs, so that the following section that treats each drug in detail can be placed in proper perspective. It is hoped that the reader can develop a general framework for the typology of drugs so that the similarities and differences in use patterns can more easily be seen. The authors regret the redundancy that results from this procedure, but they are of the opinion that it will produce a clearer presentation.

For each of the families of drugs examined, the following characteristics are presented in the order given: the physical effects of a normal dose, the common medical uses in the United States, typical and abnormal doses, including the effect of an overdose, the effects of long-term use, the presence or absence of physical dependence and any specific withdrawal symptoms, the presence or absence of tolerance, and a brief statement of the legal controls placed on the drug. Space does not permit extensive examination of any of these categories, but the information will be sufficient to give the reader an understanding of each drug.

Amphetamines

Amphetamines are stimulants that act on the central nervous system. They raise both systolic and diastolic blood pressure. Typical physical symptoms include wakefulness, euphoria, and an increased ability to concentrate. The user's speech and actions are more rapid than normal. During a period of initial use, appetite is depressed.

Physicians prescribe amphetamines for depression and fatigue, and they are often prescribed for appetite control in obesity. They are also used for combating certain diseases.

Most amphetamines are taken orally in doses of 2.5 to 5 milligrams two to three times a day. Persons habituated to the drug frequently inject it intravenously. A speed freak may inject the drug many times during the day to maintain his high for several days at a time. This "run" is then followed by an extended period of sleep. Large doses may be taken by a habitual user during a given twenty-four hour period. It has been reported that as much as 6 grams may be taken in a single day if the drug is given in relatively small doses.

Habitual use may result in emaciation and general deterioration caused by the long periods of appetite loss and sleeplessness. Paranoid delusions are common, and auditory and visual hallucinations may result from continued use. This state is often called an amphetamine psychosis. The paranoia combined with the excitability and irritability that often accompany use of this drug may account for the high degree of antisocial behavior found among amphetamine users.

Physical dependence does not occur with this drug, although the user may believe himself to be hooked. Since the drug produces a high level of activity, abstinence often results in a tired feeling accompanied by a severe depression. The user may perceive this effect as physiological withdrawal rather than actual fatigue. Tolerance develops, so that larger doses are needed by the habitual user. Joel Fort (1969) reports a case of an individual having taken 1700 milligrams (340 times the normal dose) in a single dose.

Amphetamines are legally obtained only through medical prescriptions issued by a licensed physician. They are classified as dangerous drugs, with unauthorized use carrying a federal penalty. They are, however, perhaps the most widely abused prescription drug on the market, because physicians frequently prescribe them in large quantities and people can obtain them from more than one physician at a time. In an attempt to control this, the law has recently been changed to require individuals to get only one prescription at a time. Manufacture in unlicensed laboratories is prohibited by federal law, but several such laboratories have been found by authorities.

In general, then, amphetamines produce tolerance but not physical dependence. The psychological reaction to the abrupt cessation of the drug, however, frequently appears. These drugs are stimulants that increase activity level and produce wakefulness and euphoria. Extended concentrated use will produce symptoms of paranoia and general physical deterioration. Habitual users tend to be violent; consequently, they often become isolated from others in the drug-using culture. The drugs are readily available by prescription since many physicians are not adequately informed of the problems that accompany their use. They are also easily found in the illicit market. Legal restrictions apply chiefly to the manufacture and distribution of the drugs, although there are some penalties for illegal use.

Cocaine

A drug much like the amphetamines in its abuse pattern and effects is cocaine. It is an anesthetic and, in moderate doses, a central nervous system stimulant. It increases pulse rate, blood pressure, and respiration. It enhances mental alertness and makes the user more active, talkative, and happy. In large doses, depression follows stimulation, and an overdose can kill the user because of paralysis of the respiratory system.

The chief use in contemporary American medicine is as a topical anesthetic. It is used to anesthetize the nose, throat, and adjacent areas by painting with a 10 to 20 percent solution. In 1 to 4 percent solutions it is also applied to the conjunctiva.

Cocaine has not been shown to cause physical dependence, although psychological habituation is frequently a consequence of use. Unlike the case with amphetamines, tolerance does not develop, but rather there may be the opposite effect of sensitization to the drug. The legal controls on cocaine have been the same as those on opiates.

Barbiturates

Barbiturates are depressants popularly used to produce sleep or relaxation. They have a depressing effect on the central nervous system, the skeletal muscles, the smooth muscles, and the heart muscles. They also act on all levels of the brain, producing effects similar to those seen with alcohol. There may be impairment of mental ability, confusion, and emotional instability after use. A common problem is the distortion of time perception that may result in the individual's taking more pills than intended and consequently suffering from an overdose. It has been hypothesized that many so-called suicides are actually the result of an accidental overdose.

The most common medical use is as a relaxant or sleeping pill. Phenobarbital is used as an anticonvulsant, especially in treating epilepsy. It may also be used to treat the symptoms of alcohol abuse.

Barbiturates are usually taken orally, although some users inject them. A typical dose of amobarbital is 20 to 50 milligrams several times a day. A similar dose of pentobarbitol is 30 to 60 milligrams. In general an overdose in the order of ten times the individual's usual sleep-inducing dose will produce serious effects and can result in death. Overdosing with barbiturates is one of the leading causes of accidental death or suicide.

Chronic use of barbiturates results in a condition very similar to that produced by alcohol. The individual develops a physical dependence as well as a strong desire, or psychological need, to continue taking the drug. The effects of withdrawal are severe, with the symptoms increasing over a period of several days. The individual first appears anxious and then shows a progressive weakness accompanied by dizziness and a distortion of perception. Nausea, vomiting, and a drop in blood pressure are common. In severe cases, convulsions and delirium or a major psychotic episode may occur. Usually an individual will have one or two convulsions during the first forty-eight hours and then become psychotic on the second or third night. Withdrawal from barbiturates is more dangerous for the user than withdrawal from any of the other drugs to be discussed in this chapter.

The habitual user of barbiturates develops a tolerance for the drug in a very short period of time, but there is a limit to the maintenance dose. Beyond a certain point, users do not seem to need to increase their intake continually to obtain the desired effect. This limit, however, appears to be specific to the individual and varies widely with different people. With withdrawal, tolerance is lost, and some persons become more sensitive to the drug than they were before the original habituation.

Legally, barbiturates are classified as dangerous drugs. They may be dispensed by a pharmacist with a prescription signed by a physician, but their purchase does not have to be recorded by the pharmacist. Mild penalties are defined in the law for illegal use.

In sum, barbiturates are drugs producing both tolerance and physical dependence. They are depressants that are similar to alcohol in that they cause confusion and impair mental functioning. Distortion of time perception appears to be the cause of many cases of overdose that result in coma or death. Withdrawal is severe, more so than from the narcotics, and is often accompanied by convulsions and psychotic symptoms; it may result in death. Legal restrictions mainly apply to distribution, as the drug can be legally sold only with a doctor's prescription.

Marijuana

Marijuana, or cannabis, is a plant that, when smoked or eaten, produces euphoria, changes in perception, and changes in time sense. Tetrahydrocannabinol (THC), the chief active agent so far identified in marijuana, has been shown to have a psychotomimetic effect that is dependent on the dosage (Isbell, Gorodetzsky, Jasinski, Claussen, Spulak, & Korte, 1967; Isbell & Jasinski, 1969). In smoked doses of 50 micrograms per kilogram of body weight, it produces changes in mood, chiefly euphoria, and changes in perception but no ataxia (staggering gait). In doses of 200 to 250 micrograms per kilogram, it produces hallucinations in most persons. THC has no significant effects on temperature, systolic blood pressure, and pupillary diameter, but it does increase pulse rate markedly. There is no known evidence that the drug injures body tissue or organs, although there is no research reported on the effects of long-term use.

There is no present medical use for marijuana or THC in the United States. Before marijuana was outlawed, it was used as a sedative-hypnotic, pain reliever, and a tranquilizer (Fort, 1969). Since that time, its only legal use has been in a few research studies on the drug.

When cannabis was legally prescribed as a medicine in the United States, the normal dose in extract form was 15 milligrams. Today, however, normal dosage is difficult to determine since most of the users smoke homemade cigarettes. The illegally obtained drug used in these cigarettes varies so much in quality that it is impossible to determine the actual quantity of THC taken. According to the report of the National Commission of Marihuana and Drug Abuse (1973), most marijuana coming into this country from Mexico has less than .02 percent THC, while that coming from Jamaica and Southeast Asia has from 2 to 4 percent THC. Typically the user smokes from one-half to two "joints" to gain the desired effects. Occasionally the marijuana is baked into brownies or cookies or sprinkled on top of pizza. Since the drug is not water soluble, it is not usually taken by injection.

There is no physical dependence or tolerance shown to be developed for this drug. To date, no controlled studies have shown any mental deterioration from long-term marijuana use, nor have any human deaths been reported from an overdose. With large doses of THC, hallucinations and personality disorganization may occur, although such effects seem to be rare or nonexistent among persons known to be heavy smokers of marijuana.

In the United States there is no legal way of obtaining marijuana except if the drug is to be used for scientific purposes. The penalties associated with obtaining it illegally are the same as those inflicted for other drug law violations, and they are frequently quite severe. In recent years, a number of well-known attorneys, physicians, and other public figures have advocated the legalization of the drug. Although the most recent bill passed in Congress reduces the penalties for possession of marijuana, its sale or possession may still result in imprisonment for many years.

In sum, marijuana has not been shown to produce physical dependence or tolerance. It has a euphoric effect in low doses, and hallucinations and transient psychotic states are produced in high doses. (It is,
however, only 0.7 percent as potent as LSD.) Legal restrictions concentrate primarily on the user and the dealer, both of whom are committing
a felony.

Hallucinogens

The hallucinogens, which include LSD, peyote, mescaline, and psilocybin, are a family of drugs that produce marked changes in mood and
sensory perception. LSD has been shown to produce either euphoria or
depression, visual hallucinations, and a feeling of depersonalization.
Dilation of the pupils and an increase in body temperature and blood
pressure occur. There appears to be wide variations in individual
response to all of the hallucinogens.

Presently there is no medical use for hallucinogenic drugs in the
United States. Although they have been used to treat schizophrenic
patients and autistic children, they are still considered experimental
treatment modalities.

Despite the fact that it is possible to inject it, this drug is usually
taken orally. A normal dose of LSD is between 50 and 200 micrograms,
a quantity too small to be easily seen. For this reason it is usually
combined with other drugs when taken intravenously. A single dose of
peyote is from four to twelve buttons, eaten naturally, brewed into tea,
or ground and put into capsules. Mescaline, a drug derived from
peyote, is generally taken orally in capsule form in doses of from 300 to
500 milligrams. Psilocybin, a hallucinogenic drug derived from mushrooms, is usually taken orally in doses of from 5 to 10 milligrams.
According to Fort (1969), there have been no deaths or damage to body
organs caused by the direct action of LSD, either in massive doses or
from chronic use.

The adverse effects of habitual use of hallucinogenic drugs reported
in the literature have caused considerable controversy. Psychotic or
panic reactions resulting in accidental deaths or suicides or other
damaging behavior have been reported. Fort (1969), however, estimates that such occurrences probably happen on the order of 1 in
10,000 or 100,000 experiences. Despite the fact that popular literature

has frequently suggested genetic damage from these drugs, Daniel Freedman (1969) states that neither European nor American experience in over twenty years of LSD research has clearly pointed to these drugs as causing fetal abnormalities in humans. It should, however, be noted that such damage has been demonstrated in the laboratory in animals. Juhana Idänpään-Heikkilä, Joseph Schoolar, and Alton Allen have flatly stated, "The teratogenicity of LSD in mice has been confirmed and human teratogenicity is quite possible" (1970, p. 65).

There is no evidence that physical dependence develops for any of the hallucinogenic drugs. Strong psychological dependence, however, has been reported for a minority of users. Tolerance is quickly developed but disappears rapidly (Isbell, Belleville, Fraser, Wikler, & Logan, 1956). A. B. Wolbach, Harris Isbell, and E. J. Miner (1962) have shown that there is a cross tolerance among LSD, psilocybin, and mescaline. This means that individuals cannot switch from one drug to another to gain their original high, since the substitute drug will have the effect of the one to which each is habituated. The fact that tolerance does occur also calls into question the statement made by some users that they remained high on the drug for weeks at a time.

The hallucinogenic drugs discussed here are legally classified as dangerous drugs, available only to properly licensed researchers. Manufacture, sale, and possession are controlled by federal law. When peyote is used in certain religious ceremonies by the Native American Church, it is exempt from some of the provisions of these control laws.

In sum, hallucinogens are drugs producing tolerance but not physical dependence. They cause changes in mood and often visual and auditory hallucinations. Considerably more research is still needed on the long-term physiological effects of these drugs before conclusive statements can be made about such effects. Legal restrictions concentrate primarily on the user and the dealer; unlicensed manufacture is a serious offense.

Opiates

Opiates, opioids, or narcotics, to use the common term, include such drugs as opium, morphine, heroin, meperidine (Demerol), and methadone. These are depressants that have a pronounced effect on the respiratory and central nervous systems. They are primarily used to relieve pain, although nonmedical use seems to be due to the euphoria that can accompany use. They do not have the anticonvulsant effects seen in the other types of depressant drugs and consequently do not produce impaired motor coordination. Drowsiness, however, often occurs. There is a decrease in urinary production, a constriction of pupils, and a slight drop in body temperature. Nausea and a loss of appetite may occur, especially when one is not habitually using the drug.

Narcotics are commonly used in medicine to relieve pain. Paregoric is frequently used to treat diarrhea, and codeine can be found in cough syrups. Heroin is not available for medical use in the United States, although it does have legitimate medical use in other countries. Methadone, a widely used narcotic, is often used in treatment of heroin addiction, both as a means of producing gradual withdrawal and as a long-term maintenance substitute.

Narcotics may be injected or administered orally. An average medical dose of injected morphine is from 8 to 12 milligrams; of meperidine (Demerol), 50 to 100 milligrams, depending upon method of administration; and of codeine, 30 milligrams. Injection is considerably more effective than oral administrtion, and therefore the dose tends to vary with the type of administration. A heroin user in the United States buys a "bag" of heroin, which is a small glassine envelope containing from 1 to 25 percent heroin (the remainder will be milk sugar, quinine, and any number of other adulterants). The amount of heroin in an envelope varies by region of the country and by time of year. A single bag, therefore, could contain from 3 to 75 milligrams of morphine. Fatalities resulting from overdoses are relatively common, since the individual is buying poorly controlled illegal heroin. A lethal dose of morphine is usually 120 to 250 or more milligrams, depending upon the individual's level of tolerance.

There is little or no physical deterioration resulting from continued doses of opiates. The habitual user's style of life may produce a number of physical diseases including malnutrition, hepatitis, tetanus, or chronic bronchitis. Other dangers to the physical well-being of the addict arise from the omnipresent possibility of an overdose or from the violence involved in obtaining the drug or the money to buy the drug.

Physical dependence develops rapidly from opiate use, although not, as many people believe, after the first dose. Withdrawal symptoms include anxiety, restlessness, sleeplessness, perspiration, nausea, and other general signs of discomfort. The body temperature rises, as does the respiratory rate and systolic blood pressure. Cramps and vomiting may occur. Many physicians believe these physical symptoms are accentuated by the knowledge that severe withdrawal signs should occur. Patients who become dependent upon morphine in the course of medical treatment and who are unaware of problems of withdrawal seldom show signs of more than mild discomfort during withdrawal. As with many other aspects of drug use, it is often impossible to separate the psychological and physical effects of the drug. Despite occasional "scare" articles in the popular press, Frederick Glaser and John Ball (1970) could not find a single documented case in which opiate withdrawal was the sufficient cause of death.

The habitual user develops a tolerance for narcotics. Larger and larger doses are needed to obtain the pharmacological effects of the drug. Frequently the habitual user then starts combining cocaine or amphetamines with the narcotic in an attempt to regain the original effect of the opiate. When tolerance has built up to the point where cost of the drug is prohibitive, the user will often undergo withdrawal or detoxification. This process reduces the tolerance level so that smaller doses will produce the desired reactions.

Penalties for illegal possession or sale of narcotics are severe. With the exception of heroin, most narcotics can be obtained by prescription. Some, such as codeine, are available without prescription in certain over-the-counter preparations. Physicians who actually give narcotics in the course of treatment are required by law to keep a record of all narcotics dispensed. Manufacture or sale is controlled by federal and state law.

Opiates, then, are drugs that produce both tolerance and physical dependence. They are depressants and are used chiefly in the control of pain. Little or no physical damage has been shown to result from extensive use, although the lifestyle of addicts may be dangerous. Withdrawal is less severe than from, for example, alcohol or barbiturates, although considerable discomfort may be experienced. Legal restrictions for most narcotics apply to the manufacture and distribution of the drug. Possession, sale, or manufacture of heroin is illegal in the United States except for experimental purposes, and penalties for violations are severe.

AMPHETAMINES

Henry Brill (1970) reports in his summary history of drugs that amphetamine was first synthesized by George A. Alles in 1927 to provide a
cheap form of ephedrine. It was used as a nasal decongestant in
inhalers in 1932 and shortly after that period was being used in London
as an intoxicant. The Germans developed methamphetamine prior to
World War II, and both the German and Japanese armies used this drug
as a stimulant for their troops.

Germany quickly recognized the hazards of the drug and in 1941 put
it on narcotic control. In the decade after that, the German medical
literature frequently reported a problem of habituation with the drug.
After the war Japan released its stock of methamphetamine for general
use, and by 1954 Japanese estimates of users in that country were of the
order of two million, with an estimated 10 percent considered serious
abusers. Through stringent legislation in recent years, Japan has
brought the problem under control.

In America, the realization that this drug had a high potential for
abuse was extremely slow, in the light of the experiences of Germany,
England, and Japan. In 1964 the Council on Drugs of the American
Medical Association said that the compulsive use of amphetamines was
a small problem in this country. But in 1966 this same council was
reporting that enough amphetamines were being produced in this
country to supply every man, woman, and child with from twenty-five
to fifty doses a year. Reports on the problems of amphetamine abuse
have appeared in the medical literature since that date.

The three amphetamines most frequently seen and best known as
drugs of abuse in the United States are methamphetamine (Desoxyn,
Methedrine), dextroamphetamine (Dexedrine), and d-1-amphetamine
(Benzedrine). These drugs are listed in their order of potency, with 5
milligrams of methamphetamine having the psychic effect of about 8 or
9 milligrams of dextroamphetamine.

There have been several studies that show the extent of amphetamine use in specific populations within this country. In a study of
medical students, S. N. Smith and Paul Blachly (1966) found that 26.9
percent of the students claimed that they had used the drugs at some
time. Kenneth Eells (1968) reported that 11.1 percent of the students at
the California Institute of Technology claimed some use. The study by

John Francis and David Patch (1969) at the University of Michigan showed that 24.7 percent of the students also claimed use. It seems clear, then, that a relatively large proportion of college students have used amphetamines at some time in their academic career. The mythology that relatively large numbers of students have used these drugs seems, in the light of these studies, to be well founded. The folklore suggests that they are used primarily to stay awake all night to study for a test or to write papers.

It is perhaps not well realized that amphetamine use has also developed in the secondary schools. In a publication released by the Department of Public Health and Welfare of San Mateo County, California (1971), entitled *Five Mind-Altering Drugs (Plus One)*, the authors compared survey data obtained from high school students in 1968, 1969, and 1970. The San Mateo, California, study (1971) showed in 1968 that 16 percent of high school students said that they had used amphetamines during the previous year, and 20 percent made the same claim in both 1969 and 1970. Furthermore, 5.6 percent of the students in the seventh and eighth grades in 1969 and 8.5 percent in 1970 claimed to have used amphetamines during the previous year. This would seem to indicate that amphetamine use may have stabilized in the San Mateo secondary schools but is still developing in the lower grades. This 20 percent figure on the West Coast must be compared with the findings of Betty Crowther and Terry Baumer (1971) for the same year in Southern Illinois. Their research showed that only 6 percent of the high school students reported amphetamine use. These statistics suggest a wide regional variation in the use of this drug.

Two studies on what is termed "hippy" communities have been reported. The one done by J. Fred Schick, David Smith, and Frederick Meyers (1968) in the Haight-Ashbury district of San Francisco showed that 60.5 percent of those interviewed claimed to have used the drug occasionally, 4.6 percent said they used it regularly, and 2.2 percent had used it more than thirty times during the previous month. The study by Theo Solomon (1968) in the East Village in New York City showed that 52 percent of the males and 70 percent of the females claimed to have used the drug. Perhaps the most rigorously designed of all the studies is that of Lee Robins and George Murphy (1967). Their St. Louis sample of black males showed that 17 percent had used amphetamines at some time. Most recently, a nationwide NIDA survey

(O'Donnell, Voss, Clayton, Slatin, & Boom, 1976) estimates that the current use rate of stimulants by its sample of young men is 11.5 percent.

Although these studies are not comparable, and one cannot simply pool the estimates to determine a national figure, it is clear that at least among young people from large cities the amphetamine use may go as high as 25 percent. Within particular subgroups this figure may be considerably higher. This is not a claim that 25 percent of our youths are habitual users. There is a big difference between, for example, saying that 25 percent of our young people have used amphetamines at least one time in their lives and saying that this number is habituated to drug use. It is unfortunate that most of these studies do not provide us with information about frequency of use.

There is one interesting sidelight to the history of amphetamine use that should be reported here. Interviews with large numbers of opiate addicts in the period from 1965 to 1966 showed relatively little evidence of amphetamine use, except as an additive to heroin to increase the effect of the drug. In contrast, interviews with addicts in 1968 showed that some had used amphetamines as their primary drug of abuse sometime in their career. It was seen as a pleasure-giving drug in its own right, not just a simple additive or condiment for heroin.

In the so-called hippy community, the amphetamine that is most frequently discussed is methamphetamine, known to the initiates as speed. People using this drug, especially intravenously, are known as speed freaks, and are frequently feared even by other drug users. In interviews conducted by the authors with individuals who were known as drug users, it became abundantly clear that speed freaks were seen as potentially violent, uncontrollable, and dangerous, especially when they were "crashing" (coming down from the drug). One opiate user reported seeing three assaults in one day in which people were viciously beaten by crashing amphetamine users.

The typical use pattern for speed freaks is intravenous injections of the drug in high doses for several days. This run will last for usually three or four days, but seldom as long as a week. The amphetamine may be mixed with a number of other drugs such as tranquilizers, barbiturates, and sometimes even psychedelics. When the run ends it is followed by a crash, during which the subject may sleep from twenty-four to thirty-six hours. One of the effects of the drug is suppression of appetite, and in massive doses this effect may be so powerful as to make it extremely difficult to eat or drink anything at all. Therefore at the end of the run the subject will be both extremely undernourished and dehydrated. Upon awakening after the crash, he will have a voracious appetite and may gorge himself on anything that he can find to eat. He will also be extremely thirsty due to dehydration. Psychiatric facilities report severe loss of body fluids in patients hospitalized for amphetamine psychosis. It has been suggested that at least some of the psychiatric symptoms may be due to the effect of the dehydration rather than to the direct effect of the drug.

One phenomenon frequently associated with amphetamine abuse is skin sores. Persons using speed over long periods of time will have sores typically on the arms and legs. These are not similar to the infections frequently seen in narcotic addicts; rather, they are sores that seem to the layman to be like the skinned knees of a healthy child. It has been suggested that the sores may be due to unnoticed injuries that occur when high. Another possibility is that they are due to the amphetamine users' habit of picking at various items, including their own skin. Users usually attribute the sores to the effect of the drug itself. Until such sores develop, other speed users are likely to consider a person either a novice or someone pretending to use the drug.

It was mentioned that amphetamine abusers, or speed freaks, are avoided by other drug users as dangerous. It must be recognized that amphetamines are stimulants, while alcohol, barbiturates, and narcotics are depressants having a tendency to put their users to sleep. Although alcohol in some doses reduces control and results in an increase of irritability, as the amount ingested increases, the person using it gets more and more confused and sleepy. With amphetamines, the opposite effect is seen. The drug is a central nervous system stimulant and in less than lethal doses produces both hyperexcitability and irritability. When the paranoia frequently seen with the use of the drug is added to the problem, it is easy to see how such users can be viewed as dangerous.

COCAINE

A drug in many ways similar to amphetamine is cocaine. Long before the coming of the Spaniards, cocaine was known to the Incas of Peru in the form of coca leaves, which were apparently chewed in religious rituals and court ceremonials. With the collapse of the Inca culture through the Spanish conquest, the chewing of coca leaves became almost universal in the Peruvian highlands. These users see the drug as a necessity of life that makes it possible for them to endure the heavy labor, cold, and hunger associated with life in the Andean highlands.

In 1860 Albert Niemann isolated cocaine. Sigmund Freud and other researchers claimed at first that the drug only restored the system to its original normal euphoria and was not at all dangerous. However, even at this time physicians were reporting that cocaine was being abused by morphine addicts. Interestingly enough, cocaine was tried for a short period as a treatment for morphine addiction.

Cocaine has usually been used by heroin addicts in the United States to increase the potency of heroin. For a period of about ten years, there seemed to have been a decline in cocaine use in this country. This was followed by an abrupt rise in the use of the drug in the late sixties. This can be seen in part from the reports of the law enforcement agencies. In 1962 Chester Emerick said that cocaine was not very popular, perhaps because of its high price. The Narcotic Bureau reported that it seized only 2.68 kilograms of cocaine in 1960. By 1967, the yearly total had risen to 20 kilograms, and in May 1970 the Mexican police in Tijuana discovered 15 pounds of cocaine prepared for delivery in the United States. During this year reports of seizures were made from Oakland (California), Puerto Rico, Kansas City (Missouri), Los Angeles, Philadelphia, and, of course, New York. It is clear then that by 1970 cocaine had been transported over much of the United States.

Perhaps because the drug is still relatively new compared to amphetamines and heroin, persons using it as their primary drug of abuse are not frequently seen. One person interviewed learned to use the drug from an otolaryngologist with whom he was drinking. This physician, according to the subject, offered him cocaine when they had to leave the bar at closing time. After that, the physician kept him supplied both from his own personal source and by prescription. The subject claimed the drug was both cheaper and easier on his system than alcohol.

With the advent of amphetamines, cocaine seemed almost to vanish from use. It is possible that the amphetamines, taking on the aspect of a fad, simply pushed the cocaine out of the market. In recent years, not only has cocaine use increased in the United States, but there has been a parallel increase in Britain, as evidenced by reports of 25 users in

1958 and 443 users in 1966. Since other countries have also made similar reports, it may well be that this increase in cocaine use is occurring throughout the industrialized world.

BARBITURATES

The first sedative-hypnotic drug developed for use in modern medicine was chloral hydrate in 1869. Then in 1903 the first barbiturate, barbital (Veronal), was developed. It was a relatively long time before the dangerous properties of these drugs were recognized. As Carl Essig (1970) notes, withdrawal convulsions were reported as early as 1905, but this and subsequent reports of the danger of the drug do not seem to have been heeded. The first prescription control of these drugs in the United States was not enacted until New York City passed a control act in 1922. Moreover, it was not until the publication of research indicating that the withdrawal symptoms were due to true physical dependence (Isbell, Altschul, Kernetsky, Eisenman, Flanary, & Fraser, 1950) that the serious addictive properties of barbiturates were really recognized by the medical profession. In view of the vast amount still prescribed, however, one might wonder if this profession is presently aware of the problems associated with the drugs and their abuse potential.

Although all barbiturates are abused, the ones most frequently seen are the powerful, quick-acting drugs such as pentobarbital (Nembutal, "nembies," "yellow jackets"), secobarbital (Seconal, "red devils"), amobarbital (Amytol, "blues"), and the combination known as "rainbows" or "Christmas trees." Persons primarily addicted to barbiturates characteristically eat the drugs like candy during the day and take a massive dose at bedtime. The drugs are normally taken orally in capsule form by persons whose primary addiction is barbiturates, amphetamines, or both. At times, however, opiate users who are accustomed to taking their drugs intravenously attempt to take the barbiturates in this fashion. Since these drugs are quite irritating to the skin, this mode of use can lead to a very serious ulcerous condition.

To understand the importance of barbiturates in the total drug picture, one must first look at the extent of barbiturate use. William Skinner (1969) has estimated that in 1964 2.3 billion 100 milligram doses were sold in the United States; this amount increased to 2.4

billion in 1965 and to 2.7 billion in 1967. This means that the legal sources of drugs in the United States were supplying about 17 doses per person for everyone in the United States over the age of ten. Furthermore, in 1962 Food and Drug Commissioner George P. Larrick estimated that half the barbiturates produced in the United States found their way into the illegal market. If this estimate continued to hold, then in 1967 there should have been about 34 doses per person available on the legal and the illegal market combined.

Research published by Blum (1969b) has shown that in 1965 college students who claimed that they had used sedatives ranged from 18 percent to 31 percent in the various schools studied. The study at the California Institute of Technology showed that 7 percent of the study group claimed to have used barbiturates (Eells, 1968). On May 26, 1969, the Gallup Poll reported 10 percent use among college students in a national sample. A repeat poll done six months later showed that this had increased to about 11.1 percent (Gallup Poll, October 26, 1969).

It should be noted that barbiturate use has also developed in the high schools. In his California sample of 1966, Blum (1969b) reported that 4 percent of the male high school students and 6 percent of the female high school students claimed to have used barbiturates. Fort (1969) found 10 percent of the boys and 15 percent of the girls in his California twelfth grade sample had used this drug. In 1970 the San Mateo County High School study (1971) showed that 16 percent of the students reported barbiturate use. Crowther and Baumer (1971) found 6 percent reported use among high school students in the Midwest. These figures suggest that a significant proportion of the high school population has at least experimented with these drugs.

Again, it should be remembered that each of the studies reported here is limited to a specific place and time. Without national surveys at regular intervals it is impossible to determine what the actual level of barbiturate use is or whether illegal use is increasing or decreasing in the country as a whole. It should be noted, however, that the Federal Bureau of Narcotics and Dangerous Drugs has been reporting seizures of far more illegally distributed amphetamines than barbiturates. This may be due at least in part to differential enforcement of the law or a differential allocation of police for various reasons, but it would seem indicative of the fact that illegal use of barbiturates is less than the illegal use of amphetamines. This is not inconsistent with findings of specific studies. Thus Eells (1968) who reported that 7 percent of his group used sleeping pills without medical advice, shows that 11 percent used amphetamines. Similarly, the San Mateo study found 16 percent using barbiturates and 20 percent using amphetamines, and the NIDA study (O'Donnell, Voss, Clayton, Slatin, & Boom, 1976) showed a use rate for sedatives of 8.8 percent and for stimulants of 11.5 percent. In both the Midwest studies reported here (Robins & Murphy, 1967; Crowther & Baumer, 1971), an almost identical number of subjects reported amphetamine and barbiturate use. In its report of frequency of use, however, the Robins and Murphy study showed that only 2 percent used barbiturates regularly, while 7 percent used amphetamines regularly. Sidney Cohen (1969) found that eighteen of the LSD users he studied had used amphetamines, but only seven had used barbiturates. It would therefore seem safe to state that at the present level of knowledge, barbiturates have been used at about half the rate of amphetamines.

MARIJUANA

Marijuana, Indian hemp, or cannabis—also known as pot, grass, or weed in the youth culture—is a plant that grows wild throughout much of the world. It was commercially cultivated in the United States, especially during World War II, as a source of industrial hemp. In the midwestern states, where it was grown in large areas, it went wild and can still be found growing in ditches, along the side of the roads, and in the fields within the farming areas.

Marijuana is used in various forms throughout the world. In Islamic cultures, where alcohol is forbidden by the Koran, it is widely used and socially accepted in some circles just as alcohol is in the United States. In these areas it is not only smoked, both in the form of cigarettes and in pipes, but it is also used in making small cakes or cookies and brewed in tea.

In the United States, one major source of marijuana seems to be locally grown wild plants, although law enforcement people frequently report fields where they have found the plant under cultivation. It is also imported into the United States from Mexico or Jamaica under the terms "Acapulco Gold" or "Jamaica Gold." Some of it, especially in the form of hashish, comes from the Middle East.

The most potent part of the hemp plant is the flowering top of the female plant. This flowering part and the upper leaves are processed by curing (drying) and crushing to form either a coarse or powdery substance that is usually smoked in a pipe or cigarette. Alternately, marijuana may be processed to produce hashish, a form of cannabis containing more of the resin than is usually found in marijuana. It has been estimated that hashish is about six times as potent as marijuana. Hashish, or hash as it is commonly called, is usually imported from the Middle East, not infrequently from Turkey. Marijuana from India is usually termed bhang, ganja, or charas, terms for the plant from the native languages. In Morocco, the drug is known as kif. These foreign forms are processed so that there is a greater concentration of the resin than in the marijuana usually prepared in the United States. Because of this greater potency, they are highly prized and more expensive than the forms prepared in this country from local material.

Most studies on drug use among youth in the United States find marijuana to be the most popular drug used, other than alcohol and tobacco. Estimates of use range from 0 to 90 percent, depending on the group studied. If one were to examine only newspaper reports, one might conclude that half of our high school students and all of our college students smoke pot. In controlled and serious studies, however, incidence is considerably lower. A number of studies from California suggest that the use rate for high school and college students in that area is between 30 and 50 percent, while reports from other parts of the country usually find lower percentages. The Denver study of James Barter, George Mizner, and Paul Werme (1970) reported that 26 percent of the college students surveyed had used marijuana at least once.

Since drug use differs widely throughout the country, these findings are limited to the areas where the studies were done. It should also be remembered that questionnaire surveys may provide biased estimates of use. In areas such as the Midwest where conventional norms within the schools tend to be against drug use, students are probably inhibited from reporting experimentation with drugs, while in other areas there may be peer pressure to report use, even if the individual has never tried the substance. In addition, all such surveys rely on the person's cooperation in filling out the instrument. It may be that many marijuana users, and especially the heavy users, would fail to cooperate, thus lowering the estimates of use in the area.

A nationwide survey of high-achieving high school students found that 10 percent of the group stated current use of marijuana (Merit Publishing Company, 1970). One interesting fact to be noted is that 21 percent said they would use it if it were legalized. This survey also reported use in different parts of the country. The largest use was found in the Northeast and West, with the South, Southwest, and Midwest reporting lower figures. Crowther and Baumer (1971) found that 13 percent of a large midwestern high school sample reported at least one-time marijuana use. In contrast to this relatively low figure, the 1970 San Mateo study (1971) found that 51 percent of the seniors and 34 percent of the freshmen had used marijuana at some time during the previous year.

There is some evidence that marijuana use is increasing in the United States. In the past few years law enforcement agencies have reported ever-increasing seizures of marijuana. The report by the President's Commission on Law Enforcement and Administration of Justice (1967) showed that the Bureau of Narcotics arrests for marijuana offenses doubled from 1960 to 1965. In California, there had been 4,100 adults arrested on marijuana charges in 1960. By 1964 this figure had gone to 6,055, an increase of 50 percent; by 1968 it had risen to 34,000. It is possible that this increase indicates only that law enforcement people increased their vigilance by such activities as Operation Intercept at the Mexican border. Increasing reports from school officials in both secondary schools and colleges, however, lead one to suspect that there has been an increase in the number of people using the drug.

In the San Mateo study (1971) researchers found an average 8 percent increase in use from 1968 to 1969 and another 2 percent increase the following year. They also examined the percentage increase of persons reporting frequent use (ten or more times during the past year) and found a nearly identical increase. These changes are interesting when they are compared with similar figures for other drugs. In the interval from 1968 to 1969, there was an increase in the use of all other drugs examined except tobacco, which showed a decrease. During the next year, however, marijuana and alcohol were the only drugs showing a slight positive increase, while the use of LSD and amphetamines actually decreased.

Other studies, especially in the California area, have shown dramatic increases in marijuana use during the period from 1966 to 1970. At

Stanford University, Blum (1969b) found 21 percent of his sample reporting marijuana use in 1966. One year later this figure rose to 57 percent, and the following year it jumped to 69 percent. Another study conducted at Yale University by Lillian Imperi, Herbert Kleber, and James Davis (1968) found an increase from 18 percent to 49 percent from 1967 to 1968. While such dramatic increases in use are not characteristic of the entire country, the NIDA study (O'Donnell, Voss, Clayton, Slatin, & Boom, 1976) has estimated that 37.9 percent of their total sample have used the drug. Still, it is difficult to interpret information about this subject, for use patterns are changing so rapidly that data obtained one or two years ago is almost obsolete. Furthermore, since these studies do not report frequency of use, it is difficult to know how accurately the figures reflect current use, expecially in the light of information that states that 41 percent of the adults and 45 percent of the youths who said they have used marijuana at some time are now no longer using the drug (National Commission, 1972).

When large numbers of the peer youth culture are using a drug, experimentation with the drug is no longer a high-risk exciting novelty. Norms for use develop and guide the new users into accepted patterns of behavior. This group stability and increased understanding of the effects of the drugs have apparently caused a decrease in the number of "bad trips" associated with the use of both marijuana and LSD. At the same time, the rapid change in the constitution of the drug-using group makes statements about the phenomenon problematic.

Marijuana use has often been called a middle-class white phenomenon. This statement, however, does not seem to be warranted. In Mexico and in the southwestern United States it was considered to be the drug used by peons and criminals. The article by Dario Urdapilleta Bueno (1970) contains a fascinating discussion of the development of marijuana use in Mexico. Although Blum (1969b) did find that users were most often from wealthy families, a large proportion of other students reported use. Blumer, Sutter, Ahmed, and Smith (1967) found a majority of black and Mexican-American youth of the Oakland flats used the drug on a regular basis. Robins and Murphy (1967) showed that 46 percent of their black sample admitted having used marijuana even though the sample had been chosen to be representative of the urban black population and not of the drug-using population. Crowther (1974) showed that in a population of addicts 82 percent of the Mexican-

American addicts said that they had tried marijuana before opiate use, and 88 percent had used marijuana at some time in their drug-using career. These findings show that marijuana use is not limited to middle-class white youths, but rather it may be used even more extensively in lower-class minority groups.

A more likely explanation for the middle-class myth and recent publicity about marijuana use among high school and college youth is that middle-class Americans tend to become concerned only when their own children begin using a drug. At this point, money and community action are brought to bear on the situation that is seen to be evil. Not until it began to invade, and consequently threaten, the middle-class group did a large number of people begin to take an active interest in marijuana use. It should be noted, however, that among college students marijuana use does seem to be concentrated in upper- and middle-class students.

Marijuana is not smoked only by youth. One study found that 11 percent of a sample of San Francisco adults had tried the drug, and 81 percent of the males between the ages of 18 and 29 had used it sometime in their lives (Manheimer, Melinger, & Balter, 1969). The percentages by age categories decrease rapidly, with only 1 percent of the men over 55 reporting use. The report of the National Commission on Marihuana and Drug Abuse (1973), usually known as the Shafer Report, estimates that 40 percent of the 18–21 year olds, 38 percent of the 22–25 year olds, and 6 percent of those over 50 have used marijuana at some time. In an earlier study, Blum (1969a) found that 9 percent of an urban adult population had used marijuana. Although additional studies based on adult populations are needed, these figures suggest that the drug is starting to invade the older age groups. Despite the fact that the Manheimer, Melinger, and Balter study with its high figures represents only California, it is not unlikely that adult use is increasing in other parts of the country. It is therefore not unreasonable to conclude that marijuana use appears to be increasing in every age group. It might be noted that this pattern resembles the assimilation of other innovations into a culture.

One subject on which there is much conflicting literature is the effects of marijuana. To understand at least part of the problem, one must realize that breathing any heavy vapor—smoke, gasoline, carbon tetrachloride—will reduce the oxygen supply and produce a sensation of dizziness or light-headed giddiness. If one experiences this sensation in a social situation that defines it as pleasurable, one can learn to seek this sensation. Howard Becker (1953) has emphasized the social learning of marijuana use. He argues that users learn the definition of the effects of marijuana as pleasurable from the context in which they are introduced to the use of the substance. This argument is further substantiated by the fact that users have been known to get high after smoking "marijuana" that on analysis proved to be alfalfa or other nontoxic plant leaves. In the study by Crowther and Baumer (1971), 53 percent of the students who had used marijuana said that they did not think they got high the first time they used the drug, while 25 percent said that they had never been high. In other studies it has been found that some naive subjects can be given marijuana in a laboratory setting without experiencing the subjective effects typically described by marijuana users. Marijuana, then, produces at least some of its subjective effects from this process of learning to enjoy the dizzy feeling resulting from the lack of oxygen.

Research on the effects of marijuana had long been hampered by the difficulty of finding the chemical substance that was responsible for the reported phenomena. Research using as a stimulus the material sold as marijuana on the illicit market would be much like attempting to delineate the effects of quinine by using as a stimulus chinchona bark gathered from different parts of the world, processed in an unknown manner, and containing different mixtures of impurities. It has only been within the last few years that biochemists have been able to extract the principle active ingredient of marijuana and, by controlling the effects of anoxia and impurities, demonstrate its own proper effect. Y. Gaoni and R. Mechoulam (1964) showed that delta-9-trans-tetrahydrocannabinol (hereafter called THC) occurs in hashish. F. Korte, M. Haag, and U. Claussen (1965) isolated this drug and proved its purity and structure. Research done at the Lexington Addiction Research Center in Kentucky demonstrated that when THC is smoked, it produces an effect that was identified by persons who had used natural marijuana as being marijuana-like (Isbell, Gorodetzsky, Jasinski, Claussen, Spulak, & Korte, 1967; Isbell & Jasinski, 1969).

The Lexington research on THC showed that it is a psychotomimetic whose subjective effects resembled those seen after the administration of lysergic acid diethylamide (LSD). Changes in mood, usually euphoria, were found after doses of 50 micrograms per kilogram of body weight were smoked. These changes were reported by subjects as similar to those produced by marijuana. When the smoked dose was increased to 200 to 250 micrograms, the subjects reported disturbances of visual and auditory perceptions, depersonalization, and hallucinations. Two of the subjects had to be dropped from the experiment after experiencing psychotic reactions.

Similar findings had been reported in the now classic 1944 LaGuardia Report, the popular name for the study by the Mayor's Committee on Marijuana. Among seventy-seven prisoners observed after drinking an undetermined amount of marijuana concentrate on several occasions, nine psychotic episodes were found to occur. Although inadequate controls were used in this study, it would appear that at least six of the nine psychoses were the result of extremely large doses of the marijuana concentrate.

Both of these studies have been attacked on several grounds (for example, c.f. Kaplan, 1970), particularly for their use of abnormal subjects. Isbell used known ex-opiate addicts, and the New York study used former prisoners. Isbell's group had been examined, though, and had shown no signs of serious mental disturbances. It should be noted that in both groups the psychotic episodes were transient. To the present authors' knowledge, there have been no known cases of permanent psychoses that can be directly attributed to the use of marijuana or THC, even in high doses.

Although both LSD and THC have produced alterations in perception and mood, the physical effects of these drugs are quite different. After the administration of LSD, Harris Isbell and D. R. Jasinski (1969) reported that the subjects showed an increase of body temperature, pulse rate, and blood pressure. There was also an increase of pupillary size and lowering of the threshold for the knee jerk. THC, on the contrary, had no significant effects on temperature, systolic blood pressure, pupillary diameter, or threshold for the knee jerk. Clinical observation did not detect any ataxia or staggering gait. The outstanding effect of the THC was the development of marked tachycardia, or high pulse rate. The time of the peak effect of this drug, in terms of the subjective phenomena, was one-and-a-half hours, and for the objective effect, two hours.

It is clear, then, that the known active agent in marijuana is a drug that produces both physical and psychological effects. In extreme doses it is potentially dangerous, but so are large doses of any drug, including alcohol. It must also be realized that this laboratory drug, THC, is not the same as the natural plant material usually smoked as marijuana. As of this writing the authors have found no evidence that THC is available on the street despite contrary claims by dealers and users. For example, Chauncey Leake (1969) reports that material sold as THC on the streets of San Francisco was discovered later to be amphetamines and other substitutes.

John Kaplan, after reviewing many studies on the effects of marijuana, concludes:

> [A]ll we can say at the present is, first, that if marijuana use does cause mental deterioration, it has not yet been noted in any careful look at the problem; second, that whatever damage the drug does cause must be fairly subtle at least as compared with the easily observable and fairly gross effects of long-term alcohol abuse; and finally, with reference to the calls for "more research" before any changes are made in the law, if one wished to be absolutely certain that marijuana . . . did not cause subtle, long-term brain damage, the task would take at least a generation (1970, p. 183).

A question frequently asked is whether marijuana smoking leads to heroin or other drug abuse. When Michael Pescor (1943) published his report on the early Lexington addicts, he noted that only a few addicts had used marijuana. Life history research on heroin addicts in New York, Lexington, and Fort Worth, Texas, however, shows that a very large percentage of them had previously used marijuana. Among the Fort Worth Mexican-American and Anglo sample admitted to the hospital in 1968–1969, 74 percent had reported marijuana use before heroin and other opiate use (Crowther, 1974). Still every study of addict populations known to the authors has shown that at least some of the heroin users had never previously used marijuana. It is, threfore, evident that marijuana use is not a necessary condition for future opiate use. The 1967 Robins and Murphy study reported that only 27 percent of the subjects who had used marijuana went on to try heroin, and further, that only 21 percent became addicted to heroin. In his study of college students, Blum (1969b) found that 78 percent of the opiate users had used marijuana, but that only 6 percent of the marijuana users had tried opiates. The Shafer Report (National Commission, 1972, p. 110) states that marijuana use per se does not dictate whether other drugs will be used; nor does it determine what the rate of progression will be if and when the use of other drugs does occur, or which other drugs might be used.

Examination of arrest records shows that since 1961 marijuana arrests have increased rapidly, while opiate arrests have remained about the same. If the two drugs were causally related, one would expect to see a parallel increase in use and, consequently, in arrest records. These data, then, seem to make it clear that marijuana use is neither a sufficient nor a necessary condition for heroin use in the United States. Arguing a causal relationship from the evidence that a high percentage of heroin users have also used marijuana is similar to arguing that there is a causal relationship between the use of milk and heroin, since as far as we know 100 percent of the heroin users used milk, at least as infants.

This is not to say that there is no relationship between the use of heroin and the use of marijuana. Both are illegal substances, and often the contact person for one drug can either obtain or assist the individual in obtaining the other drug. It is likely that the lifestyle associated with the use of any illegal drug increases the probability of a person coming into contact with other illegal drugs and hence makes experimentation with other drugs, including heroin, more likely. Erich Goode (1969) has pointed out that this association of marijuana with other drugs holds only when the other drugs are commonly accepted in the user's subculture. Middle-class marijuana users would be more likely to use LSD than would nonusers, but they would not use heroin if it were not used by others in their peer groups. Thus, according to this perspective, marijuana use becomes a prediction of heroin use only for those lower-class persons interacting in an environment where heroin is available.

Marijuana use, along with other drugs, has become a symbol for a large proportion of the youth in this country. Like long hair and hip clothes, marijuana smoking has become a symbol of acceptance among certain groups. Kaplan (1970) presents an interesting position when he argues that marijuana has become a symbol not only for the young people but also for the older generation. His thesis is that the older generation can place the blame on drugs for the unacceptable behavior of the younger generation and thus escape any personal responsibility for their behavior. Drugs thus can become a symbol of the moral issues separating the young from the old. In this context marijuana use has become far more important than any physical or psychological effects due to the chemical properties of the drug.

It has often been said that the most potent argument against using marijuana is the possibility of arrest and imprisonment. Since this subject is controversial at the moment, a few remarks on the legal aspects of marijuana use may be relevant here. First, however, it should be noted that sociologists have no special expertise that makes it possible for them to say what the law should or should not be. At best, when adequate research has been done, sociologists may be able to predict the probable effects of certain legal changes.

Long prison sentences have not been much more effective in halting the use of marijuana than they were effective in stopping alcohol use during Prohibition. Although one might well question whether it makes sense to legalize another intoxicant in a society that already has a large problem from the use of alcohol, one must at least look at the cost to society of the present marijuana laws. Financially, the cost of arresting and processing the thousands of marijuana offenders is staggering. There were, for example, 51,000 arrests in 1968 in the state of California alone. Further, a large proportion of marijuana offenders are not caught, and thanks to the inefficiency and leniency of our legal system, many who are arrested are not convicted and sent to prison. This discrepancy between the ideal and actual legal penalty may convince the youthful offender that the law is something that need not be respected in our society. Another problem arises in that enforcement of the law tends to discriminate against those who openly flaunt their rebellion against society through dress, hairstyle, or other signs of other deviance and those who are frequent targets for discrimination, such as members of ethnic or religious minority groups. Observation of such societal action may produce an even greater sense of alienation and injustice among young people of today.

HALLUCINOGENS

The use of hallucinogenic substances is buried in the mists of human history. Use of the sacred mushroom to obtain visions, use of peyote to obtain union with God, and use of ibogaine to promote group interaction are all so old that knowledge of their origins is lost.

The first extremely potent synthetic hallucinogen, LSD, was developed in 1938, but its hallucinogenic properties were not recognized until 1943. Its use for pleasure first developed in medical circles because it had been the subject of various types of research on mental illness by psychiatrists. From this origin, it quickly spread to college faculty and students and then into the community, where it became the symbolic drug for many so-called hippy communes.

Other drugs with effects resembling those of LSD include mescaline, psilocybin, psilocin, and a wide variety of "alphabet" drugs, including DOM, DET, and PCP. Most of these drugs are new and are considered experimental in medicine. They have not been shown to cause physical dependence, and the physical dangers of their use are poorly documented. Since the number of such substances available is so large and changes so rapidly, it would be impossible to give an account of them all. Therefore the following discussion is concerned with the hallucinogens as a group unless otherwise specified. It should be remembered, however, that respondents may be thinking only of LSD when they are asked questions about hallucinogens.

Research on California college students has shown that 6 percent of the men and 3 percent of the women have used hallucinogens (Blum, 1969b). The study by Francis and Patch (1969) at the University of Michigan showed that although 12.2 percent of the students had used hallucinogens, 81 percent of these users reported only one time use or seldom use. A study by Richard Morrison (1969) at Sacramento State College showed that 4.8 percent of the students had used LSD, and of these 52 percent had used from one to three times. Eells' 1968 study of students at California Institute of Technology showed that 5.5 percent had used LSD and 2.3 percent had used morning glory seeds.

It would seem reasonable to conclude from these data that despite newspaper reports, less than 10 percent of college students have ever used hallucinogens. When one considers regular use, it is doubtful whether more than 5 percent of the college population are users.

Hallucinogens, like other drugs, have also been used in high schools. The San Mateo study (1971) showed that in 1970, 14.4 percent of high school students had used LSD during the previous year. If one looks at the use by senior-class boys over four years, one sees that the fad seems to have peaked. In 1967, 9.6 percent reported use; in 1968, 16.6 percent; in 1969, 23.0 percent, and in 1970, 17.4 percent. The NIDA study (O'Donnell, Voss, Clayton, Slatin, & Boom, 1976, p. 57) reports that the peak year for psychedelics was 1969.

A study done in San Francisco between 1967 and 1968 showed that 3 percent of the adult population had used LSD at some time (Manheimer, Melinger, & Balter, 1969). Since few studies have focused on this population, it is impossible to provide accurate data on adult use. It is doubtful, however, that large numbers of adults have experimented with this particular drug. The previously reported study of Schick, Smith, and Meyers (1968) showed that 87 percent of the Haight-Ashbury population in his sample had used LSD. A similar study done by Solomon in 1968 in New York City showed 97 percent of the men and 80 percent of the women had used LSD at some time. Some subgroups report extremely high rates of use, suggesting that the common bond for the group may be its use of drugs. The folklore within the drug culture would suggest that this phenomenon is more likely among LSD users than among other types of drug users.

This review of some of the research literature clearly indicates a wide variation in LSD use by age and region. The secondary school data also indicates what has already been reported anecdotally: that the use of LSD and similar hallucinogens has started to decline, perhaps due to the negative effects experienced by some users.

There are several drugs that are either used with LSD or substituted for it. These are PCP (phencyclidine hydrochloric acid), DOM (called STP on the street, 4-methyl-2,5-dimethoxyamphetamine), DMT (*N,N*-dimethyltriptamine). These are usually manufactured in clandestine laboratories and sold on the street. Unlike a large number of the drugs discussed, it is rare for them to come into the illegal market from licensed laboratories.

Two of these drugs have interesting histories that will give some insight into the drug-using culture. In 1968, San Jose, California, saw a new drug on the market, "hog," that was supposed to be much better than LSD. When the drug was subjected to laboratory analysis, it was found to be PCP, a prescription anesthetic made for injection in primates. Some batches of this drug, also known as the peace pill, have been found by the Bureau of Narcotics and Dangerous Drug (BNDD) laboratories, to have been adulterated with LSD. Another interesting fact is that PCP has been reported to have been adulterated with strychnine and sold as THC.

In 1967 a new drug, STP, was widely touted as the best trip yet. When the drug was sent to the BNDD laboratories, it was found to be DOM, whose name had been changed apparently as a "put on" by the drug-using community. The illicit manufacturers apparently expected to make a fortune from it. Unfortunately, at least for the manufacturers, the drug circles quickly filled with stories of "bad trips" from the drug. As a result, sale of the drug in the illegal market has remained low.

There seem to be two distinct groups in which hallucinogen use is most likely to be found. The first, and the stereotype of the hallucinogen users, is the "hippy" group. Although not all hippy groups use LSD, those who do tend to have a number of characteristics in common. Although many members of such groups are generalized substance users, the drug of choice is LSD or drugs that they expect to have the same effect. Many of these people have moved out of such places as the Haight-Ashbury district of San Francisco because their own self-image is that of peace-loving contemplative people. When their districts became invaded by amphetamine, and sometimes even heroin, users, with the consequent increase of violence and crimes against property— theft, muggings, and purse snatchings—many moved to rural communes where people who were violent were not encouraged to come.

The second group of hallucinogen users are the professional people. College professors, physicians, and medical students were the persons originally introduced to the hallucinogens. More than twenty years ago Aldous Huxley wrote his famous work *Doors of Perception* (1954), in which he discussed his personal experimentation with mescaline. Much of the early attention to LSD came from the work of Timothy Leary, who at the time was associated with Harvard University. In this population, the drug is used occasionally and usually in association with other people, perhaps as a substitute for alcohol. Here it is almost never taken with other drugs, and the users are unlikely to use any other drugs, with the exception of alcohol, marijuana, and tobacco.

OPIATES

The use of the opium poppy as a relief for pain—both physical and mental—is almost as old as humankind. Similarly, problems associated with this drug have been known for as long. Even Homer showed awareness of its ability to lure men into a dream world. Opium use in China was seen as so destructive that the Emperor issued an edict in 1796 forbidding opium use under pain of death.

Morphine, an alkaloid extracted from opium, was developed in 1804 and, with the invention in 1885 of a practical syringe, became a widespread injected medication. After the Civil War so many veterans used the drug that morphine addiction was called the "soldier's disease." In the last decade of the nineteenth century, the medical literature contained repeated warnings about morphinomania and its treatment. In 1898 a new morphine derivative was developed that was seen as a cure for morphinomania—heroin. It required several years for the medical profession to become aware of the addictive properties of heroin, and by then morphine addicts had already started to substitute the heroin for their original drug of addiction.

Even before the development of heroin, opiate use was widespread throughout the United States. Charles Terry and Mildred Pellens (1970) estimate that there were 251,936 chronic users in 1874 and 182,215 in 1885. The authors consider both of these estimates to be well below the number of actual users at the time. They have further estimated that by 1913, one year before the passage of the Harrison Act, the number of users had risen to 782,118. If one accepts the validity of these estimates, one must conclude that there was considerable opiate use long before public demand was sufficient to legislate against the drug.

Earle Simrell (1970) reports that state and local measures of control were tried as early as 1885. By 1909 Congress had passed an act prohibiting the importation of opium for other than medical purposes. This act flatly excluded smoking opium from the country. The well-known Harrison Act was passed in 1914 to control narcotic use. It is possible that the passage of this act was at least in part a response to the "muckrakers" of the time. They wrote attacks on patent medicines and nostrums produced by the manufacturers who were making fortunes out of human misery.

Isbell (1963) points to two aspects of the opium smoking habit as contributory to the antiopium sentiment in the United States. In certain parts of the country opium smoking spread rapidly among the antisocial and delinquent elements of the society. It spread so rapidly that the importation of smoking opium increased from 20,000 pounds in 1860 to 298,000 pounds in 1883. Because so many of the known white smokers were criminals or persons living on the criminal edge of society, people soon concluded that smoking was responsible for their antisocial behavior. The second contributing element was that opium smoking was introduced by the Chinese. When these people were first imported into California, they were seen as harmless and hard-working men. As they began to compete with whites for various low-paying jobs, they quickly became regarded as dirty and immoral people attempting to corrupt white youths and lure white women into prostitution. Race riots broke out against the Chinese in California and Canada. Opium smoking became linked in the public mind with the "yellow peril." This negative vision of the opiates has maintained itself to the present time. It has, perhaps, been assisted by the great disappointment morphine caused to the medical profession, since this drug was widely touted as a cure for the opium habit. Then heroin was seen as a cure for the morphine habit. It was also seen as nonaddictive, more effective, and less toxic: the drug needed to replace morphine. By 1910, when it was recognized that these claims were untrue, the medical profession began to consider heroin more dangerous than morphine.

Under the influence of both the public's outcry against opium and quack medicines of high opiate content and the medical profession's antiheroin stand, Congress passed the Harrison Act of 1914, which has remained the basic framework for the legal control of narcotic drugs in the United States to the present time. In 1924, after lobbying by the American Medical Association, Congress prohibited the importation of opium for the purpose of making heroin. At the present time heroin is totally banned except for experimental purposes.

For the period from 1918 to 1920, shortly after the passage of the Harrison Act, Terry and Pellens (1970) give three different estimates ranging from 140,554 to 264,276, of the total number of chronic opium users in the United States. Each figure is based on different assumptions and determined from different bases. The authors note that each of these figures underestimates rather than overestimates the amount of the use. John Ball, David Englander, and Carl Chambers (1970), using extremely sophisticated techniques, have estimated the number of users for 1967 at 108,424. Since the population of the United States has increased by 70 percent since 1920, this would suggest a large decrease in the number of users. Both Ball, Englander, and Chambers (1970) and John O'Donnell (1969) point to improvements in medical practice and stricter law enforcement as responsible for at least part of this decrease.

In an article using 1963 data, the social science section of the Addiction Research Center at Lexington showed that 49 percent of the addicts admitted to the two federal hospitals at Lexington and Fort Worth came from the two most populated areas of the country: New York and Chicago (Ball, Bates, & O'Donnell, 1966). The NIDA study (O'Donnell et al. 1976) indicates that 10 percent of the sample population used heroin in either 1974 or 1975. This is a much higher use rate than ever before reported. Furthermore, over half of the addicts admitted to these two hospitals came from three states: New York, Illinois, and Texas. The highest rate of admission was for Washington, D.C., which sent to the hospital 19.3 patients for every 100,000 male residents. This was followed by New York, Puerto Rico, Illinois, and Texas, with respective rates of 14.4, 12.2, 11.5, and 7.8 per 100,000 adult males.

A large proportion of the addict population in the United States are minority group members. William Bates (1966) found that in 1964, 31 percent of all first admissions to the Lexington and Fort Worth hospitals were black. Crowther (1974) found that over 40 percent of the Fort Worth Narcotic Addicts Rehabilitation Act (NARA) admissions in a year and a half between 1968 and 1969 were of Spanish-speaking origin. The research both of Isidor Chein, Donald Gerard, Robert Lee, and Eva Rosenfeld (1964) and of Ball (1970) indicates that there is an extremely high overrepresentation of Puerto Ricans among the known narcotic addicts in the North, especially in New York City.

The research of William Bates, Paula Dubeck, and Larry Redlinger (1969) in San Antonio, Texas, shows that persons with Spanish surnames are overrepresented in the addict population. About 41 percent of the population of San Antonio has Spanish surnames, but in a study done on the patients admitted to the Fort Worth hospital from San Antonio, it was found that about 77 percent of the drug users had Spanish surnames. The population of San Antonio was 7 percent black, and the study group was also about 7 percent black. In other words, although there was no overrepresentation of blacks, more persons with Spanish surnames were admitted to the hospital than would have been expected by the population distribution.

In general it can be said, then, that in the North, narcotic drug users are more likely to be blacks or Puerto Ricans living in the large urban areas. In the South, the narcotic users are more likely to be older whites who are not living in the major metropolitan areas, as Ball (1965) and Bates (1966) have both shown. In the Southwest, users are most likely to be persons with Spanish surnames.

In addition to the geographic and ethnic distribution of the addict population, it is helpful to have some knowledge of the age distibution, since the popular literature gives the impression that most drug users are adolescents. In the previously mentioned study by Ball, Bates, and O'Donnell, it has been shown that in 1963 the youngest patient admitted to the Lexington hospital was 16 years of age and the oldest was 75. The mean age was 33.5 years, but 3 percent of the population was under 20, and 25 percent was under 25. Only about 20 percent was 40 and over. In 1935, however, when the hospital opened, nearly 50 percent of the hospital population was over 40. Thus, in the period between 1935 and 1963 a larger proportion of younger patients was admitted to the hospital. About 36 percent of the San Antonio group studied at the hospital in Fort Worth by Bates (1969) was under 25. It would not be unreasonable to say that between a quarter and third of the opiate users known to agencies are under the age of 25.

A more relevant statistic to the study of drug addiction may perhaps be the age of first narcotic use. In the San Antonio study cited above, Bates (1969) found that 62 percent of the study population started opiate use before the age of 20. Crowther (1971) found the median age of first narcotic use to be 17 for both Spanish-speaking persons and the Anglos living in the Southwest. In the research of Robins and Murphy (1967) it was shown that half their population of black addicts had started heroin use before 20. Three fourths of this sample started heroin use between the ages of 16 and 23. Chein, Gerard, Lee, and Rosenfeld reported: "Among delinquents and users, 16 seems to be the age most susceptive to experimentation with drugs" (1964, p. 153). Ball (1970) found that 63 percent of his Puerto Rican subjects had started opiate use before the age of 20.

As so often occurs when one attempts to describe characteristics of a large group of persons, generalizations are likely to be an oversimplification of existing reality. When compiling occupational data on narcotic addicts researchers often run into the problem of identifying the social class and background of the users. Most researchers agree that the use of the drug causes a change in lifestyle that makes steady employment almost impossible for many. There is some evidence, however, that many addicts, and especially those from lower-income areas, had never achieved a steady occupational pattern before their addiction. Research done by Bates (1969) indicates that among black addicts, the most characteristic occupational pattern is extensive unemployment or no steady job. Sixty percent of the addicts interviewed fell into this category. In effect, this pattern is similar to that outlined by Harold Finestone in 1957 in his frequently quoted article, "Cats, Kicks, and Color." In the study done by Chein, Gerard, Lee, and Rosenfeld (1964) in New York, the users in both high-drug-use and low-drug-use gangs were less likely to be working than nonusers in the same gang. Thus, the present state of research seems to indicate that among young people, those who are unemployed are more likely to become drug users. Those employed people who are most likely to become drug abusers are physicians and nurses and those in other medical and paramedical employments where they can actually see opiates used to end pain in human subjects.

One further note should be made here. It would be illogical to expect addicts to be hard-working individuals before their initial drug use, since it has been shown that for many the age of initial use is under twenty. It would be difficult, if not impossible, for these young initiates to have a prior history of steady employment. It is more likely that the use of opiates for many of these is simply another aspect of a deviant lifestyle developed at a relatively young age.

The data presented here are not intended to imply that all addicts have erratic job histories either before or after their addiction. O'Donnell (1969) found that his male Kentucky subjects had achieved occupational levels comparable to the 1960 census population prior to their addiction. Several studies have also shown that the largest problem of opiate addiction is in the medical and paramedical professions. Pescor (1942) reported that physicians were represented in the hospital population at Lexington at a rate of about eight times greater than their rate of representation in the nation's population. The study by Robert Rasor and James Crecraft (1955) on meperidine addiction showed that about a third of meperidine addicts studied were physicians or osteopaths. Charles Winick (1961) presents drug abuse as an occupational hazard for physicians.

A similar incidence occurs among nurses and related professions. In a sample of female addicts studied in Lexington, it was found that 15 percent had either been in nurses' training or in other paramedical training programs (Williams & Bates, 1970). Solomon Garb, in an article in *Nursing Outlook* in 1965, warned nurses that narcotic addiction must be considered an occupational hazard for them.

It has sometimes been suggested that there is a great amount of drug use among jazz and rock musicians. The classic paper by Winick (1959) shows that 53 percent of the musicians interviewed had used heroin at least once. Becker (1953) demonstrates the mechanisms by which such use develops and the value systems that emerge to make usage acceptable within small subgroups. But although the folklore of both musicians and the drug culture indicates that drug use is high among these people, there is actually little hard data to substantiate this. Furthermore, there is one bit of data that might indicate that the folklore is simply a myth. There is a belief that large numbers of the black addicts in the Lexington hospital are performing artists of various sorts. Actually, though, only 2 percent of a study group of these addicts gave this as the occupation in which they had earned their living for the longest period of time. In effect, then, this occupational category is not the one that they have used for financial support.

In sum, it would appear that chronic opiate use produces a deterioration in the individual's ability to maintain steady employment. In the medical and nursing professions there tends to be a higher rate of addiction that may be directly related to the occupational norms themselves. The typical urban addict, however, has rarely held a long-term steady job and usually has an erratic, often delinquent career before beginning opiate use.

One interesting hypothesis emerges from the occupational data on persons in the medical professions. The high incidence of drug use among this group suggests that occupational access to drugs within the human treatment context is extremely conducive to the development of drug abuse by both men and women. As might be expected, the drug of choice among this population is not heroin but Demerol, a synthetic opiate that is extensively used in medical practice as an analgesic.

Simple access to drugs, however, does not seem to be sufficient to explain the high rate among physicians. The authors could not find any evidence in the literature that would indicate that either pharmacists or veterinarians, who also have easy access to drugs, are represented in the addict group in as high a rate as are physicians and nurses.

Other evidence of the addicts' unstable lifestyle comes from studies on marital adjustment. In a study by John O'Donnell, Karst Besteman, and Judith Jones (1967), about twice as many of the male addicts had never married as might be expected. Both men and women had a high rate of divorce or separation and a low number of children. Crowther (1974) found that 29 percent of her total sample of Spanish-speaking and Anglo addicts in the Southwest had never been legally married. Of those who had, 49 percent had been married less than five years. Carl Chambers, Kent Hinesley, and Mary Moldestad (1970) found that 24 percent of their female sample reported divorce or separation. The interesting finding from this study, however, is the fact that 42 percent of the reported marriages were in fact common-law relationships rather than legal marriages. In another study, Chambers, working with Walter Cuskey and Arthur Moffett (1970), found an interesting trend in the marital history of Mexican-American addicts. In 1961 the largest proportion of his sample had never married, but in 1967 the proportion of single addicts had decreased from 45 percent to 30 percent, while the proportion of broken marriages had increased from 14 percent to 27 percent.

It is well known that addicts display a high rate of criminal activity after their addiction. The demand for money to buy drugs becomes so great that it is almost impossible for the average addict to obtain it legally. There is some evidence, however, that a large number of addicts are delinquent before their first opiate use. Ball (1970) found that 22 percent of his Puerto Rican male addicts had been arrested before their initial narcotic use. He reports that these addicts associated with neighborhood boys who were considered by the adults in the community to be a "fast crowd" or "bad boys." Thus, Ball concludes that the boys studied had a delinquent orientation before their initial opiate use. O'Donnell (1966) has shown that the proportion of persons with a criminal history prior to addiction has increased significantly since 1920. He attributes this to a change in the type of person using narcotics. He concludes: " ... [A]ddicts have been more and more recruited from among persons with prior criminal records in recent decades, and today it is probable that most new addicts were criminals before their addiction" (O'Donnell, 1966, p. 385). More recent data are available from Crowther's (1974) study. Sixty-eight percent of her Spanish-speaking sample and 67 percent of her Anglo sample reported an arrest before their first opiate use. Twenty-six percent had been institutionalized before the age of sixteen. These data argue that for at least a significant proportion of present-day addicts, opiates are simply another symptom of a delinquent and deviant style of life.

Although the opiate addiction most frequently discussed in the literature is heroin addiction, this is not the only opiate to which people become addicted. As mentioned earlier, Demerol is the drug most frequently used by physician and nurse addicts. O'Donnell (1969) found that many of his Kentucky subjects whose drugs were supplied by physicians were addicted to morphine. Ball (1965), using 1962 hospital data, showed two patterns of opiate addiction in the United States. The first, which we have focused on in this paper, consists of heroin users drawn primarily from metropolitan youth coming from minority groups. His second pattern consists primarily of middle-aged whites living in the South. In addition to morphine, many of these persons were also addicted either to paregoric or terpin hydrate and codeine, both substances that are ingested orally rather than by injection.

One opiate that is the drug of choice for some is methadone. In many parts of the United States, treatment programs for heroin addicts provide the patients with methadone maintenance; that is, another opiate, methadone, is supplied so that the patient does not crave heroin. In theory, this is done to help the patient readjust from the street life of hustling to the more socially acceptable life of the steadily employed worker. Many persons discussing these methadone programs do not seem to realize that methadone is the drug of choice for many addicts. One surprising finding from England reported by Bates (1969) is that the drug of choice for many patients attending drug clinics is methadone, even though the physicians were willing to prescribe heroin if the patient asked for it. The addicts themselves said that they preferred this drug because its effects were longer lasting and did not produce the violent ups and downs associated with heroin use.

Unlike some of the other drugs examined, the most significant aspect of heroin use is the addicts' way of life. At least two aspects of this pattern, hustling and the induction of the new initiate, will be treated here. One of the most striking features of the addict's life is that it seems to revolve entirely around the quest for drugs. This quest involves getting money for the purchase of drugs, locating the source of the drug, and "fixing," or taking the drug. The price of heroin necessary for a single shot fluctuates widely from time to time and place to place in the country. Although addicts frequently claim to have habits that cost them from $100 to $150 per day, these claims seldom survive after close questioning. A better estimate is that a person with a reasonably large habit may actually be shooting from $25 to $50 a day in drugs. Since drug users nearly always must purchase their drugs on a cash basis, the user must raise this amount of money each day. Furthermore, since most persons who are heavy heroin addicts are unemployed—and are frequently unemployable—this requires that they steal and fence enough goods each day to obtain the needed cash. They must, therefore, not only learn the techniques of stealing so that they will not be caught, but they must also learn how to dispose of what they steal. The most frequent type of stealing seems to be shoplifting, although addicts will frequently burglarize homes and offices for easily disposable items such as typewriters, dictaphones, television sets, radios, and record players. All these items can be easily fenced, and one good office burglary of perhaps four electric typewriters, two or three dictaphones, and a desk-model duplicator may bring in enough money to provide drugs for several days.

The addict is constantly anxious about a "connection," or source of drugs. This is not always easy to maintain, for connections frequently get "busted," that is, arrested. Thus, when one's connection is busted, one must locate another one. Since addicts are notoriously unreliable, it is frequently difficult for an addict to get another connection for drugs. Moreover, clients of recently arrested "pushers" are always suspect as possible informers. Contrary to popular belief, it is relatively rare for the pusher actually to seek out clients. Each seller has a specific clientele, among whom it is reasonably certain there are no police agents. Furthermore, since heroin is in sufficiently short supply in most of the United States, pushers can make an adequate living without having to seek out new clients.

After raising the money and locating the drug, the addict must "fix" or shoot himself with the drug. This involves cooking the heroin mixed with water, locating and raising a vein to shoot, and injecting with a hypodermic. Unlike swigging wine from a bottle, this ritual is relatively complicated and time consuming. The picture of the addict gained from reading the newspapers and watching television is that of a person who enjoys the evil actions in private. In truth, many addicts enjoy the company of other addicts. They prefer to take their shots in the company of others, so that shooting-up becomes a real social occasion. They will assist each other in locating the vein and passing the needle and syringe around the group—an excellent way of distributing infectious hepatitis among all the members of the group.

Since many persons who shoot heroin several times a day are using heroin so adulterated that physical dependence is minimal, the effects of the heroin itself do not seem adequate to account for their continued addiction. It has been suggested by Abraham Wikler (1961) and others that the addiction is not just to the opiate itself, but that the addict is conditioned to a whole way of life. This type of life is termed hustling. The life of the addict gains its meaning from the patterning of activities around the drug. The stealing, fencing, buying, and fixing become a pattern of life activity that must be understood to understand the addiction.

It has been suggested that one reason methadone maintenance works for some addicts is that it breaks this pattern and, in effect, forces the addict out of the hustling life even though he is still addicted to an opiate. It is possible that one reason for its failure with others is that they are more addicted to this addict role and its lifestyle than they are to the drug. For such people it is next to impossible to change their lifestyle.

How do people get introduced to this way of life and to the use of heroin? From popular discussions one gathers that evil men set out to seduce youths into drug use. This does not seem to be the usual route. Addict interviews will frequently provide such stories as these:

> "My friend was strung-out and was needing a fix. Since he was broke, he asked me to lend him the money. I told him I would if he would give me some. So we went to the connection and bought the stuff. My friend shot

most of it, and I shot what was left of the stuff. I watched him, and he helped me shoot it."

"My friend was looking for a ride to his connection. I offered to drive him if he would give me some."

"My brother was hot (i.e., police were either watching him or looking for him with a warrant) so he asked me to go to his connection with him. I did and took a little of the stuff. When he had fixed, I took his rig and tried the stuff myself."

"I was at a party, and the guys were fixing. I asked them if I could have some." Or else, "They asked me if I would like to try a shot."

In almost all the interviews the present authors conducted with heroin addicts, the addicts themselves sought out their first fix; they were not sought out by others. The only other frequent alternative was for the person to be in a social situation where heroin was being used. In this event they might be asked if they would like some, much as they might have been asked if they would like a drink.

The persons who are likely to become addicts are therefore living— and usually have been reared in—a milieu in which heroin is available. They see others under the influence of the drug; they see others fixing; they see pushers on the street and see others buying from them rela- tively openly. From these contacts they may get to know pushers—who may even be brothers or uncles or compadres—from the time they are small, so that they are known not to be police agents. As a result, initial use of the drug is about as problematic as the use of tobacco for the rest of American society.

The data of Robins and Murphy (1967) suggest that it is very unlikely for a person to be an occasional user. Although they found some persons who had tried the drug once or twice, if the subjects admitted to using more frequently, they would characteristically continue until they had become an addict. Interviews with addicts show that many of them claim to have "chipped," that is, used the drug for long periods of time without becoming a daily user. They all, however, ultimately became addicted.[6]

Unlike the previous sections, this discussion on narcotics has focused on lower-class delinquent youths whose lifestyle is quite different from that of the average middle-class American. Although there is some opiate use among high school and college students, the extent is so low as to be negligible. Fort (1969) found that in the largest metropolitan school district examined in his study, 5 percent of the boys and 8 percent of the girls in the twelfth grade had tried heroin. This does not imply that they have become addicted to the drug, but simply that they have tried it at least once. In Maryland a 1969 survey by the Joint Committee on Drug Abuse entitled "A Survey of Secondary School Students' Perceptions of and Attitudes toward Use of Drugs by Teenagers" (1970) found 1.2 percent of the senior high school students reporting any use and 0.7 percent reporting current use. In Wisconsin, Jon Udell and Robert Smith (1969) found only 0.6 percent of their high school sample reporting one- or two-time use.

Surveys of college students find similar low proportions using opiates. Blum (1969b) reports approximately 1 percent opiate use in the five colleges studied. Barter, Mizner, and Werme (1970) found 2 percent narcotic use among college students in the Denver-Boulder metropolitan area. In the Northeast, Joel Goldstein (1970) reports 0.5 percent heroin and 2.6 percent other opiate use among students at Carnegie-Mellon University. Of this group, only 1.3 percent stated that they had used other opiates as many as two to ten times, and no greater frequency was reported.

Both the high school and the college data, therefore, suggest that opiate use is low among the middle-class student population. This characteristic has probably given rise to the popular distinction between "hard" and "soft" drugs and drug users. It does suggest that the serious reader must not only distinguish between the effects of different drugs but must also realize that there are many subcultures within the drug-using community. Lower-class "hustling" addicts have little in common with physician and nurse Demerol users. Grouping all drug users into a common category and talking about the "drug culture" is like grouping the Amish and Mexican-American communities together when speaking about minority groups in the United States.

MULTIPLE DRUG USE

The term *multiple drug use* has three meanings that must be distinguished logically, although all three types may be found in a single person at different points in time. The first type is the indiscriminate use of different drugs of the same family. In this type, a person, although preferring one drug to another in the family, will be content to use whatever is easiest to obtain at the moment. A commonly seen example of this is the heroin user who prefers heroin but will use morphine. Demerol, or any other opioid when heroin is not easily available. Thus, a person may drink paregoric or cook it down for injection when heroin is in short supply. This type of multiple drug use is also found both in barbiturate and amphetamine users. If pressed, barbiturate users usually say that they prefer Seconal but that they will use any obtainable drug and will even take several kinds at one time to gain the strength of effect desired. It is actually rather rare to find drug users who will volunteer a barbiturate of choice. They are more likely to say that they use "downers," without specifying them more exactly. Amphetamine users very frequently will say they prefer Methedrine, but they will take any of the amphetamines to continue the run.

The second type of multiple drug use is the use of one drug to potentiate, or increase the effect of, the other drug. This phenomenon is known to the newspaper reader from accounts that a mixture of alcohol and barbiturates is potentially lethal. In the section on amphetamines, it was mentioned that methamphetamine has been used to increase the power of heroin. In hippy communities one frequently finds the use of a sweet wine like tokay or sherry to increase the effect of the amphetamines.

A review of some research clearly shows the existence of a third type: users of multiple drug families. It has already been mentioned that about 90 percent of the heroin users had at some time used marijuana. The data given by Robins and Murphy (1967) showed that 68 percent of their heroin users had also used amphetamines and 57 percent had used barbiturates. Furthermore, most of them had used heroin before or in the same year that they started the other drug. In other words, in this sample of St. Louis blacks, heroin use seemed to accompany other drug use. Moreover, 5 percent of the total sample had used heroin, amphetamines, marijuana, and the barbiturates.

Research by Blum (1969b) on the college patterns of drug use shows that 50 percent of the marijuana users had used amphetamines, 33 percent used sedatives, 24 percent used hallucinogens, and only 6 percent used opiates. Among Blum's opiate users, 76 percent had used marijuana, 73 percent used sedatives, 66 percent used amphetamines, and 50 percent used hallucinogens, He further reports that marijuana use preceded opiate use for the majority of his subjects.

In a hippy community studied by Theo Solomon (1968), every subject had used marijuana. In addition, 97 percent of the men and 80 percent of the women had used LSD, and 52 percent of the men and 70 percent of the women had used Methedrine. When it comes to heroin, the picture changes remarkably. Only 13 percent of the men and 20 percent of the women admitted to having used it.

The study by Schick, Smith, and Meyers (1968) in the Haight-Ashbury district of San Francisco was done with a much larger number of subjects but with fewer drugs studied. The authors found that 94 percent of the men and 98 percent of the women had used marijuana. In addition, 87 percent of the group had used LSD, while 60 percent had used amphetamines.

Goode (1969), using a sample of 200 known marijuana users, showed that 49 percent used LSD, 43 percent used amphetamines, 26 percent used DMT or DET, and 24 percent used barbiturates or tranquilizers. When the "harder" drugs were considered, though, the use was relatively infrequent: 20 percent used opium, 19 percent used heroin, and 19 percent used cocaine (1969, p. 53).

This summary of some specific studies rather clearly shows that there is in the drug-using group a relatively small number of individuals who do not seem to be addicted or habituated to any special substance. They appear to use all or any substances that they think will provide them with the change of mood or sensation desired at the time. They are looking for "new experiences," the "different and higher high." The material used to get this seems to be largely irrelevant. Emmitt Warner (1969), for example, reports that even dried sea horses and small starfish have been ingested for a new type of "trip"!

Because of the existence of this type, and because of the large overlap in the numbers of individuals using each of the drug families, it seems very important for anyone doing research in the general area of drug use *not* to study just a single drug or family of drugs. If the researcher does not include many different drugs, he runs the risk of discussing the characteristics of the class of multiple drug users. Suppose, for example, a study were to attempt to investigate the potential of DOM for street abuse. If one gathers information on DOM use excluding other drug use, the following problem arises.

Almost everyone who has shown up in studies as using DOM has been an individual who has taken a wide variety not only of hallucinogens but of other drugs as well. Such a person is usually a "generalized drug user." Therefore, the researcher would end up studying these persons rather than simply DOM users.

There are, however, a relatively large number of individuals whose only drug of abuse is marijuana. Unless the researcher collects at least some information on the use of many types of drugs, he will never discover that certain drugs are frequently drugs of abuse used by themselves. Other drugs seem to be used only in the context of multiple drug use, with little data to show that they are likely to become the drug of choice or of exclusive use for any reasonable number of people. In terms of public policy, at least, this would seem to be an important distinction. Certainly it would seem important when one is considering the various types of treatment modalities that can be used.

CONCLUSION

In this treatise we have briefly outlined some cultural considerations of the subject of drug use, presented some of the major effects of each drug class treated, and then discussed in some detail certain research findings about the extent of drug use and the population most likely to be found using the drug, with an emphasis on the American scene.

We have carefully attempted to present the material in a nonjudgmental manner so that our attitudes toward the use of various drugs would not influence our presentation and not be apparent to the reader. We have used as our basic sources research studies of some importance in the field. When the articles were of sufficient importance to require their use, we have included references to research or summary articles in which the attitudes of authors were apparent. We have, however, eschewed material that was basically oriented not to presenting data but rather to making a case for or against the use of specific substances or of drugs in general.

There seem to be two drugs that authors find difficult to discuss without presenting serious biases. These are marijuana and the hallucinogens. A very large amount of the literature, especially that written by sociologists, does not simply present data on the use of these substances or their effects. Rather, it presents data arguing either that the substances are so destructive that they must not be used at all or else that they are so innocuous that they need no controls or so wonderful that all people should be using them. We hope that our sections on these substances have been written in such a fashion that we have simply presented what is known about them without either arguing for their use or for their prohibition.

NOTES

1. Students who wish to know more about the history of drug use and abuse can find a brief introduction to the matter in O'Donnell and Ball (1966). A much more extensive review can be found in Blum (1969a). The bibliography of this latter work also provides many primary sources for the student who wishes to pursue this subject even farther.

2. This terminology is discussed in several volumes, including Wikler (1961) and Seevers (1962).

3. For a more complete discussion of common terms used by drug users, the reader is referred to Lingeman (1969).

4. A similar argument addressed to alcohol is to be found in MacAndrew and Edgerton (1969). Readers interested in a cultural comparison of the effects of alcohol and a theoretical framework extensively worked out to account for these differences in the effects of different cultures should certainly read their paper.

5. An extensive discussion of the importance of rituals in the control of drug use can be found in Blum (1969a).

6. It must be taken into account here that the sample was of addicts. Thus, the data are biased, for no one who had "chipped" and not become addicted could be represented.

BIBLIOGRAPHY

Alexander, C. Norman, Jr. "Consensus and Mutual Attraction in Natural Cliques: A Study of Adolescent Drinkers." *American Journal of Sociology,* 1964, 69:395–403.

Allegro, John M. *The Sacred Mushroom and the Cross: Fertility Cults and the Origin of Judaism and Christianity.* Garden City, N.Y.: Doubleday, 1970.

Bales, Robert Freed. "Cultural Differences in Rates of Alcoholism." *Quarterly Journal of Studies of Alcohol,* 1946, 6:480–499.

Ball, John C. "Two Patterns of Narcotic Drug Addiction in the U.S." *Journal of Criminal Law, Criminology, and Police Science,* 1965, 56:203–211.

Ball, John C. "Onset of Marijuana and Heroin Use Among Puerto Rican Addicts." In John C. Ball and Carl D. Chambers, eds. *The Epidemiology of Opiate Addiction in the United States.* Springfield, Ill.: Charles C. Thomas, 1970, pp. 167–177.

Ball, John C., and William M. Bates. "Nativity, Parentage, and Mobility of Opiate Addicts." In John C. Ball and Carl D. Chambers, eds. *The Epidemiology of Opiate Addiction in the United States.* Springfield, Ill.: Charles C. Thomas, 1970, pp. 95–111.

Ball, John C., William M. Bates, and John A. O'Donnell. "Characteristics of Hospitalized Narcotic Addicts." *Health, Education and Welfare Indicators.* Washington, D.C.: U.S. Government Printing Office, March 17, 1966.

Ball, John C., David M. Englander, and Carl D. Chambers. "The Incidence and Prevalence of Opiate Addiction in the United States." In John C. Ball and Carl D. Chambers, eds. *The Epidemiology of Opiate Addiction in the United States.* Springfield, Ill.: Charles C. Thomas, 1970, pp. 68–78.

Barter, James T., George L. Mizner, and Paul H. Werme. *Patterns of Drug Use Among College Students: An Epidemiological and Demographic Survey of Student Attitudes and Practices.* Boulder, Colo.: University of Colorado Medical School, Department of Psychiatry, 1970.

Bates, William M. "Narcotics, Negroes, and the South." *Social Forces,* 1966, 45:61–67.

Bates, William M. "Occupational Characteristics of Negro Addicts." *International Journal of the Addictions,* 1968, 3:345–350.

Bates, William M. "Some Observations on English Drug Clinics." Unpublished paper, 1969.

Bates, William, Paula Dubeck, and Larry Redlinger. "The Social Context of Urban Narcotic Use." *Proceedings of the Southwestern Sociological Association Meeting.* Houston, Tex.: Southwestern Sociological Association, 1969, pp. 199–204.

Bates, William, and Joyce E. Williams. "Towards a Typology of Female Drug Addiction." Unpublished paper, 1967.

Becker, Howard S. "Becoming a Marihuana User." *American Journal of Sociology*, 1953, 59:235–242.

Blum, Richard H., and others. *Society and Drugs*. San Francisco: Jossey-Bass, 1969a.

Blum, Richard H., and others. *Students and Drugs*. San Francisco: Jossey-Bass, 1969b.

Blumer, Herbert, Alan Sutter, Samir Ahmed, and Roger Smith. "Addiction Center Project Final Report: The World of Youthful Drug Use." Berkeley: University of California, School of Criminology, 1967. Mimeographed.

Brill, Henry. "Recurrent Patterns in the History of Drugs of Dependence and Some Interpretations." In J. R. Wittenborn, Henry Brill, Jean Paul Smith, and Sarah A. Wittenborn, eds. *Drugs and Youth*. Springfield, Ill.: Charles C. Thomas, 1969, pp. 8–25.

Bueno, Darío Urdapilleta. "The Problem of Drug Addiction in Mexico." In Robert T. Harris, William M. McIsaac, and Charles R. Schuster, Jr., eds. *Drug Dependence—Advances in Mental Science II*. Austin, Tex.: University of Texas Press, 1970, pp. 305–319.

Cahalan, Don, Ira H. Cisin, and Helen M. Crossley. *American Drinking Practices: A National Study of Drinking Behavior and Attitudes*. New Brunswick, N.J.: Rutgers Center of Alcohol Studies Publications, 1969.

Chambers, Carl D., Walter R. Cuskey, and Arthur D. Moffett. "Mexican-American Opiate Addicts." In John C. Ball and Carl D. Chambers, eds. *The Epidemiology of Opiate Addiction in the United States*. Springfield, Ill.: Charles C. Thomas, 1970, pp. 202–221.

Chambers, Carl D., R. Kent Hinesley, and Mary Moldestad. "The Female Opiate Addict." In John C. Ball and Carl D. Chambers, eds. *The Epidemiology of Opiate Addiction in the United States*. Springfield, Ill.: Charles C. Thomas, 1970, pp. 222–239.

Chambers, Carl D., Arthur D. Moffett, and Judith P. Jones. "Demographic Factors Associated with Negro Opiate Addiction." *International Journal of the Addictions*, 1968, 3:329–343.

Chein, Isidor, Donald L. Gerard, Robert S. Lee, and Eva Rosenfeld. *The Road to H*. New York: Basic Books, 1964.

Cohen, Sidney. "The Psychopharmacology of Amphetamine and Barbiturate Dependence." In J. R. Wittenborn, Henry Brill, Jean Paul Smith, and Sarah A. Wittenborn, eds. *Drugs and Youth*. Springfield, Ill.: Charles C. Thomas, 1969, pp. 135–138.

Crowther, Betty. "The Mexican-American Addict." In William Bates and Betty Crowther, eds. *Towards a Typology of Opiate Users*. Cambridge, Mass.: Schenkman, 1974.

Crowther, Betty, and Terry L. Baumer. "The Use of Drugs by Secondary School Students in the Greater Egypt Region." In Joseph F. Hupert, and others. *Drug Abuse in Middle America: Problems and Proposals.* Report submitted to the Illinois Law Enforcement Commission, 1971, pp. 7–24.

Dole, Vincent P., and Marie E. Nyswander. "A Medical Treatment for Diacetylmorphine (Heroin) Addiction." *Journal of the American Medical Association,* 1965, 193:646–650.

Durkheim, Emile. *The Rules of Sociological Method.* New York: Macmillan, 1938.

Eddy, Nathan, H. Halbach, Harris Isbell, and Maurice H. Seevers. "Drug Dependence: Its Significance and Characteristics." *Bulletin of the World Health Organization,* 1965, 32:721–733.

Eells, Kenneth. "Marijuana and LSD: A Survey of One College Campus." *Journal of Counseling Psychology,* 1968, 15:459–467.

Emerick, Chester A. "The Control Program of the U.S. Bureau of Customs." In White House Conference on Narcotics and Drug Abuse Proceedings. Washington, D.C.: U.S. Government Printing Office, 1962.

Essig, Carl. "Barbiturate Dependence." In Robert T. Harris, William M. McIsaac, and Charles R. Schuster, eds. *Drug Dependence—Advances in Mental Science II.* Austin, Tex.: University of Texas Press, 1970, pp. 129–140.

Finestone, Harold. "Cats, Kicks, and Color." *Social Problems,* 1957, 5:3–13.

Five Mind-Altering Drugs (Plus One). San Mateo, Calif.: Research and Statistics Section, Department of Public Health and Welfare, 1971.

Fort, Joel. *The Pleasure Seekers: The Drug Crisis, Youth and Society.* Indianapolis: Bobbs-Merrill, 1969.

Francis, John B., and David J. Patch. *Student Attitudes towards Drug Programs at the University of Michigan.* University Committee on Drug Education, September 1969. Mimeographed.

Freedman, Daniel X. "Drug Abuse—Comments on the Current Scene." In J. R. Wittenborn, Henry Brill, Jean Paul Smith, and Sarah A. Wittenborn, eds. *Drugs and Youth.* Springfield, Ill.: Charles C. Thomas, 1969, pp. 345–361.

Gallup Poll. *The Washington Post,* May 26, 1969.

Gallup Poll. *The Washington Post,* October 26, 1969.

Gaoni, Y., and R. Mechoulam. "Isolation, Structure and Partial Synthesis of an Active Constituent of Hashish." *Journal of the American Chemical Society,* 1964, 86:1646–1648.

Garb, Solomon. "Narcotic Addiction in Nurses and Doctors." *Nursing Outlook,* 1965, 13:30–34.

Glaser, Frederick B., and John C. Ball. "Death Due to Withdrawal from

Narcotics." In John C. Ball and Carl D. Chambers, eds. *The Epidemiology of Opiate Addiction in the United States*. Springfield, Ill.: Charles C. Thomas, 1970, pp. 263–287.

Goldstein, Joel W. *The Psychology of Student Drug Use: Report on Phase One*. Carnegie-Mellon University Drug Research Project, 1970. Mimeographed.

Goode, Erich. "Multiple Drug Use Among Marijuana Smokers." *Social Problems*, 1969, 17:48–64.

Huxley, Aldous. *The Doors of Perception*. New York: Harper, 1954.

Idänpään-Heikkilä, Juhana E., Joseph C. Schoolar, and Alton Allen. "Total Body Kinetics and Placental Transfer of Labeled LSD in Mice." In Robert T. Harris, William M. McIsaac, and Charles R. Schuster, eds. *Drug Dependence—Advances in Mental Science II*. Austin, Tex.: University of Texas Press, 1970, pp. 55–66.

Imperi, Lillian L., Herbert D. Kleber, and James S. Davie. "Use of Hallucinogenic Drugs on Campus." *Journal of the American Medical Association*, 1968, 204:1020–1024.

Isbell, Harris. "Historical Development of Attitudes in the U.S." In Seymour M. Farber and Roger H. L. Wilson, eds. *Conflict and Creativity*. New York: McGraw-Hill, 1963, pp. 154–169.

Isbell, Harris, Sol Altschul, Conan H. Kernetsky, A. J. Eisenman, H. G. Flanary, and Havelock F. Fraser. "Chronic Barbiturate Intoxication." *Archives of Neurology and Psychiatry*, 1950, 64:1–28.

Isbell, Harris, R. E. Belleville, H. F. Fraser, A. Wikler, and C. R. Logan. "Studies on Lysergic Acid Diethylamide: I. Effects in Former Morphine Addicts and Development of Tolerance During Chronic Intoxication." *Archives of Neurology and Psychiatry*, 1956, 76:468–478.

Isbell, Harris, C. W. Gorodetzsky, D. Jasinski, U. Claussen, F. V. Spulak, and F. Korte. "Effects of Trans-Tetrahydrocannabinol in Man." *Psychopharmacologia*, 1967, 11:184–188.

Isbell, Harris, and D. R. Jasinski. "A Comparison of LSD-25 with Trans-Tetrahydrocannabinol (THC) and Attempted Cross Tolerance between LSD and THC." *Psychopharmacologia*, 1969, 14:115–123.

Kaplan, John. *Marijuana—The New Prohibition*. New York: World Publishing, 1970.

Keller, Mark. "The Definition of Alcoholism and Estimation of Its Prevalence." In David J. Pittman and Charles R. Snyder, eds. *Society, Culture, and Drinking Patterns*. New York: John Wiley & Sons, 1962, pp. 310–329.

Korte, F., M. Haag, and U. Claussen. "Tetrahydrocannabinol carbonsaure, ein neuer Haschisch-Inhaltsstaff." *Angewandte Chemie* (International Edition in English), 1965, 4:p. 872.

LaGuardia Commission (Mayor's Committee on Marijuana). *The Marijuana*

Problem in the City of New York. Tempe, Ariz.: Jacques Cattell Press, 1944.

Leake, Chauncey. "Historical Aspects of Drug Abuse." In J. R. Wittenborn, Henry Brill, Jean Paul Smith, and Sarah A. Wittenborn, eds. *Drugs and Youth.* Springfield, Ill.: Charles C. Thomas, 1969, pp. 25–26.

Lingeman, Richard R. *Drugs from A to Z: A Dictionary.* New York: McGraw-Hill, 1969.

MacAndrew, Craig, and Robert B. Edgerton. *Drunken Comportment: A Social Explanation.* Chicago: Aldine, 1969.

Manheimer, Dean I., Glen D. Melinger, and Mitchell B. Balter. "Marijuana Use Among Urban Adults." *Science,* 1969, 166:1544–1545.

Merit Publishing Company. *National Survey of High School High Achievers.* Beverly Hills, Calif.: Merit, 1970.

Morrison, Richard L. "Preliminary Report on the Incidence of the Use of Drugs at Sacramento State College." May 15, 1969. Mimeographed.

National Commission on Marihuana and Drug Abuse. *Drug Use in America: Problem in Perspective.* Washington, D.C.: U.S. Government Printing Office, 1973.

O'Donnell, John A. "Narcotic Addiction and Crime." *Social Problems,* 1966, 13:374–385.

O'Donnell, John A. *Narcotic Addicts in Kentucky,* Washington, D.C.: U.S. Government Printing Office, 1969.

O'Donnell, John A., and John C. Ball, eds. *Narcotic Addiction.* New York: Harper & Row, 1966.

O'Donnell, John A., Karst J. Besteman, and Judith P. Jones. "Marital History of Narcotics Addicts." *International Journal of the Addictions,* 1967, 2:21–38.

O'Donnell, John A., Harwin Voss, Richard R. Clayton, Gerald T. Slatin, and Robin G. W. Boom. *Young Men and Drugs: A Nationwide Survey.* NIDA Research Monograph No. 4. Rockville, Md.: National Institute of Drug Abuse, 1976.

Pescor, Michael J. "Physician Drug Addicts." *Diseases of the Nervous System,* 1942, 3:173–174.

Pescor, Michael J. "A Statistical Analysis of the Clinical Records of Hospitalized Drug Addicts." *Public Health Reports,* Suppl. No. 143, 1943.

President's Commission on Law Enforcement and Administration of Justice. *The Challenge of Crime in a Free Society.* Washington D.C.: U.S. Government Printing Office, 1967.

Rasor, Robert W., and James H. Crecraft. "Addiction to Meperidine (Demerol) Hydrochloride." *Journal of the American Medical Association,* 1955, 157:654–657.

Robins, Lee N. *Deviant Children Grown Up.* Baltimore, Md.: Williams and Wilkins, 1966.

Robins, Lee N., William M. Bates, and Patricia O'Neal. "Adult Drinking Patterns of Former Problem Children." In David J. Pittman and Charles R. Snyder, eds. Society, Culture, and Drinking Patterns. New York: John Wiley & Sons, 1962, pp. 395–412.

Robins, Lee N., and George E. Murphy. "Drug Use in a Normal Population of Young Negro Men." American Journal of Public Health, 1967, 57:1580–1596.

Schick, J. Fred E., David E. Smith, and Frederick H. Meyers. "The Use of Marijuana in the Haight-Ashbury Subculture." In David E. Smith, ed. The New Social Drug. Englewood Cliffs, N.J.: Prentice-Hall, 1970, pp. 41–62.

Seeley, John R. "The Ecology of Alcoholism: A Beginning." In David J. Pittman and Charles R. Snyder, eds. Society, Culture, and Drinking Patterns. New York: John Wiley & Sons, 1962, pp. 330–344.

Seevers, Maurice H. "Medical Perspectives on Habituation and Addiction." Journal of the American Medical Association, 1962, 181:92–98.

Simrell, Earle V. "History of Legal and Medical Roles in Narcotic Abuse in the U.S." In John C. Ball and Carl D. Chambers, eds. The Epidemiology of Opiate Addiction in the United States. Springfield, Ill.: Charles C. Thomas, 1970, pp. 22–35.

Skinner, William J. "Abused Prescription Drugs: Sources of Helpful Drugs that Hurt." In J. R. Wittenborn, Henry Brill, Jean Paul Smith, and Sarah A. Wittenborn, eds. Drugs and Youth. Springfield, Ill.: Charles C. Thomas, 1969, pp. 148–158.

Small, Albion W., and George E. Vincent. An Introduction to the Study of Society. New York: American Book, 1894.

Smith, S. N., and Paul H. Blachly. "Amphetamine Usage by Medical Students." Journal of Medical Education, 1966, 41:161–170.

Solomon, David, ed. The Marihuana Papers. Indianapolis: Bobbs-Merrill, 1966.

Solomon, Theo. A Pilot Study Among East Village "Hippies." Monograph #35, Associated YM-YWHA's of Greater New York, 1968. Mimeographed.

Straus, Robert. "Alcohol." In Robert K. Merton and Robert A. Nisbet, eds. Contemporary Social Problems. New York: Harcourt Brace Jovanovich, 1966, pp. 236–280.

Straus, Robert, and Selden D. Bacon. Drinking in College. New Haven, Conn.: Yale University Press, 1953.

"A Survey of Secondary School Students' Perceptions of and Attitudes toward Use of Drugs by Teenagers." Joint Committee on Drug Abuse, Montgomery County, Maryland, 1970.

Taylor, N. Narcotics—Nature's Dangerous Gifts. New York: Dell, 1966.

Terry, Charles E., and Mildred Pellens. "The Extent of Chronic Opiate Use in the United States Prior to 1921." In John C. Ball and Carl D. Chambers, eds. *The Epidemology of Opiate Addiction in the United States.* Springfield, Ill.: Charles C. Thomas, 1970, pp. 36–67.

Udell, Jon G., and Robert S. Smith. *Attitudes, Usage, and Availability of Drugs Among Madison High School Students.* University of Wisconsin Bureau of Business Research and Service, 1969. Mimeographed.

Warner, Emmitt G. "Sources of Hallucinogenic Drugs, Including Marijuana: The Nature of Economic Significance of the Trade." In J. R. Wittenborn, Henry Brill, Jean Paul Smith, and Sarah A. Wittenborn, eds. *Drugs and Youth.* Springfield, Ill.: Charles C. Thomas, 1969, pp. 161–167.

Wikler, Abraham A. "On the Nature of Addiction and Habituation." *British Journal of Addictions,* 1961, 57:73–79.

Williams, Joyce E., and William Bates. "Some Characteristics of Female Narcotic Addicts." *International Journal of the Addictions,* 1970, 5:245–256.

Winick, Charles. "The Use of Drugs by Jazz Musicians." *Social Problems,* 1959, 7:240–253.

Winick, Charles. "Physician Narcotic Addicts." *Social Problems,* 1961, 9:174–186.

Wolbach, A. B., Harris Isbell, and E. J. Miner. "Cross Tolerance between Mescaline and LSD-25 with a Comparison of the Mescaline and LSD Reactions." *Psychopharmacologia,* 1962, 3:1–14.

Wolfe, Tom. *The Electric Kool-Aid Acid Test.* New York: Bantam Books, 1969.

SEVEN
Alcohol: use and abuse

FRED MONTANINO
Yale University

There is much concern over the recurrent tendency of the public to dissociate alcohol from conventional drugs. Official agencies, such as the Department of Health, Education, and Welfare and the National Institute on Alcohol Abuse and Alcoholism, as well as private associations, such as Alcoholics Anonymous, view alcohol as a mind-altering chemical substance in the full clinical sense. The notion that alcohol has a "spiritual" rather than chemical effect on bodily functions—indeed liquor is often referred to as "spirits"[1]—does not shield its users from chemically induced physiological repercussions, and as members of society they bring this burden into the public arena. Doctors and academicians erudite in the field raise the cry that alcoholism is our number one drug problem. Many will insist that the failure to recognize alcohol as a drug may itself be a contributing factor to its abuse.

Such assertions that seek to dispel alcohol's benign, dedrugged image are usually supported by an understanding of the basic physiological processes and consequences of alcohol consumption. The study of alcohol does not embody the divergence between physical and social sciences generally experienced in the examination of many other purer forms of social or physical phenomena. Knowledge of the physiological implications of alcohol consumption enhances rather than beclouds an understanding of its social and psychological impacts. In this sense, then, the social, psychological, and physiological aspects of alcohol use are readily collapsible into a single body of knowledge lending itself to a single mode of interpretation.

The interrelation of these three factors becomes apparent when physiological considerations are able to provide some elucidation of the user's social reality. For example, one can discern between an *alcoholic state* and a *state of alcoholism*. These conditions are usually given a social interpretation on the basis of encounter, detection, and response; indeed, one becomes socially vulnerable to categorization as an alcoholic or an inebriate if involved with social control agencies, such as police and mental health agencies. However, it is on the basis of their physiological diversity that these two states can be delineated most clearly.

Aside from various social definitions of the *state of alcoholism*, which are crucial not only for potential alcoholics but also for the communities and milieus in which they reside, a clinical definition emerges. Since alcohol is a potentially addictive drug, it has the capacity to produce a tolerance-withdrawal syndrome. As is the case with other more clandestine substances—for instance, opium and its derivatives—alcohol can be consumed in increasingly larger doses to produce the desired state of altered consciousness. Simply stated, the more one drinks, the more one can drink and needs to drink to achieve the desired state. Tolerance is most likely to come about from the daily or semi-daily ingestion of large amounts of alcoholic beverage, rather than from frequent ingestion of small amounts of the beverage; more succinctly put, tolerance is a measure of how much you drink when you drink. Those who are morning drinkers are likely to develop tolerance more quickly than those who drink at the end of the day's activity. Harold Kalant (1973) found that preactivity ingestion of alcohol leads to a more rapid development of tolerance. Additionally, tolerance towards alcohol, once developed and shed, is more easily acquired a succeeding time; this is referred to by Kalant as the *carry-over effect* (1973, p. 5). Experimental studies (Gross, 1973) have confirmed the addictive nature of alcohol. This addiction becomes literally most painfully obvious to those under its influence upon their attempt to discontinue its use. A critical alcohol level in the bloodstream, enough to create physical dependence, must be gradually reduced through a process of detoxification, or the individual will experience severe withdrawal symptoms, such as tremors, delirium, and convulsions upon an attempt to discontinue its use. These symptoms of alcohol withdrawal will usually appear a few hours after its discontinuance and will last up to a week (Fort, 1973).

The *alcoholic state*, usually referred to as intoxication, results from ingesting amounts of alcohol greater than the body's capacity to oxidize or neutralize it. When alcohol is ingested, it is absorbed through the stomach lining and intestinal tract into the bloodstream. The liver then metabolizes the alcohol and purifies the blood. The ability to absorb alcohol into the bloodstream varies among people; absorption is affected, by, among other things, the presence or absence of food in the stomach. When more alcohol is absorbed into the blood system than can be oxidized by the liver, intoxication will ensue. If one ceases to ingest and, hence, to absorb alcohol, the liver keeps working, and sobriety will eventually develop. Thus when one is told to "sleep it off," it is not the sleep but the continued activity of the liver on the alcohol level in the bloodstream, unhampered by further ingestion, that is the causative agent of sobriety (Gillespie, 1969).

Although these two states that are associated with the consumption of alcohol overlap to some degree,[2] various unique social repercussions can be attributed to each. The physiological repercussions of long-term use, or state of alcoholism, have been examined and tied to eventual pathological effects on the body organs; alcohol is suspected of acting synergistically in the development of carcinogenic ailments (Keller, 1974; Chambers, Inciardi, and Siegal, 1975). That society must bear this burden is obvious when one examines the mortality, morbidity, and hospitalization rates within the general population of chronic alcohol users. On the other hand, the threat that drunken driving engenders and the atmosphere that public intoxication fosters, as well as a myriad of social problems ranging from family discord to physically aggressive behavior, are all associated with the intoxicated condition, the alcoholic state, regardless of whether such is the individual's preferred state.[3]

Surely, not everyone who consumes alcohol is consumed by it in turn. Like any other substance with psychotropic potential, the use of alcohol exists in degrees. A critical understanding of alcohol use and abuse therefore cannot be divorced from its social setting. When, what, and how much one drinks at a sitting as well as how frequently one drinks are crucial for a comparative understanding of alcohol's place in society.[4]

Alcohol consumption per se is a widely expected and accepted behavior in society. As Don Cahalan, Ira Cisin, and Helen Crossley state, "The survey [of national drinking practices] confirmed that the use of alcohol is typical rather than unusual behavior for men and women in the United States" (1969, p. 185). In fact, it is the abstainer rather than the drinker that may experience social strain in various festive or convivial situations (Birenbaum & Sagarin, 1973). Alcohol consumption is amenable to social occasions and instrumental in at least some religious rituals (Snyder, 1958; Furst, 1972). Yet, there are occasions when the alcoholic state departs from even those normative expectations associated with its use. It is the state of drunkenness when made highly visible, indulged out of context, or combined with an activity demanding sobriety that causes concern and elicits negative reations. The formal sanctions against public intoxication and drunken driving are good examples.

This chapter will primarily concern itself with the consequences and implications of the use and abuse of alcohol in the social setting. It is no revelation that there are cultural norms associated with alcohol use. Since alcoholism and intoxication deviate from those norms and therefore harbor a high degree of social impact, they will be of most concern.

Unlike more clandestine psychotropic substances, the procurement and use of alcohol bears few important legal restrictions save those, widely evidenced as ineffectual, that aim at prohibiting its sale to or use by minors (see Maddox, 1962; Sterne, Pittman, & Coe, 1967; Jessor, 1973). This high degree of availability results in its widespread contact and influence throughout the society. Although alcohol consumption is rarely restricted on the basis of class, racial, ethnic, and religious rules, those categories are highly correlated with its use. The size of the total population of alcohol users can readily be imagined. Before delving into the various aspects of alcoholism and intoxication, an idea of the scope of its general use within the population and a view of those segments of the public disposed to its consumption is useful.

THE PERVASIVE NATURE OF ALCOHOL USE IN SOCIETY

Generally, the sociologist is little interested in chemical formulas. Yet, in the case of alcohol it proves invaluable. C_2H_5OH, or ethanol, is the active ingredient in all beverages that are considered to be alcoholic (Fort, 1973). It is present in varying degrees in beverages ranging from beer to vodka. All major studies of the incidence and prevalence of alcohol consumption within a society have had to be concerned with the entirety of this wide range of alcoholic beverages.

Authoritative research sponsored by the Rutgers Center of Alcohol Studies determined that over two thirds of the adult population in America indulge in the use of alcohol at least once a year, and that over half indulge as frequently as once a month (Cahalan, Cisin, & Crossley, 1969). The Department of Health, Education, and Welfare (HEW) has indirectly substantiated these findings with its estimate of alcoholic beverage sales, which average out to 2.63 gallons of general alcoholic beverage consumed annually per every member of the adult population (Keller, 1974, p. 3). Further, the Rutgers Center's statistics are directly consistent with earlier large-scale studies (Mulford, 1964). A higher percentage of males than females drink, and among the males consumption is negatively correlated with increasing age. In other words, the highest percentage of nondrinkers is found among the eldest age categories. This can in part be attributed to the peaking-off of alcohol consumption around the age of fifty. Findings such as these have added significantly to the social scientific knowledge of alcohol use, even if it is only that they have filled a formidable void, the scope of which had previously been of great concern to scholars.

These estimates of the general consumption rate include light, moderate, and social drinkers for whom alcohol is socially acceptable and its physiological repercussions are negligible. One of the overall findings of HEW attests to this: "Moderate consumption of alcohol is generally not harmful. In some cases, such as among the elderly, it may have beneficial physical, social and psychological effects" (Keller, 1974, p. 226).

Of more concern are the heavy drinkers: those who tend to be excessive when they do drink, and those who drink rather frequently. It was discovered that heavy drinking, evident in 12 percent of the drinking population, peaks in the age categories of 21–24 for women

and 30–34 for men, and once again at 45–49 for both (Cahala
Crossley, 1969, p. 185).

CORRELATES OF ALCOHOL CONSUMPTION

Race and Ethnicity

Alcohol is part of one's cultural milieu and as such manifests itself
differently within society's various subgroups. The comparative estimates of general and heavy consumption based on ethnicity and race
should be examined critically and should not be used to build stereotypical images. Other considerations, such as class, sex, age, and psychological profile, cannot be divorced from ethnicity and race, and the
reader should therefore view any such material that attempts to equate
alcohol use with certain ethnic groups or races with a reasonable
degree of skepticism. The vehicle by which data is collected and the
inferences and explanations that are drawn from the data, rather than
the data itself, should bear the most scrutiny, since they can be the most
misleading. Even the long-standing and seemingly legendary association between American Indians and alcoholism, replete with theories
of causation ranging from escapism to demoralization, is convincingly
questioned on the grounds that the standards associated with the collection and interpretation of data concerning them are Western European in nature and therefore somewhat inadequate when applied to the
indigenous American population (Levy & Kunitz, 1973).

In discussing white versus black consumption rates, Cahalan, Cisin,
and Crossley have seemingly succeeded in breaking the stereotypical
image of blacks as alcoholics while at the same time accounting for their
relatively higher rate of alcoholism. These researchers state, "White
and Negro men varied little in their rates of drinking. However, Negro
women differed from white women both in their much higher proportions of abstainers and in their high rate of heavy drinkers" (1969, p. 48).
Hence, they submit that the higher incidence of heavy drinkers among
blacks may in fact be due to the nature of the female consumption rate.[5]

The question remains as to why black females are on the whole more
prone to heavy drinking than their white counterparts. Some social
explanations revolve around the relatively different socioeconomic status positions of the two, while others cite differential familial stress, and

still others point to the fairly freer access white females have to other prescription drugs, such as tranquilizers, for coping with their everyday stresses and anxieties. Yet these same considerations may be employed in questioning the validity of the data from which these inferences were derived. It is feasible that familial stresses and socioeconomic status create greater pressures upon the white female respondent to underreport.

Henry Wechsler, Denise Thum, Harold Demone, and Elizabeth Kasey (1970), using breath analyzer readings of patients admitted to a hospital emergency ward, found Jews and Italian Catholics to have the lowest positive indications of alcohol in the bloodstream, while Irish, Canadians, and native-born (American) Catholics had the highest. In a similar study, William and Joan McCord (1960) noted a high relationship of the Irish to problem drinking, although both Western and Eastern Europeans and native-born Americans rated high as well. Their Cambridge-Somerville study found Italians to have a relatively weak relationship with problem drinking. Cahalan, Cisin, and Crossley, in viewing not only problem drinking but general consumption as well, state, "those with fathers born in Ireland had the highest adjusted proportion of both drinkers and heavy drinkers" (1969, p. 48). Italians, followed by Russian, Polish, and Baltic peoples, were found to have a high proportion of drinkers, although not problem drinkers. Catholics as a general ethnic grouping had high proportions of both drinkers and excessive drinkers, and the Jews, while having a high percentage of those who indulge, had a low percentage of excessive users.

Holding fast to the belief that subcultural atmospheres account for high or low percentages of both drinkers and excessive drinkers, Robert Bales, in his study of the Irish and Jewish cultural relationship to liquor, offers an explanation of the higher Irish incidence in the problem drinking category:

> The available evidence indicates that certain strictures on the eating of food have existed in the Irish culture, both situational and psychological, and that there is a tendency to substitute drinking for eating in response to certain situations (1962, p. 159).

Food famines and religious fasting, according to Bales, have taken their toll on the Irish national character. On the other hand, a separation between eating and drinking did not occur in the Jewish culture because the customary and religious strictures placed on both have been equally rigorous.

In seeking other correlates to the high rate of problem drinking among the Irish, Bales turns to an examination of the child's family and community environment. He asserts that from infancy the child is reared in an atmosphere of permissiveness concerning alcohol consumption and is taught and encouraged to participate in this activity by older role models. According to Bales, "The Irish clergy as a whole have always been inclined to be tolerant about drinking" (1962, p. 163). With this point Bales touches upon one of the major correlates of heavy drinking. Cahalan, in a multivariate community analysis of problem drinking, found that "drinking related problems will be more frequent in environments in which heavy drinking is prevalent and condoned" (1969, p. 239).

Yet a permissive culture need not lead to widespread drinking problems, and the Irish, who are professed to have the problem, are not classified by David Pittman (1967) as permissive. An atmosphere in which heavy drinking is condoned can develop in other than a permissive culture and may fail to develop in those subcultures characterized as permissive. For instance, Pittman (1967) has categorized both the Jewish and Italian cultures as permissive towards alcohol consumption. However, while both Giorgio Lolli, Emidio Serianni, Grace Golder, and Pierpaolo Luzzatto-Fegiz (1958) who studied Italians, and Charles Snyder (1958), who worked with Jews, have pointed to the high percentage in these cultures who indulge, they also found that the percentage of problem drinkers in these two groups was not as great as that of the Irish and, in the case of the Jews, was found to be extraordinarily low. Cahalan, Cisin, and Crossley (1969) have noted that there has been a shift since 1958, at least among the Italians, toward a higher proportion of problem drinkers. Ironically, in the case of the Jews, the permissive atmosphere is one in which drunkenness is highly disvalued. The Irish have been found to have a relatively larger number of abstainers as well as heavy users than either the Italians or Jews (Cahalan, Cisin, & Crossley, 1969). Pittman (1967) explains this by characterizing their culture as ambivalent: The Irish people suffer the enigma of problem drinking precisely because theirs is a culture in which alcohol is not smoothly integrated into the religious and value structures of the community. Alcohol is not used in the Irish community for religious or customary reasons but rather for convivial ones.

These ethnic correlates of alcohol consumption cannot be considered absolute. One would expect to see the continued erosion of traditional values and beliefs concerning alcoholic beverages as each succeeding generation becomes more and more adapted to "American" drinking mores.

Social Class

An important early piece of research on the topic of drinking patterns among the social classes was done by John Dollars (1945). His theories are based on the premise that drinking is primarily a learned behavior. We live in a class system, and our thoughts and behavioral patterns differ according to our position in that system. A social class for Dollard consists of "families and groups of associates who could participate together in intimate social hours"; it is a group that shares "motives, sentiments and social connections" (1945, p. 96). Dollard divides social class into six categories, two divisions in each of the upper, middle, and lower classes. In the upper-upper class, condemnation of drinking and drunkenness is minimal, but there exists a very strong censure against violent or aggressive behavior while under the influence of an alcoholic beverage. The lower-upper class is characterized by Dollard as the "cocktail set," where people drink a good deal more frequently than in the upper-upper class. The upper-middle class has a "neutral" attitude toward drinking; it is usually indulged in by men on social occasions and restricted to women of that class. The lower-middle class has a strong taboo against drinking by either sex; as a group it is motivated by a desire to assume a stance of respectability, differentiating it from the lower classes. In the upper-lower class, aggressiveness upon drinking frequently occurs, for this group has not developed the ethic of restraint of aggression and violence. Drinking in the lower-lower class is totally unrestrained, as can be seen by its high percentage of chronic drunkenness and lengthy binges; here can be found sexual equality in drinking practices. In summation, Dollard found that the lower and upper classes drink more than the middle classes. From these findings the notion of the "abstemious" middle class arose (Dollard, 1945, pp. 98–101).

The work of Cahalan, Cisin, and Crossley (1969) modified this position considerably and all but negated the notion of middle-class abstainers. Using a variant of the Hollingshead (1957) Index of Social Position (ISP), which involves such considerations as the education and occupation of the family wage earner and the status and power associated with that occupation, they found that the members of the higher statuses were more likely to be drinkers yet less likely to be heavy drinkers than those of the lower statuses. Furthermore, in controlling for sex as a variable, drinking was found to vary by social status much more among women than men. Additionally, the proportion of abstainers was much higher among lower-status groups than higher ones (Cahalan, Cisin, & Crossley, 1969, p. 26). Summing up their findings based on the ISP, these researchers state:

> Lower proportions of light and moderate drinkers were in the lower ISP groups than in the higher, while the proportion of heavy drinkers in the total sample was about the same at all social levels. Among drinkers, however, the proportion of heavy drinkers tended to be a little higher at lower social levels (1969, p. 186).

In a community study Cahalan examined the psychological and social factors of problem drinking. Out of this he developed an untested but seemingly valid explanation of the lower-class enigma:

> [L]ower sociocultural status may interact with the components of a high psychological score to bring about a higher prevalence of problems because of frustrations induced by relative deprivation (1969, p. 242).

The findings of Joseph Lawrence and Milton Maxwell (1962) are even more crucial in modifying Dollard's position. Using criteria of occupation, education, and family income, they found that 75 percent of the males in each status group from low to high were drinkers. Similarly it was discovered that the females located in the lowest status group were much more likely to be abstainers than those in the higher statuses. In general, the alcohol consumption rate varied according to social status much more among women than men. This work therefore supports the study by Cahalan and his associates in debunking the notion of the abstemious middle class, as well as notions of comparatively "wild" and reckless patterns of alcohol consumption in the lower class. Lawrence and Maxwell state:

> The present study . . . reveals no status level differences among men with regard to quantity and frequency of drinking. The significant difference[s] found among women run counter to Dollard's description (1962, p. 143).

By occupational criteria alone, the farm-owning group had the highest number of abstainers, while the highest proportion of drinkers were found in the professional, semi-professional, technical, sales, and management groups. The educational factor was found to be positively correlated with drinking. In other words, the more education people have, the less likely they are to be abstainers, with the highest proportion of nondrinkers found to be among those with a grammar school education or less. The high education, professionally skilled, high-income groups were described as consistently more indulgent (Cahalan, Cisin, & Crossley, 1969, p. 186).

Region of Residence
There is some regional variation in drinking patterns in the United States. The lowest proportion of drinkers has been found in the East South Central States, followed by other Southern areas and the Mountain states. The highest proportion of both drinkers and heavy drinkers are clustered in the urban areas of the Middle Atlantic, New England, Pacific, and East North Central United States (Cahalan, Cisin, & Crossley, 1969, p. 37). (Refer to the map in Figure 1 to see which states are included in each regional segmentation.)

Urban areas were found to possess a higher incidence of drinking. The Southern states, aside from being more rural in nature than the Middle Atlantic and Pacific regions, have the highest concentration of conservative Protestants who are very negativistic about alcohol consumption; these are two reasons that account for the lower rates of consumption there. These findings are in line with the class findings, since relatively more affluent parts of the population are located in more urban areas and these are the groups that tend to have a higher

Figure 1. The standard American regions as defined by the United States Census Bureau.

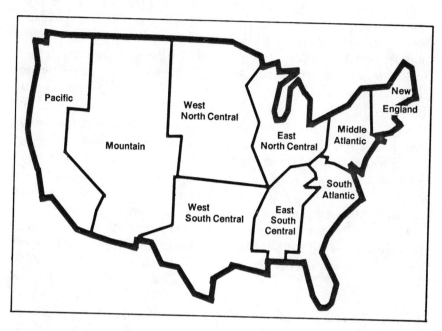

proportion of those that indulge (Cahalan, Cisin, & Crossley, 1969, pp. 38–39).

Youth

The history of alcohol in America is riddled with legal strictures barring its use by various subgroups of the society. Its general sale and use was denied by Prohibition and then reinstated upon repeal. In the early days of slavery, restrictions were placed on its sale or use by blacks, and when the nation expanded and encompassed the indigenous Indian populations, alcohol was similarly denied to them (Larkins, 1965). These regulations came and went, for they were motivated by sentiments and ideologies that changed with the passage of time. Yet perhaps the most consistent—and also most violated—type of control concerns its sale to and use by minors.

Regarding the legal prohibitions placed on alcohol use by minors,

Muriel Sterne, David Pittman, and Thomas Coe state: "Studies of teenage drinking behavior indicate that these laws fail to deter early experimentation with alcohol and often lack either parental or peer-group support" (1967, p. 55). According to Sterne and her colleagues, these legal restrictions were motivated by a belief in the intoxicating and degenerative effects of alcohol and by a desire to preserve respect for authority and order on the part of the youth. Other sentiments behind such laws involve a concern for the proper integration of youthful generations into the mainstream of American society, a feeling that the youth do not possess the developed faculty of reason that would prevent them from abusing and misusing ethanol, and lastly the recognized notion that minors are not legally responsible for their actions. Such sentiments and ideologies, unlike the others that have motivated alcohol prohibition for certain "undergroups" in the society, have remained strong and viable and a focus of concern.

Interestingly, it is the very belief that youth are not "mature" enough to become involved with alcohol consumption that does much to insure their positive sentiments toward alcohol. Alcohol for them is an adult activity; hence its consumption is sought after by youth as persistently as other societal symbols of "coming of age" (Sterne, Pittman, & Coe, 1967, p. 57; Maddox, 1962, p. 240). This youth goal is complicated by the failure of youthful segments of the population to realize that alcohol is a drug.

A false belief in the drug-free nature of alcohol, youth's association of drinking with adulthood, and the availability of alcohol in the home are reasons that George Maddox cites to support his findings that "the most frequently reported situation for the first exposure to alcohol is in the home with parents or other adults present" (1962, p. 233). Specifically, this first exposure was found to involve weak alcoholic beverages, wine or beer, and to occur at the age of fourteen or fifteen. Another estimate put forward by the National Institute of Mental Health (NIMH) (1971) places the age of first experience at ten.

The NIMH disagrees with Maddox's assessment that the first exposure to alcohol is most frequently in the home. Its report states: "Few ... [teenagers] have learned much in their own homes about its use" (1971, p. 16). The NIMH, however, seems to stand alone in this opinion. Albert Ullman (1962), Sterne, Pittman, and Coe (1967), and others seem to concur with Maddox that it is the home, replete with adult role models, in which the teenager not only learns about alcohol but comes to the false impression that it is not a drug per se but a "social elixir."

Although Maddox's view of teenage drinking is basically a social one, in the sense that he views it as a way for the teenager to identify with the adult world, he does not overlook the serious implications of early problem drinking: "For the majority of teenagers the problem is not so much whether or not they will drink but the timing and control of drinking behavior" (1962, p. 244). Undoubtedly, early excessive drinking will provide impediments to the socialization of any youth, but perhaps more alarming, at least to the adult population, is the immediate association of early drinking with serious juvenile delinquency. In dismissing the notion that all teenagers who indulge will become juvenile delinquents, the NIMH reports:

> Although a teenager who drinks is frequently assumed to be a delinquent, a recent Massachusetts investigation showed that the percentage of alcohol users is about the same among delinquents as among normal high school students. The chief difference, the study concluded, is not how many of each group drink but how they drink (1971, p. 15).

In all of these studies, teenage drinking has been characterized as an activity that is as normative as the adult counterpart behavior, and drinking among teenagers, as in the adult case, has been found to vary according to socioeconomic standing, religion, ethnicity, and other pertinent variables. It seems that the drinking that precipitates delinquent behavior tends to be excessive and involves alcoholic beverages of considerable strength. The NIMH report concludes:

> In summary, a young person's decision to drink or not to drink is usually made on the basis of a complex of forces including the practices and wishes of his parents, the attitude of his church, the influence of his peers, how much money he has to spend, and how strongly he may be impelled to assert his independence from adult authority (1971, p. 16).

In the main we may be able to identify at least two types of teenage drinking, one predominantly peer-generated and tied to the youth culture, and the other motivated in the home and tied to anticipatory socialization into adulthood. The reasons that young people may have for imbibing the alcoholic beverage may affect where, when, and with whom they drink. If, as Maddox claims, a youth is seeking to identify with the adult role, ingestion of alcohol in the presence of adults is a logical and welcomed reaffirmation. On the other hand, if the consumption of the alcoholic beverage is not identified by the youth with the adult world but is instead seen as a symbol of the youth culture that emerges anew with each successive generation, then such activity would tend not to be learned and carried out in the presence and with the permission of adults.

According to HEW (Keller, 1974), a staggering number (94 percent) of teenagers has tried alcohol previous to graduating from high school. Additionally, supporting alcohol's popularity among the youth culture, HEW found that among teenagers who smoke marijuana, 92 percent drank as well. To the extent that marijuana is associated with the youth culture among teenagers, those members who drink as well as smoke would find little value in consuming alcohol in the presence of adults. Such reasons for drinking among this group are likely not to be directed toward identification with the adult world but rebellion against it. So as not to give the impression that alcohol is predominantly associated by teenagers with the youth culture, HEW offers an estimate to the effect that of those 94 percent of the teenagers that drank, only 34 percent smoke as well. Logically, then, some 60 percent of HEW's sample of teenagers who indulge seek affirmation of their adulthood (Keller, 1974, p. 12).

Those inclined to view these estimates of teenage drinking with skepticism and to think of them as overestimates should be warned that the studies were carried out on samples drawn from schools. Omitted are those segments of the youth population who were dropouts from the formal institutions of learning and who, if included, would presumably make the figures even higher.

VIEWS OF ALCOHOLISM

Disease and Societal Dimensions of Alcoholism

Howard Jones defines alcoholism as "a disease involving either the loss of control over drinking, once drink has been taken, or the inability to abstain between drinking bouts" (1963, p. 5). Embracing the notion that definitions of alcoholism should include a social dimension, he feels that one is an alcoholic to the extent that drinking interferes not only with one's health but with one's social and economic well-being as well. Mark Keller also believes that alcoholism involves both disease and social dimensions. He defines alcoholism as "a chronic disease manifested by repeated implicative drinking so as to cause injury to the drinker's health or to his social or economic functioning" (1962, p. 316).

The National Institute of Mental Health draws on a more expanded definition that was proffered by Keller in an earlier article:

> Alcoholism is a chronic disease, or disorder of behavior, characterized by the repeated drinking of alcoholic beverages to an extent that *exceeds customary dietary use or ordinary compliance with the social drinking customs of the community,* and which interferes with the drinker's health, inter-personal relations, or economic functioning (NIMH, 1971, p. 6, emphasis added).

This definition brings the notion of community standards into play. Alcoholics, by consensus, exceed community tolerance levels both in their use of ethanol and, more importantly, in their behavior while under its influence.

Including both disease (individualistic) and community reaction (collective) concepts in approaching an understanding of alcoholism, Don Cahalan and Robin Room (1974, pp. 180–181) believe that both processes interweave to some degree to push potential alcoholics to their final destination. In probing the relationship between alcoholism and moderate or normal alcoholic use, Joel Fort asserts:

> In addition to being on a continuum with ordinary or normal alcohol use, alcoholism or problem drinking may appear at any state [point] of alcohol use; usually it appears five or more years after the use of the drug began. Once developed it may remain primarily social and mental in its impact or more commonly, produce varying degrees of damage to the liver and the brain, frequently leading to death (1973, p. 100).

Whether the alcoholic is on the road to physiological damage or social ruin is of little consequence. Both simultaneously need not occur as a result of abuse; either seems a sufficient enough consequence to make

⌐ that one is being controlled rather than being in control of ⌐ s own activity.

Phases of Alcohol Addiction

While all the researchers cited thus far have contributed to an under-standing of the reasons for and the effects of alcohol consumption, it is E. M. Jellinek who has provided the most insightful analyses of alcohol-ism. In his work on the phases of alcohol addiction, Jellinek (1962, pp. 356–368) identifies the first phase as the *prealcoholic symptomatic phase*, which lasts up to two years. This phase, according to Jellinek, is remarkably close to social, moderate, or normal drinking. Both the prospective addict and the nonaddict are socially motivated to drink in the beginning, but the prospective addict soon experiences "reward" and "relief" from his drinking and this is where he starts to differ from the "normal" drinker. The prospective alcoholic either is not able to handle stresses and tensions or has more stresses and tensions than others. Within six months to two years the alcoholic's tolerance to tension severely decreases to the point of daily alcohol ingestion. During this phase, the individual may notice the development of some tolerance to ethanol.

The second or *prodromal phase* is marked by the occurrence of episodes similar to blackouts. By this time the alcoholic, already drink-ing rather heavily, may be able to participate in fluent and cohesive social intercourse, but he has faltering memory concerning his activi-ties. This amnesia without blackout is labeled *alcoholic palimpsests.* Additionally, a fear of being adjudged by others as an alcoholic may guide his actions; he may indulge in "surreptitious drinking." Other symptoms of this phase may be preoccupation with alcohol, avid drink-ing, and guilt feelings.

The third phase of alcohol addiction is called the *crucial phase.* It is marked by loss of control, rationalization of abusive drinking, aggres-sive and grandiose behavior, loss of outside interests, social deteriora-tion, self-pity, neglect of proper nutrition, diminution of sex drive, and first hospitalization. The list could go on.

The *chronic phase* is the final one. Characteristic symptoms are permanent physiological impairment from drinking, possible loss of alcohol tolerance, tremors, possible alcoholic psychosis, psychomotor inhibition, and failure of the rationalization system. By this point the alcoholic may come to recognize and admit to his condition.

Classification of Alcoholism

Jellinek (1960) is also responsible for a comprehensive but often debated classification of alcoholism. In the state that he called *beta alcoholism*, there is degeneration of the body organs by alcohol, as is found in such conditions as cirrhosis of the liver and gastritis, but a physiological or psychological addiction to alcohol is absent. Individuals in this state have had an abnormal physiological reaction to drink. The state of alcoholism, which involves tolerance and withdrawal symptoms with uncontrolled drinking as a result, most clearly approximates *gamma alcoholism*. *Alpha alcoholism* is a purely psychological addiction to ethanol and is likely to precede gamma alcoholism. That is, where physiological dependence exists, it is likely to be accompanied by psychological dependence, although the inverse is not as definite. Gamma alcoholism would thus be characterized by both the loss of control that accompanies psychological dependence and the inability to abstain that marks physiological dependence. *Delta alcoholism* is the same as gamma alcoholism, only the loss of control is not as marked. Periodic alcoholic binges are classified by Jellinek as *epsilon alcoholism* (Chafetz & Demone, 1962, pp. 35–36).

ALCOHOLISM AND THE FAMILY

There is yet one more view on alcoholism that is of interest. Once this notion of interpersonal relationship is introduced into the discussion of alcoholism, its effect upon a purely interpersonal social institution, the family, becomes a logical line of inquiry. Such inquiry may be directed toward the alcoholic alone within the family setting or toward family members. There is much sentiment in the academic community favoring an etiological view of alcoholism in the context of the family—that is, a view of the ways in which family life places demands upon or creates anxiety within the prospective alcoholic member. Injecting their definition of alcoholism with a psychological and interpersonal perspective, Morris Chafetz and Harold Demone state:

We define alcoholism as a chronic behavioral disorder which is manifested by undue preoccupation with alcohol to the detriment of physical
and mental health, by a loss of control when drinking has begun . . . , and
by a self-destructive attitude in dealing with personal relationships and
life situations (1962, p. 4).

In his work on alcoholism and the family, Seldon Bacon (1954)
enunciates a basic incompatibility between alcoholism and family life.
His argument revolves around some noted personality characteristics of
chronic inebriates that make them inadequate in meeting interpersonal
demands that are part of family life and crucial to proper family adjustment. Alcoholics have been described as immature, at times aggressive,
and asocial. Such traits bar the development of "intimate, affectional
relationships of a reciprocal nature" (Bacon, 1954, p. 229). The contention is that intimacy and affection have evolved as major functions of
the family, which has become a haven from a complex, highly rational,
impersonal, competitive, and specialized social existence.

Similarly sympathetic to the psycho-personality approach to family
relations, Joan Jackson (1962, p. 475) cites the many personality malad-
justments of the alcoholic that account for marital failure. The alcoholic
is susceptible to varied and frequent mood changes that make interpersonal relations difficult and cannot express anger constructively in the
familial setting. Feelings of inferiority on the part of the male spouse
inebriate may undermine marital adjustment. Further, the McCords
(1962, pp. 416–417) assert that the alcoholic is unlikely to be able
satisfactorily to express affection within his family. He is likely to take a
passive role in the guidance of his family and propagate, by his own
example and rejection of affection, alcoholism among any male
children.

Jones (1963) has done research on male alcoholics and the effect of
family responsibilities that are placed upon them. He takes an alternative view, one that is much more positive in assessing the effects of
alcoholism upon marriage. Although he admits that the inebriate is
disruptive to a marriage, he found that this notion was more applicable
to those alcoholics who were law violators as well. The marriages of
those who had no history of offenses and who were involved in therapeutic management of their problem were less susceptible to disinte-

gration. The following excerpt illustrates Jones' notion of the positive effect marriage may have on the inebriate:

> It does seem as if the alcoholic who is married, and especially the alcoholic who is very dependent upon his wife, will struggle very hard to hold down a job and to meet other social demands, even to the extent of going to treatment for his alcoholism, if this seems to him to be necessary in order to save the marriage (1963, p. 153).

Chafetz and Demone point out that in the epsilon or periodic form of alcoholism, the family is often wrongly viewed as an etiological factor affecting the alcoholic's behavior: "Too often, suggestions that perhaps the family or some other social institution is responsible for the latest binge are offered" (1962, p. 200). However, families of epsilon alcoholics are less prone than families of "steady" alcoholics to accept some form of therapeutic rehabilitation for their afflicted member. While indicating that alcoholics have a much higher rate of family discord, Chafetz and Demone (1962, p. 166) hold fast to the concept that the alcoholic's family, to some extent, has an influence on his direction. In addition, the authors point to the existence of groups, such as Al-Anon, that are designed to help family members cope with the pressures and stresses an alcoholic member may impose upon them. Here, the emphasis is clearly on family members rather than the alcoholic.

Likewise concerned with alcoholism and the family, Ronald Catanzaro (1967, p. 37) focuses attention on the etiological development of alcoholism from the family background. Emphasis in this case is not on the alcoholic's relationship to his family of procreation, the one in which he stands as husband and possibly as father, but to the family of orientation, the one into which he was born and within which he experienced the process of socialization. Catanzaro cites much research describing antisocial behavior within families that gives rise to alcoholism in children: unfavorable home environments, parental inadequacy, rejection, authoritarianism on the part of the parents, strict moralism, and, last but not least, lack of a family life at all.

From the researchers cited, it can be seen that the precise effect that alcoholism may have within a particular family seems to be dependent upon a number of variables. Generally, it is viewed as having a degenerative and negative effect, the scope of which may depend upon (1) the form that the alcoholism takes, (2) the extent to which it is condoned and prevalent within the family, (3) the particular member involved, (4) the duration and stability of the marriage and home life before the onset of alcoholism and in particular the strength of the bonds of commitment between family members, (5) the specific physical and legal complications that enmesh the alcoholic as a result of the drinking problem, and (6) the degree to which the afflicted member is inclined to undergo therapy, as well as the resources the family may have to secure such therapy.

ALCOHOL AND THE COMMUNITY: THE CASE OF SKID ROW

Community notions of proper moral guidance or restraint of alcohol consumption are buttressed and imposed upon members by the formal legal rules, or criminal sanctions, placed primarily upon the alcoholic state. There is a general disapproval of and negative reaction to the state of intoxication when highly visible, as it is when it occurs in public, or overly hazardous, as it is in certain situations, such as driving, that have been defined by society as mandating sobriety. This is not to imply that there are not certain occasions, such as weddings and other festivities, that permit a fair amount of tolerance for the same state. Yet the tolerance that extends during the ritual dissipates at its end. Many people, although not really worrying, often wonder just what happened to that poor fellow at the party who showed signs of having had "one too many." The participants at such occasions will often remark as they egress, "I wonder if he'll make it home all right."

Wonderment and moderate concern turns to distress and disgust when the effect of alcohol is viewed in another social setting. Perhaps the most degenerative and blatant effect alcohol may have within a community, one that brings forth extremely negativistic and hostile reactions, is associated with its role in either bringing about or supporting a "skid row."

Jacqueline Wiseman accounts for the strong negative feelings that are harbored by members of the larger community towards skid row inhabitants by describing the popular, prevalent, and "professional" view of this inner-city phenomenon:

Skid row is seen as a prime manifestation of social pathology. The physical deterioration of the buildings and the resultant lowering of property values of adjacent areas is but one aspect of this threat. The social and psychological deterioration of its residents, inevitably resulting in added cost to the city for police surveillance and human care, is another (1970, p. 5).

A skid row is undoubtedly an unattractive, run-down area, and the highly visible, down-and-out state of the people who live there detracts from it even more. There is, however, much controversy over the role that alcohol plays in the creation and maintenance of the skid row and in the lives of its inhabitants. Harvey Siegal, David Petersen, and Carl Chambers (1975) assert that only a minority of skid row residents are driven there by excessive drinking, and few are problem drinkers. Skid row, in their view, is a community composed of social misfits who end up there because of their inability to deal with a variety of pressures, not specifically because of alcoholism. The skid row community is cohesive, rejected, and vulnerable to outside social forces that constantly modify the lifestyle of the skid rowers.

Samuel Wallace (1965) makes a fine distinction between the alcoholic and the drunk, both of whom are found on skid row. The skid row alcoholic tends to be separated from the collective drinking activity of the other denizens of that marginal world. He is not likely to share his alcohol with the cohesive group of drunks that has been called the "bottle gang," and hence he will probably not be included in its collective drinking. Yet Wallace asserts that drunkenness is a striking feature of the lifestyle of skid rowers, that it is a basic value of the skid row subculture. Members of the subculture are pressed into drinking activities that are defined as part of the group's basic norms. Wallace states:

> To be completely acculturated in skid row subculture is to be drunk—since skid rowers place strong emphasis on group drinking and the acculturated person is by definition a conformist. The drunk has rejected every single one of society's established values and wholly conformed to the basic values of skid row subculture. Food, shelter, employment, appearance, health and all other considerations are subordinated by the drunk to the group's need for alcohol (1965, p. 182).

The difference between the skid row drunk and the alcoholic, then, is that the latter is driven to alcohol by individual pathological cravings, while the former is driven by conformity to group norms. Alcohol consumption, in Wallace's view, is a very important and potent maintenance process of the skid row way of life. Whether or not one comes to skid row with an alcohol problem, he soon learns to indulge in collective drinking and drunkenness if he wishes to be accepted into the group. It is within the bottle gang that comaraderie and loyalty develop. Heavy drinking in this atmosphere is socially accepted and condoned. The absence of negative sanctions towards drinking, combined with alcohol's capacity to reduce anxiety and frustration, offers a logical and understandable way of structuring and coping with existence on this level.

The homeless, skid row, and disaffiliation have been the concern of Howard Bahr (1973), who differs from Wallace in viewing the bottle gang as a less cohesive social unit and one that is responsible for little loyalty. Bahr, however, does seem to espouse the alcohol-oriented nature of the subculture. In distinguishing between skid row and other alcoholics, he focuses on the disparity of community perceptions and reactions to them. Using as an example the increasing popularity of the medical model or the disease concept, of alcoholism, Bahr asserts that this model has served to assuage social attitudes towards other "respectable" alcoholics, but that it has only reinforced the negative view that the larger community holds of the skid rower. The clear and widely held picture of the inhabitants of skid row is that he is homeless, poverty stricken, and beset by personal problems.

> [This] homeless man is seen as dirty, defective and morally inferior; he is diseased, hopeless and non-redeemable. He tends to be treated by agents of society with intolerance and disrespect, avoidance and fearfulness, disgust and apprehension (Bahr, 1973, p. 86).

Within such a community of thought and opinion the disease concept of alcoholism becomes an excuse for showing disapproval for the derelict's condition and for restricting his freedom by forcing him to submit to involuntary institutionalization. In short, it becomes a rationale for isolating and eliminating him from the wider society.

The disease concept of alcoholism, however, does not need to have a negative effect on derelicts. It has led to a still experimental therapy for skid rowers. The National Institute on Alcohol Abuse and Alcoholism (NIAAA) (1975, p. 6) reports that therapy involving maintenance of the skid rower on the drug *disulfiram* (antabuse) within an alcohol-free environment has met with some success in the rehabilitation of New York's Bowery inhabitants.

ALCOHOLISM AS A DEVIANT MODE OF ADAPTATION IN SOCIETY

There is little dissent over the fact that the skid rower represents an acute social problem. To the extent that alcohol is associated with the skid row lifestyle, it generally comes to be viewed and treated, along with the skid rower, as a social problem. Cahalan and Room (1974) contend that viewing alcoholism as a social problem is only one of three possible approaches, for it can also be considered as a vice or a disease. Notions of alcohol as a vice are directly tied to the nature of the drinking behavior, specifically to intake or consumption that is heavy The disease concept focuses on the condition of the individual drinker (alcoholic); it is concerned with the physiological and psychological ramifications of excessive drinking. Finally, the social problem approach gives greater emphasis to the afflicted individual's relation with the wider society and culture of which he is a part (Cahalan & Room, 1974, p. 8). These approaches tend to unite in producing a picture of alcoholism as aberrant behavior that has negative repercussions for either the alcoholic, his intimate others, or the society at large.

The binge drinker, who is susceptible to bouts of drunkenness, is professed to possess a vice. Here the excessive drinking is viewed as a "bad habit" that must be overcome through self-control. Should the individual not exercise the needed control or not seek therapy that would help him to gain control, he is likely to fall subject to discipline emanating from laws and formal sanctions that deal with socially unacceptable behavior. The disease concept or medical model, like the vice model, tends to impart a moral judgment upon the alcoholic with one major modification: It is not believed that the individual has the capacity to control the drinking behavior in question. The alcoholic must face the fact that he is afflicted with a disease that he cannot control and that he cannot hope to overcome by himself. He must seek out appropriate psychological or physiological therapy in his quest for a return to normalcy or health. The social problem approach, with its focus on the expanded cultural milieu, involves the identification of the collective or social structural forces that are at work driving the individual alcoholic to his impending doom. In this view alcoholism is seen as one mode of deviant conduct in the wider society; the deviance is generated in part by social forces beyond the actor's control.

Whether viewed as a vice, a sickness, or a social problem, then, alcoholism is considered to be a deviant behavior. Therefore, differential association, anomie, and labeling theories, all of which have been used to explain various forms of social deviance, have been applied to the alcoholic experience and circumstance.

Differential Association Theory

Differential association was first advanced by Edwin Sutherland (1947) to account for various forms of juvenile delinquency and subsequent adult criminality. It is very broadly defined as a learning process. Sutherland believed that some ghetto youth learn about crime through frequency and intensity of association with the successful criminal types of their milieu (pimps, drug pushers, career criminals), and that many do not follow the rules of normative behavior because the ghetto does not provide equal frequency and intensity of association with role models who can reinforce alternative lifestyles to crime. Such youth come to aspire to deviant roles and to value and enact activities that conform to those deviant statuses. In the case of alcoholism the negative environment is likely to occur in the home and not on the street. That is, the deviant association is likely to be with one or both parents or a close adult familial relation of the prospective youthful alcoholic; the youth will probably not have a nondrinking model to supply a view of alternative behaviors. In a more general sense, differential association is provided if one's subculture takes a relatively permissive attitude toward heavy drinking (this to the extent that the individual's subculture is believed to have a serious impact on his drinking pattern). While the differential association is most likely to occur in the home, it can also be found within the larger community outside of the home. A person who begins to visit bars, saloons, or taverns will be reinforced in his drinking habits, for alcohol consumption, often heavy, is the norm in these environments. Cahalan and Room (1974, p. 9) point out that bars have inevitably come under attack during temperance movements because they are believed to sustain and encourage a subculture of heavy drinking.

The barroom environment may also provide a differential association that leads to further deviant behavior. Not only is the bar a focus of convivial drunkenness, but it is also likely to offer other "vices" to the neophyte. The prostitute often plies her trade in the saloon atmosphere, and the patrons themselves, although consuming alcohol, may be involved with or exposed to illicit drugs that, like alcohol, serve to produce an altered state of consciousness. Differential association theory allows for the possibility that a prospective alcoholic may take affiliated deviant directions, and it thereby provides flexibility for those who are disposed to working within its framework.

Practical considerations, however, demand the modification of some of the assumed results of differential association. Cahalan, Cisin, and Crossley (1969) point out that there is a very high alcohol saturation level in American society. This leads one to suspect the degree to which association with an alcoholic will provide a youth with an attractive asocial or aberrant model. However, it remains true that a youth may come to alcoholism through a great deal of association with alcoholics; that he may reject such associations because they serve as particularly unattractive models; or that he may be attracted to drinking because his subculture presents it as a rite of passage into adulthood. These are conflict-generating and anxiety-producing influences. Perhaps it is better in the case of alcoholism to stress the environmental and learning aspects of the differential association theory and leave aside notions that the association is desirable to the youth because it provides a model that is at odds with the larger society.

Anomie Theory

The concept of anomie was first introduced by Emile Durkheim, and it was most notably elaborated upon by Talcott Parsons and Robert Merton. The early work on suicide by Durkheim (1951) views group cohesion as a factor that in part accounts for suicide rates in the general population. During times of crisis (economic depression or sudden prosperity in the society), persons may experience *anomie*—a condition that, broadly defined, approximates a state of normlessness—because they feel that the society upon which they depend is disintegrating. As a result of anomie, the suicide rate climbs. The reason why social crises may lead some persons, but not others, to commit anomic suicide can be found in the fact that the former have expectations that are tied to certain social conditions. Thus, in an extreme economic depression, a person may experience anomie because of being prevented from achieving personal life goals. Many anomic suicides occurred during the stock market crash of 1929 because persons were deprived of the security that their society had previously given to them.

Parsons defines anomie as the opposite of institutionalization:

> The polar antithesis of full institutionalization is, however, *anomie*, the absence of structured complementarity of the interaction process or, what is the same thing, the complete breakdown of normative order in both senses (1951, p. 39).

Merton (1957) employed anomie to explain various forms of deviant behavior in society. His paradigm, which he refers to as a "theory of the middle range," involves the notion that success in American society is materialistically interpreted. He asserts that practically everyone aspires to material success. Yet the legitimate, normative, and accepted means of accomplishing these material goals or ends are not clearly defined, nor are these means any more readily available than the goals themselves. As a result, a condition of anomie ensues. Conformity, innovation, ritualism, retreatism, and rebellion all represent different modes of personality response to a social structure in which uneven access to prescribed goals and legitimate means is fostered.

The impact of anomie is perhaps most vividly apparent in the skid rower. Surrounded by a society with a normative way of life that he rejects, filled with a sense of anomie, the derelict's response is retreatism, and he finds whatever little solace he can in drink. In applying anomie and its psychological counterpart, anomia, to an understanding of alcoholism, Charles Snyder suggests that, as in the case of suicide, social pathologies such as inebrity and alcoholism are "sensitive indicators of the vicissitudes of the social order" (1964, p. 189). Put more simply, the anomic response of retreatism in alcohol is a telling sign of social crisis. In addition, Snyder points to the work done by David Pittman and Wayne Gordon (1962, pp. 535–546) as a persuasive application of Merton's retreatist, or "double failure," category to those who are repeatedly arrested for chronic drunkenness.

Turning to one of his own interests, alcoholism and the Jews, Snyder injects anomic considerations into an understanding of the development and impact of social drinking mores within subcultural groups:

> Without discounting the significance of specific normative attitudes towards drinking itself in thwarting drinking pathologies, it was proposed that the solidarity of the group and the relative absence of anomia seem of greater significance than has generally been acknowledged in accounting for the rarity of inebrity and alcoholism among the more traditional Jews (1964, p. 208).

Similarly, Snyder believes that the presence of anomie may, in certain instances, be at the crux of chronic inebrity. Although Snyder does not specifically do so, the theory of anomie may be applied to explain alcoholism among the American Indians. From contact with the external and dominant society, the culture of the American Indians began to decay. Further, there was no substitute culture for these people to adopt, for they were maintained in a marginal relationship to the larger society. As a result, the formerly well-adjusted members of the declining American Indian subculture were strongly impelled toward alcoholism. The same phenomenon can be seen in other cultures that are destroyed or disrupted through exposure to some other dominant society.

In his concluding remarks, Snyder expresses his belief that anomie is a fruitful frame of reference from which to understand alcoholism in society:

> This entire discussion leads to the conclusion that the approach to understanding inebrity and alcoholism via the notion of anomie—an approach heretofore seldom taken—promises to be fruitful. It would be premature to pass judgment on the importance of specific sources of anomie, such as those identified by Merton. But there are many intimations that the generic concept will prove useful, will we but use it (1964, p. 210).

Labeling Theory

Howard Becker (1963) has described deviant behavior as behavior that is so labeled. With this simple statement, emphasis is diverted from the individual "deviant actor" and focused on the community of "normals" who are assumed to partake in the labeling process. Crucial to this theory is the idea of the societal reaction to various acts and actors. Different actors, depending on their place in the social order, run dissimilar risks of being labeled deviant. What may be merely rule violation for one results in negative labeling for another. Drawing on Edwin Lemert (1951), John Kitsuse (1962), Becker (1963), and Edwin Schur (1965), Edward Sagarin (1975, p. 128) provides a concise and reasonable summary of the labeling perspective: (1) Actions derive their connotations of "badness" through the process of being defined by law abiders and rule makers. (2) Emphasis is placed upon the processes in society whereby some people gain the power to define others as deviant. (3) The assignment of a deviant label and the negative reaction to those so labeled are more dependent upon who the transgressor is than what the particular transgression might be. (4) Labeling a person as deviant results in *secondary deviation;* in other words, the labeling process itself "fixes" an individual in that status. Finally, (5) excluding the labeled from the activity and life of normals and locking common misfits into stigmatized categories aids in the development of "deviant careers."

Employing a psychological orientation in their analysis of an international sample of drinkers and abstainers, Wendell Lipscomb and Jay Holden (1974) contend that the risk of being labeled an alcoholic on the basis of drinking practices is uniform and similar for psychologically comparative groups. On the basis of their sample they state:

> In summary, the distribution and risk of being labeled "alcoholic," operationally defined in terms of drinking practices, are clearly different for various psychiatric groups (i.e., "alcoholics," "mentally ill" and "normals"), but are remarkably similar for psychiatrically comparable samples of various nationalities (1974, p. 34).

Harvey Marshall and Ross Purdy (1972) employ the labeling perspective in seeking to ascertain the dynamics of arrests for drunken driving. Using official police statistics and counterposing these to a sample of self-reports drawn from the California Division of Motor Vehicles, they assert the validity of the labeling model, for they found that arrests for drunken driving are somewhat independent of the proclaimed degree of frequency with which this aberrant behavior is enacted. Aside from their findings, their work was most supportive of the labeling perspective in the sense that it was an attempt at an empirical validation of labeling tenets in the face of the frequent criticism of labeling because of its basic incongruence with "hard data" or empirical testing.

There are other reasons why labeling as a mode of understanding and explaining deviant phenomena in society has attracted strong criticism, especially in its application to alcoholism and alcohol-related aberrant behavior. One critic, Lee Robins (1975, pp. 24–28), provides a methodical, organized assault on the labeling theory and alcoholism. She notes that the initial labelers tend to be close informal relations of the alcoholic and not outside societal authorities. The alcoholic is likely to be labeled by family members, friends, and associates before an employer, doctor, or the police make the discovery and place the label. Thus, the influence of the initial label in reinforcing an alcoholic's behavior is considerably less than it is in the case of other deviant actors, such as the juvenile delinquent and the psychotic, who are initially formally labeled deviant by official agencies of social control. Moreover, heavy drinking may persist for a considerable number of years without benefit of a label at all: The relief of anxiety and the feeling of euphoria may be sufficient reinforcement for heavy drinking patterns. Citing inaccurate police statistics on inebrity and criminal activity, falsified death certificates by compassionate physicians, and the misdiagnosis of alcohol-related physical pathology in the hospitals, Robins contends that the "official" agencies with the power to confer the formal label of alcoholic are often hesitant to do so, yet the incidence and prevalence of alcoholism remains relatively unaffected. The inverse notion that reluctance of formal agencies of social control to impart labels should result in limiting the proliferation of the deviant behavior is negated in face of soaring rates of alcoholism despite this leniency. Finally, heavy use of alcohol may result in physiological addiction, which itself provides the impetus for continued drinking, apart from negative social attitudes that at best only explain initial or original heavy drinking.

THE INCULCATION OF A LABEL: A MAJOR FORM OF THERAPY

Despite Robins' rejection, the labeling perspective has been successfully employed to help alcoholics deal with their problem. Combined with the disease concept of alcoholism, labeling forms the basis of a prevalent form of therapy that has been used most notably by Alcoholics Anonymous (AA). Labeling and disease approaches to alcoholism are able to be combined into one form of therapy, for, as Cahalan and Room (1974, p. 19) point out, they both place little emphasis on the amount of drinking a deviant actor may indulge in. That is, the fact of drinking, rather than the amount that is drunk, determines that a person will be labeled an alcoholic or seen to be suffering from a sickness.

The Philosophy and Technique of Alcoholics Anonymous

Referring back to the stages of alcoholism described by Jellinek (1962), it can be recalled that during the prodromal, or second, phase of alcoholism, the prospective alcoholic is very aware of how others perceive him, and he will indulge in surreptitious drinking to conceal his problem and prevent a negative labeling of himself by others. It is AA's contention that the road to recovery is basically contingent upon the individual alcoholic's acceptance of the label himself. Regardless of the societal reaction, a major concern of the labeling school, the alcoholic must of necessity admit that he is an alcoholic, whether he happens to be drinking or "on the wagon" at any particular moment. He is an alcoholic whether he gets drunk frequently or drinks only socially. Alcoholism exists in the absence of negative social, psychological, or physiological repercussions; a person is an alcoholic if he cannot control his propensity to drink, if he cannot say no (Gellman, 1964).

In the AA concept, accepting the label of alcoholic and society's negative judgment of that label is very crucial in learning to control the behavior. Such acceptance serves several purposes: (1) It forces an alcoholic to recognize and to resign him to the reality of his affliction; (2) it reinforces the actor's negative valuation of his own undesirable drinking activity; and (3) it shows affirmation of and solidarity with the wider, respectable, society of "normals." A member of Alcoholics Anonymous, in the absence of visible psychological, physical, or social deterioration that may accrue from drinking, has beaten society to the draw. It is as if he is saying to himself and to the world: "I have labeled myself an alcoholic. I realize my weakness and I have the strength to admit it. Therefore I am not susceptible and not deserving of your [society's] disvaluation." If the alcoholic's drinking has been visible and he has thus come to be labeled as an alcoholic within the community, he then takes the line: "You know I'm an alcoholic and I agree with you . . . yet because I agree with you and admit the errors of my ways, you should not evaluate me negatively . . . I am the first to point to the undesirable nature of alcoholism . . . and although I am helpless in coping with it alone, I am positively affirmed to overcome it with the aid of others similarly situated and equally committed to an alcohol-free, healthy social existence."

In examining the process of conversion to Alcoholics Anonymous, Michael Petrunik (1972) describes as likely converts the down-and-outers: people with serious psychological, physiological, or social problems of adjustment, who, as a result of their drinking patterns, have arrived at what they consider to be a low point in their existence. For them the AA process is one of moral regeneration, gained through an objective acceptance that their former behavior was, as a fact, immoral and asocial. The AA embraces the disease concept of alcoholism; its official view dictates that alcoholism can never be cured, only arrested, and the route one must follow is not medical but spiritual.

Criticisms of Alcoholics Anonymous

This therapy approach, which combines both disease (medical) and labeling (societal reaction) concepts of alcoholism, has been the center of much controversy. The criticism is generally aimed at the tenability, desirability, and successfulness of the AA process as a positive form of therapy.

Harrison Trice and Paul Roman (1970), although stressing the importance of the "repentant role" in AA rehabilitation, conclude that participation in the therapy does not prevent a negative evaluation of the participants. They feel that the deviant actor (the alcoholic) goes through a process whereby his identity is changed from stigmatized to reformed: that is, whereby it is "delabeled" and then "relabeled." They state:

> Alcoholics Anonymous possesses, as a consequence of the nature of the disorder of alcoholism, its uniqueness as an organization, and the existence of certain value orientations within the American society, a pattern of social processing whereby a labeled deviant can become "delabeled" as a stigmatized deviant and "relabeled" as a former and repentant deviant (1970, p. 545).

Therefore, the activity of Alcoholics Anonymous, which can be considered an organization of self-professed deviants, culminates not in a disavowel of alcoholism as a deviant mode of adaptation in society, but in a condemnation of the basically amoral, asocial, self-destructive depths of a practicing alcoholic's life. In their unswerving diligence and adamant condemnation of alcohol, the members of AA are aspiring to a "dry" existence and a more favorable reevaluation of their place in the community.

Trice and Roman point to a positive aspect of the function of the disease concept, or what they call the allergy model, of alcoholism in AA therapy:

> The significance of this [the allergy] concept is that it serves to diminish, both in the perception of AA members and their immediate significant others, the alcoholic's responsibility for developing the behavior disorder (1970, p. 540).

Limited responsibility proves efficacious in aiding the repentant alcoholic to accept and then condemn his former behavior while at the same time espousing abstinence. However, both Trice and Roman (1970) and Petrunik (1972) subscribe to the belief that the adoption of the disease or medical model of alcoholism by the AA and its members does little, in the eyes of the public, to relieve the alcoholic of responsibility for his deviant actions.

Paul Chalfant and Richard Kurtz (1970) have provided an explanation of this discrepancy. Noting the tendency of social workers to apply the disease concept of alcoholism to those alcoholics who fall under their purview, they determined that the medical model serves predominantly as an in-group function: A group to which an alcoholic belongs will be more likely to consider his deviant behavior as a disease and thus to relieve him of responsibility for his actions. Kurtz discovered that in the larger society certain personal characteristics, such as occupation, education, and familial circumstances, are taken as indicators of the alcoholic's value to the society. The more valuable he is found to be, the more likelihood there is of the disease concept being applied to his affliction by those who have the official authority to make such an application. The society's insistence, then, that AA converts bear responsibility for their actions would be explained by Petrunik's description of them as downwardly mobile in occupation and as saddled with familial and interpersonal strife. These people would not be considered valuable to their society and would thus find little sympathy among official labelers for their categorization into the medical model.

Thus, the view that alcoholism is a disease does not shield members of AA from negative valuation by others. Moreover, the AA itself, despite its espousal of the medical model, has done little to promote general acceptance of the model and thus to alter the negative public image of the practicing alcoholic. The reason for AA's inaction can also be explained by viewing the medical model as an in-group function: AA will not extend its help to alcoholics who have not entered its fold. Participation in AA activities is a requisite; the AA restricts its activity to offering sanctuary only to those who join and participate. This seeming paradox is consistent with the AA line that only it can really help the alcoholic.

Although accolades have routinely been strewn upon AA—its work praised and success attested to by social scientists and important personages—healthy criticism of its processes and philosophies cannot be ignored. The notion that one is a "life-long" alcoholic, whether he drinks or not, has been attacked as too severe. Recent research on alcoholism, sponsored by the National Institute on Alcohol Abuse and Alcoholism and the Rand Corporation (1976), has attested to the feasibility and reality of an alcoholic's return to socially acceptable drinking patterns. Sagarin (1972), in his study of organizations of deviants (Mattachine, Synanon, Little People of America, AA, and so on), similarly embraces the possibility that the problem drinker, the likes of which one may find in AA, may return to social or moderate drinking behavior. The idea that an alcoholic, self-proclaimed or otherwise, is always an alcoholic and cannot return to the ranks of the "normals" may be more an organizational mechanism, one that provides for the perpetuation of AA as an ongoing organization, than a therapeutic safeguard for its members. Additionally, AA's informal structure itself, while assuring anonymity to its members, may be an impediment to an objective estimation of its true success or even popularity.

George Lowe and Eugene Hodges (1972) have pointed to AA's total failure in reaching Southern blacks, at least those in Atlanta. They believe that either AA itself or some external agency should undertake research into AA's philosophy and image in an effort to account for this failing. Yet, AA for the most part has been able to evade unfavorable scrutiny; its basic policies and views remain intact and entrenched to the point where any attempt at modification would be difficult. This entrenchment alone may eventuate in AA's obsolescence, for breakthroughs in alcoholism rehabilitation are likely to be rejected by AA. Such discoveries are therefore left to other private or public health facilities that may be able to use them to deal more successfully than AA with the rehabilitation of the alcoholic.

CONCLUDING REMARKS

Essentially, alcohol has been identified as a chemical substance. It is one of the few drugs freely available in the society that has the capacity to produce an altered state of consciousness and, through excessive and continued use, a state of physiological or psychological addiction. Its moderate consumption is not only physiologically, psychologically, and socially beneficial but has become, to a large extent, an institutionalized feature of American life. This has made the study of alcohol consumption especially conducive to sociological investigation.[6]

Typically, sex, age, ethnic, religious, and class distinctions have been used in the identification of drinking patterns, attitudes, and values that affect the society at large. The alcoholic state and the state of alcoholism, which are associated with abuse and which stand side by side with general use in the society, are identified as major social problems predominantly because of the social costs (monetary) incurred as a result.

Family discord, community decay, and personal tragedy are hallmarks of an alcoholic or chronic drunkenness lifestyle. There is a consensus that psychological, physiological, and social deteriorations are attributes indicative of the onset of alcoholism. Yet the process of becoming an alcoholic is viewed as one that is protracted and liable to occur at almost any time in the life of any persons, except those who remain totally abstinent. The fact that some become abusers while others maintain relatively moderate consumption practices has led researchers to examine the alcoholic's environment in an attempt to isolate socio-structural and psycho-situational variables that intercede and play a part in effecting an alcoholic adjustment to society.

Numerical estimates of alcoholics in society are highly controversial but nevertheless provide some idea of the scope of those so afflicted in the nation. The National Institute of Mental Health (1971, p. 10) estimates that there are between 4 and 5 million alcoholics in the United States; NIMH (1974, p. viii) puts forth an estimate of approximately 9 million alcohol abusers and alcoholic individuals; and according to an article appearing in *The New York Times,* the head of New York City health services believes that there are some 300,000 alcoholics in that city alone, with the national figure ranging from approximately 3 to 5 million (*The New York Times,* 1971).

Taking into account lost productivity in industry, health and medical care, motor vehicle accidents, alcohol programs and research, prosecution of alcohol-related criminal offenses in the criminal justice system, and the operations of the social welfare system, NIMH (Keller, 1974, p. 50) concludes that for a one year period (1971) alcohol cost the society some $25 billion. Yet this estimate represents only the societal costs of alcoholism. Holt Babbitt (1967), using a sample of alcoholics in a midwestern rehabilitation facility, analyzed the cost of alcoholism to the individual alcoholic and asserted that alcoholism is marked by economic as well as psychological, physiological, and social deterioration. The cost of alcoholic beverages, loss of wages, destruction of home furnishings and personal belongings, expenses due to accidents, and other miscellaneous costs amount to a conservative estimate of approximately $1,000 to $1,600 per individual alcoholic per annum in maintaining addiction.

NOTES

1. Although the term *spirits* was a seventeenth century interpretation of distilled liquor whereby distilled liquor was perceived as the "spirit of the wine from which it was taken"—this is rarely realized and in its common usage it has come to be allied with liquor's effect upon users.

2. Thum, Wechsler, and Demone (1971) point to a correlation between those suffering from alcoholism and the incidence of arrest for public intoxication and drunken driving. Pittman (President's Commission, 1967, p. 8) points to the existence of the nonaddicted inebriate.

3. If the alcoholic state is a condition *preferred* by the individual, then addiction is indicated (Elinson & Nurco, 1975).

4. This notion is a mainstay of a social inquiry into alcohol consumption. Hollingshead (1956), Lolli et al. (1958), Ullman (1962), and Cahalan (1969, 1974) all give expression to this sentiment.

5. Sterne (1967) cites numerous studies from the *Quarterly Journal of Studies on Alcohol* that support these researchers' findings in this respect. Also, see Malzberg (1955), Bahn and Chandler (1961), Moon and Patton (1963), and Bailey, Haberman, and Alksne (1965).

6. This is a position taken by Cahalan, Cisin, and Crossley (1969).

BIBLIOGRAPHY

Babbitt, E. Holt. "What Does It Cost To Be an Alcoholic?" In David J. Pittman, ed. *Alcoholism.* New York: Harper & Row, 1967, pp. 45–52.

Bacon, Seldon D. "Excessive Drinking and the Institution of the Family." In Yale University Center of Alcohol Studies. *Alcohol, Science and Society.* New Haven, Conn.: *Quarterly Journal of Studies on Alcohol*, 1954, pp. 223–238.

Bahn, Anita K., and Caroline A. Chandler. "Alcoholism in Psychiatric Clinic Patients." *Quarterly Journal of Studies on Alcohol*, 1961, 22:411–417.

Bahr, Howard M. *Skid Row.* New York: Oxford University Press, 1973.

Bailey, Margeret B., Paul W. Haberman, and Harold Alksne. "The Epidemiology of Alcoholism in an Urban Residential Area." *Quarterly Journal of Studies on Alcohol*, 1965, 26:19–40.

Bales, Robert F. "Attitudes toward Drinking in the Irish Culture." In David J. Pittman and Charles R. Snyder, eds. *Society, Culture and Drinking Patterns.* New York: John Wiley and Sons, 1962, pp. 159–187.

Becker, Howard S. *Outsiders: Studies in the Sociology of Deviance.* New York: The Free Press, 1963.

Birenbaum, Arnold, and Edward Sagarin, eds. *People in Places.* New York: Praeger, 1973.

Cahalan, Don. "A Multivariate Analysis of the Correlates of Drinking-Related Problems in a Community Study." *Social Problems*, 1969, 17:234–247.

Cahalan, Don, Ira H. Cisin, and Helen M. Crossley. *American Drinking Practices: A National Study of Drinking Behavior and Attitudes.* New Brunswick, N.J.: Rutgers Center of Alcohol Studies, 1969.

Cahalan, Don, and Robin Room. *Problem Drinking Among American Men.* New Brunswick, N.J.: Rutgers Center of Alcohol Studies, 1974.

Catanzaro, Ronald J. "Psychiatric Aspects of Alcoholism." In David J. Pittman ed. *Alcoholism.* New York: Harper & Row, 1967, pp. 31–45.

Chafetz, Morris E., ed. *Proceedings of the First Annual Alcoholism Conference of the National Institute of Alcohol Abuse and Alcoholism.* Washington, D.C.: Department of Health, Education, and Welfare, 1973.

Chafetz, Morris E., and Harold W. Demone. *Alcoholism and Society.* New York: Oxford University Press, 1962.

Chalfant, Paul, and Richard Kurtz. "Social Workers and Labeling the Alcoholic." Paper presented to the American Sociological Association, Washington, D.C., September 1970.

Chambers, Carl D., James A. Inciardi, and Harvey A. Siegal. *Chemical Coping.* New York: Spectrum, 1975.

Dollard, John. "Drinking Mores of the Social Classes." In Yale University

Center of Alcohol Studies. *Alcohol, Science and Society.* New Haven, Conn.: *Quarterly Journal of Studies on Alcohol,* 1945, pp. 95–104.

Durkheim, Emile. *Suicide.* Translated by John A. Spaulding and George Simpson. Glencoe, Ill.: The Free Press, 1951.

Elinson, Jack, and David Nurco, eds. *Operational Definitions in Socio-Behavioral Drug Use Research 1975.* Rockville, Md.: National Institute on Drug Abuse, 1975.

Fort, Joel. *Alcohol: Our Biggest Drug Problem.* New York: McGraw-Hill, 1973.

Furst, Peter T., ed. *Flesh of the Gods.* New York: Praeger, 1972.

Gellman, Irving. *The Sober Alcoholic.* New Haven, Conn.: College and University Press, 1964.

Gillespie, Duff G., ed. *Alcohol, Alcoholism and Law Enforcement.* St. Louis, Mo.: Washington University, Social Science Institute, 1969.

Gross, Milton, M., ed. *Alcohol Intoxication and Withdrawal: Experimental Studies.* New York: Plenum, 1973.

Hollingshead, August B. "Views on the Etiology of Alcoholism: IV. The Sociologic View." In H. D. Kruse, ed. *Alcoholism as a Medical Problem.* New York: Hoeber-Harper Books, 1956, pp. 56–67.

Hollingshead, August B. *Social Class and Mental Illness: A Community Study.* New York: John Wiley and Sons, 1958.

Jackson, Joan K. "Alcoholism and the Family." In David J. Pittman and Charles R. Snyder, eds. *Society, Culture and Drinking Patterns.* New York: John Wiley and Sons, 1962, pp. 472–492.

Jellinek, E. M. *The Disease Concept of Alcoholism.* New Haven, Conn.: Hillhouse Press, 1960.

Jellinek, E. M. "Phases of Alcohol Addiction." In David J. Pittman and Charles R. Snyder, eds. *Society, Culture and Drinking Patterns.* New York: John Wiley and Sons, 1962, pp. 356–368.

Jessor, Richard. "Remarks on Drinking in Youth." In Morris E. Chafetz, ed. *Proceedings of the First Annual Conference of the National Institute on Alcohol Abuse and Alcoholism.* Washington, D.C.: Department of Health, Education, and Welfare, 1973.

Jones, Howard. *Alcoholic Addiction.* London: Tavistock Publications, 1963.

Kalant, Harold. "Biological Models of Alcohol Tolerance and Physical Dependence." In Milton M. Gross, ed. *Alcohol Intoxication and Withdrawal: Experimental Studies.* New York: Plenum, 1973, pp. 3–14.

Keller, Mark. "The Definition of Alcoholism and the Estimation of Its Prevalence." In David J. Pittman and Charles R. Snyder, eds. *Society, Culture and Drinking Patterns.* New York: John Wiley and Sons, 1962, pp. 310–329.

Keller, Mark, ed. *Alcohol and Health: A Report from the Secretary of Health,*

Education, and Welfare. New Knowledge. Department of Health, Education, and Welfare, 1974.

Kitsuse, John I. "Societal Reaction to Deviant Behavior: Problems of Theory and Method." *Social Problems*, 1962, 9:247–256.

Larkins, John R. *Alcohol and the Negro: Explosive Issues.* Zebulon, N.C.: Record Publishing Company, 1965.

Lawrence, Joseph J., and Milton A. Maxwell. "Drinking and Socio-Economic Status." In David J. Pittman and Charles R. Snyder, eds. *Society, Culture and Drinking Patterns.* New York: John Wiley and Sons, 1962, pp. 141–145.

Lemert, Edwin M. *Social Pathology: A Systematic Approach to the Theory of Sociopathic Behavior.* New York: McGraw-Hill, 1951.

Levy, Jerrold E., and Stephen E. Kunitz. "Indian Drinking: Problems of Data Collection and Interpretation." In Morris E. Chafetz, ed. *Proceedings of the First Annual Alcoholism Conference of the National Institute of Alcohol Abuse and Alcoholism.* DHEW NSM 73-97074. Washington, D.C.: Department of Health, Education, and Welfare, 1973.

Lipscomb, Wendell R., and Jay Holden. "Risk of Being Labeled 'Alcoholic': Significance of Psychiatric Status and Nationality." In Charles Winick, ed., *Sociological Aspects of Drug Dependence.* Cleveland, Ohio: CRC Press, 1974, pp. 15–34.

Lolli, Giorgio, Emidio Serianni, Grace M. Golder, and Pierpaolo Luzzatto-Fegiz. *Alcohol in Italian Culture.* Glencoe, Ill.: The Free Press, 1958.

Lowe, George D., and Eugene Hodges. "Race and Treatment of Alcoholism in a Southern State." *Social Problems*, 1972, 20:240–252.

Maddox, George L. "Teenage Drinking in the United States." In David J. Pittman and Charles R. Snyder, eds. *Society, Culture and Drinking Patterns.* New York: John Wiley and Sons, 1962, pp. 230–245.

Malzberg, Benjamin. "Use of Alcohol among White and Negro Mental Patients." *Quarterly Journal of Studies on Alcohol*, 1955, 16:668–674.

Marshall, Harvey, and Ross Purdy. "Hidden Deviance and the Labeling Approach: The Case of Drinking and Driving." *Social Problems*, 1972, 19:541–553.

McCord, William, and Joan McCord, with Jon Gudeman. *Origins of Alcoholism.* Stanford, Calif.: Stanford University Press, 1960.

McCord, William, and Joan McCord. "A Longitudinal Study of the Personality of Alcoholics." In David J. Pittman and Charles R. Snyder, eds. *Society, Culture and Drinking Patterns.* New York: John Wiley and Sons, 1962, pp. 413–430.

Merton, Robert K. *Social Theory and Social Structure.* Glencoe, Ill.: The Free Press, 1957.

Moon, Louis E., and Robert E. Patton. "The Alcoholic Psychotic in the New

York State Mental Hospitals, 1951–1960." *Quarterly Journal of Studies on Alcohol,* 1963, 24:664–681.

Mulford, Harold A. "Drinking and Deviant Drinking, U.S.A., 1963." *Quarterly Journal of Studies on Alcohol,* 1964, 25:634–650.

National Institute on Alcohol Abuse and Alcoholism. Information and Feature Service. United States Public Health Service. Alcohol, Drug Abuse and Mental Health. DHEW publication ADM 76–751. National Clearinghouse for Alcohol Information. Rockville Md.: Department of Health, Education, and Welfare, August 1975.

National Institute of Mental Health. First Special Report to the United States Congress on Alcohol and Health from the Secretary of Health, Education, and Welfare. DHEW Publication HSM 72-9099. Washington, D.C.: U.S. Government Printing Office, December 1971.

The New York Times, April 11, 1971, p. 7.

Parsons, Talcott. *The Social System.* Glencoe, Ill.: The Free Press, 1951.

Petrunik, Michael. "Seeing the Light: A Study of Conversion to Alcoholics Anonymous." *Journal of Voluntary Action Research,* 1972, 1:30–38.

Pittman, David J., ed. *Alcoholism.* New York: Harper & Row, 1967.

Pittman, David J., and C. Wayne Gordon. "Criminal Careers of the Chronic Drunkenness Offender." In David J. Pittman and Charles R. Snyder, eds., *Society, Culture and Drinking Patterns.* New York: John Wiley and Sons, 1962, pp. 535–546.

Pittman, David J., and Charles R. Snyder, eds., *Society, Culture and Drinking Patterns.* New York, John Wiley and Sons, 1962.

President's Commission on Law Enforcement and Administration of Justice, Task Force on Drunkenness. *Task Force Report: Drunkenness.* Washington, D.C.: U.S. Government Printing Office, 1967.

Rand Corporation. *Alcoholism and Treatment.* U.S. Public Health Service, Washington, D.C.: U.S. Government Printing Office, 1976.

Robins, Lee N. "Alcoholism and Labelling Theory." In Walter R. Gove, ed. *The Labelling of Deviance.* Beverly Hills, Calif.: Sage Publications, 1975, pp. 21–33.

Sagarin, Edward. *Odd Man In.* New York: Quadrangle, 1972.

Sagarin, Edward. *Deviants and Deviance.* New York: Praeger, 1975.

Schur, Edwin M. *Crimes Without Victims.* Englewood Cliffs, N.J.: Prentice-Hall, 1965.

Siegal, Harvey A., David M. Petersen, and Carl D. Chambers. "The Emerging Skid Row: Ethnographic and Social Notes on a Changing Scene." *Journal of Drug Issues,* 1975, 5:160–166.

Snyder, Charles R. *Alcohol and the Jews.* Glencoe, Ill.: The Free Press, 1958.

Snyder, Charles R. "Inebrity, Alcoholism, and Anomie." In Marshall B. Clinard, ed. *Anomie and Deviant Behavior.* New York: The Free Press, 1964, pp. 189–212.

Sterne, Muriel W. "Drinking Patterns and Alcoholism Among American Negroes." In David J. Pittman, ed. *Alcoholism.* New York: Harper & Row, 1967, pp. 66–99.

Sterne, Muriel W., David J. Pittman, and Thomas Coe. "Teen-Agers, Drinking, and the Law: A Study of Arrest Trends for Alcohol-Related Offenses." In David J. Pittman, ed. *Alcoholism.* New York: Harper & Row, 1967, pp. 55–66.

Sutherland, Edwin H. *Principles of Criminology,* 4th ed. Philadelphia: J. B. Lippincott, 1947.

Thum, Denise, Henry Wechsler, and Harold W. Demone, Jr. "Public Intoxication: The Arrest Records and Alcohol Levels of Emergency Service Patients." *Journal of Health and Social Behavior,* 1971, 12:259–265.

Trice, Harrison M., and Paul M. Roman. "Delabeling, Relabeling and Alcoholics Anonymous." *Social Problems,* 1970, 17:538–547.

Ullman, Albert D. "First Drinking Experience as Related to Age and Sex." In David J. Pittman and Charles R. Snyder, eds. *Society, Culture and Drinking Patterns.* New York: John Wiley and Sons, 1962, pp. 259–266.

Wallace, Samuel E. *Skid Row as a Way of Life.* New York: Harper & Row, 1965.

Wechsler, Henry, Denise Thum, Harold W. Demone, Jr., and Elizabeth Kasey. "Religious-Ethnic Differences in Alcohol Consumption." *Journal of Health and Social Behavior,* 1970, 11:21–30.

Wiseman, Jacqueline P. *Stations of the Lost.* Englewood Cliffs, N.J.: Prentice-Hall, 1970.

EIGHT

Prostitutes and prostitution

JENNIFER JAMES
University of Washington

Prostitution is a widespread phenomenon that has been studied at length and in depth. There are prostitutes in every American city of any size, and they exist under a variety of guises and in numerous styles. Their frequent arrests make up a significant percentage of the nation-wide arrests of adult women; only those for larceny, drunkenness, and narcotics violations are greater (Federal Bureau of Investigation, 1974). Prostitution violations account for approximately 30 percent of the populations of most women's jails, and the prostitutes serve long sentences compared to other misdemeanants. It has been reported that 70 percent of the women who are now inmates in American prisons were initially arrested for prostitution, indicating its possible importance as an introduction to the criminal justice system. This adds up not only to a significant impact on the lives of individual women but also to a staggering outlay of time and money by police, courts, and corrections personnel.

THE DEFINITION OF PROSTITUTION

Prostitution, as generally defined, has both moral and legal characteristics. The most common definition refers simply to the sale of sexual favors as an occupation. Kingsley Davis defines it as "the employment of sex for non-sexual ends within a competitive-authoritative system" (1937, p. 746). He specifically defines commercial prostitution in terms of the fact that the parties involved use sex for an end not socially functional: that is, for pleasure on the one hand and money on the other. Wardell Pomeroy offers a definition based on selection of partners and income: "[A]n act of prostitution is sexual activity with partners who are more or less indiscriminately selected. [The prostitute] must make a sizeable portion of her living from this activity for some period of time" (1965, p. 177). A general social definition the present author prefers is that prostitution is *any sexual exchange where the reward for the prostitute is neither sexual nor affectional.* Persons prostitute themselves when they exchange access to their bodies for material gain (clothes, apartment, promotion, entertainment) and in doing so use their bodies as commodities. Society, however, does not intercede in cases of this type of sexual exchange. The legal definition is narrower and based on four main reflections of social concern: cash, promiscuity, relationship to sexual partner, and lack of subtlety.

The legal statutes apply to women who engage in sex for money or who loiter with this intent. A woman is relatively safe in making exchanges for commodities other than cash—such as an opportunity to become a model or an evening of entertainment—that cannot be so easily recognized. Gifts from sexual partners leave more room for the assumption of affection and love. Affection as the stimulator of sexual exchange is acceptable for women and is, in fact, one of the most common rationalizations for first sexual experiences. Cash represents a nonemotional commercial exchange that society cannot modify to fit the acceptable limitations for permitting sexual access by women.

Promiscuity is an important second aspect of the legal definition. A woman is safe from being defined as a prostitute if only a few men are involved or if she knows them well and they are therefore not strangers. She is not violating the appropriate social construction of reality for women because the possibility of appropriate motivations, such as love, still exists. Her self-identification can remain more "party girl" than prostitute. The practical aspects of avoiding the appearance of promiscuity or indiscriminate sexual exchange are also important, for she is then less likely to come to the attention of public officials whose purpose is to control such behavior. A few customers will not be noticed, and if they are known to her, they are not vice squad officers or agents.

A prostitute is safe to violate the first three aspects of legal concern if she carefully accedes to the fourth—subtlety. The only women usually arrested are those who are very overt in the management of their profession. Prostitutes such as call girls who are more subtle and conform to more traditional female behavior are rarely arrested. Streetwalkers work alone on the streets late at night, a signal that they are behaving in an inappropriate manner for women. Other attributes of unsubtle prostitution provide the same signals: flashy clothes, ostentatious makeup, aggressive approaches toward male passersby, and frankly sexual verbal exchanges. The streetwalker is clearly offering herself as a commodity for sale and essentially forcing the hand of public agencies who claim they are required by the community to enforce appropriate moral standards. The concern of society reflected in the enforcement of the law is that sex for sale be invisible, or nearly so.

THE CURRENT STATUS OF PROSTITUTION

Since the end of World War II, control of prostitution throughout the world has fluctuated between toleration, licensure, and prohibition. Many countries have accepted the existence of prostitution and made various legal arrangements. Countries in the Middle East, the Far East, the Caribbean, and South America regulate it by requiring brothels to be licensed and by subjecting prostitutes to health inspections. One hundred members of the United Nations, including France, Britain, Italy, Japan, and Germany, have eliminated prostitution as a crime and have abandoned experiments at regulation (United Nations, 1951). The criminal laws in those countries seek instead to control public solicitation and to discourage the pimps and procurers who live off the earnings of prostitutes.

West Germany has become the most open of the countries in its treatment of prostitution. There, prostitution is considered a social necessity, and the government actively supports the building of pimp-free prostitution hostels where prostitutes can live and work in comfortable rooms with access to shopping centers, bowling lanes, and tennis courts and where officials can easily perform the mandatory medical inspections. Sweden has a special employment stipulation whereby a woman can work as a prostitute only if she has another full-time job in a legitimate field. The emphasis is on making sure that the woman has an alternative to prostitution and that she will have employment when she is too old to be a prostitute.

Attempts at ending prostitution have been total failures, with the apparent exception of China. Russia and Cuba also claim to have eliminated prostitution, but there is some evidence to the contrary. Journalists report that while prostitution has been reduced, it can still be found in both Moscow and Havana despite severe fines for customers and prison sentences for prostitutes. China's success seems to be based on the complete equality of the sexes in domestic, economic, and political spheres, combined with the discipline and commitment required by "pure" communist ideology. The supply of women has been eliminated by offering equal economic opportunities and the use of intensive five-year reorientation sentences. The demand has been eliminated through emphasis on discipline and heavy prison sentences.

All forms of prostitution are illegal in all areas of the United States, with the exception of some counties in Nevada. The control of prostitution is achieved in the United States through laws that make it illegal both to loiter with the intent of committing an act of prostitution and to offer and agree to the act itself. A woman who has once been convicted of offering and agreeing, regardless of the circumstances, is subject to future arrests under loitering statutes as a "known prostitute" (a woman who has been convicted of an act of prostitution within the past year). If she is seen in an area "known to be inhabited by prostitutes," she may also be arrested for loitering, a charge frequently used by enforcement agencies to control individuals labeled as deviants. A limited number of prostitution arrests are also made under sodomy and lewd behavior statutes and ordinances against keeping a "house of ill fame." Enforcement of these laws will vary from one locale to another and will depend on the resources of the particular police department and on the political pressure for either "cracking down" on prostitution or tolerating it.

FBI arrest figures list 30,166 women arrested for prostitution in 1973

(Federal Bureau of Investigation, 1974). The vast majority of these arrests are of women who are openly soliciting: obviously engaging in sexual services for money in a promiscuous and explicit manner. Attempts are occasionally made to arrest women who work in houses or in massage and sauna parlors, but these women account for less than 5 percent of the total arrests. Their prostitution is at least partially hidden by the offering of other more legitimate services. Subtle prostitutes— call girls, conventioneers—are found on all social levels and are rarely arrested because they cause no direct affront to the general public. They may irritate their apartment neighbors by their activties, but their sexuality is much less an explicit part of their behavior than it is for streetwalkers.

The most common procedure that leads to arrest is the use of police officers as decoys. An officer behaves as he assumes a customer would behave and when approached by a suspected prostitute, elicits evidence of intent. The prostitute is arrested if she mentions money and sexual service in her verbal exchange with the officer. These arrest techniques frequently involve the officer in the possibility of entrapment and questionable sexual exchanges. Therefore, some jurisdictions will use civilian agents who complete acts of sexual intercourse before the arrest is made. They view themselves as protecting society by committing immoral acts for moral reasons. The use of female agents to solicit and arrest customers is rare because it requires a violation of appropriate behavior for women. In most states customers are rarely, if ever, arrested. A few cities are now arresting customers more frequently in response to charges of discrimination under state Equal Rights Amendment (ERA) provisions, but the most likely person to be arrested is still the woman.

In some cities the object of law enforcement is just to clear the streets, and so the women are arrested regularly, kept in jail overnight, and released in the morning. This is justified on the grounds that prostitution is a threat to social order. Those prostitutes who are brought to trial will usually plead guilty because they cannot afford bail or adequate legal representation; they also believe that the judges will inevitably be biased against them. Prostitutes who can afford good attorneys plead not guilty and are less likely to serve time because juries are reluctant to convict when questionable police tactics are revealed in court.

Male homosexual prostitutes are arrested and tried in many cities under the same procedures applied to females. While the percentage of male arrests has been low, it has recently increased in some cities because of complaints and lawsuits by equal rights advocates. The arrest of males has been traditionally negligible because male prostitution could be disguised in a form in which it went relatively unnoticed by many residents not privy to knowledge of its existence. Furthermore, in some states where the ERA has not passed, only women can be found guilty of prostitution even when homosexual males are providing the same service. The author was in the booking area of a jail two years ago when a transvestite was brought in and charged with prostitution. The arresting officer had assumed the offender was a female. Later, when the jail matron pointed out that the offender was a male, he was released.

In the mid-1970s prostitution in the United States was as widespread as ever. While the demand for this service appears to have remained relatively constant since the turn of the century, the supply has diversified into many styles of operation. Prostitutes operate on all levels of society from the "jet set" call girl and the company retainer hired by large corporations to the "fleabag" on skid road. Various conservative estimates state that there are over 500,000 prostitutes working in the United States and earning a combined income of more than a billion dollars (Winick & Kinsie, 1971), but this can be only a rough estimate because of the impossibility of keeping track of sexual exchanges. Attempts to curb prostitutes through incarceration have only produced the familiar revolving door of street-jail-street. Programs of rehabilitation have generally been failures, whether based on religious conversion, job training, or psychological counseling. The basic message from corrections is that prostitutes cannot be rehabilitated until they are too old to work or until extenuating circumstances in their personal experience lead them to quit of their own accord. The failure of diversion programs seems to add up to the inability to provide women with interesting employment that pays as well as prostitution.

The failure of enforcement and rehabilitation efforts to curb prostitution have led to a reexamination of it as a problem. Its historical and cross-cultural prevalence is now being balanced against the costs of enforcement and changing concepts of the appropriate use of criminal law. Many cities find themselves spending over a thousand dollars per prostitute arrest while violent crimes soar. Civil liberties advocates and legal progressives seek a redefinition of prostitution as a victimless crime (that is, a crime without a complainant). The concept of "victimless crime" was first introduced in 1965 by Edwin M. Schur. Psychiatry, psychology, and sociology are revising their clinical and theoretical concepts of sexuality to provide more acceptance of multiple partners and to emphasize individual freedom of choice. At the same time, anthropological and sociological studies are stressing the economic in contrast to the psychologic motivations for prostitutes.

THE PROBLEM OF PROSTITUTION: REAL OR IMAGINED?

Viewpoints on Prostitution

Most government agencies are against the decriminalization of prostitution. Law enforcement agencies define prostitution as a problem because of the associated crime they say accompanies the street environment generated by the presence of prostitutes. Larceny, robbery, assault, and narcotics addiction are cited as crimes that appear in association with prostitution. Local public health officials suspect prostitution as the cause of rising venereal disease statistics.

For the general public, street solicitation is the most important problem. Many people object to activities in the street that they would tolerate in private. They find women on streetcorners offensive, much as they do public drunks. People in business feel it chases away clientele, parents want to shield their children, and passersby do not want to be subjected to sexual suggestion by glance or comment from a prostitute. This portion of the American public would tolerate prostitution if it were invisible and zoned out of their neighborhood.

Not all arguments on prostitution are as clear as these. When morality becomes an issue, the reasons for and against prostitution become confused and varied, and seemingly incompatible groups will often find themselves with similar opinions, though for different reasons. The clinical and academic definitions of prostitution as a problem historically stem from the condemnation of female promiscuity. Chastity, with sex given only in exchange for love and marriage, is the ascribed Western role for women. Commercialized sex threatens a social structure that links sexual activity to the stable relationship of marriage.

Therefore, research has concentrated on eliciting demographic variables that might contribute to a woman becoming a prostitute and on
examining the psychological trauma that produces the concomitant
personality.

Scholars, in taking this negative view of prostitution, find themselves
allied with those moralists who define promiscuity as a religious sin
and therefore prostitution as a contributor to the moral decay of American society. Other social and moral traditionalists are less concerned
about society than they are about the prostitute as victim. The women,
they state, are degraded, exploited, and abused by the business and by
the men (that is, the pimps) behind it. This group sees the total
elimination of prostitution as the only way to protect women from this
life and society from this type of woman.

Feminists are often caught between two opposing views of the
prostitute. Some are against prostitution on the gounds that it represents the ultimate degradation of a woman by requiring that she offer
her body as a commercial object. They see prostitution as based on two
cultural and sexist aspects of sexuality. The first is the traditional view
of the natural proclivities of men, and the second is the consequent
necessity of catering to their basic needs. Society must find a way to
satisfy sexual passion, for it is socially and economically important to
society that marriage not be disrupted because of sexual passion. Men
are therefore encouraged to seek prostitutes rather than some other
man's wife (K. Davis, 1937). On the other hand, many feminists argue
strongly for decriminalization of prostitution. They state unequivocally
that the prostitute is the only "honest woman," a heroine who recognizes the social reality of women as sexual objects and makes sure she
gets a fair and definite exchange for her labor. Also, in a society that
limits a woman's access to jobs and offers lower pay to women than to
men, they commend the prostitute for making a good living off of her
most salable commodity.

An Analysis of the Viewpoints

As cultural values change and arguments for the repeal of antiprostitu-
tion laws become stronger, the viewpoints of opposing groups are
becoming the subject of public debate. The question of whether or not
prostitution should be legalized is not easily resolved, for on value-
laden issues an argument becomes both personal and emotional. It is

therefore necessary to take a more objective view and analyze the question in its most basic form: in terms of the rights of the individual versus the needs of the society.

The two sides of this argument are perhaps best represented by John Stuart Mill and Patrick Devlin. In a classic statement on individual liberty, Mill wrote:

> [T]he sole end for which mankind are warranted, individually or collectively, in interfering with the liberty of action of any of their number, is self-protection. . . . [T]he only purpose for which power can be rightfully exercised over any member of a civilized community, against his will, is to prevent harm to others. His own good, either physical or moral, is not a sufficient warrant (1892, p. 6).

This contrasts sharply with Devlin's position:

> Societies disintegrate from within more frequently than they are broken up by external pressures. There is disintegration when no common morality is observed and history shows that the loosening of moral bonds is often the first stage of disintegration, so that society is justified in taking the same steps to preserve its moral code as it does to preserve its government and other essential institutions (1965, p. 13).

Should society act preventively to protect its morals, or should it only infringe on the rights of the individual when its survival is threatened? The resolution of this debate depends upon a determination of the individual behavior and human passions that actually harm the community beyond a tolerable level. Is the tolerance level to be ascertained by factual knowledge, public opinion, or political expediency? How is the balance to be maintained between the effects of individual freedom on the society at large and the erosion of freedom of choice caused by restriction of individual activities? Mill suggests that the burden of proof be shifted to those demanding restrictions. In concurring, Gilbert Geis states that "the burden that they bear should be a heavy one, perhaps one as imposing as the criminal law's demand for proof 'beyond a reasonable doubt' or the Supreme Court's standard of 'clear and present danger'" (1972, p. 13). Discussions of sexual morality rarely can be settled beyond a reasonable doubt, but the actual danger of various modes of conduct to the person or property of the community is easily determined. A precise factual view of these activities can be provided that will clarify the extent of danger to the individual and the community.

✱ *The Police View: Ancillary Crime.*   The central problem cited by the police as a danger to the community is that of ancillary crime. The argument that prostitution supports ancillary crime (larceny, robbery, assault, narcotics) is complex. It is obvious that other crimes do occur in the environment of an act of prostitution, but whether it is rational to make one activity criminal in order to reduce or control another merits serious inquiry. Assault or theft is clearly punishable as separate criminal activity. As the San Francisco Committee on Crime has pointed out:

> [S]ociety's effort to prevent crimes of violence associated with prostitution would be more effective by concentrating law enforcement efforts on the pimps rather than on the girls, on the "associated crimes" rather than prostitution (1971, p. 29).

In a well-documented opinion, Judge Charles W. Halleck of the Superior Court of the District of Columbia, also addresses the issue of ancillary crime:

> To arrest and criminally prosecute a prostitute because of a possibility that crime-related activity might be involved directly or indirectly is massively antithetical to traditional concepts of due process, equal protection, and individual liberty (1972, p. 31).

If certain activities can be curtailed because they might involve other activities that are illegal, the law is easily abused. Alcohol, for example, can lead directly to traffic deaths, yet no one seriously proposes a return to Prohibition.

Separating prostitution from the criminal code by legitimizing the service would draw a definite line between prostitution and serious crime. The question of the direction of ancillary crime could then be resolved. Is it the criminalization of prostitutes that forces them into a relationship with other criminal activity or is it an inherent part of sexual service? The data in hand, including police arrest records, supports the former as the impetus to involvement and presence in the high crime environment.

The offense reported by both arrest statistics and field research to be most frequently associated with prostitution is larceny. Many customers insist on carrying considerable amounts of money with them, and prostitutes view theft as part of the "game." This is partly due to the fact that criminalization of prostitution blurs the distinction between providing a service and committing a crime. In fact, in many criminal courts larceny is a lesser offense; loitering and offering and agreeing to an act of prostitution carry higher jail sentences and engender more police enforcement than theft. Another effect of the prohibition of prostitution is that a customer who can be prosecuted for prostitution will not report a larceny to avoid involving the police. If the prostitutes believe their victims will not report them, larceny may be encouraged. The typical case involves the lifting of the customer's money while he is distracted by the sexual act. Consumer protection in these cases would do better to educate the customer not to carry more than he wishes to spend, rather than to outlaw prostitution. The case of the drunken merchant marine who is "cleaned" at every port is sad, but the law is rarely successful in the protection of fools. Financial limits on police ability to control crime argue against extensive efforts in areas based on individual gullibility.

Robbery and assault, more serious law enforcement problems, are dangerous to the prostitute as well as to the customer. Though the instances of men who are beaten by women presumed to be prostitutes (and by their accomplices) receive more public attention, statistics on assault indicate that it is the prostitute who is more likely to be beaten by the customer. She may be more aware than the customer of her own vulnerability, but she is not free to report robbery or assault by customers or others because of the threat of a prostitution charge. Labeled as a criminal, defined by reputation as outside the protection of the law, the prostitute may be regarded by the customer as "fair game." Besides being considered as a legitimate victim, she is also a safe one, for her complaints are rarely taken seriously by law enforcement officials. It is rare, given the number of acts of prostitution, that a customer is assaulted by a prostitute or her accomplice. He has more likely been the target of a setup or con-game, with no intent of prostitution, or of a clear case of robbery. Public education and strict enforcement of the robbery and assault statutes is the most straightforward approach to dealing with these problems.

Traffic in narcotics is also cited as ancillary to prostitution, and in fact many female heroin addicts do turn to prostitution to support their habits. In the subculture they are considered "hypes" and are disassociated from professional prostitutes. A distinction between the prostitute and the addict who supports her habit through prostitution and other crimes is important. Prostitutes provide a service to support themselves and their families, and that may be the extent of their criminal involvement. Addicts, on the other hand, engage in criminal activity (prostitution) to support criminal activity (addiction). Actually, the criminal involvement of even the addict-prostitute is limited, for she rarely engages in sales of drugs, even though she may be associating with dealers or supporting an addict-pimp.

Finally, prostitution is frequently linked by the police to organized crime. It is true that during early Prohibition, the Mafia was active in running large brothels in Chicago and New York in conjunction with illicit liquor sales and speakeasies. Evidence now indicates, though, that organized crime is no longer involved in prostitution. The President's Commission on Law Enforcement and Administration of Justice has stated unequivocally that prostitution plays "a small and declining role in organized crime operations" (1967, p. 189). The writer's three years of field research in a major American city supports this statement. Recognized experts have pointed out that prostitution is not an attractive investment for organized crime because it is difficult to control. Discipline is hard to maintain because of the nature of the transaction and the relationship between pimp and prostitute (President's Commission, 1967; Winick & Kinsie, 1971). Involvement in prostitution is too visible, basically bad public relations for the legally and politically sensitive syndicates, and the return is small when compared to the severe penalties for procuring. Large brothels are no longer a viable operation, as the tastes of customers, the independence of prostitutes, and the style of the community have changed. Organized crime long ago turned to involvement in politics, investment, securities, and labor unions as more profitable ventures at less risk than earlier involvement in activities such as prostitution (N. Davis, 1971).

Concern about organized crime should be directed toward the most frequent cause of its proliferation, legal suppression of activities classified as "crimes without complainants." The criminalization of gambling, for example, creates the need for organization to restrict detection, provide protection, and control legal prosecution. The illegality of prostitution contributes to the organization that is present in the form of pimp control and circuit business. Prostitutes who are not as afraid of prosecution, such as "call girls" and women who work for entertainment agencies, rarely enter into coercive economic relationships. In contrast, women who work in the open and are frequently subject to arrest almost always depend on an agent or pimp for legal assistance and peer group protection.

The Public Health View: Venereal Disease. Citizens today are very much concerned about the spread of venereal disease, and they believe that prostitution is a major source of the problem. Venereal infections of all types are epidemic in the United States; they have showed a steady increase from a low in 1960 to the all-time high recorded in 1973. The concern about the spreading of venereal disease is therefore a valid one. The problem is in identifying prostitutes as the focus of that concern when the real causes are elsewhere.

Historically, some of the first movements against prostitution in Europe stemmed from public health concerns. In the early eighteenth century poor women who became prostitutes were a source of venereal disease, and medicine had limited methods of control. The situation in Europe was not, however, replicated in the United States. With the exception of wartime brothels, most of which were outside the continental United States, prostitutes have been found to play only a minor part in the venereal disease problem. In 1958 an international study published by the United Nations stated unequivocally that prostitution is not a major factor in the spread of venereal disease in the United States.

Public health officials who have reviewed recent research in epidemiology report that prostitutes, despite their numerous sexual contacts, account for only a small number of venereal disease cases (Idsoe & Guthe, 1967; VD Fact Sheet, 1971). Charles Winick, working with the American Social Health Association, notes: "We know from many different studies that the amount of venereal disease attributable to prostitution is remaining fairly constant at a little under 5 per cent, which is a negligible proportion compared to the amount of venereal disease we now have" (quoted in Haft, 1974, p. 18).

A poll of public health authorities on prostitution and venereal disease shows that almost all believe that most prostitutes are well educated and are watchful for the signs of venereal disease; they are also aware of precautionary techniques that include using prophylactics, checking customers, and seeking medical care. A prostitute's reputation is vitally important to her; a reputation as a VD carrier would cut down the relatively large volume of repeat business on which most prostitutes depend. It would also interfere with her health and she is therefore watchful, considering the disease a possible hazard of her profession (Haft, 1974, p. 18).

The general consensus seems to be that the increase in venereal disease is the result of the new sexual mores of young people, which have, unfortunately, not been accompanied by an improvement in their health education. The professional is aware; the amateur is not. The VD rate among high school students, aged fifteen to nineteen, is 25 percent (VD Fact Sheet, 1971). Studies indicate that up to 84 percent of all reported venereal disease is in the fifteen to thirty age group (VD Fact Sheet, 1971). The subjects in this group are rarely prostitutes or customers, for the average age of customers is well over thirty (James, 1971; Winick & Kinsie, 1971).

It can be argued that even the 5 percent disease rate attributed to prostitutes is a public health problem, but prosecution of prostitutes does not seem to be the solution. Jail facilities may provide diagnostic services after arrest, but treatment is rarely completed. In some facilities, penicillin is automatically administered without determining if venereal disease is present. Such irresponsible use of medication leads to higher tolerance levels and only aggravates the problem. Available data in European countries that have tried legalized prostitution support the argument that VD increases when prostitution is illegal and decreases when it is legalized (Willcox, 1962; Idsoe & Guthe, 1967). A possible exception to this interrelationship is in military areas where many young women engage in part-time prostitution that is tolerated but not controlled.

Police are certainly not a better source of VD control than adequate public health facilities and more intensive public education. Recognition by the public of the small role that prostitutes play in the transmission of venereal disease is necessary if proper attention is to be given to the more significant sources of the disease—promiscuity and casual sexual encounters on the part of the general public. As long as the whore myth can be used to explain the spread of venereal disease, efforts to curb its continued spread will be unsuccessful.

The General Public's View: Morality Versus the Detriments of Control. Those who hold that legalization symbolizes the moral decline of the community place great emphasis on the legal system as upholder of the values of the society. Proponents of decriminalization of prostitution and other victimless crime counter with the argument that the primary function of the criminal law is the protection of persons and property, and that even when society punishes immorality through its laws, it does not do so with consistency. They state that to seek repeal of the laws prohibiting prostitution is not necessarily to conclude that prostitution is morally good. Rather, it is to make a judgment about the appropriate use of the criminal law and the abuses that accompany the involvement of law enforcement officials in crimes without complainants.

In their efforts to regulate behavior found unacceptable by certain standards of morality, supporters of current laws often ignore the negative effects that prohibition has on police, prostitutes, and the community as a whole. Public morality is rarely served by placing law enforcement agencies in an ambivalent and discriminatory position. Prostitution forces the police to use questionable techniques. Since no citizen is a complaining victim, an officer must pose as a decoy and encourage the prostitute to solicit him. This often involves the officer himself in illicit behavior. Moreover, since most of the customers of a prostitute are not labeled criminals and are middle-aged, middle-class, white businessmen, they are rarely arrested. Law enforcement officials argue that they are less frequent violators and thus more difficult to arrest. But if curtailment of prostitution were the goal, the impact of the arrest would be significant enough to make it desirable. The hyprocrisy with which the law is enforced is not lost on rookies, who are often used as decoys when prostitutes become familiar with the vice squad officer. The new officer's image of his duty can easily become blurred. The policeman's diminished respect for his position inevitably affects the community. Further, the corruption of the police through possible payoffs and questionable professional image compromises the basic integrity of a system of justice. In a recent survey, over half (53 percent) of a metropolitan police department voted to decriminalize prostitution despite the strong opposition of their chief of police (Law and Justice Planning Office, 1973).

The effects of the enforcement procedures on the prostitute clearly are negative. Jail is not a deterrent. It contributes little to rehabilitation and often encourages criminal conduct by teaching the prostitute about genuine criminal activity. She learns that other more serious crimes may pay better; she begins to view herself as a criminal. Attaching the label "criminal" to prostitution and imposing heavy sentences blurs the distinction between the offering of an immoral service and the committing of a criminal act.

The abuse and degradation felt by the prostitute under the current system is much more a result of the arrest-incarceration process than of the act of prostitution. Interviews with streetwalkers over a three-year period noted arrest and incarceration as the point of diminished self-respect. The actual services of prostitution were "just business," involved less sex than is imagined, and were often only an increase in amount of promiscuity rather than an introduction to it. Prostitutes who are arrested repeatedly become enmeshed in a cycle of debt and degradation from which it is difficult to escape. Other employment becomes hard to find, friends and family may be alienated, and the criminal label becomes permanent. Convicted prostitutes either move elsewhere to work, commit other crimes, or continue being recycled through jails as long as they survive.

PROSTITUTES

Types of Prostitutes

The range of types of prostitution is almost endless.[1] The following categories represent the major styles of prostitution in the United States. There are other setups in Europe; for instance, women may sit at street-level windows beckoning to passersby or reside in an "Eros Center." It seems that the only limits to the possibilities are imposed by the individual's own imagination or business style.

Streetwalkers. These women work "on the block" in open view of police and customers. They usually stand on streetcorners or in doorways waiting for a customer to walk or drive by. They will wait to be approached by a man or take the initiative themselves by asking "Do you want to date?" They are easily identified just by the fact that they are alone on the street at night—unusual for a woman—and obviously looking around at passersby. Identification by bright clothing, makeup, or manner is no longer reliable, since streetwalkers in most cities prefer to be subtle to avoid unwanted attention. (Even when there is no subtlety, changing fashions for all women make identification by clothing risky.) In large metropolitan areas the women work days as well as nights, and their level of aggressiveness in contacting customers is substantially increased. The style of the streetwalkers and the money they make will usually depend on whether they work high-class or low-class sections of a city. Some streetwalkers have begun to work in suburban shopping centers to find customers and avoid police. Once she has found a customer, a streetwalker will follow him to a hotel or take him to a special "trick house" that provides cheap rooms for prostitution.[2]

Streetwalkers are the most harassed of the profession; they are frequently arrested under loitering statutes. They are most likely to be poor women, members of an ethnic or racial minority, or addicts unable to operate in more subtle systems of prostitution. They have a high incidence of drug abuse, are occasionally involved in larceny, and represent the "roughest" of the prostitutes.

Bar Girls.   One step removed from the streetwalker, the women who work bars spend their time drinking and waiting for a customer to approach. The class of their clientele and therefore the money they make is dependent on the quality of the bar. In order to work, many must make a payoff to the bar manager. In traditional B-girl situations the prostitute is also required to push drinks to raise the bar's profits. It takes longer for a prostitute to get a customer in a bar than on the street, but she is far safer in terms of arrest. The police must rely on entrapment setups that can be foiled if the bartender recognizes the vice officer.

Masseuses.   Not all massage parlors provide sexual service, but many do. The usual procedure is for the individual woman to make arrangements with the customer after entering a massage cubicle. The owner of the studio pretends he is unaware of illicit activity. The women work regular shifts and split their fees in various ways with the owner. Some provide only limited service; others provide whatever the customer desires.

Studio Models and Escorts.   Photography studios advertising nude models, sense-awareness centers, escort services, dance studios, and body-painting studios are among the potential covers for prostitution. Each type of service operates in a slightly different way. An escort may accompany her customer to a party or on a trip. Sexual service will be performed at the customer's option, at a place of his choosing. In body painting, the customer may fingerpaint the prostitute's body, or she will paint his. This activity is subject to varying regulations as to the paintable parts of the body and the medium that can be used. Generally, the medium will be tempera or baby oil and talcum powder mixtures. The body painting, as well as the activities of the other types of services that are offered within a building, will take place in private cubicles such as massage parlors have, and the possible courses of action are the same.

Stag Party Workers.   Stag parties used to be familiar scenes on campus, but they are now rare except in more conservative areas. Most stag parties are now put on by men's clubs. Men are served dinner and drinks by topless waitresses while strippers and dancers put on a show. Gambling is also a common part of the program. If the waitresses or entertainers are prostitutes the customers can make arrangements with them for sexual services. Agreements are made to meet after the party or at some later time, or phone numbers are exchanged. By working large stag parties, a new prostitute can build up a lucrative phone list. Small parties or "orgies" are also common. One woman will service a group of men in a hotel room, or two or three women will stage a party for a number of men. These arrangements may be made through an entertainment agency or through prostitutes engaged in other types of business.

Hotel Prostitutes.   In past years some hotels gave prostitutes rooms in which to live so that they would be available for guests. The most frequent arrangement now is for a prostitute to make a deal with the bellman or the manager to refer customers to her for a fee. Many second-class hotels still have "working women" living on the premises, with varying arrangements for cuts on the payments and restrictions on bringing in customers from outside the hotel.

Convention Prostitutes.   While all prostitutes take advantage of conferences in their home city that attract large numbers of out-of-town males, some prefer to obtain the schedules of major convention centers and travel the convention circuit. These prostitutes subscribe to certain views of which professions spend the most money and are the easiest to handle, and they attend conventions accordingly. The women, perhaps posing as secretaries or sales promoters, roam hotel lobbies, product display rooms, and cocktail parties. They may take a room in the convention hotel or nearby to facilitate the volume of business.

Call Girls.   The call girl business is basically a phone system. Instead of working in a studio or picking up customers on the street, in bars, or at conventions, the call girl sets up her own referral business. Many of these women have previously worked at other types of prostitution and have collected a book of names and telephone numbers. Others begin by taking the extra customers of an established call girl and paying her a share of the fee. Sometimes one woman is essentially a "madam" who acts as a central referral agency for a string of women who work for her. Almost all prostitutes do some phone business with steady customers, but the call girl does nothing else. She relies on her answering service or home phone for all her business. New customers are referred by old ones, and bored customers may exchange numbers with each other. The economic status of the prostitute depends on her class of customers, that is, on whether they are $25 or $100 tricks. This type of business is safer and steadier than the more overt types of prostitution. The police rarely arrest call girls, and slow times can always be speeded up by telephoning customers and extending invitations.

Nevada House Prostitutes.   Nevada is the only state with local county option for legalized houses of prostitution. All but the urban counties (Reno, Las Vegas, and Lake Tahoe) have opted for legalized prostitution, and the rural desert is dotted with the purple and pink trailers of such brothels as the Mustang Ranch, Miss Kitty's, Marie's, and the Pink Pussycat. Women who work in this house system are fingerprinted and checked by the local public health official. The house rules vary, but usually the women live in the trailers for three weeks and then leave for one week each month. Customers drive out from town, ring the bell on the fence surrounding the trailers, and pick a woman from the lounge display. The women pay the house owner from 50 to 60 percent of their earnings, take any customer who chooses them, and rarely leave the house area until their week off. The activities are legal and the women protected, but the outlay of energy is high and the basic charge per customer is low, which is a reflection of their controlled status.

Illegal House and Apartment Prostitutes. There are a variety of house or apartment setups that operate similarly to the Nevada houses, but on an illegal basis and with a more limited number of prostitutes and customers. Usually three or four women will share a business apartment. One will operate as an informal madam, and the business will be based on telephone, cab driver, and bartender referrals. In contrast to call girls, the women do not live in the house when they are not working.

Circuit Travelers. Some prostitutes work a more general circuit than that of the conventions, and their clientele is of a lower class than the conventioneers. Traveling in groups of two or three, these women cater to migrant labor camps, lumber camps, job-training camps, and work camps. "Road Whores," as they are sometimes called, may work an entire camp in one evening and then move on. Permission to work at a particular camp is usually secured from a foreman, who receives a cut of their earnings in return. An alternative is for the women to set themselves up nearby and let the men pass the word.

Miscellaneous Types. All possible types of prostitution styles can hardly be enumerated. They include women who work airports and the hotels surrounding them, hotel maids, manicurists, and models. One adventurous woman worked at a large toll bridge. She would hitchhike at one end, make her pitch, get the customer to pull off at the rest areas on either side of the bridge, provide the service, and then hitchhike back across.

Reasons for Choosing Prostitution as a Profession
The question of why some women choose to become prostitutes is

complex.[3] Prostitutes are not the cause of prostitution. Prostitution is, in reality, an institutionalized, if illegal, occupational choice. "The factors that account for women becoming prostitutes, just as the factors which account for a person becoming a lawyer, a doctor, or a robber, are multiple and are often on several levels" (Pomeroy, 1965, p. 183). Because of the immoral, illegal, and deviant status of prostitution in our society, however, the occupational decision for prostitution has been surrounded by social scientists with an elaborate mythology of theory and analysis that is far removed from our usual perception of such occupational choices as law or medicine. It is true that "the conscious and immediate reasons that the prostitutes themselves are capable of giving . . . must be considered in conjunction with, and as overlaying other, more deeply hidden factors" (Pomeroy, 1965, p. 183). The same would hold, of course, if we were examining why some people become lawyers. Moreover, Pomeroy continues, "[j]ust because these [conscious and immediate] reasons are easily accessible does not, of necessity, mean they are not 'real' factors" (1965, p. 183). T. C. Esselstyn states that the "avowed reasons [of prostitutes for their choice of profession] deserve a more respectful hearing than they have received in these changing times" (1968, p. 130).

The *primary* cause of women becoming prostitutes is the supply and demand equation that grows out of the sexual socialization process. Some men are socialized to view sex as a commodity that can be purchased. Quantity has traditionally had a higher value than quality of relationship in male reports of sexual encounters. Women who are socialized to view themselves as sexual objects may violate the ideal of the subtle sell for approved commodities and accept money. These women view their bodies as salable, and most prostitution does in fact pay better than other occupations available for women with limited education.

The *secondary* causes of women becoming prostitutes are those that lead them to make the shift from subtle sexual sale to overt prostitution. These include abusive family circumstances, such as incest and divorce, that lessen the female's feeling that she can be a good girl and therefore undermines her sexual self-respect. Institutionalization that labels women as deviant, economic stress engendered by the need to support children, drug addiction, and a desire for a better standard of living are other causes of prostitution. Pressures from male friends can also be significant. Girls who are popular in high school because they are physically well developed may wander into more overt sexual exchange. These secondary causes facilitate the gradual or sudden development necessary for an individual's shift to overt prostitution.

Harry Benjamin and R. Masters (1964, p. 91) posited a division of prostitutes into two general categories: voluntary and compulsive. Those in the former group are acting rationally and by free choice in opting for prostitution, while those in the latter groups are to some extent acting under compulsion by "psychoneurotic needs." In the majority of cases, however, Benjamin and Masters found that they were unable to assign prostitutes exclusively to either of these categories. Such attempts to differentiate between conscious or rational motivations and more deeply hidden or psychoneurotic influences appear again and again in the literature, as illustrated by Table 1. Conscious motivations include the factors of economics, the persuasive pimp, working conditions, and adventure. Situational motivations include early life experiences, parental abuse and/or neglect, and occupation. Psychoanalytic motivations include, along with that category itself, latent homosexuality, oedipal fixation, and retardation. These motivations are the ones that will be addressed more fully in the following discussion.

Economics. The traditional stereotype of prostitutes represents them as wretched creatures forced into their profession by extreme economic deprivation. Opposing this is a body of research showing that most of the women choose prostitution as the occupational alternative that affords them the highest attainable standard of living. Harold Greenwald studied twenty-six call girls and reported that "not one of the girls I interviewed attempted to explain her choice of profession in terms of desperate economic need" (1970, p. 199). Of the prostitutes in a 1974–1975 study, 8.40 percent claimed to have started because of economic necessity, while 56.49 percent were motivated by a desire for money and material goods (James, forthcoming).[4] It is, of course, very important in this context to recognize that money-making options are still quite limited for women in this society, especially those with little or no skill. Recognition of this basic sex inequality in the economic structure helps one to see prostitution as a viable occupational choice rather than as a symptom of the immorality of individual women.

Table 1. *Motivations of Prostitutes*

Authors	Conscious Motivations				Situational Motivations			Psychoanalytic Motivations			
	Economics	Persuasive Pimp	Working Conditions	Adventure	Early Life Experiences	Parental Abuse and/or Neglect	Occupation	General Psycho-analytic Motivations	Latent Homosexuality	Oedipal Fixation	Retardation
Benjamin & Masters (1964)	X		X	X							
Bryan (1966)	X		X	X							
Choisy (1965)										X	
Clinard (1959)					X		X	X			
Davis, K. (1937)	X										
Davis, N. (1971)	X	X		X	X						
Ellis (1936)		X				X					
Esselstyn (1968)	X				X		X	X			
Gebhard (1969)	X										
Glover (1960)					X	X		X	X	X	
Gray (1973)	X			X	X	X					
Greenwald (1958) (1970)	X		X			X		X	X	X	X
Hirschi (1962)										X	
Hollender (1964)									X		
Jackman, O'Toole, & Geis (1967)					X						

Pomeroy studied 175 prostitutes, of whom 83 to 93 percent were motivated by economic factors; he noted that "the gross income from prostitution is usually larger than could be expected from any other type of unskilled labor" (1965, p. 184). Benjamin and Masters were also aware of this sex-biased economic differential and its relationship to prostitution: "The economic rewards of prostitution are normally far greater than those of most other female occupations" (1964, p. 93). According to Esselstyn, "women are attracted to prostitution in contemporary America because the income is high and because it affords an opportunity to earn more, buy more, and live better than would be possible by any other plausible alternative" (1968, p. 129). Kingsley Davis sums this up: "Purely from the angle of economic return, the hard question is not why so many women become prostitutes, but why so few of them do" (1937, p. 750).

Some researchers claim to find an abnormal, perhaps even neurotic, materialism among prostitutes. Norman Jackman, Richard O'Toole, and Gilbert Geis, for example, state, "The rationalization by prostitutes violating social taboos against commercial sex behavior takes the form of exaggerating other values, particularly those of financial success, and for some the unselfish assumption of the financial burden of people dependent upon them" (1967, p. 138). However, as Greenwald accurately points out, "Economic factors helped to mold the entire society, the family structure, and therefore the very personalities of these [call] girls ... the girls were caught up in the worship of material success" (1970, p. 200). This desire for financial success is shared by the majority of Americans. Prostitutes are women who see their profession as their only means for moving from the poverty-level lifestyle that a low income brings to the gracious living that accompanies a possible $50,-000 a year.

A person's choice of occupation is not limited solely by external realities. Women as a class suffer from an especially narrow self-image in terms of occupational choices. Traditionally, women's roles are those of wife and mother, both of which are exclusively biological and service roles. The emphasis on service carries over into other, still traditional women's roles, such as teaching children, serving food, and keeping track of appointments for the boss. The importance of physical appearance in many of these occupations reinforces the women's self-image as physical or biological objects. As Karen Rosenblum argues:

[P]rostitution utilizes the same attributes characteristic of the female sex role, and uses those attributes towards the same ends; . . . the transition from non-deviance to deviance within prostitution requires only an exaggeration of the situation experienced as a non-deviant woman; . . . all women, to the degree to which they reflect the contemporary female sex role, are primary deviants (1975, p. 169).

Greenwald, perhaps unwittingly, demonstrates this fact in his effort to prove that the economic motivation is not the most important factor in the choice of prostitution as a profession. He claims that out of twenty prostitutes interviewed, none of whom "had skills to earn twenty to thirty thousand dollars a year in any other way," eighteen had had "chances either to marry or become the mistresses of wealthy men" (1970, p. 199). Martha Stein found in the course of a four-year study that "many of the call girls' professional techniques that had once disturbed me, began to remind me of techniques I used as a social worker" (1974, pp. 21–22).[5]

Pimps. Another erroneous myth about prostitutes sees them as defeated women cowering under the coercion of brutal pimps. Tage Kemp stated, "In many cases friendship with a pimp may be considered the immediate cause of a woman's becoming a harlot. It is the man who leads her on" (1936, p. 214). However, friendship and leading on are not necessarily coercive, and Kemp stated earlier in his book (p. 190) that the influence of a pimp was the immediate cause of prostitution for only 8.3 percent of prostitutes. Diana Gray found that the influence of pimps, when it was a factor, "was generally minimal" (1973, p. 412). Other studies support this statement (cf. James, forthcoming).

Women in this society are socialized to feel that they need a man to take care of them, to "take care of·business," to "complete" them, to love them, to make a home with them. Prostitutes are no exception. Because of their involvement in a deviant lifestyle, however, prostitutes must share their lives with men who understand the dynamics and values of their deviant subculture. Any man who lives with a prostitute will be called a pimp, although usually the key factors that distinguish a prostitute-pimp relationship from that of a normal marriage relationship are the illegality of the occupation, the woman's status as the sole breadwinner, and, often, the man's overt and simultaneous maintenance of two or more similar relationships. As is true throughout society, women's socialized need for men is reinforced by the fact that a woman's status is determined by that of her man. Prostitutes who can achieve a relationship with a high-class pimp have a higher standing in their subculture. This rise in status pays important dividends in daily interactions. Thus, in contradiction to the scenario of the coercive pimp, prostitutes will often actively seek to attach themselves to those pimps whose patronage they feel will be most beneficial.

Working Conditions and Adventure. Financial independence is a possibility not included in traditional women's roles. While roles are beginning to shift and broaden, there are still virtually no occupations available to low-skilled women that allow the independence, or provide the adventure, of prostitution. Rosenblum states that the "specific precipitating factors" that cause women to choose prostitution as a profession "can be identified simply as independence and money" (1975, p. 177). Benjamin and Masters (1964), Esselstyn (1968), Nanette Davis (1971) and James (forthcoming) specifically indicate that independence is a motivating factor in the choice of prostitution.

For many women, the "fast life" (as involvement in prostitution is called) represents more than simply independence from the conventions of the "straight" world. The lifestyle of the prostitution subculture has itself proved very attractive to a large number of women over the years. "Fondness for dancing and restaurant life" and the "tendency to vagabondage" comprised over one fourth of the immediate causes of prostitution listed by Kemp (1936, p. 190). In tabulating the factors that led three groups of prostitutes to choose their work, Pomeroy found that 3 to 19 percent were influenced by their perception of prostitution as "an easy life," 12 to 24 percent by the "fun and excitement" they found in the fast life, and 14 to 38 percent by the fact that prostitution enabled them to meet "interesting people" (1965, p. 184). Gray, in a study of "why particular women enter prostitution," reported that "many of the respondents ... felt intrigued by the description [by prostitutes] of prostitution which appeared exciting and glamorous ... the initial attraction for the girls in this study was social as well as material" (pp. 410–411). Benjamin and Masters state that the lifestyle inherent in identification with the prostitution subculture continues to be a strong attraction after women have committed themselves to the profession: "There is an abundance of evidence that on the conscious level it is the *excitement* of the prostitute's life, more than any other single factor, which works to frustrate rehabilitation efforts" (1964, p. 107). In the study by Jennifer James (forthcoming), excitement, adventure, and lifestyle were found to be significant motivating factors for a career in prostitution.

For these women, neither marriage nor extralegal monogamy seems to provide the economic independence, excitement, adventure, or social life available through prostitution. The basic fact of sexual objectification may be the same in either case, but for many women prostitution obviously has benefits that outweigh the privileges—and limitations—of socially respectable women's roles. Charles Winick and Paul Kinsie (1971) refer to a rehabilitation program for prostitutes in Japan in the 1950s that included such traditional women's activities as arts and crafts and homemaking. The program failed, they report, because the prostitutes were simply not interested. As Greenwald discovered, most prostitutes feel "overt hatred of routine, confining jobs" (1970, p. 202). The traditional female occupation of housewife can be seen as one of the most routine and confining jobs of all; it thus presents limited temptation to women who value the relative freedom of the fast life.

Early Life Experiences.　According to Rosenblum, "the only hypothesis that can be put forward is that access to prostitutes and perhaps specific incidents in the life of the individual provide the initiative to act upon the potential for prostitution inherent in the female sex role" (1975, p. 181). Maerov (1965), James Bryan (1967), and Gray (1973) also see access to prostitutes—whether through personal relationships with people in the profession or through the overt presence of prostitution in the neighborhood—as a significant factor in many women's entrance into prostitution. The study by James (forthcoming) revealed that the mean age at which the subjects became aware of prostitution was 13.73 years (standard deviation 3.23), and the mean age at which they began regular prostitution was 18.20 years (standard deviation 2.60). Girlfriends, relatives, and the neighborhood were the most important sources of their first information about prostitution.

Early sexual experience may be a significant determinant of entrance into prostitution. Of the prostitutes in one study, 44.85 percent reported that they had "gotten into trouble" because of their sexual activity while they were juveniles (James, forthcoming). Donald Carns explains, "a woman's decision to enter coitus ... implies that she is creating for herself a sexual status which will have a relatively pervasive distribution ... she will be evaluated downwardly. Such is the nature of the male bond" (1973, p. 680). Female promiscuity virtually guarantees loss of status in American society. The labeling implied by such loss of status may be an important step in the process by which a woman comes to identify with a "deviant" lifestyle such as prostitution and thus begins to see it as a viable alternative. Nanette Davis describes this process:

> The adolescent girl who is labeled a sex offender for promiscuity ... may initially experience a conflict about her identity. Intimate association with sophisticated deviants, however, may provide an incentive to learn the hustler role ... and thus resolve the status anxiety by gaining prestige through association with deviants, and later, experimentation in the deviant role (1971, p. 305).

Following the labeling impact of status loss, the girl may attempt to rebuild her self-image by moving into a subculture where the wider society's negative labeling of her will not impede her efforts toward a higher status—although that status itself will be perceived as negative by society at large.

However negative the long-term effects of juvenile promiscuity on a woman's social status may be, the short-term effects of contranormative juvenile sexual activity may often appear quite positive to the young woman involved. Young women suffering from paternal abuse or neglect—a common childhood pattern for prostitutes—may be especially susceptible to the advantages of what Greenwald calls "early rewarded sex—that is ... engaging in some form of sexual activity with an adult for which they were rewarded. [These women] discovered at an early age that they could get some measure of affection, of interest, by giving sexual gratification" (1970, p. 167). This type of positive sexual reinforcement, particularly when coupled with the cultural stereotype of women as primarily sexual beings, may cause some women to perceive their sexuality as their primary means for gaining status:

"Sex as a status tool is exploited to gain male attention" (N. Davis, 1971, p. 304). All women in Western societies must somehow come to terms with the fact that their personal value is considered inseparable from their sexual value. As Rosenblum explains:

> While men are also concerned with their sexual desirability, their opinion of themselves is not founded primarily on that desirability, for occupational achievement provides an important alternative to a self-identification based on sexual desirability. The alternatives available to females are fewer and generally carry lower social esteem, resulting in an inordinately high value being placed on sexual desirability (1975, p. 180).

Prostitution is a result of the discovery that carrying out the implications of the normal female sex role can pay off not only in a certain sort of social status but also in cold cash.

Many sexual contacts between young females and adult males have no positive aspects for the former; examples are incidences of incest and rape. Kemp (1936) and Maerov (1965) mention the prevalence of early sexual trauma among prostitute populations. In the study by James (forthcoming), 49.1 percent of the subjects answered affirmatively to the question, "Prior to your first intercourse, did any older person (more than 10 years older) attempt sexual play or intercourse with you?" The perpetrators of these attempts were 10.60 percent fathers, 12.12 percent stepfathers, 3.03 percent foster-fathers, and 15.15 percent other relatives, which makes a total of 25.75 percent for father figures and 40.90 percent for experiences that could be seen as incestuous. Further, 46.5 percent reported that they had been raped, and 16.7 percent had been raped more than once. Although the ages of the subjects when these rapes occurred is not known, 72.2 percent of the subjects of an earlier study reported having had a "forced/bad sexual experience," and 84.7 percent of these experiences occurred when the subject was aged fifteen or younger (James, 1972). Of the men responsible for these experiences, 23.1 percent were fathers and 15.4 percent were other relatives. The long-term effects of the sexual abuse of children are virtually unknown. Vincent DeFrancis (1969) found that guilt, shame, and loss of self-esteem on the part of the child victim are the immediate results of sexual abuse, and it seems likely that these reactions might have considerable impact on the victim's developing self-image and might possibly lead to an abnormal degree of sexual self-objectification.

Parental Abuse and Neglect. Parental abuse or neglect is widely considered a typical childhood experience of women who become prostitutes. Kemp (1936), Maryse Choisy (1961), Arnold Maerov (1965), Jackman, O'Toole, and Geis (1967), Esselstyn (1968), Greenwald (1970), Nanette Davis (1971), and Gray (1973) all mention unsatisfactory relationships with parents as a fact of life for these women. Whether the condition is simple neglect by absence or outright physical or psychological abuse, the result is generally considered to be the child's alienation from the parents and her consequent inability to adequately socialize into the conventional mores of society. Data from the study by James (forthcoming) seem to reaffirm the prevalence of parental abuse or neglect in the childhood experiences of prostitutes. The mean age at which the women in this study left home permanently was 16.25 years (standard deviation, 2.09), and "dispute with family" was one of the two major reasons given for leaving home.

Occupation. Some researchers believe that certain occupations lead women easily into prostitution (see, for example, Esselstyn, 1968). These occupations are those that adhere most closely to the traditional female service role, often emphasizing physical appearance as well as service. As Marshall Clinard observes, "Quasi-prostituting experiences, such as those of a waitress who after hours accepts favors from customers in return for sexual intercourse, may lead to prostitution" (1959, p. 228). It is not unusual for a woman who is required by her employer to flirt with customers and "be sexy" to find that the men with whom she must relate in business transactions consider her to be no better than a prostitute. Once she has been so labeled, her loss of status is automatic, and she may decide she might as well make the best of a negative situation by accepting the "favors"—or the money—that men are eager to give her for playing out the implications of the label. Again, these low-status service occupations are among the few occupational alternatives available to unskilled or low-skilled women.

General Psychoanalytic Motivations. The myth that women become prostitutes because they are "oversexed" has been countered by the discovery that prostitutes see their sexual activities with customers as purely business and usually get no sexual pleasure from them. Unfortunately, an opposite myth also exists: that of "the invariably frigid prostitute" (Maerov, 1965, p. 692). Responding to this, Pomeroy reports that the 175 prostitutes he studied "were more sexually responsive in their personal lives than were women who were not prostitutes and even in their contact with paid partners they were more responsive sexually than one might have anticipated" (1965, p. 183). Given this information, the search for explanations of prostitution based on the psychological effects of frigidity hardly seems worth pursuing.

There is another theory about prostitutes that pictures them as using their profession to act out their hostility toward men. Looking at this objectively, it would seem equally valid to suggest that some women become elementary school teachers in order to act out their hostility toward children. Perhaps this motivation is real for some women, both teachers and prostitutes, but documentation is very scarce. In the 1974–1975 study by James (forthcoming), only one woman mentioned hostility toward men as a motivating factor, and it was her second response, indicating that there was another, more immediate motivation. Such myths arise because of lack of objectivity in studies of prostitutes. As Stein says about her attitude at the beginning of her research on call girls, "I kept looking for signs that the women were really miserable or neurotic or self-destructive. I wanted them to be that way. I think I wanted call girls to be 'sick' because I believed that anybody—at least any woman—who sold sexual access ought to be sick" (1974, pp. 21–22). Once she had discarded these preconceptions, Stein made significant discoveries:

> The women who became successful call girls, like those who became social workers, had to be sensitive and warm. They had to like people and feel comfortable with them. Nobody who dislikes people could succeed over a period of time in a profession that requires close body contact with strangers. Within this broad framework, the call girls' attitudes to their clientele varied, much like social workers. For some girls, the call girl-client relationship was a purely business one. . . . Other call girls tended to become genuinely concerned with their clients. . . . Most of the call girls I met, like most social workers I knew, fell in between these two extremes (1974, pp. 22–23).

Latent Homosexuality. One study of prostitutes has revealed that 35.3 percent of the sample had experienced at least one lesbian relationship, 7.4 percent reported "frequent" homosexual activity, and 6.7 percent described themselves as exclusively lesbian in libidinal interest (James, forthcoming). This rate of female homosexual experience, which is certainly higher than for the general female population, is seen by some researchers as proof that latent homosexuality motivates many women to become prostitutes. Since many other explanations are possible, such reasoning is a reflection of the prejudice of the majority culture, which has a heterosexual orientation. Rather than motivating women to become prostitutes, homosexuality may be a result of being a prostitute. For instance, women already labeled deviants will more readily engage in—and admit to engaging in—other deviant sexual behavior. It is also possible that homosexuality may appear more attractive to prostitutes than it does to the majority of women because of certain aspects of the prostitute's lifestyle: the absence of conventional restraints on the open discussion of sex and sexuality, a wider experience of different sexual techniques, and the fact that in their private lives prostitutes often live more intimately with other women than with men.

Oedipal Fixation. Some researchers believe many prostitutes have an oedipal fixation. Winick and Kinsie, for example, see prostitution as atonement for guilt produced by incestuous fantasies (1971, p. 83). This theory is impossible to disprove, since we cannot accurately measure the incidence of incestuous fantasies. On the other hand, it is impossible to prove their theory, or to prove that it applies more to prostitution than to other occupations. "Money is heavily loaded with all kinds of psychological conflicts. In our civilization, among many other things . . . it symbolizes the will to power and the ensuing unconscious guilt of having taken the father's place," Choisy states (1961, p. 1). Perhaps every woman, prostitute and business executive alike, who desires economic independence is acting out oedipal fantasies. It seems unlikely, however, that many women are motivated solely or primarily by such a tenuous subconscious factor in making their occupational choice. The literature provides virtually no "hard" data to justify including oedipal fixation among the significant prostitute motivating factors.

Eighty percent of the sample in Study I (James, 1972) reported a negative childhood relationship with their fathers. In Study II (James, forthcoming), 20.5 percent reported *no* relationship with their fathers, and an equal percentage, a negative one. The fathers of 55.6 percent of the latter study's subjects were absent from the home during part or all of the subjects' childhood; 23.1 percent of the subjects in Study I and 11.7 percent of those in Study II were the victims of sexual abuse by their fathers.

Retardation.   Theories of prostitute motivation based on inherent or inherited disabilities or mental retardation have been generally unaccepted in recent years. It is simply not true that "from 30 to 50 percent of all prostitutes must be classed as feeble-minded" (Kemp, 1936, p. 126). Nor, we hope, would most present-day social scientists accept as valid the conclusions of researchers such as Cesare Lombroso and William Ferrero who stated that "even the female criminal is monotonous and uniform compared with her male companion, just as woman is in general inferior to man" (1898, p. 122); and, further on, that "women are big children; their evil tendencies are more numerous and more varied than men's" (p. 151). These are two extreme and early examples of studies of prostitution that were carried out by researchers apparently prejudiced toward their subjects, either because of their sex or their occupation. Less extreme examples of this attitude are found in other studies that seem to be attempts to discover "what is *wrong* with these women?" (see, for example, Hollender, 1964; Maerov, 1965; Greenwald, 1970; and Winick & Kinsie, 1971).

CUSTOMERS

The fact that it takes at least two people to complete a commercial sexual exchange is often ignored by social scientists as well as by police vice officers. There are numerous articles and books about the female side of prostitution but very few about their customers. The arrest statistics for prostitution mirror this imbalance.

Examination of the literature produces evidence that this concentration on the female prostitute is based on her perceived deviance in contrast to the perceived normality of the customer. Yet prostitution functions as a supply and demand economy, and the prostitute-customer transactions represent a mixture of motivations on the part of both females and males. The definition of deviance in the case of prostitution is apparently based on differential sex-role expectations, assumed personal needs, and class bias. Information on the customers of prostitutes is necessary for a full understanding of the commercial interaction of sex roles, the definitions of deviance, and the response of the legal system.

Motivations of Customers

Most articles on client motivations are limited and superficial despite estimates that the percentage of the male population having some contact with prostitutes is very substantial. The articles provide little information since they do not review client backgrounds; the exception to this is the venereal disease sample taken by T. Gibbens and M. Silberman (1960). The interest of most researchers has focused on the basic fact that men visit prostitutes and on the needs, accepted as falling within the normal range, that their visits fulfill.

Alfred Kinsey, Wardell Pomeroy, and Clyde Martin (1948), through their survey of sexuality in the human male, have provided the most comprehensive information available on intercourse with prostitutes. That survey found that about 69 percent of the white males in their total population had had some experience with prostitutes (Kinsey, Pomeroy, & Martin, 1948, p. 597). Not more than 15 or 20 percent of these, however, had regular intercourse with prostitutes. Young males were only infrequently represented in this group, with the majority of customers being between thirty-seven and forty years of age.[6] The survey further revealed an estimated 3,190 contacts per week with prostitutes in a town of 100,000 inhabitants (p. 603).

The only available book-length discussion of the customers of prostitutes is *Lovers, Friends, and Slaves* by Stein (1974). The material is drawn primarily from observations based on her training in social work, and her book is the first effort to describe the men who visit upper-class call girls. Stein outlines categories of customers to clarify her description of the male needs serviced by prostitutes. Those categories include opportunists, fraternizers, promoters, adventurers, lovers, friends, slaves, guardians, and juveniles.

There have been other attempts to determine the motivations of the customers of prostitutes. A study published by Charles Winick in 1962 reviewed customers' perceptions of themselves and prostitutes. He interviewed 732 customers and provided an extensive list of the reasons men visit prostitutes; but this analysis was primarily personal and psychoanalytic. Later, in *The Lively Commerce*, Winick and Kinsie (1971), reevaluated this client data in the context of American anecdotal material. The reasons given by Winick and Kinsie for why men visit prostitutes, along with the motivations cited by other researchers, are summarized in Table 2.

The definitions of the eleven categories of need are surprisingly uniform throughout the literature. The traveler is the classic salesman, conventioneer, or serviceman who finds himself away from home and desirous of sexual contact. The social customer desires to share the sexual experiences of his night out on the town with a group of friends. The disabled are handicapped individuals, such as paraplegics, who feel a professional is either more appropriate or their only opportunity. Men classified as specials go to prostitutes because their sexual needs might be considered perverted by other women. The impotent male seeks sexual stimulation and/or therapy. The homosexual customer seeks male prostitutes; he may find it embarrassing to find male partners other than prostitutes. Customers whose needs fall into the category of therapy often just want someone to talk with aboout personal problems. The quantity need arises when numbers of sexual contacts are required to achieve potency, and the variety need reflects the desire for different types of women as partners. The uninvolved customer desires sex without the potential problems of pregnancy, personal emotion, or courting. The final category, loneliness, overlaps other areas (as do all the categories) but basically includes individuals who find themselves in need of human contact.

Quantity. Those men who desire quantity of sexual experience adhere to the ethic that the seduction of many women provides "points" for proof of potency. The desire for quantity is apparently rooted in adolescent bull sessions and is reinforced by commercialized media images. Ordinarily seduction is a long, drawn-out affair, making quantity difficult to obtain. The prostitute provides a short cut since the exchange of cash on a direct basis eliminates the slower transaction of dinners, entertainment, and the development of rapport. A man can have hundreds of prostitutes in the time it might take to get ten other

Table 2. Customer Motivations

Authors	Travel	Social Bonding	Disablement	Special Services	Impotency	Homosexuality	Therapy	Quantity	Variety	Uninvolvement	Loneliness
Basel (1970)	X	X		X		X				X	
Bullough (1970)	X	X		X				X	X	X	X
Cave (1970)	X	X						X	X	X	X
Gibbens & Silberman (1960)	X	X	X	X	X	X					
Greenwald (1970)		X		X	X	X		X	X	X	
James (forthcoming)	X	X	X	X	X	X	X	X	X	X	X
Karpf (1953)									X	X	
Kinsey, Pomeroy, & Martin (1948)		X	X	X				X	X	X	
Kirkendall (1960)									X	X	
Liswood (1970)				X				X	X	X	
Mathis (1970)	X								X	X	
Polatin (1970)					X				X	X	X
Schimel (1970)		X							X	X	
Stein (1974)		X		X	X	X	X	X	X	X	
Winick & Kinsie (1971)	X	X		X	X	X	X	X	X	X	
Total	7	10	3	9	6	6	3	8	13	14	4

women. Moreover, the financial outlay, counting time as money, may be the same. The quantity is guaranteed; the score is easy to predict.

Variety of Women.   Most men have stereotypes of sexual attractiveness: large breasts, blond hair, long legs. Those who prefer dark women can hire black prostitutes to fill needs not satisfiable within their social circle. A penchant for very young or very old that is in conflict with the customer's place in social reality, a desire for obesity, a need for long, flowing hair: all these varieties of the female as sex object are available on the street.

Variety of Services.   The desire for a variety of sexual services is also an important customer motivation. Many men say they seek prostitutes because sexual variety cannot be obtained at home or elsewhere. This need for variety may express itself in a desire for different positions; anal intercourse; oral-genital relations; the use of oils, lotions, or liquors; a certain tone of voice; body language; or a particular direction of events. Prostitutes provide an infinite variety of possibilities that can be granted on request or introduced through experience.

Impotency.   The impotent man finds that the prostitute can help to solve his problem in a variety of ways. (1) If he subscribes to the "sex-is-dirty" school, her sexuality and its context may arouse him in a way that a "good" woman cannot. (2) Her knowledge of technique, such as the use of fellatio, may help him relax and achieve an erection. (3) The prostitute may view herself as a therapist; she may be successful in this vein and take her business seriously. She will talk with the customer, try to find his inhibitions, and work on solutions for the impotence. (4) She may provide alternative routes to help him complete the illusion that he needs for sexual gratification. She may let him orally or manually manipulate her to faked orgasm, thus proving that she is satisfied regardless of his condition. She may point out how important it is to her to have a man she can talk to instead of one who is always pawing her and treating her as a sex object. She may tell him it shows the quality of his character that he needs to get to know a girl before he responds and may urge him to return soon so that they can develop the relationship. (5) If he insists on penetration she can provide him with a brace or a dildo. On the other hand, the prostitute may just take his money and not attempt to compensate him in any way. But even then she will provide him with an excuse for his inability to achieve an erection: "Honey, you're tired, you work so hard." "You had too much to drink, you silly man." "All that tension from your job makes it difficult for you." What she will be careful never to do is let him see his lack of erection as a failure. He is safe with the professional. He has paid to be protected. He will not have to face her again in case he fails.

Therapy.   Not all customers desire sexual contact. Some want a companion to take to dinner or to a movie; others want someone to talk to for an hour. "Talkers" may have the prostitute ride out to the airport or sit in a hotel room with them while they tell her their troubles. The prostitute is the sympathetic ear in a situation where other women are too impatient or are not to be trusted. Whatever role is required—substitute mother, sister, or friend—she can play it. This is only one of the areas where the customer is, in a sense, seeking a therapist. The women frequently recognize their role as therapist with the joke that good whores and good "shrinks" always have more business than they know what to do with.

Uninvolvement.   The customer categories include men who want release of sexual tension without the problems of involvement in a relationship. A man with this motivation does not want the trouble of an affair that his wife might find out about or of a relationship with a single woman who will expect marriage or "set him up" by getting pregnant. He does not want to waste time entertaining a woman who may refuse to have sex with him, and he may also not want to assume the responsibility of providing her with sexual gratification. A prostitute is discreet, does not expect to be entertained, always says yes, and will pretend gratification regardless of his commitment to pleasuring her. He pays for access to her body to achieve ejaculation and that is what he gets, without games, problems, or the emotional expectations of other women.

Travel.   Men who travel on business or who are estranged from sexual partners because of being in the armed services or residing in work camps or construction projects also provide business for the prostitute.

The traveling salesman may express his loneliness sexually, as may the sailor, merchant marine, migrant worker, or construction worker on the Alaska pipeline. Men away from home are in a sense sexually disenfranchised because they are without a social group in which they can find an acceptable sexual outlet.

Disablement. Men who qualify as sexually disenfranchised because they are restricted or disabled may also turn to professional women to fulfill their needs. American society, in contrast to many other simpler cultures, limits sexual access to many on the basis of age, race, culture, personality, intelligence, and physical condition. Those who do not, or who feel they do not, qualify as acceptable sexual partners find it safer to pay for guaranteed acceptance by a prostitute than to risk rejection or social condemnation.

The disabled provide potential customers because of limited definitions of sexual attractiveness. Amputees seek women whom they can pay not to react to their deformities. Often, seeing prostitutes is part of a densensitization process that will enable these men eventually to attempt sexual relations with other partners. For others, their own view of their impaired sexual attractiveness will make them permanent members of the customer population. Accident victims who are burned or deformed, as well as men with birth defects, also turn to prostitutes either as a test of their sexual ability and attractiveness or as a permanent solution to the threat of rejection inherent in approaches to other women. Paraplegics and quadraplegics provide another category of permanent or learning-to-function customers.

The aged provide a classic example of men who are sexually disenfranchised. Somewhere between the ages of fifty and sixty, men are expected to discontinue sexual relations. Their spouses may insist on it; their doctor may recommend it; their widowed, divorced, or bachelor status may require it to avoid the "dirty old man" characterization. They may find women their own age unattractive, but access to younger, "ideal" sexual objects may be limited. An elderly man may live in a retirement nursing home under constant supervision or with relatives who are inimical to his having an active sex life. The only sexual alternative available to him is the professional prostitute who can be visited discreetly, who does not care about his age, and who provides the place for the meetings.

Racially or culturally disenfranchised males also face restrictions because of their perceived or actual inability to qualify as acceptable sexual partners. Variety is not the issue here as much as cultural or class limitations. For instance, white males may feel that this is the only way to satisfy their desire for access to black or Asian women, and the reverse may also be true. Or a Jewish man may want a "shicksa" but would not date a non-Jewish woman because of cultural pressures against doing so. Even if they speak English well, male foreigners who work at international occupations or travel may have problems in gaining sexual access in a socially acceptable manner.

Sexual access may be limited because of cultural history. Many Chinese men who emigrated to this country as laborers before World War II were deprived of wives because of immigration quotas on Chinese women. Unable to marry outside their culture, they were left as bachelors, living together in hotels in the international districts of cities. Prostitutes visit these hotels once or twice a month, providing sexual service for up to thirty men in a day. Often one of these men will have a relationship with an individual prostitute that may span ten years or more. Long after he has stopped receiving sexual service, he gives her money or bails her out of jail because she is "his girl." She may have been the only woman he was able to label in that way.

Special Services.   Among a prostitute's customers are those referred to as "specials" or "freaks." These are men whose means of sexual arousal fall into the category of perverse. Most people, depending on their individual experience, have special fantasies that intensify sexual pleasure; the range of fantasies extends as far as the imagination. In some cases the fantasy is necessary to achieve erection and ejaculation. A man with such fantasies may feel it is unacceptable to act them out with anyone but a prostitute, or he may feel ashamed of his needs and conceal them from a possibly willing sex partner in favor of the safety of guaranteed acceptance by a prostitute. With a professional, he may not have to do more than hint at his desires for her to understand what they are and fulfill them.

Social Bonding.   Some men view visiting prostitutes with their friends as a social-bonding mechanism. Going "with the boys" to a party or massage parlor is viewed as masculine entertainment, something men do together. Knowledge of the activity is kept from wives and other noninvolved associates. Stag parties held by members of social and business clubs are also occasions of social bonding. For an experienced, older man who wishes to introduce a younger friend or relative to sexual experience, or for two males who are seeking their first experiences together, the visit to a prostitute can provide a friendship bond.

Toward Attainment of a Need/Fulfillment Balance

The sexual needs of customers discussed above are generally considered to be within the normal range, with the exception of the "freaks" or perverts. In fact, the customers of prostitutes, and their activities as such, have enjoyed a long tradition of imputed normality. Even during the periods when intensive official attempts to end the business of prostitution were underway,[7] customers' needs were accepted as inevitable. At most, the men were chided for risking venereal disease and implored to practice self-control. The real villains, according to the reformers, were "those who made money by 'promoting' prostitution . . . not [practitioners of] 'secret or clandestine vice'" (Anderson, 1974, p. 223). Since men were considered to have a basic biological need for these "secret" sexual outlets, it was seen as somehow immoral for women to demand money for relieving that need.

Men who purchase the services of prostitutes are still considered normal and are not defined as deviant, even though their actions may be seen as unpalatable, or even immoral, according to the personal standards of the observer. Customers of prostitutes are, of course, acting outside the law, but where the law and the accepted male sex role come into conflict, the sex-role norms predominate over the power of the law. Men are expected to actively seek fulfillment of their wide variety of sexual needs. As part of that search, they are allowed to purchase the sexual services of women illegally and with relative impunity, as arrest statistics demonstrate.

The provision of sexual services to males by women is, in contrast, clearly labeled deviant. Males break few social rules in patronizing a prostitute; females break almost all the rules of their sex role in becoming prostitutes. Streetwalkers, in particular, place themselves at the wrong end of the whore-madonna spectrum: They accept money for sex, they are promiscuous, they are not in love with their customers, they are not subtle, and they engage in "abnormal" or deviant sex acts—acts that other women are not expected to perform. The location of the streetwalker's place of business also labels her as deviant. Men may walk the streets freely wherever and whenever they wish; a woman downtown late at night without a male escort is suspect.

Even more significant, however, is the fact that the independent, promiscuous, overt sexuality of the prostitute challenges the traditional assumption that female sexuality is entirely dependent on—and awakened only by—male sexuality. As Kingsley Davis (1937, p. 755) states, "Women are either part of the family system, or they are prostitutes, members of a caste set apart." Unregulated sexuality is accepted from males; from females, whose sexual stability is the *sine qua non* of our family concept, however, extrafamilial sex threatens the basic structures of society. So threatening is the idea of female sexual independence that there are laws defining young females who engage in sexual intercourse without official permission as persons "in danger of falling into habits of vice."

The differential enforcement is also a class issue. That prostitutes and their customers generally come from different classes is confirmed by statistics. It becomes important, then, to consider prostitution not only as a sex issue but also as a complex interaction between individuals from, and the institutions of, different social classes. Despite probable exceptions to the statistical generalization that customers are from the middle class and prostitutes are from the lower class, this difference in class status is traditionally assumed to be absolute:

> The professional prostitute being a social outcast may be periodically punished without disturbing the usual course of society; no one misses her while she is serving out her term—no one, at least, about whom society has any concern. The man [customer], however, is something more than partner in an immoral act; he discharges important social and business relations. . . . He cannot be imprisoned without deranging society (Flexner, 1914, p. 108).

This difference in class status, moreover, is reinforced by societal application of the deviant label to the prostitute. Her social mobility is correspondingly reduced, and the equation of prostitute to lower class becomes more nearly absolute in fact. As Davis further states, "The harlot's return is not primarily a reward for abstinence, labor, or rent. It is primarily a reward for loss of social standing" (1937, p. 750). There is no parallel social process that exists to label customers as deviant, and their higher-class status is therefore not affected by their illegal participation in prostitution.

The class status of customers also tends to protect them from the possibility of acquiring a deviant label through involvement in the criminal justice system. Judging by the arrest statistics, most customers seem to be above the law, which is quite likely since "[a]gencies of social control do not operate with impunity; they must protect themselves from public reprisal and antipathy" (Kirk, 1972, p. 24). Any attempt to routinely arrest, process, and label a large proportion of a politically powerful class can lead only to "organizational strain and trouble" (Chambliss, 1969, p. 21). On the other hand, harassment of social outcasts, with its implied confirmation of the deviant label, has always been a reasonable way to gain public approval and support.

The difference in class between the prostitute and her customers has a larger function than simple protection of the latter from social and legal labeling. One aspect of this function is that "[m]any men can achieve high sexual capacity [only] with a woman whom they regard as inferior" (Winick & Kinsie, 1971, p. 202). This supposed inferiority of the prostitute may arise from her lower-class status alone, or it may include recognition of her deviant label. Some men desire the excitement of sexual relations in an illegal, or "I'm OK, you're deviant," situation.

More importantly, the inter-class nature of prostitution is an expression of the middle-class male's need for liberation from the sexual conventions of his class. The accepted range of male sexual behavior in our society is considerably wider than the accepted behavior convention of the middle class—and especially of middle-class women. Lower-class women, then, and particularly those who have been set apart by the deviant label, must serve as substitutes for the middle-class women who are so firmly restricted by their class proscriptions. Prostitution allows men "to regress to an 'Id' state of complete freedom from all restraints of civilization and acculturation," to move briefly into the deviant subculture, secure in their class-guaranteed ability to return to their own view of normality (Winick & Kinsie, 1971, p. 97).

The more highly restricted female sex role contains almost none of the sexual motivations and behaviors allowed to the male; nor does it allow a woman to serve as a professional accompanyist for those men who would rent her participation in sexual activities. Rather than stating, then, that a prostitute is a deviant individual and her customer is a normal individual, it is actually more exact—and more telling—to say that a prostitute is a deviant *woman* and her customer is a normal *man.*

The puritan aspect of middle-class society means that the full acting out of the male sex role by middle-class males requires the existence of prostitution. As a result, the male need for purchased female sexual service is, and has long been, accepted as inevitable and therefore not to be punished. To have laws against prostitution, then, seems to imply that some aspects of the male sex role itself are intolerable—or at least dangerously at odds with the conventions of middle-class society. Women are daily jailed, stigmatized, and exiled from so-called decent society for their ability to recognize and deal with this conflict between male sexual needs and male social ideals.

Ideally, every socially accepted human need should have an equally accepted resolution. Conscious efforts at need/fulfillment balancing, then, would seem to be of especial importance to societies working toward self-betterment. In Western society—in which virtually all citizens are daily involved, both actually and symbolically, in heterosexual role playing—it obviously creates a conflict for one sex to be allowed a wide range of normal sexual behavior and the other to be narrowly restricted, for a male to be assumed to need to act out many varieties of sexual expression in which a woman is not allowed to engage under threat of being labeled deviant. The two sets of behavior patterns can never balance.

The unfortunate solution to this need/fulfillment imbalance has been the creation of a subclass of women who are simultaneously rewarded with money for participating in normal (for males) sex and punished as deviants for the same activity. The existence of prostitution depends on an exchange between a willing buyer and a willing seller. As long as men see sex as something that can be purchased, there will be women who see sexual service as a viable product. The criminal law must recognize the existence of customers and accept their motivations before a rational adjustment of the inequities inherent in the current enforcement of prostitution laws can occur.

PIMPS

There are other men in the prostitute's life besides police and customers. Friends and acquaintances within the fast life are important to the lifestyle. Streetwalkers, especially, usually do not work alone; most have a man somewhere in the background. In other prostitution styles, such as the call-girl system, a man is less necessary to business survival, but he may still be viewed as an important part of a woman's life. He may be called a pimp, although prostitutes dislike the term. He is usually referred to by the woman as "my man." This man may function as a pimp; he may be a boyfriend or husband, or a combination of pimp and boyfriend. In cases of lesbian prostitutes, this role is filled by a woman who treats her women in much the same fashion as a male would. The lesbian pimp usually works with very young girls, often runaways from home or juvenile institutions. As new girls in the business, they are afraid to work for a man and find a female is more supportive.

Characteristics of Pimps

Very few studies have been made of pimps, and no attempt has been made to determine the causes—other than the obvious ones of money and status—behind the choice of the profession of pimping. Most of what is known about pimps comes from individual biographical accounts. Iceberg Slim's book *Pimp: The Story of My Life* (1967) is a well-known account of pimping in Chicago in the thirties. Two other books, *Black Players: The Secret World of Black Pimps* (Milner & Milner, 1972) and *Gentleman of Leisure* (Hall, 1972), cover the philosophy behind "pimp ethics" and the regulations of the fast life.

In large American cities, pimps are predominately black. The few white males who operate on the West Coast utilize a black hustler model. In the Northwest an Indian will occasionally pimp, as do Chicanos in the Southwest. The East Coast supports the largest percentage of white pimps (approximately 15 percent), usually of Italian and Puerto Rican backgrounds. Explanations for the dominance of blacks are based on their unique position in American culture. With options for success limited, the pimp for many decades competed with the preacher for status in the black community. These were the only two occupations that provided opportunities for money and status in a racist society. In addition, the prostituting of black women was a common fact of life during the years of slavery, and the game of the "hustler" was one of the few ways for a black man to get ahead. Those social patterns have markedly changed, but some of the mythology and a little of the status still cling to the role of pimp. The overt display of wealth is always a guarantee of respect on some levels of society.

There is very limited information on pimps beyond their racial characteristics. A study of pimps in a West Coast city revealed an age range of 20–44 with a mean of 30.3 (James, 1972). This compares to a corresponding prostitute study with an age range of 16–40 (mean, 22.6). Most pimps are older than the women who work for them. The most successful pimps encountered were all over thirty. Differences in age between pimps and prostitutes can be explained through recourse to male-female role requirements. An older male is more likely to exercise authority over a younger female. In addition, the business of prostitution is most profitable for young women, while the age of the pimp has less economic relevance.

The educational level of men involved in pimping corresponds to that of prostitutes: 11.4 years. The interesting difference is that while most prostitutes have tried other jobs or been involved in vocational training, pimps have always been pimps. Most of them desire to be in the fast life early on in their experience and begin their careers as soon as they are old enough to talk a woman into working for them. A common pattern is to begin with a girlfriend or wife and "turn her out" into the profession. They will later recruit other women who may be already active in the profession or curious to try it out.

The Prostitute-Pimp Relationship

A pimp can be defined as someone who acts as an agent for others whom he essentially recruits and to whom he offers his services for a percentage of their earnings. In past decades the pimp took an active role as a procurer of customers for prostitutes, but this is no longer the usual case. The ideal pimp fills many roles in his relationship with the prostitute: He is substitute husband, boyfriend, surrogate father, lover, agent, and protector. As husband he may pay the bills, take care of the car, and father her children. His role as boyfriend includes taking her to parties and providing other entertainment. These two overlap in his role of lover. As father he may discipline her for inappropriate behavior and make decisions vital for her. The agent and protector provides bail money, retains the services of an attorney, and offers protection from others on the street through his reputation as a strong man whose women are not to be "hassled." How well he fills any one of these roles depends on how good a pimp he is and on his relationship with the woman.

The security of that relationship is often strained by the pressures inherent in the lifestyle, arrest, incarceration, and jealousy between women who share the same man. The ability to maintain the relationship between a single prostitute and her pimp is based on acceptance of the ethics of the lifestyle. In the life the rules are different. As long as he meets his obligations to each woman, a man may have more than one woman as his partner. Each woman may believe she will eventually be the one he will choose to settle down with when they have "made it together" and no longer need to be involved in prostitution (although this dream is rarely fulfilled). Some women are interested only in a short-term relationship because of their desire for the protection derived from association with a pimp. They pose no threat to the long-term woman because they make no demands for a position as "main lady."

Reasons for the Relationship.   The reasons offered by both pimps and prostitutes for this kind of relationship do not differ greatly from the reasons that most men and women have for marrying. Respect, business, and love—though perhaps not in that order—are major motivating factors. In reality, a detailed description of the interaction between pimp and prostitute produces a picture of a relationship that is little more than an exaggeration of the male-female relationships in the larger society. Levels of love, respect, and economic exchange vary, but the needs are the same.

RESPECT.   Regardless of how people may wish to qualify the statement, women in our society feel they need a male companion if their position is to be respected. Women alone, if they are not elderly or widowed, are viewed as needing a man. Unmarried daughters are harassed, women without men frequently feel their lives are incomplete, and friends are forever trying to make a couple out of two singles. The same feelings of need for a male associate pervade the fast life. In fact, sex-role behavior is conservative among prostitutes; a woman needs a man or she is regarded as an "outlaw," someone who is abnormal by the subculture's values. If her man is in prison or has recently been killed, she is given a period of grace, but few other excuses for being without a man are acceptable.

A man offers basic protection from harassment by other men. A prostitute without a pimp is considered fair game by other pimps who will attempt to "catch" her. She will be looked down on by her colleagues and be more open to abuse from others on the street. Her pimp's name is significant as a "keep away" sign in the same way that a wedding ring traditionally has been. On the street it becomes more important because of the threat of assault or robbery if a woman does not have a man "behind her." His reputation provides respect and therefore protection. However, he does not in fact appear on the street but instead socializes with other pimps in bars or private homes. Protection from customers is up to the prostitute and her coworkers, since the pimp is not around when she is working.

Respect has other dimensions. A woman's status among her peers in the life is directly related to the status of her pimp. Just as the banker's wife is accorded more status than the truck driver's, a prostitute's reputation in large part depends on her pimp's. If he is well dressed and handsome, drives a prestige automobile (called a pimpmobile), and handles himself well, she will be highly respected; on the other hand, if he is less than stylish and unsuccessful in playing his role, she will be looked down on. The woman is defined by the man for whom she works, and a really top pimp finds women asking and paying to be associated with him rather than waiting for him to recruit them.

BUSINESS.   A second major factor in the prostitute-pimp relationship is business. Many women feel that they need a man to take care of business details that women traditionally have not felt capable of handling. They need a man to tell them when to work and how to work, to keep them in line, to give them confidence, and to take care of them. The pimp ideally takes care of all accounts. He handles the money, pays the bills, makes the investments, and gives her an allowance. He provides a place to live, food, clothing, transportation, entertainment and medical care. He is expected to arrange for bail when she is arrested, provide a lawyer, and give her financial and moral support if she has to serve a sentence. The pimp takes care of her property and sees that her children are taken care of during the times she is working or serving a sentence. As one pimp put it, "I provide the mind and she provides the body. After all, that's the difference between a man and a woman" (James, 1972, p. 55). One of the older women interviewed put it this way:

> I gave him all of the money and, like I say, all my business was taken care of. I didn't have to worry about it. If I went to jail I'd be right out, if I needed an attorney he'd pay for it, and he sent money to my kids, and he was always buying me something. We had our little misunderstandings but nothing really serious. We did a lot of things together. We were in New York, he sent me to business school, and he went to a school of acting; we had a lot of fun. We traveled together, we even bought a house, but after the Feds were bothering me so much we had to give it up (James, 1972, p. 55).

LOVE. A third important consideration in the pimp relationship is love. Prostitutes frequently point out that everyone needs someone to come home to, and preferably it should be someone in the life. The prostitute needs a man who understands the profession and accepts her. The pimp provides the prostitute with varying degrees of affection. He may be a wonderful lover or a controlling "father." He supports her with talk of how special their relationship is and how they can make it together. To love and be loved is often stated as the motivation for staying with a pimp.

Working Arrangements. The setup of a pimp and his women is referred to as a stable. A stable can range from two to ten women who work and maintain a personal relationship with one pimp. An average stable consists of up to three women who have been with the same man for one to five years; one of these may be the pimp's legal wife. In addition, a number of younger women often come and go, some staying a year or so, and others remaining only a few weeks before looking for a better deal and perhaps a situation where they will have a chance to become the main lady, or leader of the group.

Depending on the size of the operation, a pimp will usually maintain an apartment in each of the key cities where his women work, and he will have a "driver" or other subordinate who checks on the women when he is out of town. The women of the stable will live together in this apartment, for the pimp will often feel that maintaining separate apartments for each is too expensive. A new woman simply goes to the established apartment and is given an introduction to the life by the main lady in that area. In some stables a newcomer is attracted by a woman who is already a part of the stable. Often two women in a stable will get along very well, maintain an apartment, work together, and only rarely have another woman share the facility. The relationship between members of a stable is one key to the success of a particular group in terms of economics; women who cooperate have more protection, less chance of arrest, and accumulate a higher income. A "good" pimp will attempt to keep all his women satisfied and maintain tension at a minimum in order to secure the business environment necessary for success.

This social organization is affected by pressures inherent in the lifestyle, and mobility is a frequently employed adaptive mechanism. On occasion, the relationships of women who work together and live together or who share a pimp become strained. One woman may have pulled an unfair "game" (transaction) on another, such as taking more than her share of the money after a "double" (two prostitutes servicing one customer). Reactions to arguments are often more severe among people who have an intense involvement in a deviant lifestyle or who are under the pressures of a dangerous occupation. Therefore, to avoid a buildup of tensions and hostilities that could ruin the basic working environment, the pimp will move his women in and out of town as the need for a cooling-off period arises.

Tensions may also arise between a prostitute and her man (pimp or boyfriend) because she feels that she is being mistreated or believes that he prefers someone else. If they have simply had a disagreement, she may leave temporarily to allow him to recover his temper or to avoid his sanctions. If, however, she has decided to make a change, a fast trip out of town is sometimes a necessity while the pimp recovers his dignity. A pimp's image or reputation is his most important asset. Losing a woman from his stable is an affront that requires some form of settlement. Occasionally a prostitute will pay a set fee to her old pimp; usually she will move out of town for a time to seek out another pimp to provide her with protection. If the situation is not solved by other means, the old pimp may find her through the grapevine and assault her as retribution.

Surprisingly enough, more prostitutes leave the profession successfully than do the pimps whom they support. Few pimps leave the life before they are destroyed by it through violence, imprisonment, or drug addiction (Milner & Milner, 1972). Prostitutes who have avoided alcoholism or drug addiction will drift out of the life as they get older. They take other jobs, go on welfare, and in some cases marry someone who has little knowledge of their past. Unless pimps are very successful in another status career, such as entertainment, they will rarely survive past the age of forty. Most of them find it impossible to compromise and reenter what they describe as the "square world." Only positions of fast-life status are viewed as viable alternatives.

Myths About Pimps

Pimps are described in newspaper accounts as seducers of young girls. With the exception of a few low-class pimps, this is not currently true. To most pimps, underage girls mean much more trouble than they could possibly be worth. Young girls are foolish, they cannot be trusted, and their parents check up on them. Further, the pimp can be arrested on numerous legal charges, including carnal knowledge, statutory rape, and contributing to the delinquency of a minor. In addition, while procuring may be difficult to prove with an adult woman, it is implicit with a juvenile. Some young girls, notably those recently released from institutions, seek out pimps or set up business with a boyfriend their own age. It is rare that a professional pimp would spend any time with a juvenile.

In fact, far from pimps seducing girls, the opposite is often true: Men will become pimps through seduction by an older prostitute. A young man hanging around the life will be picked up by an established prostitute who has left her pimp. She will support him and teach him to succeed in the life, how to behave, and how to control women. He becomes a pimp through being caught by the money and the style of the fast life.

Officials charge that pimps turn prostitutes into dope addicts so that they can control women, but this is seldom true. A dope addict is not a good prostitute; it is difficult to get her to work unless she needs a hit. A professional pimp will not let a heroin addict into his stable because the drug is in essence her pimp: It is what the woman is working for. Addiction reduces the pimp's control. The woman may be able to obtain her own drugs, which reduces her desire to work for the pimp and increases the chance of arrest. Many prostitutes do take amphetamines provided by their pimp or others to increase their self-confidence and ability to work long hours. While there are few professional prostitutes who turn to hard drugs after entering prostitution, there are many addicts who use the trade to support their habits; that is, they were initially addicts and secondarily turned to prostitution to pay for their drugs. There are many pimps who develop an addiction problem of their own, and involvement with heroin appears to be the most common end for a pimp. In this case they may, by example, induce one of their women to use drugs, but they would prefer, if possible, to avoid sharing their drugs and supporting two habits.

Horror stories are built around the myth that a prostitute cannot leave her pimp. In truth, however, prostitutes frequently leave pimps, and such situations are not very different from a divorce or the breakup of a love affair. If there is mutual respect and fast-life ethics are adhered to, the breakup is amicable, and the woman chooses another pimp. If not, there are fights, threats, and occasionally violence. Infrequently a pimp will beat or kill a prostitute, but it must be remembered that even in socially accepted relationships husbands will infrequently beat or kill their wives.

The lack of information and the misinformation that surround the pimp-prostitute relationship is in part due to past behavior of pimps, sensational journalism, and a protectionist policy toward women. Some pimps have been brutal and exploitative, but that interaction is changing. Prostitutes are demanding better treatment or are working alone, and pimps are discovering that they can be more successful by using psychological coercion. The women work harder if they are trying to maintain a positive relationship with their man, and the police are less likely to become involved if there is no violence. However difficult it may be to accept, many women choose to prostitute and prefer to give their money to a pimp. In the context of male-female role behavior, this relationship represents more of an exaggeration of traditional interaction than a perversion. Understanding of the pimp-prostitute relationship should be based on the recognition of these dynamics.

CONCLUSION

In the United States a number of groups are working toward changes in the prostitution and other sex laws: the National Organization of Women, the American Civil Liberties Union, sections of the American Bar Association, and the National Council on Crime and Delinquency. The main thrust of their efforts is for decriminalization and acceptance of prostitution as a victimless crime or crime without a complainant. These terms are used to refer to crimes where there is no victim to file a complaint. Examples include vagrancy, gambling, pornography, homosexuality, public drunkenness, and prostitution. With prostitution the only person who files a complaint is the police officer who, in passing as a customer, has been solicited by a prostitute. There is no victim; the customer actively seeks the prostitute's service, and she willingly agrees to sell. Those who refer to the prostitute as a victim do so in a nonlegal sense, for she is not the injured party in a crime. Rather, she is seen as a victim because of her lifestyle, her imputed degradation, or her exploitation by a pimp.

The movement to change the prostitution statutes views decriminalization as the least abusive choice. It differs from legalization in that instead of requiring more legal involvement, it removes prostitution from the criminal code entirely. Those who favor decriminalization are part of a larger movement that would put all private sexual behavior between consenting adults outside the purview of the law. Options for controls would depend upon the community's concern about the visibility of the sexual activities, possible disease problems, business and zoning regulations, and age of consent.

Taxation, health, and age requirements can be enforced in a number of ways. The least abusive to the individual woman would be a small business license with a health card requirement. Prostitutes would obtain a license much as a masseuse does; her place of business would have to conform with zoning requirements; she would be required to report her income, to be of majority age, and to keep her health card current. Violations would result in the revocation of her license and would be handled by an administrative agency other than the police. Advertisements would be limited to discreet classified ads. Houses of prostitution would not be licensed or permitted.

Regulations such as the above would, of course, still limit personal freedom in a purely private area. The unlicensed prostitute could still be prosecuted, although hers would be a civil citation, not a criminal one. To most of its proponents, decriminalization with some restrictions is regarded as only a provisional solution until the fundamental causes of prostitution can be changed.

The understanding of the causes of prostitution requires an examination of the motivations of customers and prostitutes as well as the sociocultural environment in which they operate. There are many kinds of prostitution and many types of customers. Their motivations are the significant factor in the long history of the existence of prostitution and its current status and operation. An end to prostitution is dependent not on legal reform but on a change in the sexual socialization process that produces both the supply and the demand.

Prostitution provides a population to meet the desires of some males for promiscuity. The female defines her femininity as a "good woman" by refusing to be paid, or gives it up by accepting the label "whore." The male customer buys an illusion of sexual success combined with physical release. Access to females is commensurate with success. To be a "ladies' man" is a compliment, whether the man purchases the companion overtly or subtly through less obvious favors than cash, or forces himself on women. Behind the exchange is a socialized male-female need: the male need to feel he is an attractive, competent lover; the female need to be desired as a sex object, preferably as a good woman, and receive some economic support as a result.

The sexual definition of male and female role behavior sets up the tension. Prostitution can be used to provide situations for fulfilling these role expectations: it is a business of fantasy.

Prostitution allows men an area of freedom from sexual restraints and permission to move briefly into the deviant subculture. The more highly restricted female sex role contains almost none of the sexual motivations and behaviors allowed to the male; nor does it allow a woman to serve as a professional accompanist for those men who would rent her participation in sexual activities. The prostitute is a deviant *woman* and her customer is a normal *man*.

The puritan aspect of middle-class society means that the full acting out of the male sex role requires the existence of prostitution. As a result, the male need for purchased female sexual service is, and long has been, accepted as "inevitable" and therefore not to be punished. The women, however, are in violation of their full role and dangerously at odds with the conventions of society. They are therefore stigmatized and often jailed.

Decriminalization is the least abusive method of dealing with prostitution in the United States. Decriminalization differs from legalization in that, instead of creating more legal involvement, it removes prostitution from the criminal code entirely. An ideal approach would be to put all sexual behavior in private between consenting adults outside the purview of the law, but this ideal must be balanced by the reality of public expediency. Failing the ideal, then, options for controls would depend upon concern about the overtness of sexual activities, the possible disease problems, business and zoning regulations, and age of consent. The least abusive to the individual woman would be a small business license with a health card requirement.

Decriminalization, with some restrictions, is regarded as a provisional solution only while efforts are made to change the more fundamental causes of prostitution. As long as traditional sex role expectations are retained, there will be prostitution. As long as women are socialized into the traditional female role and see their alternatives limited by that role, prostitution will remain an attractive occupational option for many women.

NOTES

1. Male prostitution, which will not be discussed here, is of growing significance. There are some researchers who estimate that there are as many male streetwalkers as there are female (Gandy & Deisher, 1970).

2. In a variation on a theme, many women will drive slowly around an area and invite men to get into their cars. The sexual service that is requested may actually be performed in the car.

3. Most of the data presented in this section were gathered from streetwalkers, who are the most flagrant and most studied of the prostitute population.

4. James' ongoing research includes a sample of 240 female offenders, 120 of whom have been identified as prostitutes. Funded by NIDA #DA 0091801, Female Criminal Involvement and Narcotics Addiction. The central focus is on drug abuse.

5. Note that social work is also a service profession.

6. Later studies have shifted the age range upward into the forties (James, 1972; Stein, 1974).

7. Anderson (1974) describes Chicago's attempts to end prostitution between the years of 1910 and 1915, and Holmes (1972) reports on nationwide efforts at about the same time.

BIBLIOGRAPHY

Anderson, Eric. "Prostitution and Social Justice: Chicago, 1910–15." *Social Service Review*, 1974, 48:203–228.

Basel, Amos S. "Why Do Married Men Visit Prostitutes?" A Panel Discussion. *Medical Aspects of Human Sexuality*, July 1970, 4:84, 87.

Benjamin, Harry, and R. E. L. Masters. *Prostitution and Morality*. New York: Julian Press, 1964.

Bullough, Vern. "History of Prostitution in the United States." *Medical Aspects of Human Sexuality*, July 1970, 4:84, 87.

Bryan, James H. "Occupational Ideologies and Individual Attitudes." *Social Problems*, 1966, 12:287–297.

Bryan, James H. "Apprenticeships in Prostitution." In John H. Gagnon and William Simon, eds. *Sexual Deviance*. New York: Harper & Row, 1967.

Carns, Donald E. "Talking About Sex: Notes on First Coitus and the Double Sexual Standard." *Journal of Marriage and the Family*, 1973, 35:677–688.

Cave, Vernal G. "Why Do Married Men Visit Prostitutes?" A Panel Discussion. *Medical Aspects of Human Sexuality*, July 1970, 4:97–98.

Chambliss, William J. *Crime and the Legal Process*. New York: McGraw-Hill, 1969.

Choisy, Maryse. *Psychoanalysis of the Prostitute*. New York: Pyramid Books, 1965.

Clinard, Marshall, *Sociology of Deviant Behavior*. New York: Holt, Rinehart, 1959.

Davis, Kingsley, "The Sociology of Prostitution." *American Sociological Review*, 1937, 2:744–755.

Davis, Nanette J. "The Prostitute: Developing a Deviant Identify." In James M. Henslin, ed., *Studies in the Sociology of Sex*. Appleton-Century-Crofts, 1971.

DeFrancis, Vincent. *Protecting the Child Victim of Sex Crimes Committed by Adults*. Final Report. Denver: American Humane Association, Children's Division, 1969, p. 215.

Devlin, Patrick, *The Enforcement of Morals*. New York: Oxford University Press, 1965.

Ellis, Havelock. *Studies in the Psychology of Sex*. Volume II. New York: Random House, 1936.

Esselstyn, T. C. "Prostitution in the United States." *Annals of the American Academy of Political and Social Sciences*, 1968, 376:123–135.

Federal Bureau of Investigation. *Crime in the United States: Uniform Crime Reports, 1973*. Washington, D.C.: U.S. Government Printing Office, 1974.

Flexner, Abraham. *Prostitution in Europe.* New York: The Century Company, 1914.

Gandy, Patrick, and Robert Deisher. "Young Male Prostitutes." *The Journal of the American Medical Association,* 1970, 212:1661–1666.

Gebhard, Paul H. "Misconceptions About Female Prostitutes." *Medical Aspects of Human Sexuality,* July 1969, pp. 28–30.

Geis, Gilbert. *Not the Law's Business?* Rockville, Md.: National Institute of Mental Health, Center for Studies of Crime and Delinquency, 1972.

Gibbens, T. C. N., and M. Silberman. "The Clients of Prostitutes." *British Journal of Venereal Disease,* 1960, 36:113–117.

Glover, Edward G. *Roots of Crime.* London: Imago Publishing Company, Ltd., 1960.

Gray, Diana. "Turning-Out: A Study of Teenage Prostitution." *Urban Life and Culture,* 1973, 1:401–425.

Greenwald, Harold, *The Elegant Prostitute.* New York: Ballantine Books, 1970.

Greenwald, Harold. "Sex Away From Home." *Sexual Behavior,* 1971, September:6–14.

Hall, Susan. *Gentleman of Leisure.* New York: The New American Library, 1972.

Halleck, Charles W. *Opinion. U.S. v. Binns, Reynolds, Adair, Fleming, Ward, Glenn.* Washington, D.C.: Superior Court of the District of Columbia, May 31. 1972.

Hirschi, Travis. "The Professional Prostitute." *Berkeley Journal of Sociology,* 1962, 7:33–50.

Hollender, Marc H. "Prostitution, the Body and Human Relatedness." *International Journal of Psychoanalysis,* 1964, 43:404–413.

Holmes, Kay Ann. "Reflections by Gaslight: Prostitution in Another Age." *Issues in Criminology,* 1972, 7:83–101.

Idsoe, O., and T. Guthe. "The Rise and Fall of Treponematoses." *British Journal of Venereal Disease,* 1967, 43:227–241.

Jackman, Norman R., Richard O'Toole, and Gilbert Geis. "The Self-Image of the Prostitute." In John H. Gagnon and William Simon, eds. *Sexual Deviance.* New York: Harper and Row, 1967.

James, Jennifer. *A Formal Analysis of Prostitution, Final Report to the Division of Research.* Olympia, Wash.: State of Washington Department of Social and Health Services, 1971.

James, Jennifer. "On the Block: Urban Perspectives." *Urban Anthropology,* 1972, 1:125–140.

James, Jennifer, and M. J. Meyerding. "Prostitution: Normal Men and Deviant Women." Forthcoming.

Karpf, Maurice J. "The Effects of Prostitution on Marital Sex Adjustment." *Marriage and Famiy Living,* 1953, February:65–71.

Kemp, Tage. *Prostitution: An Investigation of Its Causes, Especially with Regard to Heriditary Factors.* Copenhagen: Levin and Munskgaard, 1936.

Kinsey, Alfred C., Wardell B. Pomeroy, and Clyde E. Martin. *Sexual Behavior in the Human Male.* Philadelphia: W. B. Saunders, 1948.

Kirk, Stuart. "Clients as Outsiders: Theoretical Approaches to Deviance." *Social Work,* 1972, 17:24–32.

Kirkendall, Lester A. "Circumstances Associated with Teenage Boys' Use of Prostitution." *Marriage and Family Living,* 1960, May:145–149.

Law and Justice Planning Office. *Second Mile.* State of Washington, 1973.

Lemert, Edwin. *Human Deviance, Social Problems, and Social Control.* Englewood Cliffs, N.J.: Prentice-Hall, 1967.

Liswood, Rebecca. "Why Do Married Men Visit Prostitutes?" A Panel Discussion. *Medical Aspects of Human Sexuality,* July 1970, 4:84,88,92.

Lombroso, M. Cesare, and William Ferrero. *The Female Offender.* New York: Appleton, 1898.

Maerov, Arnold S. "Prostitution: A Survey and Review of 20 Cases." *The Pate Report.* In the *Psychiatric Quarterly,* 1965, 39:675–701.

Mathis, James L. "Why Do Married Men Visit Prostitutes?" A Panel Discussion. In *Medical Aspects of Human Sexuality,* 1970, 4:97–98.

Mill, John Stuart. *On Liberty.* New York: Longmans, Green, 1892.

Milner, Christina, and Richard Milner. *Black Players, The Secret World of Black Pimps.* Little, Brown, 1972.

Polatin, Phillip. "Why Do Married Men Visit Prostitutes?" A Panel Discussion. *Medical Aspects of Human Sexuality,* July 1970, 4:80–101.

Pomeroy, Wardell B. "Some Aspects of Prostitution." *Journal of Sex Research,* 1965, 1:177–187.

President's Commission on Law Enforcement and Administration of Justice. *The Challenge of Crime in a Free Society.* Washington, D.C.: U.S. Government Printing Office, 1967.

Robinson, W. J. *The Oldest Profession in the World.* Eugenic Publishing Company, 1929.

Rosenblum, Karen E. "Female Deviance and the Female Sex Role: A Preliminary Investigation." *British Journal of Sociology,* 1975, 26:169–185.

Rubin, Theodore. *In the Life.* New York: Macmillan, 1961.

San Francisco Committee on Crime. *A Report on Non-Victim Crime in San Francisco.* City of San Francisco, 1971.

Schimel, John L. "Why Do Married Men Visit Prostitutes?" A Panel Discussion. *Medical Aspects of Human Sexuality,* July 1970, 4:98,101.

Schur, Edwin M. *Crimes Without Victims.* Englewood Cliffs, N.J.: Prentice-Hall, 1965.

Segal, Morey. "Impulsive Sexuality: Some Clinical and Theoretical Observations." *International Journal of Psychoanalysis,* 1963, 44:407–417.

Slim, Iceberg. *Pimp: The Story of My Life.* Los Angeles: Holloway House, 1967.

Stearn, Jess. *Streetwalker.* New York: Viking Press, 1960.

Stein, Martha. *Lovers, Friends, and Slaves.* New York: G. P. Putman's Sons, 1974.

United Nations. *International Convention for the Suppression of the White Slave Traffic.* New York: United Nations Publishing, 1951.

VD Fact Sheet: Basic Statistics on the Venereal Disease Problem in the United States. Washington, D.C.: United States Health Education and Welfare, 1971.

Willcox, R. R. "Prostitution and Venereal Disease." *British Journal of Venereal Disease.* 1962, 38:37–42.

Winick, Charles. "Prostitutes' Clients' Perception of Prostitutes and of Themselves." *International Journal of Social Psychiatry,* 1962, 8:289–297.

Winick, Charles, and Paul Kinsie. *The Lively Commerce: Prostitution in the United States.* New York: Quadrangle Books, 1971.

NINE

Sex deviance: a view from the window of middle America

EDWARD SAGARIN
City College of New York

Probably more than any other type of behavior, sexual irregularities, transgressions, offenses, and peculiarities are triggered off in people's minds by the very mention of the words *deviate, deviant,* or *deviance* (Simmons, 1969). It is only after the sexual areas have been listed, and possibly exhausted, that people think of other kinds of deviance. Nevertheless, with the exception of a paper by Ira Reiss (1970) on premarital sex as deviant behavior,[1] almost all discussions of sexual deviance have centered around prostitution, homosexuality (male and female, and including homosexual prostitution), and child molestation or carnal knowledge of a minor. Studies of deviance will occasionally discuss such types of sexual behavior as incest, social nudity, swinging or mate swapping, transvestism, and peeping and exhibiting. The most serious types of strongly condemned sex activity—assault and rape—have most frequently been studied under violence and criminality. Despite the definition that deviance is behavior that people react to in a hostile manner (Kitsuse, 1962; Becker, 1963; Schur, 1971), the term and the concept suggested by it may be too mild, as contrasted with criminality, to permit many persons to consider forcible rape as a deviant behavior.

A brief look at some studies that specifically state, in their titles, that they are concerned with sex deviance offers an opportunity to note what is generally included under this terminology. In a book entitled *Sexual Deviance*, John Gagnon and William Simon (1967) start with an introduction that takes note of what the authors call "normal deviance" (a useful but elusive concept, to which the greater part of this chapter will be devoted), and they then proceed to a general discussion consisting of three articles, two of which deal with sex offenses. The remainder of the book is devoted exclusively to prostitution and male and female homosexuality. Erich Goode and Richard Troiden's *Sexual Deviance and Sexual Deviants* (1974) deals with pornography, prostitution, male and female homosexuality, and rape, with three miscellaneous articles covering "kinky sex": swinging, some sex-life-love letters, and pederasty. Finally, an essay on sex deviance by Kingsley Davis (1976) covers premarital and extramarital relations, but focuses particularly on prostitution and homosexuality.[2]

From this inventory it would appear that the major works on sex deviance have failed to capture some of the most pervasive and interesting areas. They have instead focused on the few that seem to be more widely shared as social concerns, that have been defined as social problems, and that come more frequently to people's attention. However, the definition of a form of behavior as deviant should not be equated with its definition as a problem for society (or a portion of society). For individuals must actively work toward the solution of a social problem, while for the behavior to be considered deviant, the members of the society need do nothing more about deviance than to show their attitudes of disapproval, contempt, stigmatization, ostracism, abhorrence, rejection, disvaluation, or the like. That is, deviance is behavior to which people react negatively (a necessary attribute of deviance) but about which they may decide to do nothing; it is behavior that is more mundane than a social problem, sometimes almost accepted, quite widespread, and yet still disapproved. Only Reiss, in the aforementioned work on premarital sex, seems to have looked at sex deviance in this light.

PROBLEMS IN THE DETERMINATION OF SEXUAL DEVIANCE

The determination of deviance is a major problem for sociologists. It involves, first, the rejection of the commonsense notion that deviance should be equated with immorality, wrongfulness, sin, or harm. Likewise, it requires the renunciation of the notion of "positive" and "negative" deviance, which goes in the opposite direction and makes no distinction between deviance and differentness. Some sociologists have defined positive deviance as being different in a socially approved manner (see Wilkins, 1965; Freedman & Doob, 1968; Scarpitti & McFarlane, 1975); such a concept can only block the way to a true understanding of deviance. Finally, one must reject the labeling thesis, which requires that an act be publicly known before its performer can be considered deviant. Even modifying this thesis in order to accommodate secret deviants cannot make it any more acceptable to the study of an area so carefully encased in both privacy and secrecy as human sexual conduct.

Deviance is not behavior (or status) that is wrong, sinful, immoral, or disvalued in the eyes of a sociologist, the deviant actor, or a social commentator. Rather, it must be so considered and so reacted to by a considerable number of persons, by important and sometimes powerful groups in a society, or at the least by meaningful and significant others in one's life, with the result that social living and interaction become difficult, embarrassing, and fraught with danger for the deviant actor. Thus, to study a form of sexual or other type of behavior as deviant involves, first, the determination of whether that behavior is condemned and, if it is, then by whom, in what way, with what consequences, and how strongly. Stated differently, the study of deviance implies the study of norms, but, more than that, it involves the location or discovery of what the norms of a society are. It is easy enough to know that it is a violation of the norms to walk along the street naked, to shout obscenities in a house of worship during a religious ceremony, to have sex with a sibling, to commit forcible rape, or to indulge in cannibalism. There is a consensus that these and innumerable other acts, some criminal and others not, are wrong, that they are not to be done. Anyone who does commit them—whether privately (and so anonymously or secretly that no one but the perpetrator and perhaps a partner knows that they have been done) or publicly—has committed an act of deviance. With many types of sexual activities, however, it is much more difficult to determine what is normative and what is deviant.

Changing Sexual Mores

One reason for this is the rapidly changing sexual mores of American society.[3] Activities once condemned are now openly accepted, at least by some important sectors of the population. Furthermore, those who do not accept them have in some instances shown a modicum of tolerance (or at least toleration) that was previously absent. Whether the activity itself is more common than it once was is not the immediate issue. What is of concern here is that hostility has been muted, and that where it does exist, it is sometimes scoffed at or dismissed as rank hypocrisy.

Never have there been changes so sweeping and rapid as in the U.S.A. during the thirty years from 1945–1975. With societal norms and modes of living changing so rapidly, it is extremely difficult to depict or even characterize something as deviant (using this as a synonym with disvalued, stigmatized, or socially condemned) if it is not universally labeled as reprehensible. For a determination of deviancy requires an evaluation of society's view on certain behaviors, and this may take much time. Before one has had an opportunity to collect one's thoughts, sift the data, and interpret the findings, the situation may have altered. Moreover, change proceeds unevenly in a society. Newly accepted standards of behavior may be reflected more in some communities, age groups, and other subgroups than elsewhere, and one cannot always predict what new categories of persons will be caught up in social movement—or what ones may initiate or support a backlash against a movement that has already taken hold.

Heterogeneity in a Society

A next obstacle to the ascertainment of sexual norms is the heterogeneity of the society, and American society probably has more varied elements than any other in the world. While sex and age groups and social classes may be found universally (although class structure takes on quite a different form in the Communist world), there can be found in the United States a tremendous racial and ethnic mixture and some regional differences (though these appear to be declining under the impact of mass media and geographic mobility). Such heterogeneity of a population gives rise to a diversity of cultural and ideological outlooks that has been fostered and encouraged, or at least made possible, by the freedom (within limits) to publish, teach, and disseminate views that may antagonize others in the nation or in one's community. Whatever value consensus there may be on rape, cannibalism, and incest, there is less on prostitution and homosexuality, and probably little on premarital sex.

There are problems in locating both the norms and the deviance when large sectors in the society hold varying opinions on what is right and what is wrong. In such an atmosphere people may openly admit to performing actions that they once did only in the most circumspect and secretive manner, for meeting with little or no ostracism, they may assume that there is wider acceptance of such behavior than may actually be the case. The toleration of some behaviors can be easily confused with the disappearance of hostility, when actually the hostility may be manifesting itself in a new, more polite, and perhaps less oppressive manner.[4]

Lack of Honesty About Sexuality

Besides rapidity of change—and of change and extent of heterogeneity—the study of sex deviance must confront yet another problem: the fact that people are unlikely to be frank and forthright about their own sexuality. This might appear to be a greater problem when one is studying behavior rather than attitudes, for quite obviously it is more risky for persons to admit, even anonymously and confidentially, to having committed certain acts than to state degrees of approval or disapproval of, indifference to, or ignorance of those acts. Nevertheless, when stating opinions as well as when relating behavior, people will not always tell the truth.

Irwin Deutscher (1973) concentrated on the dissonance between what people say and what they do, but it can be implied from his thesis that if people will say things far from the truth about what they do, they will also give incorrect information about what they believe. In the area of sexual behavior, these misleading responses can lead in many directions, and they can arise from a variety of motives. Persons may wish to present themselves as being what they consider "liberal" or "in" and may find it distasteful to express viewpoints that, at a given moment, are scoffed at because they are "square" or "reactionary." Other persons may want to show themselves as being proper and self-righteous, and they will therefore not express views that run counter to their perceived sense of respectability and propriety. Yet, both inclinations—to be considered "in" or "proper"—will be tempered by who the person is, where he resides, and what the circumstances of the survey are. Wrong answers may be given deliberately to cover up a pattern of behavior; attitudes not believed in may be offered to buttress a pattern of conduct. People who are asked about their group belonging—ethnic, racial, religious, and other—in the course of a survey may give different information than if they are not asked, for they may not wish certain viewpoints to be correlated with or associated with membership in the particular group to which they have primary loyalty.

The Double Standard

Finally, any attempt to establish certain sexual behaviors as deviant must take into account society's double standard of sexual morality. While the double standard manifests itself in many ways, in its simplest form it is the notion that nonaffectional, promiscuous heterosexual activity (consensual, of course) is quite acceptable for the male but is reprobative for the female. In its most extreme form it demands that women remain virgins until their marriage; the white bridal gown is the symbol of their virginity or "purity." Men, however, are expected to be experienced when they take a bride. Their experience, then, has to be obtained from women who are not in the market as marriageable commodities, and this means that there must be "good" women and "bad" women, the former to be loved but not touched until marriage, and the latter to be touched but not loved or married.

Feminism has spoken up strongly against the double standard, and this has resulted in a certain amount of exaggeration in two different and mutually exclusive directions: Some people declare that the double standard is dead, and others denounce the moralistic, hypocritical, male-dominated society that still lives by it. As we shall see in this chapter, the double standard is still quite prevalent in attitudes of both men and women. It therefore plays an important role in determining the deviancy or normality of any sexual behavior, whether it be premarital or nonmarital intercourse, adultery (consensual and other), nonmarital cohabitation, illegitimacy, or some other similar action.

NORMAL SEX DEVIANCE

Deviant sexual behavior cannot be considered primarily to be socially unacceptable gender or age relations, the use of sex as occupation, or even its use as part of forcible and violent activity. Instead, most sex deviance—in terms of the numbers of persons involved, the number of acts, the situations that people are likely to find in the lives of those around them, the impact on marriage and family living, and the consequences for life patterns—fall under the heading of "normal deviance," to use the phrase of Gagnon and Simon.

This is not a phrase that is easy to define. By sex deviance is meant those forms of sexual activity, behavior, desire, and conduct that meet disvaluation, hostility, punishment, ridicule, ostracism, or other negative manifestations either in society as a whole or among the significant people with whom one interacts, or that would meet with negative reaction if the otherwise private and secret acts were known. The definition of some of these acts as normal does not automatically suggest, or deny, that other deviant sex acts are abnormal, but it does signify that there is a meeting place where the norm (the sociological concept) meets the normal (a psychological concept). Some types of behavior that are frowned upon are seen by large segments of the population as normal psychological and physiological reactions that ought, nevertheless, not to be indulged in because they are improper for one reason or another. For example, a man who uses fraud to induce a woman to have sexual relations with him, making promises to her that he had no intention of keeping, would be deviant but not abnormal. Normal sex deviance, then, would be confined to adult consensual heterosexuality that violates the standards of propriety for large numbers of persons in the society and that is assumed to be committed by people who are psychologically normal and in good mental state. It is this type of sex deviance that is of concern to the grandmother who sits by her window and views the passing scene from her private home on a tree-lined street in a small town in Middle America.

PREMARITAL SEX

When Mr. and Mrs. Brown's daughter calls with the news that the family will be visiting for a few days, they are delighted. The daughter explains that five will be coming this time, because her older child, Laura, has a boyfriend. The Browns still have the big house in which their three children had been raised, so there will be enough rooms for everyone, even with the extra guest. When they arrive and Mrs. Brown shows them to their rooms, however, everyone, including Mr. Brown, is quite shocked: Mrs. Brown turns to her granddaughter and her boyfriend and says, "Now you two will stay in here. It's nice and quiet, and no one will disturb you."

Mrs. Brown is a lot more sophisticated than her family realizes. She knows that Laura and Jim have been living together for at least a year, and she has just come to accept this as a fact of life. That they have not married she likewise accepts, although she does not understand why, if they are going to live as man and wife, they refuse to give their union the benefit of church or state recognition. To have separated them when they arrived, and to have carried on a pretense of ignorance or disapproval, would have been absurd to her.

Social Acceptance of Premarital Sex

The most important change in the nature of sex deviance as viewed by the people of Middle America is the total and complete acceptance of one-to-one, young adult, heterosexual, consensual, affectional relationships. A young man and woman who are going together, who have a commitment to one another, and who give vows of faithfulness are assumed to be having sexual relations with each other, at least if they are in college or of college age. Further, acceptance of such relationships became so widespread that secrecy has been abandoned. Premarital (or nonmarital) cohabitation has become normative, and Mrs. Brown sees nothing wrong with it.

"We would never have permitted our daughter to do that when she was keeping company," Mr. Brown points out, not sure whether he approves of the arrangements that his wife has made. "So they did it without our knowing it, in a motel or something like that," she replies, adding, "just like we did a couple of times before we got married."

The change in attitudes toward premarital sex has been rapid. Virginity is no longer worshipped; if anything, it is scoffed at. One seldom hears a virgin girl referred to as "pure," and in fact, many people would not know what the word meant if used in such a context. Cohabitation carries with it no pretense: Two names are on the mailbox with no Mr. and Mrs.; parents of the young man and woman come to their apartment and see a bedroom with a double bed. One can say, from a sociological view, that premarital sex and nonmarital cohabitation have been destigmatized, taken for granted, institutionalized. If there were such a word, one might say they have been "dedeviantized," but for want of such an awkward neologism, they can be described as having been normalized (using that term in a social and not psychological sense). Nonmarital cohabitation is found not only among the young; it extends to the middle-aged and elderly as well. In the middle years, couples are finding it more convenient to form an alliance without legal entanglements, keeping separate their money and obligations to children from previous alliances (which were usually marriages) and yet having what might be called a state of "temporary permanence" that is equivalent to the concept of commitment. For the elderly, in addition to the problems of children and wills, there are social-security advantages in remaining unmarried while cohabiting in a quasi-married alliance. Such couples have been known as the "unmarried marrieds," which appears to be an accurate description, except that they are more married than "un." The situation is in some respects similar to what was proposed in the 1920s by Judge Ben Lindsay (1927) in his famous, widely hailed, and often denounced concept of companionate or trial marriage.

That this type of conduct has lost its deviant characteristic for the people of Middle America is apparent from many indicators, even in the absence of formal attitudinal surveys. Mrs. Brown's behavior on the arrival of her family is one such indicator, and the subsequent interaction of the family with her friends and relatives in town is another. But more important, it is quite common for a mother to speak to a friend about her daughter who is living with this fellow who is going for his doctorate or who has just broken up with the boyfriend she had lived with for two years. This is part of everyday conversation, and evidence of the institutionalization of the conduct can be found in the taken-for-granted manner of discussion and in the lack of raised eyebrows, as well as in the absence of gossip about such persons and events. Often, a mother or father will wistfully express the hope that the children so cohabiting will get married (or in other instances, that they will break up), and these parents will gladly spread the tidings if their children indeed do one or the other.

Whether premarital sexual relations among the young have increased remains a matter of doubt. It would appear that it has, for it is difficult to believe that the religious, familial, and educational pressures so long exerted against such activities, and the impediments placed in the way of those wishing to perform them, had no inhibitory effects whatsoever. It should be noted, though, that the increase is not as dramatic as appears on the surface. Certainly, nonmarital cohabitation, or the open flouting of the norms or laws against fornication, has dramatically increased, having once been almost unknown, except when shrouded in secrecy to which a few intimates were privy.

The New Sexual Norms

With such changes in attitude, then, what is the norm and, by extension, what is deviant? The norm demands that the act be affectional. The sexual behavior of both parties must be limited to each other; to use the everyday terminology, they must be "faithful." There must be a commitment, although it may be limited; that is, it will last only as long as each of the parties wishes it to continue (which is not greatly different from marriage when there is the alternative of no-fault and inexpensive divorce). In case of pregnancy or a decision to have a family, the union will probably be made legal (it is already legitimate) in order to give legitimacy to the offspring. Any premarital or nonmarital behavior that is not in line with these norms may be considered deviant.

PREMARITAL AND NONMARITAL PROMISCUITY

Mrs. Brown's acceptance of her granddaughter's relationship does not mean that she approves of all consensual nonmarital sex between adults. This is certainly not the case. She is greatly disturbed by stories about people who "sleep around," and she and her friends are not at all unfriendly to the double standard when it comes to nonmarital promiscuity. In fact, the most pervasive type of adult heterosexual act in which the performer is degraded in her eyes and in the eyes of most of the people around her probably involves nonmarital promiscuity on the part of the female.

The Double Standard and Attitudes Toward Promiscuity

Mrs. Brown does not use the terms, although she knows them, but she has only contempt for a girl or woman who is a "pushover" or an "easy lay" in a society of men who seek her favors and exploit her interests. Although the people of Middle America know that technically such a girl is not a prostitute, they will sometimes refer to her as a "whore," a word that men use pejoratively to describe both a woman who sells sex for money and one who gives it freely to many. While not expressing explicit approval of men who go off in constant search of sex, finding it where they can, the men and women of Middle America wink their eyes at such activity, so long as it is adult, consensual, and heterosexual, for they regard it as somehow natural and do not see anything inherently evil in it.

What this means is not only that these people adhere to the double standard (not for premarital virginity, but for nonaffectional sex and promiscuity), but that to enable men to have such outlets, there must be enough "bad" women to go around. Women who have qualified for this purpose—to serve as outlets for the unmarried men—have included those of a race or religion socially defined as inferior, prostitutes, "loose" married women, and promiscuous unmarried females. All continue to be eyed with hostility, although the men who indulge in the same or a greater amount of promiscuity can boast of the women that they "conquer." These men fear no hostility, although good taste and concepts of decency and respectability cause them to hold their tongues in the presence of Mr. and Mrs. Brown. These are just not the sort of things one discusses with the older generation. But when word gets around that they are Don Juans, wolves, Romeos, Lotharios on the prowl, or boys that good girls should beware of, they are themselves not condemned. If anything, they might be envied, or their "success stories" might be disbelieved, itself a sign that they were bragging, not confessing. There is nothing contrite about those who make such conquests.

This is not to say that the double standard remains untouched and unchallenged. Challenged it has been, and from two directions. It has been demanded either that males relinquish their right to find premarital sex, without affection, commitment, or exclusivity, wherever and whenever they can, or that the same right be granted to women. Of course, there are no legal obstacles to either course of action, except that a juvenile female might open herself to the possibility of being declared a delinquent or a person in need of supervision for the same type of behavior that is widely condoned in boys of the same age. The fact is that, socially, the promiscuous male performs his acts with impunity, something that a woman cannot do.

Looking out of her window, listening to some occasional gossip, hearing about people in college or in neighboring cities, reading, or watching television—just learning in the countless ways that people in a modern society learn—Mrs. Brown is well aware of the onslaught on the double standard. She thinks it is a pity that so many men have to "behave like beasts" (she does not know much about the behavior of beasts, but that does not stop her from using a favorite cliché), but she cannot bring herself to condemn such men with the force and opprobrium that she places upon women. After all, she says, if a woman literally throws herself at an unmarried man (she emphasizes that she is only talking of *un*married men), what can you expect him to do? And if he literally throws himself at her? Well, she can have the common sense, self-respect, and decency to say no. These are all parts of her arsenal: common sense, self-respect, decency.

In the world of many Americans, there are still good girls and bad girls, in the sexual sense of the term. What has changed is that the good girls are no longer virgins. The institutionalization of premarital sexuality also appears to have brought another change: There appears to be a diminution of the guy on the prowl, always looking for whatever he can obtain. A man, particularly a young man, courting a girl, expressing serious interest in her as a person, and finding that she reciprocates, no longer has to wait through a long period of friendship and engagement before there can be sexual consummation. The union will probably be consummated, so to speak, well before the wedding. If his commitment is strong, if the relationship is satisfactory, and if he does not carry the double standard to the point of "cheating," his relationship should remove him from the market of available young men. However, whether because of biology or culture, or some combination of both, a man still seems to be more easily tempted into enjoying sex with other women while being involved in a one-to-one affectional commitment. He finds that it still requires great willpower to resist when opportunity is thrust before him. For him, the retreat from the double standard is evidently a greater sacrifice, or a greater hardship.

This, however, is only after he has made the commitment. Before that, whatever comes his way is acceptable. While Mrs. Brown could never discuss her son's premarital sex life with him, she just assumes that he had many experiences, whether with a dozen or a hundred different partners, and has never thought the less of him for it. The same is no doubt true for her nephews, grandsons, and others as they grow into their late teens and early twenties. But it would be beyond her comprehension to believe that any of her nieces or granddaughters would be on the prowl, taking sex wherever they could find it.

For some social thinkers, this two-pronged system of making value judgments is outrageous. For others, it appears not only functional, but they argue that it actually benefits women, for it gives them the upper hand in sexual bargaining. They control the rare, scarce, and wanted commodity—heterosexual opportunity—and they are the ones to decide whether the commodity will be given away or kept. They can use it to manipulate men, to obtain stability that might otherwise be absent. Those who support such an argument exact a high price from the woman. She has no part in deciding if she wishes to gain this benefit, and she must pay for it by relinquishing either her freedom to act or her freedom from public ignominy.

Mrs. Brown's attitudes toward sexual promiscuity have been examined, and her attitudes seem to be prevalent in American culture. The sexual revolution has not been able to eliminate the double standard, although it has softened it. However, one cannot forget that the attitudes found in smaller communities, such as hers, may be different from those found in large cities, such as New York, Chicago, or New Orleans, and that even within communities these attitudes will vary according to age group, race, religion, social class, and education.

The Frequency of Promiscuous Behavior

Before leaving the topic of sexual promscuity, one more thing should be treated. Up to this point, the discussion has been about perceptions of promiscuous actions but not about the actions themselves. How many people take part in promiscuous sex, and how often? Unfortunately, there is little information on this point. Few studies of such activities have been made recently, and the figures collected by Alfred Kinsey and his colleagues are by now outdated.[5] Therefore, for lack of good evidence one relies on newspaper articles, reactions to public events, gossip and the lack of it, and talk in the social circles of Middle America. Taking all this into account, one can gain an overall picture of the incidence and frequency of promiscuous sexual behavior. Among males unmarried and not involved in a one-to-one relationship, promiscuity is rampant, accepted, and taken for granted. Moreover, it is probable that it would occur at even greater levels if men could discover acceptable sexual outlets with sufficient ease. Among females, however, once one has eliminated the prostitute, there are few who are not at least a little discriminating, and there are probably not large percentages (although the number may not be minuscule) who go with a stranger the first time they meet and who search out such encounters. Behavior is a reflection of attitudes, at least in part, and promiscuity in women will not reach the levels it has in men until the differential attitudes of Mrs. Brown and others in Middle America change.

ON THE QUESTION OF ADULTERY

People have heard of swinging in Middle America; in fact, they even mention the term when they see the little boys and girls frolicking in the playground. Still, it is beyond their comprehension that some people would indulge in adultery not only with the consent of the spouse but actually in the presence of that spouse, who is simultaneously having a session with someone else's mate.

If deviance is made synonymous with socially condemned behavior, nothing is so unmistakably deserving of that label as adultery. Many may practice it, but there is seldom a voice that is raised to condone it. The marriage vows are no longer as sacred as they once were. People can live together although not wedded, and this is acceptable; and those legally wedded can be divorced with ease and still be accepted in all social circles. While a marriage or even a marital-like relationship is in progress, however, the norm that demands exclusivity of sex is not supposed to be transgressed. The Browns have believed in this for the nearly fifty years of their marriage, they are certain that their children and all the other people who live a good life believe in it as well.

Adultery is generally defined as the sexual relationship between a man and a woman, at least one of whom is married. If they are both married, but not to each other, it is known as double adultery. In a legal sense, the term probably is not applicable to the unmarried marrieds, but socially one can say that when two people have set up a permanent relationship (or at least one they define as more or less permanent), when it has many or all of the characteristics of a marriage except the certificate, and when they have a commitment and have expectations of sexual exclusivity, then a sexual transgression on the part of either is an adulterous act.

The person who commits the act of adultery is said to have been unfaithful to or to have betrayed the spouse, and if it is done without the knowledge of the spouse, the adulterous individual is said to have cheated. Adulterous relationships may take place only once or twice or they may occur quite regularly. They may range from nonaffectional liaisons and prostitution visits to long-term love affairs with mistresses, from one-night stands and flirtations during travel or conventions to fleeting romances. Not to be excluded are the homosexual relationships of some married men and, less frequently, married women.

The Double Standard and Adultery

The social condemnation of the married woman who commits adultery has traditionally been stronger than that of the married man. This condemnation of the woman may possibly emanate from the risk of pregnancy and the confusion that would result as to the legitimacy or paternity of the child, with the concomitant emotional and financial problems. But again, the differential hostility indicates that the public sees the adulterous act as more wrong, more blameworthy, and more morally degenerate if committed by a woman than by a man. The man is just assumed to have polygamous or "varietist" needs that can be gratified with a partner under conditions that lack affection. Further, he is presumed to have the capacity to enjoy such relationships while retaining a deep sense of affection for and loyalty (although not in the strictly sexual sense of that word) to the spouse. None of this is imputed to the married female. She is either regarded as having few sexual needs of her own (a traditional view that has undergone strong change), or as being able to be satisfied entirely by one man (her husband, mate, or lover), or as being incapable of sexual gratification if she lacks affection for her partner.

Such views can be found throughout history. Although one of the Ten Commandments specifically forbids adultery, another states that "thou shalt not covet thy neighbor's wife," suggesting almost by implication that the sin would be lesser if the woman coveted were not herself married. The evil is that the man commits the act with a married woman (whether he be married or not), and although he is a sinner if he is an adulterer, the greater sin is because of the presence of an adulteress. In the annals of literature, there are no male counterparts to Madame Bovary or Hester Prynne. And while a man whose wife has been involved with another man is said to be a cuckold or to be cuckolded—a word that signifies that he has been made a fool of—no similar attitude or language describes the woman whose husband has been found with another woman. The double standard as applied to adultery is further reflected in the famous description by Kingsley Davis (1937) of the social function of prostitution—namely, that it offers the varietist-seeking and polygamous-oriented male (the assumption being that most or all males fall into this category) a sexual outlet that will not interfere with the affectional cohesion of the family. No one has suggested a corresponding reservoir of "studs" for married females, for one mate is presumed to be sexually enough for a woman, or possibly even too much. The near-institutionalized wife-mistress system in France likewise reflects the lesser (or in this case the absent) social disapproval of the husband's extramarital relations, even when they are known to the wife, so long as the household and family remain intact and the mistress is not a married woman herself.

There seems to be a practical reason for such attitudes, aside from moral expectations of women or insensitivity to their physical needs. Marriage involves what Kingsley Davis (1936) has called sexual property, and the mores are stronger in the designation of women as the property of men than the reverse. Therefore societies (male-dominated entities) have decreed that a woman is exclusive chattel of her husband for sexual purposes, and so as not to violate his rights of ownership—or his pride—she is not permitted to pursue erotic pleasures elsewhere.

The Prevalence of Adultery

In spite of these differential attitudes, there has nevertheless been a traditional hostility toward adultery committed by either party in a marriage. Such action is, in fact, an outstanding example of normal sex deviance.

Old-fashioned adultery, or cheating, may be the most common deviant act of a sexual nature, and it may perhaps be the most common deviant act of any kind. That is to say, the percentage of eligible males (all married men) who have on at least one occasion had an extramarital sexual relationship seems to be very large, and the percentage of the married females is probably only somewhat less.

Yet no one has come close to an accurate estimate of the percentage of married persons who indulge in extramarital relations. Alfred Kinsey, Wardell Pomeroy, and Clyde Martin (1948) approached this problem from two angles: the incidence, or the number of persons having had one or more such experiences, and the frequency, or the number of times such intercourse occurs, as a percentage of all intercourse that a married person has. Their data on frequency revealed that heterosexual relations other than with a wife provides

> 5 to 10 percent of the total sexual outlet of the [male] married population taken as a whole. . . . In the youngest age groups 37 percent of the males are having extramarital intercourse, but this figure cuts down to 30 percent by 50 years of age (Kinsey, Pomeroy, & Martin, 1948, p. 281).

There is a warning that appears soon after these figures:

> It should, however, be said that we are not entirely confident of the accuracy of these data on extramarital intercourse, especially among older males from upper social levels. Where social position is dependent upon the maintenance of an appearance of conformity with the sexual conventions, males who have had extramarital intercourse are less inclined to contribute to the present study. Consequently, it is not unlikely that the actual incidence and frequency figures exceed those given here (Kinsey, Pomeroy, & Martin, 1948, p. 285).

The caveat is interesting, because it could well throw into doubt all of the work by Kinsey and his colleagues, but it is invoked only when they find the figures surprisingly low, not high. If people confess, they must be telling the truth, it is implied here; if they do not, one cannot be certain. Working from their data and assuming it to be low, the researchers do hazard a guess as to the actual incidence of extramarital relationships: "allowing for the cover-up that has been involved, it is probably safe to suggest that about half of all the married males have intercourse with women other than their wives, at some time while they are married" (Kinsey, Pomeroy, & Martin, 1948, p. 585).

There are two possible ways to explain why people would not be truthful about their extramarital activities. One way is to emphasize that they want to maintain a facade of respectability and so will not admit to pursuing sexual relations outside their marriage. Society, in that case, is one big put-on; everyone is pretending to everyone else, and almost no one is capable of seeing through it, of stepping away from the game and ceasing to be an actor on a stage.

Another similar but not identical view is the idea that people are just hypocritical about their sex and moral beliefs. They are not even under self-delusion, in which the management of impression becomes confused with the real self, but they are very consciously manipulating, acting falsely. To use the term borrowed from the world of homosexuality, these people are all "in the closet"; that is, they are secret adulterers. They know this and are aware of it, but they are afraid to "come out." Instead, they condemn others in order to help in concealing their own activity.

Kinsey and his colleagues also provide information on the incidence of adultery among married women in their study of the sexuality of human females (Kinsey, Pomeroy, Martin, & Gebhard, 1953). In the 1948 study Kinsey had stated that promiscuity was the natural order for the human male, while biologically the human female was not interested in a variety of sexual partners. He found a good deal of evidence to attribute this variation between men and women to "differences in the nervous organization on which sexual behavior depends" (Kinsey, Pomeroy, & Martin, 1948, p. 589). Yet, when research into the human female was actually undertaken, it was found that sex conduct among human females did not show as marked a contrast to that of human males as had been expected. For females born in the first decade after the turn of the century, 30 percent of those married had had extramarital relations by the age of forty, a figure smaller than for the male, but not significantly.

A relaxation of the strict code that once made such relationships taboo could be seen as the researchers contrasted women born in succeeding decades. One could assume that this relaxation continued in the years since World War II, and that the influence toward increased adultery came from mass media, new sexual ideas, occasional counseling that suggested the desirability of the activity, some statements by advocates of sexual freedom, so-called "open marriage," and feminism. If such assumptions are made and applied to men as well as women, then the evidence would point to a majority of today's population having had an experience that is contrary to widely held social norms.

It may not, however, be possible to extrapolate such a large incidence of extramarital relations from Kinsey's figures, because the data may be misleading. This is not only because they may not reflect a realistic cross-section of the American populace. It is also possible that some persons in the sample had only one extramarital relationship rather than a pattern. Sometimes the one became known to the spouse, and the couple decided that they would make an effort to repair what they viewed as a damaged union, which may have been done with success. In other words, the 50 percent figure for males and the 30 percent for females might have included many whose patterns were essentially monogamous over a long period of time, despite a single episode or two. Nevertheless, to place these figures into the context of the social setting of the 1970s, one would have to hazard a view that the numbers are understated.

Consensual Adultery

During the 1960s and into the 1970s, a number of new movements arose that embodied variations of the concept of consensual adultery. That is, the consent was not limited to the two persons committing the sexual act, but the spouse of the "offender" (or both spouses, if both were married) was privy to the act and had given approval. No doubt some rare cases of this kind of adultery had occurred before, but at this time it began to take on the form of a small social movement. Consensual adultery was encouraged by a few commentators on the social and sexual scene, as well as by some counselors who suggested that such activities could assist in marital problems by helping the mental well-being of the participants. It is doubtful if there were ever large numbers of persons involved in such experiences, and therapists have generally reported that they know of very few instances, or none at all, in which such consensual extramarital relationships aided the marriage. These events were almost always carried out circumspectly and with stealth, concealed from children, other relatives, friends, and neighbors.

One of the more highly publicized types of consensual adultery came to be known as "swinging" or "wife swapping." Because of its putative sexist implication, the latter term was discarded in favor of "mate swapping." There are few authenticated studies of this phenomenon. Some estimates have suggested that as many as 15 percent of married couples were involved, together with some unmarrieds who had mate-like relationships. Many of the commentators seem to have copied from one another in making statements about the nature of these swinging groups: that the participants were for the most part suburbanite and middle-class, that the groups were never or almost never interracial, and that there was frequently some female-to-female contact that had an erotic or lesbian character to it, but that the male homosexual counterpart was entirely absent and strictly tabooed. Then, in the mid-1970s, little more was heard of this activity. The mass media, which may have been largely responsible for the spread of swinging, tired of it and went on to new and more exotic phenomena. It is not known whether the entire swinging scene disappeared, remained more or less as it had been but received less attention, or had never amounted to very much at all.

That there were such activities cannot be denied, though they seem to have been short-lived. They were probably not as suburbanite as the deliberately created stereotype that they were undertaken by very respectable people who were not at all like hippies. Mate swapping could be found in large metropolitan areas, often in the more avant-garde sections, and on college campuses, and there seem to have been many more unmarried than married couples involved. If true, this would present a rather different picture of the phenomenon: largely uncommitted couples, perhaps living together, who were drifting into promiscuous and sometimes orgiastic relationships. If one limits the figure to the legally married, it is doubtful whether more than 1 percent of all married couples in the United States ever participated. Of those who did, some did so for a very short period—one evening or one weekend—and then abandoned the activity; others found that they were unable to continue with their marriages. In short, most reports indicate that married couples who became involved in the activity either left the scene with some haste or did not remain together as husband and wife. This author has no report of a married couple whose marital difficulties were alleviated by such performances. The swinging seems to have been a fad that hit America at a time when people had not yet tired of the sexual revolution. It was the subject of widespread publicity, it remained an exotic curiosity, and it never ceased to be the subject of scorn and hostility (not merely in Middle America), while at the same time it satisfied some vicarious excitement in readers and television viewers who both envied and condemned the participants.

The people of Middle America are not much concerned about swinging. But they do feel it is wrong for a married person to stray or cheat. When adulterous relationships cause divorce and remarriage, community observers are quite upset. They see the adulterous party as having broken up a family that, they believe, might otherwise have weathered its storms. And if it is the woman who is responsible for the broken home, they are far more hostile to her than to the man who does this.

In fact, they could overlook with some admonition and considerable regret the man who strays, particularly if he does not do so frequently. While they see his action as only normal, however, they still believe that it is not right, and they react with restrained anger toward the man and with deep sympathy for the wife. If she decides that, given his action, she will not have him any longer as her spouse, the community, or at least those friends and relatives with whom she interacts, will support her, and not infrequently they will sever relationships with her husband as a sign of their own fidelity to her. But if she decides that she will not permit the one affair, or several, to disrupt their marriage, and that she will make efforts to see that he toes the line, they are more pleased. It is not that they think he deserves to be forgiven, but rather that, with all the divorce that is rampant, they retain a sense of respect for the sanctity of the family.

Not infrequently, the love affairs of a movie celebrity, a state political leader, or a teacher in a local school, become more or less common knowledge. There was a time when the movies in which the celebrity appeared would have been banned, the political leader might have retired to private life, and the teacher would have begun to search for a job in another area. Mrs. Brown and her husband have come a long way; they have not fought the tide. They disapprove, but they say it's nobody's business but the people who do these things. As long as men and women perform their jobs well, they can do what they want in bed.

"I don't have to approve of it, or mingle with such people!" she exclaims, with a sense of horror at the thought, lest her liberal defense of the right to retain employment be misunderstood.

These are normal deviants. They are normal, both the males and the females, the latter as much as the former, in a way that people who are usually thought of as sex deviants are not. No one—not Mr. or Mrs. Brown or any of their friends and neighbors, in the churches, synagogues, and rose clubs—would regard the adulterous acts described here as abnormal or the people committing them as being "psychiatric cases," "mentally unbalanced," or "perverts." But deviant they are: The moral condemnation, the social disapproval are strong. In the interests of good taste, respect for privacy, and a new liberalism and tolerance, hostility is sometimes muted, but it is there, and it is unmistakable. If either of her daughters-in-law were to come to her and say that a marriage with one of her sons was breaking up because the husband has been unfaithful, Mrs. Brown would be heartbroken, but she is sure that she would side with the daughter-in-law, not the son.

DEVIANT ACTIVITIES IN THE WORLD "OUT THERE"

What of the usual types of sexual activities identified with the concept of deviance? With television, newspapers, and particularly the women's magazines, Mrs. Brown is well aware of activities that go on in the world "out there." She has ceased using "gay" in the sense in which it had once been a favorite word; she no longer likes to think of people in her family as gay. But she gives a lot less thought to homosexuality than to the types of acts that affect the life patterns of people around her. In short, to the extent that she takes an interest in the subject of deviance at all, she is interested in normal sex deviance, not the kind that she thinks of as sick, abnormal, or intolerable.

Homosexuality

She has read of gay bars in the big cities, and cannot possibly imagine what they are, how they function, and why they would be tolerated. She does not know that there is one in her own city, or two, depending on what group of people happens to be there at the moment when one is looking. It is just as well, her husband feels, there is no need for her to know. Though Mr. Brown no longer calls homosexuals "perverts," because he has learned that it is not a nice word, he too thinks that something should be done about them. It is one thing to have them gathering in public in the larger cities, but quite another to have them in one's own community.

The Browns generally give little thought to homosexuality; they are little concerned. There is a nephew whom they have seen from time to time, the son of Mr. Brown's sister, who lives in a nearby large city (and these things happen when people live in such places). When the family gets together, no one asks any questions about the thirty-three-year-old bachelor. They used to say that he was sort of delicate or sensitive, and they still use these kind code words when talking of him to each other. There is an unwritten law that you never ask if he's going with a girl or if he'll ever get married. No one talks of such things. All the same, everyone is kind and friendly toward him, and Mrs. Brown never allows herself to articulate, even subvocally, a suspicion about his sexual preferences. Homosexuality to her is something way out there, hundreds of miles away, in other families, concerning other people; it is part of a world that does not touch her own even remotely. A sociologist who tried to define Mrs. Brown's attitude would probably conclude that she has a compassionate and sympathetic hostility, that she feels very sorry for the people involved while at the same time she sharply disapproves (or disvalues, at the least) their way of life. She would be mortified and filled with more sorrow than she could describe if she were to live to learn that one of her grandsons had become involved in such activities. But then she hastens to add, lest she be misunderstood, "I'd feel the same way if he were blind or paraplegic. I'm not condemning, I'm just saying that I don't like it."

Mrs. Brown knows little of the subculture and the lifestyle of these people. Sometimes she thinks that the denizens of the gay world must be numerous, although she cannot begin to imagine how two people of the same sex can engage in a sexual act together. On the rare occasion that she thinks of homosexual activity she is filled with a sense of repulsion, and because she cannot understand how someone could do this, or want to do it (as she can with normal deviance), she finds it difficult to believe in the numbers that she hears about. Nevertheless, there are many bits of news and pieces of information that she hears about homosexuals: there are the famous athlete who "came out," the author who made a public statement, the governor who asked that a period of time be set aside as "Gay Pride Week" ("my goodness," she demands, "what is there to be proud of?"), the revealing biography about a famous economist (an economist, not an interior decorator, mind you.) And there is the survey that revealed that homosexuality is practiced by one man out of six, making this the largest American minority. With all this information, Mrs. Brown can almost believe that homosexuality just may not be as rare as when she grew up; after all, that was a half century back. (In fact, she does not even recall ever knowing that such things existed until she heard about it several years after her marriage.) She is certain that homosexuality is on the increase and this bothers her, but all in all, her concern with the problem is small.

Child Molestation

Mrs. Brown cannot bring herself to have the same compassion for the child molester as she has for those in the gay life. On the rare occasions when she discusses these matters, she sees an inconsistency in her position, but she stays with it. She defines both kinds of deviants as people who are sick; for her they are not normal deviants but rather sufferers from an involuntary and unwanted condition that reduces personal responsibility and acts as a mitigating factor. She believes that all sick people deserve sympathy, understanding, and assistance. But even without having been directly exposed to the sociology of victimless crime (although undoubtedly some of it has trickled down to her), she cannot extend her sympathy equally to homosexuals, who hurt no one but themselves (and she is certain that they do hurt themselves, although not quite so sure that no one else is adversely affected), and child molesters, who have as their victims helpless, innocent, and potentially corruptible children.

The Browns do distinguish between statutory rape and child molestation, just as they do between forcible and statutory rape. They do not look favorably on young men, and certainly not on those slightly older, who become involved with girls fifteen to seventeen years of age or younger, even if the girls do look "like little trollops," as Mrs. Brown may comment to her husband, when they see them while they pass the schools. Nevertheless, although they are opposed to such activities, they look upon the men involved as being within the range of their purview of normality. When these acts are not forcible, and when the female is not so young as to be truly a child, the Browns may even hold the girl largely responsible. They are more likely to have this view if she is closer to the age of consent, less likely if she is closer to the social definition of a child or if the male in the case is more man than boy. In the former case, they see the girl as having been a full-fledged party to the act. In their eyes the act is consensual, a matter between two persons who, if they are not both adults, are on the verge of adulthood. Their tendency is to place greater blame upon the girl and to note that the immorality resides in the female, while expecting nothing more of a male than that he take what he can find when it is available. Only the married man is forbidden from such hedonistic pursuits in this moral code.

The child of eight is purely a victim, and despite the appellation of "sick," the perpetrator cannot be forgiven for his mental aberration. The Browns think of men who would molest children, or who would even make overtures to them, as not merely abnormal deviants but perverts and degenerates. However, they are only concerned about child molestation when they read about it in newspapers or hear of it in books. Such things are not part of their everyday world, and they never expect it to be.

Prostitution

Closer to them, involving people of their world (though not friends or relatives), is prostitution. The deviance of this type of activity is for them beyond dispute, but they do not equally condemn both the men and women who participate in it. When asked why not, they hesitate. Their immediate answer reflects the double standard: A man has natural urges, needs, and demands; a woman is immoral to sell her body to any man who will pay for it. Pressed further, the Browns do not defend the customers, but they are not revulsed at the idea that a man has performed in that role. What do they think about the pimp? Actually, they had given him no thought. The idea of a pimp sounded very bad, indeed, but maybe such a person protects the girls instead of seducing, entrapping, kidnapping, spoiling, and exploiting them. The Browns are not willing to offer similar understanding to the women who are in this profession. The Browns have only contempt for prostitutes, though they may have a faint hope that an individual may be saved now and then. Such women are promiscuous, utterly indiscriminate, degraded, and degrading, and they are seen as a disgrace to the mothers who bore them. No doubt poverty drives many women out on the street, but this hardly serves as an excuse to the Browns, no less a justification.

In the sense that it is heterosexual, adult, and consensual, prostitution is likewise a form of normal deviance. But even though it is normal, it is for Mrs. Brown more than deviant, wrong, or immoral, more than threatening to the family. (Kingsley Davis, of whom she has never heard, would of course not agree that there is a threat at all.) It has an atmosphere of moral decay and degeneracy that places it in a category apart from adultery, of which she so strongly disapproves. That the women are not sick aggrandizes the condemnation even more: They are inexcusably bad in a willful manner.

CONCLUSION

Studies on Sexual Deviants

The forms of behavior usually thought of as sex deviance have been described and analyzed, and the normality or abnormality, propriety or impropriety, of such activities have been debated with no dearth of words. On homosexuality, there are, among other works, an outstanding annotated bibliography (Weinberg & Bell, 1972), a survey essay reviewing a considerable number of books in the field (Sagarin, 1973), a near-definitive study (Karlen, 1971), and considerable literature on etiology and therapy (Bieber et al., 1962; Ellis, 1965; Ovesey, 1969; Hatterer, 1970; Socarides, 1968). Two works by Evelyn Hooker (1957, 1958) that are often cited, though their meanings are disputable, generally seem to support the position that some homosexually oriented males are psychologically indistinguishable from those with heterosexual patterns and desires. Finally, in addition to a great deal of other material, there is a brief but major statement by a government commission, headed by Hooker, that did a cursory investigation but came up with some interesting suggestions (National Institute of Mental Health, 1972) and the influential report by Wolfenden and others (1957), which dealt with both homosexuality and prostitution but which is usually considered only in regard to what it said about the former. In a number of papers and articles (Sagarin, 1974, 1976; Sagarin & Kelly, 1975), the present author has contended that homosexuality is a behavior, not a condition. Such a position was inspired by the work of Jean-

Paul Sartre and is shared in sociology by Ronald Akers (1973). The findings of Kinsey and his colleagues (1948, 1953) on the incidence and frequency of homosexuality continue to be cited, although there has been doubt cast on the accuracy of the findings by Paul Gebhard (see his comment in Sagarin, 1973) and by John Gagnon and William Simon (1973), both of whom became associated with the institute that Kinsey founded.

The literature on child molestation is certainly less abundant. Other than some psychoanalytic and some criminological material (including Bell & Hall, 1971), the major findings come from research among incarcerated offenders by Gebhard, Gagnon, Wardell Pomeroy, and Cornelia Christenson (1965), and from a study by Charles McCaghy (1966). The dearth of descriptive and analytic material in contrast to what is available on homosexuality may be attributed in part to the difference in the number of persons involved, as well as the lack of any appreciable subculture of child molesters. Probably a more important factor, though, is the lack of any significant social movement for the rights of pedophiles; the occasional statements that are made in support of them by advocates of sexual freedom are usually repudiated.

Prostitution has a considerable literature, much of which is cited by Jennifer James in her chapter in this volume. Among the better known works are the book by Harold Greenwald (1958), which deals with the call girl or "elegant prostitute," and the overall study by Charles Winick and Paul Kinsie (1971). Among the important articles that deal with self-images of the prostitutes, clients' images of prostitutes, deviant apprenticeships, deviant identities, and other aspects are those by Travis Hirschi (1962), Charles Winick (1962), Norman Jackman, Richard O'Toole, and Gilbert Geis (1963), James Bryan (1965, 1966), Kingsley Davis (1937), and Nanette Davis (1971). The Wolfenden report (1957) has already been mentioned. Homosexual prostitution has come in for a great deal of attention; it was the subject of a widely sold novel (Rechy, 1963), a study by a Danish police officer (Jersild, 1956), and other descriptive and analytic works.

Although little has been written here on rape (as it is more readily analyzed as a form of criminal violence than of sex deviance), a few remarks will be made on the literature. The literature on rape has grown with the advent of the feminist movement and its militant effort to have rapists punished and to protect victims from humiliation in court. Among the studies of importance on the subject are the sociological and data-laden work of Menachem Amir (1971), a comparison of forcible rape in two cities by Duncan Chappell, Gilbert Geis, Stephen Schafer, and Larry Siegel (1971), a major government document (Brodyaga et al., 1975), and numerous works of feminists, of which those of Susan Brownmiller (1975) and Diana Russell (1975) are particularly interesting. Brownmiller's treatise has gained greater popular renown and has no doubt stirred up more controversy.

The Future Role of Sociologists in the Study of Sexual Deviance

Sociologists may differ on some of the issues surrounding the many types of sexual deviance. They do, however, agree that if deviance is defined as that which is disliked, abhorred, reviled, or disvalued (or with equivalent words that express the gamut of feelings from mild to extreme condemnation), then all the forms of behavior that have been discussed in this chapter are deviant—and others normally thought of as criminal or psychopathic, ranging from forcible rape to exhibitionism and voyeurs—are deviant as well. That in some instances the participants see their conduct as proper and correct or as acceptable as an alternate lifestyle would in no sense affect the sociologist's view, for the latter is not making a judgment but expressing an opinion on the judgments made by others in the American society. One does not have to seek out Mrs. Brown to find the hostility against these types of behavior; negative attitudes toward sexual deviance are pervasive and significant.

What is being suggested in this chapter, however, is that traditional concerns over morality and family are uppermost in the minds of the parents and the grandparents of Middle America. They may be concerned over whether people whom they define as sick or abnormal are given sympathy, kindness, recognition, or toleration, or are prosecuted, ignored, or protected by the law, but their concern may not be so great as the social scientist imagines. These people may well give little thought to such matters as long as friends and relatives, particularly the immediate family, are not involved as participants or victims, or as long as they do not know of such involvement.

Rather, it is normal sex deviance that is of consequence to them. They have accepted with little resistance (much less than one would have anticipated a decade earlier) premarital affectional cohabitation, but the double standard for premarital nonaffectional relations has relaxed little, if at all. Adultery, consensual or not, leaves them as hostile as ever.

This chapter is mainly speculative; many of the attitudes advanced may well be hypothetical. The problem for sociologists, then, is to determine just what the sex norms and sex values are. To do this they must work out methods for testing attitudes and develop scales for quantification. They need to address the matter of deliberate dissimulation and self-delusion (see Deutscher, 1973). Such factors as age, marital status, educational level, race, religiosity, and other socially differentiating factors must be explored as sources of hostility against sexual deviance. Finally, sociologists must determine the effect that values and attitudes toward deviant sexual behaviors will have on future trends in legislation, in sexuality, in gender relations and gender roles, and in the development of the American family.

NOTES

1. I believe that Reiss was misreading the temper of the times when he so characterized it, as pointed out in my reply (Sagarin, 1971).

2. Davis (1936) has handled other sexual problems, particularly jealousy and the concept of sexual property, elsewhere, but he has not done so under the heading of deviance.

3. Standards of sexual conduct are changing in other parts of the Western world as well, although probably less than in this country. There is a real possibility that similar changes are taking place in parts of Africa and Asia and in Eastern Europe.

4. Those involved in the new etiquette of race relations, when antiblack racism has lost its intellectual and social respectability but is still highly pervasive, can readily understand this change in attitudes toward sexually deviating people.

5. Readers wishing to know what has been revealed by the studies of sex that have been conducted are referred to Kinsey, Pomeroy, and Martin (1948) and Kinsey, Pomeroy, Martin, and Gebhard (1953).

BIBLIOGRAPHY

Akers, Ronald L. *Deviant Behavior: A Social Learning Approach.* Belmont, Calif.: Wadsworth, 1973.

Amir, Menachem. *Patterns in Forcible Rape.* Chicago: University of Chicago Press, 1971.

Becker, Howard S. *Outsiders: Studies in the Sociology of Deviance.* New York: The Free Press, 1963.

Bell, Alan P., and Calvin S. Hall. *The Personality of a Child Molester.* Chicago: Aldine-Atherton, 1971.

Bieber, Irving, and others. *Homosexuality: A Psychoanalytic Study.* New York: Basic Books, 1962.

Brodyaga, Lisa, and others. *Rape and Its Victims: A Report for Citizens, Health Facilities, and Criminal Justice Agencies.* Washington, D.C.: U.S. Dept. of Justice, Law Enforcement Assistance Administration, 1975.

Brownmiller, Susan. *Against Our Will: Men, Women, and Rape.* New York: Simon & Schuster, 1975.

Bryan, James K. "Apprenticeships in Prostitution." *Social Problems,* 1965, 12:287–297.

Bryan, James K. "Occupational Ideologies and Individual Attitudes of Call Girls." *Social Problems,* 1966, 13:441–450.

Chappell, Duncan, Gilbert Geis, Stephen Schafer, and Larry Siegel. "Forcible Rape: A Comparative Study of Offenses Known to the Police in Boston and Los Angeles." In James M. Henslin, ed. *Studies in the Sociology of Sex.* New York: Appleton-Century-Crofts, 1971, pp. 169–190.

Davis, Fred. "Deviance Disavowal: The Management of Strained Interaction by the Visibly Handicapped." *Social Problems,* 1961, 9:120–132.

Davis, Kingsley. "Jealousy and Sexual Property." *Social Forces,* 1936, 14:395–405.

Davis, Kingsley. "The Sociology of Prostitution." *American Sociological Review,* 1937, 2:744–755.

Davis, Kingsley. "Sexual Behavior." In Robert K. Merton and Robert A. Nisbet, eds. *Contemporary Social Problems,* 2nd ed. Harcourt Brace Jovanovich, 1966, pp. 322–372.

Davis, Kingsley. "Sexual Behavior." In Robert K. Merton and Robert Nisbet, eds. *Contemporary Social Problems.* 4th ed. New York: Harcourt Brace Jovanovich, 1976, pp. 221–261.

Davis, Nanette J. "The Prostitute: Developing a Deviant Identity." In James M. Henslin, ed. *Studies in the Sociology of Sex.* New York: Appleton-Century-Crofts, 1971, pp. 297–322.

Deutscher, Irwin. *What We Say/What We Do: Sentiments and Acts.* Glenview, Ill.: Scott, Foresman, 1973.

Ellis, Albert. *Homosexuality: Its Causes and Cure.* Secaucus, N.J.: Lyle Stuart, 1965.

Freedman, Jonathan L., and Anthony N. Doob. *Deviancy: The Psychology of Being Different.* New York: Academic Press, 1968.

Gagnon, John H., and William Simon, eds. *Sexual Deviance.* New York: Harper & Row, 1967.

Gagnon, John H., and William Simon. *Sexual Conduct: The Social Sources of Human Sexuality.* Chicago: Aldine, 1973.

Gebhard, Paul H., John H. Gagnon, Wardell B. Pomeroy, and Cornelia V. Christenson. *Sex Offenders: An Analysis of Types.* New York: Harper & Row, 1965.

Goffman, Erving. *Stigma: Notes on the Management of Spoiled Identity.* Englewood Cliffs, N.J.: Prentice-Hall, 1963.

Goode, Erich, and Richard Troiden, eds. *Sexual Deviance and Sexual Deviants.* New York: William Morrow, 1974.

Greenwald, Harold. *The Call Girl.* New York: Ballantine Books, 1958.

Hatterer, Lawrence J. *Changing Homosexuality in the Male: Treatment for Men Troubled by Homosexuality.* New York: McGraw-Hill, 1970.

Hirschi, Travis. "The Professional Prostitute." *Berkeley Journal of Sociology,* 1962, 7:37–48.

Hoffman, Martin. *The Gay World: Male Homosexuality and the Social Creation of Evil.* New York: Basic Books, 1968.

Hooker, Evelyn. "The Adjustment of the Male Overt Homosexual." *Journal of Projective Techniques,* 1957, 21:18–31.

Hooker, Evelyn. "Male Homosexuality in the Rorschach." *Journal of Projective Techniques,* 1958, 22:33–54.

Jackman, Norman R., Richard O'Toole, and Gilbert Geis. "The Self-Image of the Prostitute." *Sociological Quarterly,* 1963, 4:150–161.

Jersild, Jens. *Boy Prostitution,* English ed. Trans. by Oscar Bojesen. Copenhagan: G. E. C. Gad, 1956.

Karlen, Arno. *Sexuality and Homosexuality: A New View.* New York: W. W. Norton, 1971.

Kinsey, Alfred C., Wardell B. Pomeroy, and Clyde E. Martin. *Sexual Behavior in the Human Male.* Philadelphia: Saunders, 1948.

Kinsey, Alfred C., Wardell B. Pomeroy, Clyde E. Martin, and Paul H. Gebhard. *Sexual Behavior in the Human Female.* Philadelphia: Saunders, 1953.

Kitsuse, John I. "Societal Reaction to Deviant Behavior: Problems of Theory and Method." *Social Problems,* 1962, 9:247–256.

Lindsey, Ben B., and Wainwright Evans. *The Companionate Marriage.* New York: Boni and Liveright, 1927.

McCaghy, Charles H. "Child Molesters: A Study of Their Careers as Deviants." Ph.D. dissertation, University of Wisconsin, 1966.

National Institute of Mental Health. *Final Report of the Task Force on Homosexuality.* In Joseph A. McCaffrey, ed. *The Homosexual Dialectic.* Englewood Cliffs, N.J.: Prentice-Hall, 1972, pp. 145–155.

Ovesey, Lionel. *Homosexuality and Pseudohomosexuality.* New York: Science House, 1969.

Rechy, John. *City of Night.* New York: Grove Press, 1963.

Reiss, Ira L. "Premarital Sex as Deviant Behavior: An Application of Current Approaches to Deviance." *American Sociological Review,* 1970, 35:78–87.

Russell, Diana E. H. *The Politics of Rape: The Victim's Perspective.* New York: Stein & Day, 1975.

Sagarin, Edward. "Premarital Sex as Normative Behavior." Paper presented to the Eastern Sociological Society, New York, 1971.

Sagarin, Edward. "The Good Guys, the Bad Guys, and the Gay Guys." *Contemporary Sociology,* 1973, 2:3–13.

Sagarin, Edward. "Homosexuality and the Homosexual: An Overview of the Former and a Denial of the Reality of the Latter." Paper presented to the American Sociological Association, Montreal, 1974.

Sagarin, Edward. *Deviants and Deviance: An Introduction to the Study of Disvalued People and Behavior.* New York: Praeger, 1975.

Sagarin, Edward. "The High Cost of Wearing a Label." *Psychology Today,* 1976, 9:25–31.

Sagarin, Edward, and Robert J. Kelly. "Sexual Deviance and Labelling Perspectives." In Walter R. Gove, ed. *The Labelling of Deviance.* Beverly Hills, Calif.: Sage Publications, 1975, pp. 243–271.

Scarpitti, Frank, and Paul T. McFarlane, eds. *Deviance: Action, Reaction, Interaction.* Reading, Mass.: Addison-Wesley, 1975.

Schur, Edwin M. *Labeling Deviant Behavior: Its Sociological Implications.* New York: Harper & Row, 1971.

Simmons, J. L. *Deviants.* Berkeley, Calif.: Glendessary Press, 1969.

Socarides, Charles W. *The Overt Homosexual.* New York: Grune & Stratton, 1968.

Weinberg, Martin S., and Alan P. Bell, eds. *Homosexuality: An Annotated Bibliography.* New York: Harper & Row, 1972.

Weinberg, Martin S., and Colin J. Williams. *Male Homosexuals: Their Problems and Adaptations.* New York: Oxford University Press, 1974.

Wilkins, Leslie T. *Social Deviance: Social Policy, Action, and Research.* Englewood Cliffs, N.J.: Prentice-Hall, 1965.

Winick, Charles. "Prostitutes' Clients' Perception of the Prostitutes and of

Themselves." *International Journal of Social Psychiatry*, 1962, 8:289–297.

Winick, Charles, and Paul M. Kinsie. *The Lively Commerce: Prostitution in the United States.* New York: Quadrangle, 1971.

Wolfenden, John, and others. *The Report of the Committee on Homosexual Offences and Prostitution.* London, England: Her Majesty's Printing Office, 1957.

TEN

Pornography and society

GEORGE D. MUEDEKING
California State College, Stanislaus

I, Ralph Ginzburg, paroled prisoner, U.S. Bureau of Prisons convict number 38124–134, do hereby accuse the United States Supreme Court of high crimes and treason, namely, of mocking the Constitution, trammeling Freedom of the Press, and playing fast and loose with one man's liberty—mine.

I have just completed eight months in prison. I face an additional four years and four months of probation and parole. I have been fined a Draconian $42,000.

For what? What is the hideous crime for which I have been so mercilessly flogged and declared an enemy of the people? I'll tell you what: I tried to give America its first beautiful, intellectual, emotionally mature, completely forthright magazine dealing with love and sex. Its name was *Eros*.

Let history mark that in the year Nineteen Hundred and Seventy-Two, in this supposedly civilized, professedly free society, a man was manacled and muzzled for trying to tell the truth about sex.
Ralph Ginzburg, (1973, pp. 33–34.)

With these words Ralph Ginzburg, convicted pornographer, expressed questions debated by an increasing number of people in our society. Is pornography harmful? In what ways? Will our magazine stands soon drown in a sea of filth?

"It can be stated that the so-called 'Danish experiment' is currently underway in the United States," announced the Commission on Obscenity and Pornography (1970b, p. 208). What is the "Danish experiment"? In 1969 Denmark repealed all laws banning pornography. Since that time officials in other countries have watched with great interest the events unfolding in Denmark in order to determine what effects such repeal would have on the society and its citizens. What led to the conclusion quoted above was the commission's investigation into the increasing availability in the late 1960s of pornography in this country.

Themes that had previously been restricted to "stag" or exploitation films have found their way into general-release motion pictures. For example, the theme is perversion in *The Damned;* drugs in *Easy Rider;* orgies in *Fellini Satyricon;* wife swapping in *Bob and Carol and Ted and Alice;* rape in *Straw Dogs;* male prostitution in *Midnight Cowboy;* and lesbianism in *The Killing of Sister George.*

Some of Europe's most famous pornographic publishing houses have recently moved their operations to the United States, specifically to southern California. Several American publishers—for instance, Grove Press—have begun publishing in earnest many of the world's classic pornographic novels. Maurice Girodias, owner of Olympia Press, an old, established pornography publisher, emigrated from Paris to the United States because of the relaxed atmosphere surrounding pornography publishing here. Peter Collier comments on this scene:

> America is a good place for publishing right now. . . . But the fact is that the small-time, gangster operators in this country—publishing everything they can lay their hands on like a pack of mad dogs regardless of its quality—could bring down the wrath of the public, first in southern California, then all over the country (1968, p. 19).

Anyone acquainted with best-seller lists in the 1960s and 1970s is aware of the large number of sexually oriented books that have dominated the fiction and nonfiction markets in the United States. In 1969, for the first time, the ten best-selling fiction books came within 2 percent of equaling sales for the ten best-selling nonfiction works. This amazing showing was almost solely due to the six sexually oriented fiction books on the top ten list (Commission, 1970b, p. 87). These included *Portnoy's Complaint, The Love Machine,* and *Naked Came the Stranger,* the latter being a semihoax perpetrated by several writers, each contributing a "formula-written" chapter.

In response to this showing by the fiction market, best-selling sexually oriented nonfiction appeared for the first time in 1970. Among these books were *Everything You Always Wanted to Know about Sex (But Were Afraid to Ask), Sensuous Woman, The Joy of Sex,* and *More Joy.* In 1968, sex newspapers came into being; the first and still most successful is *Screw,* a New York-based publication.

Estimates of the total sales of pornographic materials in this country are speculative at best because of the continued clandestine activities of the market. However a consensus of estimates puts the figure somewhere between $500 million and $1 billion annually (Commission, 1970a, pp. 7–23).

What accounts for this sudden explosion of interest in pornographic materials in this country? Several factors coalesced in the late 1960s and early 1970s to give tremendous impetus to the pornography industry. Some persons point to the phenomenal growth in international media communication, which insures that cultural developments in one country, especially any Western nation, will travel quickly to other countries. With pornography this has meant that liberalization of laws of production and distribution in one country will rapidly be felt in other countries with stricter controls. Others believe that Americans have been going through a period of significant questioning that has brought change in sexual roles and norms, with a resulting lack of standard guidelines for judging what is appropriate and inappropriate in individual sexual lifestyles. Pornography publishers themselves explain that the obscenity laws in the United States are in such an indeterminate state that officials are in a legal quagmire when it comes to enforcement. Some social scientists point to rapid social change that has led to an inability of important social institutions, such as the family and church, to preserve traditional regulations concerning sexual behavior. These factors are not mutually exclusive, nor is this list complete.

Although pornography seems to be ever-present, there are times when technological innovations or social changes appear to thrust the issue once again into the public eye, so that it is defined by many as a social problem. The social changes just enumerated were responsible for making the 1960s a time of emerging public concern about pornography. Evidence of this concern can be found in public opinion polls taken by the Gallup and Harris organizations in 1969. One showed that 85 percent of a sample of the nation's adults favored stricter laws on pornography (Gallup, 1969), while the other reported that 76 percent wanted pornographic literature outlawed (Harris, 1969). Further indications of public concern were the formation of "media watch" organizations such as Citizens for Decent Literature, the adoption by the movie industry of codes relating to sexual content, and the appearance of articles in popular magazines cataloging the rising quantity of pornography in the United States. Furthermore, in 1967 the Ninetieth Congress passed legislation that created the Commission on Obscenity and Pornography,[1] and the very next Congress introduced 197 separate bills dealing with explicit sexual material.

The reason for the creation of the Commission on Obscenity and Pornography was that the heightened public concern over pornography had raised many more questions requiring factual information than could be answered. Thus, there was a need for a commission to compile data on pornography and to offer recommendations for dealing with it. In the space of a few years, the commission financed more research in the area of pornography than had accumulated in the preceding two centuries. The questions it sought to answer were concerned with the place of pornography in our history and in the history of other civilizations, pornography's impact on both social and antisocial behavior, the place of obscenity legislation within our legal system, problems over the social control of pornography, and questions about the need for and place of sex education in society. Similar study commissions have been formed in other countries, such as Great Britain, Israel, Denmark, West Germany, Norway, and Sweden.

These efforts have resulted in a large accumulation of information that allows some empirical questions to be answered with a relatively high degree of validity. However, other questions remain that, even with large amounts of information, cannot be answered definitively because they involve personal values. It is especially in the area of sex that people have well-developed opinions and ideas that will withstand any barrage of empirical information. These opinions have their basis in theories and ideologies of the good life, mental health, ethical man, self-actualization, and they reflect human experience as interpreted and tempered by human values. It is partly through these concepts that many people define the facts and judge the validity of information.

This wide range of sexual values makes resolution of the debate on pornography difficult, because there is little agreement on what the actual effects of pornography are and whether they are harmful or beneficial. The extent of this disagreement is well-illustrated by an opinion poll that asked 2,486 citizens what they believed were the effects of pornography. The results of that poll are shown in Table 1.

Table 1. Replies to the Question: "Sexual Materials Do or Do Not Have These Effects"

Presumed Effects	Yes	No	Not sure, No answer
Sexual materials excite people sexually	67%	17%	16%
Sexual materials provide information about sex	61%	27%	12%
Sexual materials lead to a breakdown of morals	56%	30%	14%
Sexual materials lead people to commit rape	49%	29%	22%
Sexual materials provide entertainment	48%	46%	6%
Sexual materials improve sex relations of some married couples	47%	32%	22%
Sexual materials make people bored with sexual materials	44%	35%	21%
Sexual materials lead people to lose respect for women	43%	41%	16%
Sexual materials make men want to do new things with their wives	41%	28%	32%
Sexual materials make people sex crazy	37%	45%	18%
Sexual materials provide an outlet for bottled up impulses	34%	46%	20%
Sexual materials give relief to people who have sex problems	27%	46%	26%

SOURCE: Adapted from H. Abelson, R. Cohen, E. Heaton, and C. Suder. "Public Attitudes Towards and Experience with Erotic Materials." In Commission on Obscenity and Pornography. *Technical Reports*, vol. 6. Washington, D.C.: U.S. Government Printing Office, 1970, p. 191.

Still, there is some evidence that individual values are coalescing into a general public opinion. Some significant changes are appearing, and in the future the "face" of pornography should change in response. Factored into this prediction are the potential legal modifications in controlling the distribution of pornography. In fact, legislative attempts at control and court interpretations, dominating as they do the public reaction to pornography, may be the most important determinants in shaping the future content of pornography.

This chapter will examine the issue of pornography with the end that the reader will have a full understanding of the facts and feelings on the subject. Before going any further, we must first deal with a problem of terminology. Following this will be an examination of two questions that are of public concern: What are the consequences of pornography for society? What are the potential behavioral effects of pornographic material on individuals? Since legal interpretations are not only based on constitutional issues but also on beliefs about the effects of pornography, it is only after exploring these two questions that we can go on to a discussion of the legal issues associated with the social control of pornography. A final section will deal with the place of pornography in society and predictions for the continuance of the problem in the future.

A DEFINITIONAL PROBLEM

The indeterminancy of the meaning of the words *pornography* and *obscenity* has plagued not only public discussion and social scientific research but also legal scholars and justices of the Supreme Court. The definitional problem involved is that designating material as either "obscene" or "pornographic" requires a value judgment. Supreme Court Justice Potter Stewart may have illustrated this best in a 1946 decision: "I shall not today attempt to further define the types of material I understand to be embraced within the shorthand description [of obscenity] and perhaps I could never succeed in intelligently doing so. But I know it when I see it" (Beserra, Jewel, & Matthews, 1973, p. 109). In effect, obscenity is in the eye of the beholder. The result of this subjectivity is that any consensus in assigning the label requires that the designators be of like mind concerning their literary and pictorial tastes. Those who would stir the public to action over material of a sexual nature must first get community agreement on what is obscene and what is not.

Is it possible to separate these terms from their implied value judgments? For our purposes it is probably better to avoid the terms obscenity and pornography except when used in their technical senses. Generally speaking, obscenity is a legal term. It is used by legislators when constructing laws and by courts and law enforcement agencies when interpreting those laws. As such, its meaning will vary according to jurisdiction, time, and person. Pornography, on the other hand, is a term that is most often used in relation to literary and artistic enterprises. Pornography is usually contrasted with "erotic art" when speaking of the portrayal of sexual relations in art. The meaning is conveyed that pornography is "bad," or at least not "good," art, whereas erotic art is in some way artistically legitimate.

The problem of developing a value-free definition for analytic and research purposes was also encountered by the Commission on Obscenity and Pornography. Because a committee of law school deans could not achieve a consensus on definitions, the commission decided to avoid the terms pornography and obscenity and to designate any material that could be described primarily by the sexual act depicted as "erotic materials." Specifically, the commission stated:

> In the absence of well-defined and generally acceptable definitions of both obscenity and pornography, the Commission conceptualized the relevant stimuli as erotic materials, sexual materials, or sexually explicit stimuli over a range of media (photographs, snapshots, cartoons, films, and written materials in books, magazines and typewritten stories) which are capable of being described in terms of the sexual themes portrayed: e.g., "a man and woman having sexual intercourse," or "mouth-sex organ contact between man and woman" (1970a, p. 181).

The practice of the commission will be followed here. Wherever possible, the terms erotic material, erotica, or sexual material will be used. Exceptions will be where the terms obscenity and pornography are used in their specifically legal and artistic senses, respectively.

It must be noted that the terms of pornography or erotica appear in many theories or models of behavior, and that their definitions will vary according to the function the term plays in explaining the behavior in question. Where it seems crucial in understanding some viewpoint, these differences in meaning will be conveyed.

THEORIES OF THE PLACE OF EROTICA IN SOCIETY

Freudians

Does the existence of erotica harm society? Many social observers feel that sexual material is tied to the corruption of a society. As a Russian visitor to the United States, A. P. Ayasko, commented when explaining the Russian revulsion for the widespread market in pornography here: "We are convinced that the time will come in the United States when this sort of thing [porno] will be prohibited because it leads to the corruption of youth" (*San Francisco Chronicle*, 1974, p. 14). Often such viewpoints, and the justifications for intense social control of sexual materials that accompany them, are based on the "grand theories" of cultural dynamics that were developed by historians writing in the late nineteenth and mid-twentieth centuries. In the broadest possible framework, entire cultural configurations are compared and contrasted, and conclusions are drawn about the positive or negative contributions that a particular element of culture makes for the whole society. Two theorists who have singled out sexual lifestyles and commented on them are Pitirim Sorokin (1957) and Arnold J. Toynbee (1961).

Sorokin classified cultures according to two major types: *sensate* and *ideational*. According to Sorokin, an ideational society is functionally integrated around spiritual or religious concerns, and it therefore denies the primacy of individual feelings or pleasures, including sexual pleasure. Such a culture will be characterized by the repression of sex. Sensate culture is just the opposite, and it thus places an emphasis on sexual pleasure and fulfillment. From his study of cultures that promote sensual concerns at the expense of spiritual ones, Sorokin concluded that the pattern of sexual behavior strongly influences the culture's progress or regress: "Excessive sexual activity, particularly when it is illicit, has markedly deleterious effects" (1956, p. 57).

A similar viewpoint is taken by Toynbee, who emphasized the factors involved in the genesis and growth of civilizations. His studies showed that economic and militaristic domination has been associated with those civilizations that postpone heterosexual encounters among their youth until well after sexual maturity is reached. As Toynbee explained:

> I myself believe, on the historical evidence, that the later we can postpone the age of sexual consciousness, the better able we are to educate ourselves. As I see it, this feature in the mores of the Western people has been one of the causes of their comparative success during the last centuries" (quoted by Packard, 1968, pp. 420–421).

These theories of the relationship between sexual practice and cultural success fail to explain one basic question: Why should the sexual practices of individuals be functionally related to cultural progress, domination, or success? No psychological or biological theory was offered by these men and other well-known social scientists (such as J. D. Unwin, Carle C. Zimmerman, and David Mace) to explain why the relationship between sexual practice and cultural change was considered more important than the thousands of other possible causal relationships. The probable reason for this emphasis, however, is that at the time these men were being educated, Sigmund Freud was having a great influence on thoughts concerning society and sex. Psychoanalytic theory is very relevant to questions about erotica and its existence in society.

Freud's writings were so comprehensive and wide-ranging that they prohibit easy summaries. However, of relevance here is the seminal work of Freud, *Civilization and Its Discontents* (1930). Freud based his psychological notions on the biological concept of instincts. He felt that instincts to fulfill the body's basic needs provide the impetus for the development of certain wishes. These wishes lead a person to seek certain object choices that will provide fulfillment of those needs. The energy necessary for this search is derived from the *id*, the source of all psychic energy. Freud emphasized especially the sexual instinct that impelled the organism to find object choices to fulfill its need for sex. In *Civilization and Its Discontents* Freud developed the concept of *sublimation*. This is the process by which primitive object choices are inhibited and the energy that would normally be used to search for them is instead diverted to work that will advance society and be of benefit to it. In other words, sexual energy can be diverted to projects that contribute to the advancement of the culture. For example, Leonardo da Vinci painted many madonnas because, according to Freud, his original object choice, his mother, had been separated from him at an early age (Hall & Lindzey, 1957, p. 48). The task for society is to insure that blocked choices are replaced with socially useful ones. Contemporary psychoanalysts, such as Bruno Bettelheim, have carried on in Freud's tradition. Bettelheim writes, "If a society does not taboo sex, children will grow up in relative sex freedom. But so far history has shown that such a society cannot create culture or civilization; it remains primitive" (Commission, 1970a, p. 625).

Psychoanalytic theory, based as it is on particular cases, is difficult to apply cross-culturally. Researchers have discovered that many of Freud's propositions do not hold when applied to cultures very much different from Western European ones.[2] If one approves of the general results of sexual sublimation in the West, then it is a positive practice. But such approval would seem to depend on one's social class position, that is, on whether one is reaping the benefits of Western cultural dominance or whether one is suffering the consequences (as did, for example, Southeast Asian peasants). Wilhelm Reich, a student of Freud's who later broke with him over these and other issues, did not agree that sexual gratification was postponed to divert energy to constructive social contributions. Rather, he felt that sublimation was simply a social class phenomenon based on attempts by the higher social classes to control the marital selections of their children in order to preserve class position through inheritance lines (MacBean, 1972). This notion seems to fit the data just as well as Freud's explanations.

Structural Functionalists

Thus far, the social thinkers cited have pointed to the benefits of severe control of erotica. In their view, such material harms society because it promotes sexual license that is culturally unproductive. But what if it can be shown that erotica exists because it is somehow socially beneficial? Studying the contributions of various social institutions and cultural practices has been the particular focus of the school of American sociology known as structural-functionalism.[3]

Theoreticians of this school contend that for society to operate adequately, certain functions (tasks) must be performed. They study how various cultures fulfill these functions through social institutions (such as the family) and how cultural practices support those institutions.

Functionalists often find that things normally considered socially harmful may actually promote stability in a society. Kingsley Davis (1937), for example, has written that the "world's oldest profession," prostitution, must be socially usful or it would not have lasted for so long in so many different societies. Davis has argued that man's sexual instincts are not naturally regulated, and that it is the job of society to connect sex to socially important ends, such as bearing and raising children within an institution like the family. The moral restrictions of sex must be inculcated to individuals so that society can survive. But what is to be done with the natural human sexual inclinations? Some safety valves must be developed to deal with the potential for antisocial sexual behavior. Prostitution is such a safety valve: It promotes the stability of the family, which is necessary for the adequate functioning of society, by offering the human male an outlet for his promiscuous needs in a manner that does not compete with his permanent and affectional relationship with his wife.

Ned Polsky (1969) has argued that Davis' explanation for the existence of prostitution fits pornography or erotica just as well. Erotica, according to Polsky, is a "functional alternative" for prostitution because it does the same thing for society—promotes the stability of the family—as does prostitution. That is why one finds erotica in all cultures that have developed techniques of reading and writing. In fact, prototypes of erotica are even found in the legends and myths of preliterate peoples. According to Polsky, erotica performs its functions in at least two ways. First, it facilitates masturbation, which relieves sexual tension that might otherwise find a socially harmful outlet.[4] Second, it allows for the portrayal of "weird" or perverse sex that would otherwise be forbidden, even within the institution of marriage.

There is evidence to support Polsky's argument, for a connection does in fact seem to exist between erotica and masturbation. Males deprived of sex because they are in restrictive social environments do tend to turn to masturbation for the release of sexual tension, and they will look at erotic materials to facilitate this act. Distinctions between "art" and "pornography" are unnecessary in this argument. If, as Polsky's argument defines it, erotica is any visual aide to masturbation, then Sears catalogs, National Geographic magazines, medical dictionaries, and history of art textbooks can all be pornographic at times. Yet, much is left unanswered by this line of thought. Societies do make distinctions between art and pornography, and when large numbers of people are concerned about the problem of pornography, they are talking about an increase in certain types of material.

Polsky's explanation is inadequate in other respects. It does not delineate how much or how little erotica is necessary for the adequate functioning of society. It gives no explanation of why public concern about erotica magnifies at certain times and diminishes at others. Moreover, according to the functional argument one would expect that those societies with the most restrictive sexual norms—with legitimate sex confined only to marriage—would be those with the most stable and viable industries of erotica. In fact, an examination of cross-national trends brings forth an alternative question, "Why is it that societies that have the most permissive sexual norms are also those where erotic materials represent a highly productive and stable industry?"

Conflict Theorists

Answers to such questions are offered by the conflict sociologists.[5] These theorists assume that society consists of groups of persons with varying interests that may often come in conflict. The focus of their study is the conflict of economic interests and its consequences for social life, with special attention given to conflict over the content of cultural institutions; school policies, church social doctrines, and conditions in the work-place. In modern society, law is of primary importance in social control, and conflict theorists consider the control of the legal institution to be the primary vehicle by which one group's interests gain ascendancy over those of another group.

Furthermore, Joseph Gusfield (1967) has drawn attention to the subtle, *symbolic* importance of law, in addition to its overt *instrumental* purpose. Instrumentally, law is meant to influence peoples' behavior directly by requiring them to refrain from some acts or to perform others. Symbolically, the law expresses the public worth of the norms and values of one culture or subculture over or against others.

In a pluralistic society such as the United States, many groups appear from time to time with norms and interests different from those of dominant groups. Differences may stem from generational differences (for instance, youth culture), economic needs (welfare mothers), ethnic origin (immigrants), or other factors that produce changes in lifestyles. Shifts in public morality usually signify that demographic and other changes have taken place and that older, established attitudes and norms are being displaced by newer, emerging ones.

The dissent over erotica arises from a conflict of economic interest and societal norms. Many people desire the liberalization of law and social norms surrounding erotica. Those directly involved include authors, movie makers, publishers, bookstore owners, and others who earn a living by producing and distributing erotica. Less directly interested in liberalization are persons holding unorthodox ideas about sex who find their views and practices in regard to sexual behavior to be in conflict with older traditions.

In the face of these interest groups, people with conservative opinions about erotica find that their ability to define sexually explicit material as harmful is diminished. They therefore turn to the courts and to legislatures to seek protection of their power in the cultural marketplace. Once the law is brought into the conflict, the struggle is irretrievably joined and a winner must emerge who will have cultural dominance.[6]

While the overall desire has been to suppress depictions of sexual acts, the focus of antiobscenity movements has often changed over the years as modern cultures have moved toward secularization. Original campaigns were more interested in the use of sexual metaphor to blaspheme the Church or propose sedition against the state. Later, the repression of erotica surrounded the dissemination of birth control information. More recent, and yet unresolved, campaigns have been concerned with sex education of youth. Generally, these cultural conflicts have been resolved in favor of liberalization, but not without significant legal battles.

As a general principle toward understanding the periodic designation of sexual material as a social problem, one should remember that when established norms are threatened and consensus in the community does not exist, moral crusades are pushed by people committed to those lifestyles that are losing legitimacy. As Gusfield states, "it is when [community] consensus is least attainable that the pressure to establish legal norms appears to be the greatest" (1967, p. 73).

In reviewing these social-scientific theories of the place of erotica in society, one concludes that a consensus does not exist among social observers regarding the positive or negative contributions that erotica imparts to the social fabric. Of course, these theories are not mutually exclusive; they may all be partly correct. Erotica, like political ideologies, can mean different things to different people. The Freudians see erotica as associated with cultural decline, and the functionalists cannot conceive of societies without it. The conflict theorists forsake both of these "normative" orientations and try to describe the incidence of pornography and the rise and fall of social concern about it in terms of interest groups. In the end, then, judgments about the social good or harm of pornography must rest largely on evidence concerning the actual effects of erotica on the behavior of individuals.

THE EFFECT OF EROTICA ON PEOPLE

Assumptions about the effect of erotica on one's fellow citizens appear to be the most important factor in determining a person's opinion about societal control of such materials. More than one-half of the respondents in a public opinion poll sponsored by the Commission on Obscenity and Pornography (1970a, p. 190) reported that they would be in favor of removing controls on erotica if it could be shown that such material produces no harmful effect on the user. And, almost 80 percent said that they would favor controls if they were convinced that erotica was harmful. The amount and validity of the evidence concerning harm is thereby considered to be of great importance to many in developing useful solutions to the problem of erotica.

Public opinion appears to support an *imitation model* to explain the effects of erotica on individuals. Many persons tend to believe that seeing certain types of sexual activities will cause people to go out and do that very thing. Such an effect is generally assumed for other people; most will say that erotica does not have that effect on them personally. For example, 41 percent of those interviewed by the commission (1970a, p. 192) reported a belief that erotica "makes men want to do new things with their wives," but only 7 percent said that it had ever had this effect on them. Of the 56 percent who felt that erotica leads "to a breakdown of morals" only 1 percent reported this effect on themselves, and only 13 percent declared that this had happened to someone they knew. Almost half, or 49 percent, felt that erotica leads to rape, but no one reported that it had influenced them to commit this act, and few (9 percent) knew someone whom it had influenced in this way. Interestingly, the commission reported that the more exposure to erotica persons had had, the less likely they were to report the conviction that it had harmful consequences.

Until recently there was not much evidence that could help determine whether erotica did indeed have the effects that were generally attributed to it. Because of this dearth of information, the commission had to conduct numerous experiments, surveys, and extended interviews to accumulate a much larger body of knowledge. One persistant problem in researching the power of erotica to sexually arouse people concerns measurement. Arousal involves physiological reactions such as blood pressure and temperature changes, pupil dilation, and respiratory changes. But these are affective changes characteristic of other emotions, such as love, trust, and disgust that should also be measured in such studies. The subjects can be asked to explain their reactions, but these self-reports are rather unreliable unless accompanied by extensive questioning. While these problems exist in measuring responses to erotica, they are not insurmountable, and the following information on the effects of erotica on individuals is the most reliable and valid that exists today.

Factors Affecting Arousal by Erotica

Somewhere between 60 and 80 percent of the people studied reported arousal when reading or viewing erotic stimuli (Commission, 1970a, p. 201). These figures are contingent on the *medium of presentation.* Males appear to be more aroused by visual stimuli (pictures and movies), whereas females report more arousal from general literature. Both sexes appear to show the greatest arousal from use of their own imaginations (pp. 206–207).

The theme of the erotic material also appears to be a factor in determining sexual arousal (p. 210). Most people report conventional sexual activities to be more sexually stimulating than those that are unconventional (homosexual relations, sadism). Reports indicate that depictions of males either nude or in homosexual encounters are more stimulating to females than to males, and that depictions of females in this way are more stimulating to males than to females (p. 210).

As common sense might lead a person to expect, one's own sexual orientation has considerable effect on the type of material that leads to arousal (pp. 210–211). Heterosexual females and males report that depictions of heterosexual activity arouse them more than homosexual portrayals, while for homosexuals the opposite effect is reported. Age also seems to be significant (pp. 212–213), with arousal being less likely as age increases.

The context of exposure is another factor in determining arousal (pp. 213–214). Persons tend to report more arousal when viewing material alone than in the presence of others. More arousal occurs in informal than in formal settings. Also of interest are findings that show that filling out a questionnaire inquiring about sexual response produces arousal, as does attaching electrodes designed to measure sexual arousal (pp. 213–214).

Long-term viewing of erotica has a satiation effect. Both experiments and interviews show that prolonged viewing of erotica leads to increasingly less sexual arousal. In the first experiment of its kind, J. L. Howard, C. B. Reifler, and M. B. Liptzin (1970, pp. 214–215) had male college students view erotica for ninety minutes a day, five days a week, for three weeks. As the experiment continued, the subjects showed less interest in erotica and, correspondingly, the degree of their sexual arousal from the material decreased.

Erotica and Sexual Behavior

What is the relationship between the amount of exposure to erotic stimuli and the frequency and amount of sexual behavior? Studies in both the United States and Sweden have rendered consistent evidence that those persons who have experienced early and frequent exposure to erotica report earlier masturbatory and heterosexual activity. They also had higher rates of sexual behavior at the time of the research (Commission, 1970a, pp. 228–231). This fact alone does not help in evaluating the effect of erotica, however, so it is necessary to explore the relationship between erotica and sexual behavior more fully.

The Commission financed several studies to determine the exact effect of erotica on sexual behavior. Some of these studies specifically wanted to determine if exposure to erotica causes higher rates of sexual behavior. It was consistently shown that

> [exposure] to sex stimuli increases the frequency of masturbation among minorities of various populations, and principally among individuals with either established masturbatory patterns or established but unavailable sexual partners (p. 212).

Effects appear to disappear within forty-eight hours. Similar conclusions were made from studies of the effects of exposure on heterosexual coitus. The commission concluded:

> In general, these experiments indicate that when masturbatory and coital responses to exposure do occur, they tend to be mutually exclusive, and the occurrence of one rather than the other appears to be determined principally by the availability of an established sexual partner (p. 224).

Other experiments were designed to explore whether exposure led to new, untried types of sexual behavior. No relationship was found between exposure and new forms of sexual behavior (p. 227). In short, exposure to erotica affects behavior by emphasizing preestablished attitudes and patterns of sexual activity.

Important questions remained unanswered, however. Some findings of the commission's studies were unexpected, especially those relating to male-female responses. Researchers discovered that the measured physiological reactions of females upon exposure to erotica were quite similar to those of males, although attitudinal and emotional responses were different. The commission could provide no explanation for this finding. Therefore, for information that sheds more light on how this and other questions that hinge on the relationship between factors might affect both behavior and exposure—we must turn to other researchers.

Human sexual behavior had not been extensively studied from sociological perspectives until recent years. As Edward Sagarin (1971) pointed out, early scientific work in this field had been conducted by physicians with a strong biological outlook (Richard von Krafft-Ebing, Havelock Ellis, and then Sigmund Freud), which more recently could be found in the experimental research of William Masters and Virginia Johnson (1966). Alfred Kinsey and his colleagues (1948, 1953), however, made a great breakthrough with their sociological study of human sexual behavior. Two sociologists who were associated with the Institute for Sex Research (founded by Kinsey), John Gagnon and William Simon, have continued with that sociological orientation by concentrating their attention on social learning. A major contribution they have made is to emphasize characteristics of the social organization of sexual behavior that are unrelated to, or at least do not directly stem from, sexual needs (Gagnon & Simon, 1973). Biological accounts emphasize sexual needs and the many ways in which humans satisfy them; Freud was fond of pointing out the unconscious sexual sublimation and repression evident in everyday life. But it is in the reverse sense—in the contribution of socialization to sexual lifestyles—that one may better understand the part that erotica plays.

First, socialization can help to explain the strong relationship between gender and use of erotica. Users of erotica tend exclusively to be males, or at least this was true until rather recent times. For the most part, erotica has presented a male point of view and male fantasies about sex. In erotica, sex seems to be just around the corner; willing female partners who will perform even the most erotic sexual acts are everywhere. Females, on the other hand, tend to be more aroused by descriptions of sex that take place in a fuller context, such as can be found in general literature.

To explain this difference, Simon and Gagnon (1969) point out that in our society women and men do not receive the same type of sexual training. Women are taught that sex is part of a romantic relationship, whereas men acquire values that relate more closely to sexual inter-course as tension release. In a study of "romance magazines," which are directed toward females, David Sonenschein (1972) discovered that explicit descriptions of sex encounters were usually of the type socially tabooed and that the outcomes were disastrous, thus reinforcing con-ventional notions about the consequences of disapproved sexuality. In addition, women are protected from heterosexual learning (Simon & Gagnon, 1969). Although there are exceptions, it may be that for a young woman the problem in becoming a sexual human is not so much fighting sexual repressions as it is simply learning to be sexual. Thus, the commission findings that physiologically women tended to be as aroused as males but consciously they were not can be explained, first, by the lack of romantic sexual encounters portrayed in erotica and, second, by the lack of recognition of sexual feelings by females.

Second, socialization can help account for the considerable guilt and anxiety that has usually accompanied sex education and practice in Western societies. These feelings are not so much caused by social disapproval; rather, they stem from the fact that sexual matters are rarely discussed in families, with the result that a child has little understanding of the process and effects of sexual maturation. Gagnon and Simon (1967) assert that guilt and anxiety may come to be so closely associated with sexual behavior—for example, masturbation or premarital intercourse—that the two types of sensations become confused. This confusion may account for one of the primary attractions that erotica has for males: its production of feelings closely associated with sex. For middle-aged males whose routine sex lives may have lost excitement, erotica can reactivate feelings of guilt and fear (besides sexual fantasies) that were once closely associated with their earlier, more intensified sexual strivings. Studies show that one of the major reasons for the interest people have in erotica is its forbidden nature. Gagnon and Simon (1967) have reported that the label *pornography* triggers responses that are quite close to the reaction brought on by actual sexual material. The commission's findings that when confronted frequently with erotica, persons become quickly satiated with it, lose interest in it, and develop benign attitudes toward it would be explained by the loss of feelings associated with "forbidden fruit" and illegal "sexual goings-on."

Finally, several studies show a social class relationship to the use of erotica (Commission, 1970a; Nawy, 1973), the patrons of distributional outlets for erotica being predominately white middle-class males. This relationship can be explained by other evidence that points to erotica's importance for sexual fantasy involved in male masturbation (Polsky, 1969; Commission, 1970a; Goldstein & Kant, 1973). Studies show that masturbation is more important in the sexual styles of middle-class than lower-class males. "Manliness" is an important value for lower-class males, and masturbation is less frequent in this group because it is considered to be unmanly (Simon & Gagnon, 1969). Desiring admiration of other males, the lower-class male is more interested in showing his manliness through sexual prowess with women, considering masturbation to be a sign of weakness. Studies of middle-class males, on the other hand, show that not only is masturbation more regularly practiced in adolescence, but it also continues during marriage. For these reasons erotica, with its contribution to sexual fantasy, is more likely to be found in the behavior patterns of middle-class males.

Erotica and Sexual Deviance
What part does erotica play in the lifestyles of sexual deviants? Does erotica cause sexual deviance? These are important questions in the

study of erotica, for the public will be opposed to anything that encourages behavior that is at odds with accepted norms. It is not enough, however, to determine if pornography causes deviance. The decision must then be made if that deviance is harmful to the community.

Results of the public opinion poll done for the Commission on Obscenity and Pornography (1970a, p. 191) showed that 47 percent of the males and 51 percent of the females questioned believed that sexual materials lead people to commit rape. This belief is no doubt at the root of many attempts to suppress erotica, including decisions by the Supreme Court supporting censorship of sexual materials.

Prior to the formation of the commission, few studies existed to provide information on any correlation between erotica and rape. The most important previous research was a comprehensive investigation of sexual offenders by Paul Gebhard, John Gagnon, Wardell Pomeroy, and Cornelia Christenson (1965) of the Kinsey institute. They could find no differences between sex offender and control groups in their uses of erotica, and sex offenders even reported less arousal from sexual materials than did the controls.

The studies that were conducted for the commission all came to similar conclusions. The experience with erotica of sexual offenders is substantially less in both frequency and extent than that of offenders convicted of nonsexual crimes and adult nonoffenders. Michael Goldstein and H. S. Kant (1973) reported that experience with erotica in childhood appears to be about the same for the various subgroups in their study sample—institutionalized sex offenders, homosexuals, transsexuals, pornography users, and controls. However, they found that with adolescence, divergences in experiences with erotica begin to show up, with sex offenders reporting less exposure to erotica.

Rapists, especially, are reported to have come from sexually repressive environments (Goldstein & Kant, 1973, pp. 144–146). There was no discussion of sex in their homes, and little nudity occurred. When interviewed, rapists had great difficulty in discussing sex and reported little enjoyment in heterosexual activities due to heavy feelings of guilt. Similar patterns were found among child molesters (p. 146).

Both homosexuals and adult heavy users of erotica report little exposure to sexual materials during childhood and adolescence and increasingly greater use of them in adulthood (Goldstein & Kant, p. 146). The homosexuals who were interviewed showed an almost obsessive interest in homosexual erotica, especially if they were involved in a homosexual community. Adults who used sexual materials heavily appeared to be compensating for the little exposure they had to erotica in childhood and adolescence. These findings all tend to support the conclusion of Gebhard, Gagnon, Pomeroy, and Christenson (1965) that preexisting interests create a particular orientation toward erotica.

In summary, a person's use of erotica appears to reflect deep-seated, acquired attitudes and feelings about sexuality in general. If an individual has severe feelings of guilt about sex, if he is ambivalent about his own sexuality, or if he has confusion about members of the opposite sex, then his use of erotica will reflect such tendencies and aversions, as will his reactions upon exposure.

It appears that the normal pattern is for adolescent males to be interested in erotica and to seek it out in response to their own sexual maturation. Erotica provides information about sex and stimulates sex drives that are associated with pleasure. The commission studies report that erotica and the peer group are practically the exclusive source of sex education for a high percentage of adult males in our society. However, as the male grows older, he substitutes actual sexual gratification for erotica and develops relationships with the opposite sex. The use of erotic materials will tend to drop off until middle age, when a renewed interest in erotica may be touched off by further modification in sexual lifestyle.

Returning to the original questions concerning effects of erotica on deviant or antisocial behavior, then, we can see that these effects are, if anything, negative. Contrary to what common sense might suggest, there is a negative correlation between exposure to erotica and development of a preference for a deviant form of sexuality. The evidence even indicates that exposure to erotica is salutary, probably providing one of the few sources in society for education in sexual matters.

The experience of Denmark is interesting in this regard. As mentioned earlier, Denmark has removed all restrictions on the sale of erotic materials to persons sixteen years of age and older. Studies of sex crimes in that country have shown that with increased availability of erotica, all forms of sex crimes have decreased. Overall, heterosexual offenses showed a decrease of 61 percent, with rape showing a decline of 48 percent (Commission, 1970a, p. 274). These decreases have not been traced to changes in legislation or in police reporting practices.

Because too many uncontrolled variables are involved, these data cannot be used as evidence to support the hypothesis that the decline in sex crimes was due to increasing availability of erotica. However, the data do offer strong support for the hypothesis that increasing availability does not lead to greater amounts of sex crimes.[7]

THE LEGAL CONTROL OF EROTICA

What legal efforts has American society made to control the existence and distribution of erotica? Are these attempts consistent with American beliefs about pornography? And are they consistent with research findings concerning the potential harm of pornography?

One of the main sources of social control in modern societies is through the institution of law. Disputes over proper social behavior tend to be decided by the enactment of new laws or the reemphasis of old ones. Law, the most formal of various social control mechanisms, generally stands in opposition to less formal means of control; that is to say, law encroaches on customary informal means of handling disputes. The history of legal control of erotica exemplifies this process.

Early Prohibitions on Erotica

Erotica seems to have played an important role in the literature of civilizations and also to have been a considerable source of controversy (see Ginzburg, 1958; Haight, 1970). It is recorded that in 378 *B.C.* Plato urged that youth be allowed to read only an expurgated version of *The Odyssey*.[8] In another historically related case, Ovid was permanently exiled from Rome in *A.D.* 7 by Emperor Augustus Caesar for writing the classic sex instruction manual, *The Art of Love*.

It appears that by the time the English language evolved, erotica was fairly well accepted in Western societies. Early works in English literature carry riddles, stories, and poems that are considered part of the legacy of erotica. *The Exeter Book*, the oldest extant example of Anglo-Saxon literature, contains bawdy riddles that were compiled by a monk (Commission, 1970a). Chaucer's *Canterbury Tales* have been expurgated reading for the young for many decades. Most of this literature was written in a humorous vein. Full-fledged erotica does not appear in English works until the late sixteenth and seventeenth centuries, when the first attempts at legal control were made. Ginzburg (1958) has argued that erotica received a tremendous boost from legal control. There is an analogy to this in modern attempts to control "victimless" crimes through law, which, many contend, only exacerbates the problem when the law is at odds with the behavior of a substantial portion of the population.[9]

The earliest prosecutions for publishing and distributing erotica were based on charges of sedition against the Crown or blasphemy against the Church. Roman Catholicism especially was the target of early erotica, with a major dispute arising over a book entitled *Venus in the Cloister, or the Nun in Her Smock*, by Edmund Curll. It was against this work that the Crown, in 1728, gained its first obscenity conviction. Earlier, in 1708, a case had been brought against *The Fifteen Plagues of a Maidenhead*, but the prosecution had lost because of the legal defense that the book libeled no one. In fact, public acceptance of erotica seems to have been so well ensconced that when Curll's sentence—a pillorying at Charing Cross—was carried out, not one person did him ill in any way. In fact, after he was taken down, the mob carried him off in triumph to a nearby tavern (Ginzburg, 1958, p. 44).

During the latter part of the nineteenth century, Victorian England displayed great concern over public morals and behavior. The first obscenity legislation, which prohibited the dissemination of works because of their lewd content rather than their libel of the Church of the Crown, was enacted in 1824 as part of the Vagrancy Act. In 1853 a statute aimed at prohibiting the importation of erotica from France was enacted. And in 1857 Lord Campbell's Act, the first general statute aimed exclusively at obscenity was passed.

Such legal measures generally follow two developments that contribute to the spread of erotica: the advance in printing techniques and the increasing literacy of that population. Polsky (1969) points out that in the first decade of the nineteenth century, England perfected the Fourdrinier machine for cheap papermaking. In addition, while England's population grew four-fold in ensuing decades, the literate portion of the population increased thirty-two fold. There are several other factors that encouraged erotica and thus gave impetus to legal control of erotica in Victorian England: the rise of the state (Crown) and the decline of the Church as the supreme institution and the corresponding necessity for the state to replace custom with uniform laws for the control of behavior; the fear of satirical erotica undermining the authority of the state; and the development of a lucrative underground market in erotica (which, interestingly enough, arose out of the very existence of antipornography laws).

Antiobscenity Legislation in the United States

These processes had their counterpart in the United States. During the eighteenth century there was no prosecution corresponding to the antireligious obscenity precedent set by the Curll case. The only state that had a law resembling obscenity legislation was Massachusetts, with its Puritan tradition, and there were no recorded convictions under this law until the *Fanny Hill* case in 1821. It was not until the nineteenth century that state obscenity statutes began to proliferate. The Commission on Obscenity and Pornography has found parallels in the forces that led to enactment of British and American antiobscenity laws:

> The proliferation . . . coincided with an increase in literacy among the American population, the beginnings of free universal education, and a decline in the direct influence of the Church over community life (1970a, p. 353).

Howard Becker (1963) has written that wherever rules are instituted, either formally or informally, an investigator should be able to find a person or group that has coordinated the efforts of diverse groups and used the communication media to develop a positive climate of opinion for that rule.[10] This principle is nowhere better illustrated than with the enforcement, beginning in the latter half of the nineteenth century, of obscenity statutes. Becker has applied the term *moral entrepreneur* to enterprising legalists, and America's chief moral entrepreneur in the case of obscenity was Anthony Comstock. Largely at the urging of Protestant groups, New York had passed an obscenity statute in 1868. Few convictions were brought, however, until Comstock, a grocery store clerk, began on his own to investigate local retailers, report them to the prosecutors, and agitate for more restrictive legislation. Comstock joined with other groups, notably the Young Men's Christian Association, and became the chief Washington lobbyist of the Committee for the Suppression of Vice. This group pressured Congress into broadening the 1865 Federal Mail Act to include a prohibition on using the mails for sending lewd or obscene material. Comstock was appointed by President Ulysses S. Grant to an unsalaried position with the Post Office Department, where he was authorized to open any material passing through the mails and personally judge if its content was obscene.

Following the federal legislation against sending erotica through the mails, states that had not yet passed obscenity statutes did so. From 1868 until 1957, most of these statutes were based on a common law test for obscenity that had been taken from *Queen* v. *Hicklin*, an 1868 British case in which material was ruled obscene when "the tendency of the matter charged as obscenity is to deprave and corrupt those whose minds are open to such immoral influences, and into whose hands a publication of this sort may fall."

Until 1957 the Supreme Court did not question the right of the government to control material deemed obscene. Obscenity became a constitutional issue beginning with the Roth decision in 1957, when the court declared that obscene material is outside the protection of the First and Fourteenth Amendments. But the court, by narrowly defining what is obscene and superseding of the definition, undermined existing general obscenity statutes. An important precedent to the Roth case had occurred in the *Ulysses* case of 1933. In the decision by Judge John Woolsey of the U.S. District Court, James Joyce's highly esteemed work was not held to be pornographic because

> in any case where a book is claimed to be obscene it must first be determined, whether the intent with which it was written was what is called, according to the usual phrase, pornographic,—that is, written for the purpose of exploiting obscenity. . . .
>
> But in *Ulysses*, in spite of its unusual frankness, I do not detect anywhere the leer of the sensualist. I hold, therefore, that it is not pornographic.

Likewise, in the Roth case the court decided that the *context* in which allegedly obscene material is presented is just as important as the depictions themselves in determining what is and what is not obscene. The Roth test required that a work be examined "as a whole" in order to

judge whether the "dominant theme" is obscene. Cases since Roth
have attempted to clarify the meaning and application of the terms in
the Roth decision.

In *Memoirs* v. *Massachusetts*, the successful modern effort to publish and distribute *Fanny Hill* legally, three justices developed a tripartite test that came to be used generally by prosecutors in bringing cases
of alleged obscenity to trial.

> Three elements must coalesce: it must be established that (a) the domi-
> nant theme of the material taken as a whole appeals to a prurient interest
> in sex; (b) the material is patently offensive because it affronts contempo-
> rary community standards relating to the description or representation of
> sexual matters; and (c) the material is utterly without redeeming social
> value (Commission, 1970a, p. 369).

Important questions remained unanswered. What is a "community"?
What counts as a "social value"? What is meant by "redeeming"? And
who is qualified to decide the applicability of the tests? If any consistent trend could be found in cases since Roth, it was that legal attempts
to specify distributional activities were constitutionally justified, but
that statutes restricting the access of consenting adults to sexual materials must be so carefully drawn that they are practically ineffectual.

When the Burger Court decided to hear a new group of obscenity
cases in 1972, the legal community anticipated that these problems
with the law of obscenity would be significantly reduced. With the 1973
decision in *Miller* v. *California*, the majority opinion held that material
could be deemed obscene if it met the following test: (1) The average
person, applying contemporary community standards, found that the
work, taken as a whole, appealed to the prurient interest; (2) the work
depicted or described, in a patently offensive way, sexual conduct
specifically defined by the applicable state law, as written or authorita-
tively construed; and (3) the work, taken as a whole, lacked serious
literary, artistic, political, or scientific value. The decision removed the
requirement that the material must be shown to be utterly without
redeeming social value, and it stated that specifically drawn laws
designating which depictions are illegal would serve as fair warning as
to what activities will bring prosecution. Finally, the majority opinion
stated that "contemporary community standards" refers to community

as opposed to national standards, but it did not define the term community. This is where the law on obscenity stands at the present time. The court majority has steadfastly refused to grant writs of *certiorari* (the court requests a case from a lower court) to cases resulting in convictions under the new interpretation in lower courts. Many would say that rather than clear away entangling legal debris, this decision simply added some anew.

The Social Climate and Obscenity Legislation

The legal questions surrounding the control of erotica are interesting to review, but it may be more important to note the social conditions and conflicts of which these legal problems are a manifestation. For several centuries nation-states evolved law as the most important arbitrator of disputes, until it became practically the only means of justice standing between the individual and other citizens. This process is well illustrated by the growing incursion of federal courts into the area of obscenity. Originally, federal courts had left control up to local jurisdictions. By 1957, however, interest groups representing businessmen, publishers, writers, artists, critics, professors of art and literature, and others involved in the manufacture, sale, and consumption of erotic material had generated enough conflict to force the Supreme Court to redress their grievances.

The Supreme Court was aware, however, that local jurisdictions had been bowing to local pressure groups, that public opinion polls showed that a majority of adults desired strict controls, and that decisions favoring a wide dissemination of erotica would be unpopular. The Supreme Court's decisions in these matters have reflected the difficulty of the federal government within the confines of the Constitution to control published material. The court has attempted to limit itself to making "definitions of obscenity" and has left the impetus for control up to local law enforcement. Of course, this is where the problem was in the first place.

Congress tried to gather information on obscenity legislation through the formation of the Commission on Obscenity and Pornography. The commission findings, however, did not support the "social or individual harm" hypothesis that had been the chief justification for legislative control. Reacting to the report of this finding, and without waiting to become acquainted with the research and scholarship on which it was based, President Richard Nixon and congressional leaders announced that they would disregard the commission's recommendations as a basis from which to repeal obscenity legislation. In one of the obscenity cases heard in 1973, Chief Justice Warren Burger voiced an implicit objection to the commission's findings when he stated:

> Although there is no conclusive proof of a connection between antisocial behavior and obscene material, the legislature of Georgia could quite reasonably determine that such a connection does or might exist (1973, p. 459).

At this point, American governmental institutions seem to be caught in the middle of the conflict. There are organized pressure groups urging for tighter controls on erotica, other groups, bolstered by the commission's findings, arguing for repeal of the present laws, and a Supreme Court unwilling to intervene in matters they feel are local issues. Into this limbo have stepped enterprising publishing companies that are literally glutting the urban market with erotica, while law enforcement agencies in smaller communities seek political support from local constituencies by moving against relatively mild forms of sexual display.

What is the outlook? It is quite possible that Congress and lesser legislative bodies are misreading public opinion. The group opposing free access to erotica by adults is large, but the commission discovered that its size is overestimated by legislators, due to the severe pressure that it has generated. Public opinion in favor of strict control is based on the harm hypothesis. Now that the commission has found that adults can have direct experience with erotica without harmful consequences, public opinion will no doubt change toward the acceptance of access to erotica for consenting adults. A similar process has recently been observed in Western European countries that have liberalized their obscenity laws (Kutschinsky, 1970).

It is possible, however, that obscenity laws will not be abolished in the United States. As long as behavioral-scientific findings are systematically disregarded by political leaders, justifications for repealing the laws are missing. More likely, these laws will fall either gradually or quickly, depending on the region, into nonenforcement. For antipornography legislation lacks a wide base of public support, and it is difficult to justify the heavier-than-average expenditure of court resources and law enforcement funds required to bring an obscenity case to court if convictions are not likely.

Indeed, in one of the first cases brought under the newest Supreme Court guidelines—*County of Stanislaus v. Swinging Door Adult Bookstore* (in Modesto, California)—the jury acquitted the defendants because they felt that "local community" standards are equally as hazy as "national" standards. Further, the chief prosecutor in Sacramento announced that he would no longer prosecute obscenity cases because of the expenses involved and the lack of convictions.

CONCLUSIONS: WILL PORNOGRAPHY CONTINUE TO BE A PROBLEM?

The problem of public depiction of sexuality is not a new one. Myths and legends containing explicit descriptions of sexual activities, excretion, and urination occur frequently in preliterate and ancient civilizations. As long as these tales are passed by word of mouth and are therefore subject to informal social controls and customs, erotica does not appear as a social problem. There is speculation as to why public issue develops when these stories are written or published. Censorship of literature, of course, would not be an issue if techniques of writing and publishing had not developed, for ideas can more easily be regulated through the simple control of the individuals possessing the ideas. Imprisonment or exile becomes a major means of control. However, ideas and conceptions are inherently uncontrollable and become an integral part of a culture when they are able to be widely disseminated.

When erotic elements in a culture are reduced to writing, as in the cases of *The Odyssey* or *The Art of Love*, they become separated from the speaker, move further from the control of the state or the governmental institution, and force the latter to develop new types of formal legal control. The development of literacy in the general population is thus a factor that hastens the emergence of censorship. The expansion of modern law from the general areas of libel and breach of the peace to specific censorship of sexual materials follows trends toward mass literacy.

The founders of the United States recognized the power that traditional ways of thought and censorship of ideas had in preventing adaptation and change. For these reasons the Constitution was ratified only after assurances that the adoption of a Bill of Rights would guarantee freedom of the press, speech, and religion. The Supreme Court, however, has long interpreted many of the guarantees of the Bill of Rights as applying only to federal and not state restrictions, and it has held that the founders never believed that speech should be absolutely unbridled in society. Traditionally, freedom of speech does not include nonpolitical or nonreligious expressions that have the potential to produce physical harm. (The classic example of this is the prohibition against yelling "fire" in a crowded theater.) In the case of erotica, though, it is interesting to note that the definition of obscenity long used in legislation was based in a restriction on religious expression, for in the Hicklin case the tract in question, *The Confessional Unmasked,* was clearly an anti-Catholic publication. In finding the material obscene, the court had to choose between the value of freedom of speech and the value of protection of religion.

The political uses of erotica have not disappeared. In defending a tasteless sketch appearing in the student newspaper of the City College of New York, the editor proclaimed that one can only test the validity of freedom of press guarantees by publishing what is certain to be offensive to authorities (Sagarin, 1974). Certainly a purpose of the underground newspaper movement during the latter 1960s was to push out the boundaries of freedom of the press by publishing articles with detailed sexual advice, photos and drawings of sexual scenes, advertisements soliciting group sex and mate swapping, and sexually "kinky" comics, such as *Zap.* Erotica can definitely be a tool for antiestablishment speech and press. Paul Krassner has for years used sexual metaphor for political purposes in his magazine, *The Realist.* And many see the criminal conviction of Ginzburg as a reaction not so much against sexual contact *per se* but against interracial sexual contact. It is this use of sexual metaphor for political ends that causes defenders of the Bill of Rights to recoil at attempts to separate censorship of sexual material from political comment.

Norms change. What is acceptable for publication at one time in history may change drastically in the next generation. The development of obscenity statutes in this country in the latter 1800s was in direct response to publications dealing with sex education and providing birth control information. Today these areas would not be included in a definition of obscene material. The confusing and contradictory decision of the Supreme Court since the Roth decision in 1957 can be understood in terms of the protection of some social values over others, with the court trying to balance the right of individuals to have free access to ideas of all sorts against the feeling that some values have to be defended against public attack. The United States seems to have come to the point where blasphemous speech against religion and seditious comments against the state are generally protected, except where "clear and present danger" can be proved, but sexual depictions are illegal unless it can be shown that they are somehow "redeeming."

Why is sex singled out for this special treatment? Even where no clear and present danger exists, for sexual material to be acceptable it must be shown to have socially redeeming value, according to the standards of the Roth case, or not to "lack serious literary, artistic, political, or scientific value," as stated in the Miller decision. Most of the support for censorship laws must come from people who believe that erotica is socially or individually damaging or that it does involve a clear danger, if not a present or immediate one. Justice William Douglas' comment in his dissenting opinion in *Miller* correctly points out: "As is intimated by the Court's opinion the materials before us may be garbage. But so is much of what is said in political campaigns, in the daily press, on TV or over the radio." Furthermore, the weight of evidence is that erotica does not cause antisocial acts or individual pathologies.

Instead, the evidence tends to support the opposite hypothesis. Early exposure to information and portrayals of sex are associated with normal sexual development. The suppression of sex information or the encouragement of attitudes of "dirtiness" about sex are associated with feelings of guilt and confusion that later promote problems of sexual adjustment. Evidence from the public opinion polls taken by the commission's researchers showed that a surprisingly high percentage of respondents received their own sexual education from erotica. The commission (1970a, p. 315) concluded that (1) most people learn about sex from their peers, and (2) exposure to pornography occurs within the context of the peer group.

As a result of these and other findings from the survey, the commission advocated more frequent and massive sex education in our society. This suggestion was based on the principle that "good" sex information should have a tendency to drive out the "bad." As young people's curiosity about sex is satisfied by sources more acceptable to adults, the influence and interest in erotica should decline, a conclusion supported by findings that persons from families that discussed sex showed less interest in erotica than those persons who received most of their sex information from peer groups (Commission, 1970a, pp. 315–316). Thus, one would expect that public acceptance of sex as a topic of discussion and the increasing availability of erotica would lessen the public influence and need for erotica.

But who will provide the needed sex education? A considerable majority of the public advocates that information first come from parents and then from public schools, physicians, and the clergy, in that order.[11] At this time, however, these groups appear woefully inadequate to the task. The commission found that parents are still rather reluctant to speak of sex to their children. School systems come under attack from right-wing organizations that associate sex education with the "Communist menace" and with moral degeneracy. (Curiously, the Communist countries have been anything but libertarian on this question.) Because of such pressures, several school systems that have undertaken sex education programs have had to cancel or seriously curtail them (Commission, 1970a, p. 319). The commission discovered that very few doctors had received an education in the area of human sexuality, although this may be changing. The training of the clergy has likewise been deficient. The commission found only one seminary in the United States that required courses in human sexuality for its students.

Changes are taking place, though, that should help to increase the number of adults who are willing and able to speak intelligently to children on sexual matters. The tremendous public interest in sexuality, probably a reaction to the many years of hushed talk and secrecy about sex, is making parents more comfortable in talking about sex and is causing medical schools and seminaries to realize how necessary a knowledge of human sexuality is to their students. Sensitive, well-written books about human sexuality are now available that can help adults both to experience sexually fuller lives and to teach their children about sex. Such openness in sexual matters is even likely to affect ultraconservatives who are opposed to both erotica and public discussion of sex. For, as reported earlier in this chapter, persons who are exposed to erotica subsequently are less likely to believe that it has harmful effects. This can be no better illustrated than by the experience of William B. Lockhart, who had written extensively about the harm of erotica and the need for restrictive legislation. Upon serving as chairman for the Commission on Obscenity and Pornography, however, he changed his views about erotica sufficiently to be able to agree with the commission's basic recommendations, including the removal from legislative control of provisions restricting the distribution of erotica to adults.

The increasing openness about sexual matters may not only help erotica to become more acceptable; it may also affect the character of the sexual materials published. One of the most persistent values in American society has been the double standard, which specifies different sexual values and behavior for men and women. Commission studies showing that women advocate stricter controls on all forms of sexual depictions than men do can be explained by the traditional image of woman as the protector of important social values and the "cement" that holds the family together. Paula Johnson and Jacqueline Goodchilds (1973, p. 236) feel that women may show more disgust with pornography not because it turns them off sexually but because it often turns them on! What are they to do, faced with the value that women are not supposed to have the sexual needs that men have and should therefore not need to seek out sexual gratification?

With the new sexual frankness, however, the double standard seems to be disappearing. According to Ira Reiss (1969), the new norm that is increasingly replacing it is one of permissiveness with affection for both men and women. Sexual attitudes of men and women are becoming more similar because women are accepting their own sexuality and men are recognizing that sex is or can be a part of social relationships. Such attitudes cannot help but affect erotica, which has always reflected the male-oriented sexual values of the society. The material portrayed in erotica has stemmed from male sexual fantasies, with the women being either "lily white" innocents or sexually promiscuous "ladies of the night" (Johnson & Goodchilds, 1973, p. 235). Thus, traditional pornography themes have been concerned with sexually ignorant maidens who, forced into sex, experience utter joy, or with sexually promiscuous individuals who become "tamed" by "real men." If sexual values of men change, these images of female sex in pornography can be expected to decline as well. Furthermore, as women become—and are allowed to become—more sexually assertive, pornography will probably reflect female as well as male concerns, and a market for female-centered erotica may well develop.

Other changes in the character of erotica can be expected. There will probably be a trend toward what is termed erotic art and away from hard-core pornography. Depictions of sexuality may increasingly incorporate human feelings and take place more often in the context of everyday social living. What this trend embodies is a return to the acceptance of erotica as a central part of culture and social living. As people turn away from depictions of male fantasies and myths about female sexual masochism and subservience, and turn toward more realistic portrayals of sex that reflect both the concerns of the culture and general entertainment values, erotica may once again be regarded in a benign fashion.

These trends assume, though, that erotica will be able to evolve in a free atmosphere. This may not happen. As erotica has become increasingly acceptable, counterforces have been mustered that attempt to keep erotica under the control of the more conservative elements in the community. Armed with moral convictions and legal precedents set by a Supreme Court dominated by Nixon appointees, local citizens and district attorneys are once again attempting to suppress erotica. For instance, the Georgia courts are presently reviewing the obscenity conviction of a local theater manager who showed the movie *Carnal Knowledge* (rated R), considered by many critics to be one of the best movies of 1971. Citizen groups that crusade against erotica may misjudge the attitudes of the community and consider public opinion against erotica to be much greater than it actually is (Commission, 1970a, p. 38). They will usually win their case, though, because persons in the community are generally reluctant to speak out in favor of the free trade in erotica for fear of social condemnation. It is difficult to defend the view that erotica appears, on the basis of existing evidence, to be harmless and even socially beneficial when the weight of traditional points of view is against one.

If the forces of suppression win out, then the "problem of pornography" will remain with Americans for the foreseeable future. The underground market, spurred by promises of large profits, will continue to operate, and in order to satisfy the continuing curiosity of the public, the pornography producers will put on the market erotica depicting less socially acceptable themes than could have been expected if restrictions on erotica were lifted. Indeed, A. B. Smith and Harriet Pollack, commenting on a poll (Yankelovich, 1973) showing that 53 percent of the sample favored stricter enforcement against pornography, assert:

> These responses can mean only one thing: that despite our signal failure to control this kind of behavior punitively the general public knows of no other response but more of the same—more of the same unsuccessful punitive approaches that have failed in the past. The public needs to be shown that there is a way out of the frustration, fear, and failure that are the results of the criminalization of modes of conduct that should be handled nonpunitively. Our blind use of the penal code is self-defeating. There are other ways, decent, kindlier, more compassionate and above all, more effective ways. It is time to try them (1975, p. 162).

NOTES

1. Readers interested in a summary of the legislative steps that led to the formation of the commission and the role that behavioral science was to play in its creation are referred to Wilson (1973).

2. This discovery emerged with the study by Malinowski (1960) of the Trobriand Islanders.

3. For a review of the logic and procedures of functional analysis, see Merton (1968).

4. The French writer Mirabeau once wrote an aside to readers in one of his pornographic novels, "Eh bien, lis, dévore, et branle-toi." Translated: "And now, read, devour, and masturbate" (Collier, 1968, p. 23).

5. For analysis of the theoretical divergences between structural-functionalism and conflict theory, see Chambliss (1973, pp. 1–38).

6. According to Gusfield, the struggle for cultural dominance is not the only motivation of the liberalization forces. He points out that "the permissive and legitimizing movement must also be seen as a prevalent way in which deviants throw off the onus of their actions and avoid the sanctions associated with immoral activities" (1967, p. 72).

7. Evidence shows that the availability of erotica and rates of violent crime will vary from time to time and place to place, thus indicating that other variables are at work. But the data from Denmark indicate that the two variables are not necessarily related.

8. Incidentally, Ginzburg (1958, p. 22) points out that Senator Estes Kefauver suggested the same censorship approximately two thousand years later.

9. These are consensual crimes in that the parties are willing participants. Since the illegal behavior is considered to hurt no one but themselves, the justification for legal control lacks a primary element of the common-law tradition, that is, the existence of a party whose person or property has undergone injury. For a discussion, see Schur (1965).

10. Lemert (1972, p. 19) has pointed out that Becker's proposition cannot be applied to all legal definitions. Instead, it most nearly illustrates legal attempts

to solve public issues characterized by ambivalence, value conflict, and the absence of victimization. Examples of such issues are pornography, drug use, gambling, and prostitution.

11. Public opinion poll information reported that 57 percent of the males and 54 percent of the females would support dissemination of sex information by the schools.

BIBLIOGRAPHY

Abelson, H., R. Cohen, E. Heaton, and C. Suder. "Public Attitudes Towards and Experience with Erotic Materials." In Commission on Obscenity and Pornography. *Technical Reports*, vol. 6. Washington, D.C.: U.S. Government Printing Office, 1970, pp. 1–137.

Becker, Howard S. *Outsiders: Studies in the Sociology of Deviance.* New York: The Free Press, 1963.

Becker, Howard, and Harry E. Barnes. *Social Thought from Lore to Science,* vol. 2. New York: Dover, 1961.

Beserra, Sarah S., Nancy M. Jewel, and Melody W. Matthews. *Sex Code of California.* A report of the Public Education and Research Committee. Sausalito, Calif.: Graphic Arts of Marin, 1973.

Burger, Warren. "Decision." *Paris Adult Theatre I.* v. *Slaton,* 37 L Ed 2d 446, 1973.

Chambliss, William J. *Sociological Readings in the Conflict Perspective.* Reading, Mass.: Addison-Wesley, 1973.

Collier, Peter. "Pirates of Pornography." *Ramparts,* 1968, 7:17–23.

Commission on Obscenity and Pornography. *Report.* New York: Bantam Books, 1970a.

Commission on Obscenity and Pornography. *Technical Reports,* vol. 3. Washington, D.C.: U.S. Government Printing Office, 1970b.

Davis, Kingsley. "The Sociology of Prostitution." *American Sociological Review,* 1937, 2:744–755.

Erikson, Kai T. "Notes on the Sociology of Deviance." *Social Problems,* 1962, 9:307–314.

Freud, Sigmund. *Civilization and Its Discontents.* London: Hogarth Press, 1930.

Gagnon, John H., and William Simon. "Pornography—Raging Menace or Paper Tiger?" *Trans-action,* 1967, 4:41–48.

Gagnon, John H., and William Simon. *Sexual Conduct: The Social Sources of Human Sexuality.* Chicago: Aldine, 1973.

Gallup, George. "Pornography." *Gallup Opinion Index: Political, Social and Economic Trends,* Report No. 49. Princeton, N.J.: Gallup International Inc., 1969, pp. 16–24.

Gebhard, Paul H., John H. Gagnon, Wardell B. Pomeroy, and Cornelia V. Christenson. *Sex Offenders: An Analysis of Types.* New York: Harper & Row, 1965.

Ginzburg, Ralph. *An Unhurried View of Erotica.* New York: Helmsman Press, 1958.

Ginzburg, Ralph. *Castrated: My Eight Months in Prison.* New York: Avant-Garde Books, 1973.

Goldstein, Michael J., and Harold S. Kant. *Pornography and Sexual Deviance.* Berkeley, Calif.: University of California Press, 1973.

Gusfield, Joseph R. "Moral Passage: The Symbolic Process in Public Designations of Deviance." *Social Problems,* 1967, 15:175–188.

Haight, Anne. *Banned Books,* 3rd ed. New York: Bowker, 1970.

Hall, Calvin S., and Gardner Lindzey. *Theories of Personality.* New York: John Wiley and Sons, 1957.

Harris, Louis. *Time Morality Poll.* New York: Harris and Associates, May 1969.

Howard, J. L., C. B. Reifler, and M. B. Kiptzin. "Effects of Exposure to Pornography." *Technical Reports,* vol. 8. Commission on Obscenity and Pornography, Washington, D.C.: U.S. Government Printing Office, 1970, pp. 214–215.

Johnson, Paula, and Jacqueline D. Goodchilds. "Pornography, Sexuality, and Social Psychology." *Journal of Social Issues,* 1973, 29:231–238.

Kinsey, Alfred C., Wardell B. Pomeroy, and Clyde E. Martin. *Sexual Behavior in the Human Male.* Philadelphia: Saunders, 1948.

Kinsey, Alfred C., Wardell B. Pomeroy, Clyde E. Martin, and Paul H. Gebhard. *Sexual Behavior in the Human Female.* Philadelphia: Saunders, 1953.

Kutschinsky, Berl. "Pornography in Denmark: Pieces of a Jigsaw Puzzle Collected Around New Year 1970." In Commission on Obscenity and Pornography. *Technical Reports,* vol. 4. Washington, D.C.: U.S. Government Printing Office, 1970, pp. 263–288.

Lemert, Edwin M. *Human Deviance, Social Problems, and Social Control,* 2nd ed. Englewood Cliffs, N.J.: Prentice-Hall, 1972.

MacBean, James Roy. "Sex and Politics." *Film Quarterly,* 1972, 25:2–13.

Malinowski, Bronisław. *Argonauts of the Western Pacific.* New York: E. P. Dutton, 1960.

Masters, William H., and Virginia E. Johnson. *Human Sexual Response.* Boston: Little, Brown, 1966.

Merton, Robert K. *Social Theory and Social Structure.* New York: The Free Press, 1968.

Nawy, Harold. "In the Pursuit of Happiness?: Consumers of Erotica in San Francisco." *Journal of Social Issues,* 1973, 29(3):147–161.

Packard, Vance. *The Sexual Wilderness.* New York: David McKay, 1968.

Polsky, Ned. *Hustlers, Beats, and Others.* New York: Doubleday, Anchor Books, 1969.

Reiss, Ira L. "Premarital Sexual Standards." In Carlfred B. Broderick and Jessie Bernard, eds. *The Individual, Sex, and Society.* Baltimore: Johns Hopkins Press, 1969, pp. 109–118.

Sagarin, Edward. "Sex Research and Sociology: Retrospective and Prospective." In James M. Henslin, ed. *Studies in the Sociology of Sex.* New York: Appleton-Century-Crofts, 1971.

Sagarin, Edward. "On Banning the Beautiful and Showing the Ugly." *The Humanist,* 1974, 34(2):22–25.

San Francisco Chronicle, June 4, 1974, p. 14.

Schur, Edwin M. *Crimes Without Victims: Deviant Behavior and Public Policy—Abortion, Homosexuality and Drug Addiction.* Englewood Cliffs, N.J.: Prentice-Hall, 1965.

Simon, William, and John H. Gagnon. "Psychosexual Development." *Transaction,* 1969, 6:9–17.

Smith, A. B., and Harriet Pollack. *Some Sins Are Not Crimes.* New York: Franklin Watts, 1975.

Sonenschein, David. "Love and Sex in the Romance Magazines." In George H. Lewis, ed. *Side-Saddle on the Golden Calf: Social Structure and Popular Culture in America.* Pacific Palisades, Calif.: Goodyear, 1972, pp. 66–74.

Sorokin, Pitirim. *The American Sex Revolution.* Boston: Sargent, 1956.

Sorokin, Pitirim. *Social and Cultural Dynamics.* New York: E. P. Dutton, 1957.

Toynbee, Arnold J. *A Study of History.* London: Oxford University Press, 1961.

Wilson, W. Cody. "Pornography: The Emergence of a Social Issue and the Beginning of Psychological Study." *Journal of Social Issues,* 1973, 29:7–17.

Yankelovich, Daniel, and others. *The New Morality.* New York: McGraw-Hill, 1974.

ELEVEN
Suicide

NORMAN L. FARBEROW
Veterans Administration Wadsworth Hospital Center, Los Angeles

Suicide is deceptively easy to define. A suicide occurs when a person kills himself; thus it is death by one's own hand. *Webster's Third New International Dictionary* defines suicide as "the act or instance of taking one's own life voluntarily." This definition, nevertheless, leads to confusion when we consider all the situations to which we apply the term. For example, Nero ordered an attendant to kill him, so his "suicide" was not death by his own hand. Seneca was ordered by Nero to take his own life, so his death was not voluntary. Finally, *seppuku* (often called *hara-kiri*) was practically obligatory for Japanese nobility and samurai when their failure caused loss or defeat to their emperor or lord.

Even more confusion arises with the word *suicidal*. Unlike the word from which it is derived, suicidal can refer to some state of being or feeling other than death. Further, the word suicidal is used to describe a wide variety of situations. For example, suicidal might refer to an overt act, such as physical self-injury, or to a verbal statement, such as a threat to do away with oneself, or to obsessive ruminations on how life has lost its meaning. Suicidal is also used in confusing temporal contexts. It might describe a person who has injured himself in the past, who is engaging in self-injury right now, or who, it is predicted, will be self-destructive in the future. It may also be any combination of these.

Some progress has been made in defining suicide by using the criterion of intention—that is, whether a person intends by his actions that death or self-injury should occur. Difficulties still occur, however, such as when we must take unconscious intention into account (Shneidman, 1963).

Suicide includes a wide range of behavior. The continuum of suicidal activities covers total self-destruction, or death; nonlethal self-injury, such as crippling, maiming, stabbing, cutting, swallowing corrosive materials, and the like; threats and other verbal statements of intention toward self-destruction; feelings of despair, depression, and unhappiness; and thoughts of separation, departure, absence, and relief and release. Somewhere along this continuum the thought or impulse becomes translated into action.

The clinical impression is that once the defenses have been breached for the first time and the action has occurred, the possibility exists that acting-out will occur more readily on another, future occasion of severe emotional tension and strain. At one time it was assumed that increasingly serious (lethal) behavior results in repeated attempts at self-destruction. However, research has indicated that this is not always true. Psychiatric treatment after the first attempt often significantly reduces the seriousness of subsequent attempts. In a reported study it was found that if treatment was obtained at the time of the first attempt, subsequent attempts were less lethal; if no treatment or minimal treatment was received, the later attempts were likely to be more serious (Worden & Sterling-Smith, 1973).

Suicide is only one kind of death the coroner must certify. It differs from the other kinds of death—natural, accident, and homicide—in that to certify a death as suicide, the coroner must determine that the victim initiated the act for the purpose of dying and with the awareness that his actions would cause his own death. In other words, the role of the person in his own death is maximal. In contrast, the person supposedly plays no role in his own death when he dies from natural causes (for instance, pneumonia), from homicide (perhaps as the victim of an armed assault), or from a car accident. There is, however, good clinical evidence suggesting that many deaths certified as natural, accident, or homicide involve a significant contribution by the deceased. Examples are the heart patient who shovels heavy snow, the traffic accident victim who was driving at high speeds, and the armed robber who deliberately resists police fire. Nevertheless, deaths during such events are not certified as suicide.

There are also people who live borderline, self-destructive lives, shortened by self-neglect or self-abuse. They may disregard doctor's orders or fail to follow a medical regimen recommended for control of a chronic condition such as diabetes or heart trouble (Farberow, Stein, Darbonne, & Hirsch, 1970). Likewise, they may engage in excessive risk taking, as in compulsive gambling. These are some of the reasons that social scientists view with great caution published statistics on suicide deaths.

Another important reason for caution in interpreting suicide statistics is the emotion evoked by a suicide. The mere mention of the word suicide today in most of the Western world arouses attitudes of guilt, shame, or embarrassment or ideas of cowardice, dishonor, and weakness. Suicide is a taboo subject, often talked about only in whispers. A suicide in the family is rarely admitted, and the survivors often feel they have been bequeathed a heavy burden. Interestingly enough, people in other parts of the world, such as Scandinavia or Japan, do not have the same feelings about suicide. There have even been some parts of the world where suicide has been unknown, as in some of the South Sea islands and in the Hindu Kush Mountains of India.

SUICIDE IN HISTORY

An overview of suicide in history indicates that the suicide rate has varied in inverse proportion to the extent of social controls and the accompanying emphasis on the value of the individual in comparison with the state (Farberow, 1972b). Put more simply, when the controls were great, the rate was lower; when the individual was more free, the rate was higher. In the high-control eras the attitudes toward suicide stemmed from emotional, nonrational aspects; in the low-control periods rationality, individuality, and democratic processes were idealized.

In primitive and precivilized cultures, which are characterized by a highly structured society, death, and especially suicide, has always been a taboo subject. One consequence was the development of rituals to ward off the evil of the transgression. Many of these rituals have carried over into later customs. For example, the English custom of burying a suicide victim at a crossroads (not legally abolished until 1823) was directly linked to the primitive custom of burying at a crossroads an infant who had been born feet first and so was considered unclean.

Two other reasons for the growth of the strong feeling of revulsion surrounding suicide were, first, the fact that a man was rejecting all the things he prized showed a contempt for society, compelling society to question everything it valued. Second, a suicide deprived the tribe of a useful warrior or a potential mother.

Oriental sacred writing contained many contradictions about suicide. While it was encouraged in some religions, it was vigorously condemned in others. Brahmanism institutionalized and sanctioned *suttee*, a ceremonial sacrifice of widows that was as common in China as in India. The Brahman doctrine was sympathetic to suicide, for this act was consonant with denial of the flesh, a common objective in philosophies of the Orient. By divorcing the body from the soul, the soul might occupy itself only with supersensual realities. Buddhism accepted suicide as a means by which to extinguish craving or passion so that life's chief purpose of acquisition of knowledge could be achieved. In Japan suicide became embedded in the national tradition and eventually developed into the highly ritualized act of *seppuku*, as well as *shuniju*, or lovers' suicide, and *junshi*, the practice of following one's master into death (Porterfield, 1968, p. 40). On the other hand, Mohammedanism always condemned suicide with the utmost severity, for one of the cardinal teachings of Mohammed was that the Divine Will was expressed in different ways and man must submit himself at all times.

Suicide among the Jews was generally rare. The Old Testament emphasized the value of life for the Jew, who was permitted to transgress every religious commandment to save his life, with but three exceptions: murder, the denial of God, and incest. According to the law set forth in the Torah, suicide was wrong, and the victim and his family were punished by denial of a regular burial and the customary rituals of mourning. However, suicide was acceptable under extreme conditions, such as in apostasy, ignominy, and disgrace of capture or torture.

While the Old Testament does not specifically condemn suicide, neither does it promise a happy afterlife, which may be one reason that it notes only five suicides: Abimelech (Judges 9:54), who killed himself to avoid having it recorded that he was mortally wounded when hit by a rock thrown by a woman; Samson (Judges 16:28–31), whose hair grew back, allowing him to regain strength to pull down the pillars of the temple of the Philistines, killing them and himself in the process; Saul (Samuel 31:1–6) and his armor bearer, who killed themselves rather than be taken captive after the victory of the Philistines; and Ahitophel (Samuel 17:1), whose betrayal of David failed.

The first known document dealing entirely with suicide is an ancient Egyptian text entitled *The Dialogue of a Misanthrope with His Own Soul,* in which a man tired of life tries to convince his soul to accompany him in death. The soul hesitates because it is afraid the man will be deprived of a proper funeral and thus will ruin the soul's chances of a blissful afterlife.

The early Greeks, especially the Stoics and Epicureans, considered suicide a natural and fitting solution to many unhappy situations, such as dishonor or unrequited love. One of the better known is the suicide of Dido, the founder and queen of Carthage, who killed herself when Aeneas, one of the outstanding defenders of Troy, left her. Suicide to avoid the pain of sickness or old age was also considered acceptable. Pliny the Elder viewed the existence of poisonous herbs as a proof of a kindly Providence because it allowed men to die painlessly and quickly. Zeno, the founder of Stoic philosophy, lived until he was ninety-eight, apparently without meeting a situation to warrant taking his own life. At that age, however, he fell and put a toe out of joint, disgusting him enough to go home and hang himself.

Among the Romans, suicide induced by pain, sickness, or grief was exempt from punishment, but suicide committed "without cause" was punishable. It was especially forbidden when interests of the state were involved or property rights were affected, as when soldiers deprived the state of their services by killing themselves or when a slave committed suicide. Suicide to avoid execution was frequent inasmuch as the property of those officially executed was confiscated by the state. Nero's order to his teacher Seneca to commit suicide (Seneca was suspected of plotting against him) thus appears as a kindness, since it allowed his family to keep his considerable fortune.

The advent of Christianity brought marked changes in attitudes toward suicide. At first there were many suicides by early Christians, especially by martyrs who found the attraction of an afterlife in paradise greater than the hardships of their life on earth. The Church could ill afford to lose so many of its supporters at that time, and a quick halt to the rash of suicides was brought about in the fourth century by St. Augustine, who codified the Church's official disapproval of suicide by placing it in a moral framework and condemning it as a grievous sin. As a result, in the Middle Ages, from about the fourth to the thirteenth centuries (when the Catholic Church held great sway in Europe), suicide became practically unknown. In the thirteenth century, in his great writings about Church and God, *Summa Theologica*, Thomas Aquinas (1947) further specified the Church's attitude toward suicide, condemning it as an unnatural act and a usurpation of God's power to dispose at His discretion man's life, death, and resurrection.

The Renaissance in the fourteenth and fifteenth centuries brought about a new awareness of life's beauties at the same time that it brought home the transitory nature of life. An emergence of individualism led to an increasing emphasis on personal freedom, including the decision to end one's own life. Shakespeare's eight tragedies contain no less than fourteen suicides. This period also found social attitudes developing from economic values. Poverty, which had been accepted as a natural state during the Middle Ages, began to be associated with sin and unworthiness as a result of the rise of Puritanism, the industrial revolution, and the incorporation of the Protestant Ethic into Anglo-Saxon culture.

Although suicide continued to be condemned throughout the next era, there were some philosophers who challenged this attitude. In his 1644 work, *Biothanatos*, John Donne (1930) argued that the power and mercy of God were great enough to remit the sin of suicide. David Hume (1929) stated in 1777 that a suicide does not do society any harm; the person only ceases to do good. And Merian (1763) saw suicide as neither a sin nor a crime nor evidence of weakness, but rather as a disease. He thus introduced for the first time the idea of mental derangement and emotional disturbance as significant factors in suicide.

Legal attitudes toward suicide have developed from canonical law. Changes indicating a softening in attitude toward suicide have been slow in appearing, with most changes being relatively recent. In the fourteenth and fifteenth centuries, the laws in many countries reflected the horror that suicide aroused. For example, in England early law directed that a stake be driven through the heart of any suicide and the body be buried at a crossroads. Desecration of the corpse and forfeiture of estate were practiced in Germany. It was 1961 before England repealed its law making attempted suicide a crime, and Canada repealed its similar law in June 1972. In the United States, which inherited its legal code from England, attempted suicide is still a crime in nine states, while aiding and abetting suicide is a crime in eighteen states.

THEORIES OF SUICIDE

No one theory as yet satisfactorily explains the wide range of self-destructive behavior subsumed under suicide. In the search for "causes" or correlated variables, researchers have turned up literally hundreds of factors, sometimes singly, sometimes in combination. In a bibliography on suicide (Farberow, 1972a), among the correlates of suicide listed were abortion, alcoholism, climate, cranial injury, depressive states, diabetes, drug addiction, epilepsy, heredity, Huntington's chorea, impulse, insanity, menstruation, obsession or compulsion, pathological anatomy, pregnancy, schizophrenia, sex and its perversions, sunspots, tuberculosis, twilight affective state, weather, and many others (Porterfield, 1968, p. 35). Obviously, there is a great need for synthesizing approaches that would look for common denominators. Since suicide is recognized as stemming from personal problems, it is clearly a problem for psychology; and since it is also recognized as directly related to social conditions, it is an appropriate problem for sociology. The two great names that emerge in these fields are Sigmund Freud, who took the psychological approach, and Emile Durkheim, who presented a sociological view.

Psychological Theories

Freudian Approaches.   Freud's early psychoanalytic conceptualization of suicide (1950b) described it as the result of extreme depression combined with rage. A close relationship with another person results in the introjection of that person into one's own personality, a kind of process in which the other person becomes a "part of the self." However, any intimate relationship with another person involves ambivalence—that is, contradictory feelings, such as like and dislike, love and hate, toward that person. These feelings are also introjected. If the love object has been lost and anger or frustration results, the person may act against this introjected component of himself. Thus, suicide is retroflexed rage, that is, anger directed at the introjected lost love object but acted out against the self. Of course, most people suffer loss of love objects and do not kill themselves, although they will mourn, grieve, and even go through a depression. However, the suicidal person is postulated as narcissistic and generally less mature and therefore as unable to transfer an attachment to another object without great difficulty.

This formulation of the dynamics of suicide, derived from studies of mourning and depression, did not completely satisfy Freud. Later, he developed his more complicated and highly developed theory of suicide as an expression of the death instinct (see Freud, 1950a). Freud argued that humans were born with two basic instincts—the life instinct, *Eros*, and the death instinct, *Thanatos*—and that these exerted their hierarchically organized psychic forces at all times. According to Freud, everyone is somewhat vulnerable to suicide, for the pressure of the death instinct might increase at any time, depending upon internal and external events. The extreme helplessness of the human ego, he felt, is never completely overcome, so that there is always a readiness under conditions of great stress to regress to more primitive ego states (Litman & Tabachnick, 1968).

Karl Menninger (1938) became the best-known protagonist of Freud's death instinct proposal. He hypothesized suicide as the winning out of the death instinct over the life instinct, of the destructive tendencies over the constructive tendencies, under conditions of stress and conflict. Menninger believed that three elements could be found in varying degrees in all self-destructive behavior: (1) the wish to kill, derived from primary aggressiveness; (2) the wish to be killed, modified from primary aggressive impulses; and (3) the wish to die, derived from primary aggressiveness and additional sophisticated motives. Menninger also categorized other forms of self-destruction, including those that did not end in immediate death but rather that resulted in life-shortening, life-negating behavior. There are, for example, *chronic suicides*, involving asceticism, invalidism, and drug and alcohol addiction; *focal suicides*, in which the self-destructive force is focused on a particular part, organ, or system of the body, as seen in self-mutilations, polysurgery, purposive accidents, malingering, impotence, and frigidity; and *organic suicides*, wherein some forms of organic disease represent unconscious conflicts between aggression, self-punishment, or guilt and erotic components of the tendency toward self-destruction. In such cases, the parts, organs, or systems of the body seem to be "used" by the person against himself to form symptoms severe enough to indicate that more is operative than merely the physiological components themselves.

Other Psychoanalytic Explanations. Alfred Adler (1937) put forward an individual psychology describing the person's strivings to overcome his innate inferiority. As he fails in this, he attacks others, casts reproach upon those he feels are responsible for his loss of self-esteem, and attempts to hurt others by hurting himself. By his act of self-destruction, the suicide hopes to evoke sympathy for himself. Adler described the potential suicide as the inferiority-ridden person who "hurts others by dreaming himself into injuries or by administering them to himself." The potential suicide thinks too much of himself and too little of others, and as a result he is unable sufficiently to play, function, live, and die with others. He has an exaggerated estimate of his own worth and always expects results that are favorable for him. Social interest, an important element in mature development, is lacking.

As explained by Bruno Klopfer (1961), Carl Jung considered the self-destructive act to be an effort at rebirth, to reflect an unconscious longing for spiritual regeneration. Suicide would thus be a way of escaping the intolerable conditions of the present. Jung's conceptualization contains the symbolism of the crucifixion—death brings its reward of new life with resurrection. Klopfer adds his own notion of a "floating island" ego, in which impulsive, completely unanticipated, self-destructive urges might erupt because of the lack of controls.

James Hillman (1964), a Jungian psychoanalyst, and Thomas Szasz (1972), a psychiatrist, forcefully defend the individual's right to kill himself. They deplore the moralistic attitudes and the "ridiculous idea" that suicide must be prevented at all costs. They feel that religious and legal traditions have prevented active thought about suicide and hence a full understanding of it. Hillman believes that "[b]ecause suicide is a way of entering death and because the problem of entering death releases the most profound fantasies of the human soul, *to understand a suicide we need to know what mythic fantasy is being enacted*" (1964, pp. 51–52).

Harry Stack Sullivan (see Green, 1961) and Karen Horney (see De Rosis, 1961) have more interpersonal orientations. Sullivan postulated an interpersonal theory of psychology in which the subject evaluates himself in terms of the reactions of significant others toward him. When his security is threatened and his unresolved conflicts and attitudes become unbearable, the individual wishes to transfer the "bad me" into the "not me." Suicide represents the individual's hostile attitude toward other people—the outer world—redirected against the self.

Horney felt that culture, religion, politics, and other similar forces conspire to distort the child's self-development, engendering a state of basic anxiety. Because of this basic anxiety, the world is a hostile place to live in. Suicide results from a childish dependency and from deep-rooted feelings of inferiority. The suicide may be a "performance suicide," arising from a sense of failure to meet the standards expected by society.

Gregory Zilboorg (1936) felt that suicide is a way of thwarting outside sources that are making living impossible. Suicide also illustrates the paradox of "living by killing oneself." By this act one may gain immortality and fame, thus maintaining the ego rather than destroying it. William O'Connor (1947–1948) also stressed the immortality aspect, stating that the suicide of the depressed patient is a kind of return to early power-narcissism and omnipotence.

Nonpsychoanalytic Theories.   Some of the nonpsychoanalytic psychological theorists have focused on other factors. Hugh Crichton-Miller (1931) saw suicide as a failure of adaptation and a final regression from reality. There are many exaggerated fears, doubts, and dreads that people must live with throughout their lives. For suicidal persons, the anticipation of pain is much more powerful than the pain itself. Joseph Teicher (1947) argues that individuals who attempt suicide have developed aggressive patterns of reaction to situations provoking insecurity; they then turn these aggressions inward because of their insecurities. Suicide thus becomes an infantile, exhibitionistic protest and an act of hostility against a harsh, restraining figure. Lauretta Bender and Paul Schilder (1937) studied attempted suicide in children under thirteen and found that the most common motivating factor was spite. Suicide for children was an attempt to escape an unbearable situation involving the deprivation of love. Aggressive tendencies were provoked that in turn aroused guilt feelings. The aggressive feelings then were directed against the self. The attempts also constituted a punishment against the children's surroundings and a method of obtaining a greater amount of love. Nolan Lewis (1933, 1934) attributed suicide to the final breakdown of the adaptive process in psychobiological development. For him suicide was not being able to adapt in the midst of so-called higher-level contradictions because of some lack of compensatory adjustment.

George Kelly (1961) approached suicide from the framework of his theory of personal constructs, which assumes that we impose on life's events the uniqueness of our own thinking. Thus, every person makes his own "reality" and in turn validates it in relation to his own personal constructs. For each suicide, the question has to be asked: What was he trying to validate by his action? The choice of death by any one person can be understood only from the point of view of that person's constructs. Important in the understanding of suicide are (1) the basic postulate and choice corollary, or the psychological channeling of a person's processes by the way in which he anticipates events, with the tendency to choose alternatives that seem to provide more validity to his construct system; (2) dilation versus constriction, or overinclusion versus overexclusion of pertinent events in the hope of making better sense out of what is happening; (3) a sense of chaos and anxiety with feelings of helplessness; (4) a sense of threat that emanates from finding oneself on the brink of deeply significant change; (5) efforts to extort evidence of validity from the environment in order to preserve the status quo; and (6) guilt, resulting from the feeling that one no longer has any significant, meaningful role to play.

The Suicide Note.   Much of suicidal behavior can be viewed as a distorted, desperate attempt to communicate feelings, mood, and state of mind. The clinical impression is that the suicidal person is looking for a way in which to emphasize the suffering and anguish that he is experiencing. Not only is the suicidal act itself a communication, but often the person will leave a suicide note. Suicide notes have been studied in detail by a number of investigators (Shneidman & Farberow, 1957; Osgood & Walker, 1959; Capstick, 1960; Tuckman, Kleiner, & Lavell, 1960; Jacobs, 1967; Darbonne, 1969; and Frederick, 1969). In general, investigators report that the proportion of suicide cases leaving notes ranges from 10 to 25 percent. However, the study by Norman Farberow and Edwin Shneidman (1961b) indicated an incidence of approximately 37 percent.

The content of the note is directed to a significant other—the person with whom the suicidal individual is most involved—or to the community in general. The content will depend to a large degree on the target of the communication. Thus, it may contain statements of despair; explanations for the act; expiation of guilt and responsibility; relief of culpability in others; placement of blame; description of thoughts, feelings, and attitudes while going through the experience; or some other content. The message may vary from "the cry for help" epitomized in the title of the book by Farberow and Shneidman (1961a) to statements of despair and "the end of hope" (Kobler & Stotland, 1964).

Sociological Theories

The sociologist approaches problems such as suicide by examining what roles and statuses a person in the social system has and how they organize, or fail to organize, that person's life. While the sociologist is aware of individual states of mind, the contention is that these are derived from the collective features of society.

The classic sociological study of suicide is Emile Durkheim's work of 1897, from which most later theories have sprung as attempts either to modify or to reformulate his original concepts. Durkheim's work has been so influential that it has been erroneously regarded as the first major sociological treatise on the subject. Actually, there were earlier essays on suicide (see, for example, Esquirol, 1845; Morselli, 1882), and in fact Durkheim was writing primarily in response to these works.

Durkheim's Theory of Suicide. Durkheim's emphasis was on the forces of cohesiveness and consensus. Nineteenth-century writers before him had either taken a moralistic and individualistic approach to suicide and emphasized nonsocial factors, such as psychopathology, climate, or race, or had attempted to show a link between suicide and individual social factors, such as economic status, fluctuations in the economy, rural versus urban residence, and others. In contrast, Durkheim attempted to integrate all the social factors into a general theory. He thus eliminated the need for a number of special theories to account for differences among specific populations. For Durkheim, two characteristics of society are primary: social integration and social regulation. Together or singly, and most especially at their extremes, these two variables determine social conditions that in turn determine suicide rates.

The first type of suicide that Durkheim suggested is based on the factor of social integration. A high rate of *egoistic suicides* occur in social groups that have the lowest degrees of social integration and, consequently, an excessive amount of individuation. Egoism generally characterizes unmarried people and Protestants, for example.

Social integration also plays the most important role in Durkheim's second group of suicides, *altruistic suicides.* This is the polar opposite of egoistic suicide and is attributed to insufficient individuation; that is, it occurs when social integration is too strong. Examples of altruistic suicide are women killing themselves on their husbands' deaths (the now-forbidden practice of *suttee* in India) and sacrifices of self for religious or nationalistic purposes (*kamikaze* pilots).

Durkheim also presents a third group in which social integration is the determining factor of suicide rates. In this group social integration lies midway between egoism and altruism. Since Durkheim did not name this etiological type, and for want of a better term, we will refer to this condition as moderate social integration. Where social integration is moderate, the suicide rate is low. Examples that Durkheim gave of groups in this situation are Catholics and Jews.

The other basic social factor in Durkheim's scheme is social regulation. This is crucial in his concept of *anomic suicide.* This type of suicide occurs under conditions of weak social regulation in which the activities, behaviors, attitudes, and feelings of the individual are relatively unrestrained. Durkheim pointed to the suicides of businessmen in times of financial crisis and those of women who have been divorced as examples of anomic suicide. *Fatalistic suicide* is the polar opposite of anomic suicide and occurs under conditions of intense social regulation. Suicide of a slave or of the very poor, who are caught up in inescapable social conditions or in extreme poverty, are examples. Fatalistic suicide is relatively little discussed or cited in reference to Durkheim's work. It is egoism, altruism, and anomie that have become most widely associated with his name.

As was the case with social integration, there is a third group of suicides associated with social regulation. This level lies midway between anomie and fatalism and is best termed moderate social regulation. Durkheim never states specifically that where the level of social regulation is low, the suicide rate is low, but he does imply that this is the case by the examples he provides. One such example is his statement that less-regulated older married males have a lower incidence of suicide than younger married males, who are prone to fatalistic suicide.

In summary, although Durkheim names two types of social integration and two types of social regulation, there are actually three principal levels of integration and three of regulation, and to each of these levels Durkheim assigned either a high or low suicide rate. He stressed that at any given time a society is both integrated and regulated to some degree and that these two variables act *together* to determine the suicide rates. Durkheim illustrated this again by his examples of mixed types such as the egoistic-anomic and the altruistic-anomic.

Modifications of Durkheim's Theory.   In relation to mixed types, Barclay Johnson (1965) recognized that Durkheim made no mention of either egoism-fatalism or altruism-fatalism. Subsequently, he incorporated these two additional mixed types in his extension of Durkheim's thesis. This extension implies that while high suicide rates occur when either social integration or social regulation is high or low, they are very high when both conditions are present, with social regulation being high and social integration either high or low.

Johnson attempted to simplify Durkheim's theory by reducing his four types of suicide to one. He claimed that the categories of altruism and fatalism could be dispensed with, since most of the examples of these types of suicide were derived from studies of premodern and nonwestern societies. Also, he claimed that Durkheim based these classes primarily on psychological considerations rather than on social variables. Finally, Johnson attempted to prove that anomie and egoism were simply two different aspects of one social state and thus were identical conceptually. For Johnson, egoism meant a lack of interaction among members of a society, a lack of common conscience, purposes, and goals. Also, it implied a lack of social regulation. Johnson ultimately reformulated Durkheim's theory as follows: "The more integrated (regulated) a society, group, or social condition is, the lower its suicide rate. Another way to say exactly the same thing is this: The higher the level of egoism (anomie) prevailing in a society, group, or social condition, the higher the suicide rate" (1965, p. 886).

Maurice Halbwachs (1930) conducted an extensive review of Durkheim's findings and in general confirmed them. However, Halbwachs was critical of Durkheim's tendency to consider each social factor in relation to suicide independently, and he argued that the social factors were highly correlated and should be considered in combination. The most important factors were those that isolated the individual from stable social relationships. Durkheim's concepts of anomie and egoism were rejected in favor of "social isolation." For example, Halbwachs felt that urban life was most characterized by social isolation factors.

Andrew Henry and James Short (1954) attempted to account for both suicide and homicide within the same theoretical framework by focusing on status and strength of relationships. As the basis for their theory, they used the frustration-aggression hypothesis developed by John Dollard, Leonard Doob, Neal Miller, and Robert Sears (1939). Henry and Short's theory proceeds on the basis of three main assumptions: (1) Aggression is often a consequence of frustration; (2) business cycles produce variation in the hierarchical ranking of persons and groups; and (3) frustrations are generated by interference in the "goal response" of maintaining a constant or rising position, relative to the status of others, in a status hierarchy. Two additional assumptions are made: (4) High-status persons lose more status relative to low-status persons during business contraction; low-status persons lose more status relative to high-status persons during business expansion; (5) suicide occurs mainly in high-status persons; homicide occurs mainly in low-status persons. Henry and Short investigated the relationship between the business cycle and suicide and homicide rates and concluded that their predictions of the rise and fall of these rates from the above assumptions were confirmed. They predicted that: (1) suicide rates will vary negatively with the business cycle, and that homicide rates will vary positively with business conditions; and (2) the correlations between suicide rates and the business cycle would be higher for high-status than for low-status groups, while the correlation between homicide rates and business conditions would be higher for low-status than for high-status groups. Henry and Short decided that the assumption that frustration is produced by variation in the business cycle and is expressed by suicide or homicide was supported by their data.

Henry and Short tried to specify the processes by which the aggression would be expressed toward either the other or self. The general assumption is that frustration, and subsequent aggression, varies directly with the presence of external restraints. The more these restraints are codified and applied, the more readily are transgressions against the other accepted. They argue that when behavior must conform rigidly to the demands and expectations of others—that is, when external restraints are strong, with stringently enforced laws—the expression of aggression against others is legitimized. When external restraints are weak, it is no longer legitimate to direct aggression against others, and the individual must bear responsibility for his behavior. In general, therefore, suicide varies directly and homicide inversely with position in the status hierarchy, and suicide varies inversely and homicide directly with the strength of external restraints on behavior.

Support for Henry and Short's approach came from Arthur Wood (1961), who examined suicide and homicide in Ceylon, and found that suicide was less frequent among people of lower overall status and lower occupational status. He also found that higher classes were more strongly committed to the moral code and thus were subject to a higher suicide rate in the presence of external restraints. There are, however, some data for which Henry and Short's theory does not account. For example, whites have higher prestige in the United States than Asian-Americans, yet the suicide rate is generally higher for the latter. Also, the suicide rate for persons sixty-five years and over in the United States is usually higher than that for persons fifteen to sixty-four, despite the assertion that there is a loss of prestige after age sixty-five. In addition, Ronald Maris (1967) found, when he examined different segments of the population in Cook County, Illinois, that members of high-status categories and persons who are relatively free from external restraints do not always have the highest suicide rates. Maris also criticizes the use of high- and low-status categories by Henry and Short as obscuring important relationships that might have existed between social status and suicide rates. For example, he found in Cook County that within the lower class suicide rates varied widely with occupation and race.

Several other researchers have also concentrated on the ideas of Henry and Short. Martin Gold (1958) felt that they were mistaken in using absolute rates of homicide and suicide, since these did not allow for a control on the total number of aggressive acts committed by any social group. He suggested using instead a ratio, the suicide rate divided by the combined suicide and homicide rate, and found that his predictions were confirmed. James Teele (1965) felt that Henry and Short's notion that other-directed aggression becomes legitimized as the strength of external restraints increases was too simple. Teele suggested that the notion applied to familial and religious relational systems but not to voluntary ones (such as interaction with friends and participation in voluntary associations).

Elwin Powell (1958) felt that suicide varied with social status in society. The latter defines the individual's goals and motives; anomie results when the individual cannot accept these goals.

Powell reformulated Durkheim's concept of anomie by proposing two distinct forms: anomie of dissociation and anomie of envelopment. Anomie of dissociation is disengagement of the self from the goals of the culture and is found mostly among the lower classes. Anomie of envelopment, characteristic of the upper classes, is an absorption of the self into the culture, with a deficit of spontaneity as result of uncritical shouldering of the burdens of the prevailing cultural framework. Either form of anomie increases the probability of suicide in an individual. In general, the two forms of anomie proposed by Powell are similar to Durkheim's original concepts of anomie and fatalism.

Jack Gibbs and Walter Martin (1964), finding Durkheim's concepts of stability and durability of social relations too difficult to apply, developed from them the concept of status integration, a social characteristic that could be measured. Status integration reflects the extent to which members of a population conform to socially sanctioned demands and expectations. Gibbs and Martin define a status as a social identification and postulate that every member of society is identified by his inclusion in various recognized categories, such as man, husband, and laborer. The degree to which the role of one status conflicts with conforming to the role of another determines the degree to which the statuses are incompatible. If two statuses have conflicting roles, they will be less frequently occupied simultaneously than will two statuses with roles that do not conflict. The relative frequency with which a set of statuses is occupied is the degree of status integration. The extent to which individuals occupy incompatible statuses in a population varies inversely with the degree of status integration in that population. Gibbs and Martin postulate that the greater the status integration in a population, the lower the suicide rate. They have conducted a series of tests on the theory in several societies and report that of 175 coefficients of correlation between statuses or roles, such as occupation, religion, marital status, age and sex distribution, rural-urban location, and others, 160, or 91 percent, were in the direction predicted by the theory.

In focusing on the status integration theory of Gibbs and Martin, other researchers offered criticisms, mostly of the difficulty in defining the concept operationally. William Chambliss and Marion Steele (1966) felt the operational definition of status integration was not a plausible one and questioned the empirical support for the theory. Douglas (1967) expressed doubts over the operational definition of status integration, pointing out that a status configuration may be infrequently occupied not because of a role conflict but rather because society restricts entry into that particular status configuration. He also felt that the operational definition is poor because it is static and does not measure the individual's relationships over time. However, it is possible to sample the variable in different populations at any given time, so this argument is readily overcome. Naroll [1965] also objected to the measure of status integration, calling it a measure of status association or popular combination. Statuses that are satisfying are likely to be more popular, which will make them highly associated, producing low suicide rates in those occupying them.

John Douglas' (1967) orientation led him to reject official statistics on suicide and to propose a very different sociological theory. Douglas sought to identify the "meanings" of suicidal behavior derived from close observation of the behavior in question. He first picked out general meanings, properties that were found in most instances of suicide, and then inferred that most suicidal actions (1) are meaningful, (2) imply that something is fundamentally wrong with the situation, and (3) indicate something fundamental about the actor himself. Among less general meanings of suicide phenomena, Douglas identified suicide as (1) a means of transforming the soul from this world to another world, (2) a means of transforming one's image in this world from one state to another, (3) a means of achieving identity with others in one's society, and (4) a means of getting revenge. Criticisms of Douglas' theory are based primarily on the difficulty of defining meanings and measuring their occurrence.

A number of sociologists have proposed special points in relation to Durkheim's theory. Hugh Whitt (1969) concluded that part of Durkheim's thinking on suicide suggested that he partially supported a theory of suicide based on happiness or psychological equilibrium. Unhappiness is caused by the failure of the individual to resolve conflicts between two antagonistic aspects of the self: the individual self and the social self. Bruce Dohrenwend (1959) felt that the basic concept involved in Durkheim's four types of suicide is that of norms or rules. The categories egoism, fatalism, and altruism differ from anomie in that the last is the only one of the four that implies that there are no norms or rules; the other three categories involve the existence of norms of some kind. In egoism the rules are individualistic, while in altruism the rules are collective; in fatalism the authority is external, whereas in egoism and altruism the authority is internal. Ralph Ginsberg (1966) reinterpreted Durkheim's notion of anomie in terms of levels of aspiration. He noted that anomie arises from dissatisfaction of the individual, which is a direct function of discrepancy between the reward that the individual is receiving and his level of aspiration. In the normal process the level of aspiration is proportional to the rewards; in the anomic process the level of aspiration runs away from the rewards, resulting in unhappiness. Ginsberg related his concepts to different points in the business cycle and was able to predict the observed association between business prosperity and the suicide rate.

The Influence of Suggestion on Suicide. A final area of sociological investigation has been concerned with the influence of "suggestion" or "imitation" on suicide. The increase in the number of suicides after one has been reported in the newspapers has been called the *Werther effect,* a term taken from Goethe's novel, *The Sorrows of Young Werther,* in which the hero committed suicide. A wave of suicides swept over Europe after publication, causing authorities in Rome, Leipzig, and Copenhagen to become so apprehensive as to ban the book.

Explorations of the phenomenon of suggestion in suicide have been few, probably because Durkheim (1897) asserted that imitation of suicide did not occur in sufficient numbers to affect the national level of suicides. David Lester reviewed the half dozen or so published studies on suggestion in suicide and concluded:

> On the whole, therefore, contagion and suggestibility are equally difficult both to document and to rule out. . . . The problem for research on this topic is to distinguish imitation and suggestion, and the likelihood of temporally contiguous suicidal actions in two individuals who are both potential suicides and who have a suicidogenic relationship (1972, pp. 188–189).

To document the influence of suggestion, David Phillips (1974) hypothesized that more suicides should occur in the month after the suicide of a prominent person than usual. He calculated the "usual" number of suicides that could have been expected in this month by averaging the number of suicides for the same time period in the year preceding and the year following the suicide. On studying what happened after thirty-four publicized suicides appeared on the front page of *The New York Times* between 1948 and 1967, Phillips found that twenty-eight were followed by a rise in the observed over the expected number. The greatest rises occurred, as expected, after the most prominent and most widely publicized deaths. Phillips found that the more days the story remained on the front page, the larger the rise; that the rise was greater when the stories were publicized in both the *Times* and the *New York Daily News;* that suicides of local familiar subjects were followed by greater proportional rises in the New York area than in the rest of the country; and that the percentage rise in suicide deaths after stories always publicized in the United States and occasionally in England was generally greater in the United States.

Phillips speculates that there is a theoretical relationship between suggestibility and anomie: Anomic individuals, in looking for ways to reduce their loneliness, may choose to commit suicide, and thus "join" a person who preceded them in this act, or to involve themselves in a religious or political movement. Either path would be a solution to the problem of finding meaning in their lives. Why some anomic individuals would elect suicide as their solution while others would choose a regenerative collective solution like a social movement is a question still to be answered. However, Phillips felt that the predictions deduced from this hypothesis substantiated the fact of suggestion if not the explanation for it, and he pointed the way to further potentially productive explorations.

A General Criticism of the Sociological Theories.   One of the most common general criticisms of sociological theories of suicide is that they have ignored the consideration of individual cases and the way in which these affect the resulting suicides rates. A Japanese sociologist makes this point in a general study of suicide rates in Japan. Minoru Uematsu (1961) investigated the suicide rate in a portion of the population as it grew older. First, he correlated the suicide rate of the fifteen- to nineteen-year-old age group with the suicide rate of the twenty- to twenty-four-year-old age group five years later. This is, of course, essentially the same group of people. He did the same thing for each year from 1920 to 1941 and found correlations of −0.45 for males and −0.48 for females. There was thus a strong negative correlation between the suicide rates of the same group of people at different periods in their lives. He therefore argued that there must be predispositional individual factors that influence certain individuals to commit suicide. When these individuals have completed their suicides and dropped out of the group, the suicide rate of that group will decline. In looking for those individual factors, Uematso focused on the question of why suicide was so high in the Japanese adolescent and youth age groups, especially among so many who "appear to be healthy without any mental diseases and, at the same time, tend to commit suicide" (1961, p. 28). Without defining them, he assumed the presence of predispositions in the susceptible individuals in order to account for his results. However, his explanation of predisposing factors in the host applies only to a declining rate, such as he studied, not to an increasing one, such as is often found. In addition, he would have to assume that the predispositions would become operative (without significant contribution from environmental factors) at different times. Until this theory is tested, it remains more description than explanation.

SUICIDE STATISTICS

Suicide Rates and Factors Affecting Their Accuracy

A suicide rate is a statistic that indicates the number of suicide deaths per 100,000 of the living population in which they occurred. This statistic, like the rates of death from causes such as circulatory diseases, diabetes, and cancer, is used by most countries in the world today. Death certifications are classified for statistical purposes according to International Classification of Diseases. This system of classification and its supporting rules were developed by the World Health Organization in Geneva and are revised approximately every ten years. The rates are generally determined within each country and then reported to the World Health Organization, which collects data from its member nations. The individual countries also publish data concerning causes of death, permitting a continuous overview of changing patterns in the health of the nation. In the United States, these data are collected and published by the National Center for Health Statistics, Public Health Service, Department of Health, Education, and Welfare. This agency receives data from each of the states, which collate data obtained from the counties within each state.

Suicide rates have always played an important role in suicide research. Because of their "objectivity" (based on death as an incontrovertible behavioral fact), they have been looked upon as a highly reliable set of data for measuring and comparing the magnitude of the suicide problem in various populations. For the sociologist they have been the chief source of evidence in the study of suicide and development of theory. For the public health specialist they have been one of the primary indicators of the mental health status of any community. For organizations and individuals engaged in suicide prevention, they are the obvious instrument for evaluating preventive measures.

Only in recent years has the reliability of mortality statistics in general and of suicide rates in particular been questioned. According to Louis Dublin (1963), who is well-known for his work on suicide statistics, the United States suicide rates understate the true incidence of suicide by about one fourth to one third. Social scientists in other countries have expressed similar doubts about the accuracy of suicide statistics in their own countries.

The reasons for the variations in suicide rates are many. One of the most significant is the difference in attitudes and feelings about suicide found in different countries. Another source of variability is to be found in the methods of certification used in various countries. If the procedures and criteria for certification of suicide vary widely from country to country, then the rates are not entirely comparable. Erwin Stengel and Norman Farberow (1968), after surveying the countries reporting to the World Health Organization to learn their procedures in certifying suicide, substantiated the need to interpret suicide rates with great caution because of differences in criteria, procedures, and personnel involved.

Certification of Suicide.   In the United States there are in general two kinds of death certifications: natural deaths, which are certified by a physician, and coroner's or medical examiner's office deaths, which require an investigation. The certification of natural death is usually a simple process if a person dies from an illness in the hospital or at home; the attending physician simply fills out the death certificate. But if no physician has attended the patient, if the physician is unable to ascertain the cause of death, or if there is a suspicion of death by violence, the case becomes the responsibility of a legal functionary such as the coroner, the medical examiner, the public prosecutor, the district attorney, or a lay magistrate. In a small number of countries— for example, in Scandinavia and Japan—no member of the judiciary is involved, and the final responsibility rests with a police physician or a specialist in forensic medicine.

In the case of questionable death, the medical examiner must follow special procedures laid down by law. In the majority of countries, there must be an investigation to determine intent (to commit suicide) as well as the circumstances and manner of the injury, for a case cannot be certified as suicide unless "foul play"—that is, homicide or manslaughter—has been excluded first. This means that the first steps to be taken are identical with those required by the criminal law in cases of suspected murder. Depending on the intent, or lack of it, the death is certified as an accident, a suicide, or a homicide. The thoroughness with which the investigation is conducted depends upon the nature of the case and upon the competence of the staff.

While in all countries some public official has the final responsibility for the certification of suicide, the functions of this official vary. The criteria on which a legal functionary bases a suicide verdict may differ considerably from the criteria used by a physician. Whereas a physician may make an inference as to cause of death based on his medical knowledge, a coroner insists on positive, unambiguous evidence of self-destructive intent before certifying a death as suicide. Since a degree of uncertainty is an inherent feature of most suicide acts, the coroner's criteria would exclude many typical suicide acts.

Because the responsibility for the vital statistics system in the United States lies with each state and not with any central authority, a certain degree of diversity of practice exists within the system (Moriyama & Israel, 1968). The cases that generally fall under medicolegal jurisdiction are deaths resulting from or suspected to result from violence (that is, accident, suicide, or homicide); deaths without a physician in attendance; deaths resulting from known or suspected industrial diseases; deaths in which the cause cannot be determined; deaths in which the identity of the deceased is not established; and deaths occurring in hospitals within twenty-four hours after admission. To further complicate matters, the qualifications and experience of the medicolegal officer may vary according to state and local laws. This official may be a layman or a physician, and in the latter case the law may or may not require specialized training in pathology and forensic medicine. Furthermore, the position of medicolegal officer may be either appointive or elective.

Thus, it can be seen that suicide statistics are affected by the criteria as to what constitutes a medicolegal case, the manner in which the investigations are conducted, and the procedures by which causes of death are ascertained. In addition, a serious problem arises in the reporting of accident, suicide, or homicide. Generally, coroners and medical examiners are reluctant to certify a death as suicide or homicide without substantial evidence, even though they may have strong suspicions of suicide or homicide. The possibility of becoming involved in litigation may be a strong deterrent to expressing opinions unsupported by evidence on a legal document. Another possible factor

affecting the certification of accident rather than suicide is that the
survivors of the deceased might receive double indemnity in the event
of an accident or perhaps no benefits in the event of a suicide. All these
factors are in addition to the social or cultural pressures that operate in
the United States to favor certification of an accidental death rather than
a suicide. There is yet one more factor on which the accuracy of the
reported suicide rates depends, one that is not even related to suicide—
that is, the reliability of the population census. Even if there were no
resistance to the reporting of suicides, the suicide rates would be quite
useless unless the incidence figures were related to correct population
figures. In a number of countries the population census procedures may
also be suspect.

The Psychological Autopsy. In Los Angeles a procedure has been
developed to try to improve the accuracy of certification of suicide. It is
based on the assumption that suicide is most accurately certified when
the intent of the deceased is known. Did he intend that his actions
should bring about his death? Intention is a part of motivation, a
psychological area that in turn is probably best evaluated by behavioral
scientists. It thus seems useful for each coroner's office to have on its
staff professionals from the behavioral science area as well as from the
medical (pathologist and autopsy surgeon), forensic (legal), toxicologi-
cal, and investigatory disciplines (Curphey, Shneidman, & Farberow,
1970).

The behavioral scientists conduct investigations in cases of equivocal
death in which the certification decision falls between suicide and
another mode; such as accident, homicide, or natural death. The aim is
to obtain as much information as possible about the personality and
state of mind of the victim. Explorations focus on the person's lifestyle,
characteristic ways of handling conflicts, personality defenses and coping mechanisms, relationships with significant others, communications
in the recent past, previous suicidal behavior (if any), state of physical
health, work status, and state of mind and mood. Persons interviewed
may be members of the immediate family, relatives, employer or
employees, physician, clergy, friends, and neighbors.

Over the years the efforts of behavioral scientists working as part of
coroners' offices have increased our confidence in the accuracy of the
certifications of suicide. An evaluation of the psychological autopsies

done in two periods, fiscal years 1959–1961, when the procedure was first started, and 1964–1966, five years later, indicated increasing reliance on the information provided by behavioral scientists (Farberow & Neuringer, 1971). The coroner followed the recommendations of the investigations in 88 percent of the cases in the first period and in 96 percent of the cases in the second period. It was apparent from the disproportionate number referred for investigation that it was young males below age thirty whose mode of death troubled the coroner most often. As for specific methods, it was the ingestion of various substances by females of middle age and older that were most difficult to evaluate. The authors concluded that the advantages of having a behavioral scientist on the coroner's staff include more accurate certifications of suicide and other deaths, a more accurate picture of the mental and public health of the community, and more effective service to the members of the community.

In addition, the community profits from the knowledge that all possible effort and expertise has been expended in the attempt to certify the death accurately. An unexpected but clearly valuable benefit of the investigations is the cathartic effect of the interviews. The investigators frequently find themselves listening to distraught survivors such as the parents of an adolescent suicide, who have had no opportunity to discuss with any trained person the overwhelming residue of guilt, shame, self-blame, doubt, and anger that has been left behind.

International Suicide Rates

The World Health Organization publishes the statistics for suicide for about a third of the countries in the United Nations. The source is volume one of *World Health Statistics Annual: Vital Statistics and Causes of Death*. Some countries in Eastern Europe, like Yugoslavia, Rumania, and the German Democratic Republic, do not separate the categories found in Section E XVII Accidents, Poisonings, and Violence (External Causes) of the International Classification of Diseases, such as suicide (E950–E959), accidents (E800–E949), homicides (E960–E978), and other external causes (E980–E999); instead, they publish a combined figure for all external causes. At this writing, the latest published data are available in the *World Health Statistics Annual, 1972* (1975). Some of these data are shown in Table 1.

Table 1. *1972 International Rates for Death by Suicide and Self-inflicted Injury (per 100,000 Population).*

Countries	Total	Male	Female	Ratio Male/Female
Africa				
Mauritius	2.3	3.4	1.2	2.83
America				
Canada	12.2	17.4	6.9	2.52
Chile	5.5	9.0	2.2	4.09
Iceland	8.6	11.3	5.8	1.95
Mexico	0.7	1.1	0.3	3.67
United States	12.0	17.5	6.8	2.57
Venezuela	6.0	8.4	3.5	2.40
Asia				
Hong Kong	11.4	13.3	9.4	1.41
Israel	7.5	8.4	6.5	1.29
Japan	16.8	19.4	14.2	1.37
Philippines	0.6	0.9	0.4	2.25
Thailand	4.5	5.0	3.9	1.25
Western Europe				
Austria	23.4	33.3	14.5	2.30
Belgium	15.4	21.5	9.6	2.24
Denmark	23.9	30.2	17.7	1.71
Finland	24.0	39.0	10.0	3.90
France	16.1	23.3	9.3	2.51
Germany, Federal Republic of	19.9	26.3	14.1	1.87
Greece	2.7	3.9	1.5	2.60
Ireland	3.0	4.3	1.7	2.53
Italy	5.8	8.2	3.6	2.28
Luxembourg	14.9	20.4	9.6	2.12
Netherlands	8.2	10.0	6.5	1.54
Norway	9.0	13.0	5.1	2.55
Portugal	8.2	13.4	3.6	3.72
Spain	4.4	6.7	2.3	2.91
Sweden	20.3	29.4	11.2	2.62
Switzerland	19.5	28.2	11.2	2.52
United Kingdom				
England and Wales	7.7	9.2	6.2	1.48
North Ireland	3.0	4.1	2.0	2.05
Scotland	8.1	9.5	6.8	1.40

Table 1. 1972 International Rates for Death by Suicide and Self-inflicted Injury (per 100,000 Population) (cont.).

Countries	Total	Male	Female	Ratio Male/Female
Eastern Europe				
Bulgaria	11.4	15.8	6.9	2.29
Czechoslovakia	24.6	36.3	13.5	2.69
Hungary	36.9	53.4	21.4	2.50
Poland	12.0	20.3	4.1	4.95
Oceania				
New Zealand	8.8	11.7	6.0	1.95

SOURCE: World Health Statistics Annual, 1972. Vol. 1. Vital Statistics and Causes of Death. Geneva, Switzerland: World Health Organization, 1975.

The highest suicide rates among the different countries are all in Europe: Hungary, Czechoslovakia, Finland, Denmark, Austria, Sweden, Germany (Federal Republic), Switzerland, and so on. Most of these same countries also had the highest suicide rates in 1962 and in 1969. Hungary, the country with the highest rate in 1969, 33.1, continues to top the list, having increased to 36.9 in 1972. The Scandinavian countries continue to present the same paradox of high rates in Finland (24.0), Denmark (23.9), and Sweden (20.3) and a moderate to low rate in Norway (9.0). The United States' rate of 12.0 falls in about the middle of the range of rates reported.

The lowest rates have generally been found in predominantly Catholic countries, such as Mexico (0.7), the Philippines (0.6), Greece (2.7), and Ireland (3.0). Rates among Arab countries, though not shown in the table, are also known to be very low. Both Catholicism and Mohammedanism strongly condemn suicide. Some social scientists in Catholic and Arab countries, however, have expressed doubts about the accuracy of the low rates, implying that a suicide may be hidden by the family or certified in another mode because of the strong cultural and religious feelings against this act.

In none of the countries does the female rate of suicide exceed the male rate. The highest ratios of male to female suicides occur in Poland (4.95:1), Chile (4.09:1), Finland (3.90:1), Portugal (3.72:1), and Mexico

(3.67:1). The rates for the sexes have drawn very close in other countries, for instance, in Thailand (1.25:1), Israel (1.29:1), Japan (1.37:1), Scotland (1.40:1), and Hong Kong (1.41:1). Most of the countries in Europe, along with the United States, show ratios of between two and three males to one female.

Suicides rates broken down by age and sex for a few countries are shown in Table 2. The United States rate rose to its highest point in the 55–64 age group and then leveled off. The rates for males rose through all age groups, starting at 14.1 in the 15–24 age group and rising to 43.6 in the 75+ age group. Israel, Japan, and Chile show a bimodal course with peaks at 25–34 for Israel and Japan and 15–34 for Chile, and then again 65–74 for Israel and Chile and 75+ for Japan. Japan's 75+ rate of 75.3 is one of the highest recorded; it is exceeded only by Hungary's 96.2.

Sweden's rate, like Hungary's and England and Wales', almost doubles from the age group 15–24 (11.9) to 25–34 (20.8). Hungary's climbs precipitously throughout each successive decade, most markedly among the males. The male 75+ rate (151.0) is 50 percent higher than the rate for the decade immediately preceding it (99.0). In contrast, West Germany's rate also rises throughout each decade but much less steeply. Among the males, its highest rate is also in the 75+ age group (62.6).

Suicide Rates of the United States, 1900–1974

The suicide rates for the United States have fluctuated widely since the turn of the century (see Figure 1). The highest recorded rate was 17.4 per 100,000 in 1932, the depth of the Great Depression years; the lowest rate, 9.8 per 100,000, occurred in 1957, at a time when the economic status of the country was bright. One period of high suicide rates extended from 1908 through 1916, encompassing the years prior to the United States' entry into World War I; another period was the decade 1930–1940, the years of deep economic recession and the buildup toward World War II.

Since the end of World War II and the Korean War, from about 1952 through 1974, there has been a general and gradual rise in the suicide rate. These years include the period of the Vietnam war, which, in contrast to most of the other wars in which the United States was

Table 2. Rates for Death by Suicide and Self-inflicted Injury (per 100,000 Population): Rates by Sex and Age for Selected Countries in 1972.

Countries	All Ages	5–14	15–24	25–34	35–44	45–54	55–64	65–74	75+
Chile	5.5ᵃ	0.7	9.5	9.5	7.5	8.0	8.3	10.0	8.7
	9.0	0.8	13.7	15.2	13.0	15.1	16.8	17.0	21.6
	2.2	0.7	5.4	3.2	2.4	1.7	0.7	4.0	—
England and Wales	7.7	0.1	4.6	7.3	9.2	12.2	13.5	14.6	13.2
	9.2	0.1	6.3	9.6	11.6	14.0	15.5	19.2	19.0
	6.2	—	2.9	5.0	6.8	10.5	11.8	11.3	10.6
Germany, Federal Republic of	19.9	0.6	13.5	18.6	24.7	30.4	33.3	34.7	38.9
	26.3	0.9	20.4	26.1	34.1	41.3	43.1	48.7	62.6
	14.1	0.3	6.3	10.5	14.5	22.1	26.3	25.1	27.0
Hungary	36.9	0.8	17.4	30.1	46.7	59.4	60.0	69.9	96.2
	53.4	1.4	26.3	47.7	72.3	89.2	89.9	99.0	151.0
	21.4	0.2	8.1	12.5	22.3	32.6	34.6	47.5	64.6
Israel	7.5	—	5.3	7.9	7.1	14.6	16.8	22.6	17.7
	8.4	—	7.0	10.4	8.1	15.9	11.6	32.4	18.7
	6.5	—	3.5	5.3	6.2	13.4	21.8	12.5	16.7

Japan								
16.8	0.5	15.5	18.0	16.3	18.9	27.9	47.3	75.3
19.4	0.8	18.5	22.0	20.6	23.5	33.1	52.8	83.4
14.2	0.3	12.4	14.0	11.9	15.0	23.5	42.5	70.0
Sweden								
20.3	0.1	11.9	22.8	28.6	34.4	31.4	26.6	27.2
29.4	0.2	16.1	31.9	40.9	48.4	46.5	42.7	50.0
11.2	—	7.5	12.9	16.0	20.3	16.8	12.9	11.3
United States[b]								
11.7	0.3	9.4	13.7	17.2	19.8	21.6	21.5	20.9
16.7	0.5	14.1	19.0	22.3	26.7	32.8	36.4	43.6
6.8	0.2	4.7	8.6	12.3	13.4	11.7	9.9	6.4

[a]Each group of three figures, read from top to bottom, gives the total rate, the rate for males, and the rate for females.

[b]Rates for the United States are for 1971.

SOURCE: *World Health Statistics Annual, 1972.* Vol. 1. *Vital Statistics and Causes of Death.* Geneva, Switzerland: World Health Organization, 1975.

Figure 1. Suicide Rates for All Races (per 100,000 Population): United States, 1900–1974.

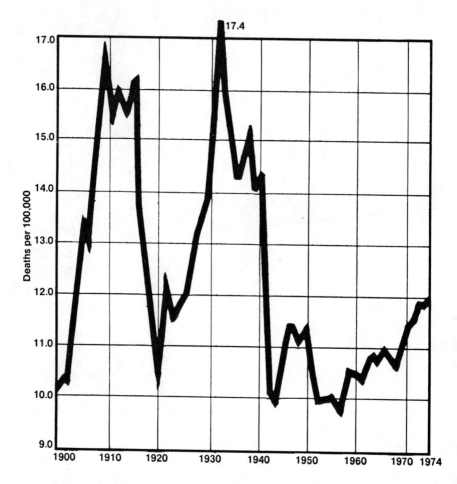

SOURCE: National Center for Health Statistics, Mortality Statistics Branch, Rockville, Md.

involved, did not seem to lower the suicide rate to any noticeable degree.[1] While some concern has been voiced over the gradual but continuing rise in the rates, it is also possible that the rates have been seeking their own mean because they were unusually low for the United States during the fifties.

Demographic Data on Suicides in the United States

Data for the Entire United States. Table 3 presents the death rates for adults in the United States for 1974, excluding early injury mortality. Suicide ranks tenth on this list with a rate of 12.1 per 100,000. Diseases of the heart continues to rank first by a wide margin (349.2), followed by malignant neoplasms (170.5) and cerebrovascular diseases (98.1). In succession we find accidents (49.5), influenza and pneumonia (25.9), diabetes (17.7), cirrhosis of the liver (15.8), arteriosclerosis (15.3), bronchitis, emphysema, and asthma (12.7), and suicide.

Among males, suicide rises to the eighth rank with a rate of 18.1, while among females it ranks ninth even though the rate drops to 6.5. Whites kill themselves almost twice as often as other races (12.0 as opposed to 6.5). The suicide rate of white males is 19.2 and of white females, 7.1, while among other races males have a rate of 10.2 and females, a rate of 3.0.

The course of suicide by age (Table 4) indicates that the rate for all races and both sexes below age 15 is very low (0.3), but that it jumps about 340 percent, to 10.2, for the adolescent and youth group, ages 15–24. It rises gradually to 19.9 and 21.4 through the middle years, for the age groups 45 through 64, varies only slightly down (20.4) then up (to 22.2) in the next two decades through 84 years of age, and then goes down to 20.5 for the years 85 and over.

For the method of suicide (Table 5), both white and nonwhite males favored firearms and explosives. The second most popular method for all males was hanging, strangulation, and suffocation. White females showed equal preference for firearms and explosives and poisoning by solids or liquids. (which includes the well-known sleeping pills). For nonwhite females firearms and explosives were used most often, followed by poisoning by solids and liquids and then hanging, strangulation, and suffocation.

Table 3. *Death Rates for Selected Causes (per 100,000 Population): United States, 1974.*

	All Races			White			All Other		
	Total	Male	Female	Total	Male	Female	Total	Male	Female
Disease of the heart	349.2	399.7	301.2	362.7	415.5	312.3	258.0	291.0	227.9
Malignant neoplasm	170.5	191.1	151.0	174.4	193.7	156.1	144.1	173.5	117.2
Cerebrovascular diseases	98.1	87.8	107.9	99.2	87.6	110.3	90.9	89.4	92.3
Accidents	49.5	71.1	29.0	48.5	69.1	28.9	56.0	85.3	29.3
Influenza and pneumonia	25.9	28.9	23.0	25.9	28.4	23.6	25.7	32.9	19.2
Diabetes mellitus	17.7	14.7	20.5	17.0	14.5	19.5	21.9	16.3	27.1
Cirrhosis of the liver	15.8	21.2	10.6	15.1	20.4	10.0	20.4	26.7	14.7
Arteriosclerosis	15.3	12.9	17.5	16.2	13.5	18.9	8.5	8.3	8.7
Bronchitis, emphysema, and asthma	12.7	19.6	6.2	13.7	21.1	6.7	6.0	9.2	3.1
Suicide	12.1	18.1	6.5	12.0	19.2	7.1	6.5	10.2	3.0

SOURCE: *Monthly Vital Statistics Reports, Final Mortality Statistics, 1974.* National Center for Health Statistics, Vol. 24, No. 11, Supplement, Feb. 3, 1976.

Table 4. Suicide Rates by Race, Sex and Age (per 100,000 Population): United States, 1972.

Race and Sex	All Ages	5–14	15–24	25–34	35–44	45–54	55–64	65–74	75–84	85+
All races	12.0	0.3	10.2	14.7	16.8	19.9	21.4	20.4	22.2	20.5
Male	17.5	0.4	15.7	20.9	22.2	28.0	31.5	35.9	45.0	50.0
Female	6.8	0.2	4.7	8.8	11.6	12.4	12.4	8.5	7.6	5.4
White	12.8	0.3	10.1	15.0	17.7	21.3	22.9	21.9	23.3	22.2
Male	18.5	0.5	15.5	20.9	23.0	29.7	33.5	38.4	48.0	54.5
Female	7.3	0.2	4.6	9.2	12.6	13.4	13.3	9.2	7.8	5.9
All other	6.6	0.1	11.0	12.7	10.0	8.2	7.5	6.1	8.1	3.0
Male	10.3	—	16.7	20.9	15.8	13.2	11.9	11.6	12.4	7.8
Female	3.3	0.2	5.6	5.7	5.2	3.8	3.7	1.5	5.0	—

SOURCE: *Vital Statistics of the United States, 1972*. Vol II. *Mortality*, Part A, Rockville, Md.: National Center for Health Statistics, 1976.

Table 5. *Suicide Rates by Race, Sex, and Method of Suicide (per 100,000 Population): United States, 1972.*

Method of Suicide	Both Sexes	All Races Male	All Races Female	White Male	White Female	All Other Male	All Other Female
Firearms and explosives	6.4	10.7	2.3	11.3	2.5	6.4	1.3
Poisoning by solids or liquids	1.9	1.5	2.3	1.6	2.5	0.6	1.2
Hanging, strangulation, and suffocation	1.6	2.5	0.7	2.6	0.8	1.8	0.3
Poisoning by gas (other than domestic)	1.2	1.7	0.7	1.9	0.8	0.3	0.1
Submersion or drowning	0.3	0.3	0.3	0.3	0.3	0.3	0.1
Jumping from high place	0.3	0.4	0.2	0.4	0.2	0.4	0.2
Cutting and piercing	0.2	0.3	0.1	0.3	0.1	0.2	0.0

SOURCE: *Vital Statistics of the United States, 1976.* Vol. II. *Mortality,* Part A, Rockville, M National Center for Health Statistics, 1976.

Experts in suicide prevention who have been watching variations in suicide rates have noted some changes that are beginning to occur, such as an increase in rates for the young, a decrease in rates for the old, a lessening of the male–female ratio, and an increase in black suicides. While these trends have not yet appeared in the national statistics, they have begun to show in local statistics. Nancy Allen (1973) has reported an intensive study of suicide trends in California. Some of Allen's data are reported here so that the reader can see the basis for such trends. It will be interesting to see whether they are duplicated in other states.

Data for California. There are fifty-eight coroners in the state of California, representing a variety of backgrounds and range of responsibilities. At the time the survey was completed (1972), thirty-two were sheriffs, nineteen were public administrator-public guardians, four were medical doctors (three forensic pathologists), and three others were combinations of the above. Personal interviews with fourteen coroners indicated that they generally felt their primary responsibility was ruling out foul play (homicide); practically every case was approached as a potential homicide when a suicide intent could not be established. Some coroners would not certify a death as a suicide unless there was a suicide note.

California's suicide rate per 100,000 population increased from 15.9 in 1960 (2,502 cases) to 18.8 in 1970 (3,744 cases). Suicide has ranked among the top ten leading causes of death in California since 1910. In 1970 suicide overall ranked seventh; in the 15–34 age group it ranked second among causes of death for both sexes, and in those 35–44 it ranked no lower than fifth.

California's crude death rate due to suicide does not fit the pattern described by other states, that is, higher suicide rates in cities than in rural areas. The number of suicides in the greater metropolitan areas is high (16.7 in 1960 and 20.5 in 1970), but the isolated rural areas have the highest suicide rate (20.0 in 1960 and 29.0 in 1970).

California appears to be ahead of national figures in reducing the male–female ratio. The male–female ratio for suicide in the United States for 1969 was 2.6 to 1; in California the ratio for the same year was 1.7 to 1 (males 23.4, females 14.2). This smaller ratio has been explained as part of the movement toward equality between men and women, which has been more rapid in California than in the United States as a whole. Women are becoming more involved outside the family and are experiencing an increase in stress relative to men.

Suicide in California, as nationally, increases in frequency and rate with advancing years. This is especially true of white males (with the exception of a lower peak in the 20–24 age group). The peak for white females in 1970 was in the 55–64 age group; the rate declined after age 65. There has been a significant increase in the number of suicides among young people. Comparing 1960 and 1970 (Table 6), change is most evident among those aged 15–19 and 20–24, for whom the rates have more than doubled. In the early ages, where suicide ranks high among the leading causes of death, it does so in part because other killers, such as heart disease and cancer, are relatively absent. Some

Table 6. *Suicide Death Rates by Race, Sex, and Age (per 100,000 Population): California, 1960 and 1970.*

		1970								
Race and Sex	All Ages	Under 15	15–19	20–24	25–34	35–44	45–54	55–64	65–74	75+
All races	18.8	0.3	12.0	24.0	22.5	25.1	29.7	34.9	33.1	35.1
Male	23.4	0.5	15.0	33.5	28.5	28.2	33.3	43.9	48.6	65.1
Female	14.2	a	8.9	14.4	16.5	22.1	26.2	26.5	21.2	16.9
White	19.9	0.4	12.7	23.9	23.1	26.6	31.2	37.2	34.9	35.9
Male	24.9	0.6	15.9	34.1	28.9	29.9	35.2	47.0	51.4	68.0
Female	15.0	a	9.2	13.6	17.1	23.4	27.4	28.3	22.4	17.0
Black	10.4	—	9.4	32.0	19.2	16.8	13.3	7.9	a	a
Male	12.9	—	10.0	33.9	26.2	19.3	16.9	14.5	a	a
Female	8.1	—	8.8	30.2	12.7	14.4	10.0	a	—	—
All other	9.0	—	a	12.6	16.9	8.1	15.6	a	19.1	34.1
Male	10.2	—	a	20.1	23.2	a	a	a	27.0	a
Female	7.7	—	a	a	11.0	10.0	20.9	a	a	a

1960

All Races	15.9	0.2	5.5	10.9	14.8	22.7	31.6	36.1	29.8	40.0
Male	21.9	0.3	8.6	17.3	19.3	28.0	40.2	55.3	48.3	68.9
Female	10.0	a	2.1	4.2	10.2	17.5	22.8	17.8	14.3	19.4
White	16.6	0.2	5.6	11.4	15.4	23.6	32.9	37.2	30.2	39.7
Male	22.9	0.3	8.7	17.9	20.0	29.1	41.8	57.6	49.8	69.6
Female	10.5	a	2.3	4.6	10.7	18.2	24.0	18.1	14.0	18.9
Black[b]	4.4	—	a	a	7.5	7.7	5.6	17.8	a	a
Male	7.1	—	a	a	12.2	10.9	a	28.5	a	a
Female	1.8	—	—	—	a	a	a	a	—	—
All other	15.7	—	a	a	13.0	22.6	35.2	21.4	48.6	104.8
Male	19.1	—	a	a	14.8	24.9	43.8	a	a	a
Female	11.6	—	—	—	a	20.0	a	a	a	a

[a]Rates are not calculated for fewer than five deaths.

[b]Black population for 1960 is based on 25 percent sample.

SOURCE: State of California, Department of Public Health, Death Records (1973).

authorities, though, feel that suicides in youth are more underreported than those in adults because of the additional stigma and emotional trauma that they entail and for insurance reasons.

The pattern of methods of suicide used in the United States—that is, first firearms and explosives and second hanging, strangulation, and suffocation—does not hold true in California. Looking at males and females together, there are more suicides by means of poisoning by solids, liquids, and gases than any other, with firearms and explosives a close second, and hanging, strangulation, and suffocation third.

However, when we look at the rates broken down by sex, firearms and explosives were the leading means of suicide for the male population in California, accounting for 46.1 percent of male suicides in both 1960 and 1970. Solids, liquids, and gases accounted for 60.6 percent of female suicides in 1960 and 65.4 percent in 1970. This pattern holds for males and females in each age group for 1960 and 1970.

During the past decade there has been a significant increase in black suicides in California. The black suicide rate increased from 4.4 in 1960 to 10.4 in 1970, whereas the white suicide rate increased from 16.6 to 19.9. The 136 percent increase for black suicides in California probably understates the increase in some counties because of the concentration of blacks in urban areas. There are many theories to account for this increase. Some behavioral scientists believe it is an outcome of frustration and rage in reaction to life in urban ghettos, other feel it is the exposure to new and unfamiliar stresses as a result of migrating to large cities.

SUICIDE PREVENTION: CLINICAL ASPECTS

History

Although suicide, with its needless, often tragic, waste of life, has been a known part of civilization throughout recorded history, organized efforts to prevent it are relatively recent. Among the earliest efforts were agencies established in Austria in the late 1890s and 1900s; they included the Lemberger Freiwilligen Rettungsgesellschaft (the Lemberg Volunteer Rescue Society) in Lemberg and Budapest, the Welfare Department of the Vienna Police Department, Lebensmüdenstelle der

Ethischen Gemeinde (Ethical Society Agency for Suicidal Persons), and Jugendberatung (Youth Counseling Service). In England the Anti-Suicide Bureau of the Salvation Army was established around 1906 and operated for several years, and in New York in 1906 Reverend Harry M. Warren, a Baptist preacher, founded the National Save-A-Life League, an agency still in operation today (Farberow & Shneidman, 1961b).

In more recent years the Lebensmüdenfürsorgestelle (Suicide Prevention Agency) was established by the Catholic Archdiocese in Vienna under Doctor Erwin Ringel in 1948, and a group called the Samaritans was begun in England in 1953 by Reverend Chad Varah. The Samaritans have spread throughout the British Commonwealth and now number over two hundred separate agencies that are not only in England, Wales, and Scotland but also in other parts of the world, such as Hong Kong, Singapore, and Rhodesia. Such agencies, usually church supported and offering a telephone counseling service manned by volunteer, nonprofessional personnel, have formed a federation with other agencies on the European continent called the International Federation of Telephonic Emergency Services, which has its headquarters in Geneva.

In the United States, the Los Angeles Suicide Prevention Center was the pioneer professionally organized and operated center specifically set up for the prevention of suicide. It was established in 1958 with support from the federal government by means of a grant from the National Institute of Mental Health to determine the feasibility of such an organization to save lives, conduct research, train personnel, and serve as a model for other communities. The success of the center as a pilot project is indicated by the fact that there are now over two hundred suicide prevention and crisis intervention centers in the United States, most of them patterned, in part at least, after the model of the Los Angeles center. The worldwide movement in suicide prevention has spread with the establishment of a number of national associations, such as the American Association of Suicidology and the French Groupement d'Études et de Prevention du Suicide. Canada at this time is planning a national association. An international organization, called the International Association for Suicide Prevention, with headquarters in Vienna, has been founded to provide a common forum for the individuals and associations working in the area of suicide prevention.

Crisis Theory and Intervention

Suicide has been characterized as the epitome of crisis, the best example of an emotion-laden psychiatric emergency, which is heightened by the fact that a life is at stake. *Webster's Third New International Dictionary* indicates that the word "crisis" comes from the Greek *krisis* or *krinein* and from the Latin *cernere*, both of which mean "to separate." It defines crisis as a turning point in time, a decisive or crucial time, event, or happening. It is interesting that the Chinese ideogram for crisis contains the symbols for both danger and opportunity, emphasizing the possibility for positive change as well as the negative element of possible catastrophe or disaster.

Crisis theory had already begun to emerge in the late 1940s, and suicide theory and prevention were readily incorporated into its theoretical framework. The first article to deal specifically with crisis intervention was the report by Eric Lindemann (1944) on the behavior of the survivors of the 1943 Coconut Grove Club fire. Lindemann developed the concept of "grief work" and outlined the phases of mourning through which an individual generally passes. In 1946 in Cambridge, Massachusetts, Gerald Caplan, with Lindemann, established the Wellesley Human Relations Service, a community-wide program of mental health focusing on the development of procedures for crisis intervention.

Caplan has defined crisis as a state "provoked when a person faces an obstacle to important life goals that is for a time insurmountable to the utilization of customary methods in problem-solving" (1961, p. 18). Crisis theory is based on the concept of homeostasis (Caplan, 1964). The individual maintains a balance in his emotional functioning through the use of coping techniques learned throughout his life. However, these usual coping techniques may not be sufficient if the problems encountered are too difficult. Four phases in crisis have been distinguished: (1) An initial rise in tension occurs that produces the usual problem-solving reaction; (2) an increase in tension upset and feelings of incapability appear as a result of the failure of the usual problem-solving approaches; (3) additional hasty, defensive behaviors are mobilized as tension mounts; and (4) if the problem remains unsolved, there is increasing tension, which can cause major disorganization and panic states.

Crisis intervention has been defined as one or more activities initiated to influence the course of crisis in an individual so that a more adaptive outcome will result. Merton Gill (1954) differentiated crisis intervention from other kinds of therapeutic work by emphasizing that the patient focuses on "derivative conflicts" without attempting to work on "basic conflicts." The therapist, though generally aware of the latter, which are used to help formulate a treatment plan, does not attempt to identify them and work on them with the patient. Lydia Rapaport (1962) identified the principles of crisis intervention as (1) keeping the focus explicitly on the crisis, (2) helping the patient with cognitive mastery, (3) offering basic information and education, and (4) creating a bridge to other community resources.

Crisis intervention and suicide prevention services may be seen from another viewpoint. Using the systematic framework employed in public health, that of tertiary, secondary, and primary stages of activity, work in the crisis and suicide areas can be understood as focusing primarily on the secondary stage of intervention. That is, it is activity applied at the time of outbreak or shortly thereafter. Mental health prior to World War II had been almost entirely in the tertiary or remediation stage, as was apparent from its large conglomeration of mental hospitals and its pattern of one-to-one treatment in private offices. Since World War II mental health has moved into the secondary stage and thus, necessarily, into the community. This move has provided opportunity for early intervention and quick remediation by making trained personnel available for dealing with emotional disturbances at the time they first occur. The primary stage, prevention, has not yet been achieved in mental health, although it is a natural development to be expected from the current emphasis on community psychology and psychiatry.

Suicide Prevention Centers

Until very recently, suicide prevention services developed primarily as emergency phone-in centers. As listed by Farberow (1969), the basic concepts in suicide prevention activities were as follows:

(1) *Accessibility and availability.* Services were to be available at any time without waiting, twenty-four hours a day, seven days a week.

(2) *Place in the network of community helping agencies.* Because

many of the patients need to seek treatment in other helping resources in the community, the suicide prevention center must be a part of the mental health complex of the community.

(3) *Transferral rather than referral of clients.* The suicide prevention service is not an information or referral center. Each call is considered a therapy interview, and responsibility is maintained until the client can be transferred to a subsequent treatment resource. The transfer in effect extends the treatment offered by the center, which has served an important purpose in locating and providing the next resource needed in the sequential treatment program.

(4) *Crisis intervention theory and practice.* The aim is to relieve the immediate emergency situation so that the individual can regain a level of adequate functioning insofar as is possible.

In establishing itself as a helping agency in the community, the suicide prevention center has to effect adequate liaison with a number of other organizations and agencies in the community. Some of these are essential and others desirable. The essential liaisons are with community psychiatric hospitals, emergency hospital services, police, local medical examiner or coroner's office, professional mental health workers, medical practitioners, and the "gatekeeper" groups in the community (such as teachers, clergy, and law enforcement officials). It is also desirable to have contacts with the Association for Mental Health, local universities, and insurance companies.

In general the worker answering the telephone in a suicide prevention center takes the following steps:

1. *Establishes rapport and maintains contact with the caller.* Efforts are begun as early as possible to combat feelings of helplessness and hopelessness. The caller needs to feel that he has come to the right place, that the person to whom he is talking is experienced and can help him, and that there is hope for him.

2. *Clarifies the caller's immediate need and less urgent problems.* The patient, in his chaos and confusion, frequently is unable to concentrate on any one of his problems but tends to get lost in all of them. The worker is of most assistance in helping the person to appraise each problem and to assign priorities to them.

3. *Evaluates suicide or danger potential.* A question of major concern at all times is: How close is the caller to acting out self-destructive impulses? If the danger is not immediate, the interview can continue by telephone. If the danger is imminent or the caller has already initiated a suicide attempt, the primary responsibility of the worker is either to provide constructive ways of preventing the suicide act or to obtain medical care, such as immediate emergency hospitalization. The caller may be at any point along this continuum of "no immediate danger," and a set of criteria has been developed into a schedule, with items such as age, sex, suicide plan, symptoms, stress, resources, physical illness, and previous suicidal behavior.

4. *Evaluates resources available to the caller.* The suicidal person's tendencies toward isolation and detachment need to be halted. His interpersonal, financial, and physical resources are explored and used where possible. These may include family or relatives, a significant other, friend, neighbor, employer, clergy, professional, hospital, or other.

5. *Sets up a treatment plan.* A plan is worked out with the caller that tries to involve him in doing something for himself. The program is action oriented and frequently involves manipulating his environment as well as providing general support.

Crisis Intervention Versus Long-term Psychotherapy

Crisis intervention differs in obvious ways from traditional hospital and office psychotherapy. Crisis therapy is short-term and emergency oriented, while traditional therapy is usually long-term (six months and longer) and rehabilitation oriented. Table 7 summarizes the differences between the two types of treatment.

The goals of the crisis intervention and traditional therapy are a first source of dissimilarity. Crisis therapy attempts to help the patient to regain his ability to meet and solve his immediate problems as quickly as possible. The aim is to provide relief from symptoms and to resolve any pressing emotional conflicts that have produced his current disorganized state. This is most often achieved by leading the patient to cognitive mastery or intellectual insight. In contrast, long-term psychotherapy aims at helping the patient fashion new ways of feeling and

Table 7. *Comparison of Crisis Intervention and Long-term Psychotherapy.*

	Crisis Intervention	Long-term Psychotherapy
A. Goals	"Reconstitute" the person	Rehabilitation; "reconstruct" the person
	Cognitive mastery (intellectual insight)	Emotional mastery (integrated insight)
	Symptom relief	Restructuring of personality
	Resolution of derivative conflicts	Resolution of basic conflicts
B. Characteristics		
Length	Short-term (1 to 6 contacts); resolution within 1 to 2 months	Long-term (6 months or more)
Treatment process	Usually only part of a plan involving transfer or referral	Does not usually involve transfer
Information elicited and used	May be limited; gathered quickly	Extensive; accumulated slowly
Other persons involved	May involve many others	May or may not involve others; most often a one-to-one relationship
Telephone consultations	Typically caller and worker never see each other	Avoided; patient and therapist are physically in same room
Resources	Any help available is freely used	May or may not be used; therapist helps patient to use his relationships optimally
Availability	Available 24 hours a day, 7 days a week	Regularly scheduled appointments of specified length

C. Therapeutic aspects
Activity of helping agent

	High	Low
Role of authority	Willing to be directive, controlling; expert role	Generally does not direct; may or may not suggest
Precipitating event	Often a single incident, e. g., separation, loss, failure	Often no one event but a buildup
Presenting symptoms	Chaos, disorganization, immobilization, high anxiety level, overwhelming guilt, shame, anger	Discomfort, curiosity, generalized feeling of unhappiness, inadequacy, obessive-compulsive symptoms, and the like
Transference	Deliberately seeks patient's dependency and positive transference	Allows what will to develop and uses it for patient's insight
Focus	Clearly defined; readily resolvable problems	Not always clear; changes periodically with progress
Treatment plan	Action oriented	Insight or support oriented

behaving through providing corrective emotional experiences that, if accompanied by insight, can be integrated into his everyday behavior. This frequently requires a restructuring of his personality and the resolution of basic conflicts that the individual has developed over many years.

The structural and temporal characteristics of the two treatments show significant differences. In crisis intervention the period of time is generally short, involving only one to six contacts and attempting resolution within one or two months. This means that the caseworker is often forced to work with very limited information about the patient and his problems. Steps taken are understood to be stopgap measures rather than complete therapy. Transfer of the patient as soon as the emergency has subsided is intended. Frequently others are involved, and outside resources are readily used.

In psychotherapy, the length of time spent in treatment is generally no less than six months, which means that the therapist has much more extensive information on which to base interpretations. Generally, one therapist treats the patient for all or most of the problems presented, and transfer to another therapist or agency is not part of the treatment plan. Significant others may or may not be involved. Most often treatment occurs on a one-to-one basis. The therapist is very selective in using outside resources to help the treatment process. The telephone is rarely used for treatment; indeed, it is avoided as much as possible. The general procedure is to schedule one or more regular appointments of specified length per week.

The final major category of differences involves therapeutic aspects. Crisis intervention generally entails a high level of activity by the caseworker, who must be willing to be directing and controlling, to be an authority. A dependent relationship may be deliberately sought and then used to help the patient to solve his immediate crisis. The most urgent need is kept clearly in focus. The treatment plan is action oriented, generally intended to resolve the critical, precipitating event that evoked the suicidal feelings or acts. The symptoms presented by the patient will generally be a high level of anxiety, overwhelming guilt, shame, and poorly controlled anger.

In long-term psychotherapy the therapist generally takes a role of minimal activity and does not try to assume a directive or authoritative role. The therapeutic content is not usually determined by the precipitating event but rather by an accumulation of emotions and circumstances that have brought discomfort, curiosity, and generalized feelings of unhappiness. These may or may not have developed into characteristic symptoms. The therapist focuses the content but often does so indirectly through reflections, confrontations, and interpretations. The treatment plan is most often insight oriented but may also aim at giving support to the patient. The feelings developed by the patient are used by the therapist to help the patient to achieve insight.

Who Calls the Suicide Prevention Center?

The people who call suicide prevention centers fit no stereotype. They present a great variety of symptoms and syndromes, are troubled by complex conflicts, and are looking for a wide range of responses. While there is no single type of "suicidal person" that is readily identifiable, there are general characteristics that emerge when a large number of callers are examined. By 1967 files had been accumulated on approximately 26,000 persons calling the Los Angeles Suicide Prevention Center (Wold, 1970). From these files a sample of 1,000 cases was determined by a table of random numbers. When the actual case files were drawn, 984 of the 1,000 cases were found; the 16 remaining were either missing or proved to be duplicates of other files. The 984 cases were reviewed and the data categorized.

Similar information was culled from the files of 42 Suicide Prevention Center patients who had later committed suicide. These people, who had had some contact with the Suicide Prevention Center (SPC) prior to their suicide, represented all the known SPC patients (up to 1967) who had later killed themselves. Table 8 shows the percentages of patients in these two groups who had the characteristics listed.

Of the larger patient sample, about two thirds are female and one third are male. Depression is a very common symptom, with the affective type occurring in 85 percent of the callers. Among the other symptoms found are confusion in 38 percent, a drinking problem in 25 percent, and drug problems in about 13 percent. Approximately two thirds are thinking or threatening suicide, and one third have made or are in the process of making a suicide attempt. About 50 percent have a history of at least one suicide event. About one out of every ten has been in trouble with the law. More than half the individuals called the Suicide Prevention Center themselves; the callers for the remaining 45

Table 8. *Characteristics of Los Angeles Suicide Prevention Center Cases.*

Characteristics	Percent of General Sample (N = 984)	Percent of Suicide Deaths (N = 42)
Sex		
Male	36	64
Female	64	36
Depression		
Somatic	67	88
Affective	85	95
Social	62	92
Confusion		
Yes	38	44
Yes, and psychotic	14	10
Current drinking problem	25	31
Current drug problem	13	20
Current suicide problem		
Suicidal ideas	31	19
Suicidal threats	33	55
Suicidal behavior	5	0
Suicide attempt	31	26
No prior suicidal problems	28	12
Prior suicidal problems	52	60
Homicide component	12	15
Pregnant	2	0
Recent professional contact	59	34
Current living arrangement		
Alone	32	51
With friends	9	2
With family	58	44
Interpersonal loss	48	40
Health loss	20	8
Repeated marriages (2 or more)	19	40
Prior inpatient treatment	33	27
Prior outpatient treatment	50	42
Trouble with the law	11	12
Who called SPC		
Self	52	47
Friend	15	21
Family	17	18
Professional	16	14

Table 8. Characteristics of Los Angeles Suicide Prevention Center Cases (cont.).

Characteristics	Percent of General Sample (N = 984)	Percent of Suicide Deaths (N = 42)
Current acute suicide potential rating		
High	19	45
Moderate	38	45
Low	43	10
Our recommendation		
Hospital	16	35
Back to therapist	10	0
Outpatient	34	32
None	11	3

SOURCE: Adapted from Carl I. Wold, "Characteristics of 26,000 Suicide Prevention Center Patients." *Bulletin of Suicidology,* Spring 1970; pp. 24–28.

percent were evenly distributed among friends, family, and professional persons. Ratings of suicide potential indicate approximately 40 percent were low, 40 percent moderate, and 20 percent high.

The characteristics of the callers who later committed suicide are markedly different. The proportion of men to women is reversed, two-thirds male and one-third female (this is the ratio found in the general population of suicides). Depression, whether somatic, affective, or social, was an even more prominent characteristic for all of them. Marked confusion was present in 44 percent, while those having current drinking and drug problems were up to 31 and 20 percent, respectively. At the time they called, 55 percent threatened suicide (versus 33 percent in the larger, general sample), and 90 percent were considered either high or moderate in suicide potential. Another indication of seriousness is the recommendation of immediate hospitalization for over twice as many in this group of suicide deaths as in the patient sample (35 percent versus 16 percent, respectively). Approximately one out of every two was living alone at the time of the call.

Later, using sets of empirically derived items describing the callers to a suicide prevention center, Wold (1971) was able to derive clinically meaningful subgroups. Identification of these subgroups was based on primary characteristics rather than standard psychiatric categories. Wold observed the following subgroups[2]:

(1) *Discarded women.* About 8 percent of the SPC callers were young women who had been repeatedly discarded by lovers or spouses. They were generally hysterical and overdramatic, and they showed exaggerated emotional responses alternating with denial of feeling. They frequently felt that they had been abandoned by their parents as well. Suicide risk was generally low or at most moderate, and they did not appear among the suicides, although they may have made many attempts.

> Ms. L, a 31 year old woman, first called the SPC four years ago when she broke up with her boy friend. She was crying, threatening suicide, and begging the worker to help her get her lover back. When questioned about how she intended to kill herself she talked vaguely of jumping from a downtown high building. She had no sleeping pills on hand and no gun. She reluctantly agreed to her parents being notified and they persuaded her to give up her apartment and stay with them during the crisis. Two other contacts with Ms. L occurred in the years following, each time when she was in difficulty with her current boy friend. On one of these occasions she had taken a small number of sleeping pills, which resulted in having her stomach pumped.

(2) *Discarded, stable (I can't live without you).* This group was made up of two-thirds women and one-third men, ranging in age from the twenties through the fifties, who had become suicidal in response to the breakup of a love relationship in which they had become overly dependent on the other person. Job and residence history were relatively stable; neither alcohol nor drugs was ever a problem. The stress was caused by close personal loss and included severe mourning reactions. They were seen as high suicide risks, with about 67 percent rated high or moderate. This category accounted for 12 percent of SPC patients and 20 percent of SPC suicides.

> Mr. B, a 43 year old man, called in a severe depression, marked by agitation, sleeplessness, and loss of interest in his job. His wife had told him five months previously that she had been having an affair with her

employer and wanted to end their marriage of eighteen years. She had agreed to terminate the affair but insisted that she wanted a divorce. However, she did not want to desert him and stated she would wait until he had adjusted to their new relationship. B felt betrayed by the affair but was willing to forgive his wife if she would stay and they "could start their life over." If she left, however, he would kill himself. The wife stayed with the condition that B seek therapy. She agreed to marital counseling for both of them, but remained adamant on the eventual divorce. B quit his engineering job to stay home with her and try to change her mind. When the wife finally left, B made a very serious suicide attempt from which he was barely saved. He continues to be very depressed.

(3) *I can't live with you.* Two thirds of this group were women, ranging in age from twenty to fifty. They accounted for 7 percent of the SPC patients and about 10 percent of the patient suicides. They were seen as high suicide risks, with about 90 percent rated either as high or moderate. Most of these people were severely confused and disorganized in their thinking, with 35 percent seen as psychotic. About 15 percent were rated as alcoholic, and the same percentage used drugs abusively.

Mr. T is a short order cook who has had many problems holding on to his jobs because of drinking. T's wife has been in and out of the hospital many times. He was always glad at first when his wife was released from the hospital, but her demands on him would soon begin to weigh heavily and his drinking would increase. On the occasions when his wife returned to the hospital, he would be overwhelmed with conflicting feelings, relief from his wife's psychotic unpredictable behavior and guilt that he had contributed to its reappearance. T's reaction to the pressures resulted in mild overdoses of pills, although on one occasion he used a knife to cut his arms. The Center worked with him to agree to call before he injured himself and to relieve his feelings through talking rather than pain.

(4) *Down-and-out, unstable.* While this group accounted for only 3 percent of the SPC patients, they contributed 22 percent to the patient suicides. Two thirds of the callers were men, mostly between the ages of forty and sixty; all of the suicides were men. They showed a pattern of failure and loss in love and jobs, and their residence had been unstable

for some years. Symptoms were alcoholism, drug abuse, and poor physical health. They were generally chronic, high suicide risks.

> Mr. J, a 48 year old man, has been on a progressively downward course for the past eight years, ever since his wife died. He had invested her with all the wonderful qualities a woman could possess, and her death by cancer after three lingering years devastated him. He had given up his job in an accounting firm in order to nurse her and after her death was unable to return to work. He felt all meaning had gone from his life and began to drink heavily. He stopped periodically, but was unable to control his drinking even though he joined Alcoholics Anonymous. He found several jobs with accounting firms, but his drinking habit got him fired each time. He then tried a succession of jobs in ever-decreasing status, such as selling, clerking, and labor, but was unable to hold on to any of them. His depression has continued. He has been unable or unwilling to establish a relationship with another woman.

(5) *Malignant masochism.* The SPC patients in this group were primarily in their twenties or thirties and were mostly women. There was a chronic pattern of omnipresent suicidal feelings, relatively independent of stress or current symptoms. Death and suicide were looked upon with peaceful and pleasurable fantasies. These callers made up 4 percent of the patients and 5 percent of the patient suicides; 90 percent had shown chronic suicidal problems. Almost all were rated as high or moderate risks.

> Miss A was 23 years old when she was first referred to the Suicide Prevention Center for therapy in fulfillment of condition of her parole. She had just finished her third prison term for drug abuse. Ms. A's past history also showed several stays in a mental hospital and a series of treatment by psychotherapists ever since she was ten years old. Her past history was filled with violence, chaos, and disorganization. Her step-father had been extremely cruel and, when she became a teenager, had beaten her mercilessly, accusing her of sexual promiscuity. Her mother had given her little support, but had provided her with a weak ally in the intrafamily conflicts. Miss A had become a drug addict, used alcohol when drugs were not available, and lived in a continuously chaotic relationship with a succession of boy friends. Very bright, Miss A also had remarkable sensitivity and awareness of her unconscious. She wrote poetry filled with longings about death; death was eroticized and made

into a fanciful lover into whose arms she tenderly surrendered herself. She was treated both in individual and group psychotherapy and successfully completed her parole. It was not without incident, however, including several serious suicide attempts and a number of brushes with the law.

(6) *Violence*. This pattern was found in 4 percent of the patients and 10 percent of the suicides. Of the patients in this category, approximately 55 percent were male and 45 percent female, distributed evenly among those in their twenties, thirties, and forties. These patients showed episodes of violent rage toward themselves or others that were frequently associated with heavy drinking and followed by strong guilt and remorse. There was a good social involvement and high job investment. Impulsiveness, however, was difficult to control.

When Mr. B, a 34 year old white male, first attended group psychotherapy in the Suicide Prevention Center, he showed marks of a recent fist fight. His knuckles were bandaged, he wore a bandaid on his face and there were bruises and discolorations. He reported having been in a bar two nights ago and "taking on half a dozen fellows." Mr. B had been drinking heavily over the past several years. His wife had recently started divorce proceedings, giving as one of the reasons his continually getting into fights. In the course of therapy Mr. B revealed he had a gun at home. However, he refused to dispose of it although he recognized that he was impulsive and might get into trouble using it. He claimed that his "connections" with the underworld required that he keep it. On several occasions he became belligerent in the therapy sessions and had to be reminded that physical violence was not acceptable and that he would not be permitted to return if he struck anyone. Although he made no suicide attempt during his contact with the Center, his continuing depression, impulsivity, and contradictory feelings toward his wife made it continually uncertain whether he would act against his wife or himself.

(7) *Middle-age depression*. About 3 percent of the patients and 12 percent of the suicides fell into this group, which is characterized by acute symptoms of depression appearing in stable, middle-aged people, ages thirty to sixty. Very few had made a recent suicide attempt. Most of them either threatened to kill themselves or were troubled with suicidal thoughts and ideas. The majority were seen as moderate suicide

risks, with about 8 percent rated as high risks. For most of the group, achievements and goals had lost their meaning. Symptoms included mostly somatic depression—fatigue, inability to feel pleasure, vague physical complaints, and concern about impotence—as well as social withdrawal. Often these callers were ashamed and guilty about their symptoms and therefore were not communicative at first.

> Mr. G began to call the Center daily when his back pains increased and he was unable to obtain any relief. He had been mildly depressed since he had divorced his wife four years ago "because she was not contributing equally to their partnership." He had asked for a leave of absence from his school where he was a manual arts teacher in order to concentrate on improving his physical condition and overcoming his depression. Rigid in his ways he approached every situation looking for the "perfect solution" and finding great difficulty understanding why people behaved so unpredictably. Every attempt at a relationship ended in failure because the other person could not be trusted to live up to expectations. Further pressure was exerted on him by his school, which did not seem to understand his problems and kept insisting that he return to work or resign. However, his back pains did not subside and he finally resigned. His depression deepened as he felt he had little to look forward to either in his profession as a teacher or his relationships with people.

(8) *Adolescent turmoil.* This group, made up of teenagers and those in their early twenties, accounted for 10 percent of the patient sample and about 8 percent of the suicides. About half of the patient sample were females, while among the deaths 80 percent were male. Most of the symptoms involved current turmoil, such as agitation, confusion, and chaotic or impulsive behavior. These patients were generally struggling with adolescent problems of identity and independence and separation from the family.

> Mr. W was 18 when he first appeared at the Center. He was in psychotherapy in a community mental health center but felt they were unable to help him with his depression and suicidal impulses. He had dropped out of school in the past year, the second time in the last three years. He was living with his mother with whom he was in constant conflict. Several attempts in the past to move out and live independently had

resulted in wild threats of suicide on her part if he stayed away. He was angry and bitter toward his mother but was afraid she would take pills if he stayed away. His father had committed suicide six years ago and his mother had made him feel guilty by telling him it was problems with him that had so depressed his father. Mr. W was persuaded to return to school and was given support in establishing his own apartment again. However, follow-up six months later indicated he was living once more with his mother and that he was again having problems with his school work. He was urged to resume psychotherapy, which provided him with much-needed support when he became suicidal.

(9) *Chaotic, psychotic, and borderline.* This group accounted for 9 percent of the patients and 12 percent of the patient suicides. All were rated as severely confused and disorganized in their thinking. Two thirds had a history of multiple suicide attempts. The chronic symptom pattern was of current and recurrent severe confusion, agitation, and chaotic or impulsive behavior relatively independent of stress. The group consisted mostly of young adults or older persons with long histories of personal difficulties.

Ms. V is a 24 year old white girl with a long history of disturbed relationships. She is unpredictable and frequently infantile in her behavior, and is constantly seeking assurance and direction. Unable to resist male advances she finds herself repeatedly being "used" by men who seem to have little regard for her as a person. She cries in ready sympathy when another group member recounts a difficult experience, but exhibits no understanding of others' needs in the group discussion. She demands detailed instructions on how to behave in her relations with others. She has been helped by the control in her group interactions but still finds it difficult to apply what she has learned to her activities outside the Center. A board and care home provides more structure for her, but short periods of relative calm are continually punctuated by impulsive behavior and a short-lived crisis. Ms. V is seen as probably needing close supervision and control for most of her life.

(10) *Old and stable.* Accounting for 3 percent of the patients, this group made up 10 percent of the suicides. Most of the group were sixty or older, living alone and suffering from severe depression. In general, they showed a stable life history and were suicidal in response to stress—recent loss of a loved person or loss of health or finances.

Mr. M had run a small business successfully in the East. He moved to the West with his wife of 27 years in order to retire and live out the rest of his life in the sunshine of Southern California. However, the stocks in which he had invested most of his money had depreciated and he found it necessary to look for employment. He has found that very few business or industries are willing to employ a 63 year old man with a small hardware store experience. His wife is sympathetic but unable to help because of her arthritic condition, which makes movement painful. Two married children still in the East send small sums of money monthly but Mr. M feels this to be degrading. He continues to be bitter and angry about his deprived life and to talk about ending it all for both his wife and himself.

Effectiveness of the Suicide Prevention Center

The question has been raised whether a suicide prevention center actually succeeds in preventing suicides. Answers to this question have been sought primarily through follow-up studies conducted at varying periods. The first question is whether the individuals calling the center are generally higher risks than the population at large. Robert Litman (1972) has estimated that unselected Suicide Prevention Center cases in general are pathologically higher risks. The average suicide rate for the United States is about 11 suicides per year per 100,000 population. In contrast, the suicide probability for unselected Suicide Prevention Center cases was estimated by Litman to be about 1,000 per 100,000 population, or approximately one hundred times as great. This estimate is based on follow-up studies from suicide prevention centers in Los Angeles (Litman, 1970), Chicago (Wilkins, 1970), and Cleveland (Browning, Tyson, & Miller, 1970), which indicate a suicide rate of 1 to 2 percent per year for the first and second year after contact. A short-term follow-up study conducted in the Los Angeles Suicide Prevention Center in May 1970 attempted to obtain follow-up information on callers by recontacting them within five to seven days. Approximately 50 percent of the original callers (325 out of 652) were available and cooperated. At the call-back, workers evaluated the suicide potential as lower in 70 percent of the cases, higher in 12 percent of the cases, and the same in 18 percent of the cases. Eleven callers had made suicide attempts in the intervening week. To the question, "Were you helped by the Suicide Prevention Center?" 87 percent of the subjects responded yes, 11 percent responded no, and 2 percent gave no answer. To the question, "Did the Suicide Prevention Center save your life?" 32 percent of those who said they had been helped said yes, 31 percent said no, and 37 percent said maybe.

Christopher Bagley (1968) attempted to evaluate the effectiveness of the Samaritans' service in preventing suicide by comparing changes in the suicide rates of fifteen English towns that initiated Samaritan services with other control towns that did not. He found an average reduction of 5.8 in the rates in the Samaritan towns compared with an average increase of 7.3 in the control towns. The evidence suggested to him the possibility that Samaritan activities lowered local suicide rates. One of the major questions that arises in evaluating this study is the variability in processes by which suicides were certified in the various localities.

Crisis Versus Chronic Response

Kenneth Stein (1969) and Wold (1971) have indicated that half to two thirds of the callers to a suicide prevention center are likely to be chronically disturbed, tenuously adjusted individuals in whom the current suicidal crisis is an exacerbation of ongoing conflicts and problems. The usual techniques and procedures of crisis intervention practiced in the suicide prevention center can help persons who are in acute stress and who are acutely suicidal. However, there is some question whether crisis intervention procedures are effective in preventing suicide in chronically disturbed people.

Crisis intervention is appropriate for suicidal patients who have had a previous period of stable adjustment and who have fallen into disequilibrium because of some acute stress. Supplementary types of intervention are needed for patients who do not conform to the crisis model. Two programs to meet the needs of the chronically suicidal individual are currently under examination.

A program of "continuing relationship maintenance" is being used with some suicidal individuals who call a prevention center and are evaluated as high risks. A patient is assigned to a group of paraprofessional volunteers, who establish a relationship with the patient and develop this relationship under the supervision of the professional staff. The program includes regular telephone calls initiated by the volunteer, home visits, and individual and group meetings at the suicide prevention center or other meeting place. The patient is encouraged and helped to use all available community and personal resources. The emphasis in this intervention model is on rehabilitating rather than on coping with a single crisis. The goals are developing increased self-confidence, increasing communication with others, lessening of isolation, and improving socialization capacities.

In a second program suicidal persons are invited to participate according to need in group psychotherapy of various types. Group psychotherapy seems especially suited for suicidal persons in light of their tendencies toward isolation and detachment. The group provides a ready-made arena for social interaction and development of interpersonal skills (Farberow, 1973). One of the different kinds of groups is the long-term, insight-oriented group, which is conducted in traditional fashion with closed membership and which is focused on dynamics, motivation, and self-understanding. These long-term groups meet once a week under the leadership of two professional therapists. The primary focus is the social and interpersonal relationships of the patients. The interaction in the group is used as a reflection of the experiences with others outside. Depression, anxiety, and suicidal behavior are the most frequent themes. The most common concern is self-concept and self-esteem—who am I and am I worthy of love?

> Thus, Ms. K lost her husband to another woman, and felt it was appropriate because the other woman would be a much better wife than she. Ms. O could not allow herself to succeed in her work (office manager) for to do so was to be aggressive and therefore not feminine. Nevertheless, being successful had always been held up to her by her family as the most important goal in life.

A post-crisis-oriented, time-limited group led by two certified group therapists meets twice a week for a specified period of eight weeks for each patient. The focus is a set of objectives mutually agreed upon by patients and therapists to reestablish functioning and to reconstitute relationships and coping mechanisms.

> For example, Ms. A, a 32 year old woman in the process of divorce, attempted suicide twice within two months following the break-up of her marriage. She was now running around frantically with a number of men and was close to being fired from her job because of neglecting her work. The goal was set as helping her to reestablish herself at work. She had denied her feelings of rage against her husband. In group she learned that she was directing those feelings of rage against herself

instead of the person really provoking them. As she became more able to tolerate these previously unacceptable feelings, the suicidal impulses subsided and her work performance improved.

A creative expression group led by two psychology graduate students uses nonverbal expressive procedures, such as painting, clay, movement, and other techniques. A socialization group under two psychology graduate students meets once a week with a focus on ease in interrelationships and the development of social skills. Therapy as such is avoided, and instead the emphasis is on techniques for feeling comfortable with oneself and for facilitating interactions with others.

A drop-in group meets every day of the week and is open to any person who calls and is considered in need of an immediate resource consisting of acceptance, understanding, and tolerance from both staff and other patients. The patients are informed that the drop-in group is available to them any time they wish to attend and that they need not commit themselves to regular attendance, although some of them do. No responsibility for any other person is demanded, although many begin to assume interest in and to develop relationships with other patients who attend. The groups are led by different volunteers each day, so that the patients do not become dependent upon any one individual but rather relate to the Center as the primary resource.

A 56 year old woman lost her job as a bookkeeper she had held for twenty years. She overdosed once, called the Center and was invited to the drop-in group. She attended eight sessions reporting severe anxiety and somatic symptoms. The group members encouraged her to go out on job interviews despite her anxiety. After two weeks, she found another job and all her symptoms subsided. Although the majority of patients use the drop-in group during crisis, a number have become "regulars," attending almost every day for extended periods. A 53 year old male had called the Center often when drunk and suicidal. He frequently became abusive over the phone. Invited to attend the drop-in group, he came to 85 sessions, 80 of them consecutively, and remained sober throughout. His suicidal ideation diminished and he seemed to enjoy helping others in the group. He left after he found a job, the first in many years.

Both the continuity relationship maintenance program and the group therapy program are new, and their effectiveness is yet to be evaluated.

The aim is to reduce and eliminate often unnecessary anguish and torment. Those working in the field of suicide believe that this act will yield in part to the dissemination of information and the reduction of taboos. The most constructive help is the unhesitating showing of genuine interest, care, and concern.

NOTES

1. Wars are assumed to provide a missing sense of purpose and meaningfulness to suicidal people, contributing to a lower rate (Dublin, 1963). The fact that the rate did not decrease during the Vietnam war years tempts the speculation that the country never developed a sense of unified purpose about this war.

2. Percentages reported do not total 100. Some cases in both groups could not be classified; others were counted in more than one subgroup.

BIBLIOGRAPHY

Adler, Alfred. "Selbstmord (Suicide)." *Internationale Zeitschrift für Individual Psychologie,* 1937, 15:49–52. (Reprinted in *Journal of Individual Psychology,* 1958, 14:57–61.)

Allen, Nancy H. *Suicide in California 1960–1970.* State of California Department of Health, 1973.

Aquinas, Thomas. *Summa Theologica.* New York: Benziger Brothers, 1947. (Reprint of the first edition.)

Bagley, Christopher. "The Evaluation of a Suicide Prevention Scheme by an Ecological Method." *Social Science and Medicine,* 1968, 2:1–14.

Bender, Lauretta, and Paul Schilder. "Suicidal Preoccupations and Attempts in Children." *American Journal of Orthopsychiatry,* 1937, 7:225–234.

Browning, Charles H., Robert L. Tyson, and Sheldon I. Miller. "A Study of Psychiatric Emergencies. II. Suicide." *Psychiatry in Medicine,* 1970, 1:359–366.

Caplan, Gerald. *An Approach to Community Mental Health.* New York: Grune & Stratton, 1961.

Caplan, Gerald. *Principles of Preventive Psychology.* New York: Basic Books, 1964.

Capstick, Alan. "Recognition of Emotional Disturbance and the Prevention of Suicide." *British Medical Journal,* 1960, 1:1179–1182.

Chambliss, William J., and Marion F. Steele. "Status Integration and Suicide." *American Sociological Review,* 1966, 31:524–532.

Crichton-Miller, Hugh. "The Psychology of Suicide." *British Medical Journal,* 1931, 2:239–241.

Curphey, Theodore J., Edwin S. Shneidman, and Norman L. Farberow. "Drugs, Deaths, and Suicides—Problems of the Coroner." In William G. Clark and Joseph del Guidice, eds. *Principles of Psychopharmacology.* New York: Academic Press, 1970, pp. 523–536.

Darbonne, Allen R. "Study of Psychological Content in the Communiations of Suicidal Individuals." *Journal of Consulting and Clinical Psychology,* 1969, 33:590–596.

De Rosis, Louis. "Suicide: The Horney Point of View." In Norman L. Farberow and Edwin S. Shneidman, eds. *The Cry for Help.* New York: McGraw-Hill, 1961, pp. 236–254.

Dohrenwend, Bruce P. "Egoism, Altruism, Anomie, and Fatalism." *American Sociological Review,* 1959, 24:468–473.

Dollard, John, Leonard W. Doob, Neal E. Miller, and Robert R. Sears. *Frustration and Aggression.* New Haven, Conn.: Yale University Press, 1939.

Donne, John. *Biothanatos.* Facsimile-Text Society, 1930. (Reprint of the first edition, 1644.)

Douglas, John D. *The Social Meanings of Suicide.* Princeton, N.J.: Princeton University Press, 1967.

Dublin, Louis I. *Suicide: A Sociological and Statistical Study of Suicide.* New York: Ronald Press, 1963.

Durkheim, Emile. *Le Suicide: Étude de Sociologie (Suicide: Sociological Study).* Paris: Felix Alcan, 1897. (Translated by John A. Spaulding and George Simpson. Glencoe, Ill.: The Free Press, 1951.)

Esquirol, Jean Étienne Dominique. *Mental Maladies: A Treatise on Insanity.* Translated by E. K. Hunt. Lea and Blanchard, 1845. (Reprinted by New York: Hefner, 1965.)

Farberow, Norman L. "Concepts and Conceptions of a Suicide Prevention Center." In Erwin Ringel, ed. *Selbstmordverhütung (Suicide Prevention).* Vienna: Hans Huber, 1969, pp. 179–194.

Farberow, Norman L. *Bibliography on Suicide and Suicide Prevention, 1897–1957, 1958–1970.* DHEW Publication No. 72–9080. Washington, D.C.: U.S. Government Printing Office, 1972a.

Farberow, Norman L. "Cultural History of Suicide." In Jan Waldenström, Tage Larsson, and Nils Ljungstedt, eds. *Suicide and Attempted Suicide.* Stockholm: Nordiska Bokhandelns Förlag, 1972b, pp. 30–44.

Farberow, Norman L. "Group Psychotherapy for Self-Destructive Persons." Paper presented at the National Institute for Mental Health Continuing Education Seminar on Emergency Mental Health Services, Washington, D.C., June 1973.

Farberow, Norman L., and Charles Neuringer. "The Social Scientist as Coroner's Deputy." *Journal of Forensic Sciences,* 1971, 16:15–39.

Farberow, Norman L., and Edwin S. Shneidman, eds. *The Cry for Help.* New York: McGraw-Hill, 1961a.

Farberow, Norman L., Edwin S. Shneidman. "A Survey of Agencies for the Prevention of Suicide." In Norman L. Farberow and Edwin S. Shneidman, eds. *The Cry for Help.* New York: McGraw-Hill, 1961b, pp. 6–18.

Farberow, Norman L., Kenneth Stein, Allen L. Darbonne, and Sophie Hirsch. "Indirect Self-Destruction in Diabetic Patients." *Hospital Medicine,* 1970, 6:123–153.

"Final Mortality Statistics, 1974." *Monthly Vital Statistics Report,* vol. 24, no. 11, supplement. Rockville, Md.: National Center for Health Statistics, February, 3, 1976.

Frederick, Calvin J. "Suicide Notes: A Survey and Evaluation." *Bulletin of Suicidology,* March 1969, pp. 17–26.

Freud, Sigmund. *Beyond the Pleasure Principle*. London: Hogarth Press, 1950a.

Freud, Sigmund. "Mourning and Melancholia." In *Collected Papers*, vol. 4. London: Hogarth Press, 1950b, pp. 152–170.

Gibbs, Jack P., ed. *Suicide*. New York: Harper & Row, 1968.

Gibbs, Jack P., and Walter T. Martin. *Status Integration and Suicide: A Sociological Study*. Eugene, Ore.: University of Oregon Books, 1964.

Gill, Merton. "Psychoanalysis and Exploratory Psychotherapy." *Journal of American Psychoanalytic Association*, 1954, 2:771–797.

Ginsberg, Ralph B. "Anomie and Aspirations." *Dissertation Abstracts*, 1966, 27a:3945–3946.

Gold, Martin. "Suicide, Homicide, and the Socialization of Aggression." *American Journal of Sociology*, 1958, 63:651–661.

Green, Maurice R. "Suicide: The Sullivanian Point of View." In Norman L. Farberow and Edwin S. Shneidman, eds. *The Cry for Help*. New York: McGraw-Hill, 1961, pp. 220–235.

Halbwachs, Maurice. *The Causes of Suicide*. Paris: Felix Alcan, 1930.

Henry, Andrew F., and James F. Short, Jr. *Suicide and Homicide*. Glencoe, Ill.: The Free Press, 1954.

Hillman, James. *Suicide and the Soul*. New York: Harper & Row, 1964.

Hume, David. *An Essay on Suicide*. Yellow Springs, Ohio: Kahoe, 1929. (Reprint of the first edition, 1777.)

Jacobs, Jerry. "A Phenomenological Study of Suicide Notes." *Social Problems*, 1967, 15:60–72.

Johnson, Barclay D. "Durkheim's One Cause of Suicide." *American Sociological Review*, 1965, 30:875–886.

Kelly, George A. "Suicide: The Personal Construct Point of View." In Norman L. Farberow and Edwin S. Shneidman, eds. *The Cry for Help*. New York: McGraw-Hill, 1961, pp. 255–280.

Klopfer, Bruno. "Suicide: The Jungian Point of View." In Norman L. Farberow and Edwin S. Shneidman, eds. *The Cry for Help*. New York: McGraw-Hill, 1961, pp. 193–203.

Kobler, Arthur, and Ezra Stotland. *The End of Hope: A Social-Clinical Study of Suicide*. New York: The Free Press of Glencoe, 1964.

Lester, David. *Why People Kill Themselves*. Springfield, Ill.: Thomas, 1972.

Lewis, Nolan D. C. "Studies on Suicide. I. Preliminary Survey of Some Significant Aspects of Suicide." *Psychoanalytic Review*, 1933, 20:241–273.

Lewis, Nolan D. C. "Studies of Suicide. II. Some Comments on the Biological Aspects of Suicide." *Psychoanalytic Review*, 1934, 21:146–153.

Lindemann, Eric. "Symptomatology and Management of Acute Grief." *American Journal of Psychiatry*, 1944, 101:141–148.

Litman, Robert E. "Suicide Prevention Center Patients: A Follow-Up Study." *Bulletin of Suicidology*, Spring 1970, pp. 12–17.

Litman, Robert E. "Experiences in a Suicide Prevention Center." In Jan Waldenström, Tage Larsson, and Nils Ljungstedt, eds. *Suicide and Attempted Suicide*. Stockholm: Nordiska Bokhandelns Förlag, 1972, pp. 217–230.

Litman, Robert E., and Norman D. Tabachnick. "Psychoanalytic Theories of Suicide." In Harvey L. P. Resnik, ed. *Suicidal Behaviors: Diagnosis and Management*. Boston: Little, Brown, 1968, pp. 73–81.

Maris, Ronald. "Suicide, Status, and Mobility in Chicago." *Social Forces*, 1967, 46:246–256.

Menninger, Karl A. *Man Against Himself*. New York: Harcourt, Brace, 1938.

Merian, "Sur la Crainte de la Mort, sur le Mépris de la Mort, sur le Suicide, Mémoire." *Histoire de l'Académie Royale des Sciences et Belles-Lettres de Berlin*, 1763, 19:385, 392, 403.

Monthly Vital Statistics Report. National Center for Health Statistics, Vol. 24, No. 11, Supplement, February 3, 1976.

Moriyama, Iwao M., and Robert A. Israel. "Problems in Compilation of Statistics on Suicides in the United States." In Norman L. Farberow, ed. *Proceedings of the Fourth International Conference for Suicide Prevention*. Los Angeles: Suicide Prevention Center, 1968, pp. 16–21.

Morselli, Henry. *Suicide: An Essay on Comparative Moral Statistics*. New York: Appleton-Century, 1882.

Naroll, Raoul. "Status Integration and Status Association." Unpublished paper, Northwestern University, 1965.

O'Connor, Willaim A. "Some Notes on Suicide." *British Journal of Medical Psychology*, 1947–1948, 21:222–228.

Osgood, Charles E., and Evelyn G. Walker. "Motivation and Language Behavior: A Content Analysis of Suicide Notes." *Journal of Abnormal and Social Psychology*, 1959, 59:58–67.

Phillips, David P. "The Influence of Suggestion on Suicide: Substantive and Theoretical Implications of the Werther Effect." *American Sociological Review*, 1974, 39:340–354.

Porterfield, Austin L. "The Problem of Suicide." In Jack P. Gibbs, ed. *Suicide*. New York: Harper & Row, 1968, pp. 31–57.

Powell, Elwin H. "Occupation Status and Suicide." *American Journal of Sociology*, 1958, 23:131–139.

Rapaport, Lydia. "The State of Crisis: Some Theoretical Considerations." *Social Service Review*, 1962, 36:211–217.

Shneidman, Edwin S. "Orientations toward Death: A Vital Aspect of the Study of Lives." In Robert W. White, ed. *The Study of Lives: Essays on Personality in Honor of Henry A. Murray.* New York: Atherton Press, 1963, pp. 200–227.

Shneidman, Edwin S., and Norman L. Farberow. *Clues to Suicide.* New York: McGraw-Hill, 1957.

Shneidman, Edwin S., and Norman L. Farberow. "Statistical Comparisons between Attempted and Committed Suicides." In Norman L. Farberow and Edwin S. Shneidman, eds. *The Cry for Help.* New York: McGraw-Hill, 1961, pp. 19–47.

Stein, Kenneth. "A Challenge to the Role of the Crisis Concept in Emergency Psychotherapy." Ph.D. dissertation, University of Oregon, 1969.

Stengel, Erwin, and Norman L. Farberow. "Certification of Suicide Around the World." In Norman L. Farberow, ed. *Proceedings of the Fourth International Conference for Suicide Prevention.* Los Angeles: Suicide Prevention Center, 1968, pp. 8–15.

Szasz, Thomas. "The Ethics of Suicide Prevention." *Audio-Digest: Psychiatry,* 1972, Vol 1, No. 2.

Teele, James E. "Suicidal Behavior, Assaultiveness, and Socialization Principles." *Social Forces,* 1965, 43:510–518.

Teicher, Joseph D. "A Study in Attempted Suicide." *Journal of Nervous and Mental Disease,* 1947, 105:283–298.

Tuckman, Jacob, Robert J. Kleiner, and Martha Lavell. "Credibility of Suicide Notes." *American Journal of Psychiatry,* 1960, 116:1104–1106.

Uematsu, Minoru. "A Statistical Approach to the Host Factor of Suicide in Adolescence." *Acta Medica et Biologica,* 1961, 8:279–286.

Vital Statistics of the United States, 1972, vol. 2. Mortality, part A. Rockville, Md.: National Center for Health Statistics, 1976.

Whitt, Hugh T. "The Lethal Aggression Ratio and the Suicide Murder Ratio." *Dissertation Abstracts,* 1969, 29b:2624–2625.

Wilkins, James. "A Follow-up Study of Those Who Called a Suicide Prevention Center." *American Journal of Psychiatry,* 1970, 127:155–161.

Wold, Carl I. "Characteristics of 26,000 Suicide Prevention Center Patients." *Bulletin of Suicidology,* Spring 1970, pp. 24–28.

Wold, Carl I. "Sub-groupings of Suicidal People." *Omega,* 1971, 2:19–29.

Wood, Arthur L. "A Socio-Structural Analysis of Murder, Suicide, and Economic Crime in Ceylon." *American Sociological Review,* 1961, 26:744–753.

Worden, J. William, and Robert S. Sterling-Smith. "Lethality Patterns in Multiple Suicide Attempts. *Life-Threatening Behavior,* 1973, 3:95–104.

World Health Statistics Annual, 1972, vol. 1. Vital Statistics and Causes of Death. Geneva: World Health Organization, 1975.

Zilboorg, Gregory. "Suicide among Civilized and Primitive Races." *American Journal of Psychiatry,* 1936, 92:1347–1369.

Contributors

William Bates is professor of sociology at Loyola University. He is co-author with Betty Crowther of *Towards a Typology of Narcotic Addiction* and many papers and articles on drug use and other forms of deviance. He worked at the federal government's narcotics hospital at Lexington and Fort Worth for 5 years, and he was director of Social Research at the NIMH Clinical Research Center at Fort Worth, Texas. He received his bachelor's degree from Gonzaga University, masters from the College of the Pacific, and doctorate from Washington University. He is particularly interested in methodology, statistics, and deviant behavior.

Betty Crowther is professor of sociology at Southern Illinois University, Edwardsville. She is co-author with William Bates of *Towards a Typology of Narcotic Addiction* and many papers and articles on drug use and social psychology. She was a Research Social Psychologist at the NIMH Clinical Research Center at Fort Worth, Texas, and an assistant to William Bates. She received her bachelor's degree from Brown, master's from Cornell, and doctorate from the University of Wisconsin. Her interests are in methodology, statistics, and social psychology.

Norman L. Farberow is principle investigator of the Central Research Unit of the Veterans Administration Wadsworth Hospital Center, Los Angeles, and Co-Director of the Los Angeles Suicide Prevention Center. He is author of numerous papers, articles, and monographs on self-destruction. He is co-editor, with Edwin Shneidman, of *The Cry for Help,* and *Clues to Suicide,* and editor of *Suicide in Different Cultures.* He received his doctorate from the University of California at Los Angeles.

Jennifer James is assistant professor of psychiatry and behavioral sciences at the University of Washington, and has done extensive research in the fields of prostitution and female addiction. She received her bachelor's degree in history and master's in anthropology, both from Washington State University, and a doctorate in anthropology at the University of Washington.

Carl Klockars is adjunct associate professor of sociology at the University of Delaware. He is author of *The Professional Fence,* a life history of a major dealer in stolen property, and of numerous articles on crime and the ethics of criminological research. He is engaged in a two year ethnographic study of detective-level police work. He received his bachelor's degree from the University of Rhode Island, and master's and doctoral degrees from the University of Pennsylvania.

Lowell L. Kuehn is on the faculty of Evergreen State College, where he is engaged in designing and teaching interdisciplinary courses in the social sciences. He received his bachelor's degree from University of Redlands, and master's and doctorate at University of Washington. He has done research on the perception of violent crime, the methodology of social action program evaluation, and on decision-making in small claims courts.

David F. Luckenbill received his bachelor's degree from California State College at Fresno, and his master's degree from the University of California at Santa Barbara. He is a Ph.D. candidate at the University of California at Santa Barbara. His interests are in crime, criminal justice, and social psychology.

Edwin I. Megargee is professor of psychology at Florida State University. He received his bachelor's degree from Amherst and a doctorate in clinical psychology from the University of California at Berkeley. He is past president of the American Association of Correctional Psychologists, was a consultant to the President's Commission on the Causes and Prevention of Violence, and has been consultant for many years to the Federal Bureau of Prisons.

Fred Montanino received his bachelor's and master's degrees from City College of New York, and is currently a doctoral student at Yale University. He is assistant to the editors of *Criminology: An Interdisciplinary Journal,* co-author of a study of anthologies and readers in deviance, and has done research on a variety of subjects. including small claims courts, alternatives to the criminal justice system, and the sociology of possession.

George D. Muedeking is associate professor of sociology and coordinator of criminal corrections studies at California State College at Stanislaus. He received his doctorate from Washington State University, and has published articles on prisons, skid row, and popular culture.

Edward Sagarin is professor of sociology at City College of New York, and co-editor of *Criminology: An Interdisciplinary Journal.* He received his bachelor's degree from Brooklyn College and his doctorate from New York University. He is former president of the American Society of Criminology; associate editor of *Journal of Sex Research;* editorial consultant of *Journal of Criminal Law and Criminology;* and author of many books and essays on crime, deviance, sexual behavior, and other subjects.

William Sanders is assistant professor of sociology at the University of

Florida. He received his bachelor's degree from the University of California at Santa Barbara, master's from San Francisco State, and then returned to Santa Barbara where he received a doctorate. He is author of several books and articles on delinquency, criminal justice, and crime, and on the methodology of field research in the study of police and detectives.

Name Index

Subject Index